Belay Seyoum, PhD

Export-Import Theory, Practices, and Procedures

Second Edition

Pre-publication
REVIEWS,
COMMENTARIES,
EVALUATIONS . . .

"This book covers a number of significant gaps that are not addressed elsewhere. By focusing specifically on trade rather than other forms of international expansion, Dr. Seyoum has achieved the near-impossible—in-depth and thorough coverage of both the theory and the practice of exporting, and significantly broader coverage of importing than is the norm, thus offering the most complete coverage of all facets of trade that I have seen. It excels by integrating theory with practice and exports with imports. The fact that this book starts with a brief history of international trade and concludes with a sample distributorship agreement, speaks to the singular achievement of this book: true cover-to-cover, and top-to-bottom, coverage of all relevant issues in exporting and importing."

Dr. Nicolas Papadopoulos, PhD
Professor of Marketing and International Business; Associate Dean (Research); Director, International Business Study Group, Eric Sprott School of Business, Carleton University, Ottawa, Canada

More pre-publication
REVIEWS, COMMENTARIES, EVALUATIONS . . .

"International Trade has always been a hands-on subject and the few books that are out there do not address anywhere near the width and depth that *Export-Import Theory, Practices, and Procedures: Second Edition,* does. Each of the twenty chapters in this book closes with a great summary. The student here is also provided with enough references, case studies, and international perspectives on the subject matter covered within the chapter. There are even review questions for further self-study. The chapters on import regulations is especially valuable to the student of international trade and the section on export licensing and regulations of the Commerce Department is a boon to any new or seasoned export manager. The useful presentation of typical import and export transactions as well as samples of distributor agreements and business plans put this book way above any other in its class."

Ashok Sadhwani, BCom, GDMM, CHB
*President and CEO, ASMARA USA INC.;
Instructor, Business and Legal Programs,
UCLA Extension, Los Angeles;
Associate Professor, International Trade,
Chulalongkorn University,
Bangkok, Thailand;
Consultant for the Government
of The Philippines, Airport Cargo
Operations*

Export-Import Theory, Practices, and Procedures

Second Edition

Export-Import Theory, Practices, and Procedures

Second Edition

Belay Seyoum, PhD

Routledge
Taylor & Francis Group

NEW YORK AND LONDON

First published 2000 by The Haworth Press
This edition published 2009
by Routledge
270 Madison Ave, New York, NY 10016

Simultaneously published in the UK
by Routledge
2 Park Square, Milton Park, Abingdon, Oxon OX14 4RN

Routledge is an imprint of the Taylor & Francis Group, an informa business

© 2000 The Haworth Press

© 2009 Taylor & Francis

Printed and bound in the United States of America on acid-free paper by Edwards Brothers, Inc.

Cover design by Jennifer M. Gaska

Library of Congress Cataloging in Publication Data
  Seyoum, Belay, 1953–
  Export-import theory, practices, and procedures / Belay Seyoum, editor.—2nd ed.
    p. cm.
  ISBN: 978-0-7890-3419-9 (hard : alk. paper)
  ISBN: 978-0-7890-3420-5 (soft : alk. paper)
  1. Exports. 2. Imports. 3. Export marketing. 4. International trade. I. Title.
  HF1414.4.S49 2007
  382—dc22

                                                                2007034264

ISBN10: 0-7890-3419-0 (hbk)
ISBN 10: 0-7890-3420-4 (pbk)
ISBN 10: 0-2038-8930-4 (ebk)

ISBN13: 978-0-7890-3419-9 (hbk)
ISBN 13: 978-0-7890-3420-5 (pbk)
ISBN 13: 978-0-2038-8930-5 (ebk)

CONTENTS

About the Author	**xiii**
Preface	**xv**
Strengths and Features of this Book	xv
Changes in the Second Edition	xv
Acknowledgments	**xvii**
Introduction: A Brief History of International Trade	**1**
Ancient Period	1
Colonial Period (1500-1900)	2
1900 to the Present	3

SECTION I: OVERVIEW OF INTERNATIONAL TRADE

Chapter 1. Growth and Direction of International Trade	**7**
Importance of International Trade to the Global Economy	7
Determinants of Trade	9
Volume and Direction of Trade	9
Important Developments in Trade	10
Chapter Summary	14
Review Questions	15
Case 1.1. The Limitations of Export-Led Growth	15
Chapter 2. International and Regional Agreements Affecting Trade	**19**
The GATT and WTO	19
Regional Integration Agreements (RIAs)	22
The North American Free Trade Agreement (NAFTA)	25
The European Union	32
Chapter Summary	36
Review Questions	37
Case 2.1. The Benefits and Costs of Free Trade	37

SECTION II: EXPORT MARKETING AND STRATEGY

Chapter 3. Setting Up the Business   41

Ownership Structure   41
Business or Trade Name   48
Bank Accounts, Permits, and Licenses   49
Location and Use of Professional Services   49
Organizing for Export: Industry Approach   50
General Principles of Taxation   52
Taxation of Export-Import Transactions   54
International Transfer Pricing   61
Chapter Summary   65
Review Questions   66
Case 3.1. Globalization and the Shrinking Tax Base   66

Chapter 4. Planning and Preparations for Export   69

Assessing and Selecting the Product   69
International Market Research   72
International Market Assessment   75
Developing an International Business Plan   77
Export Counseling and Assistance   78
Overseas Travel and Promotion   83
Chapter Summary   91
Review Questions   92
Case 4.1. Developing Export Markets   92

Chapter 5. Export Channels of Distribution   95

Indirect Channels   99
Direct Channels   105
Locating, Contacting, and Evaluating Agents
    and Distributors   108
Contracts with Foreign Agents and Distributors
    (Representatives)   110
Major Clauses in Representation Agreements   110
Maintaining and Motivating Overseas Representatives   115
Chapter Summary   115

Review Questions   116
Case 5.1. Export Channel Decisions of Two U.S.
    Companies   117
Case 5.2. The Internet and Exporting: A Focus
    on Developing Countries   118

Chapter 6. International Logistics, Risk, and Insurance   121

International Logistics   121
External Influences on Logistics Decisions   123
Typical Logistics Problems and Solutions   125
The International Logistics Process   126
Logistics Functions   129
Risks in Foreign Trade   131
Marine and Aviation Insurance   135
Claims and Procedures   140
Chapter Summary   145
Review Questions   147
Case 6.1. Marine Insurance   147
Case 6.2. Marine Insurance: Inchmaree Clause   148

SECTION III: EXECUTING THE TRANSACTIONS

Chapter 7. Pricing in International Trade   153

Determinants of Export Prices   154
Pricing in Export Markets   156
Terms of Sale   158
Chapter Summary   174
Review Questions   176
Case 7.1. Incoterms (CIF)   177
Case 7.2. Incoterms (C&F)   177

Chapter 8. Export Sales Contracts   179

Harmonization of Contract Law   179
CISG: Essential Elements   180
Pertinent Clauses in Export Contracts   185
Chapter Summary   193

Review Questions 194
Case 8.1. CISG 195
Case 8.2. China National Products versus Apex Digital Inc. 195

Chapter 9. Trade Documents and Transportation 197

Documentation in Export-Import Trade 197
Transportation 201
Air Transportation 201
Ocean Freight 205
The Role of Freight Forwarders in Transportation 214
Chapter Summary 217
Review Questions 219
Case 9.1. What Constitutes a Package Under COGSA? 220
Case 9.2. The Container Revolution 221

SECTION IV: PAYMENT TERMS AND PROCEDURES

Chapter 10. Exchange Rates and International Trade 225

Foreign Exchange Transactions 225
Protection against Exchange Rate Risks 229
Chapter Summary 236
Review Questions 236
Case 10.1. Will the U.S. Dollar Maintain Its Key
    Currency Status? 237

Chapter 11. Methods of Payment 239

Consignment Sales 239
Open Account 241
Documentary Collection (Documentary Draft) 242
Documentary Letter of Credit 247
Cash in Advance 258
Other Letters of Credit 259
Chapter Summary 265
Review Questions 268
Case 11.1. Dishonoring Letters of Credit 269
Case 11.2. The Independent Principle in Letters of Credit 270

Chapter 12. Countertrade   **271**

Origins of Countertrade   271
Benefits of Countertrade   273
Theories on Countertrade   274
Forms of Countertrade   276
Countertrade and the WTO   284
Countertrade and the International Monetary Fund   285
Governments' Attitudes Toward Countertrade   286
Chapter Summary   287
Review Questions   290
Case 12.1. The Bofors-India Countertrade Deal   290
Case 12.2. Offsets in U.S. Defense Trade   291

SECTION V:
FINANCING TECHNIQUES AND VEHICLES

Chapter 13. Capital Requirements and Private Sources of Financing   **297**

Capital Sources for Export-Import Businesses   299
Private Sources of Export Financing   306
Chapter Summary   314
Review Questions   316
Case 13.1. Tadoo's Sales to Belgium   316

Chapter 14. Government Export Financing Programs   **319**

Export-Import Bank of the United States (Ex-Im Bank)   320
Small Business Administration   332
Overseas Private Investment Corporation (OPIC)   334
Private Export Funding Corporation   337
U.S. Department of Agriculture   337
Chapter Summary   338
Review Questions   340
Case 14.1. Trade Finance for Small and Medium-Sized
    Enterprises in Transition Economies   341
Case 14.2. Ex-Im Bank Financing: Selected Cases   342

SECTION VI:
EXPORT REGULATIONS AND TAX INCENTIVES

Chapter 15. Regulations and Policies Affecting Exports   **347**

Export Licensing and Administration   347
Antiboycott Regulations   360
Foreign Corrupt Practices   363
Antitrust Laws and Trade Regulation   368
Incentives to Promote Exports   373
Chapter Summary   377
Review Questions   380
Case 15.1. Export Trade Certificate of Review   381
Case 15.2. Enforcement of Export Regulations   383

SECTION VII:
IMPORT PROCEDURES AND TECHNIQUES

Chapter 16. Import Regulations, Trade Intermediaries, and Services   **389**

Import Restrictions in the United States   389
U.S. Free Trade Agreements   394
U.S. Trade Preferences   396
Trade Intermediaries and Services   398
Chapter Summary   403
Review Questions   404
Case 16.1. Tax Deduction for Processing in Maquilas:
     Mere Assembly or Fabrication   406

Chapter 17. Selecting Import Products and Suppliers   **407**

Types of Products for Importation   407
Finding the Product   409
What Determines Import Volume?   411
Selecting the Supplier   412
International Sourcing   414
Pricing the Imported Product   417
Import Marketing Channels   417

Financing Imports   419
Chapter Summary   420
Review Questions   421
Case 17.1. The ATA Carnet: Unlocking Customs
    for Temporary Entry of Goods   421
Case 17.2. Maytag's Triad Strategy   423

Chapter 18. The Entry Process for Imports   **425**

The Entry Process   428
The Harmonized Tariff Schedule of the United States   432
Customs Valuation   433
Rules of Origin and Other Marking Requirements   438
Chapter Summary   439
Review Questions   441
Case 18.1. Deemed Liquidation by Customs   444
Case 18.2. Product Classification   445

Chapter 19. Import Relief to Domestic Industry   **447**

Antidumping and Countervailing Duties   447
Antidumping and Countervailing Duty Proceedings   453
Other Trade Remedies   456
Chapter Summary   461
Review Questions   462
Case 19.1. Similar Products and Dumping   463

Chapter 20. Intellectual Property Rights   **465**

What Are IPRs?   465
IPRs and International Trade   468
Protection of IPRs   469
International/Regional Protection   473
Chapter Summary   476
Review Questions   476
Case 20.1. Patents and Access to Lifesaving Drugs   477

Appendix A: Trading Opportunities in Selected Countries   **479**

Appendix B: Importing into the United States   **521**

Appendix C: Trade Profiles of Selected Nations (2004)
(Million U.S. Dollars)   531

Appendix D: Average Tariff Rates of Selected Countries
(2002-2004)   535

Appendix E: Ex-Im Bank Programs   537

Appendix F: Sample Export Business Plan: Donga Michael
Export Company   561

Appendix G: Sample Import Business Plan: Otoro Import
Company   567

Appendix H: Export Sales Contract (Basic Clauses)   573

Appendix I: Sample Distributorship Agreement   585

Appendix J: Sample Sales Representative Agreement   593

Appendix K: North American Free Trade Agreement   601

Appendix L: Trade Documents   619

References   627

Index   649

ABOUT THE AUTHOR

Belay Seyoum, PhD, is Associate Professor of International Business Studies at Nova Southeastern University in Fort Lauderdale, Florida, where he teaches a variety of courses in international business and economics. Prior to coming to Nova Southeastern, Dr. Seyoum taught international business at Concordia University and McGill University in Montreal, Canada. Dr. Seyoum has published four books as well as numerous articles in the area of international trade in several prestigious academic journals such as the *International Business Review,* the *Journal of World Trade, Multinational Business Review,* the *International Trade Journal,* the *Columbia Journal of World Business,* and the *Journal of Global Business.* He is recipient of the Fulbright Scholar award for 2007 and lives in Florida.

Preface

This book resulted from the author's realization of the inadequacy of existing books to serve the needs of the academic/professional audience. Most of the books published in this area lack substance and provide only soft coverage of international trade operations. Another problem is that they hardly discuss theoretical issues such as the role of exports/imports in the global economy or pertinent regulatory and policy issues. Current books are almost exclusively devoted to export activities and provide only cursory treatment of import processes. Furthermore, most offer no discussion of current research information in the area.

STRENGTHS AND FEATURES OF THIS BOOK

1. *Conceptual and theoretical approach:* The book develops a conceptual/theoretical framework to explain international trade operations. Important scholarly studies are adequately treated in each chapter. Sufficient attention is also given to important legal and policy issues affecting export/import trade.
2. *Depth and breadth:* The book provides a comprehensive and analytical treatment of pertinent topics in the area. In addition to exports, the book provides an in-depth examination of import trade. Adequate coverage is also given to emerging areas such as intellectual property, countertrade, the role of logistics and transportation, regional trade arrangements, and so forth. No book on the market comes close in terms of scholarly substance.
3. *Presentation:* The book is written in a pedagogically sound manner by including end-of-chapter summaries, a reference section, and Internet sources, as well as learning aids such as vignettes, figures, and tables.

CHANGES IN THE SECOND EDITION

1. *Current coverage:* Important developments in the area of international trade since the publication of the first edition are discussed.

Export-Import Theory, Practices, and Procedures, Second Edition

This includes, but is not limited to, trends in regional integration agreements, international transfer pricing, terms of sale, U.S. export regulations, and export financing programs.

2. *Expanded coverage:* The book has expanded the coverage of certain topics, such as taxation of international trade operations, export counseling, export channels of distribution, export sales contracts, transportation, and import procedures and techniques.

3. *Review questions and cases:* Every chapter summary is followed by review questions and cases, many of which were written for this book.

4. *Learning package:* The text is accompanied by instructor's manual, test bank, and answers to review questions.

Acknowledgments

It would have been impossible to produce this book without the assistance of many people. I would like to thank the leadership team: Dr. Randy Pohlman, dean; Dr. Preston Jones, executive associate dean; and Dr. Russell Abratt, associate dean at the Huizenga School of Business, Nova Southeastern University, for creating a supportive intellectual environment. Many thanks to the librarians at the Alvin Sherman library, especially Lia Hemphill, for opening up their resources. I would like to acknowledge the valuable research assistance of Bina Patel. I thank her for assisting me in completing the book and instructor's manual in time for publication. I also thank the following people for their helpful feedback on the book: Ralph Jagodka, San Antionio College, California; Ron Mesia, Microsoft, Florida; Hoon Park, University of Central Florida; Ashok Sadhwani, Chulalongkorn University, Thailand; Habte Selassie, University of Bedforshire, UK; and Randi Sims, Nova Southeastern University, Florida.

This book could not have been written without the help, support, and encouragement of my wife, Muwen Seyoum.

Writing a book is a major undertaking. However, the reward comes not only from its publication but from its useful contribution to those in the field (students, professors, professionals, researchers, etc.), not only in understanding international trade policies and practices, but also in encouraging additional research and dialogue.

Introduction:
A Brief History of International Trade

ANCIENT PERIOD

International trade based on the free exchange of goods started as early as 2500 BC. Archaeological discoveries indicate that the Sumerians of Northern Mesopotamia enjoyed great prosperity based on trade by sea in textiles and metals. The Greeks profited by the exchange of olive oil and wine for grain and metal somewhere before 2000 BC.

By around 340 BC, many devices of modern commerce had made their appearance in Greece and its distant settlements: banking and credit, insurance, trade treaties, and special diplomatic and other privileges.

With the decline of Greece, Rome became powerful and began to expand to the East. In the first century AD, the Romans traded with the Chinese along the Silk Road and developed many trade routes and complex trading patterns by sea. However, the absence of peace made traveling unsafe and discouraged the movement of goods, resulting in the loss of distant markets.

By the time of the breakup of the Roman Empire in the fifth century, the papacy (papal supremacy) had emerged as a strong institution in a new and unstable world. The church's support (sponsorship) for the crusades in the eleventh century revived international trade in the West through the latter's discovery and introduction of new ideas, customs, and products from the East. New products such as carpets, furniture, sugar, and spices brought from Egypt, Syria, India, and China stimulated the markets and the growing commercial life of the West. This helped Italian cities such as Venice and Genoa to prosper and to replace Constantinople as the leading center of international commerce. Letters of credit, bills of exchange, and insurance of goods in transit were extensively used to accommodate the growing commercial and financial needs of merchants and travelers.

By the end of the fifteenth century, the center of international commerce had moved from the Mediterranean to Western Europe. Spain, Portugal, and later Holland became the focal points of international commercial activity.

Export-Import Theory, Practices, and Procedures, Second Edition

The more developed areas of Europe were changing from a subsistence economy to one relying heavily on imports paid by money or letters of credit.

COLONIAL PERIOD (1500-1900)

With the discovery of America in 1492, and sea routes to India in 1498, trade flourished and luxury goods and food products such as sugar, tobacco, and coffee became readily available in the markets of Europe.

The principal motivations behind global expansion (colonization) in the fifteenth century had been to enhance national economic power (mercantilist policy) by exploiting the colonies for the exclusive benefit of the mother country. Colonies were regarded as outposts of the home economy that would reduce trade dependence on rival nations and augment national treasure through exports as well as discoveries of precious metals. This first phase of colonization, which lasted until the advent of the Industrial Revolution in England in 1750, was characterized by the following general elements with respect to commerce:

1. All commerce between the colonies and the mother country was a national monopoly, meaning all merchandise exports/imports had to be carried by ships of the mother country and pass through specified ports.
2. Little encouragement was provided toward the development or diversification of indigenous exports. For example, in 1600, precious metals constituted 90 percent of colonial exports to Spain. In the mid-1650s, British imports from its colonies were mainly concentrated in three primary products: sugar, tobacco, and furs. To protect domestic producers, competing colonial exports were restricted or subject to special duties. The patterns of economic relations were fashioned on the basis of dissimilarity, that is, noncompetitiveness of colonial and metropolitan production.
3. Certain enumerated products could be exported only to the mother country or another colony. The policy ensured a supply of strategic foodstuffs and raw materials.
4. Private companies in the metropolis received a charter from the government that granted them (i.e., the companies) a monopoly of trade in the colonies. In most cases, the charter also granted complete local administrative authority, ranging from the making of laws and administration of justice to imposition of taxes. Examples of this include the British East India Company (1600), the Dutch West India Company (1621), and Hudson's Bay Company (1670).

The second historical phase of overseas expansion (1765-1900) was dictated more by commercial considerations than by mere territorial gains. Britain emerged as the dominant colonial power, and by 1815 it had transformed its empire into a worldwide business concern. By the 1860s, the Industrial Revolution had transformed the social and economic structure of England, and mass production dictated an expansion of the market for goods on an international scale. The political economy of mercantilism that had proliferated over the preceding century was gradually replaced by that of free trade. By 1860, Britain had unilaterally repealed the Corn Laws, abolished the Navigation Act restrictions (foreign ships were permitted to take colonial goods anywhere) and the commercial monopolies given to particular companies. Preferential duties on empire goods were gradually abolished. In trade, as in foreign policy, Britain led the free trade ideology based on nondiscrimination. At the time, Britain was most likely to benefit from free trade because of its industrial and commercial lead over other nations.

1900 TO THE PRESENT

The major characteristics of economic relations from 1900 until the outbreak of World War I were the further development of trade and the emergence of a world economy. These were also the result of the international migration of people and capital from Europe, particularly Britain, since the 1850s, to other countries such as the United States, Australia, Argentina, Brazil, and Canada. This pattern of world economy provided the industrial economies with new sources of food and raw materials and new markets for exports of manufactures. For example, by 1913, Brazil was the source of two-thirds of German coffee imports, whereas North Africa supplied over half of French imports of wine. However, much of the import trade in Europe was subject to trade restrictions, such as tariffs, to secure home markets for local producers. Even within Britain there were mounting pressures for the abolition of free trade.

The post–World War I recovery was further delayed by the disruption of trading links, as new nations were created and borders were redrawn. State intervention and restrictive economic policies had been consolidated in Europe and other countries by the end of the war. The U.S. government introduced the Fordney-McCumber Tariff in 1922, which imposed high tariffs on agricultural imports, and later the Smoot-Hawley Tariff in 1930, which provoked widespread retaliation. Britain imposed high duties on various industrial products, such as precision instruments and synthetic organic chemicals, to encourage domestic production under the Safeguarding of Industries Act, 1921. The volume of world trade in manufactures fell by 35 percent between 1929 and 1932, and prices also fell by a similar amount. The volume of trade in primary products fell by 15 percent, but prices fell by about 50 percent. To alleviate the worst effects of the Depression, countries resorted to more protectionism. This wave of protectionism produced a massive contraction of international trade and further aggravated the Depression. Many of the barriers placed on trade included tariffs and quotas, a variety of price maintenance schemes, as well as arbitrary currency manipulation and foreign exchange controls and management.

To avoid a repetition of the economic situation of the previous two decades, Allied countries met even before the war to discuss the international financial arrangements that should govern trade and capital movements in the postwar world. In 1944, they established the International Monetary Fund (IMF) and the International Bank for Reconstruction and Development (IBRD). The IMF was to be concerned with facilitating the growth and expansion of global trade through the system of fixed exchange rates, while IBRD was established to promote long-term investment. This was followed by an agreement (the General Agreement on Tariffs and Trade, or the GATT) in 1948 to permit the free flow of goods among nations.

SECTION I:
OVERVIEW OF INTERNATIONAL TRADE

Chapter 1

Growth and Direction of International Trade

International trade is the exchange of goods and services across national boundaries. It is the most traditional form of international business activity and has played a major role in shaping world history. It is also the first type of foreign business operation undertaken by most companies because importing or exporting requires the least commitment of, and risk to, the company's resources. For example, a company could produce for export by using its excess production capacity. This is an inexpensive way of testing a product's acceptance in the market before investing in local production facilities. A company could also use intermediaries, who will take on import-export functions for a fee, thus eliminating the need to commit additional resources to hire personnel or maintain a department to carry out foreign sales or purchases (Daniels and Radebaugh, 2004).

International trade in services has grown over the past decade at an annual rate of about 18 percent compared to that of approximately 9 percent for merchandise trade. Trade in services constitutes 25 percent of overall world trade in 2004 (WTO, 2004a). In some countries, such as Panama and the Netherlands, services account for about 40 percent or more of total merchandise trade. Typical service exports include transportation, tourism, banking, advertising, construction, retailing, and mass communication.

IMPORTANCE OF INTERNATIONAL TRADE TO THE GLOBAL ECONOMY

International trade allows manufacturers and distributors to seek out products, services, and components produced in foreign countries. Companies

Export-Import Theory, Practices, and Procedures, Second Edition

acquire them because of cost advantages or in order to learn about advanced technical methods used abroad; for example, methods that help reduce the cost of production lower prices and in turn, induce more consumption thus producing increased profit. Trade also enables firms to acquire resources that are not available at home. Besides providing consumers with a variety of goods and services, international trade increases incomes and employment. In 1990, the number of U.S. jobs supported by merchandise exports to all foreign markets reached 7.2 million. U.S. merchandise exports to all foreign markets contributed to 25 percent of the growth in U.S. civilian jobs between 1986 and 1990 (Davies, 1992). It is estimated that each billion dollars of merchandise exports supports about 25,000 jobs. A survey of 3,032 small- and medium-sized manufacturing enterprises in Canada over a three-year period (1994-1997) strongly indicates that growth in exports is associated with an increase in jobs (Lefebvre and Lefebvre, 2000). Even though imports are associated with loss of jobs due to plant closings or production cutbacks of domestic industries, the export job-generation effect is about 7.5 percent larger than the import job-loss effect (Belous and Wyckoff, 1987). During the 1979-1999 periods, about 6.4 million U.S. jobs were displaced due to import competition. Such losses are largely concentrated in electrical/nonelectrical machinery, apparel, motor vehicles, and blast furnaces. A quarter of displaced workers reported earning losses of about 30 percent, while 36 percent indicated comparable or higher earnings than from their previous job (Kletzer, 2001). Most occupations show a net job gain from an equal amount of exports and imports except for blue-collar occupations, which are shrinking in most developed countries due to increasing pressure from low-wage imports.

Exports create high-wage employment. In a study of recent wage statistics, the U.S. Trade Representative's Office found that U.S. workers employed in export-related jobs earn 17 percent more than the average worker in the United States. Export-related wages are higher for manufacturing and service sector jobs. While service-related jobs generally pay less than manufacturing jobs, service jobs in the export sector were found to pay more on average than manufacturing jobs in the overall economy (U.S. Department of Commerce, 1994). A recent study on wages and trade finds a strong positive correlation between export intensity and wages. This could be partly explained by the fact that export intensive sectors tend to show higher levels of productivity than other firms. It is also consistent with economic theory, as industries in which a nation enjoys comparative advantage are likely to be those in which workers are more productive and therefore receive higher wages. It also shows that greater import penetration is associated with greater demand elasticity, which reduces workers' bargaining power (Harless, 2006).

DETERMINANTS OF TRADE

Why do some countries export or import more than others? Several studies have been conducted to establish major factors that influence exports. The trade and exchange rate regime (import tariffs, quotas, and exchange rates), presence of an entrepreneurial class, efficiency enhancing government policy, and secure access to transport (and transport costs) and marketing services are considered to be important influential factors of export behavior (Kaynak and Kothavi, 1984; Fugazza, 2004). A study on the nature, composition, and determinants of Singapore's technology exports suggests that the country's open trade and investment regime and development-oriented economic policy have been the key factors in enhancing the country's exports. Singapore's economy has shown continued and remarkable growth in exports for over thirty years with only two brief and mild recessions in the mid-1970s and mid-1980s. Its total trade as a proportion of GDP remains one of the highest in the world, over 300 percent of GDP in 2003 (Fong and Hill, 1991; WTO, 2004b). A recent study on the determinants of export performance underlines the importance of foreign direct investment (FDI) and the general quality of the institutional framework. Foreign direct investment contributes to capital formation and helps promote the development and export of knowledge-based industries (Fugazza, 2004).

Much of the research literature on imports underlines the importance of high per capita incomes, price of imports, and the exchange rate in determining import levels (Lutz, 1994). For developing countries, however, determinants of import demand also include factors such as government restrictions on imports and availability of foreign exchange. A study examining the factors influencing import demand in Pakistan from 1959 to 1986 found that the policy of devaluation or the policy of raising tariffs was not significant in reducing imports except in the case of imports of machinery and equipment (Sarmand, 1989).

VOLUME AND DIRECTION OF TRADE

The growth in the volume of world merchandise trade has always exceeded the growth of output (1870-2004) except for the period 1913-1950, which was marked by global political and economic instability. Since 1950, while world economic output has shown steady growth, world exports increased at an average annual rate of more than ten times the estimated rate for 1913-1950 (Rostow, 1978, 1992). The volume of world trade in 2004 was about three times what it was in 1990 and approached eleven trillion

U.S. dollars (WTO, 2004a). The dollar value of total world trade in 2004 was greater than the gross national product of every nation in the world except the United States. Another measure of the significance of world trade is that one-fourth of everything grown or made in the world is now exported.

The rapid increase in the growth of world trade after World War II can be traced to increased consumption of goods and services as more people joined the middle class in many countries of the world. Trade liberalization, both at the regional and international level, has created a global environment that is conducive to the growth and expansion of world trade. New technologies such as computers, telecommunications, and other media also assisted in the physical integration of world markets.

Small countries tend to be more dependent on international trade than larger ones because they are less able to produce all that they need. Larger countries (in terms of population) import less manufactured goods on a per capita basis because such countries tend to have a diversified economy that enables them to produce most of their own needs. The previous statement can be exemplified by the case of the United States, Japan, India, and China, which have low import propensities compared to countries such as Belgium or the Netherlands.

Merchandise trade currently accounts for about four-fifths of world trade. The top seven exporters accounted for just over one-half of world merchandise exports (United States, Germany, Japan, France, United Kingdom, Italy, and Canada). Merchandise trade includes three major sectors: agriculture, mining, and manufactures. Trade in manufactured goods has been the most dynamic component of world merchandise trade. In 2004, the value of world merchandise exports was estimated at $8.91 trillion (U.S.) compared to that of $2.12 trillion (U.S.) for services. Growth in service exports has lagged behind that of merchandise trade for the past few years. However, during 2000-2004, both merchandise and service exports rose at an average of 9 percent (WTO, 2004a).

Industrial market economies account for the largest part of world trade. Trade among these countries is estimated to be greater than 67 percent of global trade. In view of their role in world trade, Western countries also account for major shares of trade with developing countries and an increasing share of trade with transition economies.

IMPORTANT DEVELOPMENTS IN TRADE

- In 1994, the World Trade Organization (WTO) was established replacing the GATT under the Final Act of the Uruguay Round. Member countries of the GATT as of the enforcement date of the WTO agreement became original members of the WTO. World Trade Organization became the principal agency of the United Nations (UN) with responsibility for international trade.

- The Final Act of the Uruguay Round was signed in 1994 by 124 governments providing for a global reduction in trade barriers, establishment of a multilateral framework of discipline for trade in services, and protection of trade-related intellectual property rights. The agreement also strengthened existing multilateral rules in agriculture, textiles, and clothing and provided for a more effective and reliable dispute-settlement mechanism. After the implementation of the Uruguay Round, WTO members launched a subsequent round in Doha, Qatar, in 2001 to further reduce trade barriers. The focus of this round has been the reduction of trade distorting agricultural subsidies provided by developed countries and the introduction of equitable trade rules for developing nations.

- There has been a steady growth in the role of developing countries in world trade. In 2004, developing countries accounted for over a third of the world's top twenty-five exporters and importers. Since the 1980s, a number of newly industrializing countries (NICs), particularly the four in the Pacific Rim (Hong Kong, Singapore, South Korea, and Taiwan), and China have greatly increased their roles in world trade. Another significant development is the opening up of China and Eastern Europe for trade and investment.

- China joined the WTO in 2001. Within three years its exports doubled and the country is now the world's third largest exporter/importer of goods and services.

- Over the past few decades, the major emphasis of many developing countries had been on the liberalization of world markets for their exports. Their focus has now shifted from demanding tariff cuts by wealthy countries for their exports to requesting technical assistance to increase production and exports. In 2004, thirty-six countries depend on a single commodity and fifty-two on two commodities for over 50 percent of their export revenue. In view of their domestic economic conditions, the emphasis is on increasing supply/productive capacity and exports.

- There has been a marked increase in the establishment of common markets and free trade areas, thus further increasing economic linkages among nations through trade, investment, and the operation of multinational companies. The most notable examples are the North American Free Trade Agreement (NAFTA), the Asian Free Trade Area, the

Preferential Trade Area for Eastern and Southern American Common Market (MERCOSUR), U.S.–Central America–Dominican Republic Free Trade Agreement (CAFTA-DR), and so on. Many scholars believe that such agreements are inferior to the multilateral, nondiscriminatory approach of the WTO. Bilateral/regional trade arrangements discriminate against nonmembers and create a maze of trade barriers that vary for every exporting country: rules of origin, tariff schedules, nontariff barriers such as quotas, etc. There are concerns that such agreements also work in favor of powerful nations that will sneak in reverse preferences such as protection of intellectual property rights or labor standards.

- Export trade is no longer limited to the big multinational firms. Small and medium-sized businesses are increasing their share of exports and already account for almost a quarter of all exports in the United States. Such firms still represent the largest pool of potential exporters and can play a significant role in improving the U.S. balance of trade, while at the same time enhancing their competitiveness and increasing their profits. These firms also have the advantage of developing much more flexible structures than the big multinational enterprises.

- Given the dynamic role of services in today's economy, trade in services has shown continued growth in most countries. Even though services trade takes place mainly among the industrialized nations, some developing countries have established strong service sectors that are competitive on a global scale in areas such as engineering, construction, tourism, or financial services. The liberalization of services trade (under NAFTA, EU, and WTO), in tandem with the advent of communication and information technology, will inevitably induce an upsurge in services trade. Among the developed countries, the United States has had a healthy surplus in service trade for some years. In 2005, for example, U.S. service exports exceeded imports by $66 billion, offsetting 8 percent of the deficit in merchandise trade. A few developing nations such as Egypt, India, and Pakistan also have a surplus in their service account, largely resulting from tourism and workers' remittances.

- Today's integration of the world economy is driven by advances in communications and information technology as well as government policies to reduce obstacles to the flow of trade and capital flows. This growing integration of nations has intensified competitive pressures partly because countries have access to similar pools of knowledge and technology. Traditional notions of comparative advantage do not squarely fit with present patterns of production and trade. For example, even though U.S. comparative advantage lies in high-skilled, high value–added activities, many developing countries such as China and India (with high-skilled, low-cost workforce) are competing in the very products for which the United States has had a global competitive advantage. Such competitive pressures have resulted in the reorganization and relocation of the firm's basic activities overseas, either to affiliate firms or independent contractors. With the reduction of trade barriers and transportation costs, many U.S. firms have outsourced labor intensive work to overseas firms and reimport for final assembly and sale. A number of Western service industries have also started to migrate to low cost locations overseas. This process of outsourcing is likely to have major implications for employment and the structure of international trade flows.

- The U.S. current account deficit reached 7 percent of GDP in the last quarter of 2005. Imports are 60 percent higher than exports. At the same time, the East Asian economies (including Japan) held about $2.4 trillion (U.S.) in official foreign exchange reserves out of a global total of $4 trillion. China's foreign currency reserves alone reached $1 trillion (U.S.) by the end of 2006. The Southeast Asian countries' heavy reliance on exports as a way of sustaining domestic economic growth, weak currencies, and high savings has resulted in unsustainable global imbalances. Global imbalances cannot diminish without, inter alia, reducing such excess savings through currency adjustments and/or increased imports in the surplus countries.

- About 60 percent (by value) of total world trade in goods is carried by sea and a substantial increase in fuel costs could act as a disincentive to exports by raising transportation cost. In air transportation (more fuel sensitive than shipping), rising oil prices could severely damage trade in time-sensitive products such as fruits and vegetables, or parts in just-in-time production, etc. Faster economic growth in emerging economies is also putting pressure on the limited supply of other raw materials such as copper, coal, etc.

- After the terrorist attacks of 9/11, there was a marked decline in transpacific freight container rates for 2001 and 2002. Since 2002, however, demand for container shipping has grown by over 10 percent per year compared to the thirty-year average of 8 percent. Programs were introduced at domestic and foreign ports to screen the containers. Extra security costs are estimated at about $18 per typical container. The volume of trade has since grown and traders appear to have coped with new guidelines without sacrificing efficiency or market share.

CHAPTER SUMMARY

Major Benefits of International Trade

To acquire a variety of goods and services, to reduce cost of production, to increase incomes and employment, to learn about advanced technical methods used abroad, and to secure raw materials.

Determinants of Trade

Major determinants of exports. Presence of an entrepreneurial class; access to transportation, marketing, and other services; exchange rates; and government trade and exchange rate policies.

Major determinants of imports. Per capita income, price of imports, exchange rates, government trade and exchange rate policies, and availability of foreign exchange.

Volume of Trade

1. World trade approached eleven trillion (U.S.) in 2004 and was triple what it was in 1990.
2. Services trade accounts for about 25 percent of total trade.
3. Since 1970, average annual growth in world merchandise exports is estimated at about 12 percent.
4. The industrial market economies account for 70 percent of global trade.

Major Developments in Trade

1. The establishment of the World Trade Organization (WTO) as a permanent trade organization.
2. The introduction of rules under the WTO to govern trade in services, trade-related intellectual property, and investment measures.
3. The marked increase in the establishment of regional trading arrangements such as NAFTA, MERCOSUR, etc.
4. Growing role of developing countries in world trade.
5. Increasing participation of small and medium-sized businesses in export trade.
6. The dynamic role of services in today's economy and continued growth in trade in services.
7. Globalization, competitive pressures and the reorganization/relocation of value-added activities.

8. The increasing U.S. current account deficit and global imbalances.
9. Fast economic growth in many countries and pressure on limited resources. Business adjustment to security costs after 9/11.

REVIEW QUESTIONS

1. Discuss the importance of international trade to national economies.
2. What are the major determinants of exports? Why do some countries trade more than others?
3. What is the volume of trade?
4. What are some of the major developments in trade over the past two decades?
5. What are the implications of the increasing U.S. trade deficit for global production and exports?
6. What is the reason behind the increase in common markets and free trade areas over the past few decades?
7. What are the limitations of export-led growth?
8. Why are small countries more dependent on international trade than larger ones?

CASE 1.1. THE LIMITATIONS OF EXPORT-LED GROWTH

International trade played an important role in the economic development of North America and Australia in the nineteenth century and that of East Asian economies in the second half of the twentieth century. East Asia's growth contributed to improve living standards and reduced inequality as the new prosperity was widely shared among its population. In Malaysia and Thailand, for example, the level of poverty was reduced from almost 50 percent in the 1960s to less than 20 percent by 2000.

Central to the success of these countries is the promotion of exports. Governments provided credits, restricted competing imports, and developed export marketing institutions. As they increased their exports to wealthy countries, their economies grew at 7 to 8 percent per year.

The export-led model may have worked for a few countries during the time when most developing countries pursued import substitution policies—substituting domestic production of manufactured goods with the exportation of raw materials. There are a number of limitations to export-led growth when many countries including China begin to use it. Here are some of its potential limitations:

- It is difficult for all countries to increase exports by 8 to 10 percent per year when the world economy grows at 2 or 3 percent per year. It is not possible for every country to have a trade surplus.
- The major importing nation, the United States, cannot continue to run large trade deficits. U.S. current account deficit set a record of $790 billion in 2005 (nearly 6.5 percent of GDP). Other potential destinations for global exports, Japan and the European Union, also rely on an export promotion policy to sustain economic growth and are not willing to run large deficits.
- China and other East Asian economies have not taken measures to open their markets in order to absorb increasing exports from the rest of the world. Foreign currency reserves of China, Japan, South Korea, Taiwan, Malaysia, Singapore, and Indonesia were estimated at $2.22 trillion in 2005. In the absence of other sources of economic growth, focusing on the U.S. market is unsustainable in the long run.
- Many multinational corporations are already experiencing flat or shrinking revenue growth due to reduced demand reflecting the natural limitations of export growth (see Table 1.1).

TABLE 1.1. Average Rate of Revenue Growth for Selected Sectors in the 1990s and 2000s (%)

Sectors	Industries	Average Rate of Growth, 1990s	Average Rate of Growth, 2000s
Consumer goods	Beverages, tobacco, food items, personal care products	4.98	1.95
Technology	Software, hardware, semiconductors	13.59	3.67
Communications	Telephone service, equipment, cellular/wireless, long distance	12.53	1.53
Health care	Biotechnology, pharmaceuticals, medical products	14.3	9.82
Financial	Banks, investment brokerages	22.64	5.37

TABLE 1.1 *(continued)*

Sectors	Industries	Average Rate of Growth, 1990s	Average Rate of Growth, 2000s
Energy	Oil, drilling	2.21	20.39
Transport	Air freight, rail, airlines	5.08	2.44
Capital goods	Equipment, aerospace, manufacturing	9.84	1.92
Basic materials	Chemicals, paper, aluminum	7.53	4.69
Utilities	Electric, gas, water	7.48	6.39

Source: Adapted from SEC Fillings, Moody's Industrial manuals, 2004.

Questions

1. Do you agree with the author's view on the limitations to export-led growth?
2. What other alternatives are available to export-led growth?

Chapter 2

International and Regional Agreements Affecting Trade

THE GATT AND WTO

The General Agreement on Tariffs and Trade (GATT) was established in 1945 as a provisional agreement pending the creation of an International Trade Organization (ITO). The ITO draft charter, which was the result of trade negotiations at the Havana Conference of 1948, never came into being due to the failure of the U.S. Congress to approve it. Other countries also declined to proceed with the ITO without the participation of the United States. Thus, the GATT continued to fill the vacuum as a de facto trade organization, with codes of conduct for international trade but with almost no basic constitution designed to regulate its international activities and procedures. The GATT, in theory, was not an "organization," and participating nations were called "contracting parties" and not members (Jackson, 1992; Hoekman and Kostecki, 1995).

Since its inception, the GATT has used certain policies to reduce trade barriers between contracting parties (CPs):

- *Nondiscrimination:* All CPs must be treated in the same way with respect to import-export duties and charges. According to the most favored nation treatment, each CP must grant to every other CP the most-favorable tariff treatment that it grants to any country with respect to imports and exports of products. Certain exceptions, however, are allowed, such as free trade areas, customs unions, or other preferential arrangements in favor of developing nations. Once imports have cleared customs, a CP is required to treat foreign imports the same way as it treats similar domestic products (the national treatment standard).

Export-Import Theory, Practices, and Procedures, Second Edition

- *Trade liberalization:* The GATT has been an important forum for trade negotiations. It has sponsored periodic conferences among CPs to reduce trade barriers (see International Perspective 2.1). The Uruguay Round (1986-1993) gave rise to the establishment of a permanent trade organization (World Trade Organization or WTO). The most recent round (the Doha Round) hopes to reach agreement on other trade distortions, such as agricultural subsidies and trade barriers imposed by developing countries on imports of manufactured goods.
- *Settlement of trade disputes:* The GATT/WTO has played an important role in resolving trade disputes between CPs. In certain cases where a party did not follow GATT's recommendations, it ruled for trade retaliation that is proportional to the loss or damage sustained. It is fair to state that the existence of the GATT/WTO has been a deterrent to damaging trade wars between nations.
- *Trade in goods:* The GATT rules apply to all products both imported and exported, although most of the rules are relevant to imports. It was designed primarily to regulate tariffs and related barriers to imports such as quotas, internal taxes, discriminatory regulations, subsidies, dumping, discriminatory customs procedures, and other nontariff barriers. The Uruguay Round (1994) resulted in a new general agreement on trade in services, trade-related aspects of intellectual property (TRIPs) and trade-related investment measures (TRIMs). Thus, CPs have moved beyond the original purpose of the GATT to achieve unrestricted trade in goods, to reduce barriers to trade in services, investment, and to protect intellectual property (Collins and Bosworth, 1995).

The Uruguay Round and WTO

In 1982, the United States initiated a proposal to launch a new round of GATT talks. The major reasons behind the U.S. initiative were (1) to counter domestic pressures for protectionism precipitated by the strong dollar and rising trade deficit, (2) to improve market access for U.S. products by reducing existing tariff and nontariff barriers to trade, (3) to reverse the erosion of confidence in the multilateral trading system, (4) to extend GATT coverage to important areas such as services, intellectual property, and investment, and (5) to bring developing nations more effectively into the international trading system.

Despite the initial reluctance of many developing nations, the effort culminated in the conclusion of a successful trade negotiation (the Uruguay Round) in 1994. The results of the Uruguay Round are summarized in the following sections.

INTERNATIONAL PERSPECTIVE 2.1.
GATT Negotiations (1947-2006)

GATT Round	Explanation
Geneva (1947)	Twenty-three countries participated in establishing the GATT in 1947. Average tariff cut of 35 percent on trade estimated at $10 billion.
Annecy, France (1949)	Thirty-three countries participated in tariff reductions.
Torquay, UK (1951)	Thirty-four countries participated in tariff reductions.
Geneva (1956)	Twenty-two countries participated in tariff reductions on trade estimated at $2.5 billion.
Dillon (1960-1961)	Forty-four countries participated in tariff reductions on trade estimated at $5 billion.
Kennedy (1962-1967)	Forty-eight countries participated in tariff reductions on trade estimated at $40 billion.
Tokyo (1973-1979)	Ninety-nine countries participated in reductions of tariff and non-tariff barriers on trade valued at $155 billion.
Uruguay (1986-1994)	Broadening of the GATT to include services, intellectual property, and investment. It also resulted in the establishment of WTO. One hundred and twenty-four countries participated on reductions of tariff and non-tariff barriers on trade valued at $300 billion.
Doha (2001)	Reduction of agricultural subsidies and other trade barriers on agricultural exports, broadening of international rules in services, lowering trade barriers by developing nations. More than 124 countries participate in this round.

Trade Liberalization

Significant progress was made toward reducing trade barriers in the areas of agriculture and textiles that had long been resistant to reform. Tariff reductions of about 40 percent were achieved. The agreement also opened access to a broad range of government contracts (Government Procurement Agreement). It also provided for the liberalization of the textiles and apparel sector by the end of 2004. Textiles quotas have been removed except for occasional safeguards used to protect a sudden increase in imports.

Trade Rules

The Uruguay Round added new rules relating to unfair trade practices (dumping, subsidies) and the use of import safeguards.

New Issues

The agreement broadened the coverage of the GATT to include areas such as trade in services, TRIPs, and TRIMs. The GATT establishes rules to liberalize trade in services, which in 2002 was estimated to be almost $1.6 trillion (Wild, Wild, and Han, 2006). The TRIPs agreement establishes new trade disciplines with regard to the protection and enforcement of intellectual property rights. TRIMs provides for the elimination of trade distorting investment requirements such as local content, limitation of ownership, or exports of certain shares of domestic production.

Institutional Reforms

In the area of institutional reform, the Uruguay Round strengthened the multilateral dispute settlement mechanism and established a new and permanent international institution, the World Trade Organization, responsible for governing the conduct of trade relations among its members. The new dispute settlement procedure instituted an appeals procedure, expedited decision making, and encouraged compliance with GATT decisions. Members of WTO are required to comply with the GATT rules as well as various agreements (rounds) negotiated under GATT auspices.

REGIONAL INTEGRATION AGREEMENTS (RIAs)

WTO members are permitted to enter into RIAs under specific conditions. Regional integration agreements must be consistent with the WTO rules, which require that the parties to the agreement (1) establish free trade on most goods in the regional area within ten years and (2) refrain from raising their tariffs against countries outside the agreement.

The number of RIAs and their share in global trade has been steadily rising over the past decade (see Tables 2.1 and 2.2). Since January 1995, approximately 196 RIAs have been notified to the WTO with 112 currently in

TABLE 2.1. Notifications of RIAs in Force to GATT/WTO (June 15, 2006)

	Accessions	New RIAs	Total
Free trade areas	4	122	126
Customs union	5	6	11
Enabling clause[a]	1	21	22
Free trade in services	2	36	38
Total	12	185	197

[a]Agreements between developing countries.

Source: Adapted from WTO, 2006.

TABLE 2.2. Merchandise Exports, 1993, 2002 (Billion U.S.$)

Source	Destination	1993	2002
U.S. exports to	Canada	100	161
	Mexico	42	97
Canadian exports to	USA	117	220
	Mexico	0.64	1.54
Mexican exports to	USA	42	143
	Canada	1.57	2.81
Total intra-NAFTA trade		303.82	625.8
NAFTA trade with rest of world		535.68	761.51

Source: Adapted from UNCTAD, 2002.

effect. During the period 2004-2005 alone, about forty-three RIAs were notified to the WTO (WTO, 2006). A large percentage of these agreements (over 80 percent) are mostly bilateral free trade deals intended for market access and do not require a high degree of policy coordination between participating countries. Less than 10 percent of the agreements provide for high levels of integration as well as harmonization of trade policies (customs union; see International Perspective 2.2).

Small countries enter into RIAs not only for market access but also to deal more effectively with larger economies in multilateral trade talks and other areas. Although RIAs are not often considered a potential threat to multilateralism, some scholars believe that (1) they lead to large volumes of

INTERNATIONAL PERSPECTIVE 2.2.
Stages of Economic Integration

Preferential Trade Arrangements: Agreement among participating nations to lower trade barriers. *Example:* British Commonwealth preference scheme, 1934.

Free Trade Area: All barriers are removed on trade among members but each nation retains its own barriers on trade with nonmembers. *Example:* The European Free Trade Area (EFTA) formed in 1960 by Austria, Denmark, Norway, Portugal, the U.K., Sweden, and Switzerland.

Customs Union: In addition to an agreement to lower or remove trade barriers, members establish a common system of tariffs against nonmembers (common external tariff). *Example:* The Andean Common Market, MERCOSUR.

Common Market: A common market includes all the elements of a customs union and allows free movement of labor and capital among member nations. *Example:* The European common market achieved common market status in 1970.

Economic Union: Economic union goes beyond a common market and requires members to harmonize and/or unify monetary and fiscal policies of member states. *Example:* Benelux, which includes Belgium, The Netherlands, and Luxembourg, formed in the 1920s and also forms part of the EU; the European Union.

trade diversion often leading to substantial welfare losses, (2) they create lobbies and interest groups against multilateral trade liberalization, and (3) their differing regulatory regimes including rules of origin pose a challenge to the multilateral trading system (Das, 2004).

The major drivers of RIAs are stated as follows:

- Consolidation of peace, regional security, and free market reforms in many countries
- Promotion of deeper levels of economic integration than what is available under the WTO (issues pertaining to competition, investment, labor, and the environment)
- Market access and a means of attracting foreign direct investment (FDI). Discriminatory liberalization in favor of partner countries is likely to provide firms (from these countries) with competitive advantages
- Sluggish progress in multilateral trade talks

THE NORTH AMERICAN
FREE TRADE AGREEMENT (NAFTA)

The North American Free Trade Agreement (NAFTA) established a free trade area among Canada, the United States, and Mexico. The agreement came into effect on January 1, 1994, after a difficult ratification by the U.S. Congress and approval by the Canadian and Mexican legislatures. The North American Free Trade Agreement gave rise to the second largest free trade zone (in terms of population) in the world after the European Union—439 million people and a joint gross domestic product exceeding $14 trillion— and constitutes one of the most comprehensive free trade pacts ever negotiated among regional trading partners. It is also the first reciprocal free trade pact between a developing nation and industrial countries (Hufbauer and Schott, 1994). Canada and the United States agreed to suspend the operation of the Canada–U.S. Free Trade Agreement so long as both countries are parties to NAFTA and to establish certain transitional arrangements.

Negotiating Objectives

The United States

Since World War II, the United States has advocated trade liberalization and the elimination, on a reciprocal and nondiscriminatory basis, of measures that restrict commercial transactions across national boundaries. To achieve this, it had relied on the GATT, now the WTO, and had demonstrated its commitment through its active participation in the successive rounds of trade negotiations under the GATT framework. However, the GATT process has been slow and ineffective in liberalizing trade in general, particularly in certain sectors such as agriculture. The regional approach was thus considered an attractive alternative to the multilateral framework for achieving rapid progress in trade liberalization. Second, the proliferation of regional common markets and the continued expansion of the European Union are considered to be important factors in influencing the United States to enter into a regional free trade agreement, as a response to the prevailing trend in international economic relations. Third, it was logical to embark on a free trade arrangement with Canada and Mexico, not only due to their geographical proximity but also because they are the most important trading partners to the United States. The United States is the destination for over 80 percent of Canadian and Mexican exports. Both countries also import about one-third of U.S. exports. The United States is also the largest investor in both countries. It was in the interest of the United States to maintain and expand existing trade and investment opportunities through a regional trade arrangement.

Canada

The North American Free Trade Agreement permits Canadian firms to achieve economies of scale by operating larger and more specialized plants. It also provides a secure access to a large consumer market. Even though tariff rates between United States and Canada have declined over time, there had been an increase in protectionist sentiment and use of aggressive trade remedies to protect domestic industries in the United States. These measures created uncertainty for producers with respect to investment in new facilities. The North American Free Trade Agreement reduces this uncertainty since it provides rules and procedures for the application of trade remedies and the resolution of disputes.

Mexico

The North American Free Trade Agreement provides secure access to the U.S. and Canadian markets for Mexican goods and services. Its low labor costs and access to the U.S. market attracts FDI to Mexico (Echeverri-Carroll, 1995; Lederman, Maloney, and Serven, 2005). In view of the adverse impact of its import substitution policy in the 1980s and the debt crisis, trade liberalization was considered to be an effective means of fostering domestic reform and achieving sustainable growth. Ostry briefly describes Mexico's objectives:

> So NAFTA is a means of consolidating an export-led growth path both by improving secure access to the U.S. market and encouraging a return of flight capital as well as new investment. (Quoted in Randall, Konrad, and Silverman, 1992, pp. 27-28)

Overview of NAFTA

Market Access for Goods

The North American Free Trade Agreement incorporates the basic national treatment obligation of the GATT. This means that goods imported from any member country will not be subject to discrimination in favor of domestic products. It provides for a gradual elimination over fifteen years of tariffs for trade between Mexico and Canada, as well as between Mexico and the United States, except for certain agricultural products. Under the Canada–U.S. Free Trade Agreement, tariffs between the two countries were eliminated in January 1998.

By January of 1998, tariffs had been phased out on about 65 percent of all U.S. exports to Mexico. For certain import-sensitive sectors in which quotas are imposed, the agreement provides for a replacement with a sliding tariff quota over ten or fifteen years. The North American Free Trade Agreement also provides for a gradual elimination of nontariff barriers such as customs user fees, import licenses, export taxes, and duty drawbacks on NAFTA-made goods. Since NAFTA would gradually phase out tariffs within the free trade area, such drawbacks will no longer be necessary. To qualify for preferential market access, however, goods must be wholly or substantially made or produced within the member countries. For example, farm goods wholly grown or substantially processed within the NAFTA region would qualify for NAFTA treatment.

Services

The agreement governs financial, telecommunications, trucking, and rail services. With respect to financial services, NAFTA commits each party to treat service providers such as banks and insurance companies from other NAFTA parties no less favorably than its own service providers in like circumstances. It also commits members to gradually phase out, during the transition period, limits on equity ownership by foreign individuals or corporations and on market share by foreign financial institutions. Mexico was allowed to set temporary capital limits for banks, securities firms, and insurance companies during the transition period. The agreement allows members to take prudential measures to protect the integrity of the financial system or consumers of financial services. It includes a freeze on restrictions governing cross-border trade in financial services and also provides for consultations and a dispute settlement mechanism.

The North American Free Trade Agreement commits members to impose no conditions (i.e., reasonable and nondiscriminatory terms) on access to, or use of, public telecommunication networks unless they are necessary to safeguard the public service responsibilities of the network operators or the technical integrity of the networks. It also imposes an obligation to prevent anticompetitive conduct by monopolies in basic services.

The agreement (1) removes most limitations on cross-border trucking and rail, and liberalizes Mexican investment restrictions in these sectors, and (2) preserves existing cabotage laws, that is, laws that allow a truck to carry goods to and from a given destination but not to make additional stops unless the vehicle and cargo are registered in the country.

Investment

Investment includes majority-controlled or minority interests, portfolio investments, and investments in real property from member countries. All three countries agree to (1) provide national treatment to investors from member countries, a treatment that is not less favorable than that given to an investor from a non-NAFTA country; (2) prohibit the imposition and enforcement of certain performance requirements in connection with the conduct or operation of investments, such as export requirements or domestic content; and (3) severely restrict or prohibit investment in their most strategic industries, such as energy (Mexico), cultural industries (Canada), nuclear energy, and broadcasting (all three countries). Both Canada and Mexico reserve the right to screen potential investors in certain cases. The parties also agree to subject disputes raised by foreign investors to international arbitration.

Intellectual Property

The North American Free Trade Agreement mandates minimum standards for the protection of intellectual property rights (IPRs) in member countries and requires each country to extend national treatment to IPRs owned by nationals of other countries. The scope of IPR protection includes patents, trademarks, trade secrets, copyright, and industrial designs. It also extends to semiconductors, sound recordings, and satellite broadcast signals. Patents are to be provided for products or processes that are new, useful, and nonobvious. They are valid for twenty years from the date of filing, or seventeen years from the date of grant. The agreement permits the use of compulsory licensing (i.e., a requirement to grant licenses to local companies or individuals if the patent is not used in the country) in limited circumstances. The North American Free Trade Agreement protects registered trademarks for a term of no less than seven years, renewable indefinitely. It harmonizes members' laws on trademark protection and enforcement. The agreement prohibits "trademark-linking" requirements in which foreign owners of trademarks are to use their mark in conjunction with a mark owned by a national of that country. The North American Free Trade Agreement requires adequate protection for trade secrets and does not limit the duration of protection. Copyright protection is extended to computer software and provides owners of computer programs and sound recordings with "rental rights" (i.e., the right to authorize or prohibit the rental of programs or recordings). It ensures protection of copyright for a minimum period of fifty years and gives effect to the 1971 Berne Convention on artistic and literary works.

Government Procurement

Purchase of goods and services by government entities in member countries is estimated at over one trillion dollars. The North American Free Trade Agreement extends the national treatment standard (equal treatment to all member country providers) for all goods and services procured by federal government entities unless specifically exempted. Procurement contracts must, however, meet certain minimum value thresholds: $50,000 for contract of goods, and/or services and $6.5 million for construction contracts procured by federal government entities. For government enterprises, the threshold is $250,000 for contract of goods and/or services and $8 million for construction services. For U.S. and Canadian entities, the Canada–U.S. Free Trade Agreement maintains the threshold at $25,000 for goods contracts. It provides tendering procedures and bid-challenging mechanisms to seek a review of any aspect of the procurement process by an independent authority.

Safeguards

If a surge in imports causes serious injury to domestic producers, a member country is allowed to take emergency action temporarily, for up to four years, to protect the industry. A request for emergency action is usually initiated by a domestic industry. A number of factors are considered by the investigating tribunal in arriving at a decision on injury: the level of increase in imports, market share of the imports, changes in sales, production, profits, employment, and other pertinent variables.

Technical and Other Standards

The North American Free Trade Agreement requires a member to provide sixty days notice before adopting new standards to allow for comments before implementation. It prohibits members from using standards as a disguised restriction to trade. Working groups are established to adopt or harmonize technical and other standards pertaining to specific sectors.

Other Areas

The agreement (1) requires members to create and maintain rules against anticompetitive business practices, (2) allows for temporary entry of businesspersons and certain professionals who are citizens of another member country—NAFTA does not create a common market for the movement of labor, (3) establishes institutions such as the Free Trade Commission (FTC) to supervise the implementation of the agreement and resolve disputes, and (4) creates a secretariat, composed of national offices in each country, to support the commission. The agreement also allows any country or group of countries to join NAFTA, subject to approval by each member country and on such terms as agreed upon by the FTC.

Dispute Settlement

Disputes arising over the implementation of the agreement may be resolved through (1) consultations; (2) mediation, conciliation, or other means of dispute resolution that might facilitate an amicable resolution; or (3) a panel of nongovernmental experts. If the decision is made by a binding panel (binding dispute settlement), the parties are required to comply within thirty days or else compensation/retaliation may result. If the decision is reached by a nonbinding panel, parties shall comply or agree on another solution within thirty days or else compensation/retaliation may result. Panel reports are not automatically enforceable in domestic law.

Separate dispute settlement mechanisms are in place for certain specialized areas, such as financial services, investment, environment, standards, and private commercial disputes, as well as dumping and subsidies.

Preliminary Assessment of NAFTA

The full impact of NAFTA can only be determined in the long term after the necessary economic adjustments have taken place. Although a short-term assessment of such a comprehensive agreement is often inadequate and sometimes misleading, a cursory discussion will be made on economic conditions since NAFTA.

Overall Increase in Trade between Members

There has been a marked increase in trade among the three member countries since the agreement went into effect in January 1994 (U.S. Census, 1993-2003). Intra-NAFTA trade jumped from $304 billion in 1993 to $626 billion in 2002 compared to NAFTA's trade with the rest of the world, which increased by only 42 percent (from $536 billion to $762 billion) during the same period. An increasing portion of Canadian and Mexican trade is conducted with the United States. The United States accounted for 86 percent of Canadian exports (76 percent of its imports) and 89 percent of Mexican exports (62 percent of its imports) in 2005. During the same year, the two countries accounted for about 36 percent of U.S. exports (23 percent for Canada and 13 percent for Mexico; see Table 2.3).

TABLE 2.3. Gross Inward FDI Flows 1994, 2001 (Billion U.S. $)

Country	1994	% of world FDI flows	2001	% of world FDI flows
Canada	8.2	3.2	27.46	3.7
Mexico	10.64	4.2	25.33	3.4
USA	45.1	17.6	124.44	16.9

Source: Adapted from UNCTAD (2002)

Increase in the U.S. Trade Deficit

The U.S. merchandise trade deficit with Canada and Mexico quadrupled since NAFTA. By 2005, U.S. exports to Canada and Mexico had grown to $330 billion. However, this was not sufficient to offset the growing trade deficit with both countries. The U.S. trade deficit with Canada and Mexico stands at $76.4 and 50 billion (U.S.), respectively in 2005.

NAFTA's Impact on Jobs is Uncertain

There is no conclusive evidence on the effect of NAFTA on jobs. There are certain indications, however, that NAFTA may have had a negative effect on jobs. Between 1994 and 2002, the U.S. Department of Labor certified 525,000 workers for income support and training due to loss of jobs arising from shifts in production to Mexico or Canada. In view of its narrow eligibility criteria, the program covers a small number of workers who lost their jobs due to NAFTA. Most of the job dislocations appear to be concentrated in apparel and electronic industries. This may be attributed to the growing trade deficit with both countries, which often leads to declines in production and employment. There are also some studies that show the negative effects of NAFTA on agricultural employment and real wages in manufacturing in Mexico. The Canadian Center for Policy Alternatives states that the Canadian government reduced social spending (such as qualification for unemployment insurance) to enhance competitiveness (Campbell, 2006).

Substantial Increase in Foreign Investment in all Countries

Since NAFTA, there has been a substantial growth in inward FDI flows in member countries (Weintraub, 2004; see Table 2.4).

TABLE 2.4. NAFTA and EU: Major Differences

NAFTA	EU
NAFTA does not provide for a common external tariff	EU has a common external tariff
NAFTA has no provision for economic assistance or economic/monetary union	EU provides for economic assistance to members and economic/monetary union
NAFTA does not provide for free movement of labor	EU allows for free movement of labor

THE EUROPEAN UNION

The European Union (EU) is the oldest and most significant economic integration scheme, involving twenty-seven Western and Eastern European countries: Austria, Belgium, Bulgaria, Cyprus, Czech Republic, Denmark, Estonia, Finland, France, Germany, Greece, Hungary, Ireland, Italy, Latvia, Lithuania, Luxembourg, Malta, the Netherlands, Poland, Portugal, Romania, Slovakia, Slovenia, Spain, Sweden, and the United Kingdom. One of the most important developments is the recent EU enlargement from fifteen to twenty-five countries in May 2004, with the admission of Cyprus, Malta, and eight East European countries. In January 2007, Bulgaria and Romania also joined the EU, increasing the number to twenty-seven countries. Turkey and other East European countries will be considered for admission in the coming years based on certain criteria such as stable democratic institutions, free markets, and ability to assume EU treaty obligations (Van Oudenaren, 2002; Poole, 2003).

Even though the European economic integration dates back to the Treaty of Rome in 1957, the European Union is the outcome of the Maastricht treaty in 1992. The European Union has an aggregate population of about 456 million and a total economic output (GDP) of $12 trillion (U.S.) (2005), and involves the largest transfer of national sovereignty to a common institution. In certain designated areas, for example, international agreements can only be made by the European Union on behalf of member states (Wild, Wild, and Han, 2006).

The pursuit of such integration was partly influenced by the need to create a lasting peace in Europe as well as to establish a stronger Europe that could compete economically against the United States and Japan (see Table 2.5). Since the countries were not large enough to compete in global markets, they had to unite in order to exploit economies of large-scale production.

TABLE 2.5. Other Major Regional Trade Agreements

The European Free Trade (EFTA, 1960)	*Members:* Iceland, Liechtenstein, Norway, Switzerland *Objectives:* Removal of customs barriers and differing technical standards. Free trade with EU strictly limited to commercial matters
The Preferential Area for Eastern and Southern American Common Market (MERCOSUR, 1991)	*Members:* Argentina, Brazil, Paraguay, Uruguay, Venezuela. Chile and Bolivia joined as associate members *Objectives:* Free trade and industrial cooperation
The Central American Common Market (CACM, 1960)	*Members:* Costa Rica, El Salvador, Guatemala, Honduras, Nicaragua *Objectives:* Free trade and a common external tariff
The Andean Pact, 1969	*Members:* Bolivia, Colombia, Ecuador, Peru, Venezuela *Objectives:* Free trade and industrial development
The Association of Southeast Asian Nations (ASEAN, 1967)	*Members:* Brunei, Cambodia, Indonesia, Laos, Malaysia, Myanmar, Philippines, Singapore, Thailand, Vietnam *Objectives:* Reduction of trade barriers, industrial cooperation
The Caribbean Common Market (CARICOM, 1973)	*Members:* Antigua and Barbuda, The Bahamas, Barbados, Belize, Dominica, Grenada, Haiti, Guyana, Jamaica, Montserrat, St. Kitts and Nevis, St. Lucia, St. Vincent and the Grenadines, Trinidad and Tobago, Suriname *Objectives:* Political unity, economic cooperation
The Southern African Customs Union (SACU, 1969)	*Members:* Botswana, Lesotho, Namibia, South Africa, Swaziland *Objectives:* Free movement of goods, common external tariff
The Economic Community of West African States (ECOWAS, 1974)	*Members:* Benin, Burkina Faso, Cape Verde, Cote d'Ivoire, the Gambia, Ghana, Guinea, Guinea-Bissau, Liberia, Mali, Niger, Nigeria, Senegal, Sierra Leone, Togo *Objectives:* Economic and monetary union
Asia Pacific Economic Cooperation (APEC, 1989)	*Members:* Australia, Brunei, Canada, Chile, China, Japan, S. Korea, Malaysia, Mexico, New Zealand, Papua New Guinea, the Phillippines, Peru, Russia, Singapore, Taiwan, Thailand, USA, Vietnam *Objectives:* Strengthen the multilateral trading system, simplify and liberalize trade and investment procedures among members

The objectives of European integration as stated in the Treaty of Rome (1957) are as follows:

- To create free trade among member states and provide uniform customs duties for goods imported from outside the EU (common external tariff).
- To abolish restrictions on the free movement of all factors of production, that is, labor, services, and capital. Member states are required to extend the national treatment standard to goods, services, capital, etc., from other member countries with respect to taxation and other matters (nondiscrimination).
- To establish a common transport, agricultural, and competition policy.

A number of the objectives set out in the Treaty of Rome were successfully accomplished. The Common Agricultural Policy (CAP) was established in 1962 to maintain common prices for agricultural products throughout the community and to stabilize farm incomes. Tariffs between member nations were eliminated and a common external tariff established in 1968. However, efforts to achieve the other objectives, such as a single internal market (elimination of nontariff barriers), free movement of services or capital, and so forth, had been slow and difficult. Coordinated or common policies in certain areas such as transport simply did not exist (Archer and Butler, 1992).

The European Commission (for other EU institutions, see International Perspective 2.3) presented a proposal in 1985 to remove existing barriers to the establishment of a genuine common market. The proposal, which was adopted and entitled The Single European Act (SEA), constitutes a major revision to the Treaty of Rome. The SEA set the following objectives for its members:

- To complete the single market by removing all the remaining barriers to trade such as customs controls at borders, harmonization of technical standards, liberalization of public procurement, provision of services, removal of obstacles to the free movement of workers, and so on. In short, efforts involved the removal of physical, technical, and fiscal (different excise and value added taxes) barriers to trade.
- To encourage monetary cooperation leading to a single European currency. The Maastricht Treaty of 1992 further reinforced this and defined plans for achieving economic and monetary union.
- To establish cooperation on research and development (R & D) and create a common standard on environmental policy.
- To harmonize working conditions across the community and improve the dialogue between management and labor.

INTERNATIONAL PERSPECTIVE 2.3.
Institutions of the European Union

The European Council: Composed of representatives (ministers) of member states, the council sets out general direction of the union. The council approves legislation and international agreements, acting on a proposal from the commission and after consulting with the European Parliament.

The European Commission: Members of the commission are chosen by the mutual agreement of national governments and serve four-year terms. Larger nations appoint two while smaller nations appoint one commissioner. They neither represent nor take orders from member states. The commission initiates policies and ensures members' compliance with the treaty.

The European Parliament: Composed of 732 representatives directly elected, the European Parliament supervises the commission, adopts the community budget, and influences the legislative process. Any agreement concerning international cooperation must be reviewed and accepted by Parliament before it is concluded. The parliament, however, does not have express legislative powers.

The Court of Justice: Settles disputes arising from the treaty (i.e., interprets and applies the EU treaty). The judges are appointed by mutual agreement of member states and serve six-year terms. The court ensures uniform interpretation and application of community law, evaluates legality of legislation adopted by the council and the commission, and provides rulings on community law when requested by national courts in member states.

The Single European Act established a concrete plan and timetable to complete the internal market by 1992. It is fair to state that most of the objectives set out under the SEA were accomplished: border checks are largely eliminated, free movement of workers has been achieved through mutual recognition of qualifications from any accredited institution within the EU, free movement of capital (banks, insurance, and investment services) has been made possible with certain limitations, and the single currency (the Euro) was introduced in 1999. The Euro has helped reduce transaction costs by eliminating the need to convert currencies and made prices between markets more transparent. There still exist a number of challenges in completing and sustaining the single market, expanding EU policy responsibilities in certain controversial areas such as energy policy, and undertaking appropriate structural reforms to take advantage of the economic and monetary union.

CHAPTER SUMMARY

The GATT/WTO

Principal objectives of the GATT: Nondiscrimination, trade liberalization, and settlement of trade disputes between members.

The Uruguay Round of the GATT and the Birth of WTO

Important results of the Uruguay Round trade negotiations (1986-1994): Reductions in tariffs, adoption of new trade rules on unfair trade practices, GATT coverage extended to trade in services, intellectual property, and trade-related investment measures, and the birth of WTO.

The North American Free Trade Agreement (NAFTA)

Scope of coverage: Market access for goods, services, investment, protection of intellectual property, government procurement, safeguards, standards, and dispute settlement.

NAFTA: Preliminary Assessment

Increases in overall trade between members, increase in the U.S. trade deficit on merchandise trade with members, and a rise in foreign investment.

The European Union (EU)

Major objectives of the EU: To create free trade and a common external tariff between members, to abolish restrictions on the free movement of all factors of production, to establish common policies in the area transport, agriculture, competition, etc.

Institutions of the EU: The European Council, the European Commission, the European Parliament, the Court of Justice.

Other Regional Trade Agreements

The European Free Trade Area (EFTA), MERCOSUR, The Central American Common Market (CACM), The Andean Pact, The Association of Southeast Asian Nations (ASEAN), The Caribbean Common Market (CARICOM), The Southern African Customs Union (SACU), The Economic Community of West African States (ECOWAS).

REVIEW QUESTIONS

1. What were the major achievements of the Uruguay Round of the GATT/WTO?
2. Distinguish between the most-favored nation and national treatment standard in international trade.
3. Discuss the major drivers of regional trade agreements.
4. Compare and contrast the negotiating objectives of Canada and Mexico behind NAFTA.
5. Discuss NAFTA pertaining to services and investment. Has it increased trade between the member countries?
6. What are the various stages of economic integration?
7. What are the objectives of European integration? Which countries joined the EU in 2004?
8. Discuss the major differences between NAFTA and the EU.
9. What were the major achievements of the Single European Act?
10. What is the role of the EU commission?

CASE 2.1. THE BENEFITS AND COSTS OF FREE TRADE

Since 1980, the orthodox recipe for economic growth has been the re-duction of barriers to the free flow of commerce and capital. International institutions such as the IMF and the World Bank have contended that the free market approach to development will create faster levels of economic growth and alleviate poverty. The integration of markets has been largely achieved through regional free trade agreements and unilateral liberaliza-tion. It has also been facilitated by deregulation, the shrinking costs of com-munications and transportation, and the IT revolution.

Some developing countries benefited from trade liberalization. China's ratio of trade to GDP doubled. Brazil, Mexico, and other middle-income countries registered large increases in their volume of trade. They managed to export a range of manufactured goods often as part of global production net-works. In China, the number of poor people (earning less than $0.70 a day) decreased from 250 million in 1978 to 34 million in 1999. Similarly in India, the number decreased from 330 million in 1977 to 259 million in 1999.

In the case of many other nations, however, the laissez-faire approach appears to have worsened growth rates and income distribution. In 1980, for example, the medium income in the richest 10 percent of countries was seventy-seven times greater than in the poorest 10 percent. By 1999, this gap had grown to 122 times (see Table 2.6). Many studies show that trade

TABLE 2.6. Distribution of World Income[a]

	1980	1990	1999
By Countries			
Ratio of average incomes	86.20	125.90	148.80
Ratio of medium incomes	76.8	119.6	121.8
By Population			
Ratio of average incomes	78.9	119.7	117.7
Ratio of medium incomes	69.6	121.5	100.8
By Population, Excluding China			
Ratio of average incomes	90.3	135.5	154.4
Ratio of medium incomes	81.1	131.2	153.2

Source: Adapted from IMF, 2000.

[a]Ratio of income of the richest 10 percent of countries/population to that of the poorest 10 percent of countries/population.

liberalization in Latin America, for example, led to widening wage gaps, falling real wages for unskilled workers, and rising unemployment. In many countries, trade liberalization and deregulated markets have induced rapid structural changes often leading to declining wages, working conditions, and living standards. The challenge today is to make trade liberalization work for the poor. This requires a wide-ranging reform in national institutions and policies.

Questions

1. How can trade liberalization be made to work for the poor?
2. Select a country or region and evaluate its performance (GDP per capita, distribution of income, etc.) before and after trade liberalization.

SECTION II:
EXPORT MARKETING
AND STRATEGY

Chapter 3

Setting Up the Business

Whether it is a new or existing export-import business, the legal form, or structure, will determine how the business is to be conducted, its tax liability, and other important considerations. Each form of business organization has its own advantages and disadvantages, and the entrepreneur has to select the one that best fulfills the goals of the entrepreneur and the business. (For questions to consider before starting a business, see International Perspective 3.1.)

Selection of an appropriate business organization is a task that requires accounting and legal expertise and should be done with the advice of a competent attorney or accountant.

OWNERSHIP STRUCTURE

In this section, we examine different forms of business organizations: sole proprietorships, partnerships, corporations, and limited liability companies.

Sole Proprietorships

A sole proprietorship is a firm owned and operated by one individual. No separate legal entity exists. There is one principal in the business who has total control over all export-import operations and who can make decisions without consulting anyone. The major advantages of sole proprietorships are as follows:

1. They are easy to organize and simple to control. Establishing an export-import business as sole proprietorship is simple and inexpensive and requires little or no government approval. At the state level,

Export-Import Theory, Practices, and Procedures, Second Edition

registration of the business name is required, while at the federal level, sole proprietors need to keep accurate accounting records and attach a profit or loss statement for the business when filing individual tax returns (Schedule C, Internal Revenue Service Form 1040). They must operate on a calendar year and can use the cash or accrual method of accounting.

2. They are more flexible to manage than partnerships or corporations. The owner makes all operational and management decisions concerning the business. The owner can remove money or other assets of the business without legal or tax consequences. He or she can also easily transfer or terminate the business.

3. Sole proprietorships are subject to minimal government regulations versus other business concerns.

4. The owner of a sole proprietorship is taxed as an individual, at a rate lower than the corporate income tax rate. Losses from the export-import business can be applied by the owner to offset taxable income from other sources. Sole proprietors are also allowed to establish tax-exempt retirement accounts (Harper, 1991; Cheeseman, 2006a).

The major disadvantage of running an export-import concern as a sole proprietorship is the risk of unlimited liability. The owner is personally liable for the debts and other liabilities of the business. Insurance can be bought to protect against these liabilities; however, if insurance protection is not sufficient to cover legal liability for defective products or debts, judgment credi-

INTERNATIONAL PERSPECTIVE 3.1.
Establishing an Appropriate Business Organization:
Pointers

- Does the entrepreneur intend to be the sole owner of the export-import business? If not, how many people have an ownership interest?
- Does the entrepreneur need additional capital and/or expertise?
- What legal form provides the greatest flexibility for management?
- What legal form affords the most advantageous tax treatment for the business concern and individual entrepreneurs?
- Which legal structure is easy and less expensive to establish and subject to a low degree of government regulation?
- How important is it to limit personal liability of owners?
- Which legal structure is the most appropriate in light of the goals and objectives of the export-import business?

tors' next recourse is the personal assets of the owner. Another disadvantage is that the proprietor's access to capital is limited to personal funds plus any loans that can be obtained. In addition, very few individuals have all the necessary skills to run an export-import business, and the owner may lack certain skills. The business may also terminate upon the death or disability of the owner.

Partnerships

A partnership is an association of two or more persons to carry on as co-owners of a business for profit. "Persons" is broadly interpreted to include corporations, partnerships, or other associations. "Co-ownership" refers to a sharing of ownership of the business and is determined by two major factors: share of the business profits and management responsibility. The sharing of profits creates a rebuttable presumption that a partnership exists. The presumption about the existence of a partnership is disproved if profits are shared as payment of a debt, wages to an employee, interest on a loan, or rent to a landlord.

> *Example:* Suppose Gardinia Export Company owes Kimko Realty $10,000 in rent. Gardinia promises to pay Kimko 20 percent of its business profits until the rent is fully paid. Kimko realty is sharing profits from the business but is not presumed to be a partner in the export business.

Although a written agreement is not required, it is advisable for partners to have some form of written contract that establishes the rights and obligations of the parties. Since partnerships dissolve upon the death of any partner that owns more than 10 percent interest, the agreement should ascertain the rights of the deceased partner's spouse and that of surviving partners in a way that is least disruptive of the partnership.

A partnership is a legal entity only for limited purposes, such as the capacity to sue or be sued, to collect judgments, to have title of ownership of partnership property, or to have all accounting procedures in the name of the partnership. Federal courts recognize partnerships as legal entities in such matters as lawsuits in federal courts (when a federal question is involved), bankruptcy proceedings, and the filing of informational tax returns (profit and loss statement that each partner reports on individual returns). The partnership, however, has no tax liability. A partner's profit or loss from the partnership is included in each partner's income tax return and taxed as income to the individual partner (Cooke, 1995; Cheeseman, 2006b).

Partners are personally liable for the debts of the partnership. However, in some states, the judgment creditor (the plaintiff in whose favor a judgment is entered by a court) must exhaust the remedies against partnership property before proceeding to execute against the individual property of the partners.

What are the duties and powers of partners? The fiduciary duty that partners owe the partnership and the other partners is a relationship of trust and loyalty. Each partner is a general agent of the partnership in any business transaction within the scope of the partnership agreement. For example, when a partner in an import business contracts to import merchandise, both the partner and the partnership share liability unless the seller knows that the partner has no such authority. In the latter case, the partner who signed the contract will be personally liable but not the partnership. A partner's action can bind the partnership to third parties if his or her action is consistent with the scope of authority, that is, expressed or implied authority provided in the partnership agreement (Cheeseman, 2006a).

Limited Partnerships

A limited partnership is a special form of partnership which consists of at least one general (investor and manager) partner and one or more limited (investor) partners. The general partner is given the right to manage the partnership and is personally liable for the debts and obligations of the limited partnership. The limited partner, however, does not participate in management and is liable only to the extent of his or her capital contribution. Any person can be a general or limited partner, and this includes natural persons, partnerships, or corporations. Limited partners have no right to bind the partnership in any contract and owe no fiduciary duty to that partnership or the other partners due to the limited nature of their interest in the partnership.

Whereas a general partnership may be formed with little or no formality, the creation of a limited partnership is based on compliance with certain statutory requirements. The certificate of limited partnership must be executed and signed by the parties. It should include certain specific information and be filed with the secretary of state and the appropriate county to be legal and binding. The limited partnership is taxed in exactly the same way as a general partnership. A limited partner's losses from an export-import business could be used to offset income generated only by other passive activities, that is, investments in other limited partnerships (passive loss rules). They cannot be used against salaries, dividends, interest, or other income from portfolio investments. Both types of partnership can be useful in international trade. They bring complimentary assets needed to distribute and/or commercialize the product or service. The combination of skills by different partners usually increases the speed with which the product/service enters a market and generally contributes to the success of the business. Limited partners may also be useful when capital is needed by exporters or importers to prepare a marketing plan, expand channels of distribution, increase the scope and volume of goods or services traded, and so on. However, potential exists for conflict among partners unless there exists a partnership agreement that eliminates or mitigates any sources of conflict. If limited partners become involved in marketing or other management decisions of the export-import firm, they are considered general partners and, hence, assume unlimited risk for the debts of the partnership (Anderson and Dunkelberg, 1993; Cheeseman, 2006a).

Corporations

A corporation is a legal entity separate from the people who own or operate it and created pursuant to the laws of the state in which the business is incorporated. Many export-import companies prefer this form of business organization due to the advantage of limited liability of shareholders. This means that shareholders are liable only to the extent of their investments. These companies could be sued for any harm or damage they cause in the distribution of the product, and that incorporation limits the liability of such companies to the assets of the business. Other advantages of incorporation are *free transferability of shares, perpetual existence, and ability to raise additional capital by selling shares in the corporation.* However, most of these companies are closely held corporations; that is, shares are owned by few shareholders who are often family members, relatives, or friends, and not traded on national stock exchanges.

Export-import corporations as legal entities have certain rights and obligations: they can sue or be sued in their own names, enter into or enforce contracts, and own or transfer property. They are also responsible for violation of the law. Criminal liability includes loss of a right to do business with the government, a fine, or any other sanction.

If an export-import company that is incorporated in one state conducts intrastate business (transacts local business in another state), such as selling merchandise or services in another state, it is required to file and qualify as a "foreign corporation" to do business in the other state. Conducting intrastate business usually includes maintaining an office to conduct such business. Using independent contractors for sales, soliciting orders to be accepted outside of the state, or conducting isolated business transactions do not require qualification to do business in another state. The qualification procedure entails filing certain information with the secretary of state, payment of the required fees, and appointing a registered agent that is empowered to accept service of process on behalf of the corporation.

The process of forming a corporation (incorporating) can be expensive and time consuming. A corporation comes into existence when a certificate of incorporation, signed by one or more persons, is filed with the secretary of state. The corporation code in every state describes the types of information to be included in the articles of incorporation. Generally, they include provisions such as the purpose for which the corporation is organized, its duration, and powers of the corporation.

Many businesses incorporate their companies in the state of Delaware even when it is not the state in which the corporation does most of its business. This is because Delaware has laws that are very favorable to businesses' internal operations and management. It is even more ideal for companies that plan to operate with little or no surpluses or that have a large number of inaccessible shareholders, making obtaining their consent difficult when needed (Friedman, 1993).

One of the main disadvantages of a corporation as a form of business organization is that its profits are subject to double taxation. Tax is imposed by federal and state governments on profits earned by the company, and later, those profits are taxed as income when distributed to shareholders. Companies often avoid this by increasing salaries and bonuses for their owners and reporting substantially reduced profits. In this way, the income will be subject to tax when the owners or shareholders receive it rather than at the corporate level *and* the individual level.

It is important that export-import companies maintain a separate identity from that of their owners. This includes having a separate bank account, export/distributor contracts in the name of the company, hold stockholders meetings, and so on. In circumstances in which corporations are formed without sufficient capital or when there is a nonseparation of corporate and personal affairs, courts have disregarded the corporate entity. The implication of this is that shareholders may be found personally liable for the debts and obligations of the company. The corporate entity is also disregarded in cases in which the corporation is primarily used to defraud others and for similar illegitimate purposes, such as money laundering, trade in narcotics, or funneling money to corrupt officials (bribery).

Directors and officers of export-import companies owe a duty of trust and loyalty to the corporation and its shareholders. Directors and officers must act within their scope of authority (duty of obedience) and exercise honest and prudent business judgment (duty of care) in the conduct of the affairs of the corporation. In the absence of these, they could be held personally liable for any resultant damages to the corporation or its shareholders. Breach of duty of obedience and care by directors and officers of an export-import company could include one or more of the following:

- *Investment of profits:* Investment of profits from export-import operations in a way that is not provided in the articles of incorporation or corporate bylaw.
- *Corporate decisions:* Making export-import decisions without being adequately informed, in bad faith, and at variance with the goals and objectives of the company.

S Corporations

The subchapter S Revision Act of 1982 divides corporations into two categories: S corporations and C corporations, that is, all other corporations. If an export company elects to be an S corporation, it has the best of advantages of a corporation and a partnership. Similar to a corporation, it offers the benefits of limited liability, but still permits the owner to pay taxes as an individual, thereby avoiding double taxation. One advantage of paying taxes at the level of the individual shareholder is that export-import companies' losses could be used to offset shareholders' taxable income from other sources. It is also beneficial when the corporation makes a profit and when a shareholder falls within a lower income tax bracket than the corporation. However, the corporation's election to be taxed as an S corporation is based on the following preconditions:

1. *Domestic entity:* The corporation must be a domestic entity, that is, it must be incorporated in the United States.
2. *No membership in an affiliated group:* The corporation cannot be a member of an affiliated group (not part of another organization).
3. *Number of shareholders:* The corporation can have no more than seventy-five shareholders.
4. *Shareholders:* Shareholders must be individuals or estates. Corporations and partnerships cannot be shareholders. Shareholders must also be citizens or residents of the United States.
5. *Classes of stock:* The corporation cannot have more than one class of stock.
6. *Corporate income:* No more than 20 percent of the corporation's income can be from passive investment income (dividends, interest, royalties, rents, annuities, etc.).

Failure to maintain any one of the previous conditions will lead to cancellation of the S corporation status. Another election after cancellation of status cannot be made for five years.

Limited Liability Companies

This form of business organization combines the best of all the other forms. It has the advantages of limited liability and no restrictions on the number of owners or their nationalities (as in the case of S corporations). It is taxed as a partnership, and, unlike limited partnerships, it does not grant limited liability on the condition that the members refrain from active participation in the management of the company. To be taxed as a partnership, a limited liability company (LLC) can possess any of the following attributes: two or more persons as associates, objectives to carry on business and divide gains, limited liability, centralized management and continuity, and free transferability of interests (Cheeseman, 2006b). Such a company can be formed by two or more persons (natural or legal) and its articles of incorporation filed with the appropriate state agency. Limited liability companies provide the advantage of limited liability, management structure (participation in management without being subject to personal liability), and partnership tax status. It has become a popular form of business for subsidiaries of foreign corporations as well as small-scale and medium-sized businesses (August, 2004).

BUSINESS OR TRADE NAME

A sole proprietorship or partnership that is engaged in an export-import business can operate under the name of the sole proprietor or one or more of the partners. There are no registration requirements with any government agency. However, if the sole proprietorship or partnership operates under a fictitious name, it must file a fictitious business name statement with the appropriate government agency. Most states also require publication of the trade name in a local newspaper serving the area where the business is located.

> *Example:* Suppose John Rifkin wants to operate an export-import business (sole proprietorship) under the name "Global." This is commonly stated as: "John Rifkin doing business as Global."

Corporations are required to register their business name with the state. It is important to obtain permission to use a trade name before incorporation. This is intended to ensure that (1) the trade name does not imply a purpose inconsistent with that stated in the articles of incorporation, and (2) the trade name is not deceptively similar to registered and reserved names of other companies incorporated to do business in the state. The secretary of state or other designated agency will do a search before authorizing the party to use the name (Cheeseman, 2006a).

Unlike the effect of corporate name registration, registration of fictitious names does not prevent the use of the same name by others. This is because most states do not have a central registry of fictitious business names and that registration of such names is simply intended to indicate the person doing business under the trade name. To avoid registration of a similar trade name, it is advisable to check records of counties as well as local telephone directories for existing fictitious business names (McGrath, Elias, and Shena, 1996).

Another important issue is the potential problems that ensue when such names are used as trademarks to identify goods or services. Suppose John Rifkin intends to use the trade name "Global" to market his perfume imports. It is important to ensure that the same or similar name is not being used or registered with the U.S. Patent and Trademarks Office by another party prior to Rifkin's use of "Global" as a mark. The basic principles also apply in the case of corporations. If Rifkin used "Global" as a trademark in connection with his trade or business for some time, he acquires exclusive use of the mark regardless of the previous registration of the same or similar mark by others. Once a trader acquires a reputation in respect of his mark, then it becomes part of his goodwill, which is regarded by law as part of personal property that may be sold or licensed.

BANK ACCOUNTS, PERMITS, AND LICENSES

An export-import firm must open a bank account with an international bank that can accommodate specialized transactions such as letters of credit, foreign exchange payments, forfeiting, and so on. Some international banks have subsidiaries in importing countries that can verify the creditworthiness of foreign buyers. Sole proprietors and partnerships can open a bank account by submitting an affidavit of the fictitious business name statement to the bank with the initial deposit. In the case of a corporation, banks often require articles of incorporation, an affidavit that the company exists, and its tax identification number. It is important to check with the city or county to determine if permits or business licenses are required.

LOCATION AND USE OF PROFESSIONAL SERVICES

When the export-import business is small, it is economical to use one's home as an office during the early phase of the operations. Besides saving money and travel time, using a portion of a home provides opportunities for deduction of expenses related to the business. All of the direct expenses for the business part of the home, for example, painting or repairs, are deductible expenses. The business use of a home may, however, provide the wrong impression to credit-rating agencies or clients who may decide to pay an impromptu visit. Another problem with using one's home is that it may violate a city's bylaws that prohibit the conduct of any trade or business in an area that is zoned strictly for residential purposes. Homeowner's insurance coverage may not cover business equipment, merchandise, or supplies. It may be advisable to rent from a company with extra space or rent an office with basic services.

The use of professional services (use of attorneys, accountants, and consultants) is important not only during the early stages of the business but throughout its operation as an informal source of guidance on liability, expansion, taxes, and related matters. If the entrepreneur does not have sufficient resources to pay for such services, many professionals are willing to reduce rates, defer billing, or make other arrangements.

ORGANIZING FOR EXPORT: INDUSTRY APPROACH

The Small Business Administration (SBA) states that, besides multinational firms such as General Motors or IBM, there are many small-scale industries that export their output. For many of these companies, there are a number of organizational issues that need to be addressed to achieve an optimal allocation of resources. Some of the issues include (1) the level at which export decisions should be made, (2) the need for a separate export department, and (3), if the decision is made to establish a separate department, its organization within the overall structure of the firm including coordination and control of several activities. Such organizational issues involve three related areas:

1. *Subdivision of line operations based on certain fundamental competencies:* This relates to functional (production, finance, etc.), product, and geographical variables. A firm's organizational structure is often designed to fit its corporate strategy, which is in turn responsive to environmental realities (Albaum, Stradskov, and Duerr, 2002).
2. *Centralization or decentralization of export tasks and functions:* Centralization is generally advantageous for firms with highly standardized products, product usage, buying behavior, and distribution outlets. Advantages from centralization also tend to accrue to firms

(1) with few customers and large multinational competitors, and (2) with high R & D to sales ratio and rapid technological changes.

3. *Coordination and control:* Coordination and control of various activities among the various units of the organization is determined by the information-sharing needs of central management and foreign units.

Conventional business literature suggests that the choice of organizational structure determines export performance. The development of formal structures becomes important as the firm grows in size and complexity as well as to respond to internal and external changes. The adoption of flexible organizational structure can partly offset the disadvantage arising from formal organizational structure (Enderwick and Ranayne, 2004).

A study by Beamish et al. (1999) shows that the organizational structure within which a firm manages its exports has a significant impact on export performance. It also suggests that management commitment to internationalize by establishing a separate export department increases firms' export performance.

Organizational Structures

An international company can organize its export-import department along functional, product, market, or geographical lines. Some firms organize their international division at headquarters based on functional areas. Under this arrangement, functional staff (marketing, finance, etc.), located at the head office, serve all regions in their specialties. Such a structure is easy to supervise and provides access to specialized skills. However, it could lead to coordination problems among various units as well as duplication of tasks and resources. It is generally suitable for companies that produce standardized products during the early stages of international operations.

Organization of export operations along product lines is suitable for firms with diversified product lines and extensive R & D activities. Under this structure, product division managers become responsible for the production and marketing of their respective product lines throughout the world. Even though this structure poses limited coordination problems and promotes cost efficiency in existing markets, it leads to duplication of resources and facilities in various countries and inconsistencies in divisional activities and procedures.

Organization along geographical lines is essentially based on the division of foreign markets into regions that are, in turn, subdivided into areas/subsidiaries. The regions are self-contained and obtain the necessary resources for marketing and research. This structure is suitable for firms with homogenous products that need efficient distribution and product lines that have similar technologies and common end-use markets (Albaum, Stradskov, and Duerr, 2002). It allows firms to respond to the changing demands of the market. This organizational approach makes coordination of tasks difficult when new and diverse products are involved. It also leads to duplication of certain tasks at the regional level. Certain companies adopt a mixed structure to manage international marketing activities. This structure combines two or more competencies on a worldwide basis. This approach is described as follows:

> Instead of designating international boundaries, geographical area divisions or product divisions as profit centers, they are all responsible for profitability. National organizations are responsible for country profits, geographical area divisions for a group of national markets and product divisions for worldwide product profitability. (Albaum et al., 1994, pp. 469-470)

A separate export department within a firm may become necessary as overseas sales volume increases. However, the provision of additional resources for a separate department is not warranted at the early phase of market entry, since such activities can often be handled by domestic marketing units.

GENERAL PRINCIPLES OF TAXATION

The United States levies taxes on the worldwide income of its citizens, residents, or business entities. The United States, the Netherlands, and Germany are some of the few countries that impose taxes on the basis of worldwide income; most other countries tax income only if it is earned within their territorial borders. For U.S. tax purposes, an individual is considered a U.S. resident if the person (1) has been issued a resident alien card (green card), (2) has been physically present in the United States for 183 days or more in the calendar year, or (3) meets the cumulative presence test: this test may be met if the foreign individual was present in the United States for at least 183 days for the three-year period ending in the current year. In establishing cumulative presence, days present in the current year are added to one-third of the days present in the preceding year and one-sixth of the days in the second preceding year. An alien is treated as a resident if the total equals or exceeds 183 days.

Example of cumulative presence test: If Jim (a U.K. citizen) was in California for sixty-six days in 2003, thirty-three days in 2004, and 162 days in

2005, he would be considered a U.S. resident for 2005 (162 + [33 ÷ 3] + [66 ÷ 6] = 184 days). Jim may, however, rebut this presumption by showing that he has a closer connection to the United Kingdom than the United States, or that his regular place of business is in the United Kingdom.

A company incorporated in the United States is subject to tax on its worldwide income, as in the case of U.S. citizens and residents. A partnership is not treated as a separate legal entity, and, hence, it does not pay taxes. Such income is taxed in the hands of the individual partners, whether natural or legal entities.

Example 1

Suppose Joan, a U.S. citizen, has an export-import business as a sole proprietor and also works as manager in a fast-food restaurant. The profit from the business is added on to her employment income. If the business operates at a loss, the loss will be subtracted from her employment or other income thus reducing the tax payable.

Example 1A: Joan's Income Tax Liability as Sole Proprietor

	Year 1	Year 2
Joan's salary	30,000	31,500
Export-import profit (loss)	12,000	(8,500)
Total income	42,000	23,000
Personal exemption	(2,500)	(2,500)
Itemized deduction	(10,000)	(10,000)
Taxable income	29,500	10,500

Example 1B: Joan's Income Tax under A Corporation

Taxable income of export-import company	48,000
Less corporate income tax (15%)	(7,200)
Distributed dividend to Joan	40,800
Dividend tax on Joan's individual tax return	(11,887)
Total corporate and individual income tax	19,087

As illustrated in Example 1B, a corporation's income is subject to double taxation, first at the corporate level and then on the individual income tax return. Such incidences of double taxation are often reduced when deductions and other allowances are applied against taxable income. If earnings are left in the business, the tax rate may be lower than what would be paid by a sole proprietor. If the export-import business is incorporated as an S corporation, earnings are taxed only once at the owner's individual tax rate. Payment of Social Security tax is also avoided by withdrawing profits as dividends.

TAXATION OF EXPORT-IMPORT TRANSACTIONS

Taxation of U.S. Resident Aliens or Citizens

U.S. citizens and resident aliens are taxed on their worldwide income. In general, the same rules apply irrespective of whether the income is earned in the United States or abroad. Foreign tax credits are allowed against U.S. tax liability to mitigate the effects of taxes by a foreign country on foreign income. It also avoids double taxation of income earned by a U.S. citizen or resident, first in a foreign country where the income is earned (foreign source income) and in the United States. Such benefits are available mainly to offset income taxes paid or accrued to a foreign country and may not exceed the total U.S. tax due on such income.

Example 2

Nicole, who is a U.S. resident, has a green card. She exports appliances (washers, dryers, stoves, etc.) to Venezuela and occasionally receives service fees for handling the maintenance and repairs at the clients' locations in Caracas and Valencia. Last year, she received $9,000 in export revenues (taxable income) and $3,500 in service fees (taxable income). No foreign tax was imposed on Nicole's export receipt of $9,000. However, she paid $2,200 in taxes to Venezuela on the service fees. Nicole also received $15,000 from her part-time teaching job at a community school (taxable income). Assume a 30 percent U.S. tax rate.

Source of Income	Taxable Income	Tax Liability
Venezuela	9,000	2,700
Venezuela	3,500	2,200
United States	15,000	4,500
Total income	**27,500**	**9,400**

Foreign tax limit 5 U.S. tax liability 3 $\dfrac{\text{Taxable income from all foreign sources}}{\text{Total taxable worldwide income}}$

The credit is the lesser of creditable taxes paid ($2,200) or accrued to all foreign countries (and U.S. possessions) or the overall foreign tax credit limitation ($3,750). The foreign tax credit limitation = 30 percent (27,500) × 12,500 ÷ 27,500 = $3,750.

If the foreign tax credit limitation is lower than the foreign tax owed (i.e., suppose the foreign tax was greater than $3,750), the excess amount can be carried back two years and forward five years to a tax year in which the taxpayer has an excess foreign credit limitation.

Taxation of Foreign Persons in the United States (Nonresident Aliens, Branches, or Foreign Corporations)

Foreign firms use different channels when marketing their products in the United States. They often commence to sell goods through independent distributors until they gain sufficient resources and experience. As their export volume grows, they may wish to directly export to their U.S. customers and market their products by having their employees occasionally travel to the United States in order to contact potential clients, identify growing markets, or negotiate sales contracts. As the company becomes more successful in the market, it may decide to establish a branch or subsidiary in the United States.

Foreign persons engaged in U.S. trade or business are subject to U.S. taxation on the income that is "efficiently connected" with the conduct of U.S. trade or business. This includes U.S.–source income derived by a nonresident alien, foreign corporation, or U.S. branch from the sale of goods or provision of services. "Effectively connected income" may be extended beyond U.S.–source income to include certain types of foreign-source income that was facilitated by use of a fixed place of business or office in the United States.

> *Example:* Amin, a Brazilian software exporter, opens a small sales office in Hammond, Indiana, in order to sell in the United States and Canada. Canadian sales (foreign-source income) are generally considered "effectively connected" since income is produced through the U.S. sales office in Indiana. Amin's sales in the United States (through U.S. branch or subsidiary) are also subject to U.S. tax due to permanent establishment in the United States or income from U.S. trade or business.

A foreign corporation or nonresident alien that exports goods/services to the United States through a fixed place of business or office can claim deductions for expenses, losses, foreign taxes or claim a tax credit for any foreign income taxes, that is, foreign- and U.S.–source effectively connected income. The credits are not used to offset U.S. withholding or branch profits tax and allowable only against U.S. taxes on "effectively connected income." While a tax deduction reduces taxable income by the amount of a given expense, tax credits are a dollar for dollar reduction of U.S. income tax by the amount of the foreign tax.

Model tax treaties that the United States entered with many trading nations contain the following common provisions:

- Foreign person's (nonresident alien, foreign corporation, U.S. branch) export profits are exempt from U.S. tax unless such profits are attributable to a permanent establishment maintained in the United States, that is, a fixed place of business, or when U.S.–dependent agents have authority to conclude sales contracts on behalf of the company.

  Example: Donga Inc., a trading company incorporated in Monaco, exports ceiling fans to the United States. Its sales agents spend two months every year traveling across the United States to market/promote sales with major clients. When they receive orders, they forward them to the home office for final approval. The agents do not sign purchase orders or sales contracts.

  Donga Inc. is not subject to U.S. taxes since (1) the agents do not have contracting authority and (2) the company does not have permanent establishment in the United States.

- Marketing products in the United States through independent agents or distributors does not create a permanent establishment and thus no tax liability in the United States.
- Income from personal services provided by nonresident aliens in the United States are normally exempt unless the employee is present in the United States for over 183 days or paid by a U.S. resident. Income derived by professionals (accountants, doctors, etc.) are exempt unless attributable to a fixed place of business in the United States.

Taxation of U.S. Exports

In general, U.S. companies that export their goods overseas will incur no tax liability in the importing country if:

1. They undertake their exports through independent distributors (they have non taxable presence in the importing country).
2. Their agents/employees overseas do not have authority to conclude sales contracts on behalf of the U.S. exporter.
3. The services performed are attributable to a fixed place of business in the host country.

An export-import firm may enter a foreign market by establishing a branch in a foreign country. Branches are often used to retain exclusive control of overseas operations or to deduct losses on initial overseas activities. However, they can be incorporated abroad when such operations become profitable, to enable the firm to defer any U.S. income taxes owed on profits until they are remitted to the United States. A branch is not a separate corporation; it is considered an extension of the domestic corporation. One of the major disadvantages of operating a branch is that it exposes the domestic firm to liability in a foreign country. Foreign branch taxes are paid when they are earned (not when remitted to the United States, as in the case of a foreign corporation), and losses are reported when incurred. Foreign taxes paid or accrued on branch profits are eligible for foreign tax credits (see Figure 3.1).

An export-import firm can enter a foreign market by establishing a separate corporation (subsidiary) to conduct business. The parent corporation and subsidiary are separate legal entities and their individual liabilities are limited to the capital investment of each respective firm. Foreign taxes are paid when the subsidiary receives the income, but U.S. taxes are paid when distributed to shareholders as a dividend. Foreign taxes paid (a ratable share) are eligible for a tax credit at the time of distribution of dividend to the U.S. taxpayer. A U.S. shareholder (parent firm) can also claim a proportional share of a dividends-received deduction.

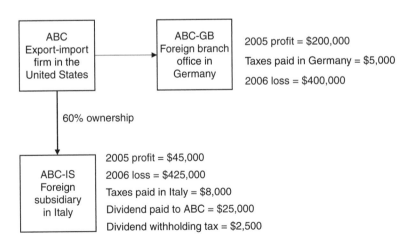

FIGURE 3.1. Taxation of Foreign Subsidiaries and Branches

Example

1. The 2005 profit ($200,000) of the German branch is taxable to ABC export-import firm in 2005. Remittance of reported earnings to the United States is not required for tax purposes. However, 2005 profits earned by the Italian subsidiary are subject to tax in the United States only when remitted; that is, taxes could be deferred until remitted to the U.S. parent.
2. The 2006 losses by ABC-GB can be used to offset ABC's 2006 taxable income from its U.S. operations. However, ABC-IS's losses cannot be used to reduce ABC's 2006 taxable income. The $425,000 loss incurred can only be used to reduce profits earned in other years and distributed as dividend to ABC company.
3. Taxes paid by ABC-GB to Germany can be claimed to offset ABC's U.S. taxes due on its profits. In the case of ABC-IS's taxes paid on its profits to Italy, ABC can claim a foreign tax credit for the taxes withheld on its dividend receipts for the given year. This does not reduce all or most of the foreign taxes incurred or paid on the subsidiary's profits, since it is limited only to taxes withheld from a foreign subsidiary's dividend remittances. The introduction of the "deemed paid foreign tax credit" was intended to remedy this inequity. Under this method, the U.S. shareholder (ABC) will be deemed to have paid a portion of ABC-IS's foreign taxes, corresponding to the proportion of dividends received and not on any withholding taxes on the dividends distributed. However, the deemed paid foreign tax credit is available to U.S. companies that own at least 10 percent of the foreign subsidiary's voting stock at the time of distribution and is based only on actual dividends paid. It is also limited only to corporate U.S. shareholders.

Deemed paid tax credit (DPTC) is calculated as follows:

$$DPTC = \frac{\text{Dividends paid to U.S. corporate shareholders from post-1986 undistributed earnings}}{\text{Accumulated post-1986 undistributed earnings}} \times \text{Post-1986 creditable taxes paid or accrued by foreign subsidiary}$$

$$DPTC = \frac{\$25,000}{\$45,000} \times 8,000 = \$4,444$$

ABC's U.S. Tax Liability:

Dividend	$25,000
DPTC	$4,444
Gross income	$29,444
Corporate tax (35%)	$10,305
Gross U.S. tax liability	$10,305
Less DPTC	($4,444)
Less dividend tax withheld	$2,500
Net ABC tax liability	$3,361.00

Taxation of Controlled Foreign Corporations

A controlled foreign corporation (CFC) is a foreign corporation in which U.S. shareholders own more than 50 percent of its voting stock or more than 50 percent of the value of its outstanding stock on any of the foreign corporation's tax year. Rules governing CFCs are concerned with preventing U.S. businesspersons from escaping high marginal tax rates in the United States by operating through controlled corporations in a foreign country that imposes little or no tax. The parent company could sell goods or services to a foreign subsidiary and manipulate prices so that most of the profits are allocated to the subsidiary in a country that imposes little or no tax, thus avoiding U.S. and foreign taxes. The CFC could also be used as a base company to make sales outside its country of incorporation or as a holding company to accumulate passive investment income such as interest, dividends, rent, and royalties.

U.S. shareholders must report their share of CFC's subpart F income each year. Subpart F income includes foreign base company income (foreign base sales, services, shipping, and personal holding company income), CFC's income from insurance of U.S. and foreign risks, boycott-related income and bribes, and other illegal payments.

A U.S. shareholder is subject to tax on the subpart F income only when the foreign corporation is a CFC for at least thirty days during its tax year. A U.S. shareholder of a CFC must then include his or her pro rata share of the subpart F income as a deemed dividend that is distributed on the last day of the CFC's tax year or the last day on which CFC's status is retained (McDaniel, Ault, & Repetti, 1981; Ogley, 1995).

Example: Monaco corporation, located in Hong Kong, is a CFC owned by XYZ Company of San Diego, California. Monaco corporation buys computer parts from XYZ Company and sells about 80 percent of the parts in other Asian countries. The remainder is sold to retailers in Hong Kong. Profits earned from sales in foreign countries are foreign base sales income, that is, subpart F income, and taxable to XYZ Company during the current year. Sales to foreign countries of goods manufactured by Monaco in Hong Kong would not constitute foreign base sales income.

Taxation of Domestic International Sales Corporations

Taxation of domestic international sales Corporations (DISCs) is discussed in Chapter 15.

Deductions and Allowances

Export-import businesses may deduct ordinary and necessary expenses. Ordinary and necessary expenses are defined by the Internal Revenue Service as follows:

> An ordinary expense is one that is common and accepted in your type of business, trade, or profession. A necessary expense is one that is helpful and appropriate for your trade, business, or profession. An expense does not have to be indispensable to be considered necessary. (Internal Revenue Service, 1996a, p. 6)

When one starts the export-import business, all costs are treated as capital expenses. These expenses are a part of the investment in the business and generally include

1. the cost of getting started in the business before beginning export-import operations, such as market research, expenses for advertising, travel, utilities, repairs, employee's wages, salaries, and fees for executives and consultants; and
2. business assets such as building, furniture, trucks, etc., and the costs of making any improvements to such assets, for example, a new roof, new floor, and so on. The cost of the improvement is added to base value of the improved property.

The cost of specific assets can be recovered through depreciation deductions. Other start-up costs can be recovered through amortization; that is, costs are deducted in equal amounts over sixty months or more. Organizational costs for a partnership (expenses for setting up the partnership) or corporation (costs of incorporation, legal and accounting fees etc.) can be amortized over sixty months and must be claimed on the first business tax return. Once the business has started operations, standard business deductions are applied against gross income. Standard business deductions include the following:

1. *General and administrative expenses:* Office expenses such as telephones, utilities, office rent, legal and accounting expenses, salaries, professional services, dues, and so forth. These also include interest payments on debt related to the business, taxes (real estate and excise taxes, estate and employment taxes), insurance, and amortization of capital assets.
2. *Personal and business expenses:* If an expense is incurred partly for business and partly for personal purposes, only the part that is used for business is deductible. If the export-import business is conducted from one's home, part of the expense of maintaining the home could be claimed as a business expense. Such expenses include mortgage interest, insurance, utilities, and repairs. To successfully claim such limited deductions, part of the home must be used exclusively and regularly as the principal place of business for the export-import operation or as a place to meet customers or clients. Similarly, automobile expenses to conduct the business are deductible. If the car is used for both business and family transportation, only the miles driven for the business are deductible as business expenses. Automobile-related deductions also include depreciation on the car; expenses for gas, oil, tires, and repairs; and insurance and registration fees (Internal Revenue Service, 1996b).
3. *Entertainment, travel, and related business expenses:* Expenses incurred entertaining clients for promotion, travel expenses (the cost of air, bus, taxi fares), as well as other related expenses (dry cleaning, tips, subscriptions to relevant publications, convention expenses) are tax deductible (Internal Revenue Service, 1996c).

If deductions from the export-import business are more than the income for the year, the net operating loss can be used to lower taxes in other years. All of the previously listed expenses have to be specifically allocated and apportioned between foreign- and domestic-source income.

INTERNATIONAL TRANSFER PRICING

Transactions between unrelated parties and prices charged for goods and services tend to reflect prevailing competitive conditions. Such market prices cannot be assumed when transactions are conducted between related parties, such as a group of firms under common control or ownership. If a parent company sells its output to a foreign marketing subsidiary at a higher price, it moves overall gains to itself. It if charges a lower price, it will shift more of the overall gains to the subsidiary. Even though transfer prices do not affect the combined income or absolute amount of gain or loss among related persons or "controlled group of corporations," they do shift income among related parties in order to take advantage of differences in tax rates.

In the following example, the combined income remains at $1,000 for the steel export regardless of the transfer price used to allocate income between the parent and subsidiary. If the tax rate is 30 percent in United States and 40 percent in Spain, the U.S. parent company can use higher transfer price for its controlled sale (Option B) to reduce its worldwide taxes:

Option A: 1,000 × 40 percent = $400 (Spain's rate)
Option B: 1,000 × 30 percent = $300 (U.S. rate)

In cases where U.S. companies operate in low-tax jurisdictions, income can be shifted to a low-tax subsidiary. This has the advantage of U.S. tax deferral until the foreign subsidiary repatriates its earnings through dividend distribution.

Example

	U.S. Parent Co. (Steel Co.) in Detroit, Michigan	U.S. Subsidiary in Madrid, Spain
Option A	Production Cost = 1,000	Cost of sales = 1,000
		Selling expense = 200
	Sale to subsidiary = 1,000	Sales revenue = 2,200
	Net Profit = $0	Net Profit = $1,000
Option B	Production cost = 1,000	Cost of sales = 2,000
		Selling expense = 200
	Sales to subsidiary = 2,000	Sales revenue = 2,200
	Net Profit = $1,000	Net Profit = $0

U.S. regulation (Section 482) on transfer pricing is largely intended to ensure that taxpayers report and pay taxes on their actual share of income arising from controlled transactions. The appropriateness of any transfer price is evaluated on the basis of the arm's length or market value standard (see International Perspective 3.2). For example, in the case of loans extended by a U.S. parent company to its overseas subsidiary, the Internal Revenue Service has successfully imposed an arm's length interest charge (a charge that would be paid by unrelated parties under similar circumstances).

Tax Treaties

Income tax treaties are entered into by countries to reduce the burden of double taxation on the same activity and to exchange information to prevent

INTERNATIONAL PERSPECTIVE 3.2.
Transfer Pricing Methods

A number of factors are considered in the determination of comparable prices between parties dealing at arm's length transactions: contractual terms, such as provisions pertaining to volume of sales, warranty, duration or extension of credit, functions performed such as marketing, R & D, etc., and risks assumed including responsibility for currency fluctuations, credit collection, or product liability. Other factors include economic market conditions (similarly of geographical market, competitive conditions in industry and market) as well as nature of property or services transformed.

In the case of sale of tangible goods between related parties, arm's length charge is determined by using the following methods:

- The comparable uncontrolled price method: prices on the sale of similar goods to unrelated parties.
- Resale price method: resale price to unrelated parties using gross profit margin.
- Cost plus method: cost plus method is used in situations in which products are manufactured and sold to related parties.
- Comparable profits method: this method uses profit level indicators such as rate of return on operating assets, etc., of uncontrolled parties to adjust profit levels of each group.
- Profit split method: allocation of profit between related parties based on the relative value of the contribution to the profit of each party.

In the performance of services to related parties, the regulations do not require that a profit be made on the change for services unless the services are an integral part of the business activity of the providing party, that is, the principle activity of the service provider is that of rendering such services to related or unrelated parties.

tax evasion. Tax treaty partners generally agree on rules about the types of income that a country can tax and the provision of a tax credit for any taxes paid to one country against any taxes owed in another country.

The United States has entered into a number of tax treaties with approximately sixty countries. They include Canada, China, EU countries, India, Japan, South Korea, Mexico, New Zealand, South Africa, and many transition economies of Central and Eastern Europe. In most countries, the treaty prevails over domestic law. In the United States, if there is a conflict between a treaty provision and domestic law, whichever is recently enacted will govern the transaction.

The following are some of the common treaty provisions with regard to business profits.

- The export profits of an enterprise of one treaty country shall be taxable only in that country unless the enterprise carries on business in the other treaty country through a permanent establishment situated therein. The importing country may tax the enterprise's profits that are attributable to that permanent establishment (U.S. Model Income Tax Treaty, 7.1).
- Permanent establishment is meant to describe a fixed place of business through which the business of an enterprise is wholly or partially discharged. It includes a place of management, a branch, an office, a factory, a workshop, a mine, or any other place of extraction of natural resources. It is assumed to be a permanent establishment only if it lasts or the activity continues for a period of more than twelve months (U.S. Model Income Tax Treaty, 5.3).
- Permanent establishment shall not include certain auxiliary functions such as purchasing, storing, or delivering inventory (U.S. Model Income Tax Treaty, 5.4).
- An enterprise is deemed to have a permanent establishment in a treaty country if its employees conclude sales contracts in its name. If a Canadian exporter sends its sales agents to enter into a contract with a U.S. firm in New York, the Canadian company shall be deemed to have a permanent establishment in the United States even if it does not have an office in the United States (U.S. Model Income Tax Treaty, 5.5).
- Permanent establishment is not imputed in cases where a product is exported through independent brokers or distributors, regardless of whether these independent agents conclude sales contracts in the name of the exporter (U.S. Model Income Tax Treaty, 5.6).

CHAPTER SUMMARY

Ownership Structure

The forms of business organizations are sole proprietorship, partnership, and corporation.

Business or Trade Name

Corporations are required to register their trade name with the state. Sole proprietorships and partnerships are required to register with the appropriate government agency if they operate under a fictitious name.

Bank Accounts, Permits, and Licenses

1. Opening a bank account: It is advisable to open an account with an international bank.
2. An export/import firm can be operated from a home during the early phase of the business. All direct expenses related to the business are tax deductible.
3. The use of professional services is important as a source of guidance on liability, taxes, expansion, and related matters.
4. Permits and licenses: It is important to check with the city or county to determine if permits or business licenses are required.

Organizational Issues

Export decisions should be made regarding the need for a separate export department, coordination and control of various activities, organizational structure of the export-import department.

Common Organizational Structures

These are organizations along functional lines, organizations along geographical lines, and organizations based on product or market.

Taxation of Export-Import Business

Foreign persons' export profits are exempt from U.S. tax unless such profits are attributable to a permanent establishment maintained in the United States. Similarly, U.S exports will not be subject to tax in the importing country unless the firm has a fixed place of trade or business in the importing country or its agents in the latter country have authority to conclude contracts on behalf of the U.S. exporter.

Deductions and allowances include organizational costs, general and administrative expenses, personal and business expenses, entertainment, travel, and other related business expenses.

Transfer pricing is intended to ensure that taxpayers report and pay tax on their actual share of income arising from controlled transactions. There are several methods used to estimate an arm's length charge for transfers of tangible property: the comparable uncontrolled price method, the resale price method, the cost plus method, the comparable profits method, and the profit split method.

REVIEW QUESTIONS

1. What are the major disadvantages of running an export-import business as a partnership?
2. Are partnerships recognized as legal entities? Discuss.
3. Both general and limited partnerships may be useful forms of organization for export-import businesses. Why/why not?
4. What is an S corporation?
5. What types of professional services are needed when you start an export-import business?
6. State three typical organizational structures of firms that are engaged in international trade. Is a separate export department necessary for a manufacturing firm with limited exports?
7. ABC Company is incorporated in Florida although all its business activities are done in France. Its management office is located in Amsterdam, where the board of directors holds their regular meeting. The shareholders are from U.K. and Denmark and hold their annual meeting in Vienna. What is ABC's residence for tax purposes?
8. Are U.S. exporters subject to income tax in importing countries? What are the tax implications of establishing a trading firm as a branch (as opposed to a subsidiary) in foreign countries?

CASE 3.1. GLOBALIZATION
AND THE SHRINKING TAX BASE

Many developed countries are confronted with declining tax revenues from multinational corporations. The recent European Commission proposal attempts to harmonize the tax base in the EU to limit the shrinking corporate tax yield. In view of the pressure to increase shareholder value, multinationals feel obligated to use complex tax avoidance strategies. In high tax jurisdictions, such as the United Kingdom, for example, investment inflows tend to lead to an increase in debt and a reduction in equity of the acquired firms. This often leads to large payments in tax allowable interest to foreign parent companies thus reducing taxable income. Thin capitalization rules intended to limit repatriation of profits through high interest charges on intragroup borrowings does not appear to be effective. These rules have not been able to prevent multinationals from transforming preinterest profits into pre-tax losses in high tax jurisdictions.

A study by the *Financial Times* noted that eight of the top twenty non-oil multinationals operating in the United Kingdom paid little or no tax to the U.K. treasury in 2002. It indicates that in many cases, profits are being reduced by transfer pricing and intergroup charges. This includes, but is not limited to, overinvoicing imports and underinvoicing exports. A multinational, for example, sells goods to other group companies at below market prices while the subsidiary resells it at market prices, thereby ensuring that profits are made in low tax jurisdictions. Enforcement of existing rules has proven difficult. Comparing operating margins between sister companies and other competitors, etc., is often difficult because of the multinational company's different regional structures and mixes of product. Tax authorities do not have sufficient information relative to their multinational clients to effectively enforce the rules. One study estimates the total tax losses to the U.S. treasury from artificial transfer pricing at approximately $53 billion in 2001 (see Tables 3.1 and 3.2).

Here are other examples:

> The Asda Group, which was acquired by Wal-Mart (United Kingdom), declared pre-tax profits of £608 million in 2002. This shrinks at Asda's parent (Wal-Mart United Kingdom) to £209 million due to interest and amortization of goodwill on the acquisition. Not taking into account deferred taxation, the tax charge was at £88 million despite Asda profits of over £405 million.

> Deferred tax assets of the four largest investment banks in the United Kingdom amounted to over $1.1 billion in 2002. This allows them to pay less tax in the future by carrying forward their losses.

> In January 2002, Glaxo Smith Kline, the pharmaceutical firm, was presented with $5.2 billion bill for extra taxes (not paid due to transfer pricing) and interest by the U.S. government pertaining to revenues owed since the late 1980s.

Questions

1. Do you think countries' efforts to limit transfer pricing are effective?
2. What other ways are available to limit transfer pricing?

TABLE 3.1. Top Ten Sources of Lost U.S. Taxes Due to Overinvoicing of Imports/Underinvoicing of Exports, 2001

U.S. Export (Import)	Tax Loss at 34% (Million U.S. $)	Income Shifted (Million U.S. $)
Japan	10,154 (2,591)	29,864 (7,622)
Germany	3,475 (2,072)	10,221 (6,093)
Netherlands	2,484 (1,446)	7,299 (4,254)
Canada	2,375 (1,164)	6,987 (3,425)
Mexico	2,365 (1,095)	6,954 (3,220)
United Kingdom	2,237 (767)	6,578 (2,255)
Philippines	1,451 (653)	4,269 (1,921)
France	1,217 (537)	3,579 (1,578)
S. Korea	1,039 (465)	3,055 (1,368)
China	970 (449)	2,853 (1,322)

Source: Pak and Zdanowicz, 2002.

TABLE 3.2. Selected List of Abnormally Low Export/High U.S. Import Prices (2001)

U.S. Export	Destination	Price ($)
Bovine animals—live	Mexico	20.65/unit
Multivitamins	Finland	1.34/kg
Dynamite	Canada	1.24/kg
Radial tires—bus/truck	United Kingdom	11.74/unit
Diamonds	India	13.45/carat
Aluminum ladders	Hong Kong	1.75/unit

U.S. Import	Source	Price ($)
Multivitamins	China	1,868.77/kg
Plastic buckets	Czech Republic	973/unit
Fence posts—treated	Canada	1,853.50/meter
Wood Moldings	Bolivia	1,124/meter
Toilet/facial tissue	China	4,121/kg
Briefs and panties	Hungary	739/dozen

Source: Pak and Zdanowicz, 2002.

Chapter 4

Planning and Preparations for Export

ASSESSING AND SELECTING THE PRODUCT

Although the basic functions of exporting and domestic selling are the same, international markets differ widely because of great variations in certain uncontrollable environmental forces. These include currency exchange controls/risks, taxation, tariffs, and inflation, which happen to originate outside the business enterprise. Such variations require managers who are aware of global threats and opportunities.

If a company already manufactures a product or service, it is reasonable to assume that its product or service is what will be exported. However, companies must first determine the export potential of a product or service before they invest their resources into the business of foreign trade. To establish the export potential of a product, firms must consider the following factors: *the success of the product in domestic markets, participation in overseas trade shows, advertising, and market data.*

If a product is successful in the domestic market, there is a good chance that it will be successful in markets abroad. However, a careful analysis of a product's overseas market potential is needed. One could start by assessing the demand for similar products domestically and abroad, as well as determining the need for certain adaptations or improvements. Trade statistics provide a preliminary indication of markets for a particular product in most countries. For products or services that are not new, low-cost market research is often available that can help determine market potential. Products that are less sophisticated and that have a declining demand in developed countries' markets often encounter a healthy demand in developing nations because the goods are less expensive and easy to handle (Weiss, 1987).

Participation in overseas trade shows is a good way to test the export potential of products or services. A recent study commissioned by American Business Media found that seven out of ten business executives purchased or

Export-Import Theory, Practices, and Procedures, Second Edition

recommended the purchase of a product or service after looking at an advertisement or promotion at a trade show (Schwartz, 2006). However, if an assessment of the actual and potential uses of the product or service indicates that it satisfies certain basic needs in the market place, initial sales can be made to establish demand as well as to determine potential improvements.

To achieve success, there must be a strong and lasting management commitment to the export business. The long-term commitment is necessary to ensure the recovery of high market entry costs related to product modification, legal representation, and advertising, as well as the development of an agent/distributor network (see Table 4.1).

Companies already operating in the domestic market need to consider the development of export markets through the allocation of financial and personnel resources or through the use of outside experts. In the absence of

TABLE 4.1. The Export Decision: Management Issues

Experience
- With what countries is trade being conducted?
- Which product lines are most in demand and who are the buyers or likely buyers?
- What is the trend in sales?
- Who are the main domestic and international competitors?
- What lessons have been learned from past experience?

Management and Personnel
- Who will be responsible for the export department's organization and staff?
- How much management time should or could be allocated?
- What organizational structure is suitable?

Production Capacity
- What is the firm's production capacity?
- What is the effect of exports on domestic sales and production capacity and cost?
- Is a minimum order quantity required?
- What are the design and packaging requirements for exports?

Financial Capacity
- What amount of capital is tied up in exports?
- What level of export department operating costs can be supported?
- What are the initial expenses of export efforts to be allocated?
- When should the export effort pay for itself?

---

sufficient knowledge about exporting, it is often advisable for companies to hire consultants who would be engaged in the establishment of the department and the training of personnel.

An individual entrepreneur, acting as a middleman between the manufacturer and importer, can pick any product or service. The following are two approaches to selecting a product or service.

Systematic Approach

The systematic approach involves selection of a product or service based on overall market demand. An individual entrepreneur often selects a product line or service based on demand and growth trends by observing trade flows. A variety of statistical sources provide data (for products and services) pertaining to the major export markets, projected total demand, and U.S. exports in each market, along with the rank of the countries based on the projected import value. This process of collecting and analyzing information will enable the potential exporter to draw conclusions on the best line of products or services as well as promising markets. It is, however, important to select products or services based on familiarity and skill. A computer technician is in a more advantageous position to export computers, computer parts, software, and computer services than a graphic designer because of the former's prior knowledge about the product/service. This individual is more likely to be familiar with product and/or service-specific issues such as quality, technical specifications, adaptability to overseas requirements, and maintenance or after-sales service.

Other important factors to consider in product/service selection include proximity of the producer or manufacturer to one's home or office in order to maintain close personal contact and closely monitor/discuss product quality, production delays, order processing, and other pertinent matters. Once a potential product (service) for export has been identified, the individual must undertake market research to select the most promising markets based on import value and growth trends. Both in the case of manufacturing companies and individuals, one must consider if a given product has export potential before substantial time, effort, and capital are invested (Ball et al., 2006).

Reactive Approach

The reactive approach involves selecting a product based on immediate market need. Even though it is quite common to select the product and identify possible markets, certain exporters initially identify the consumer need and then select a product or service to satisfy the given market demand. A plethora of publications advertise products/services (exporters can also advertise) that are needed in foreign countries by public- or private-sector importers. The first step would be to contact potential importers to indicate one's interest in supplying the product and to obtain other useful information. Once there is a reasonable basis to proceed (based on the importer's response), potential suppliers of the product/service can be identified from the various directories of manufacturers. In the United States, for example, the *Thomas Register of Manufacturers* is considered to be a comprehensive source of U.S. manufacturers.

In both cases (systematic or reactive), selection of the manufacturer depends on a number of factors including price, quality, proximity to home or office, as well as the manufacturer's commitment to export sales. There must be a long-term commitment from management to encourage the development of export markets, and this cannot be motivated by occasional needs to dispose of surplus merchandise. It is also important to consider the existence of export restrictions that limit the sale of these products to specific countries and their implications for sales and profits. Manufacturers may also impose certain restrictions when they have an agent/distributor or a subsidiary producing the goods in the market (see International Perspective 4.1).

The reactive approach to selecting a product has certain disadvantages for the individual entrepreneur who acts as an intermediary between the manufacturer and importer:

1. *Lack of focus on a given product or market.* Chasing product orders in different markets impedes the development of a systematic export strategy. This approach ignores the idea of niche exporting, which is critical to the success of any export-import enterprise. It leads to exports of unfamiliar products and/or sales to difficult markets, which hampers the long-term growth and profitability of export businesses.
2. *Absence of long-term relationship with the importer.* Selling different products to different markets impedes the development of a long-term relationship with importers. It also creates suspicion on the part of importing firms about the long-term reliability and commitment of the firm to exporting.

INTERNATIONAL MARKET RESEARCH

International market research deals with how business organizations engaged in international trade make decisions that lead to the allocation of resources in markets with the greatest potential for sales (Ball et al., 2006). This process of market screening helps to maximize sales and profits by identifying and selecting the most desirable markets.

INTERNATIONAL PERSPECTIVE 4.1. Important Factors to Consider in Selecting the Export Product

Shifting spending patterns: Basic determinants of how much a consumer buys of a product are the person's taste and preference, as well as the price of the product relative to the price of other products. Another major influence is the consumer's income. If the consumer's income increases, demand for most goods will rise. However, the demand for goods that people regard as necessities, such as fuel, tobacco, bread, or meat, tends to decline and exporters of such products are not likely to greatly benefit from rising consumer incomes in other countries. The demand for luxuries, such as new cars or expensive food, expands more rapidly. Therefore, exporters should generally put more emphasis on goods that consumers regard as "luxuries," due to shifting spending patterns in response to rising incomes.

Products to be excluded from the list: Individuals starting an export-import trade should initially work with small to medium-sized manufacturers because large companies, such as Motorola, have their own export departments or overseas subsidiaries that produce the goods in those markets. Products that compete with such large companies should not be considered at this stage. It is also important to avoid products/services that require too many export/licensing requirements as a condition of executing an international business transaction. Also, the fashion-oriented market is too volatile and unpredictable to warrant a full commitment until a later stage. This also extends to multimillion-dollar contracts for overseas government projects, as well as sophisticated products that often require the development of training facilities and a network of technicians for after-sales service.

Emphasis on quality and niche marketing: Several studies on export-import trade indicate that firms that have shown a sustained increase in their sales and overall profits have often emphasized quality and concentrated on niches. In this age of diversity, marketers are being awakened to the erosion of the mass market. Traditional marketing methods are no longer as effective as they used to be and a new emphasis on quality and niche marketing is proving successful. Even after the elimination of textile quotas in 2005, many European textile producers have maintained steady growth in their exports because of their emphasis on high fashion items with special brand identity.

Why Conduct International Market Research?

International market research is needed because export/investment decisions are often made without a careful and objective assessment of foreign markets and with a limited appreciation for different environments abroad. This is often a result of the perception of other markets as an extension of the domestic market and that methods/practices which work at home also work abroad. The cost of conducting international research is seen as prohibitively high and managers make export decisions based on short-term and changing market needs (reactive approach). Environmental scanning is viewed as a prerequisite for the successful alignment of competitive strategies (Subramanian, Fernandes, and Harper, 1993; Beal, 2000).

The purpose of international marketing research is to: (1) identify, evaluate, and compare the size and potential of various markets and select the most desirable market(s) for a given product or service, and (2) reassess market changes that may require a change in a company's strategy. A firm may research a market by using either primary or secondary data sources.

Primary research (using primary data) is conducted by collecting data directly from the foreign marketplace through interviews, focus groups, observation, surveys, and experimentation with representatives and/or potential buyers. It attempts to answer certain questions about specific markets such as sales potential or pricing. Primary research has the advantage of being tailored to the company's market and therefore provides specific information. However, collection of such data is often expensive and time-consuming.

Secondary market research is based on data previously collected and assembled for a certain project other than the one at hand. Such information can often be found inside the company or in the library, or it can be purchased from public or private organizations that specialize in providing information, such as overseas market studies, country market surveys, export statistics profiles, foreign trade reports, or competitive assessments of specific industries. Although such data are readily available and inexpensive, certain limitations apply to using secondary sources:

1. The information often does not meet one's specific needs. Because these materials are collected by others for their own purpose, they may be too broad or too narrow in terms of their scope of coverage to be of much value for the research at hand. Also, such information is often out of date.
2. There could be differences in definition of terms or units of measure that make it difficult to categorize or compare the research data.
3. It is difficult to assess the accuracy of the information because little is known about the research design or techniques used to gather the data.

INTERNATIONAL MARKET ASSESSMENT

International market assessment is a form of environmental scanning that permits a firm to select a small number of desirable markets on the basis of broad variables. Companies must determine where to sell their products or services because they seldom have enough resources to take advantage of all opportunities. Not using scanning techniques may create the tendency to overlook growing markets. For example, European companies have often neglected the fastest growing markets in Southeast Asia while expanding their traditional markets in North America. Assessment of foreign markets involves subjecting countries to a series of environmental analysis with a view to selecting a handful of desirable markets for exports. In the early stages of assessment, secondary data are used to establish market size and level of trade, as well as investment and other economic and financial information.

Preliminary Screening (Basic Need and Potential)

The first step in market assessment is the process of establishing whether there is a basic need for the company's products or services in foreign markets. Basic need potential is often determined by environmental conditions such as climate, topography, or natural resources. In situations in which it is difficult to determine potential need, firms can resort to foreign trade and investment data to establish whether the product and/or service has been previously imported, its volume, its dollar value, and the exporting countries.

After establishing basic need potential, it is important to determine whether the need for the product or service has been satisfied. Needs may be met by local production or imports. If there are plans for local production by competitors, imports may cease or be subject to high tariffs or other barriers. Market opportunities still exist for competitive firms if a growing demand for the product cannot be fully met by local production in so far as governments do not apply trade restrictions in favor of local producers or imports from certain countries. If the research indicates that market opportunities exist, it is pertinent to consider the market's overall buying power by examining country-specific factors such as population, gross domestic product, per capital income, distribution of wealth, exports, and imports. While considering these factors, one should note that (1) per capita income might not be a good measure of buying power unless the country has a large middle class and no profound regional disparities, and (2) imports do not always indicate market potential. Availability of foreign currency, as well as change in duties and trade policies, should be monitored to ensure that they are conducive to the growth of imports in the country.

Secondary Screening (Financial and Economic Conditions)

Secondary screening involves financial and economic conditions such as trends in inflation, interest rates, exchange rate stability, and availability of credit and financing. Countries with high inflation rates (as well as controlled and low interest rates) should be carefully considered because they may limit the volume of imports by restricting the availability of foreign exchange. There is also a need to verify the availability of commercial banks that can finance overseas transactions and handle collections, payments, and money transfers.

Economic data are also used to measure certain indicators such as market size (relative size of each market as percentage of total world market), market intensity (degree of purchasing power), and growth of the market (annual increase in sales). Countries with advanced economies, such as the United States or Germany, account for a large percentage of the world market for automobiles, computers, and televisions. Their high per capita incomes reflect the attractiveness of the market and the degree of purchasing power. Such information will help in selecting countries with rapidly growing markets and high concentrations of purchasing power.

Third Screening (Political and Legal Forces)

It is important to assess the type of government (democratic/nondemocratic) and its stability. Countries with democratic governments tend to be politically stable and favor open trade polices, and are less likely to resort to measures that restrict imports or impede companies' abilities to take certain actions. Political instability may also lead to damage to property and/or disruption of supplies or sales. It could be as a result of wars, insurrections, takeover of property, and/or change of rules. Consideration should also be given to legal forces in these countries that affect export/import operations. These include the following:

- *Entry barriers:* Product restrictions, high import tariffs, restrictive quotas, import licenses, special taxes on imports, product labeling, and other restrictive trade laws.
- *Limits on profit remittances and/or ownership:* Imposition of strict limits on capital outflows in foreign currencies, restrictions on or delays in remittance of profits, and ownership requirements to establish a business.
- *Taxes and price controls and protection of intellectual property rights:* The existence of high taxes, price controls, and lack of adequate protection for intellectual property rights should be considered.

Fourth Screening (Sociocultural Forces)

This involves consideration of sociocultural forces such as customs, religion, and values that may have an adverse effect on the purchase or consumption of certain products. Examples include sales of pork and its derivatives and alcohol in Muslim countries.

Fifth Screening (Competitive Forces)

It is important to appraise the level and quality of competition in potential markets. The exporter has to identify companies competing in the markets, the level of their technology, the quality and price of the products and/or services, and their estimated market shares, as well as other pertinent matters.

Final Selection (Field Trip)

This stage involves a visit to the markets that appear to be promising in light of the market assessment technique. Such visits could be in the form of trade missions (a group of business and government officials that visit a market in search of business opportunities) or trade fairs (a public display of products and services by firms of several countries to prospective customers). The purpose of such visit is to:

- corroborate the facts gathered during the various stages of market assessment; and
- supplement currently available information by doing research in the local market, including face-to-face interviews with potential consumers, distributors, agents, and government officials.

This will facilitate final selection of the most desirable markets as well as the development of a marketing plan, product modification, pricing, promotion, and distribution.

DEVELOPING AN INTERNATIONAL BUSINESS PLAN

A business plan involves a process in which an entity puts together a given set of resources (people, capital, materials) to achieve defined goals and objectives over a specific period of time. In addition to providing the direction necessary for success, a sound business plan should be flexible to take advantage of new opportunities or to allow adjustments when certain assumptions or conditions change. This plan should be reviewed and progress assessed (perhaps once every three or four months) to ensure that implementation is consistent with overall goals and objectives laid out in the business plan.

Developing a business plan is an important factor for success regardless of the size, type, or time of establishment of the business. Even though some export-import companies start a business plan after they have reached a certain stage, planning is needed at all stages of business development from inception to maturity (Williams and Manzo, 1983). It is a roadmap to one's targeted destination. By allowing for critical evaluation of different alternatives, a business plan forces entrepreneurs to set realistic goals, predict resource allocation, and project future earnings. Such a practice assists in avoiding costly mistakes and enhances the decision making abilities of businesses (Silvester, 1995). A written business plan is the basis on which other parties (e.g., bankers, potential partners, etc.) assess the overall business concern. It is used for obtaining bank financing, seeking investment funds, obtaining large contracts to supply governments or companies, or arranging strategic alliances to conduct joint marketing and other activities.

The structure of a typical business plan includes the following components (see Figure 4.1): executive summary, description of the industry and company, target market, present and future competition, marketing plan and sales strategy, management and organization, long-term development and exit plan, and the financial plan (Cohen, 1995). Some plans also include critical risks/problems and community benefits.

EXPORT COUNSELING AND ASSISTANCE

A number of assistance sources are available to U.S. exporters.

The U.S. Department of Commerce

Through the local district office, the exporter has access to all assistance available through the International Trade Administration (ITA) and to trade information gathered overseas by the U.S. and foreign commercial services. The U.S. Trade Information Center serves as a single source of research support, trade information counseling, and industry consultation. A valuable source of trade information while conducting foreign market research is the National Trade Data Bank (NTDB). The NTDB provides specific product and country information as well as a list of foreign importers in specific product areas. The Department of Commerce also has the Trade Opportunities Program (TOP), which helps U.S. exporters with current sales leads from foreign companies that are interested in buying U.S. products or representing

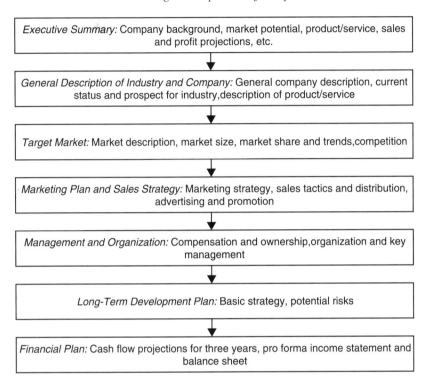

FIGURE 4.1. Structure of An International Business Plan

U.S. firms (STAT-USA). U.S. exporters can also advertise in *Commercial News USA,* a bimonthly magazine that promotes U.S. products and services overseas. It is distributed throughout the U.S. embassies and consulates in over 140 countries (International Perspective 4.2).

The following is a list of some of the major programs offered by the Department of Commerce.

- *Market Access and Compliance (MAC):* MAC specialists monitor foreign country trade practices and help U.S. exporters deal with foreign trade barriers.
- *U.S. and Foreign Commercial Service (U.S. & FCS):* U.S. commercial officers in foreign countries provide important trade and investment information on foreign companies. This includes but is not limited to conducting market research, finding foreign representatives, etc.

- *Trade Development:* This unit offers extensive support to U.S. exporters by providing critical information on market and trade practices overseas, including industry analysis and trade policy. Industry-specific trade development includes aerospace, automotive, consumer goods, e-commerce, and energy, and so on. Industry officers identify trade opportunities by product or service, develop export marketing plans, and conduct trade missions.
- *Gold Key Service:* This services U.S. exporters by prescreening potential distributors, professional associations, etc. It is available in many countries.
- *Trade events:* The Department of Commerce organizes various trade events (trade fairs, trade missions, international catalog exhibitions, etc.) in order to help market U.S. products or locate representatives abroad.

INTERNATIONAL PERSPECTIVE 4.2.
Contact Programs for U.S. Exporters

The United States government provides several services to U.S. exporters. The business contact programs provided by the Department of Commerce include:

Agent/Distributor Service (ADS): The commercial officers of ADS act on behalf of U.S. export firms in order to locate foreign agents and distributors. U.S. firms provide ADS with their product information, who then search and prepare reports that include six foreign prospects or firms who have expressed an interest in the product(s). The ADS then provides U.S. exporting firms with the proper contact information of the interested agents.

Commercial News USA (CNUSA): The CNUSA program allows U.S. firms to receive global exposure through its catalogs, magazines, and electronic resources. The catalog and magazines are distributed throughout the U.S. embassies and consulates among 152 countries, specifically for business readers. All published products must be 51 percent U.S. made (parts), with 51 percent U.S. labor. The leads obtained by the program are redirected to the U.S. exporting firms and include detailed contact information, including sales, representation, distributorships, and joint ventures or licensing agreements that help these firms identify potential markets. Inquiries from abroad do not come through the CNUSA channels as they are directly reached to the exporting firms.

(continued)

(continued)

Gold Key Service: The Gold Key Service is a matching service that sets appointments in foreign markets with prescreened partners for U.S. exporters. The service provides orientation briefing, market research, a debriefing with trade professionals after meetings to discuss the results of the meetings, and also offers assistance in generating follow-up strategies for exporting firms. The service is offered by the Commercial Service with a fee ranging from $150-$600.

International Company Profiles (ICP): The commercial officers of the ICP prepare background reports of foreign firms who are interested in working with U.S. exporters. Each report includes information on a foreign organization's bank and trade references, principles, key officers and managers, product lines, number of employees, financial data, sales volume, reputation, and market outlook. The ICP is only offered to countries that are in need of providers who offer background information on local companies in the private sector. Credit reports from private-sector resources are generally available on nearly all foreign firms.

Trade Opportunities Program (TOP): This is a service program that is headquartered in Washington, DC, where U.S. commercial officers attend international trade shows to gather leads through several local channels on foreign firms that seek to purchase or represent U.S. products and services. The leads normally include specifics on quantities and end use. The reports are available electronically. In order to help U.S. exporting firms expose their products, the Department of Commerce holds trade events on an annual basis that allow foreign firms to examine the products in person, especially those that are difficult to sell due to their nature. Trade events include trade shows, fairs, trade missions, matchmaker delegations, and catalog exhibitions.

Small Business Administration (SBA)

The SBA provides free export counseling services to potential and current small business exporters (through its field offices) throughout the United States.

- *SCORE/ACE programs:* Members of the Service Corps of Retired Executives (SCORE) and the Active Corps of Executives (ACE), with years of practical experience in international trade, assist small firms in evaluating export potential, developing and implementing export marketing plans, identifying problem areas, etc. "SCORE" has a new acronym, Counselors to America's Small Business or "CASB." Since its inception, the organization has worked with over seven million entrepreneurs.

- *Small Business Development Centers (SBDCs):* Additional export counseling and assistance is offered through the Small Business Development Centers (SBDCs), which are located within some colleges and universities. The centers are intended to offer technical help to exporters by providing, for example, an export marketing feasibility study and an analysis for the client firms. There is also an initial legal assistance program for small exporters on the legal aspects of exporting.
- *U.S. Export Assistance Centers (EACs):* These are intended to deliver a comprehensive array of export counseling and trade finance services to U.S. firms. They integrate the export marketing know-how of the Department of Commerce with the trade finance expertise of the Small Business Administration and Export-Import Bank. EAC-trade specialists help U.S. firms enter new markets and increase market share by identifying the best markets for their products; developing an effective marketing strategy; advising on distribution channels, market entry, promotion, and export procedures; and assisting with trade finance. They are generally located with state promotion agencies, local chambers of commerce and other local export promotion organizations.

U.S. Department of Agriculture

The U.S. Department of Agriculture (USDA) provides a wide variety of programs to promote U.S. agricultural exports. Some of the trade assistance programs include promotion of U.S. farm exports in foreign markets, services of commodity and marketing specialists, trade fairs, and information services. Programs are available to expand dairy product exports, provide technical assistance for specialty crops, and so on.

State Government and City Agencies

Many states, cities, and counties have special programs to assist their own exporters. Such programs generally include export education, marketing assistance, trade missions, and trade shows.

Private Sources of Export Assistance

Commercial banks, trading companies, trade clubs, chambers of commerce, and trade associations, as well as trade consultants, provide various forms of export assistance (see Table 4.2).

TABLE 4.2. Private Sources of Export Assistance

Private Sources	Services
Commercial banks	Advice on export regulations, exchange of currencies, financing exports, collections, credit information and assistance
Trading companies	Market research and promotion, shipping and documentation, financing sales, facilitating prompt payment, appointing overseas distributors, etc.
World trade clubs	Education programs on international trade and organization of promotional events
Chambers of commerce and trade associations	Chambers of commerce provide the following services: Export seminars, trade promotion, contacts with foreign companies and distributors, issuance of certificates of origin, transportation routing, and consolidating shipments. U.S. chambers of commerce abroad are also a valuable source of marketing information. Trade associations provide information on market demand and trends and other information on pertinent trade issues through newsletters
Trade consultants	Advice on all aspects of exporting ranging from domestic/foreign regulations to market research and risk analysis

OVERSEAS TRAVEL AND PROMOTION

Once market research is conducted and the target countries are selected, the next step is to visit the countries in order to locate and cultivate new customers or to develop and maintain relationships with foreign distributors. As we enter the twenty-first century, the world has become one market, and this has naturally given rise to more intercultural encounters. The exporter has to be aware of certain important factors before embarking on a trip, not only to avoid embarrassment but also to be able to conclude a successful business arrangement (International Perspective 4.3).

Planning and Preparing for the Trip

Making Prior Arrangements

The most important meetings should be confirmed before leaving the United States. One should avoid traveling during national holidays, or

INTERNATIONAL PERSPECTIVE 4.3.
The Twelve Most Common Mistakes of Potential Exporters

- Failure to obtain qualified export counseling and to develop a master international marketing plan before starting an export business.
- Insufficient commitment by top management to overcoming the initial difficulties and financial requirements of exporting
- Insufficient care in selecting overseas distributors
- Chasing orders from around the world instead of establishing a basis for profitable operations and orderly growth
- Neglecting export business when the U.S. market booms
- Failure to treat international distributors on an equal basis with domestic counterparts
- Assuming that a given market technique and product will automatically be successful in all countries
- Unwillingness to modify products to meet regulations or cultural preferences of other countries
- Failure to print service, sale, and warranty messages in locally understood languages
- Failure to consider use of an export management company
- Failure to consider licensing or joint venture agreements
- Failure to provide readily available servicing for the product

political elections in the host countries. Contacts can be made with the Department of Commerce country desk officers in Washington, DC, and/or U.S. embassies abroad to obtain current and reliable information about the target countries.

Acquiring Basic Knowledge of the Host Country

Exporters should know some basic facts about the history, culture, and customs of the host countries. Several books and magazines cover business manners, customs, dietary practices, humor, and acceptable dress in various countries. It is essential to exercise flexibility and cultural sensitivity when doing business abroad. The exporter should also obtain prior information on such important areas such as weather conditions, health care, exchanging currency, and visa requirements. Various travel publications provide such information (for a typical export procedure, see International Perspective 4.4).

INTERNATIONAL PERSPECTIVE 4.4.
Typical Export Transaction

Step 1: The exporter establishes initial contact by responding to an overseas buyer's advertisement for a product that she or he can supply. Such ads are available in various trade publications. The exporter's letter briefly introduces the company and requests more information on the product needed as well as bank and trade references.

Step 2: The prospective buyer responds to the exporter's letter or fax by specifying the type and quantity of product needed, with a sample where appropriate. The potential importer also sends his or her trade references.

Step 3: The exporter checks with the consulate of the importer's country to determine (1) whether the product can be legally imported and if any restrictions may apply, and (2) any requirements that need to be met. The consulate may indicate that a certificate of origin is needed to clear shipment at the foreign port. The exporter also verifies the buyer's bank and trade references through its bank and other U.S. government agencies, such as the Department of Commerce.

Step 4: The exporter (if an agent) contacts manufacturers of the product to (1) establish if the given product is available for export to the country in question, and (2) obtain and compare price lists, catalogs, and samples.

Step 5: The exporter selects the product from responses submitted by manufacturers based on quality, cost, and delivery time. The sample selected is sent by airmail to the overseas customer to determine if the product is acceptable to the latter. In the meantime, the exporter prepares and sends a price quotation suggesting the mode of transportation and letter of credit terms. The price quotation should include commission and markup.

Step 6: The exporter obtains a positive response from the overseas customer and is requested to send a pro forma invoice to enable the latter to obtain an import and foreign exchange permit. The exporter sends the pro forma invoice.

Step 7: The overseas customer receives the pro forma invoice, opens a confirmed irrevocable letter of credit for the benefit of the exporter, and sends an order to the latter to ship the merchandise.

Step 8: The exporter verifies with its bank about the validity of the letter of credit and finds that it meets the agreed conditions in the export contract and that it will be honored by the bank if the exporter meets the terms. The exporter ships the merchandise and submits the required documents (such as bill of lading, commercial invoice, consular invoice, certificate of origin, packing list etc.) to the bank with a request for payment. The exporter is paid, the merchandise is in transit, and the transaction is completed.

Obtaining the ATA Carnet

For exporters who take product samples, duties and burdensome customs formalities can be avoided by obtaining the ATA (Admission Temporaire-Temporary Admission) carnet. The United States is a member of the ATA carnet system, which permits U.S. commercial and professional travelers to take material to member countries of the ATA carnet system for a temporary period of time without paying duty. An exporter should check whether a host country is member of the ATA convention. The U.S Council for International Business handles applications for carnets. A bond, a letter of credit, or a cash equivalent (as guarantee for 40 percent of the value), will, however, be required to cover outstanding duties in case the samples are not returned to the United States.

Business Negotiations

Negotiations should be entered into with sufficient planning and preparation. The exporter should establish the line or boundary below which he or she is not willing to concede. It is also advisable to draft the agreements since it will enable the exporter to include terms and conditions with important implications into the contract.

Documentation

The exporter should document the various meetings at the end of the day to avoid confusing one market with another. It also provides a record for company files. Once the trip is over and the exporter returns home, there should be an immediate follow-up, with a letter confirming the commitments and timetable for implementation of these commitments.

Overseas Promotion

Overseas promotion of exports is often designed to open new markets, maintain and increase existing market share, and obtain market intelligence. Such efforts must meet strategic marketing goals and achieve the greatest impact at the lowest possible cost. Effective promotion should go beyond enabling the potential buyer to receive the desired information. It must be strong enough to motivate him or her to react positively. This requires the conveying of a message that does not offend cultural sensibilities and one that is uniquely designed for each market. The exporter can choose one or a combination of promotional tools: direct mail, advertising, trade fairs/

missions, and publicity. The choice will depend on the target audience, company objectives, the product or service exported, the availability of internal resources, and the availability of the tool in a particular market (Czinkota, Ronkainen, and Moffett, 2003). Exporters may use the same promotional strategy in different foreign markets if the target markets vary little with respect to product use and consumer attitudes. In some cases, the product and/or promotional strategy must be adapted to foreign market conditions. For example, Tang sold in Latin America is especially sweetened and promoted as a drink for mealtime. In the United States, people drink it in the morning and the product is promoted as a drink for breakfast (Ball et al., 2006).

In certain developing countries where the rate of illiteracy is high, advertising in periodicals does not reach a broad audience. However, if the product or service marketed is intended for a small part of the population, such as the middle- or high-income consumers, using periodicals could be an effective way of reaching the target market. For products that are intended for a broader audience, such as soap or cooking oil, radios or billboards could be an effective way of reaching many consumers in these countries.

It is often stated that adapting a product to local conditions and accentuating the local nature of a certain aspect of the product in the promotional material tend to create a favorable image among the public and stimulate product sales. This means that exporters should consider ways and means of localizing a certain part of their activity, such as product adaptation to local conditions or assembly of parts, in the host countries. Such activities not only increase product sales, but also create employment opportunities in the local economy. For less sophisticated products, a firm could export the necessary ingredients or components into a host country, preferably into a free trade zone, and use local labor to produce or assemble the final product. In addition to being a good promotional tool for the product, such localization will enhance the competitiveness of the product by reducing cost.

Advertising

Advertising is any paid form of nonpersonal presentation and promotion of ideas, goods, or services by an identified sponsor. Typically, no one vehicle reaches an entire target audience and hence, exporters must evaluate the many alternatives so as to meet their desired objectives. One or a combination of vehicles can be used (magazines, newspapers, TV, radio, direct mail, or billboards) to carry the advertisements to target audiences.

Exporters should be aware of regulations in various countries that govern advertising. In some European countries, for example, television stations allow only a certain percentage (12 to 18 percent) of advertising per hour. In many developed countries, the advertising of tobacco and alcoholic beverages is heavily regulated. In some Latin American countries, such as Peru, commercial advertising on national television should be domestically produced.

The advertising process involves: (1) budgeting—how much it will cost and how much the exporter can afford, (2) determining the most effective and least expensive media to reach the potential customer, and (3) preparing the appropriate advertising package that emphasizes the important, but minimal, number of points.

Small exporters often use direct mail (correspondence and brochures) to reach their overseas customers. In Southeast Asian markets, direct mail is the most effective way of promoting the sale of industrial goods. Brochures have to be translated into the local language and accurate mailing lists have to be obtained. Mailing lists can be purchased from private firms—most libraries have various resources, such as trade publications and journals of various trade associations, from which a list of potential overseas customers can be obtained. In addition, such lists are available from the directory and catalog of trade shows and other government publications, such as *Foreign Trades Index, The Export Contact List Service,* and the *World Traders Data Reports* (WTDR).

The exporter can use one or a combination of the following media to advertise the product or service:

Foreign media. A product can be advertised in an overseas retailer's or distributor's catalog, or trade publication. Cooperative advertising, that is, a group advertising program, can be arranged by business associations and local chambers of commerce. Cooperative advertising is more effective for noncompeting and/or complementary products. The advantage of such advertising is that it reduces expenses, especially for small exporters, and also enables exporters to combine advertising budgets to reach a larger audience than is normally possible individually.

Government-supported advertising. There are many government-supported (federal and state) promotional programs for U.S. exporting firms that facilitate the marketing of U.S. products overseas.

Commercial publications. Many U.S. trade publications are widely read in many parts of the world. Advertising in such journals or magazines will enable the exporter to reach a broader market. Some of these publications include *Showcase U.S.A., Export,* and *Automobile and Truck International*.

The Internet. The Internet provides the exporter with an additional global medium. Potential consumers can be reached through Web sites in key languages and e-mails. A number of products are being made available online. Data collected from customers can also be used for future marketing efforts.

Tuller describes the reasons that certain overseas promotional tools, such as advertising, fail to deliver: (a) the expected results were ill defined, (b) the time frame within which results could be expected was too short, (c) advertisements were inappropriately presented, or (d) the wrong media was used (Tuller, 1994, p. 225).

Personal Selling

Personal selling is often used during the first stages of internationalization. It is also used for the marketing of industrial, especially high-priced goods. Personal selling entails oral presentations by sales personnel of the organization or agents to prospective overseas purchasers. Salespeople also collect information on competitive products, prices, services, and delivery problems that assist exporters in improving quality and service. In short, such media are used in cases in which advertising does not provide an effective line with target markets, the price is subject to negotiation, and the product/service needs customer application assistance. Avon and Unilever, for example, use personal sellers in rural villages in many developing countries to market their products.

Sales Promotion

Sales promotion refers to marketing activity other than advertising, personal selling, or publicity. It includes trade shows, trade fairs, demonstrations, and other nonrecurrent selling efforts not in the ordinary routine (Asheghian and Ibrahimi, 1990). Trade shows are events at which firms display their products in exhibits at a central location and invite dealers or customers to visit the exhibits. They are a cost-effective way of reaching a large number of customers who might otherwise be difficult to reach. Adding to their benefit, from a cost and efficiency standpoint, is that trade shows help exporters to contact and evaluate potential agents and distributors. Trade fairs also provide an important opportunity for exporters to introduce, promote, and demonstrate new products, cultivate new contacts, and collect market intelligence, as well as close deals with a number of attendees who often have direct responsibility for purchasing products and services.

Trade fairs can be organized by certain industries, trade associations, or chambers of commerce. For example, the Hanover Trade Fair in Germany organizes regional and national fairs and exhibitions in various product sectors targeted at specialized audiences as well as the general public. Every year it organizes around fifty trade fairs and exhibitions which attract over 28,000 exhibitors and 2.5 million visitors from over 100 countries around the world. The Seoul International Gift and Accessories Show is one of the largest trade fairs for gift and fashion accessories in Asia. It attracts approximately 32,000 local and overseas visitors resulting in about $15 million in sales.

Trade shows are also supported or organized by governments in order to promote exports. In the United States, the Department of Commerce (DOC) organizes various export promotion events such as exhibitions, seminars, trade missions, and other customized promotions for individual U.S. companies. Under the International Buyer program, the DOC selects leading U.S. trade exhibitions each year in industries with high export potential. Offices of the DOC abroad recruit foreign buyers and distributors to attend these shows, while program staff help exhibiting firms make contact with international visitors at the show to achieve direct export sales and/or international representation. The DOC, through the certified trade fair program, supports private-sector organized shows. Exhibitors use U.S. pavilions to create enhanced visibility and also receive the support of commercial services from U.S. embassies and consulates. The DOC and state agencies also jointly organize U.S. company catalogs/product literature to present to potential customers abroad and send the trade leads directly to participating U.S. firms. Many developed countries have similar programs to promote the sale of their products abroad.

Trade missions are another export sales promotion tool. Under a trade mission, a group of business people and/or government officials visits foreign markets in search of business opportunities. Missions typically target specific industries in selected countries. Events are also organized by private organizations or government agencies so that foreign buyer groups can come to the United States to meet individually with U.S. companies, exporters, or relevant trade associations. At these events, foreign businesses buy U.S. products, negotiate distributor agreements, find joint venture partners, or learn about current industry trends.

Publicity

Publicity is communicating with an audience by personal or nonpersonal media that are not explicitly paid for delivering the messages. This is done by planting commercially significant news about the exporter and/or products in a published medium or obtaining favorable presentation on the local media without sponsoring it. A carefully managed advertising and public relations program is essential to the long-term success of an export firm. The public relations (publicity) program could include charitable donations to schools, hospitals, and other social causes; sponsorship of youth athletic teams; participation in local parades; or inviting the media to cover special events sponsored or supported by the export company.

CHAPTER SUMMARY

Assessing and Selecting the Product

In order to establish market potential for a product/service, it is important to consider: Success of the product in the domestic market, participation in overseas trade shows, advertising in foreign media, market data.
Approaches to selecting a product for exports:

1. *Systematic approach:* Product selection based on overall market demand.
2. *Reactive approach:* Selection of a product based on immediate (short-term) market need.

International Market Research (IMR)

IMR helps business organizations in making business decisions that lead to the proper steps.

Developing an Export/Import Business Plan

Typical structure of a business plan: Executive summary, general description of industry and company, target market, marketing plan and sales strategy, management and organization, long-term development plan, and financial plan.

Sources of Export Counseling

Public sources: The U.S. Department of Commerce, U.S. Export Assistance Centers, and The Small Business Administration.
Private sources: Commercial banks, trading companies, world trade clubs, chambers of commerce and trade associations, trade consultants.

Business Travel and Promotion Abroad

Planning and preparing for the trip: Making prior arrangements, acquiring basic knowledge of host country, using the ATA carnet, preparing for business negotiations, and documentation.

Overseas promotion: Advertising, personal selling, sales promotion, and publicity.

REVIEW QUESTIONS

1. Discuss the two major approaches to selecting a product for exports. Why is it important to participate in overseas trade shows?
2. What are the disadvantages of the reactive approach to selecting a product for exports?
3. Explain the importance of the following factors in the selection of products for exports: shifting spending patterns, quality, and niche marketing.
4. Do a country's imports completely measure the market potential for a product? Discuss.
5. Why should an export firm consider financial and economic conditions in importing countries?
6. What is the importance of political and legal forces in international market assessment?
7. Identify the public sources of export counseling in the United States.
8. Discuss three private sources of export assistance. What is the gold key service?
9. Explain the steps involved in a typical export transaction.
10. What is SCORE?

CASE 4.1. DEVELOPING EXPORT MARKETS

A recent survey by Babson College and the London Business School on entrepreneurship noted that middle-income countries have a larger share of individuals engaged in business ventures with high growth potential than high-income countries. The study also notes that these countries have higher percentages of people starting businesses. This is partly attributed to the deployment of existing technologies to exploit their comparative advantages. High rates of early stage entrepreneurship, however, do not necessarily translate into high rates of established business. Rich countries such as Japan, for example, have low levels of early stage entrepreneurial activity but a large number of established businesses. This is because the start-ups are opportunity-driven companies with lower rates of business failures than those in middle-income or poor countries that are largely motivated by the necessity to earn a living. In rich countries, there is also a tendency for entrepreneurial activity to shift from the consumer, such as retailing, to business services.

Export of luxury tea from Argentina. During the worst financial crisis in Argentina (2001), three young entrepreneurs founded a luxury tea business with just $10,000. They focused on quality with a view to selling in high value export markets. The bags are a hand-tied sack of muslin that does not alter the flavor of the tea, containing one of the five types of organic tea: cedron, black-leaf tea, peppermint, patagonian rosehip, and mate lightened, for the overseas market. They traveled to different parts of Argentina to locate the best growers. After finding suitable suppliers, the partners agreed to create a premium product to be sold in up-market outlets and trendy stores. Over 75 percent of the output is sold in overseas markets: the United States, United Kingdom, Continental Europe, the Middle East, and Asia. Over the past few years, the company has registered substantial increases in sales.

The partners note that (1) exporting maximizes the benefits of selling from countries with weak currencies, (2) it is necessary to focus on quality materials, production, and packaging to charge premium prices, (3) high quality products should be sold in high quality outlets, and (4) it is important to disprove national stereotypes such as lack of punctuality, dishonesty, etc., with buyers and distributors.

Exports by Rwanda's nascent entrepreneurs. Rwanda is a small landlocked country with a population of eight million located in the Great Lakes Region of East-Central Africa. Despite the legacy of genocide and war, the country is showing signs of rapid development. J. Nkubana, one of a number of women entrepreneurs, sells over 5,000 Christmas ornaments and baskets to Macy's in New York. Another rising entrepreneur, Beatrice Gakuba, founder of Rwanda Floral, is the nation's largest exporter of roses. She sells over five tons of flowers a week at auctions in Amsterdam. Exporters, however, face a number of challenges in Rwanda: (1) regular electricity outages resulting in lost productivity, (2) Rwanda's landlocked status requires use of ports in neighboring countries and this delays shipments and delivery of exports, and (3) borrowing costs are high (17 percent interest on loans) and banks require 100 percent collateral. Public funding is almost nonexistent to promote exports.

Questions

1. Comment on the statement that "exporting maximizes the benefits of selling from countries with weak currencies."
2. Based on the information provided, what is your advice to the government of Rwanda to increase exports?

Chapter 5

Export Channels of Distribution

Global competition is motivating firms to seek innovative ways of entering new markets. Export managers have to decide which marketing functions are to be delegated to other intermediaries or partners and which are to be performed internally. Selecting and managing the right distribution systems is the key to successful internationalization. They provide a competitive advantage in global markets by helping identify market opportunities. Channels are also more difficult to change and thus require careful planning.

Williamson (1991) argues that contracting is determined by the governance mechanism that seeks to minimize transaction costs. He states that "assets specificity, uncertainty, and frequency" determine the efficient transaction governance form. Specific assets are involved in investments made in market research, branding, product design, and human assets. "Uncertainty" refers to changes in market forces stemming from individuals' limited information or opportunistic motives of other actors. "Frequency" concerns frequency and volume of transactions. Studies indicate that asset specificity, uncertainty, and frequency in volume of transactions are associated with direct forms of market entry (vertical integration). There is an incentive to integrate distribution channels to minimize transaction costs (McNaughton, 1996; Tesfom, Lutz, and Ghauri, 2004). In many developing countries, direct entry may be needed, in spite of their limited market size, due to the problem of asset specificity and lack of contract enforcing institutions.

Export firms can be involved in two principal channels of distribution when marketing abroad:

Indirect channels. With indirect channels, the firm exports through an independent local middleman who assumes responsibility for moving the product overseas. Indirect exporting entails reliance on another firm to act as a sales intermediary and to assume responsibility for marketing and shipping the product overseas. The manufacturer incurs no start-up cost, and this

Export-Import Theory, Practices, and Procedures, Second Edition

method provides small firms with little experience in foreign trade access to overseas markets without their direct involvement. However, using indirect channels has certain disadvantages: (1) the manufacturer loses control over the marketing of its product overseas, and (2) the manufacturer's success totally depends on the initiative and efforts of the chosen intermediary. The latter could provide low priority to, or even discontinue marketing, the firm's products when the competitor's product provides a better sales or profit potential.

Direct channels. With direct channels, the firm sells directly to foreign distributors, retailers, or trading companies. Direct sales can also be made through agents located in a foreign country. Direct exporting can be expensive and time consuming. However, it offers manufacturers opportunities to learn about their markets and customers in order to forge better relationships with their trading partners. It also allows firms greater control over various activities. Heli Modified, Inc., of Maine, which manufactures custom-made handles for motorcycles, attributes much of its export success to U.S. government agencies as well as its international network of sales agents and distributors. The company now exports to approximately twenty-five countries on four continents.

The decision to market products directly or use the services of an intermediary is based on several important factors.

International Marketing Objectives of the Firm

The marketing objectives of the firm with respect to sales, market share, profitability, and level of financial commitment will often determine channel choice. Direct exporting is likely to provide opportunities for high profit margins even though it requires a high degree of financial commitment.

Manufacturer's Resources and Experience

A direct channel structure may be neither feasible nor desirable in light of the firm's limited resources and/or commitment. Small to medium-sized firms appear to use indirect channels due to their limited resources and small export volumes, whereas large firms use similar channels because of trade barriers in the host country that may restrict or prohibit direct forms of ownership (Kogut, 1986). Firms tend to use independent intermediaries during the early phases of their internationalization efforts compared to those with greater experience (Anderson and Coughlin, 1987; Kim, Nugent, and Yhee, 1997).

Availability and Capability of Intermediary

Every country has certain distribution patterns that have evolved over the years and are complemented by supportive institutions. Firms that have used specific types of distribution channels in certain countries may find it difficult to use similar channels in other countries. This occurs in cases in which distributors have exclusive arrangements with other suppliers/competitors or when such channels do not exist.

Customer and Product Characteristics

If the number of consumers is large and concentrated in major population centers, the company may opt for direct or multiple channels of distribution. In Japan, for example, over half of the population lives in the Tokyo-Nagoya-Osaka market area (Cateora, 1996). Another factor is that customers may also have developed a habit of buying from a particular channel and are reluctant to change in the short term.

Direct exporting is often preferable if customers are geographically homogeneous, have similar buying habits, and are limited in number, which allows for direct customer contact and greater control (Seifert and Ford, 1989). The choice of channel structure is primarily dictated by market considerations. However, in certain situations, the nature of the product determines channel choice. In a study on export channels of distribution in the United States, 52.7 percent of the respondents indicated that the distribution was primarily dictated by the market, while 15.5 percent stated that the choice was dictated by the nature of the product exported (Seifert and Ford, 1989). For example, industrial equipment of considerable size and value that requires more after-sales service is usually exported to the user or through the use of other direct channels. Direct channels are also frequently used for products of a perishable nature or high unit value (since it will bring more profit) or for products that are custom-made or highly differentiated. Smaller equipment, industrial supplies, and consumer goods, on the other hand, tend to have longer channels. In Canada, for example, consumer goods are purchased by importing wholesalers, department stores, mail-order houses, chain stores, and single-line retailers.

Marketing Environment

The use of direct channels is more likely in countries that are more similar in culture to the exporter's home country. For example, U.S. sales to Canada are characterized by short (direct) marketing channels compared to the indirect channels used in Japan and Southeast Asia. In certain cases, firms have limited options in the selection of appropriate channels for their products. In the lumber industry, the use of export intermediaries is the norm in many countries. In Finland, over 90 percent of distribution of nondurable consumer goods is handled by four wholesale chains. Exporters have to use these distribution channels to gain a significant penetration of the market (Czinkota, Ronkainen, and Moffett, 2003). Legislation in certain countries requires that foreign firms be represented by local firms that are wholly owned by nationals of the country. Exporters must market their goods indirectly by appointing a local agent or distributor. Some studies support the use of direct/integrated channels when there is a high degree of environmental uncertainty. The establishment of integrated channels is intended to place the firm closer to the market so as to react and adapt to unforeseen circumstances (Klein, Frazier, and Roth, 1990).

Control and Coverage

A direct or integrated channel affords the manufacturer more control over its distribution and its link to the end user. However, it is not a practical option for firms that do not have adequate foreign market knowledge or the necessary financial, operational, and strategic capabilities.

Firms that use indirect channels are still able to exercise control mechanisms to coordinate and influence foreign intermediary actions. Two types of controls are available for the manufacturer/exporter: process controls and output controls. Under process controls, the manufacturer's intervention is intended to influence the means intermediaries use to achieve desirable ends (selling technique, servicing procedure, promotion, etc.). Output controls are used to influence indirectly the ends achieved by the distributor. The latter includes monitoring sales volume, profits, and other performance-based indicators (Bello and Gilliland, 1997). It is important to note the following salient points with respect to manufacturers' coordination and control of independent foreign intermediaries:

- Manufacturers must rely on both unilateral and bilateral (collaboration) control mechanisms in order to organize and manage their export relationships with independent foreign intermediaries.
- The use of output controls tends to have a positive impact on foreign intermediaries' overall performance. Process controls, however, do not appear to account for performance benefits, largely due to manufacturers' inadequate knowledge of foreign marketing procedures.

- Firms that export highly technical and sophisticated products tend to exercise high levels of control (process and output controls) over foreign intermediaries in order to protect their proprietary rights (trade secrets/know-how) as well as to address unique customer needs.

In terms of coverage, firms that use longer channels tend to use different intermediaries (intensive coverage). However, recent studies show a positive relationship between channel directness and intensive coverage. This means that firms employing direct methods to reach their overseas customers tend to use a large number of different types of channel intermediaries.

Types of Intermediaries

One of the distinguishing features of direct and indirect channel alternatives is the location of the second channel. If the second channel is located in the producer's country, it is considered an indirect channel, whereas if it is located in the buyer's country, it is assumed to be a direct channel. This means that agents, distributors, or other middlemen could be in either category, depending on whether they are located in the buyer's or seller's country. Channel alternatives are also defined on the basis of ownership of the distribution channel: a direct channel is one owned and managed by the company, as opposed to one in which distribution is handled by outside agents and middlemen. A firm's channel structure is also defined in terms of the percentage of equity held in the distribution organization: majority ownership (greater than 50 percent) is treated as a direct or integrated channel, while less than majority ownership is considered an indirect channel. The first definition of channel alternatives is used in this chapter.

INDIRECT CHANNELS

Several intermediaries are associated with indirect channels and each type offers distinct advantages. Indirect channels are classified here on the basis of their functions.

Exporters That Sell on Behalf of the Manufacturer

Manufacturer's Export Agents (MEAs)

Manufacturer's export agents usually represent various manufacturers of related and noncompeting products. They may also operate on an exclusive basis. It is an ideal channel to use especially in cases involving a widespread or thin overseas market. It is also used when the product is new and demand conditions are uncertain. The usual roles of the MEA are as follows:

- Handle direct marketing, promotion, shipping, and sometimes financing of merchandise. The agent does not offer all services.
- Take possession but not title to the goods. The MEA works for commission; risk of loss remains with the manufacturer.
- Represent the manufacturer on a continuous or permanent basis as defined in the contract.

Export Management Companies (EMCs)

Export management companies act as the export department for one or several manufacturers of noncompetitive products. Over 2,000 EMCs in the United States provide manufacturers with extensive services that include, but are not limited to, market analyses, documentation, financial and legal services, purchase for resale, and agency services (locating and arranging sale). An EMC often does extensive research on foreign markets, conducts its own advertising and promotion, serves as a shipping/forwarding agent, and provides legal advice on intellectual property matters. It also collects and furnishes credit information on overseas customers.

Most EMCs are small and usually specialize by product, foreign market, or both. Some are capable of performing only limited functions such as strategic planning or promotion. Export management companies solicit and carry on business in their own name or in the name of the manufacturer for a commission, salary, or retainer plus commission. Occasionally, they purchase products by direct payment or financing for resale to their own customers. Export management companies may operate as agents or distributors. The following are some of the disadvantages of using EMCs:

- Manufacturer may lose control over foreign sales. To retain sufficient control, manufacturers should ask for regular reports on marketing efforts, promotion, sales, and so forth. This right to review marketing plans and efforts should be included in the agreement.
- Export management companies that work on commission may lose interest if sales do not happen immediately. They may be less interested in new or unknown products and may not provide sufficient attention to small clients.
- Exporters may not learn international business since EMCs do most of the work related to exports.

Despite these disadvantages, EMCs have marketing and distribution contacts overseas and provide the benefit of economies of scale. Export management companies obtain low freight rates by consolidating shipments of several principals. By providing a range of services, they also help manufacturers to concentrate on other areas.

Export Trading Companies (ETCs)

Trading companies are the most traditional and dominant intermediary in many countries. In Japan, they date back to the nineteenth century and in Western countries, their origins can be traced back to colonial times. They are also prevalent in many less developed countries. They are demand driven; that is, they identify the needs of overseas customers and often act as independent distributors linking buyers and sellers to arrange transactions. They buy and sell goods as merchants taking title to the merchandise. Some work on a commission. They may also handle goods on consignment.

In the United States, an ETC is a legally defined entity under the Export Trading Company Act. It is difficult to set up ETCs unless certain special certifications and requirements are met: the U.S. Export Trading Act allows bank participation in trading companies thus facilitating better access to capital and more trading transactions. Antitrust provisions were also relaxed to allow firms to form joint ventures and share the cost of developing foreign markets. By 2002, about 186 individual ETCs covering more than 5,000 firms had been certified by the U.S. Department of Commerce. Trade associations often apply for certification for their members. To be effective, ETCs must balance between the demands of the markets and the supply of the members (trade association; see International Perspective 5.1).

Trading companies offer services to manufacturers similar to those provided by EMCs. However, there are some differences between the two channels:

*   Trading companies offer more services and have more diverse product lines than export management companies. Trading companies are also larger and better financed than EMCs.
*   Trading companies are not exclusively restricted to export-import activities. Some are also engaged in production, resource development, and commercial banking. Korean trading companies, such as Daewoo and Hyundai, for example, are heavily involved in manufacturing. Some trading companies, such as Mitsubishi (Japan) and Cobec (Brazil), are affiliated with banks and engaged in extension of traditional banking into commercial fields (Meloan and Graham, 1995).

The disadvantages of ETCs are similar to the ones mentioned for EMCs.

INTERNATIONAL PERSPECTIVE 5.1.
Export Trading Companies in Global Markets

Trading companies have been the most traditional channels for international commercial activity. Trading companies supported by governments, such as the English East India Company (1600), the Dutch East India Company (1602), and the French Compagme des Indes Orientales (1664), were established and enjoyed not only exclusive trading rights but also military protection in exchange for tax payments. Today, trading companies also perform the important function of exporting, importing, investing, and countertrading. In Japan, for example, the Sogo Shosha, which includes the top nine trading companies such as Mitsubishi and Mitsui, conducts about two-thirds of the country's imports and a half of its exports. In Korea, trading companies similar in scope to the Sogo Shosha (Daewoo, Hyundai, Samsung) are responsible for a substantial part of the country's exports and imports. In addition to trade, trading companies in these countries are involved in mega projects, participate in joint ventures and act as financial deal makers. The success of these conglomerates is due to: (1) extensive market information that allows for product or area diversification, (2) economies of scale that allows them to obtain preferential freight rates, etc., and (3) preferential access to capital markets that makes it easy to undertake large or risky transactions.

In view of the success of these trading companies, Brazil, Turkey, and the United States have enacted domestic legislation that allows the establishment of trading companies. The Brazilian Decree (No. 1298) of 1972, for example, sets up conditions for the registration of new enterprises with the government and allows local producers to export by selling to a trading company without losing their export incentives. In the United States, the Export Trading Company Act of 1982 allows businesses to join together to export goods and services or to assist unrelated companies to export their products without fear of violating antitrust legislation. Bank participation in trading companies was permitted to enable better access to capital. The legality of any action can be ascertained by precertification of planned activities with the U.S. Department of Commerce.

Exporters That Buy for Their Overseas Customers

Export Commission Agents (ECAs)

Export commission agents represent foreign buyers such as import firms and large industrial users and seek to obtain products that match the buyer's preferences and requirements. They reside and conduct business in the exporter's country and are paid a commission by their foreign clients. In certain cases, ECAs may be foreign government agencies or quasi-government firms empowered to locate and purchase desired goods. They could operate from a permanent office location in supplier countries or undertake foreign government purchasing missions when the need arises. In some countries, the exporter may receive payment from a confirming house when the goods are shipped. The confirming house may also carry out some functions performed by the commission agent or resident buyer (making arrangements for the shipper, and so on). For the exporter, this is an easy way to access a foreign market. There is little credit risk, and the exporter has only to fill the order.

Another variation of the ECA is the resident buyer. The major factor that distinguishes the resident buyer from other ECAs is that in the case of the former, a long-term relationship is established in which the resident buyer not only undertakes the purchasing function for the overseas principal at the best possible price, but also ensures timely delivery of merchandise and facilitates principal's visits to suppliers and vendors. This allows foreign buyers to maintain a close and continuous contact with overseas sources of supply. One disadvantage of using such channels is that the exporter has little control over the marketing of products (Onkvisit and Shaw, 1997).

Exporters That Buy and Sell for Their Own Accounts

Export Merchants

Export merchants purchase products directly from manufacturers, pack and mark them according to their own specifications, and resell to their overseas customers. They take title to the goods and sell under their own names, and, hence, assume all risks associated with ownership. Export merchants generally handle undifferentiated products or products for which brands are not important. In view of their vast organizational networks, they are a powerful commercial entity dominating trade in certain countries.

When export merchants, after receiving an order, place an order with the manufacturer to deliver the goods directly to the overseas customer, they are called export drop shippers. In this case, the manufacturer is paid by the drop shipper, who in turn, is paid by the overseas buyer. Such intermediaries are commonly used to export bulky (high-freight), low-unit value products such as construction materials, coal, lumber, and so forth.

Another variation of export merchant is the export distributor (located in the exporter's country). Export distributors have exclusive rights to sell manufacturers' products in overseas markets. They represent several manufacturers and act as EMCs.

The disadvantage of export merchants as export intermediaries relates to lack of control over marketing, promotion, or pricing.

Cooperative Exporters (CEs)

These are manufacturers or service firms that sell the products of other companies in foreign markets along with their own (Ball et al., 2004). This generally occurs when a company has a contract with an overseas buyer to provide a wide range of products or services. Often, the company may not have all the products required under the contract and turns to other companies to provide the remaining products. The company (providing the remaining products) could sell its products without incurring export marketing or distribution costs. This helps small manufacturers that lack the ability/resources to export. This channel is often used to export products that are complementary to that of the exporting firm. A good example of this is the case of a heavy equipment manufacturer that wants to fill the demand of its overseas customers for water drilling equipment. The heavy equipment company exports the drilling equipment along with its product to its customers (Sletten, 1994). Companies engage in cooperative exporting in order to broaden the product lines they offer to foreign markets or to bolster decreasing export sales. In the 1980s, for example, the French chemical company Rhone-Poutenc sold products of several manufacturers through its extensive global sales network.

Export Cartels

These are organizations of firms in the same industry for the sole purpose of marketing their products overseas. They include the Webb-Pomerene Associations (WPAs) in the United States, as well as certain export cartels in Japan. The WPAs are exempted from antitrust laws under the U.S. Export Trade Act of 1918 and permitted to set prices, allocate orders, sell products, negotiate, and consolidate freight, as well as arrange shipment. There are WPAs in various areas such as pulp, movies, sulphur, and so on. Webb-Pomerene Associations are not permitted for services and the arrangement is not suitable for differentiated products because a common association label often replaces individual product brands. In addition to member firms' loss of individual identity, WPAs are vulnerable to lack of group cohesion, similar to other cartels, which undermines their effectiveness. Under the Export Trade Act, the only requirement to operate as a WPA is that the association must file with the Federal Trade Commission within thirty days after formation (see International Perspective 5.2).

INTERNATIONAL PERSPECTIVE 5.2.
Indirect Channel Structures

Advantages

- Little or no investment or marketing experience needed. Suitable for firms with limited resources or experience.
- Helps increase overall sales and cash flow.
- Good way to test-market products, develop goodwill, and allow clients to be familiar with firm's trade name or trademark before making substantial commitment.

Disadvantages

- Firm's profit margin may be dwindled due to commissions and other payments to foreign intermediaries.
- Limited contact/feedback from end users.
- Loss of control over marketing and pricing. Firm totally dependent on the marketing initiative and effort of foreign intermediary. Product may be priced too high or too low.
- Foreign intermediary may not provide product support or may damage market potential.
- Limited opportunity to learn international business know-how and develop marketing contacts. Creates difficulty in taking over the business after the relationship has ended.

DIRECT CHANNELS

A company could use different avenues to sell its product overseas employing the direct channel structure. Direct exporting provides more control over the export process, potentially higher profits, and a closer relationship to the overseas buyer and the market place. However, the firm needs to devote more time, personnel, and other corporate resources than needed in the case of indirect exporting.

Direct Marketing from the Home Country

A firm may sell directly to a foreign retailer or end user, and this is often accomplished through catalog sales or traveling sales representatives who are domestic employees of the exporting firm. Such marketing channels are a viable alternative for many companies that sell books, magazines, housewares, cosmetics, travel, and financial services. Foreign end users include foreign governments and institutions such as banks, schools, hospitals, or businesses. Buyers can be identified at trade shows, through international publications, and so on. If products are specifically designed for each customer, company representatives are more effective than agents or distributors. The growing use of the Internet is also likely to dramatically increase the sale of product and/or services directly to the retailer or end user. For example, Amazon.com has become one of the biggest bookstores in the United States with over 2.5 million titles. Its books are sold through the Internet. Direct sales can also be undertaken through foreign sales branches or subsidiaries. A foreign sales branch handles all aspects of the sales distribution and promotion, displays manufacturer's product lines, and provides services. The foreign sales subsidiary, although similar to the branch, has broader responsibilities. All foreign orders are channeled through the subsidiary, which subsequently sells to foreign buyers. Direct marketing is also used when the manufacturer or retailer desires to increase its revenues and profits while providing its products or services at a lower cost. The firm could also provide better product support services and further enhance its image and reputation.

A major problem with direct sales to consumers results from duty and clearance problems. A country's import regulations may prohibit or limit the direct purchase of merchandise from overseas. Thus it is important to evaluate a country's trade regulations before orders are processed and effected.

Marketing Through Overseas Agents and Distributors

Overseas Agents

Overseas agents are independent sales representatives of various noncompeting suppliers. They are residents of the country or region where the product is sold and usually work on a commission basis, pay their own expenses, and assume no financial risk or responsibility. Agents rarely take delivery of and never take title to goods and are authorized to solicit purchases within their marketing territory and to advise firms on orders placed by prospective purchasers. The prices to be charged are agreed on between the exporters and the overseas customers. Overseas agents usually do not provide product support services to customers. Agency agreements must be drafted carefully so as to clearly indicate that agents are not employees of the exporting companies because of potential legal and financial implications, such as payment of benefits upon termination. In some countries, agents are required to register with the government as commercial agents.

Overseas agents are used when firms intend to (1) sell products to small markets that do not attract distributor interest, (2) market to distinct individual customers (custom-made for individuals or projects), (3) sell heavy equipment, machinery, or other big ticket items that cannot be easily stocked, or (4) solicit public or private bids. Firms deal directly with the customers (after agents inform the firms of the orders) with respect to price, delivery, sales, service, and warranty bonds. Given their limited role, agents are not required to have extensive training or to make a substantial financial commitment. They are valuable for their personal contacts and intelligence and help reach markets that would otherwise be inaccessible. The major disadvantages of using agents are: (1) legal and financial problems in the event of termination (local laws in many countries discriminate against alien firms [principals] in their contractual relationships with local agents), (2) firms assume the attendant risks and responsibilities, ranging from pricing and delivery to sales services including collections, and (3) agents have limited training and knowledge about the product and this may adversely impact product sales.

Overseas Distributors

These are independent merchants that import products for resale and are compensated by the markup they charge their customers. Overseas distributors take delivery of and title to the goods and have contractual arrangements with the exporters as well as the customers. No contractual relationships exist between the exporters and the customers and the distributors may not legally obligate exporters to third parties. Distributors may be given exclusive representation for a certain territory, often in return for agreeing not to handle competing merchandise. Certain countries require the registration and approval of distributors (and agents) as well as the representation agreement.

Distributors, unlike agents, take possession of goods and also provide the necessary pre- and postsales services. They carry inventory and spare parts and maintain adequate facilities and personnel for normal service operations. They are responsible for advertising and promotion. Some of the disadvantages of using distributors are: (1) loss of control over marketing and pricing (they may price the product too high or too low), (2) limited access to or feed-back from customers, (3) limited opportunity to learn international business know-how and about developments in foreign markets, and (4) dealer protection legislation in many countries that may make it difficult and expensive to terminate relationships with distributors (see International Perspectives 5.3 and 5.4).

INTERNATIONAL PERSPECTIVE 5.3.
The Japanese Distribution System

Distribution channels in Japan are very different from our own; they are as inefficient as they are complex. The system is characterized by multiple layers of wholesalers who have developed close, personal relationships with other wholesalers, manufacturers, importers, and retailers. Moreover, these intimate relationships often serve as an informal barrier to U.S. companies wishing to sell directly to end users or retailers.

Many American exporters find retailers/end users unwilling to disrupt their longstanding, personal relationships with Japanese suppliers even when the U.S. company can offer a product of superior or equal quality at a cheaper price. Many Japanese retailers/end users are unwilling to make the switch to an "unreliable" foreign supplier. They fear a lack of commitment on the part of the foreign supplier will lead to problems. This system, although inefficient, does offer some important advantages for the participants. First, these close business relationships make it far easier for retailers/distributors to suggest product modifications and improvements. Second, this system encourages the sharing of information on product trends, innovations, competition, and overall market opportunities. Third, it contributes to a more cooperative business relationship.

The number of retail outlets in Japan is nearly the same as in the United States, despite the fact that the population of Japan is roughly half that of the United States and Japan is slightly smaller in geographical size than California. Distribution channels vary considerably from industry to industry and product to product, with particular differences between consumer and industrial goods. A foreign firm must understand existing distribution channels in order to utilize them or develop an innovative approach.

LOCATING, CONTACTING, AND EVALUATING AGENTS AND DISTRIBUTORS

Once the firm has identified markets in which to use agents and distributors, it could locate these intermediaries by using various sources: government trade offices (The Department of Commerce in the United States), chambers of commerce, trade shows, international banks and other firms, trade and professional associations, and advertisements in foreign trade publications. After identifying potential agents and distributors in each desired market, the firm should write directly to each, indicating its interest in appointing a representative and including a brochure describing the firm's history, resources, product line, personnel, and other pertinent information.

INTERNATIONAL PERSPECTIVE 5.4.
Parallel versus Multiple Exporters

Parallel (gray) market goods are products that enter a country outside regular, authorized distribution channels. They differ from black market products since they often enter the market legally. Factors contributing to the rise of parallel exports include:

- Substantial differences in the prevailing prices of the same product between two national markets.
- Differences in marketing and administrative expenses between the authorized distributor and the parallel distributor.
- Sale of distressed merchandise at deep discount to overseas markets sometimes gives rise to re-exports to the home market.
- Price discounts to distributors in the home market but not to nearby foreign markets.
- The authorized foreign distributor may have restrictive credit terms or unable (or unwilling) to carry sufficient inventory to service the market.

There is a flourishing market in parallel market goods in the United States in cars, watches, etc., estimated at over $6 billion (U.S.). The major problems created by parallel export channels is (1) reduction in sales and profits for the authorized distributor, (2) disruption in manufacturer-distribution relations, and (3) difficulty in maintaining a consistent image, quality, and reputation of a product.

Companies recognizing these problems should develop appropriate corporate policies such as creating product differentiation between the domestic and exported product, flexibility in the export price of the product sold to the foreign distributor.

Multiple channels are used by many firms in order to gain long-term sustainable advantages in global markets. A firm could supplement agents with their own salespersons to prevent lock-in and establish a credible alternative. A few strategic markets can be identified and developed by integration, while other markets are served by third parties, thus spreading the risk. Such channels are common in sectors where transaction costs and uncertainty are high (knowledge-intensive sectors like software development).

Evaluation and selection of potential representatives (agents or distributors) is often based on some of the following factors: local reputation and overall background, experience with a similar product or industry and adequate knowledge of the market, commitment not to represent competing brands, genuine interest and ability to devote sufficient time and effort to the product line. In the case of distributors, it is also important to evaluate sales organization; financial, marketing, and promotion capability; installation and after-sales service; timely payments; and similar characteristics. Once the firm has selected an agent or distributor based on the aforementioned criteria, the next step will be to negotiate a formal agreement. Foreign representatives are also interested in firms that are committed to the market and willing to provide the necessary product support and training. They also want to protect their territory from sales by third parties or the firm itself.

CONTRACTS WITH FOREIGN AGENTS AND DISTRIBUTORS (REPRESENTATIVES)

It is estimated that about 50 percent of global trade is handled through overseas agents and distributors. Laws governing agents and distributors are complex and vary from country to country. In certain countries, protective legislation favors local representatives with respect to such matters as market exclusivity and duration or termination of contracts. In the event of termination without good cause, for example, a Belgian distributor is entitled to an indemnity.

Similar laws exist in France, Germany, and other countries. In Germany, maximum compensation payable to agents usually equals one year's gross commissions based on an average over the previous five years or the period of existence of the agency, whichever is shorter. In countries such as Egypt, Indonesia, Japan, and South Korea, representation agreements must be formally registered with and their contents must be approved by the appropriate authority. In many Latin American countries, local law governs service contracts if the services are to be performed in local jurisdictions and any representative agreement that is not in conformity with local law will be invalid and unenforceable. Thus, it is important that in the negotiation and drafting of such agreements, sufficient attention is given to the impact of local laws and other pertinent issues.

MAJOR CLAUSES IN REPRESENTATION AGREEMENTS

Definition of Territory

The contract should define the geographical scope of the territory to be represented by the agent or distributor and whether the representative has sole marketing rights. In exclusive contracts, the agreement has to clearly specify whether the firm reserves the right to sell certain product lines to a specific class of buyers such as governments or quasi-government agencies.

If agreements do not explicitly state that they are exclusive, they will often be deemed exclusive if no other representatives have been appointed within a reasonable time. The contract should also state whether the representative could appoint subagents or subdistributors and the latter's status in relation to the firm. It is also important to explicitly state the intention of the parties not to create an employer-employee relationship due to financial and tax implications.

Definition of Product

The contract should identify those products or product lines covered by the agreement as well as the procedures for the addition of successive products. It should also provide for the alteration or deletion of certain product lines based on the exporter's continued production, representative's performance, or other events.

Representative's Rights and Obligations

The agreement should state that the representative will do its best to promote and market the product and cooperate to attain the objectives of the exporting firm. It should also include (1) the representative's commitment to periodically inform the exporter of all pertinent information related to market conditions and its activities; (2) the parties' agreement to provide due protection to each other's confidential information as defined in the contract, which often includes seller's patents, trade secrets, and know-how, as well as the representative's marketing information including customer lists; (3) a provision as to whose responsibility it is to arrange for all the necessary approvals, licenses, and other requirements for the entry and sale of goods in the foreign country; and (4) the right of the representative to carry noncompetitive and complementary products.

An agency agreement should state the nature and scope of an agent's authority to bind the exporter (which is often denied) as well as the agent's discretion with respect to pricing. All sales of products are to be in accordance with the price list and discount structure as established in the contract. The parties could also agree on mechanisms to implement changes in prices and terms. It is also important to stipulate the amount of compensation (commission) when it accrues to the account of the agent, and the time of payment. Most agreements state that all commissions shall not become due and payable until full settlement has been received by the firm. The agent could also be given the responsibility for collection with respect to sales it initiated.

Distributor agreements should state clearly that the overseas distributor acts as a buyer and not as an agent of the seller. The agreement could require the distributor to maintain adequate inventories, facilities, and competent personnel. The exporter could sometimes stipulate that orders representing a minimum value or quantity shall be placed within a fixed time. The agreement also defines the advertising and promotion responsibilities of the distributor, including an undertaking to advertise in certain magazines or journals a minimum number of times a year at its own expense, for example:

> The distributor agrees during the lifetime of this contract to provide and pay for not less than seven full-page advertisements per year, appearing at regular monthly intervals in the national journals or magazines of the industry circulating generally throughout the territory.

Exporter's Rights and Obligations

In agency contracts, the exporter is often required to provide the agent with its price schedules, catalogs, and brochures describing the company, its product and other pertinent features. In distributor contracts, the exporter is required to provide the distributor and his or her personnel with training and technical assistance as is reasonably required in order to service, maintain, and repair products. In both agency and distributor agreements, the exporter should warrant that the product complies only with the specified standards of quality and also state the party that will be responsible for warranty service.

The exporter is also required to provide sufficient supplies of the product and new developments in products, as well as marketing and sales plans.

Definition of Price

In agency agreements, all sales of products are made in accordance with the price list and discount structure agreed upon between the parties. However, the seller reserves the right to change prices at any time, usually upon a thirty- or sixty-days' prior notice.

Distributor agreements also contain provisions relating to the price to be charged by the seller upon purchase of goods by the distributor. Any discounts available are also stated. In the case of products that are affected by inflation, the parties could set a definite price ruling on a specific date, such as the date of the sales contract or shipment. The parties could also agree that the exporter charge the distributor the best price it provides other customers at the time of sale (the most-favored-customer price) except for those products supplied to a holding company, subsidiary, or other associated companies of the supplier. The distributor agreement should also stipulate the terms of shipment such as FOB (free on board) or CIF (cost, insurance, and freight), as well as the method of payment (open account, letter of credit, etc.), for example:

> The prices specified are in U.S. dollars, exclusive of taxes and governmental charges, freight, insurance and other transportation charges. Payment shall be on consignment. The product will be shipped FOB (Miami) to the buyer's address in Colombia.

Renewal or Termination of Contract

In many countries, issues relating to appointment, renewal, or termination of representatives are largely determined by local law. Many foreign representation agreements provide for a short trial period followed by a longer-term appointment if the representative's performance proves satisfactory. It is important to state the duration of appointment and the basis for renewal or termination. Any renewal or termination requires an act of notification to the representative.

In certain countries, the longer the period the representative has been appointed, the more difficult and expensive it is to terminate the contract. Representative agreements are terminated in cases when one of the parties is guilty of nonperformance or of not performing to the satisfaction of the other party, for example:

> In the event that either party should breach any term or condition of this agreement or fail to perform any of its obligations or undertakings, the other party may notify the defaulting party of such default, and if such default is not rectified within sixty days, the party giving notice shall have the right, at its election, to terminate the agreement.

The previous clause is often used to terminate nonperforming representatives. It is, however, important to set certain targets and objective performance criteria against which representative's performance will be measured: sales volume, inventory turnover rates, advertising, and market share. It is also advisable to include other causes of termination, such as the following:

Right to Terminate Without Cause

A significant number of contracts allow for termination of the contract by either party with no prerequisite of action or omission by the other party upon giving advance notice, for example:

Either party shall have the right to terminate the agreement at any time by giving not less than 180 days prior written notice of termination to the other party.

Force Majeure

Most contracts state the occurrence of specific events beyond the control of the parties as a basis for termination of the contract. The enumerated actions or events fall into four major categories: (1) acts of God, (2) wars and civil disorder, (3) acts of government such as exchange controls or host government regulations, and (4) other acts beyond the parties' control.

Other Causes of Termination

Some contracts provide for termination of the contract in cases such as bankruptcy or liquidation of either party, assignment of contractual rights or duties, change of ownership or management, and nonexclusivity, or the firm's decision to establish its own sales office or assembly operations.

In most countries, the exporter can terminate a representative in accordance with the contractual terms and without payment of indemnity. In situations lacking reasonable ground for termination, courts impose a liability for unjust termination that is often based on the volume of sales, goodwill developed by the representative, and duration of the contract. A typical formula is to award a one year's profit or commission to the distributor or agent based on an average over the previous five years or the duration of the contract, whichever is shorter. It may also include cost of termination of the representative's personnel.

Applicable Law and Dispute Settlement

The parties are at liberty to agree between themselves as to what rules should govern their contract. Most contracts state the applicable law to be that of the manufacturer's home state. This indicates the strong bargaining position of exporters and the latter's clear preference to be governed by laws about which they are well informed, including how the contract will function and its repercussions on the whole commercial and legal situation of the parties. In cases with no express or implied choice of law, courts have to decide what law should govern the parties' contract based on the terms and nature of the contract. Many factors are used to settle this issue in the absence of an express choice of law, including the place of contract, the place of performance, and the location of the subject matter of the contract, as well as the place of incorporation and place of business of the parties. The contract should also provide for a forum (court) to settle the dispute relating to the validity, interpretation, and performance of the agreement.

Many representative contracts also provide that any dispute between the parties shall be submitted to arbitration for final settlement in accordance with the rules of the International Chamber of Commerce.

MAINTAINING AND MOTIVATING OVERSEAS REPRESENTATIVES

Agents and distributors can be motivated in many ways to do the best possible job of marketing and promoting the firm's product. This could be accomplished by, for example, developing good communications through regular visits from the home office, the organization of conferences, or providing inexpensive free trips for representatives during a given period. It is also important to inform representatives of company's goals and principles and to keep them abreast of new developments in the product line, supplies, and promotion strategies, and to assist in training and market development. Firms could also motivate representatives through provision of better credit terms or price adjustments based on sales volume or other performance-based criteria.

CHAPTER SUMMARY

Introduction

Channels of distribution used to market products abroad:

1. *Indirect channels:* Exports through independent parties acting as sales intermediary.
2. *Direct channels:* Direct sales to foreign distributors, retailers, or trading companies.

Determinants of Channel Selection to Market Products Abroad

1. International marketing objectives of the firm
2. Manufacturer's resources and experience
3. Availability and capability of intermediary
4. Customer and product characteristics

5. Marketing environment
6. Control and coverage

Indirect Channels

Types of indirect channels:

1. *Exporters that sell on behalf of the manufacturer:* Manufacturer's export agents, export management companies, international trading companies
2. *Exporters that buy for their overseas customers:* Export commission agents
3. *Exporters that buy and sell on their own account:* Export merchants, cooperative exporters, WPAs

Direct Channels

Types of direct channels:

1. Direct marketing from the home country
2. Marketing through overseas agents and distributors: Overseas agents, overseas distributors

Major Clauses in Representation Agreements

1. Definition of territory and product
2. Representative's rights and obligations
3. Exporter's rights and obligations
4. Definition of price
5. Renewal or termination of contract

REVIEW QUESTIONS

1. Distinguish between direct and indirect channels of distribution. What are the advantages and disadvantages of using indirect channels?
2. Discuss three major determinants of channel selection to market products abroad.
3. Do firms that export high-technology products exercise high levels of control?
4. Discuss the role and function of manufacturer's export agents.

5. Discuss the disadvantages of using export management companies.
6. What are the differences between export trading companies and export management companies?
7. Briefly describe Webb-Pomerene Associations (WPAs).
8. What are some of the disadvantages of using overseas distributors?
9. State some of the clauses (provisions) in representation agreements.
10. Briefly describe force majeure.

CASE 5.1. EXPORT CHANNEL DECISIONS OF TWO U.S. COMPANIES

Wayne Engineering: Wayne Engineering, Inc., is a leading manufacturer of side loaders, recycling vehicles, and recycling and garbage trucks. It uses Tradesur, Inc., to handle the promotion, marketing, and distribution of its products in overseas markets.

TradeSur is an export management company (EMC) located in San Diego, California, with over eighteen years of experience in the export market. It has established distribution channels in several countries. As an EMC, its major functions include the following: (1) promotion, marketing, and distribution of U.S.–made construction equipment in Latin America and Europe; (2) handling complex logistics and outsourcing of various phases of the production process when necessary; (3) managing complex construction and infrastructure requirements by coordinating with multiple manufacturers of equipment worldwide and assembling the end product; (4) establishment of links with several financial institutions to help overseas buyers to finance their purchases, enhance their cash flows, and expand U.S. exports; and (5) arrangement of independent financing of turnkey projects for qualified government agencies and corporations from eligible foreign countries.

Farouk Systems: Farouk Systems, Inc. (FS), a Houston-based manufacturer of natural hair care and spa products wanted to get a foothold in Southeast Asia, following its successful entry in over sixty countries including China. The company sought distributors in Singapore to market its products. With the help of the U.S. Commercial Service, which locates potential buyers and distributors for U.S. firms, the company was able to appoint a distributor from a list of prospective candidates.

Singapore was considered a good market for U.S. beauty care products because Singaporean women spend an average of nearly $80 a year on such goods, compared with 17 cents spent by women in China. There is, however, intense competition from various providers in the market.

Final selection of the distributor (True Line Beauty) was based on a number of factors: experience within the Southeast Asian market, solid foundations within the industry, experience in conducting hair shows and educational seminars, sound financial position, personal chemistry, and gut instinct. They also considered the extent to which the potential candidates were willing to look at the long-term perspective and invest in the brand.

The distributor, True Line Beauty (TLB) was formed twelve years ago and has twenty employees. True Line Beauty asked for and received exclusive distribution rights in a number of other countries including Malaysia and Taiwan. Its sales force travel across the country explaining the benefits of the product, such as natural ingredients that are environmentally friendly, and offering incentives, such as refunds if the product does not sell or one free bottle for every so many sold. Once a new beauty shop or spa has shown interest, TLB provides training for stylists, demonstrates new cutting and coloring techniques using FS products.

Efforts have been quite slow in developing markets outside Singapore. True Line Beauty's approach appears to focus on tackling one market at a time. If certain specified performance benchmarks (such as sales, profit margins) as stated in the contract remain unmet over a given period of time, the U.S. company has the option of finding another distributor with the requisite capability to do the job. However, flexibility is the key in evaluating performance expectations and establishing goodwill.

CASE 5.2. THE INTERNET AND EXPORTING: A FOCUS ON DEVELOPING COUNTRIES

A business that would like to succeed in export markets needs information about market prospects and must continually fine tune its marketing skills, which includes the use of the Internet and Web-based resources to sell and promote products as well as generate new clients. For example, an export company that plans to participate in an international trade fair in an overseas market should do some Internet research on the prospective market to evaluate demand.

Analysts predict that about 10 percent of total business-to-consumer sales of U.S. retailers will be online. Business-to-business sales volume is also expected to outpace business-to-consumer sales by a factor of twenty within the next few years. The Internet enables exporters to interact directly with overseas customers. Furthermore, it facilitates product customization and the provision of extended services. Even though these new possibilities pose a serious threat to export intermediaries, a virtual market presence is not likely to be a substitute for existing networks since physical distribution channels still have several positional advantages compared with virtually organized ones. A number of value added services, for example, can only be provided via traditional distribution outlets. The Internet will not entirely replace the need for interpersonal relations and trust building. The Internet also poses organizational and managerial challenges (Peterson, Welch, and Liesch, 2002). It is plausible to contend that the Internet provides an infrastructure for carrying information and digital services, which is complementary to the existing marketing channel structure, improving performance (Anderson, 2005). In industries characterized by a high degree of information content such as publishing, travel, and financial services, export intermediation is undergoing a radical change. It has also given rise to new channels of export intermediation (e-Bay, Amazon, etc.), which were not previously available.

A study by Freund and Weinhold (2000) on the effect of the Internet on international trade shows its increasing and significant impact from 1997 to 1999. The study shows that a 10 percent increase in the relative number of Web hosts in one country would lead to about 1 percent greater trade. It also finds the effect of the Internet to be stronger for poor countries than for rich ones. However, the Internet does not seem to have reduced the impact of distance on trade. Clarke and Wallsten (2004) also find a positive correlation between Internet penetration in developing countries and their increasing exports to developed countries.

In many countries, global business-to-business Web sites have already been set up in a number of industries. Daimler-Chrysler, GM, and Ford have started an Internet-based market (COVISINT) for car parts worldwide; e-steel is established to link buyers and sellers of steel products around the world. In Egypt, some seventy-five products are marketed on the Internet. Adelphi, a leather products maker in Kenya, started a Web site with the intention of expanding into the global market. Global orders are executed through international courier firms such as DHL.

In spite of the increase in the number of users, Internet penetration rates in most developing countries remain low (see Table 5.1). Online trade is limited. Other factors contributing to lower than average e-commerce activity include low per capita incomes, low credit card usage, lack of relevant products or services, or poor logistics and fulfillment services.

In more advanced developing nations such as Taiwan, for example, the Internet is widely used in most sectors of the economy. Taiwanese firms are more concerned with improving forward linkages to their customers than

TABLE 5.1. Internet Users (Thousands) and Hosts (Thousands) by Region

Region	Internet Users	Internet Hosts
Africa	7,943	281
Latin America and Caribbean	35,459	3,412
North America	170,200	109,084
Asia	201,079	10,803
Western Europe	166,387	18,363
Oceana (Australia, New Zealand, and others)	10,500	3,035
Developing Countries	189,882	7,279
Developed Countries	401,686	137,700

Source: Adapted from International Telecommunications Union (ITU), 2003.

improving backward linkages to their suppliers. In spite of the diffusion of the Internet, concerns over security and privacy in online trading represent the most significant barrier to its use in international business transactions.

Questions

1. Would you advise Wayne Engineering to use overseas distributors to market its products abroad?
2. What are some of the limitations of the Internet in facilitating the expansion of exports from developing countries?

Chapter 6

International Logistics, Risk, and Insurance

INTERNATIONAL LOGISTICS

Logistics is a total systems approach to management of the distribution process that includes the cost-effective flow and storage of materials or products and related information from point of origin to point of use or consumption.

There are two categories of business logistics:

1. *Materials management:* In the context of export-import trade, logistics applies to the timely movement or flow of materials/products from the sources of supply to the point of manufacture, assembly, or distribution (inbound materials). This includes the acquisition of products, transportation, inventory management, storage, and the handling of materials for production, assembly, or distribution. For example, products can be assembled in Canada for distribution in Canada and the United States.
2. *Physical distribution:* The second phase relates to the movement of the firm's product to consumers (outbound materials). It includes outbound transportation, inventory management, and proper packaging to reduce damage during transit and storage.

Materials management primarily deals with inbound flow, whereas physical distribution is concerned with the outbound flow of materials or products (Guelzo, 1986). Both inbound and outbound activities are interdependent and influence the company's objective of reducing cost while conforming to customer needs. The interdependence of such activities can be illustrated

Export-Import Theory, Practices, and Procedures, Second Edition

by the example of U.S. flower imports from Latin America. Atlantic Bouquet, a U.S. company, purchases most of its flowers from its sister company that has flower farms in Latin America. Continental Air freights the flowers from company-owned farms in Latin America to a warehouse in Miami before they are moved nationwide by air, or by truck for distances of less than 300 miles. A proper management of the logistics system, that is, the unique combination of packaging, handling, storage, and transportation, will ensure that the product is imported and made available to the customer at the right time and place and in the right condition.

The interdependence of functional activities has been articulated through various new approaches or concepts:

1. *The systems approach:* The systems concept is based on the premise that the flow of materials within and outside the firm should be considered only in the context of their interaction (Czinkota, Ronkainen, and Moffett, 1998). This approach puts more emphasis on maximizing the benefits of the corporate system as a whole as opposed to that of individual units.
2. *Total cost approach:* This is a logistics concept based on evaluation of the total cost implications of various activities.
3. *The opportunity cost approach:* This approach considers the trade-off in undertaking certain logistic decisions. For example, the benefits and costs of sourcing components abroad versus buying from domestic sources. Additional costs associated with transportation, increases in safety stock inventory, warehousing costs, and so forth, are examined to ensure that the total opportunity cost of outsourcing abroad is not greater than other available options.

What is the importance of logistics to international trade? One of the major contributions of logistics to international trade is in the area of efficient allocation of resources. International logistics allows countries to export products in which they have a competitive advantage and import products that are either unavailable at home or produced at a lower cost overseas, thus allowing for efficient allocation of resources. For example, natural resource advantages and low-cost labor has enabled Colombia to export flowers to the United States and to import technology. Colombian flower exports have driven less efficient U.S. producers out of their own markets and forced the Dutch out of the rose and carnation markets in the United States (Thuermer, 1998). Such advantages from international trade cannot be realized without a well-managed logistics system. To the extent that logistics facilitates international trade, it contributes to the expansion of economic growth and employment. As import firms expand their ability to procure needed raw materials or components for their customers, international logistics management becomes a critical source of competitive advantage for both the firms and the customers. Such material procurement and sourcing decisions include the number and location of warehouses, levels of inventory to maintain, as well as selection of the appropriate transportation mode and carrier (Christopher, 1992). The development of advanced logistics systems and capabilities has also increased the efficient production, transportation, and distribution of products. For example, by outsourcing logistics to third-party operators, pharmaceutical and health care companies can reduce costs associated with inventory, overhead, labor, and warehousing. The use of various transportation modes facilitates rapid and consistent delivery service to consumers, which in turn reduces the need for safety stock inventory. Transportation cost is also reduced through shipment consolidation and special contracts with carriers for large shipments without adversely affecting delivery time. In short, a well-managed international logistics system can result in optimal inventory levels and optimal production capacity (in multiplant operations), thereby maximizing the use of working capital. All this helps to strengthen the competitive position of domestic companies in global trade.

EXTERNAL INFLUENCES ON LOGISTICS DECISIONS

A number of external factors influence international logistics decisions.

Regulations

Governments in many countries encourage their domestic carriers to handle their exports or imports since the provision of such transportation services contributes to the nation's balance of payments. This can be illustrated by U.S.–China trade, which is mostly transported by Chinese vessels. This occurs because the Chinese Foreign Trade Agency insists, whenever possible, on terms that allow it to control most of the transportation and thus use its state-run transport companies (Davies, 1987).

International logistics activity in the form of overseas transportation, handling of shipment, and distribution management also creates jobs. Besides the need to earn or save foreign currency and the creation of employment opportunities, governments support their national carriers to ensure national shipping capacity during war or other emergencies. Governments also control or limit the export and import of certain commodities through a host of devices, such as export controls, import tariffs, and nontariff barriers, for example, quotas or cumbersome import clearance procedures. There are also bilateral negotiations between countries on airline routes and the provision of various services, such as insurance. All this has an influence on international logistics and transportation. The process of privatization and deregulation in transportation and communications has reduced shipping costs and increased productivity. This has also increased the possibilities for different prices and services, thus underscoring the need to integrate marketing and logistics functions.

Competition

The proliferation of new products and services and short product life cycles creates pressures on firms to reexamine their logistics systems. This often requires the need to reduce inventory, lower overall costs, and develop appropriate logistics networks and delivery systems to retain and enhance their customer base. Crucial to the success of any logistics system is also a holistic examination of the relationship among transportation, warehousing, and inventory costs in order to adapt to the changing competitive environment. Such a reexamination of its various logistics functions resulted in a substantial reduction in inventory costs and delivery time for Cisco Systems of San Jose, California, in 1997. The company ships routers to Europe and needed to let customers know when orders would arrive and to be able to reroute an order to fill urgent requests. It hired UPS Worldwide Logistics to handle the various logistics functions. Using its expertise, UPS can now track Cisco's routers from San Jose to European customers in less than four days as opposed to three weeks. In cases in which UPS's planes or trucks cannot offer the quickest route, it subcontracts the job to other carriers such as KLM or Danzas, a European trucking firm. This resulted in more savings in inventories (Woolley, 1997).

Technology

Technology improvements, added to the deregulation of transportation and communications, have transformed the logistics industry. They have helped to increase logistics options, improve performance, and decrease costs. The use of communications technology has now integrated marketing and distribution activities with overseas customers, enabling the latter to know the date of shipment, the location of the cargo on transit, and the expected date of arrival. Importers have achieved total visibility of goods in transit and can make adjustments when a shipment is running late. Such tracking and tracing of cargo has the added advantage of synchronizing promotions and long-term inventory decisions for customers. Federal Express has recently developed a user-friendly software that tracks and traces shipments, eliminates the preparation of air waybills by hand, and allows printing on bar-coded shipping documents. Rates can be computed by plotting both origin and destination points. Vastera Incorporated, a software firm based in Dulles, Virginia, has also developed a multilingual logistics software package that handles multitask functions such as regulatory compliance and tariff information, documentation, shipment tracking, and letter of credit and duty drawback support (Fabey, 1997).

TYPICAL LOGISTICS PROBLEMS AND SOLUTIONS

Each export-import firm must use a logistics system that best fits its product line and chosen competitive strategy (see Table 6.1 for differences between domestic and international logistics).

Example 1

Arturo Imports, Incorporated, a firm based in Boca Raton, Florida, specializes in the importation of gift articles from South America and the Caribbean. It sells its products through company-owned retail stores in thirty U.S. states. The company has distribution centers in twenty locations all over the country and spends over $650,000 a year in warehousing costs. Over the past few years, it has come under increasing attack from competitors and has lost about 20 percent of its market share. Its profits also declined by over 15 percent in 2005 alone. The firm hired a consultant to advise it on

TABLE 6.1. Differences Between Domestic and International Logistics

Domestic Logistics	International Logistics
• Domestic currency used	• Different currency and exchange rates
• One national regulation on customs procedures, documentation, packaging, and labeling requirements	• Different national regulations and many intermediaries participating in the distribution channel (customs brokers, forwarders, banks, etc.)
• Most goods transported by truck or rail	• Most goods transported by air or sea
• Generally, short distances, short lead times, and small inventory levels	• Long distances, longer lead times, and the need for higher inventory levels

how to reverse the situation. Based on the advice it received, Arturo Imports consolidated its operations in six distribution centers; reduced dead, obsolete, and slow-moving stock; and decreased the likelihood of stock-out (an item that is out of stock) for products customers want to buy. It centralized its purchasing functions and switched to an intermodal air and truck (from ocean and rail) combination to ensure rapid delivery. The company began to see its market share and profit margin grow six months after implementing its new logistics systems.

Example 2

A U.S.–owned export firm in Bangor, Maine, serves a narrow product line in eastern Canada from two distribution centers located in Montreal and Toronto. The company began to reexamine its logistical infrastructure in response to its loss of profits and market share to competitors. It increased the number of branch warehouses and level of fast-moving inventory while reducing the market area served by each warehouse. It also extended its product line. In spite of the additional expenses incurred, the company began to see a marked increase in its profits and sales volume.

THE INTERNATIONAL LOGISTICS PROCESS

In export-import transactions, the following steps represent the approximate order of physical movement and distribution of goods to a foreign buyer.

Step 1

As a result of previous correspondence between the prospective seller and buyer, the prospective customer (buyer) places an order to purchase the desired merchandise, including such essential items as terms of sale, payment method, and other conditions. The parties must ensure that there are no restrictions on the export or import of the merchandise in question. The prospective exporter confirms receipt of the order and commits to fill the order based on the given terms and conditions. The seller's acceptance without modification of the terms creates a binding contract. In the event of any modification by the prospective seller, a binding contract is created only upon acceptance of the proposed modification by the prospective customer. A pro forma invoice is then prepared by the exporter, stipulating the essential terms and conditions of sale, and when accepted by the overseas customer, it may also serve as a contract. The prospective exporter must meet packaging, labeling, and other documentary requirements. In cases in which the exporter has inventory in different locations or countries, a determination has to be made as to which goods should be supplied on the basis of proximity to customer, tariff benefits, and so on. The exporter prepares the order for transportation. The order is then picked, packed, and labeled.

Step 2

A freight forwarder arranges for goods to be picked up and delivered to a carrier. The freight forwarder selects the transportation mode (airline, ship, truck, etc.) and the carrier, as well as books the necessary space for the cargo. Such decisions will influence packing and documentation requirements. The forwarder confirms booking with the supplier, who will in turn confirm with the overseas customer. If the consignee is different from the buyer, the forwarder notifies the consignee.

Step 3

The carrier loads the cargo and the merchandise is transported to the customer. Unless otherwise stipulated in the contract, the buyer is responsible for the cost of preshipment inspection. Many developing countries have adopted this practice primarily to conserve foreign currency earnings and to control illegal flights of currency through transfer pricing, that is, overinvoicing of imports and underinvoicing of exports. Preshipment inspection also ensures that the shipment conforms to the contract of sale. However, it is costly and time-consuming for exporters and delays the physical movement and distribution of merchandise. Appropriate precautions should be taken to detect and control possible diversion of merchandise into the gray market. Export products may be sold below domestic prices if domestic advertising or R & D is not allocated to the export price. Such export products, if diverted to the domestic market, could potentially undermine the exporter's market position. Some of the warning signs of potential diversion include offers of cash payment when the terms of sale would normally call for financing, little or no background in the particular business, vague delivery dates, or shipping instructions to domestic warehouses. After the merchandise is transported, the forwarder sends the necessary documentation, that is, the commercial invoice, customs invoice, packing list, bill of lading or air waybill, and certificate of origin, to the customs broker who clears goods for the overseas customer at the port of destination.

Step 4

The customs broker submits documents to customs to obtain release of the merchandise. In some countries, assessed taxes and duties have to be paid before release of the merchandise. Customs may also physically examine the merchandise. Penalties may be imposed if any serious errors or problems are found in the documentation or with the imported merchandise. The customs broker informs the forwarder of the release of the merchandise.

Step 5

If the terms of sale provide for the seller to obtain release of merchandise from customs and deliver to the consignee, the forwarder picks up the merchandise from customs and arranges for delivery to the consignee. This step depends on the terms of sale. The consignee signs the bill of lading or air waybill, noting any irregularities, and accepts the merchandise (for attributes of a good logistics system, see International Perspective 6.1).

INTERNATIONAL PERSPECTIVE 6.1.
Attributes of a World Class Logistics System: Denmark

Denmark held the world's top spot in logistics. Its excellence in logistics is attributed to a number of factors:

- *Investment in infrastructure:* International airport within about thirty minutes of ten international ports and free trade zones. It provides direct access to European rail and highway network with direct connections to many European cities. It has international forwarders and integrators with bonded warehouse facilities. It provides substantial investment for infrastructure maintenance and development (bridges, airport, and seaport). It has efficient air cargo handling facility. Customs clearance of goods is done before payment of duties, with minimum red tape. Information technology helps streamline procedures for exports or imports and links shippers and consumers.
- *Human resources:* Highly skilled and motivated labor force, twenty-four-hour/seven-day operations and good management–labor relations (walkouts or strikes are virtually nonexistent).
- *Business environment:* Availability of free trade zones and bonded warehouses, low trade restrictions with a stable economic/political environment.

LOGISTICS FUNCTIONS

Labeling

Importers are required to comply with domestic labeling laws. Even though an imported product may comply with the labeling requirements of the country where it was manufactured, it may not comply with the labeling laws of the importing country. Labeling requirements are imposed in many countries to ensure proper handling (e.g., "do not roll"; "keep frozen") or to identify shipments (e.g., "live animals"). Exporters need to be aware of certain labeling requirements to avoid unnecessary delays in shipping. The cartons or containers to be shipped must be labeled with the following: shipper's mark or purchase order number, country of origin, weight in both pounds and kilograms, the number of packages, handling instructions, final destination and port of entry, and whether the package contains hazardous material. Markings should appear on three faces of the container. It is also advisable to repeat the instructions in the language of the importing country.

Under the U.S. Clean Air Act (amended in 1990), all products containing ozone-depleting substances are required to be labeled. More detailed and specific regulations can be obtained from freight forwarders, since they keep track of changing labeling laws in various countries.

Packing

The rigors of long-distance transportation of goods require protection of merchandise from possible breakage, moisture, or pilferage. This means that goods in transit must be packed not only to allow the overseas customer to take delivery of the merchandise but also to ensure its arrival in a safe and sound condition. Consumers in many countries often prefer packaging with recyclable or biodegradable containers due to environmental concerns. For example, about 70 percent of packaging material used in any of the federal states in Germany must be recycled or reused. Packaging cost has an influence on product design. In certain cases, it is considered less costly to ship disassembled parts or dense cargo to save shipping cost.

Merchandise should be packed in strong containers, adequately sealed, and filled, with the weight evenly distributed. Goods should be packed on pallets if possible, to ensure greater ease in handling, and containers should be made of moisture-resistant material. Packing must be done in a manner that will ensure safe arrival of the merchandise and facilitate its handling in transit and at its destination (see International Perspective 6.2 for an example of product packing tips).

INTERNATIONAL PERSPECTIVE 6.2.
Packing Handicraft Exports: Important Pointers

Prior to packaging: Dusting, cleaning, removing fingerprints, and drying items.
Major problems to consider in packaging: Tarnishing, corrosion, staining, decay, breakage, moisture.
Preventing moisture: Use of a drying agent (silica gel) to reduce humidity, reducing surface area of package, drying items, and packaging materials in packages with a moisture tight seal.
Preventing damage: Cushioning fragile or high-cost handicrafts. Handicrafts exported in large quantities should be palletized when possible.
Heavy items: For heavy handicrafts, wooden boxes are recommended.
Small items: Bulk packaging with separators to protect individual items.
Outer packaging: Corrugated fiber-board and wooden boxes are recommended.

Insufficient packing not only results in delays in the delivery of goods but will also entitle the customer to reject the goods or claim damages. Export products must be packed to comply with the laws of the importing country. For example, Australia and New Zealand prohibit the use of straw or rice husk as packaging materials. The United Nations has adopted standards for packaging hazardous materials and provides for training of personnel, use of internationally accepted standards, and certain other conditions. Freight forwarders and marine insurance companies can advise on packaging.

Traffic Management

Traffic management is the control and management of transportation services. Such functions include selection of mode of transportation carriers, consolidation of small cargo, documentation, and filing of loss and damage claims. The international logistics manager's selection of a given mode of transportation depends on a number of factors. First, for products that are perishable, such as cut flowers, delivery speed is of the essence. Speed may also be required in cases involving important delivery dates or deadlines. In such cases, airfreight becomes the only viable mode of transport to successfully deliver the product to the overseas customer on time. Airfreight is also more reliable than other modes of transport that have more cumbersome unloading operations, which could expose the cargo to loss or damage. Second, the selection of transportation mode is influenced by cost considerations.

Since airfreight is more expensive than other modes of transport, the international logistics manager has to determine whether such high costs are justified. Export firms tend to transport compact products or high-priced items by air because such products are more appropriate for airfreight or because the price justifies the cost. Third, government pressures could be imposed on exporters to transport by national carriers, even when other more economical alternatives exist. The choice of airport or port may be another important decision to be made. Such choices may be influenced by the desire to consolidate cargo or the presence of adjoining highways (to the port) on which weight limits are not rigorously enforced (Guelzo, 1986).

Inventory and Storage

The proper management of an export-import firm's inventory is a critical logistics function. The costs associated with holding inventories can easily account for 25 percent or more of the value of the inventories themselves and could potentially create liquidity problems for many firms. In addition to this are the cost of storage, interest paid on borrowed money, and the risks of deterioration and obsolescence. It is important to establish certain guidelines with respect to such issues as maximum holding period, time of shipment of inventories to the supplier, and other related factors. Acceptable levels of inventory can still be maintained to serve overseas customers on time without unduly increasing costs and creating storage problems. To reduce warehousing costs, it may be necessary to store inventory in distribution centers based on customer needs. Inventories that are slow moving (no activity for six to twelve months) can be shipped from the exporter or manufacturer. Appropriate inventory planning and control will reduce the number of storage facilities as well as carrying and freight costs.

In certain situations, accumulating inventories may have its own benefits. In countries that have certain macroeconomic problems, inventory may be a good edge against inflation and devaluation of currency.

RISKS IN FOREIGN TRADE

Businesses conducting export-import trade face a number of risks that may adversely impact their operations, such as the following:

- Actions of legitimate government authorities to confiscate cargo, war, revolution, terrorism, and strikes that impede the conduct of international business (political risk)
- Nonpayment or delays in payment for imports (foreign credit risk)

- Loss (partial/total) or damage to shipment during transit (transportation risk)
- Depreciation of overseas customer's currency against the exporter's currency before payment or the nonavailability of foreign currency for payment in the buyer's country (foreign exchange/transfer risk)

Political Risks

Many export-import businesses are potentially exposed to various types of political risks. War, revolution, or civil unrest can lead to destruction or confiscation of cargo. A government may impose severe restrictions on export-import trade, such as limitation or control of exports or imports, restrictions of licenses, currency controls, and so on. Even though such risks are less likely in Western countries, they occur quite frequently in certain developing nations. Such risks can be managed by taking the following steps.

Monitoring Political Developments

Private firms offer monitoring assistance to assess the likelihood of political instability in the short and medium term. Such information can be obtained from specialized sources for specific countries such as political risk services (e.g., Political Risk Services of Syracuse, a unit of International Business Communications, Incorporated), the Economic Intelligence Unit, Euromoney, and Business International Corporation. Public agencies such as the Export-Import Bank of the United States (Ex-Im Bank) and the Department of Commerce also provide country risk reports.

Insuring Against Political Risks

Most industrialized nations provide insurance programs for their export firms to cover losses due to political risks. In the United States, Ex-Im Bank offers a wide range of policies to accommodate many different insurance needs of exporters. Private insurers cover ordinary commercial risk, but Ex-Im Bank assumes all liability for political risks (see Chapter 14 on government export financing).

Foreign Credit Risks

A significant percentage of export trade is conducted on credit. It is estimated that approximately 35 to 50 percent of exports of the United States and the United Kingdom are sold on open account and/or consignment

(Seyoum and Morris, 1996). This means that the risk of delays in payment or nonpayment could have a crucial effect on cash flow and profits. Payment periods vary across countries, and even within countries that have close economic relations, such as the European Common Market, payment periods range from forty-eight days in the Netherlands to ninety days in Italy. Payments are, on average, eighteen days overdue in Germany, twenty-three in the United Kingdom, nineteen in France, and twenty in Italy (Luesby, 1994). Payment practices appear to be a function of the global/local economic conditions as well as the local business culture. In many developing countries, delays may be due to foreign exchange shortages, which in turn result in delays by central banks in converting local currencies into foreign exchange. The likelihood of bad debt from an overseas customer (0.5 percent of sales) is generally less than that for an American company. However, this does not provide comfort to an exporter whose cash flow and profit could be adversely affected by late payments and default. Beans Industries, once part of the British Leyland group, which makes automotive components, was taken into receivership in 1994, despite increased demand for its products, due to bad debts and late payments that had a dramatic effect on cash flow (Cheeseright, 1994). A default by an overseas customer is costly even when the exporter has insurance to cover commercial credit risks. The exporter must follow strict procedures to obtain payment before insurance claims will be honored. The following measures will help export companies in dealing with problems of defaults and/or delays in payment.

Appropriate Credit Management

Appropriate credit management involves the review of credit decisions based on current and reliable credit reports on overseas customers. Credit reports on foreign companies can be obtained from international banks that have affiliates in various countries and private credit information sources such as Dunn and Bradstreet, Graydon America, Owens Online, TRW Credit Services, and the NACM (National Association of Credit Management Corporation). A number of foreign credit information firms also provide accurate and reliable information on overseas customers. Government agencies such as the U.S. Department of Commerce, the Ex-Im Bank, and FCIA (Foreign Credit Insurance Association) also offer credit reporting services on foreign firms. Export firms also need to have a formal credit policy that will help them recover overdue or bad debts and substantially reduce the occurrence of such risks in future.

Requiring Letters of Credit and Other Conditions

A confirmed, irrevocable letter-of-credit transaction avoids risks arising from late payments or bad debts because it ensures that payments are made before the goods are shipped to the importer. However, such requirements (including advanced payments before shipment) do not attract many customers, and exporters seeking to develop overseas markets often have to sell on open account or consignment to enable the foreign wholesaler or retailer to pay only after the goods have been sold. The exporter can also require the payment of interest when payment is not made within the time period agreed or, failing that, within a given number of days. The introduction of a similar measure in Sweden in the mid-1970s is believed to have substantially reduced the delinquency of late payments to fewer than seven days. The European Commission submitted a draft recommendation to discourage late payments in cross-border trade (European Commission, 1994). Another safeguard would be to secure collateral to cover a transaction.

Insuring Against Credit Risks

Many export firms do not insure trade receivables, and yet, such cover is as necessary as fire or car insurance. It is estimated that in most developed countries, less than 20 percent of trade debts are insured. Credit insurers tend to have extensive databases that allow them to assess the credit worthiness of an insured's customer. This helps export companies to distinguish those buyers with the money to pay for their orders from those which are likely to delay payments or default. A credit insurance policy also provides confidence to the lender and may help exporters obtain a wide range of banking services and an improved rate of borrowing.

Few private insurance firms cover foreign credit risk: American Credit Indemnity, Continental Credit Insurance, Fidelity and Deposit Company, and American Insurance Underwriters are among those that provide such coverage. Such firms could be contacted directly or through brokers stationed in various parts of the country. Policies often cover commercial and political risks, although, in some cases, they are limited to insolvency and protracted default in eligible countries. Minimum premiums range from $1,250 per policy year to $10,000.

Ex-Im Bank provides various types of credit insurance policies: credit insurance for small businesses (umbrella policy, small business policy), single and multibuyer policies, Overseas Private Investment Corporation, the bank letter-of-credit policy, and so on. Its major features are U.S. content requirements and restrictions on sales destined for military use or to communist nations (see Chapter 14, "Government Export Financing Programs").

Foreign Exchange Risks

Export-import firms are vulnerable to foreign exchange risks whenever they enter into an obligation to accept or deliver a specified amount of foreign currency at a future point in time. These firms could face a possibility that changes in foreign currency values could either reduce their future receipts or increase their payments in foreign currency. Different methods are used to protect against such risks, for example, shifting the risk to third parties or to the other party in an export contract (for details, see Chapter 10 on exchange rates and trade).

MARINE AND AVIATION INSURANCE

Export-import firms depend heavily upon the availability of insurance to cover against risks of transportation of goods. Risks in transportation are an integral part of foreign trade, partly due to our inability to adequately control the forces of nature or to prevent human failure as it affects the safe movement of goods. Insurance played an important part in stimulating early commerce. In Roman times, for example, money was borrowed to finance overseas commerce, whereby the lender would be paid a substantial interest on the loan only if the voyage was successful. The loan was canceled if the ship or cargo was lost as a result of ocean perils. The interest charged in the event of a successful voyage was essentially an insurance premium (Greene and Trieschmann, 1984; Mehr, Cammack, and Rose, 1985).

The primary purpose of insurance in the context of foreign trade is to reduce the financial burden of losses arising from the movement of goods over long distances. In export trade, it is customary to arrange extended marine insurance to cover not only the ocean voyage but also other means of transport that are used to deliver the goods to the overseas buyer. According to W. R. Vance, there are five essential elements to an insurance contract:

1. The insured must have an insurable interest, that is, a financial interest based on some legal right in the preservation of the property. The insured must prove the extent of the insurable interest to collect, and recovery is limited by the insured's interest at the time of loss.
2. The insured is subjected to risk of loss of that interest by the occurrence of certain specified perils.
3. The insurer assumes the risk of loss.

4. This assumption is part of a general scheme to distribute the actual loss among a large group of persons bearing similar risks.
5. As a consideration, the insured pays a premium to a general insurance fund. (Vance, 1951)

Since insurance is a contract of indemnity, a person may not collect more than the actual loss in the event of damage caused by an insured peril. An export firm, for example, is not permitted to receive payment from the carrier for damages for the loss of cargo and also recover for the same loss from the insurer. On paying the exporter's claim, the insurer stands in the position of the exporter (insured party) to claim from the carrier or other parties who are responsible for occasioning the loss or damage. This means that the insurer is subrogated to all the rights of the insured after having indemnified the latter for its loss. This is generally described as the principle of subrogation. Another point to consider is whether an exporter, as an insured party, can assign the policy to the overseas customer. It appears that assignment is generally allowed insofar as there is an agreement to transfer the policy with the merchandise to the buyer and the seller has an insurable interest during the time when the assignment is made.

Marine Insurance

Marine policy is the most important type of insurance in the field of international trade. This is because (1) ocean shipping remains the predominant form of transport for large cargo, and (2) marine insurance is the most traditional and highly developed branch of insurance. All other policies, such as aviation and inland carriage, are largely based on principles of marine insurance. Practices and policies are also more standardized across countries in the area of marine insurance than in insurance of goods carried by land or air (Day and Griffin, 1993).

Term of Policy

Cargo policies may be written for a single trip or shipment (voyage policy), for a specified period (time policy), usually one year, or for an indefinite period (open policy), that is effective until canceled by the insured or insurer. The majority of cargo policies are written on open contracts. Under the latter policy, shipments are reported to the underwriter as they are made and premium is paid monthly based on the shipment actually made. The time policy differs from the open contract not just in the term of the policy, but also with respect to the premium payment method. Under the time policy, a premium deposit is made based on an estimated future shipment and adjustments are later made by comparing the estimates with the actual shipment. Another version of open policy is one that is generally available to exporters/importers with larger shipments. It covers most of the shipper's needs and has certain deductibles (blanket policy). Under a blanket policy, the insured is not required to advise the insurer of the individual shipments and one premium covers all shipments.

Types of Policies

There are two general types of marine cargo insurance policies:

1. Perils-only policy: This policy generally covers extraordinary and unusual perils that are not expected during a voyage. The standard perils-only policy covers loss or damage to cargo attributable to fire or explosion, stranding, sinking, collision of vessel, general average sacrifice, and so on. Such policies do not generally cover damage due to unseaworthiness of vessel or pilferage. An essential feature of such a policy is that underwriters indemnify for losses that are attributable to expressly enumerated perils. The burden is on the cargo owner to show that the loss was due to one of the listed perils.

   Export-import companies have the option of purchasing additional coverage (to include risk of water damage, rust, or contamination of cargo from oil, etc.) or take an all-risks policy that provides broader coverage.

2. All-risks policy: The all-risks policy provides the broadest level of coverage except for those expressly excluded in the policy. A typical clause reads:

   To cover against all risks of physical loss or damage from any external cause irrespective of percentage, but excluding, nevertheless, the risk of war, strikes, riots, seizure, detention, and other risks excluded by the F.C. & S. (free of capture and seizure) (losses due to war, civil strife, or revolution) warranty and the S.R. & C.C. (strikes, riots, and civil commotion) warranty, excepting to the extent that such risks are specifically covered by endorsement.

In the case of all-risks policy, the burden to prove that the loss was due to an excluded clause rests with the underwriter. Additional coverage can be provided through an endorsement on the existing all-risks policy or through a separate war-risks policy.

Extent of Coverage for Cargo Loss/Damage

Marine insurance policies generally specify the extent of coverage provided under the policy. Levels of cargo coverage fall into two broad categories: with average (WA) and free of particular average (FPA). This indicates whether the policy covers less than total losses (WA) or only total losses (FPA). With average covers total as well as partial losses. Most WA policies limit coverage to those losses that exceed 3 percent of the value of the goods. A standard WA coverage may read:

> Subject to particular average if amounting to 3 percent, unless general or the vessel and/or craft is stranded, sunk, burnt, on fire, and/or in collision, each package separately insured or on the whole.

This policy provides protection against partial losses by sea perils if the damage amounts to 3 percent or more of the value of the shipment. If the vessel is stranded, sunk, etc., the percentage requirement is waived and the losses are recovered in full.

Free of particular average provides limited coverage. This clause provides that in addition to total losses, partial losses from certain specified risks such as stranding or fire are recoverable. A standard FPA clause reads:

> Free of particular average (unless general) or unless the vessel or craft be stranded, sunk, burnt, on fire, or in collision with another vessel.

Exporters that sell on credit and use terms of sale where the buyer is responsible for insurance (free alongside ship [FAS], free on board [FOB], and so on) should consider taking out contingency insurance for the benefit of the overseas buyer in case the latter's insurance becomes inadequate to cover the loss. By paying a small premium for such insurance, the exporter creates a favorable condition for the buyer to pay for the shipment. Contingency insurance is supplementary to the policy taken out by the overseas buyer, and recovery is not made under the policy unless the buyer's policy is inadequate to cover the loss.

Marine cargo insurance covers only the period when the goods are on the ship. The marine extension (warehouse to warehouse clause) extends the standard marine coverage to the period before the loading of the goods and the period between off loading and delivery to the consignee.

Insurance Policy versus Certificates

An insurance company may issue an insurance policy (policy) or a certificate. If the insurer issues only policies, an application must be completed by the insured for each shipment and delivered to the insurer or agent before a policy is prepared and sent to the former. This can be time-consuming. However, in the case of certificates, the insurer provides a pad of insurance certificates to the exporter or importer, and a copy of the completed certificate (with details of goods, destination, type and amount of insurance required, etc.) is mailed to the insurance company whenever a shipment is made. Certificates save time and facilitate a more efficient operation of international business transactions.

Open policies for import/export shipments are often reported by using declaration forms which require the completion of certain particulars such as points of shipment and destination, description of units, amount of insurance, etc. When full information is not available at the time a declaration is made, a provisional report may be submitted to the insurance agent (this is closed when value is finally known). They are prepared by the assured and forwarded daily, weekly, or as shipments are made. The premium is billed monthly based on the schedule of rates provided in the policy.

Insurance policies or certificates are often used in the case of exports since the exporter must provide evidence of insurance to banks, customers, or other parties in order to permit the collection of claims abroad. Besides what is often included in declarations, policies/certificates include additional information such as names of beneficiary (usually assured or "order") thus making the instrument negotiable upon endorsement by the assured. Whether the policy/certificate is prepared by the assured, freight forwarder, or agent, it is important to describe the shipment in sufficient detail.

General Average: Illustration

A vessel carrying a cargo of copper was stranded and part of the cargo had to be sacrificial (thrown away) to lighten the vessel. The vessel had sustained certain damage and a salvage vessel was employed to refloat it. Adjustment of the general average will be as follows:

Value of the cargo (thrown away) less duty and handling charges	10,000
Cost of repairs for vessel (chargeable to general average)	40,000
Services for salvaging vessel	35,000
Disbursement at port and other charges	15,000
Total "vessel" sacrifice	*90,000*
Amount to be allowed in general average	100,000

Value of cargo (including sacrifice)	100,000	
Value of vessel (including sacrifice)	300,000	
Total contributory value	*400,000*	
Rate of general average contribution	100,000/400,000	25%
Cargo's contribution	25% (100,000)	
	= 25,000	
Vessel's contribution	75% (300,000)	
	= 75,000	

Cargo owner's liability = Assigned contribution 2 value of cargo sacrificed
   Thus, 25,000 – 10,000 = 15,000 (to pay)
Vessel's liability = Assigned contribution 2 vessel's sacrifice
   Thus, 75,000 – 90,000 = 15,000 (to receive)

Air cargo insurance: A modified form of marine insurance coverage is issued for air cargo insurance. Some airlines sell their own coverage.

CLAIMS AND PROCEDURES

Claims

Shippers can claim from carriers or insurers with respect to loss or damage to their cargo. Shippers often attempt to recover from carriers when they have a reasonable basis to believe that the loss or damage was caused by the negligent act or omission of the carriers that was easily preventable through exercise of due diligence in the transportation and handling of the cargo. Another motivating factor for the insured to obtain a satisfactory settlement with carriers could be to maintain a healthy loss to premium and keep premiums low. It could also be that the loss or damage is not covered by the insurance policy. However, in most cases, shippers claim from their insurers partly because carriers reject claims received from the insured or because the shippers find that the adjustment for loss or damage is inadequate due to liability limitations. It may also be that some shippers find it more convenient and efficient to handle claims with insurance companies.

Settling losses under insurance contracts is the function of claims management. Claims management is often accomplished through employed (in-house) or independent adjusters who negotiate settlement with the insured. The claims department is responsible for ascertaining the validity of the loss, investigating, estimating the extent and amount of the loss, and finally approving payment of the claim. It is important to note the following in relation to insurance claims:

- To recover, the loss or damage incurred by the insured must be covered by the insurance policy. The insurer will avoid liability if the particular risk is specifically excluded or is not reasonably attributable to the risk insured against.
- The burden of proof falls on the insured to show that the loss or damage to the cargo is covered by the policy.
- The insured must take prudent measures to protect the merchandise from further loss or damage. Under the sue and labor clause that is incorporated in most cargo insurance contracts (see International Perspective 6.3 for other typical clauses), the insured is required to take all necessary steps to safeguard the cargo and save it from further damage, without in any way prejudicing its rights under the policy. The underwriter agrees to pay any resulting expense (for types of cargo loss/damage, see Table 6.2 and International Perspective 6.4).
- Once the insurance company settles the insured's claim, it could exercise its subrogation right to claim from parties responsible for the loss or damage. Under the principle of subrogation, the right to recover from carriers and other parties who are responsible for the loss or damage passes from the insured to the insurer on payment of the insurance money. Since the insurer stands in the shoes of the insured in claiming from third parties, the insurer does not have a better right than what the insured possessed. Any payments obtained by the insured shipper from the carrier or other parties must be transferred to the insurer (after settlement with insurer) because under the principle of subrogation, the insured is not allowed to recover more than once for the same loss.

Claims are generally valid for two years from the date of arrival for air shipments and one year in the case of ocean shipments. Claims are invalid if not initiated within this period unless legal action is pursued.

Typical Steps in Claim Procedures

Step 1

Preliminary notice of claim: The export-import firm (insured) must file a preliminary claim by notifying the carrier of a potential claim as soon as the loss is known or expected. A formal claim may follow when the nature and value of the loss or damage is ascertained.

INTERNATIONAL PERSPECTIVE 6.3.
Typical Clauses in Cargo Insurance Contracts

1. *Inchmaree clause:* This clause covers any loss or damage to cargo due to the bursting of boilers, breakage of shafts, or any latent defect in the machinery, as well as from negligence of the captain or crew when it is the proximate cause of a loss.
2. *Free of particular average clause:* This relieves the insurer of liability for partial cargo losses, except for those caused by the stranding, sinking, burning, or collision of the vessel with another.
3. *The labels clause:* In the case of damage to labels, capsules, or wrappers, the insurer is not liable for more than the cost of the new items and the cost of reconditioning the goods.
4. *The delay clause:* This relieves the insurer of liability for loss of market due to delay in the delivery of the cargo.
5. *The general average clause:* A general average loss occurs when a sacrifice is voluntarily made or an expense is incurred in times of imminent peril to preserve the common interest from disaster. Payments of apportioned losses are secured by a general average deposit before goods are released by the carrier. When the actual shipper's share is established, appropriate adjustments are made and any excess is returned. A general average clause covers the amount of the insured shipper's contribution.
6. *Craft and lighter clause:* In this clause, the insurer agrees to provide lighters or other craft to deliver cargo within the harbor limits.
7. *Marine extension clause:* Under this clause, no time limit is to be imposed on the insurance coverage at the port of discharge while goods are delayed in transit to final destination insofar as the delay is occasioned by circumstances beyond the control of the insured.
8. *Shore clause:* This covers certain risks to cargo, such as collision, hurricane, floods, and so on, while the goods are on docks, wharves, or elsewhere on shore.
9. *Warehouse to warehouse clause:* This covers cargo while on transit between the initial point of shipment and the point of destination, subject to terms of sale and insurable interest requirement. The policy is effective from the time the goods leave the warehouse/store named in the policy for the commencement of transit to the final warehouse at the point of destination stated in the policy.

Step 2

Formal notice of claim: The consignee must file a formal claim with the carrier and the insurance company once the damage or loss is ascertained. The claim should include costs such as the value of the cargo, inland freight,

TABLE 6.2. Types of Losses

Total Loss	
1. Actual total loss	Goods are completely damaged or destroyed or so changed in their nature as to be unmarketable.
2. Constructive total loss	Actual loss is inevitable (such as frustration of voyage for an indefinite time), or damaged cargo can only be saved at considerable cost (i.e., cost greater than its value).
Partial Loss	
1. General average loss	These are goods sacrificed as part of a general average act or as a cargo owner's contribution for the general average loss of others.
2. Particular charges	These are expenses incurred to prevent loss or damage to insured cargo from risk that is insured against. *Example:* expenses for extra fodder for a cargo of horses while the ship is under repair for hurricane damage that was covered under the policy.
3. Particular average loss	This includes partial losses that are not covered by general average and particular charges.

ocean/airfreight, documentation, and other items. If the insurance policy is 110 percent of the cost in freight (CIF) value, the insured could add 10 percent of the value of the goods to the claim. Assuming that the insured intends to claim from the insurer (not the carrier), the insured should arrange for a survey with the claims agent of the insurance company. The formal claim form should be submitted with certain documents: a copy of the commercial invoice; a signed copy of bill of lading/air waybill; the original certificate of insurance; a copy of the claim against the carrier, or reply thereto; the survey report, if done by the surveyor; the packing list; and a copy of the receipt given to the carrier on delivery of the merchandise. It could also include photographs, repair invoice, and an affidavit from the carrier, if possible.

Step 3

Settlement of claim: If the claim is covered by the policy and claims procedures are appropriately followed, the insurance company will pay the insured. If the insurance company declines to approve payment, the insured could pursue arbitration or other dispute settlement procedures as provided in the insurance contract.

INTERNATIONAL PERSPECTIVE 6.4.
Cargo Loss or Damage

A number of factors contribute to the loss or damage of cargo in transit. It is often stated that over 80 percent of all cargo losses are preventable. We examine some of the major preventable causes for cargo loss or damages as well as some ways of minimizing it.

A. *Theft:* Appropriate packing, use of shrink-wrapping, strapping and branding, specifically patterned sealing tapes (enables quick detection of tampering), and use of coded markings. Containerized shipments should be sealed after loading. Theft accounts for 20 percent of cargo loss.

B. *Handling and storage:* Internal blocking and bracing to distribute weight, cushioning to absorb shocks and vibrations, palletizing the cargo, use of cautionary markings and handling instructions, and not exceeding the weight/volume capacity of package and/or container. Poor handling and storage account for 40 percent of cargo loss.

C. *Water damage:* Waterproof wrapping and waterproof linings on the interior of outer packages, elevating cargo above any drainage area, drain holes for containers to prevent accumulation of water. Water damage accounts for 15 percent of cargo loss.

The claim is filed by the party that assumes the risk of loss on transit. For example, in CIF contracts, the exporter takes out an insurance policy for the benefit of the buyer and the risk of loss is transferred to the buyer once goods are put on board the vessel at the port of shipment. The exporter will send the necessary documents and detailed instructions to the overseas customer (consignee) to follow in the event of loss or damage. The consignee should be instructed to examine the goods upon delivery to determine any apparent or concealed loss or damage to cargo. Any loss or damage discovered upon such inspection should be noted on the carrier's delivery receipt or air waybill. Once the carrier obtains a clean receipt from the consignee, it becomes difficult for the latter to successfully make a claim.

The best way to deal with claims is to prevent the occurrence of loss or damage to cargo as much as is practically feasible. It is estimated that proper packing, handling, and stowage can prevent about 70 percent of cargo loss or damage. The frequent occurrence of damage or loss to cargo not only becomes a source of friction or suspicion on the part of insurance companies but also discourages the growth and expansion of trade. It could also have the effect of reducing sales abroad if overseas customers are discouraged by the frequency of such occurrences, since it could consume the parties' time and effort. If payment has already been made to the exporter, the buyer's capital is tied up with merchandise that cannot be sold.

CHAPTER SUMMARY

Logistics

The process of planning, implementing, and controlling the flow and storage of materials from the point of origin to the point of consumption.

Two categories of logistics:

1. *Materials management:* The timely movement of materials from sources of supply to point of manufacture, assembly, or distribution.
2. *Physical distribution:* Movement of a firm's products to consumers.

Logistics concepts:

1. The systems approach: Emphasis on maximizing benefits of the corporate system as a whole as opposed to that of individual units.
2. The total cost approach.
3. The opportunity cost approach.

Importance of logistics to international trade:

1. Efficient allocation of resources.
2. Expansion of economic growth and employment.

External influences on logistics decisions:

1. Regulations: Export controls, tariffs, nontariff barriers, privatization and deregulation of transportation and communications.
2. Competition: Competitive pressures on firms to examine logistics systems, that is, to reduce costs etc.
3. Technology: New technologies now enable importers to know the date of shipment, location of cargo on transit and expected date of arrival. It also handles other logistics functions.

Logistics functions:

Labeling, packing, traffic management, inventory, and storage.

Risks in Foreign Trade

1. *Political risks:* Actions of government authorities, war, revolution, terrorism, strikes.
   Managing political risk: Monitoring political developments, insuring against political risks.
2. *Foreign credit risk:* Risks of buyer's default or delay in payment.
   Managing foreign credit risk: Appropriate credit management, letter of credit and other conditions, insurance.
3. *Foreign exchange risk:* Changes in currency values that could reduce future exporter's receipts or increase importer's payments in foreign currency.
   Managing foreign exchange risk: Shifting the risk to the other party or to third parties.
4. *Transportation risk:* Loss or damage to merchandise during transit.

Insurance

Two essential principles:

1. *The principle of insurable interest:* A financial interest based on some legal right in the preservation of the insured property.
2. *The principle of subrogation:* On paying the insured's claim, the insurer stands in the position of the former (the insured) to claim from other parties who are responsible for the loss or damage.

Marine Insurance

Term of policy:

1. *Voyage policy:* Policy for a single trip
2. *Time policy:* Policy for a specified trip
3. *Open policy:* Policy for an indefinite period of time

Policies for cargo loss/damage:

1. *Free of particular average:* Policy covers total loss and partial loss from certain specified risks insured against.
2. *Within average policy:* Policy covers total loss and partial losses greater than a given percentage and insurer liable for the total amount lost.

Claims and Procedures

Claims for loss or damage to shipment on transit can be claimed from carriers or insurers. Most cargo claims are settled with insurance companies.

Typical claims procedures: Preliminary notice of claim, formal notice, and settlement.

REVIEW QUESTIONS

1. Discuss the importance of logistics to international trade.
2. What is the systems approach to logistics?
3. State the external factors that influence international logistics decisions.
4. What is materials management and how does it differ from physical distribution?
5. State some of the differences between domestic and international logistics.
6. What are political risks in foreign trade? How can it be managed?
7. What kinds of risks does marine insurance cover? How does an FPA policy differ from WA policy?
8. A shipper obtains a marine policy covering the shipment of textiles from China to Poland. The declared value of the shipment was $15,000 although the real (market) value of the merchandise was $7,500. If the goods are lost at sea, is the insurance company liable for $15,000?
9. How does actual total loss differ from constructive total loss? What is general average loss? You receive compensation from a marine insurance company because your goods were jettisoned from a ship as a general average act. Does the insurance company have a claim for general average against the ship owner and the other cargo owners?
10. Discuss typical steps followed in claims from carriers or insurers with respect to loss or damage to cargo.

CASE 6.1. MARINE INSURANCE

Actual total loss versus constructive total loss: Goods are regarded as having become an *actual total loss* as soon as they cease to be goods of the kind insured from a commercial point of view. It occurs where a ship or goods have been actually lost and the freight can no longer be recovered. The three elements that constitute actual total loss include the following:

1. Destruction of subject matter: Destruction of cargo ship by fire, sinking, or enemy attack.
2. The subject matter ceases to be of the kind insured: *Example:* A cargo of dates is damaged by water in the cargo hold that makes it unfit for human consumption. A cargo of tobacco is rendered worthless by the stench of rotten hides that are damaged by the entry of sea water into the cargo hold.
3. The insured is deprived of the subject matter: *Example:* Capture or seizure of a ship by an enemy could amount to irretrievable deprivation.

There is *constructive total loss,* where the subject matter insured is reasonably abandoned on account of its actual total loss appearing to be unavoidable or because it could not be preserved from actual total loss without an expenditure which would exceed its value. Constructive total loss occurs under any of the following circumstances:

1. The insured is deprived of the possession of the ship or goods by a peril insured against. *Example:* A cargo of goods is detained by the enemy and there is no likelihood of recovery within a reasonable time.
2. The cost of repair is in excess of the value of the property. In the case of damage to the ship, the cost of repairing the damage would exceed the value of the ship when repaired. *Example:* An old cargo vessel was being towed to a particular location to be dismantled and broken apart. During the passage, the vessel ran aground on the Florida coast. The owner contends that it will be quite expensive to bring it to the shore. He intends to hire a company to rescue the cargo ship. The ship had no cargo on board when it ran aground.

CASE 6.2. MARINE INSURANCE: INCHMAREE CLAUSE

A forty-foot wooden hull fishing vessel sprang an unexpected leak a few days after leaving port. As more water entered the vessel, the engine was flooded and the vessel eventually sank. Inspection of the vessel during the leak showed that the water was coming from underneath a refrigerated space in the front part of the vessel. In view of its construction style, the bilge underneath the vessel was inaccessible. The underwriter refused to indemnify the insured for the loss of the vessel by claiming that the latter had not exercised diligence to make the vessel seaworthy prior to the developing of the leak (as provided under the Inchmaree clause). The owner/master of the ship had no knowledge of the leak before the ship started its voyage.

Questions

1. Is this actual or constructive total loss? Explain your answer (Case 6.1).
2. In Case 6.2, do you think the loss is covered under the policy (see International Perspective 6.3)?

SECTION III:
EXECUTING THE TRANSACTIONS

Chapter 7

Pricing in International Trade

Price is an important factor in determining a firm's ability to compete in world markets. For many companies, pricing policies and procedures are secret information and not easily available to outsiders. Export prices should be high enough to make a reasonable profit and yet low enough to be competitive in the market. Products rarely sell on one factor alone, and the exporter should be competitive on nonprice factors of different kinds. Sources of nonprice competition include reliable delivery, short delivery time, product reliability, and product quality, as well as any other feature considered unique by customers. This form of product differentiation based on specific characteristics of a product or service gives firms a competitive advantage (Dussauge, Hart, and Ramanantsoa, 1987). Apple Computer increased its market share in Japan not only by slashing prices but also by broadening distribution outlets and through the addition of Japanese software packages.

The crucial element in determining price relates to the value consumers place on the product. Value results from consumers' perceptions of the total satisfaction provided by the product (Hiam and Schewe, 1992). Companies can charge high prices and manage to remain competitive if the price charged is lower than, or in alignment with, the perceived value of the product or service. In competitive markets, high prices represent an indication of the social desirability of producing the product or service. They may also be justified in export markets if the sale also involves transfers of technology or training.

Pricing in world markets is often used as an instrument of accomplishing the firm's marketing objectives. The firm could use price to achieve certain levels of market share, profits, or returns on investments, or to reach some other specific goal. The following policies for pricing and markups generally apply to both domestic and export markets:

Export-Import Theory, Practices, and Procedures, Second Edition

- High markups are common in industries with relatively few competitors. Markups are also higher in industries in which companies produce differentiated products rather than homogeneous ones. The high markups could be taken as rent arising from market power. For example, in the chemical industry, the biggest profits lie in specialty chemicals designed and produced for particular industrial uses (Reich, 1991). High markups may also be due to R & D expenditures and costs of increasing the skills of the workforce.
- Export prices tend to be relatively low in sectors in which there is increased competition. Changes in competitors' prices or the state of demand are more likely to trigger a reduction in export prices. Markups are relatively low for textiles, food, electric machinery, and motor vehicles; they remain high in industries such as medicines, computers, industrial chemicals, and television and communications equipment (Martens, Scarpetta, and Pilat, 1996). The low markups for the former are due to the fragmented and nondifferentiated nature of these industries, which makes it difficult to exercise market power.

A company needs to develop a workable guideline with respect to pricing of its product or service in export markets. Its pricing policy should be firm enough to achieve the targeted level of profits or sales, while maintaining some flexibility to accommodate the overall marketing objectives of the firm. Flexibility is seen as an absolute necessity for optimizing profits, and a firm may use all pricing methods according to the type of product being sold, the class and type of customer, and the competitive situation in the marketplace. Mismanagement of export pricing could often lead to pressures for price reductions or the development of parallel markets. Parallel, or gray, markets are created when the product is purchased at a low price in one market and sold in other markets enjoying higher prices. For example, Eastman Kodak prices its films higher in Japan than in other countries. An importer in Japan can purchase the product at a discount in a foreign country and sell it in the Japanese market at a price lower than that charged by authorized Kodak dealers. Appropriate pricing and control systems of quality and distribution outlets are important in reducing such incidences of parallel markets.

DETERMINANTS OF EXPORT PRICES

A number of variables influence the level of export prices. Some of these are internal to the firm; others are factors that are external to the firm. A major internal variable is the cost that is to be included in the export price. The typical costs associated with exports include market research, credit checks, business travel, product modification, special packaging, consultants, freight forwarders, and commissions (Anonymous, 1993). An additional cost is the chosen system of distribution. The long distribution channels in many countries are often responsible for price escalation. The use of manufacturers' representatives offers greater price control to the exporter. Another internal variable is the degree of product differentiation, that is, the extent of a product's perceived uniqueness or continuance of service. Generally, the higher the product differentiation a firm enjoys, the more independent it can be in its price-setting activities.

The external forces that influence export pricing include the following:

- *Supply and demand:* The pricing decisions for exports are subject to the influence of the supply of raw materials, parts, and other inputs. In a competitive economy, any increase in demand is followed by a higher price, and the higher price should, in turn, moderate demand. It is often stated that exports of manufactured goods exhibit the same price characteristic as primary products, their prices varying with the state of world demand and supply (Silberston, 1970). The classical supply-and-demand approach—whereby price acts as an allocating device in the economy and supply equals demand at an equilibrium price—is largely based on certain assumptions: perfect buyer information, substitutability of competing goods, and marginal cost pricing. The classical assumption that reducing prices increases demand ignores the interpretation of price changes by buyers. Studies have shown that consumers perceive price as an indicator of quality and may interpret lower product prices as a sign of poor quality (Piercy, 1982). If a product has a prestigious image, price can be increased without necessarily reducing demand.
- *Location and environment of the foreign market:* Climatic conditions often require product modification in different markets, and this is reflected in the price of the export product. Goods that deteriorate in high-humidity conditions require special, more expensive packaging. For example, engines that are to be exported to countries in the tropics require extra cooling capacity.
- *Economic policies such as exchange rates, price controls, and tariffs also influence export pricing:* Exchange rate depreciation (a drop in the value of a currency) improves price competitiveness, thus leading to increased export volumes and market shares. For example, in 1984 to 1985, when the dollar had appreciated to roughly double its 1980

value against the German mark, luxury German cars were selling for lower prices in the United States than in Germany. In export markets where buyers are used to negotiating prices, a flexible price is preferable over one that uniformly applies to all buyers.

- *Government regulations in the home country:* Different regulations in the home country have a bearing on export pricing. For example, U.S. government action to reduce the impact of its antitrust laws on competition abroad has enhanced the price competitiveness of American companies.

PRICING IN EXPORT MARKETS

The export price decision is distinct from the domestic price decision in the home market. The export decision has to consider variations in market conditions, existence of cartels or trade associations, and the existence of different channels of distribution. The presence of different environmental variables in export markets militates against the adoption of a single export-pricing policy (ethnocentric pricing) around the world. Another factor against uniform pricing is that different markets may be at different stages in the life cycle of a product at any given time.

It is customary to charge a high price during the introduction and growth stages of a product and to progressively reduce the price as the product matures. Other pricing alternatives include (1) polycentric pricing, which is pricing sensitive to local conditions, and (2) geocentric pricing, whereby a firm strikes an intermediate position. There are four approaches to export pricing.

Cost-Based Pricing

The most common pricing approach used by exporters is one that is based on full-cost-oriented pricing. Under this procedure, a markup rate on full cost is determined and then added to the product's cost to establish the price. The markup rate could be based on the desired target rate of return on investment.

The Marginal Approach to Pricing

Marginal pricing is more common in exporting than in domestic markets. It is often employed by businesses that have unused capacity or to gain market share. In this case, the price does not cover the product's total cost, but instead includes only the marginal (variable) cost of producing the product to be sold in the export market. This will result in the sale of a product at a lower price in the export market than at home and often leads to charges of dumping by competitors.

Skimming versus Penetration Pricing

Skimming, or charging a premium price for a product, is common in industries that have few competitors or in which the companies produce differentiated products. Such products are directed to the high-income, price-inelastic segment of the market.

Penetration-pricing policy is based on charging lower prices for exports to stimulate market growth. Increasing market share and maximizing revenues could generate high profits.

Demand-Based Pricing

Under this method, export prices are based on what consumers or industrial buyers are willing to pay for the product or service. When prices are set by demand, market surveys will help supply the data to identify the level of demand. The level of demand generally establishes the range of prices that will be acceptable to customers. Companies often test-market a product at various prices and settle on a price that results in the greatest sales.

A firm does not have to sell a product at or below market price to be competitive in export markets. A superior or unique product can command a higher price. Cartier watches and Levi's jeans are examples of products that, despite their high prices, generate enormous sales worldwide due to their reputation. These are products for which consumers feel a strong demand and for which there are few, or no, substitutes (products with inelastic demand). In cases in which demand for the product is elastic, consumers are sensitive to changes in price. For example, rebates and other discount schemes often revive lagging export sales in the auto industry (which is characterized by elastic demand). A few years ago, Toyota launched a special sales campaign in Tokyo to give away money (about one million yen to 100 customers) to some of the customers of the competitor car it sells in Japan on behalf of General Motors.

Competitive Pricing

Competitive pressures are important in setting prices in export markets. In this case, export prices are established by maintaining the same price level as the competition, reducing prices or increasing the price with some level of product improvement. However, price-cutting is generally a more effective strategy for small competitors than for dominant firms. An important factor in establishing a pricing strategy is also a projection of likely responses of existing and potential competitors (Oster, 1990).

TERMS OF SALE

Despite wide differences among national laws, there is a high degree of uniformity in contract practices for the export and import of goods. The universality of trade practices, including terms of sale, is due to the development of the law merchant by international mercantile custom. The law merchant refers to the body of commercial law that developed in Europe during the medieval period for merchants and their merchandise (Brinton et al., 1984).

Trade terms are intended to define the method of delivery of the goods sold and the attendant responsibilities of the parties. Such terms also help the seller in the calculation of the purchase price (Anonymous, 1993). A seller quoting the term of sale as FOB, for example, will evidently charge a lower price than if quoting CIF because the latter includes not only the cost of goods but also expenses incurred by the seller for insurance and freight to ship the goods to the port of destination. The national laws of each country often determine the rights and duties of parties with respect to terms of sale. In the United States, the Revised American Foreign Trade Definitions (1941) and The Uniform Commercial Code govern terms of sale. Since 1980, the sponsors of the Revised American Foreign Trade Definitions recommend the use of Incoterms. Parties to terms of sale could also agree to be governed by Incoterms, published by the International Chamber of Commerce in 1953 (latest revision, 2000, which now enjoys almost universal acceptance [Herman, 1989]). The ICC is a nongovernmental entity. Incoterms is neither a national legislation nor an international treaty. It applies when the parties expressly indicate their intention to incorporate it into their export sales contract. If the parties do not explicitly agree to be governed by Incoterms, it could be made an implicit term of the contract as part of international custom.

Incoterms are periodically revised every ten years to represent contemporary commercial practice (Incoterms, 1980, 1990, 2000). In order to avoid any misunderstanding, parties to export contracts should always state the application of the current version of Incoterms. The Uniform Commercial Code (UCC) and Incoterms complement each other in many areas. Trade terms are not understood in the same manner in every country and it is important to explicitly state the law that governs the contract. For example, a contract should state FOB New York (Incoterms) or "CIF Liverpool (Uniform Commercial Code)" (see Table 7.1).

TABLE 7.1. Major Differences Between Incoterms, 2000 and Uniform Commercial Code (UCC)

Terms of Sale	Incoterms, 2000	UCC
Commercial terms	There are many new commercial terms in Incoterms which are not found in UCC (FCA, CPT, CIP, DAF, DES, DEQ, DDU, DDP)	Many of the new terms in Incoterms are generally covered by existing UCC terms (Using a different name, definition, etc.)
Ex Works	Seller needs only to tender the goods to buyer by placing them at the buyer's disposal at a named place of delivery and notifying the buyer the time/place. The seller has no obligation to deliver the goods to carrier or load them on a vehicle. The seller has no obligation to arrange transportation or insurance	Where a third party carrier is not involved, risk of loss passes not upon mere tender of delivery but when buyer receives the goods. There is no provision for transportation and insurance. When third party carrier is involved, transfer of risk occurs upon tender of goods to enable buyer to take delivery. It requires seller to arrange for transportation and insurance
FOB	Exclusively used for waterborne transportation	Not exclusive to waterborne transportation unless it is FOB (vessel). In FOB (place of shipment) seller arranges for transportation and insurance. UCC's FOB (place of destination) is equivalent to DDU term under Incoterms
	FCA (Incoterms), seller arranges for transportation only in special circumstances. There is no obligation for insurance	UCC's FOB (place of shipment) equivalent to FCA under Incoterms
	There is no requirement for payment against documents	Requires payment against documents
FAS and CIF	There is no requirement for payment against document or use of negotiable bill of lading	UCC requires payments against tender of documents

All trade terms are classified into four groups based on the point of transfer of risk (delivery) from seller to buyer (see Table 7.2):

1. *Group E term (Ex Works):* This grouping has only one term and represents the seller's minimum obligation, that is, to place the goods at the disposal of the buyer. There are no contractual arrangements between seller and buyer with regard to insurance, transportation, or export.

2. *Group F terms (FCA, FAS, FOB):* The seller is expected to bear the risk and expense of delivery to a nominated carrier. It is the buyer's responsibility to arrange and pay for the main carriage to the point of destination.

3. *Group C terms (CRF, CIF, CPT, CIP):* C-terms establish the point of delivery (transfer of risk) from seller to buyer at the point of shipment. However, it extends the seller's obligation with regard to the costs of carriage and insurance up to the point of destination. This means that the seller bears certain costs even after the critical point for the division of the risk or damage to the goods. They are often referred to as shipment terms.

4. *Group D terms (DAF, DES, DEQ, DDU, DDP):* The seller's delivery obligation extends to the country of destination. This means that the seller could be held liable for breach of contract if the goods are lost/damaged after shipment but before arrival at the agreed point of destination. The seller may be required to provide substitute goods or other forms of restitution to the buyer. They are often referred to as arrival terms (see Table 7.3).

Group E (Ex Works, Ex Warehouse, and Ex Store)

Ex Works, Ex Warehouse, Ex Store (named place): Under this term, the buyer or agent must collect the goods at the seller's works, warehouse, or store. The seller bears all risk and expenses until the goods are placed at the

TABLE 7.2. Group of Incoterms, 2000

Group E (Departure)	Group F Main Carriage Unpaid	Group C Main Carriage Paid (Shipment Terms)	Group D Arrival Terms
Ex Works (EXW) (AMT)[a]	Free Carrier (FCA) (AMT)	Cost and Freight (CFR) (STO)	Delivered at Frontier (DAF) (AMT)
	Free Alongside Ship (FAS) (STO)[a]	Cost, Insurance and Freight (CIF) (STO)	Delivered Ex Ship (DES) (STO)
	Free on Board (FOB) (STO)	Carriage Paid To (CPT) (AMT)	Delivered Ex Quay (DEQ) (STO)
		Carriage and Insurance Paid To (CIP) (AMT)	Delivered Duty Unpaid (DDU) (AMT)
			Delivered Duty Paid (DDP) (AMT)

[a]AMT: All modes of transport; STO: Sea transport only.

TABLE 7.3A. Responsibilities of Parties under Incoterms, 2000

Responsibility	Sea Transport Only					
	FAS	*FOB*	*CFR*	*CIF*	*DES*	*DEQ*
Loading at seller's premises	SR	SR	SR	SR	SR	SR
Domestic precarriage (local cartage)	SR	SR	SR	SR	SR	SR
Contract of carriage and dispatch	BR	SR	SR	SR	SR	SR
Trade documentation (country of export)	SR	SR	SR	SR	SR	SR
Customs clearance (country of export)	SR	SR	SR	SR	SR	SR
Export charges	SR	SR	SR	SR	SR	SR
Transshipment at carrier's terminal	BR	BR	SR	SR	SR	SR
Transport (cargo) insurance				SR		
Int. main carriage	BR	BR	SR	SR	SR	SR
Transshipment at terminal	BR	BR	SR	SR	BR	SR
Trade documentation (country of transit/import)	BR	BR	BR	BR	BR	BR
Customs clearance (country of import)	BR	BR	BR	BR	BR	BR
Import charges	BR	BR	BR	BR	BR	BR
Local cartage/domestic oncarriage	BR	BR	BR	BR	BR	BR
Unloading at buyer's premises	BR	BR	BR	BR	BR	BR

disposal of the buyer at the time and place agreed for delivery, normally the seller's premises, warehouse, or factory. The purchase price becomes payable at the time of delivery.

Risk is not transferred to buyer if damage or loss is attributed to the failure on the part of the seller to deliver the goods in conformity with the contract (e.g., damage due to inadequate packing of goods).

The buyer bears all risk and charges pertaining to preshipment inspection, export/import licenses, and customs duties/taxes needed for exportation. The buyer is also responsible for clearance of goods for exports, transit, and imports since the seller makes the goods available to the buyer in the country of export.

This term of sale is similar to a domestic sales transaction, although the product is destined for export.

Group F (FCA, FAS, and FOB)

Free carrier (FCA), named place: The seller bears the risk and costs relating to the goods until delivery to the carrier or any other person nominated by the buyer. The place of delivery could be the carrier's cargo terminal or a vehicle sent to pick up the goods at the seller's premises. The seller is

TABLE 7.3B. Responsibilities of Parties under Incoterms, 2000

Responsibility	All Modes of Transport															
	EXW	FCA1	FCA2	CPT1	CIP1	CPT2	CIP2	CPT3	CIP3	CPT4	CIP4	DAF	DDU1	DDP1	DDU2	DDP2
Loading at seller's premises	BR	SR	SR	SR	SR	SR	SR	SR	SR	SR	SR	SR	SR	SR	SR	SR
Domestic precarriage (local cartage)	BR	BR	SR	SR	SR	SR	SR	SR	SR	SR	SR	SR	SR	SR	SR	SR
Contract of carriage and dispatch	BR	SR	SR	SR	SR	SR	SR	SR	SR	SR	SR	SR	SR	SR	SR	SR
Trade documentation (country of export)	BR	SR	SR	SR	SR	SR	SR	SR	SR	SR	SR	SR	SR	SR	SR	SR
Customs clearance (country of export)	BR	SR	SR	SR	SR	SR	SR	SR	SR	SR	SR	SR	SR	SR	SR	SR
Export charges	BR	SR	SR	SR	SR	SR	SR	SR	SR	SR	SR	SR	SR	SR	SR	SR
Transshipment at carrier's terminal	BR	BR	BR	SR	SR	SR	SR	SR	SR	SR	SR	SR	SR	SR	SR	SR
Transport (cargo) insurance					SR		SR		SR		SR					
Int. main carriage	BR	BR	BR	SR/BR	SR/BR	SR/BR	SR/BR	SR	SR	SR	SR	SR	SR	SR	SR	SR
Transshipment at terminal	BR	BR	BR	BR	BR	BR	BR	SR	SR	SR	SR	SR	SR	SR	SR	SR

TABLE 7.3B *(continued)*

	All Modes of Transport															
	EXW	FCA1	FCA2	CPT1	CPT2	CPT3	CPT4	CIP1	CIP2	CIP3	CIP4	DAF	DDU1	DDP1	DDU2	DDP2
Trade documentation (country of transit/import)	BR	BR	BR	BR	BR	BR	BR	BR	BR	BR	BR	BR	BR	SR	BR	SR
Customs clearance (country of import)	BR	BR	BR	BR	BR	BR	BR	BR	BR	BR	BR	BR	BR	SR	BR	SR
Import charges	BR	BR	BR	BR	BR	BR	BR	BR	BR	BR	BR	BR	BR	SR	BR	SR
Local cartage/domestic on carriage	BR	BR	BR	BR	BR	BR	SR	BR	BR	BR	SR	BR	BR	BR	SR	SR
Unloading at buyer's premises	BR	BR	BR	BR	BR	BR	BR	BR	BR	BR	BR	BR	BR	BR	BR	BR

CIP1: Carriage and Insurance Paid To (named frontier point in country of dispatch); CIP2: Carriage and Ins. Paid To (named frontier point in country of destination); CIP3: Carriage and Ins. Paid To (named terminal); CIP4: Carriage and Ins. Paid to buyer's premises; CPT1: Carriage Paid To(named frontier point in country of dispatch); CPT2: Carriage Paid To (named frontier point in country of destination); CPT3: Carriage Paid To (named terminal); CPT4: Carriage Paid To buyer's premises; DDP1: Delivered (named terminal) Duty Paid, exclusive of (named tax); DDP2: Delivered buyer's premises Duty Paid, exclusive of (named tax); DDU1: Delivered (named terminal) Duty Unpaid; DDU2: Delivered buyer's premises Duty Unpaid; FCA1: Free carrier seller's premises; FCA2: Free carrier (named terminal).

responsible for loading the goods onto the buyer's collecting vehicle. If the place of delivery is the carrier's cargo terminal, the seller is only required to bring the goods to the terminal (not obligated to unload them). It is sought that the carrier is likely to have the necessary personnel and equipment to unload the goods at its own terminal rather than the seller.

Upon delivery of the goods to the carrier, the seller receives (from the carrier) a receipt, which serves as evidence of delivery and contract of carriage made on behalf of the buyer. Neither party is required to insure under FCA. However, the seller must provide the buyer (upon request) with the necessary information for procuring insurance.

Besides payment of the purchase price as provided in the contract, the buyer has the following obligations:

- Obtain at his or her own risk and expense any import license and other official authorization necessary for importation of the goods as well as for their transit through another country.
- Contract at his or her own expense for carriage of the goods from the named place of delivery.
- Pay the costs of any preshipment inspection except when such inspection is mandated by exporting country.

Free alongside ship (FAS), named port of shipment: This term requires the seller to deliver the goods to a named port alongside a vessel to be designated by the buyer (ICC, 2000). "Alongside the vessel" has been understood to mean that the goods be within reach of a ship's lifting tackle. The risks to the goods pass to the buyer upon seller's delivery alongside the ship. This implies that all charges and risks for the goods are borne by the buyer from the time they have been effectively delivered alongside the vessel.

The seller must obtain at his own risk and expense any export license and other official authorizations, including customs formalities that are necessary for the export of the goods. The seller's obligation to clear the goods for export is similar to that of FOB contracts. There is an implied duty on the part of the seller to cooperate in arranging a loading and shipping schedule, and to render at the buyer's request and expense every assistance in obtaining necessary documents for the import of the goods and their transit through another country. The seller must provide the buyer (at his or her own expense) with the usual proof of delivery.

The buyer must contract (at his or her own expense) for the carriage of goods from the port of shipment. Since the buyer has to nominate the ship, he or she has to pay any additional costs incurred if the named vessel fails to arrive on time or the vessel is unable to take the goods. In such cases, a premature passing of risk will occur. Costs of any preshipment inspection are borne by the buyer except when such inspection is mandated by the exporting country.

The use of FAS is appropriate in cases where sellers took their shipment to the pier and deposited it close enough for loading. However, today most of the outbound cargo is delivered to ship lines days before placement alongside the vessel. It is also not applicable in cases of rolling cargo (cars, trucks) that can be driven aboard vessel, or in ports with shallow harbors that do not allow for vessels to come alongside the pier.

Free on board (FOB), named port of shipment: The central feature of FOB contracts is the notion that the seller undertakes to place the goods on board the ship designated by the buyer. This includes responsibility for all charges incurred up to and including delivery of the goods over the ship's rail at the named port of shipment (ICC, 2000). The buyer has to nominate a suitable ship and inform the seller of its name, loading point, and delivery time. If the ship that was originally nominated is unable or unavailable to receive the cargo at the agreed time for loading, the buyer has to nominate a substitute ship and pay all additional charges. Once the seller delivers the goods on board the ship, the buyer is responsible for all subsequent charges such as freight, marine insurance, unloading charges, import duties, and other expenses due on arrival at the port of destination. Unless otherwise stated in the contract of sale, it is customary in FOB contracts for the seller to procure the export license and other formalities necessary for the export of the goods since the latter is more familiar with licensing practices and procedures in the exporting country than the buyer. Transfer of risk occurs upon seller's delivery of the goods on board the vessel. Seller's responsibility for loss or damage to the goods terminates on delivery to the carrier. The ship's rail is thus considered the dividing line between the seller's and buyer's responsibility in terms of transfer of risk (see Table 7.4).

Free on board does not appear to be consistent with current practice except for shipments of noncontainerized or bulk cargo, as well as shipments by chartered vessel. In many other cases, sellers are required to deliver their outbound cargo to ship lines days before actual loading of the cargo. The seller, however, remains responsible for the goods until delivery on board the vessel (see International Perspectives 7.1 and 7.2).

Group C (CIF, CFR, CPT, and CIP)

Cost, insurance, and freight (CIF), named port of destination: The CIF contract places upon the seller the obligation to arrange for shipment of the goods. The seller has to ship goods described under the contract to be delivered at the destination and arrange for insurance to be available for the

TABLE 7.4. Price Determination Worksheet (UCC)

Price (or cost) per unit _____ 3 _____ unites 5 total	1
Profit (or mark up)	1
Commissions	1
Financing costs	1
Ex factory	5
Crating/containerization charges (if done at factory)	1
Labeling and marking costs (if done at factory)	1
Drayage charges (usually associated with movement of containers from railroad ramp to plant and back to ramp)	1
Loading charges, if applicable	1
Demurrage and detention charges, if applicable	1
Other charges (specify)	1
Free on board (FOB) truck or rail car at point of origin	5
Inland freight charges (including fuel surcharges)	1
Unloading charges at port facilities	1
Drayage to packer (crater/containerized), if applicable	1
Containerization/crating charges (if done at port)	1
Labeling and marking (if done at port)	1
Freight forwarding and documentation charges (includes charges associated with consular fees, export license, postage, telex, and telephone/telegram use, etc.)	1
Drayage to warehouse and unloading, if applicable	1
Warehousing charges, if applicable	1
Loading and drayage to pier from packer or warehouse, if applicable	1
Wharfage charges	1
Terminal notification charges	1
Demurrage/detention at port	1
Free alongside vessel at port of _____	5
Vessel loading charges	1
Heavy lift or extra-length charges, if applicable	1
Other charges (specify)	1
Free on board vessel at port of _____	5
Ocean freight charges	1
Bunker or other surcharges, if applicable	1
Cost and freight to _____	5
Insurance	1
Cost, insurance and freight to _____	5

benefit of the buyer or any other person with insurable interest in the goods. In the absence of express agreement, the insurance shall be in accordance with minimum of cover provided under the Institute of Cargo Clauses or similar set of guidelines. The cost of freight is borne by the seller and the

INTERNATIONAL PERSPECTIVE 7.1.
Incoterms: Salient Features

A. *Incoterms 1990 versus Incoterms 2000:* Important differences:
- Incoterms 2000 places the responsibility for export clearance on the seller in FAS contracts. This obligation was borne by the buyer in Incoterms 1990.
- Incoterms 2000 requires the buyer to clear imports at his or her own expense (seller's responsibility in Incoterms 1990) under delivered at quay (DEQ) term.
- Incoterms 2000 obligates the seller to load the goods on the buyer's collecting vehicle under FCA term. In Incoterms 1990, the seller is not responsible for placing the goods on board the carrier (plane, truck, etc.) nominated by the buyer.

B. *Recognizing the limitation of Incoterms:* Incoterms only deal with matters pertaining to the interpretation of terms of delivery. The rules do not deal with transfer of property rights in the goods, exemptions from liability, or consequences in cases of breach of contract. They deal with obligations in connection with delivery, provision of documents, insurance, and clearance of goods for export/import operations.

C. *Thirteen terms in Incoterms 2000:* Incoterms attempts to reflect contemporary commercial practice and offers a variety of terms ranging from Ex Works, which entails minimal obligation for the seller to extended obligations (FCA, FAS, FOB). It also provides for maximum obligations for the seller (DAF, DES, DEQ, DDU, DDP). Incoterms are often used in contracts of sale and contracts of carriage.

D. *Insurance:* Seller's obligation to take out insurance to the benefit of the buyer applies only under CIP and CIF terms. Parties have to arrange insurance as they see fit under all other terms.

buyer undertakes to pay upon arrival of the merchandise (ICC, 2000). The seller must notify the buyer that the goods have been delivered on board the vessel to enable the buyer to receive the goods.

The seller has to tender the necessary documents (commercial invoice, bill of lading, policy of insurance) to the buyer so that the latter could obtain delivery upon arrival of the goods or recover for their loss. The buyer must accept the documents when tendered by the seller when they are in conformity with the contract of sale and pay the purchase price. Import duties/licenses, consular fees, and charges to procure a certificate of origin are the responsibility of the buyer, while export licenses and other customs formalities necessary for the export of the goods have to be obtained by the seller.

INTERNATIONAL PERSPECTIVE 7.2.
Incoterms and Business Strategies

- *Which Incoterms are appropriate?* The choice is dependent on the type of cargo and the buyer's intention to sell the goods in transit. It also depends on the ability of the parties to obtain the most favorable contract of carriage.
- *Appropriateness of C versus F term:* In cases where the seller can procure marine insurance at a competitive price and where there are government regulations to use national shipping lines, it may be appropriate to use CFR and CIF. If the parties prefer the seller to procure carriage (CPT) and insurance, CIP may be appropriate. When the buyer can procure insurance at a competitive rate, the parties may prefer to use FAS or FOB.
- *Manufactured goods:* Exporters of manufactured goods often sell on extended terms using DDU and DDP (seller makes goods available to buyer at the cargo terminal) to remain competitive. Since such goods are normally containerized, the parties can also use FCA, CPT, or CIP.
- *Use of Ex Works, FCA:* Large buyers such as wholesalers, department stores may find it advantageous to arrange for transportation in order to ensure just-in-time deliveries.

The CIF contract may provide certain advantages to the overseas customer because the seller often possesses expert knowledge and experience to make favorable arrangements with respect to freight, insurance, and other charges. This could be reflected in terms of reduced import prices for the overseas customer (see Table 7.5).

Under a CIF contract, risk passes to the buyer upon delivery, that is, when the goods are put on board the ship at the port of departure.

Rejection of documents versus rejection of goods: When proper shipping documents that are in conformity with the contract are tendered, the buyer must accept them and pay the purchase price. The right to reject the goods arises when they are landed and, after examination, they are found not to be in conformity with the contract. It may also happen that while the goods conform to the contract, the documents are not in accordance with the contract of sale (discrepancies between documents such as bill of lading, commercial invoice, draft and the letter of credit, or contract of sale). In this case, the buyer could accept the goods but reject the documents and claim damages for a breach of condition relating to the goods. Thus, under a CIF contract, the right to reject the documents is separate and distinct from the right to reject the goods.

TABLE 7.5. Items to Be Included in the Calculation of the Price Using Various Terms and Required Documents

	Incoterms, 2000													
	Ex Works	FCA[1]	FCA[2]	FAS	FOB	CPT	CIP	CFR	CIF	DAF	DDU	DDP	DES	DEQ
Invoice Items														
Total items	X	X	X	X	X	X	X	X	X	X	X	X	X	X
Export packing		X		X	X									
Precarriage[a]			X	X	X					X			X	X
Vessel loading												X	X	X
Main carriage[b]						X	X	X	X			X	X	X
Forwarding fees						X	X	X	X					
Total carriage										X	X			
Insurance							X		X					X
Unloading														X
Total	X	X	X	X	X	X	X	X	X	X	X	X	X	X
Required Documents														
Commercial invoice	X	X	X	X	X	X	X	X	X	X	X	X	X	X
Buyer's receipt	X													
Delivery receipt[c]		X	X											
Export license		X	X	X	X	X	X	X	X					
Clean receipt[d]				X	X									
Transport document						X	X	X	X	X				
Insurance							X		X					

TABLE 7.5 (continued)

Incoterms, 2000

	Ex Works	FCA[1]	FCA[2]	FAS	FOB	CPT	CIP	CFR	CIF	DAF	DDU	DDP	DES	DEQ
Document to take Delivery														
Import license												x		
Suggested Payment Terms														
Cash in advance	x	x	x	x	x	x	x	x	x	x	x	x	x	x
Letter of credit		x	x	x	x	x	x	x	x		x	x	x	x
Documentary collection		x	x	x	x	x	x	x	x	x	x	x	x	x
Open account	x	x	x	x	x	x	x	x	x	x	x	x	x	x

Note: CIA: Cash in advance; L/C: Letter of credit; DD: Documentary draft; OA: Open account.

[1]Seller's place
[2]Carrier's terminal
[a]precarriage: inland freight to the point of departure i.e., port etc.
[b]Main carriage: Transportation to the overseas customer, normally by air or ship
[c]delivery receipt: certificate of carriage given by carrier
[d]clean receipt: receipt by carrier to show that the goods bear no damage or loss.

Payment is often made against documents. Tender of the goods cannot be an alternative to tender of the documents in CIF contracts. The buyer's acceptance of conforming documents does not impair subsequent rejection of the goods and recovery of the purchase price if on arrival the goods are not in accordance with the terms of sale.

Loss of goods: If the goods shipped under a CIF contract are destroyed or lost during transit, the seller is entitled to claim the purchase price against presentation of proper shipping documents to the buyer. Since insurance is taken for the benefit of the buyer, the buyer can claim against the insurer in so far as the risk is covered by the policy. If the loss is due to some misconduct on the part of the carrier not covered by the policy, the buyer could recover from the carrier.

The only difference between CIF and CFR terms is that the latter does not require the seller to obtain and pay for cargo insurance.

Carriage paid to (CPT), named place of destination is similar to the CFR term, except that it may be used for any other type of transportation. Even though the seller is obligated to arrange and pay for the transportation to a named place of destination, he or she completes delivery obligations and thus transfers risk of loss/damage to the buyer when the goods are delivered to the carrier at the place of shipment.

The seller must notify the buyer that the goods have been delivered to the carrier (first carrier in the case of multimodal transportation) and also give any other notice required to enable the buyer to take receipt of the goods. The term is appropriate for multimodal transportation. When several carriers are involved (e.g., carriage by road or rail from the seller's warehouse for further carriage by sea to the destination), the seller has fulfilled his or her delivery obligation under CPT term when the goods have been handed over for carriage to the first carrier. In CFR and CIF contracts, delivery is not completed until the goods have reached a vessel at the port of shipment.

In the absence of an explicit agreement between the parties, there is no requirement to provide a negotiable bill of lading (to enable the buyer to sell the goods in transit). The buyer must pay the costs of any preshipment inspection unless such inspection is mandated by the exporting country. Given the absence of postinspection provisions in the Incoterms 2000, the CPT does not appear to restrict inspection before payment.

The CPT term is similar to the CIP term, except that the seller is not required to arrange or pay for insurance coverage of the goods during transportation.

Group D (DAF, DES, DEQ, DDU, and DDP)

Among the Group D terms, delivery Ex Quay (DEQ) and delivery Ex Ship are used for waterborne transportation while the other three can be used for any type of transportation including multimodal transport. All D terms share certain common features:

1. They are arrival/destination terms.
2. The seller is required to arrange for transportation, pay freight, and bear the risk of loss to a named point of destination.
3. The seller must place the goods at the disposal of the buyer (varies according to term).
4. There is no requirement for use of negotiable bill of lading and delivery occurs only after arrival of the goods.
5. Incoterms do not require insurance during transportation. Seller may have to arrange and pay for insurance or act as self-insurer during transportation.
6. The buyer must pay the costs of any preshipment inspection except when such inspection is mandated by the exporting country. There are no provisions for postshipment inspection.

Delivery at frontier (DAF), named place: DAF is frequently used in continental export trade (USA-Canada) where rail or road transportation is involved. It should specify not only the frontier but also the place of delivery (e.g., delivered at U.S.–Canada frontier, Vancouver). The frontier refers to a geographical or customs frontier. It can be that of the country of export, import, or some intermediate frontier.

The seller's obligations under DAF term have been defined as follows:

- To obtain at his or her own expense any export license and other documents necessary for placing the goods at the buyer's disposal
- To contract at his or her own expense for the carriage of the goods to the named point at the place of delivery at the frontier.
- To place the goods at the disposal of the buyer on the arriving means of transport, not unloaded at the named place of delivery. The risk of loss is on the seller until the goods reach the place of delivery at the frontier. The risk of loss passes to the buyer on arrival, without unloading. If there is no designated place of delivery, it may be determined by customs. (Incoterms, 2000)
- To provide the buyer (at seller's expense) with the necessary documents to enable the latter to take delivery of the goods (invoice, export

license, transport document). The seller must provide customary packaging which is required for the delivery of the goods at the frontier.

The buyer must bear all risk of loss or damage to the goods from the time they have been delivered at the frontier.

Delivery ex ship (DES), named port of destination: The DES term is applied only for waterborne transportation and almost always used with charter vessels. The seller is responsible for the carriage of the goods to the named port of destination. Transfer of risk from seller to buyer occurs when the goods are placed at the buyer's disposal on board ship at the named port of destination. The seller delivers when the goods are placed at the disposal of the buyer on board the vessel not cleared for import at the named port of destination. This means that the seller bears all the risk and expense involved in bringing the goods to the named port of destination (before discharging) that is, the goods should be made available to the buyer on board the vessel at the unloading point to enable them to be removed from the vessel by unloading equipment.

The seller is also obligated to notify buyer of the estimated time of arrival of the vessel and provide the necessary documents, such as invoice and bill of lading, as well as procure export license and other customs familiarities necessary for the export of the goods and their transit through another country. The buyer is responsible for unloading the goods and import clearance.

Delivered ex quay (DEQ), named port of destination: The DEQ term is used for waterborne transportation. A central feature of this term is that the seller arranges and pays for transportation to the named port of destination. Delivery occurs when the goods are placed at the buyer's disposal on the quay or wharf at the named port of destination, that is, the seller discharges goods on the quay or wharf. The buyer is required to clear the goods for import and handle other formalities and charges necessary for importation. With regard to other issues such as notice to buyer, provision of documents, packing, etc., it is similar to DES term. If the parties wish to extend the seller's obligations to handling of the goods (risk and expense to be incurred by the seller) from the quay to a warehouse or terminal in or outside the port of destination, it is appropriate to use delivery duty paid (DDP) or delivery duty unpaid (DDU) term. In DDP, delivery occurs when the goods are placed at the buyer's disposal on any means of transport not unloaded at the named port of destination. Unlike DDU, the seller pays for import duties and other charges necessary for importation at the port of destination. In other areas, such as notice to the buyer, provision of documents, packing, the DEQ term is similar to DDU and DDP terms.

The major differences between arrival contracts and a CIF contract are as follows:

- In arrival contracts, delivery is effected when the goods are placed at the disposal of the buyer. In CIF term, delivery is effected upon loading the goods on board the vessel at the port of departure.
- In arrival contracts, the buyer is under no obligation to pay the purchase price if the goods are lost on transit. In CIF contracts, the buyer is required to pay against documents. However, the loss of goods gives the buyer the right of claim from the carrier or the insurance company depending on the circumstances.

CHAPTER SUMMARY

Sources of Export Competitiveness

Price and nonprice factors such as reliable delivery, short delivery time, product reliability, product quality, design flexibility, support services, financial services

Export Pricing Objectives

Market share, profits, a targeted level of return on investment

Pricing and Markup Policy

1. High markups are common in industries with relatively few competitors and which produce differentiated products.
2. Low markups are common in sectors of increased competition.

Determinants of Export Prices

Internal Variables

Cost of production, cost of market research, business travel, product modification and packing, consultants, freight forwarders, and level of product differentiation

External Variables

Supply and demand, location and environment of foreign market, and home country regulations

Approaches to Export Pricing

1. *Cost-based pricing:* Export price is based on full cost and markup or full cost plus a desired amount of return on investment.
2. *Marginal pricing:* Export price is based on the variable cost of producing the product.
3. *Skimming versus penetration pricing:* Price skimming is charging a premium price for a product; penetration pricing is based on charging lower prices for exports to increase market share.
4. *Demand-based pricing:* Export price is based on what the market could bear.
5. *Competitive pricing:* Export prices are based on competitive pressures in the market.

Groups of terms of sale, 2000

1. *Group E (Ex Works):* Buyer or agent must collect the goods at the seller's works or warehouse.
2. *Group F*
   A. *FCA, free carrier:* Place of delivery could be the carrier's cargo terminal (seller not obligated to unload) or a vehicle sent to pick up the goods at the seller's premises (seller required to load the goods on the vehicle).
   B. *FAS, free alongside ship (named port of shipment):* Requires the seller to deliver goods to a named port alongside a vessel to be designated by the buyer. Seller's responsibilities end upon delivery alongside the vessel.
   C. *FOB, free on board (named port of shipment):* Seller is obliged to deliver the goods on board a vessel to be designated by the buyer.
3. *Group C*
   A. *CIF, cost, insurance, freight:* This term requires the seller to arrange for carriage by sea and pay freight and insurance to a port of destination. Seller's obligations are complete (transfer of risk) when the goods are put on board the ship at the port of departure.
   B. *CFR, cost and freight:* It is similar to CIF term except that the seller is not obligated to arrange and pay for insurance.

C. *CPT, carriage paid to:* It is similar to CFR term except that it may be used for any mode of transportation.

D. *CIP, carriage and insurance paid to:* It is similar to CPT term except that the seller is required to arrange and pay for insurance.

4. *Group D*

A. *DAF, delivery at frontier:* Seller bears all risk of loss to the goods till the time they have been delivered to buyer at the frontier.

B. *DES, delivery ex ship:* Applied only for waterborne transportation. This term requires the seller to deliver goods to a buyer at an agreed port of arrival.

C. *DEQ, delivery ex quay:* Seller is required to deliver goods at the quay at the port of destination.

D. *DDP, delivered duty paid:* Goods placed at the buyer's disposal on any means of transport not unloaded at the port of arrival.

E. *DDU, delivered duty unpaid:* Similar to DDU except that the seller pays for import duties.

REVIEW QUESTIONS

1. High markups are common in industries with relatively few competitors. Discuss and provide examples.

2. The large influx of shrimp imports into the United States from Asia and Latin America depressed wholesale prices by over 40 percent between 1997 and 2002. Despite such lower prices, shrimp entrées at some seafood restaurants in the United States rose by about 28 percent during the same period. Discuss why prices (shrimp prices at sea food restaurants) are not aligned with costs.

3. What is the difference between marginal and cost-based pricing?

4. Seller agreed to deliver 300 tons of coffee to buyer DES port of Montreal, Canada. The goods were transported and unloaded at the port and kept at customs shed for inspection and payment of duties. The buyer was notified of the arrival of the merchandise and its location. Before the buyer picked up the goods, the customs shed (including the merchandise in it) was destroyed by fire. The buyer claims refund of the purchase price stating that she did not receive the goods. Is the seller responsible?

5. In reference to question 4, would the outcome be different if the contract had been DEQ port of Montreal?

6. Seller in New York agrees to ship goods to buyer in Lima, Peru, under a CIF contract. The goods were loaded on the ship and seller tendered the necessary documents to buyer for payment (in New

York). The buyer refused payment claiming that it will only pay after inspection upon arrival of the goods at the port of destination. Is the seller entitled to payment before arrival of the goods?

7. Discuss the major differences between CIF and arrival contracts such as DES.
8. State the major differences between Incoterms 1990 and Incoterms 2000.
9. What are the limitations of Incoterms? Compare and contrast Incoterms with the Uniform Commercial Code.
10. In what cases would export-import managers prefer to use Group C (shipment) terms?

CASE 7.1. INCOTERMS (CIF)

A contract of sale was entered between an American company, BAT, Inc., of Calumet City, Illinois (buyer), and a German scientific equipment manufacturing firm, Tola (seller), for the sale of a mobile MRI. Tola sent the requested MRI machine to buyer aboard the ship, *Superior Carrier,* in good working condition. However, when it reached its final destination, it had been damaged and was in need of extensive repair. The buyer and its insurance company believe that the MRI was damaged in transit. BAT's insurance company, St. Guardian Insurance, covered the cost of the damage, which was $350,000. In turn, the insurance company intends to recover from Tola. However, Tola claims that, since the goods were shipped under CIF (New York) term, they were under no obligation for the loss, that is, its contractual obligation with regard to risk of loss ended when it delivered the machine to the vessel at the port of shipment. The buyer (its insurance company) contends that Incoterms were inapplicable since they were not specifically incorporated into the contract. They also argue that the seller's explicit retention of title modified the risk of loss.

Question

1. Do you agree with BAT and St. Guardian Insurance? Why/why not?

CASE 7.2. INCOTERMS (C&F)

In August 2006, International Commodities Export Corporation (ICEC) entered into an agreement for the sale of 230 tons of Chinese white beans to North Pacific Lumber company (NPL). According to the agreement, the beans were to conform to sample pc-16 and the shipment was to be made on the basis of C&F. Thirteen separate containers of beans were loaded on board two vessels at the port of Hong Kong to Portland, Oregon. An independent surveyor of quality found the bean quality to be in conformity with the description of the goods in the shipper's invoice.

The U.S. Food and Drug Administration (FDA) detained the shipment on arrival in Portland, Oregon, on the grounds that the goods contained filth and were unfit for human consumption. The beans were stored in a warehouse under federal government detention. After efforts to obtain release of the cargo, the buyer rejected the shipments for failure to conform to the contract (sample pc-16).

Questions

1. Did title pass from seller to buyer? If so, when?
2. Is the seller responsible for the goods under C&F when the goods are on board the vessel? How about after delivery to buyer?

Chapter 8

Export Sales Contracts

HARMONIZATION OF CONTRACT LAW

Export sales contracts are central to international commercial transactions and around it revolves a series of connected, but distinct, relationships, including cargo insurance, transportation, and payment arrangements. The rules and practices governing such contracts vary from one export transaction to another, based on the agreement of the parties as well as the legal system. National legal systems on contracts may differ, but the basic principles of contracts, such as good faith and consideration, are generally recognized and accepted in many countries. There is also a movement toward convergence among the world's different legal systems in the area of international commercial law (Lubman, 1988; DiMatteo, 1997). Today, it is almost difficult to identify any examples of substantial divergence that produce important and predictable differences in the outcome of commercial disputes (Rosett, 1982). Certain differences in theory or approach are often offset by the countervailing force of international usage or custom, which brings about a predictable and harmonious outcome in commercial dispute resolution. It is pertinent to identify the motives behind the move toward harmonization of international contract law:

- *Increase in trade and other economic relations between nations*
- *The growth of international customary law:* Commercial custom and usage have often been used in the drafting and interpretation of commercial law. Today, certain customs and practices, derived from merchants in Europe, regarding documentary drafts, letters of credit, and so forth, are universally accepted and form the basis for domestic and international commercial law.
- *The adoption of international conventions and rules:* There have been several attempts at unification of international contract law. The most

Export-Import Theory, Practices, and Procedures, Second Edition

recent attempt at progressive harmonization of the law of international trade is one undertaken by the United Nations Commission on International Trade Law (UNCITRAL). The UNCITRAL produced a set of uniform rules (Convention on International Sale of Goods or CISG) on international trade that are a product of different national legal systems. The CISG, which came into force on January 1, 1988, governs the formation of international sales contracts and the rights and obligations of parties under these contracts. Many important trading nations, such as France, Germany, Italy, The Netherlands, Singapore, and the United States, have signed or ratified the convention (CISG, 1994). As of September 2004, sixty-three countries accounting for over two-thirds of world trade have adopted the convention. The CISG is largely identical to the provisions of the U.S. Uniform Commercial Code. However, there are several important distinctions (see Table 8.1). The CISG applies to contracts for the commercial sale of goods between parties whose "place of business" is in different nations that have agreed to abide by the convention. "Place of business" is often interpreted to mean the country that has the closest relationship to the contract and is closest to where it will be performed, for example, the place where the contract is to be signed or the goods delivered. Parties to a sales contract are at liberty to specify the application of a law of some third country that recognizes the convention in the event of a dispute. The CISG does not apply to certain types of contracts, such as sales of consumer goods, securities, labor services, electricity, ships, vessel, aircraft, or to the supply of goods for manufacture if the buyer provides a substantial part of the material needed for such manufacture or production (see International Perspective 8.1). The CISG is intended to supersede the two Hague conventions (UNIDROIT rules) on international sales.

CISG: ESSENTIAL ELEMENTS

Oral Contracts/Statements

A contract need not be concluded in or evidenced in writing. Import companies that negotiate contracts by phone may be under the impression that the agreement will not be enforceable since it is not made in writing. However, they could be held liable under CISG if they either verbally accept an offer or their verbal offer is accepted by the other party. The CISG,

TABLE 8.1. The CISG versus the Uniform Commercial Code

	CISG	Uniform Commercial Code
Oral testimony	The provisions of a written contract can be modified by a prior or contemporaneous oral agreement.	A written sales contract between the parties cannot be modified by prior or contemporaneous written or oral agreement
Enforceability of oral contracts	CISG does not require that contracts for sale of goods be in writing to be enforceable. That is, agreements made on the phone, in a meeting are enforceable.	Oral contracts for the sale of goods worth $500 or more are not enforceable unless the existence of contract is admitted or that there has been payment or delivery and acceptance
Perfect tender rule	A buyer may not reject the goods or cancel the contract unless the nonconformity constitutes a fundamental breach of the contract. Buyer can demand substitute goods in the event of a fundamental breach of contract by seller.	A buyer may reject the goods and cancel the contract even if the defects are not serious and the buyer would have received substantial performance
Specification of quantity/price	A contract is not sufficiently definite if it fails to indicate the goods and does not expressly or implicitly fix or make provisions for determining the quantity and price.	A contract is valid despite missing terms on provisions pertaining to performance and price in so far as the parties intend to be bound by the contract
Revocability of an offer/terms of acceptance	An offer to sell goods becomes irrevocable if it indicates a fixed time for acceptance or states that it is irrevocable or someone acts by relying on the statement. Acceptance of sale offer by buyer/seller occurs upon receipt by seller/buyer, respectively.	A firm offer to buy or sale goods made in writing, promising to keep the offer open for a period (no longer than 3 months) is valid and enforceable. Acceptance of sales offer by buyer/seller occurs when it is mailed or transmitted by seller/buyer, respectively
Additional terms	Expression of acceptance of the contract by buyer or seller that has additions, limitations, or other modifications is considered to be a rejection and a counteroffer.	Expression of acceptance by buyer or seller of contract terms is valid even if it contains additional terms to that expressed in the offer. In the absence of any objections, the additional terms that do not materially alter the offer (other than quantity, price, and warranty) become part of the contract

INTERNATIONAL PERSPECTIVE 8.1.
Chicago Prime Packers versus Northam Trading Co.

Chicago Prime, a Colorado Corporation (seller), and Northam Trading, a partnership under the laws of Ontario, Canada (buyer), entered into an agreement for the sale of pork back ribs. In March 2001, Chicago Prime contracted to sell 40,500 pounds of pork back ribs to Northam for $178,200 with payment due within seven days of the shipment. Chicago Prime purchased the ribs specified in the contract from Brookfield Farms (Brookfield) and Northam's carrier (Brown Trucking was hired by Northam) picked up the ribs from Brookfield and signed a bill of lading acknowledging that the goods were in apparent good order. The bill of lading also indicated that the "contents and condition of contents of packages were unknown." Brown Trucking delivered the goods to Northam's customer, Beacon Premium Meats, which also signed a second bill of lading indicating that they had received the shipment in "apparent good order."

As Beacon Premium Meats noticed some unusual conditions with the quality of the meat, it requested inspectors at the U.S. Department of Agriculture (USDA) to examine the product. The inspectors concluded that the inspected product was rotten (that it arrived to Beacon in rotten condition) and condemned the entire shipment. Even after Northam informed Chicago Prime of the results of the USDA's inspection, Chicago Prime continued to demand payment and later filed suit.

At trial, Northam submitted that it was relieved of its payment obligation because the product was spoiled when Brown Trucking received them for delivery to Beacon Prime Meats. The district court awarded Chicago Prime the contract price on grounds that the damage to the goods occurred after the risk had passed to the buyer. It also held that the contract was governed by CISG. Northam appealed stating that: (1) the court erred in placing the burden of proof on Northam to show that the ribs were spoiled at the time of transfer, and (2) the evidence did not support the court's finding.

The court of appeal affirmed the ruling of the district court. It agreed that the contract at issue was governed by CISG. Second, it stated that the CISG did not clearly provide as to which party bore the burden of proving that the product conformed to the contract. Given the similarity of the CISG with the provisions of the UCC, the court interpreted the CISG by comparing it with the general principles of the UCC. It stated that, as the buyer bears the burden of proving breach of implied warranty of fitness under the UCC, the buyer needs to prove nonconformity at the time of transfer to Brown Trucking. Also, Northam did not provide credible evidence to show that the ribs were spoiled at the time of delivery to the trucking company. (408 F.3d 894. 2005 U.S. App.)

however, allows members to opt out of this provision (in favor of domestic law that requires writing).

Example. ABC Inc., a cellular phone manufacturer in Florida, contacts various suppliers of semiconductors. The import manager negotiated an oral contract with suppliers in Italy and Germany. Both suppliers orally accepted the offer made by ABC Inc. (type, quality, quantity, price of semiconductors). A few days later, the import manager was advised that a Russian company makes similar goods at lower prices and that the price includes transportation costs to ABC Inc. in Florida. The import manager of ABC Inc. called the suppliers in Italy and Germany to cancel the contract. He thought that oral contracts were not valid and thus unenforceable.

Since each party is located in a different CISG country, CISG applies. The oral contracts with the German and Italian suppliers are enforceable. This means that ABC Inc. is obligated to buy the semiconductors or pay damages.

Parole Evidence

Prior oral statements (including witness testimony) are potentially enforceable and can be used to challenge the provisions of a written contract. Thus, exporters-importers have to be cautious about representations made during the negotiations which are not intended to be part of the written contract, since oral statements could be construed as part of the written contract (if used to prove intent). One solution is to include an integration clause which states that the written contract was the entire agreement and that no other agreements or evidence, which is contradictory, would be admissible.

> *Example.* An Australian supplier of dairy products orally agreed to pay the cost of insurance during transportation of the goods to the buyer's warehouse in Portland, Oregon. However, the written terms of the contract explicitly provided for payment by the U.S. buyer.

The prior oral statement by the supplier is admissible and can be used to modify the terms of the written contract. The supplier would be obligated to pay the cost of insurance.

Battle of the Forms

A reply to a sales offer which purports to be an acceptance but contains additions or modifications is a rejection of the offer and constitutes a counteroffer. However, if the counteroffer does not materially alter the terms of the offer, it constitutes an acceptance unless objected and notified by the offeror. Material terms include price, payment, quantity, and quality of goods; place and time of delivery; and liability.

> *Example.* A manufacturer of leather shoes in Italy sends a purchase order for 500 pounds of polished leather from New Zealand at $10 per pound and three year warranty. The supplier in New Zealand accepted the order but modified the terms: "$12 per pound and two year warranty." The terms added by the supplier are material to the contract, and hence constitute rejections of the offer or are considered a counteroffer.

Duty to Inspect and Proper Notice

In the event that the buyer receives nonconforming goods, he or she must give timely (within as short a period as is practicable) and effective notice of nonconformity (specify the nature of nonconformity). The buyer's notice, such as "the goods are rancid" or "poor workmanship and improper fitting of the goods," were considered by courts as being insufficiently specific and regarded as no notice.

Right to Remedy Deficiencies

The CISG permits the seller to remedy the delivery of defective goods after the time of performance has expired unless such delivery would cause the buyer "unreasonable inconvenience and uncertainty." The buyer reserves the right to sue for damages caused by the delay or buy the initial delivery of nonconforming goods.

Exemptions from Liability

The CISG exempts a party from liability for failure to perform any of his or her obligations due to reasons beyond his or her control and not foreseeable at the time of the contract formation. Prompt notice of the impediment is required to avoid damages. The following circumstances do not give rise to exemptions from liability: financial difficulties of seller's supplier, buyer's inability to obtain foreign currency, increases in the cost of goods, and delivery problems due to production stoppages.

Limitation Period

There are no provisions in the CISG on limitation period (the time within which a buyer must bring a court action or seek arbitration). Another United Nations (UN convention), "Convention on the limitation period in the International Sale of Goods," provides rules on limitation period and has been ratified by eighteen countries including the United States in 1994. The convention provides a four-year limitation period for most claims.

The International Chamber of Commerce (ICC) has also published several valuable documents on international trade. The Uniform Rules for Contract Guarantees (1978) deals with the issue of performance and bank guarantees supporting obligations arising in international contracts. The ICC also has rules on adaptation of long-term contracts to changing economic and political circumstances.

Standard contract forms are often used in certain types of international commercial transactions, such as trade in commodities or in capital goods. These contracts are prepared by trade associations, such as The Cocoa Association of London, The Refined Sugar Association, or certain agencies of the United Nations (model contracts for supply of plant, equipment, and machinery for export, or for the export of durable consumer goods and engineering articles).

PERTINENT CLAUSES IN EXPORT CONTRACTS

An export contract is an agreement between a seller and an overseas customer for the performance, financing, and other aspects of an export transaction. An export transaction is not just limited to the sale of final products in overseas markets but extends to supply contracts for manufacture or production of the product within a given time period. Parties should have a well-drafted and clear contract that properly defines their responsibilities and provides for any possible contingencies. This is critical in minimizing potential conflicts and allowing for a successful conclusion of the transaction.

Although many export contracts are concluded between the seller and an overseas buyer (the main contract), the buyer may also enter into a contract with an independent consultant for technical assistance and with a lender for financing in the case of complex projects. The exporter as prime contractor may enter into joint venture agreements with other firms, such as subcontractors or suppliers, to bid on and perform on a project. Parties could also establish a partnership, corporation, or a consortium in order to bid on and undertake different aspects of the transaction while assuming joint responsibility for the overall project. Such collaboration is common when one firm lacks the financial or technical resources to perform the contract.

It is relevant to state briefly how these joint venture arrangements differ from one another. Members may form a partnership for the purpose of undertaking the export contract. Each of the members remains responsible for the entire transaction even though the parties may be carrying out different portions of the export transaction. Parties could also establish a new corporation to act as exporters or prime contractors. In the case of a consortium, each partner of the venture has a separate contract with the customer for performance of a portion of the work and, hence, is not responsible to the other members.

Scope of Work Including Services

The goods to be sold should be clearly spelled out in the contract. There is also a need to include the scope of work to be performed by the exporter, such as installation, training, and other services. The scope of work to be performed is usually contained in the technical specification, which should be incorporated into the main contract (by listing it with the other documents intended to form the contract). It is also important to specify whether the agreed price covers certain services, such as packaging, special handling, or insurance. Any contribution by the overseas customer should be explicitly stated as to the consequences of the failure to perform those services to enable the exporter to complete the transaction on time. Such contributions could include provision of office space and other support services, such as secretarial and translation, government licenses, permits, and personnel necessary for the performance of the contract.

Price and Delivery Terms

The total price could be stated at the time of the contract, with a price escalation clause that provides for increases in the price if certain events occur. Such provisions are commonly used with goods that are to be manufactured by the exporter over a certain period of time and when inflation is expected to affect material and labor costs. Such a clause also extends to increases in costs arising from delays caused by the overseas customer. It is important to draft the contract with a clear understanding between the parties as to whether such a clause applies when there is an excusable delay. In many contracts, the price escalation clause is in force in cases of excusable delay in performance by the exporter.

The contract should also specify the currency in which payment is to be made. Foreign exchange fluctuations could adversely affect a firm's profit. In addition, government exchange controls in the buyer's country may totally or partially prevent the exporter from receiving payment for goods and services. Hence, it is important to provide the necessary protection against such contingencies. The following contract provisions would be helpful to the exporter.

Shifting the Risk to the Overseas Customer

An exporter may shift the risk by providing in the contract that payment is to be made in the exporter's country and currency. This ensures protection against currency fluctuations and exchange controls.

Payment in Importer's Currency

Even though the seller will generally prefer payment in U.S. dollars, such a requirement may be difficult to comply with if U.S. dollars are not readily available in the buyer's country. The exporter may have to accept payment in the importer's currency. In such a situation, the exporter could fix the exchange rate in the invoice and would thus be compensated in the event of devaluation. Suppose Smith, Incorporated, of California, exports computers to Colombia; the price could be stated as follows: "300 million Colombian pesos at the exchange rate of $1 5 1,000 pesos. The importer will compensate the exporter for any devaluation in the peso from the rate designated in the contract."

Another method of protection against fluctuations in the importer's currency is to add a risk premium on the price at the time of the contract. Yet another method is to establish an escrow account in a third country in an acceptable (more stable) currency from which payments would be made under the contract.

The contract should clearly indicate the delivery term (e.g., FOB, New York, or CIF, London) since there are different implications in terms of risk of loss, insurance, ownership, and tax liability. The seller would ideally prefer to be paid cash in advance (before delivery of goods or transfer of title) in its own currency or by using a confirmed irrevocable letter of credit. The buyer would often desire payment in its own currency on open account or consignment. Hence, the provision to be included in the contract has to accommodate the competing interests of both parties.

Delivery, Delay, and Penalties

The most common type of clause included in export contracts is one that provides for a fixed or approximate delivery date and that stipulates the circumstances under which the seller will be excused for delay in performance and even for complete inability to perform. Most contracts state that either party has the right to cancel the contract for any delay or default in performance if it is caused by conditions beyond its control, including, but not limited to, acts of God and government restrictions, and that neither of the parties shall be liable for damages (force majeure clause). The force majeure clause may also cover a number of specified events, including the inability of the exporter to obtain the necessary labor, material, information, or other support from the buyer to effect delivery. It should also include certain warranty obligations, such as delays in manufacture of replacement components. It is important to state that the force majeure (excusable delay) clause will apply even if any of the causes existed at the time of bidding, were present prior to signing the contract, or occurred after the seller's performance of its obligations was delayed for other causes. Some force majeure clauses provide for the temporary suspension of the contract until the causes for the nonperformance are removed; others state that the agreement will be terminated at the option of either of the parties if performance remains impossible for some stated period.

Contracts often provide for damages if the delay is caused by one of the parties. In the event that the delay is caused by the exporter (i.e., unexcused delay), some contracts specify that the importer will be entitled to recover liquidated damages (even in the absence of actual damages), whereas others provide that payment would be limited to damages actually incurred by the buyer (see International Perspective 8.2).

The converse of the seller's obligation to deliver is the buyer's obligation to accept delivery as stipulated in the contract. If delay in delivery is caused by the buyer, most contracts provide that the seller will be entitled to direct damages incurred during the delay, such as warehousing costs, salaries and wages for personnel kept idle, or loss of profit. Some contracts even provide for payment of indirect (consequential) damages, such as loss of productivity or loss of future profits due to delays caused by the buyer. Both parties can possibly eliminate or reduce potential risks of excusable delay by inserting (1) a best-efforts clause, without expressly providing for consequences in the event of delay, or (2) an overall limitation of liability clause. In cases in which the contract does not expressly impose the previous obligation on the customer, the customer remains responsible for delays caused personally or by someone for whom the customer is responsible. In most legal systems a party has an implied duty to cooperate in the performance of the work by the other party or to not interfere with the performance of the other party.

Quality, Performance, and Liability Limitations

Most contracts state that the seller warrants to the buyer that the goods manufactured by the seller will be free from defects in material, workmanship, and title and will be of the kind and quality described in the contract. It is not uncommon to find deficiencies in performance, even when the exporter

INTERNATIONAL PERSPECTIVE 8.2.
Acceptance of Standard International Contracts

In 1982, a buyer in Indonesia contracted to buy from a seller in England 400,000 metric tons of white sugar (C&F, Indonesian port for delivery in 1983/1984). The contract provided for payment under an irrevocable letter of credit against shipping documents in London. The contract was to be governed by English law and provided for arbitration of disputes in London under the Rules of the Refined Sugar Association. It was also expressly stated in the contract that the buyer was to be totally responsible for obtaining the necessary license and that failure to obtain the license was not to be considered sufficient ground for invoking force majeure.

As sugar prices collapsed during 1982/1983, the buyer declined to open a letter of credit in order to pay the seller in London. In June 1984, the seller commenced arbitration proceedings in London, as provided in the contract claiming damages for breach of contract. The buyer initiated two lawsuits against the seller in London, seeking the court to declare the contracts to be illegal since the Indonesian government declined to buy the sugar and it refused to provide an import license. The seller was awarded $27 million in damages to be paid in three installments. The buyer paid the first installment and brought a lawsuit against the seller in Indonesia, seeking a court order declaring the contract illegal because it violated a decree stating that only the government agency could import sugar into Indonesia. The Indonesian court held that the contract violated the decree (local law) and was therefore illegal. The court ignored the following:

1. The contracts provided only for shipment to an Indonesian port, not importation into Indonesia, and the risk of not being able to import was expressly assumed in the contract by the buyer.
2. Under English law, delivery of shipping documents does not require that the goods be imported into the country of destination.

Source: Adapted from Hornick, 1990, pp. 8-10.

provides a product with state-of-the-art design, material, and workmanship. Hence, it is advisable to use certain approaches to limit risk exposure:

- Specify in the contract the performance standards that are to be met, and provide warranties for those which can be objectively tested, such as machine efficiency, for a specified period, usually a year.
- Stipulate the kinds of damages that may be suffered by the buyer, for which the seller is not responsible, such as loss of profit for machine

downtime, extra costs of acquiring substitute services, as well as other damages that are incidental or consequential.

- Limit the liability, especially in exports of machinery and equipment, to a specific amount expressed either in reference to the total contract price or as a certain sum of money. This limit should cover all liability or liabilities arising from product quality or performance.
- Carefully evaluate the cost implications of an extended warranty or an evergreen warranty provision before agreeing to include it in the contract. An evergreen warranty is automatically renewed each time a failure protected under the warranty provision is corrected.

Taxes and Duties

In the United States, Canada, and other developed countries, an exporter will not be subject to any taxes (i.e., when products are exported to these countries) if business is not performed through an agent, a branch, or a subsidiary. However, when the price includes a breakdown for installation and other services to be performed in the importing country, such income could be taxable as earnings from services. In some cases, it may be advisable to reserve the right to perform these services through a local affiliate to restrict exposure to foreign taxes. It is thus important to consider the tax and customs duty implications of one's pricing and other export decisions relating to shipment of components or assembly of (final) products. It is also helpful to evaluate the impact of tax treaties with importing countries.

Guarantees and Bonds

It is quite common for overseas importers to require some form of guarantee or bond against the exporter's default. Public agencies in many countries are often prohibited from entering into major contracts without some form of bank guarantee or bond. Guarantees are more commonly used than bonds in most international contracts. These are separate contracts and independent of the export agreement.

Bid guarantees or bonds are often provided at the first stage of the contract from all bidders (potential exporters) to provide security to the overseas customer. Then, performance guarantees or bonds are provided by the successful bidder(s) to protect the overseas customer against damages resulting from failure of the seller to comply with the export contract. Last, payment guarantees or bonds are provided so the importer can secure a refund of the advance payment in case of the exporter's default.

In the case of a bank guarantee, a standby letter of credit is issued by a bank, under which payment is made to the importer on demand upon failure of the exporter to perform its obligation under the export contract. Most importers favor a contract provision that allows them to obtain payment from the bank by simply submitting a letter that the exporter has defaulted and demanding payment. However, it may be advisable to stipulate in the standby credit that the amount of the credit becomes payable to the importer only upon the finding by a court or arbitration tribunal that the supplier of goods or services is in default of the contract.

A bank guarantee (standby credit) and a bond are similar in that both instruments are a form of security provided by a third party (a bank in the case of a guarantee; a surety company in the case of a bond) to the importer against the exporter's default. Both instruments are issued only if the exporter has a good credit standing, and they both specify the amount payable in the event of default, the period within which such claims can be made, as well as the fee charged for such services (see International Perspective 8.3).

In export trade, there is a tendency to make standby credits payable on the submission of a letter by the importer that simply alleges default by the exporter and demands payment. This is not usually the case with bonds, which are payable only when the importer has shown that the exporter is in default under the export contract. Bonds also usually require that the importer has met its obligations under the contract before realizing any benefits from the bond. In short, the surety company will conduct an investigation on the conduct of the parties before making a decision about payment. Second, the bank in the case of a standby letter of credit does not have the option of performing the contract (e.g., completing delivery of goods not made by exporter, paying losses incurred by exporter, etc.), as in the case of a surety company. The bank guarantor is required to pay the full amount of the standby credit without regard to the actual damages suffered. Under a bond, the surety is obliged to make good on only the actual damages suffered by the overseas buyer. In both cases, the exporter has to reimburse the bank or the surety company for any payments made under the guarantee or bond, respectively. In view of the widespread use of guarantees (standby credits) in international trade and the possibility of abuse, many countries provide their exporters an insurance program that protects them against wrongful drawing on the credit. In 1978, the International Chamber of Commerce adopted the "Uniform Rules for Contract Guarantees," which deals with guarantees, bonds, and other undertakings given on behalf of the seller and applies only if the guarantee or bond explicitly states the intentions of the parties to be governed by these rules. In view of the limited acceptance of the Uniform Rules for Contract Guarantees, the ICC adopted, in 1992, the "Uniform

INTERNATIONAL PERSPECTIVE 8.3.
Tendering for Export Contracts

In many countries, government purchases over a certain size are required to be awarded under tender. Purchase of goods under tender is common in cases involving goods and services purchased in large volumes and the likelihood of price competition. Tenders are also offered in the case of contracts for purchase or installation of complex projects that involve the purchase of goods and services. Tenders provide the purchaser the unique advantage of selecting the best supplier from among a large pool of bidders in terms of quality, price, and other factors, allowing the purchaser to avoid charges of patronage and favoritism.

The tendering process begins with a purchaser of goods and services inviting potential suppliers for submission of tenders (bids). However, with important projects, bidders are prequalified before submitting tenders to ensure that they satisfy the basic criteria that are critical for awarding the contract: necessary technical qualifications and compliance with local laws in submitting the bid. The invitation to submit bids (for prequalification or final selection) is usually announced in newspapers and this guarantees a fair, competitive, and transparent tendering process and affords some protection against corruption and nepotism by civil servants.

The invitation to submit tenders is announced in the newspapers to the public or to selected bidders who are prequalified. This stage in the tendering process is often called a request for proposal (RFP). At this stage, potential bidders are invited to submit tenders with certain conditions (e.g., technical specifications, commercial terms, etc.) that are to be included in the proposal. Suppliers may be requested to submit bid bonds to ensure that a supplier will not decline to sign the contract when the bid is accepted.

Once a proposal is accepted, the successful supplier is awarded the contract. In most cases, however, the award is just a first step prior to negotiation of the contract. In the event of failure to conclude the final contract, the customer would have to negotiate with the second bidder on the list.

Rules for Demand Guarantees," which attempts to standardize existing guarantee practice. As in the case of contract guarantees, the parties have to state their intention to be subject to these rules.

Applicable Law and Dispute Settlement

The fundamental principle of international contract law is that of freedom of contract. This means that the parties are at liberty to agree between themselves as to what rules should govern their contract. Most contracts state the applicable law to be that of the exporter's country. This indicates the strong bargaining position of exporters and their clear preference to be governed by laws about which they are well informed. It may be possible to arrange a split jurisdiction, whereby the portion of the contract to be performed in the customer's country will be interpreted under the importer's laws and the portion to be performed in the exporter's country will be governed by the laws of that country.

In cases where there is no express or implied choice of law, it may be the role of the courts to decide what law should govern the contract based on the terms and nature of the contract. The factors to be considered often include the place of negotiation of the contract, the place of performance, location of the subject matter, place of business, and other pertinent matters.

For several reasons, a large and growing number of parties to export contracts provide for arbitration to settle disputes arising under their contracts. Despite the wide use of arbitration clauses, the superiority of arbitration over judicial dispute resolution is not quite clear-cut, and parties considering arbitration should also be aware of the disadvantages in this choice, such as lack of mandatory enforcement mechanisms and difficulty obtaining recognition and enforcement of the award, which requires a separate action of law. It is also stated in some contracts that the parties agree to abide by the award and that the award is binding and final and enforceable in a court of competent jurisdiction.

CHAPTER SUMMARY

Export Contract

An export contract is an agreement between a seller and an overseas customer for the performance, financing, and other aspects of an export transaction. It also includes supply contracts for the manufacture of a product within a given period.

Factors Behind the Move Toward Harmonization of International Contract/Commercial Law

1. Increases in global trade and economic relations between nations
2. The growth of international customary law
3. The adoption of international convention and rules
   - The Vienna Convention on international sale of goods
   - The ICC rules on contract agreements
   - Standard contracts developed by trade associations

CISG: Essential elements: (1) oral contracts, (2) parole evidence, (3) battle of the forms, (4) duty to inspect and proper notice, (5) right to remedy deficiencies, and (6) limitation period.

Major Clauses in Export Contracts

- Scope of work
- Price and delivery terms
- Quality, performance, and liability
- Taxes and duties
- Guarantees and bonds
- Applicable law and dispute settlement

REVIEW QUESTIONS

1. What are some of the factors that militate in favor of harmonization of international contract law?
2. State the major differences between the CISG and the Uniform Commercial Code.
3. In certain transactions involving transfer of technology, the contract provides for the sale of goods and services. Does the CISG apply to such contracts?
4. The CISG does not apply to certain types of contracts. Discuss.
5. An Italian seller agreed to produce and supply 250 pieces of leather furniture to a buyer in the United States. The contract included certain specifications and was signed by the parties. It further stated that any changes may only be made in writing and signed by both parties. A few days after the contract was signed, both parties agreed by phone to change the specifications. A couple of months later, when the seller delivered the furniture pieces, with the modified specifications, the buyer refused to accept them, stating that the latest agreement was not binding since it was not part of the written (original) contract. Does the CISG apply? If it does, is the buyer obligated to accept the furniture?
6. A manufacturer in California, United States, and distributor in British Columbia, Canada, agreed for the delivery of routers. The contract choice of law clause adopted "California Law." In the event of a dispute, does it mean that the CISG will not apply?
7. What is the battle of the forms under CISG?
8. Discuss a typical tendering process for export contracts.

9. What are some of the provisions in a typical export contract?
10. How does an exporter protect against foreign exchange fluctuations?

CASE 8.1. CISG

Wombat, Inc., is a Florida corporation engaged in the rental and sale of tiles, while Pinochet, Inc., is an Italian corporation engaged in the manufacture of ceramic tiles. Representatives of Wombat negotiated an agreement with Pinochet to purchase tiles based on samples examined at a trade show in Bologna, Italy. After finalizing an oral agreement on important terms of the contract such as price, quality, delivery, and payment, the parties recorded these terms on one of Pinochet's preprinted order forms and the president of Wombat signed the contract. The agreement provided for the sale of high grade ceramic tiles at specific discounts as long as Wombat purchased sufficient quantities.

Wombat delayed payments for some of the shipments since it was not satisfied with the quality of the tiles. Pinochet stopped shipments and cancelled the contract with Wombat, claiming that the provisions on the printed form gave him the right to cancel or suspend the contract in the event that the buyer defaulted or delayed payment. Pinochet was not informed of the defects in writing, although the contract provided for notification of any defects in writing by means of certified letter within or no later then ten days after receipt of the merchandise. Wombat argued that the parties never intended the terms printed on the reverse of the order form to apply to the agreement. It also submitted affidavits from translators and Pinochet's representatives that the parties subjectively intended not to be bound by the terms on the reverse of the order form.

Questions

1. Is the contract governed by CISG?
2. Are the parties bound by the terms on the reverse side of the print form?

CASE 8.2. CHINA NATIONAL PRODUCTS VERSUS APEX DIGITAL INC.

China National is a Beijing-based corporation organized under the laws of China with specific foreign trading rights. It facilitates the import and export of goods between Chinese and foreign companies. Apex is a company incorporated in Ontario, California, and engaged in the import and distribution of consumer electronic goods. In 2000, China National entered into a purchase agreement with Apex for the export of DVD players. The purchase agreement was formalized with the conclusion of several but substantially identical written contracts for the different types of players. Each contract contained two significant provisions: (1) in the event of nonconformity of the goods with the contract, Apex should claim for quality discrepancy within thirty days after arrival of the goods at the port of destination, and (2) all disputes arising from the contract shall be submitted to certain arbitration tribunal specified in the contract and the award is final and binding on both parties.

Apex imported and sold the products to major retailers such as Circuit City, Best Buy, and K-Mart. Soon after distribution of the imported goods, Apex began receiving reports from its retailers that consumers were dissatisfied with the quality of the DVD players: disk loaders did not open, the disk did not load after it was inserted, the player did not recognize certain music files, the front panel of the loader fell off, etc. Some were returned. In spite of these problems, Apex continued to place more orders with China National. It did, however, express its concerns to China National. Apex declined to pay China National, claiming "financial troubles" as well as China National's refusal to correct the defects. In an effort to obtain payment, China National wrote several letters to Apex threatening legal action. It eventually filed suit in California.

The central issue to be decided by the court was whether Apex rejected the goods or if it did not, whether it later would be relieved of liability. The court stated that if buyers accept nonconforming goods and do nothing, the law deems them to have accepted those goods. Apex's actions in continuing to order and sell known defective goods constituted an acceptance of those goods. Such conduct of ordering and selling of defective goods was inconsistent with the seller's ownership and acceptance. It ordered Apex to pay for all unpaid invoices. (Source: 141 F. Supp. 2nd 1013. 2001 U.S. Dist.)

Questions

1. Is the contract governed by CISG?
2. Do you agree with the decision of the court? Why/why not?

Chapter 9

Trade Documents and Transportation

DOCUMENTATION IN EXPORT-IMPORT TRADE

A number of documents are used in export-import trade. The completion and submission of required documents is critical to the successful shipment, transportation, and discharge of cargo at the port of destination. The documents used depend on the requirements of both the exporting and importing countries. Much of the documentation is routine for freight forwarders or customs brokers acting on the firm's behalf, but the exporter is ultimately responsible for the accuracy of the documentation. Information on documentation requirements in importing countries can be obtained from overseas customers, foreign government embassies and consulates, as well as various export reference books, such as the *Export Shipping Manual* and *Air Cargo Tariff Guide*. In the United States and other developed countries, government departments have specialists on individual foreign countries and can advise on country conditions and documentation requirements.

Air Waybill

The air waybill is a contract of carriage between the shipper and air carrier. It is issued by the air carrier and serves as a receipt for the shipper. When the shipper gives the cargo to a freight consolidator or forwarder for transportation, the air waybill is obtained from the consolidator or forwarder. Air waybills are nonnegotiable and cannot be issued as a collection instrument. Air waybills are not particular to a given airline and can be from any other airline that participates in the carriage (Wood et al., 1995).

Bill of Exchange (Draft)

A bill of exchange is an unconditional written order by one party (the drawer) that orders a second party (the debtor or drawee) to pay a certain sum

Export-Import Theory, Practices, and Procedures, Second Edition

of money to the drawer (creditor) or a designated third party. For example, Hernandez Export Incorporated of Lawton, Oklahoma, sends an importer in Uzbekistan a draft for $30,000 after having shipped a truckload of autoparts. The company's draft orders the overseas buyer in Uzbekistan to pay $30,000 to its agent, Expotech, in Uzbekistan. In this scenario, Hernandez Incorporated is the drawer, the importer is the drawee, and Expotech is the payee. In many cases, the drawee is the overseas buyer and the drawer/payee is the exporter. When a draft is payable at a designated future date, it is a time draft. If it is payable on sight, it is a demand or sight draft.

Bill of Lading (B/L)

A bill of lading is a contract of carriage between the shipper and the steamship company (carrier). It certifies ownership and receipt of goods by the carrier for shipment. It is issued by the carrier to the shipper. A straight bill of lading is issued when the consignment is made directly to the overseas customer. Such a bill of lading is not negotiable. An order bill of lading is negotiable, that is, it can be bought, sold, or traded. In cases in which the exporter is not certain about payment, the exporter can consign the bill of lading to the order of the shipper and endorse it to the buyer on payment of the purchase price. When payment is not a problem, the bill of lading can be endorsed to the consignee (Zodl, 1995; Wells and Dulat, 1996).

Clean/Claused Bill of Lading

The bill of lading form is normally filled out in advance by the shipper. The carrier will check the goods loaded on the ship to ensure that they comply with the goods listed (quantity, condition, etc.) on the bill of lading. If all appears proper, the carrier will issue a clean bill of lading certifying that the goods have been properly loaded on board the ship. However, if there is a discrepancy between the goods loaded and the goods listed on the bill, the carrier will issue a claused bill of lading to the shipper. Such bill of lading is normally unacceptable to third parties, including the buyer under a CIF (cost, insurance, and freight) contract or bank that is expected to pay under documentary credit on receipt of the bill of lading and other documents.

Inland Bill of Lading

An inland bill of lading is a bill of lading issued by the railway carrier or trucking firm certifying carriage of goods from the place where the exporter is located to the point of exit for shipment overseas. This document is issued by exporters to consign goods to a freight forwarder who will transport the goods by rail to an airport, seaport, or truck for shipment.

Through Bill of Lading

A through bill of lading is used for intermodal transportation, that is, when different modes of transportation are used. The first carrier will issue a through bill of lading and is generally responsible for the delivery of the cargo to the final destination.

Consular Invoice

Certain nations require a consular invoice for customs, statistical, and other purposes. It must be obtained from the consulate of the country to which the goods are being shipped and usually must be prepared in the language of that country (U.S. Department of Commerce, 1990).

Certificate of Origin

A certificate of origin is required by certain countries to enable them to determine whether the product is eligible for preferential duty treatment. It is a statement as to the origin of the export product and usually is obtained from local chambers of commerce.

Inspection Certificate

Some purchasers and countries may require a certificate attesting to the specifications of the goods shipped, usually performed by a third party. Such requirements are usually stated in the contract and quotation. Inspection certificates are generally requested for certain commodities with grade designations, machinery, equipment, and so forth.

Insurance Certificate

When the exporter provides insurance, it is necessary to furnish an insurance certificate that states the type, terms, and amount of insurance coverage. The certificates are negotiable and must be endorsed before presentation to the bank.

Commercial Invoice

A commercial invoice is a bill for the merchandise from the seller to the buyer. It should include basic information about the transaction: description of the goods, delivery and payment terms, order date, and number. The overseas buyer needs the commercial invoice to clear goods from customs, prove ownership, and arrange payment. Governments in importing countries also use commercial invoices to determine the value of the merchandise for assessment of customs duties.

Dock Receipt

This receipt is used to transfer accountability when the export item is moved by the domestic carrier to the port of embarkation and left with the international carrier for export. The international carrier or agent issues it after delivery of the goods at the carrier's dock or warehouse. A similar document, when issued upon receipt of cargo by a chartered vessel, is called a mate's receipt.

Destination Control Statement (DCS)

This statement appears on the commercial invoice, bill of lading, air waybill, and shipper's export declaration. It is intended to notify the carrier and other parties that the item may only be exported to certain destinations.

Shipper's Export Declaration (SED)

A shipper's export declaration (SED) is issued to control certain exports and to compile trade data. It is required for shipments valued at more than $2,500. Carriers and exporters are also required to declare dangerous cargo.

Pro Forma Invoice

A pro forma invoice is a provisional invoice sent to the prospective buyer, usually in response to the latter's request for a price quotation. A quotation usually describes the product, and states the price at a specific delivery point, the time of shipment, and the terms of payment. A pro forma invoice is also needed by the buyer to obtain a foreign exchange or import permit. Quotations on such invoices are subject to change without notice partly because there is a lag between the time when the quotation is prepared and when the shipment is made to the overseas customer.

Export Packing List

An export packing list itemizes the material in each individual package and indicates the type of package (e.g., box, carton). It shows weights and measurements for each package. It is used by customs in the exporting and importing countries to check the cargo and by the exporter to ascertain the total cargo weight, the volume, and shipment of the correct merchandise. The packing list should be either included in the package or attached to the outside of a package in a waterproof envelope marked "packing list enclosed."

Manifest

A manifest is a detailed summary of the total cargo of a vessel (by each loading port) for customs purposes. It covers condition of the cargo, and summarizes heavy lifts and their location.

TRANSPORTATION

Three modes of transportation are available for exporting products overseas: air, water (ocean and inland), and land (rail and truck). Whereas inland water, rail, and truck are suitable for domestic transportation and movement of goods between neighboring countries (the United States to Canada, France to Germany, etc.), air and ocean transport are appropriate for long-distance transportation between countries that do not share a common boundary.

Export-import firms may use a combination of these methods to deliver merchandise in a timely and cost-efficient manner. The exporter should consider market location (geographical proximity), speed (e.g., airfreight for perishables or products in urgent demand, etc.), and cost when determining the mode of transportation. Even though air carriers are more expensive, their cost may be offset by reduced packing, documentation, and inventory requirements. It is important to establish with the importer the destination of the goods, since the latter may wish the goods to be shipped into a free-trade zone that allows for exemption of import duties while the goods are in the zone.

AIR TRANSPORTATION

Airfreight is the least utilized mode of transportation for cargo and accounts for less than 1 percent of total international freight movement (see Table 9.1 for advantages and disadvantages of this transportation type). However, it is the fastest growing mode and not just confined to the movement of high-value products. A 1996 study by McDonnell Douglas forecast that oversized freight business would increase tenfold to $1.5 billion per year by 2010. A similar study by Boeing also found that about 4.5 million tons of

TABLE 9.1. Advantages and Disadvantages of Air Transportation

Advantages	Disadvantages
• Faster delivery of perishable commodities, production parts, etc.	• Generally expensive for high-bulk freight. Value must be high enough to justify higher freight cost.
• Shipments do not require heavy packing (standard domestic packing is sufficient).	• Inefficient for shorter distances, which are handled faster by trucks. Only the express air services, such as UPS or DHL, have equally competitive services.
• Reduces inventory and storage costs.	• Shipping containers must be small enough to fit into an air carrier.
• Reduces insurance cost and documentation.	• Not suitable for products that are sensitive to low pressures and variations in temperature.
• Achieves savings in total transportation cost and provides reliability of service.	

heavy, outsized freight worldwide could be transported by air (Anonymous, 1998a). A number of factors are likely to contribute to such growth in airfreight:

1. In view of the heavy infrastructure investment being made in many developing countries, the potential need exists for imports of heavy equipment and services. It is estimated that such imports could amount to about $17.8 billion in surface transport, sea, and airport projects in South America alone. Certain types of equipment exports to these countries, such as bulldozers, buses, or oil-drilling equipment, often do not fit in a standard ocean container (Anonymous, 1998a; Reyes and Gilles, 1998).

2. Since many of these projects are built from supplies shipped to the sites on a just-in-time basis, delays in delivering cargo can lead to heavy financial losses or penalties for the suppliers. Such needs cannot be accommodated by using the traditional modes of carriage for heavy freight. Airfreight becomes the only viable means of moving such cargo to ensure timely delivery.

3. Technological changes over the past two decades have significantly altered the size and design of aircraft to handle heavy cargo. For example, the recent version of the Boeing 747 can carry more freight (even with passengers) than all-cargo versions of the previous generation

of jets. The all-cargo plane has a weight capacity of about 122 tons (Anonymous, 1998a; Reyes and Gilles, 1998). Furthermore, improvements in terminal facilities in many countries have also contributed to increased speed and better handling and storage of shipments at airports, thus minimizing loss or damage to merchandise.

4. Integrators and forwarders have also played a role. The development of air carriers that provide integrated services (DHL, UPS) has increased the amount of air cargo. For example, UPS Sonic Air Service offers a guaranteed door-to-door service to most international destinations, regardless of size or weight limitations, within twenty-four hours. In addition, the role of forwarders as consolidators of small shipments makes it easier for shippers to send their merchandise by air without being subject to the minimum charge for small shipments. The forwarder consolidates various small shipments and tenders them to the airline in volume in exchange for a bill of lading furnished as the shipper of the cargo. The role of a forwarder is similar to that of a non-vessel-operating carrier in ocean freight.

Air Cargo Rates

Determinants of air cargo rates. Distance to the point of destination as well as weight and size of the shipment are important determinants of air cargo rates. The identity of the product (commodity description) and the provision of any special services also influence freight rates. If a product is classified under a general cargo category (products shipped frequently) a lower rate applies.

Products can also be classified under a special unit load (for shipments in approved containers) or a commodity rate (negotiated rates for merchandise not classified as general cargo). Special services such as charter flight or immediate transportation could substantially increase the freight rate.

Rate setting. The International Air Transport Association (IATA) is the forum in which fares and rates are negotiated among member airlines. Over the past few years, such fares and rates have been set by the marketplace, and tariff conference proposals have tended to become reference points. The service conferences of IATA also promote among members the negotiation of certain standards and procedures for cargo handling, documentation and procedures, shipment of dangerous goods, etc.

International air express services (the integrators). The big carriers are under increasing competitive pressure from the integrated air service providers such as Federal Express or UPS. While the traditional carriers provide airport-to-airport service, the integrators have the added advantage of furnishing direct delivery services to customers, including customs clearance and payment of import duties at foreign destinations. Even though the strength of integrators had been in the transportation of smaller packages, they are now offering services geared to heavyweight cargo.

Carriage of Goods by Air

The international transportation of goods by air is governed by the Warsaw Convention of 1929 (original convention) and the amended convention of 1955. In certain cases, neither convention applies. Many countries, including the United States, are members of the original Warsaw Convention and did not accede to the amended convention. The major differences between the two conventions relate to the carrier's liability and limits of that liability (see International Perspective 9.1). The important aspects of the original Warsaw Convention are detailed in the following material.

Scope of the convention. The convention governs the liability of the carrier while the goods are in its charge, whether at or outside an airport. It applies when the departure and destination points set out in the contract of carriage are in two countries that subscribe to the original Warsaw Convention (i.e., both are not members of the amended convention).

Air consignment note (air waybill). A consignment note (air waybill) is a document issued by the air carrier to a shipper that serves as a receipt for goods and evidence of the contract of carriage. However, it is not a document of title to the goods, as in the case of a bill of lading. The carrier requires the consignor to make out and hand over the air waybill with the goods. The consignor is responsible for the accuracy of the statements relating to the

---

INTERNATIONAL PERSPECTIVE 9.1.
The Two Warsaw Conventions and Air Carriage:
Major Differences

- **Carrier's Liability:** Under the amended convention, defense of negligent pilotage or negligence in the handling and navigation of aircraft is no longer available to carriers. The amendment also extends the benefit of liability limitations to the agents and servants of the carrier.
- **Limitation of Action:** The time to give a written notice of loss or damage by consignee has been extended from seven days to fourteen days.
- **Required Particulars:** Required particulars on the air waybill are fewer under the amended convention.

goods stated in the air waybill. The carrier's receipt of the consignor's goods without an air waybill or all particulars relating to the goods will not entitle the carrier to exclude or limit liability under the convention. The carrier notifies the consignee as soon as the goods arrive and hands over the air waybill upon compliance by the consignee with the conditions of carriage.

Liability of carrier. The carrier is liable for loss or damage to cargo and for damage arising from delay unless it proves that: (1) the damage was occasioned by negligent pilotage or negligence in the handling of the aircraft, and (2) the carrier and its agents have taken all necessary measures to avoid such damage. An airline can escape liability if it proves that the shipper was negligent regardless of its own negligence. In the case of intermodal transport where more than one carrier is involved, each carrier is responsible for the part of the carriage performed under its supervision. All the carriers are, however, jointly and severally liable to the consignor or consignee in the event of loss, damage, or delay to cargo.

Limitation of liability. The liability of the carrier with respect to loss or damage to the goods, or delay in delivery is limited to a sum of $9 per pound ($20 per kilogram) unless the consignor has declared a higher value and paid a supplementary charge. Any agreement to lower or exclude liability is void.

Limitation of action. The right to damages will be extinguished if an action is not brought within two years after the actual or supposed delivery of cargo. Notice of complaint must be made within seven days from the date of receipt of goods (in the case of damage) or within fourteen days from the date on which the goods have been placed at the consignee's disposal (in the case of delay).

The most recent amendment to the Warsaw Convention is the Montreal Convention adopted in 1999. The Montreal Convention has been adopted by about thirty countries including the United States. The convention provides protection for air travelers and amends existing limitations on liability for death and bodily injury for damages. It also provides for electronic waybills and tickets. Liability of carriers for cargo losses are still governed by the Warsaw Convention.

OCEAN FREIGHT

Ocean shipping is the least expensive and the dominant mode of transportation in foreign trade. It is especially suitable for moving bulk freight such as commodities and other raw materials. Today, almost all ocean freight travels by containers, which results in minimal handling at ports. If a full-container-load cargo is to be shipped, a freight forwarder arranges for the container to be delivered to the shipper's premises. Once the container is fully loaded, it is moved by truck to a port to be loaded onto a vessel. Less-than-container-load freight is usually delivered at the port for consolidation with other shipments.

Types of Ocean Carriers

The following are the three major types of ocean carriers (see also International Perspective 9.2).

Private fleets. These are large fleets of specialized ships owned and managed by merchants and manufacturers to carry their own goods. Apart from its cost advantages, ownership of a private fleet ensures the availability of carriage that meets the firm's special needs. Such ships can occasionally be leased to other firms at times of limited activity. Some firms in certain industries, such as oil, sugar, or lumber, own their own fleets.

Tramps (chartered or leased vessels): Tramps are vessels leased to transport, usually, large quantities of bulk cargo (oil, coal, grain, sugar, etc.) that fill the entire ship (vessel). Chartered vessels do not operate on a regular route or schedule. Charter arrangement can be made on the basis of a trip or voyage between origin and destination or for an agreed time period, usually several months to a year. The vessel could be leased with or without a crew (bare-boat charter). The major factors for the continued existence of tramp shipping are that (1) it provides indispensable ocean transportation at the lowest possible cost, and (2) it is adaptable to the changing and/or unanticipated requirements for transportation. When charter rates are low, commodity traders tend to move materials in advance of actual delivery time to take advantage of low transportation costs (Wood et al., 1995). The just-in-time system that delivers products when they are needed is not often feasible in cases in which transport and distribution could be impeded by severe winter weather. A commodity trader's decision to purchase and export a product is influenced by the spread between the export and purchase price, the charter rate, and any warehousing or storage cost. This means that an exporter can purchase and export a product even before delivery time if the charter rate and storage cost are substantially less than the spread to allow for a reasonable profit margin.

Conference lines. A shipping conference line is a voluntary association of ocean carriers operating on a particular trade route between two or more countries. Shipping conferences date back to the nineteenth century when such associations were established for trade between England and its colonies. One of the distinguishing features of a liner service is that sailings are

INTERNATIONAL PERSPECTIVE 9.2.
Types of Ocean Cargo/Vessels

Types of Ocean Cargo

Containerized: Cargo loaded at a facility away from the pier, or at a warehouse into a metal container usually 20 to 40 feet long, 8 feet high, and 8 feet wide. The container is then delivered to a pier and loaded on to a "containership" for transportation. Some cargo cannot be containerized, for example, automobiles, live animals, bulk products.

Bulk: Cargo that is loaded and carried in bulk, without mark or count, in a loose unpackaged form, having homogenous characteristics. To be loaded on a containership, bulk cargo would be put in containers first. It could also be stowed in bulk instead of being loaded into containers. Example: coal, iron ore, raw sugar, etc.

Break-Bulk: Packaged cargo that is loaded and unloaded on a piece-by-piece basis, that is, by number or count. This can be containerized or prepared in groups of packages covered by shrink wrap for shipment. Example: coffee, rubber, steel, etc.

Neo-Bulk: Certain types of cargo that are often moved by specialized vessels. Example: autos, logs.

Types of Ocean Vessels

Tankers: Vessels designed to carry liquid cargo such as oil in large tanks. They can be modified to carry other types of cargo such as grain or coffee.

Bulk Carriers: Vessels that carry a variety of bulk cargo.

Neo-Bulk Carriers: Vessels designed to carry specific types of cargo such as autos, logs, etc.

General Cargo Vessels: These include: (1) Containerships: vessels that carry only containerized cargo, (2) roll-on and roll-off (RO/RO) vessels: vessels that allow rolling cargo such as tractors and cars to be driven aboard the vessel, and (3) LASH (lighter Aboard Ship) vessels: vessels that can carry very large containers such as barges. It enables cargo to be loaded on barges in shallow waters and then loaded on board a vessel.

Barges: Unmanned vessels generally used for oversized cargo and towed by a tugboat.

Combination Carriers: Vessels that carry passengers and cargo, oil and dry bulk, or containers and bulk cargo. Other combinations are also possible.

regular and repeated from and to designated ports on a trade route, at intervals established in response to the quantity of cargo generated along that route. Even though the sailing schedule is related to the amount of business available, it is general practice to dispatch at least one ship each month (Kendall, 1983). The purpose of a shipping conference is the self-regulation of price competition, primarily through the establishment of uniform freight rates and terms and conditions of service among the member shipping lines. In spite of its cartel-like structure, it is considered to be a necessary evil to ensure the stability and growth of international trade by setting rate levels that are more stable and predictable and by reducing predatory price competition.

Conference agreements become effective between carriers unless rejected, the forty-fifth day after filing with the Federal Maritime Commission (FMC), or the thirtieth day after publication of notice of filing in the Federal Register, whichever day was later.

Conferences serving U.S. ports must be "open," that is, they must admit any common carrier willing to serve the particular trade or route under reasonable and equal terms and conditions. This is generally intended to preclude conferences from using membership limitations as a means of discriminating against other U.S. carriers. Conferences are also allowed to form an exclusive patronage contract with a shipper, allowing the latter to obtain lower rates by committing all or a fixed portion of its cargo to conference members. Vessels engaged in liner service may be owned or leased. Conferences compete with independent lines, chartered vessels, and each other, although the same carrier could belong to several conferences.

> *Example:* An exporter in Taiwan intends to arrange for shipment of its textiles by a conference carrier to New York. A case for a lower (tariff) rate for large shipments can be made to a conference rate-making committee that consists of member lines. If the conference elects to reject the application for a lower rate, several options are available to the exporter: (1) the exporter may request a member of the conference to establish the rate independently of the conference, (2) the product could be shipped through nonconference carriers (independent or other conference lines) that offer a reasonably low tariff, (3) the product could be shipped through other ports using other conference carriers, or (4) the shipper could consider non-vessel-operating common carriers (NVOCC) or tramp vessels, depending on the amount of cargo. Non-vessel-operating common carriers take possession of smaller shipments from several shippers and consolidate them into full-container loads for shipment by an ocean carrier. They charge their own tariff rates and obtain a bill of lading as the shipper of the consolidated merchandise.

Carriage of Goods by Sea

International transportation of cargo by sea is governed by various conventions. The Hague Rules of 1924 have won a certain measure of global support. The U.S. law on the carriage of goods by sea is based on the Hague Rules. Subsequent modifications have been made to the Hague Rules (the

Hague-Visby Rules, 1968), which are now in force in most of Western Europe, Japan, Singapore, Australia, and Canada. In 1978, the United Nations Commission on International Trade Law (UNCITRAL) was given the task of drafting a new convention to balance the interests of carriers and shippers. Although the Hague-Visby Rules were intended to rectify the procarrier inclination of the Hague Rules, many developing countries felt that the Hague-Visby rules did not go far enough in addressing the legitimate concerns of cargo owners or shippers. The commission's deliberations led to an agreement in 1978 (the Hamburg Rules). It came into effect in 1991, and its impact remains to be seen. Unlike the Hague and Hague-Visby Rules, which have been ratified by many developed and developing nations, the Hamburg Rules are mostly followed by developing nations, except Austria (Flint and O'Keefe, 1997). In view of the widespread acceptance of the Hague Rules, it is important to briefly examine some of their central features (see International Perspective 9.3).

Scope of application. The application of the rules depends on the place of issuance of the bill of lading; that is, the rules apply to all bills of lading issued in any of the contracting states. If the parties agree to incorporate any

---

INTERNATIONAL PERSPECTIVE 9.3.
The Hague, Hague-Visby, and Hamburg Rules: Overview

All three rules define the rights and duties of parties in a contract of carriage of goods by sea, insurance for goods, and transfer of title. The Hague and Hague-Visby Rules are generally identical except for provisions dealing with limitations of liability, third parties, and a few minor areas. The Visby amendments to the Hague rules increase the limits of carrier's liability, change the method of expressing the limitation amount (by weight), and protect third parties acting in good faith.

The Hamburg rules have been criticized by carriers and their insurers as favoring shippers (cargo interests). The prominent differences between the Hamburg rules and Hague/Hague-Visby are as follows: (1) The Hamburg rules have higher limits of liability and set higher damages against carriers; (2) under the Hamburg rules, the carrier is liable for delays in delivery, in addition to loss or damage to goods; (3) any loss or damage to goods in transit imposes a burden of proof on the carrier to show that the latter was not at fault, whereas such burden is only triggered when the loss/damage resulted from an unseaworthy condition of the ship under the Hague and Hague-Visby rules; and (4) the limits of carrier's liability may not extend to acts of independent contractors unlike the other two rules.

one of the previous rules in their contract, such rules will govern the contract of carriage even when the countries where the parties reside subscribe to different rules. However, this will not be allowed if the parties are required to apply certain rules adopted by their countries. These rules apply only to bill of lading (B/L).

The carrier's duties under B/L. A carrier transporting goods under a B/L is required to exercise "due diligence" in (1) making the ship seaworthy; (2) properly manning, equipping, and supplying the ship; (3) making the ship (holds, refrigerating chambers, etc.) fit and safe for reception, carriage, and preservation of the goods; and (4) properly and carefully loading, handling, stowing, carrying, and discharging the goods. Whenever loss or damage has resulted from unseaworthiness, the burden of proving the exercise of due diligence falls on the carrier. When different modes of transportation are used, the issuer of the bill of lading undertakes to deliver the cargo to the final destination. In the event of loss or damage to merchandise, liability is determined according to the law relative to the mode of transportation at fault for the loss. If the means of loss is not determinable, it will be assumed to have occurred during the sea voyage.

Basis of carrier's liability and exemptions. The carrier's liability applies to loss of or damage to the goods. It does not extend to delays in the delivery of the merchandise. The rules exempt carriers from liability that arises from actions of the servants of the carrier (master, pilot, etc.) in the management of the shipment, fire and accidents, acts of God, acts of war, civil war, insufficient packing, inherent defects in the goods, and other causes that are not the actual fault of the carrier. That loss or damage to the goods falls within one of these exemptions does not automatically absolve the carrier from liability if the damage/loss could have been prevented by the carrier's exercise of due diligence in carrying out its duties (Yancey, 1983).

Period of responsibility. The period of responsibility begins from the time the goods are loaded and extends to the time they are discharged from the ship.

Limitations of action. All claims against the carrier must be brought within one year after the actual or supposed date of delivery of the goods. This means that lapse of time discharges the carrier and the ship from all liability in respect to loss or damage. The Hague Rules also stipulate that notice of claim be made in writing before or at the time of removal of the goods.

Limits of liability. The maximum limitation of liability is $500 per package. Under the Hague-Visby rules, it is $1,000 per package. In most cases, a container is considered as one package, and the carrier's liability is limited to $500. To ensure the application of liability limits to their agents and employees, carriers add the "Himalaya Clause" to their bills of lading. The clause entitles such agents and employees the protection of the Hague Rules. Exporters can, however, obtain full protection against loss or damage by paying an excess value charge or by taking out an insurance policy from an independent source (Force, 1996; see also International Perspective 9.4 for accepted principles in ocean transportation).

INTERNATIONAL PERSPECTIVE 9.4. Generally Accepted Principles and Practices in Ocean Transportation

A. **Freight Forwarders:** The freight forwarder acts as an agent for the shipper in selecting a common carrier and booking cargo space. It does not issue a bill of lading and is not liable for damage to the goods while in the possession of the carrier. Liability may, however, arise in cases where the freight forwarder was negligent in selecting the carrier or customs broker.

B. **Removal of Limitation to Carrier's Liability:** The carrier shall become liable for any loss or damage in connection with the transportation of goods in an amount not exceeding $500 per package or in cases of goods not shipped in packages, per customary freight unit or the equivalent of that sum in other currency unless the nature and value of such goods have been declared by shipper on the bill of lading. The carrier can be held fully responsible for all damages (without the benefit of the liability limitation) in the following cases: (1) material deviation (carrier's geographical departures from course, unauthorized on-deck storage); (2) failure to give shipper fair opportunity to declare a higher value; (3) misdelivery—the carrier that issued the bill of lading is responsible for releasing the cargo only to the party who presents the original bill of lading, unless otherwise agreed with the shipper.

C. **Burden of Proof for Shipper and Carrier**: The initial burden of proof falls on the shipper to prove that the goods delivered to the carrier were in sound condition. This burden can be met by providing a "clean" bill of lading. The provision of a clean bill of lading shifts the burden to the carrier to prove that the damage or loss to the merchandise was not caused by its negligence.

D. **Four Parameters to Establish Seaworthiness of Ship**:

   1. Is the ship appropriate for the type of cargo?
   2. Is the ship properly equipped for the goods (for reception, carriage, preservation of goods)?
   3. Is the ship staffed with a competent crew?
   4. Did the carrier properly load, handle, stow, and discharge the goods carried? Proper storage varies according to the types of goods transported.

Land Transport and Intermodal Service

Land transportation carriers (trucks, trains) are mainly used to transport exports to neighboring countries as well as to move goods to and from an airport or seaport. A substantial volume of U.S. exports to Canada and Mexico is moved by rail and/or trucks. Compared to rail transport, trucking has the advantage of flexibility, faster service, lower transportation costs, and less likelihood of damage to merchandise on transit. Rail transport has its own unique advantages: capacity to handle bulk cargo, free storage in transit, as well as absorption of loading, unloading, wharfage, and lighter charges. With the proliferation of free-trade agreements in various regions, there is likely to be a marked growth in the role of land carriers in transporting exports among countries that are in the same geographical area. For example, in eastern and southern Africa, an agreement that allows movement of land carriers across countries would make trucks and trains the dominant mode of transportation for exports. This is because land transport already accounts for over 80 percent of the region's freight movements and with a regional arrangement, these transportation services could easily be extended to neighboring countries with limited capital investment.

The use of land transportation is considered economically justifiable for large flows of cargo over distances greater than 500 kilometers (310 miles). A recent Swedish study on intermodal techniques (rail/truck) in transportation found that improving the competitiveness of intermodal transport for short-distance trips requires the operation of "corridor trains" that make short stops every 100 or 200 kilometers along a route (Anonymous, 1998b). Intermodal transport is not just limited to moving goods between rail and truck; it is also used for any service that requires more than one means of transportation (e.g., rail and ocean, truck and ocean) under one bill of lading. Such arrangements, ideally, must seek the fastest and least costly transportation for the shipper. The essence of intermodal contract is an agreement between different types of carriers (steamship lines, railroads, trucking firms, airlines, etc.) to achieve certain well-defined and carefully described functions. The advantages of such a mode of transport is simplicity for the shipper and consignee (one bill of lading and no other arrangements necessary), reduced damage because of fewer handlings, and reduced pilferage due to limited exposure of cargo. Such services are already offered by the integrators in the airline industry.

Examples of Intermodal Service

A truck will move merchandise from the exporter's warehouse outside New York City to a railroad yard some fifty miles away. The railroad will take the container to a New York port where it will be placed aboard a ship to Rotterdam, Holland. The whole movement would be covered by a single contract of carriage issued by the trucker as the initiating carrier.

Fresh oranges that arrive by sea from Chile in Miami, Florida, are then distributed to a network of inland points by air and then delivered door to door to customers by truck.

Inland Carriage

Transportation of merchandise almost always involves the use of an inland carrier (a trucking or rail company) to move merchandise from the exporter's warehouse to the seaport or airport. Inland transportation is governed by domestic legislation unless goods are shipped to a different country or such movement of cargo from warehouse to port is the first part of intermodal transportation to a foreign country. In the United States, different laws, including the Carmack Amendment, govern domestic transportation. Under the Carmack Amendment, rail and motor common carriers are liable for the full value of the goods lost, damaged, or delayed in transit. However, there are certain exceptions to this strict liability: act of God, act of shipper, inherent vice (defects in the goods), act of a public enemy, and intervention of law. Even though there are no universal agreements, a few regional treaties regulate transportation of goods by road and rail (Schmitthoff, 1986). Prominent among these is the Convention on the Contract for the International Carriage of Goods by Road (Convention relative au Contract de Transport International de Merchandises par Route, or CMR, 1956) and the Convention Concerning International Carriage by Rail (Convention relative au Transport Internationaux Ferroviares, or COTIF, 1980). Members include most European countries, and a few Middle Eastern nations in the case of COTIF. The respective conventions cover areas such as scope of application, liability of the carrier, the use of multiple carriers, and time limits:

- The conventions generally apply to contracts for the carriage of goods by road or rail between two countries, of which at least one is a contracting party. The convention also applies to carriage by states or public institutions.
- A carrier is required to issue a consignment note (nonnegotiable) as evidence of contract of carriage and condition of the goods. The consignee has a right to demand delivery of the goods in exchange for a receipt and to sue the carrier in its own name for any loss, damage, or delay for which the carrier is responsible. The shipper can change the

place of delivery or order delivery to another consignee at any time before the delivery of the consignment note or cargo to the first consignee.
- In cases involving multiple carriers, each carrier is responsible for the entire transaction.
- Carriers are liable for loss, damage, or delays up to a liability limit insofar as the contract is governed by the CMR or COTIF. There are, however, certain exceptions to liability in cases such as inherent vice in the goods, circumstances that the carrier could not avoid, and the consequences of which he was unable to prevent, or negligence on the part of the shipper.
- There is a limitation period for bringing action (one year) and for notice of reservations (i.e., notice of damage or loss).

THE ROLE OF FREIGHT FORWARDERS IN TRANSPORTATION

A freight forwarder is the party that facilitates the movement of cargo to the overseas destination on behalf of shippers and processes the documentation or performs activities related to those shipments. Freight-forwarding activity dates back to the thirteenth century when traders employed middlemen, or "frachtors," to cart and forward merchandise throughout Europe. The frachtor's responsibility later extended to provision of long-distance overseas transportation and storage services, issuance of bills of lading, and collection of freight, duties, and payment from consignees (Murr, 1979).

In the United States, the forwarding industry developed in the latter part of the nineteenth century. It started in New York, where the bulk of U.S. export trade was handled, to provide various transportation services to shippers. Ullman succinctly points out the changing role of the ocean freight forwarder in the United States:

> Many forwarding concerns originally started as freight brokers, but with the continuing increase in manufactured shipments, the forwarding work took precedence over the broker activity. Today, some forwarders handle ship loads of large parcels either on a common carrier or tramp vessels as brokers, but for the most part, forwarders deal with individual shipments varying in size or containers. (Ullman, 1995, p. 130)

Role and Function of Freight Forwarders

The freight forwarder (1) advises the exporter on the most economical choice of transportation and the best way to pack and ship the cargo to minimize cost and prevent damage, and (2) books for air, ocean, or land transportation (or intermodal movement of cargo) and arranges for pickup, transportation, and delivery of the goods. The forwarder also ensures that the goods are properly packed and labeled and documentation requirements are met so the cargo is cleared at the port of destination. When a letter of credit is used, the forwarder ensures that it is strictly complied with to enable the exporter to receive payment. Thus, the advantage of a forwarder goes far beyond moving freight. Forwarders help shippers and consignees by tracking and tracing cargo. They can also negotiate better rates with carriers because they can purchase space on airlines or ships at wholesale prices. The wide array of services they provide also helps shippers save time and money.

Freight forwarders are a significant part of U.S. commerce and facilitate the growth and expansion of international trade. A U.S. Senate report on the industry describes freight forwarding as follows:

> a highly important segment of the economy of the United States in that its functioning makes possible participation in the nation's foreign commerce by many industries and businesses whose lack of familiarity with the complexities and formalities of exporting procedures might hinder or even preclude such participation if forwarding services were not freely available. (Ullman, 1995, p. 133)

Today, it is generally estimated that over 90 percent of export firms use the services of an international freight forwarder. Most of the forwarding activity is still concentrated in ocean shipping, although some diversification into air and land transportation has occurred.

A forwarder is distinguishable from a NVOCC. Non-vessel-operating common carriers are international ocean carriers that do not operate their own vessels. They fulfill the role of the shipper with respect to carriers and that of a carrier with respect to shippers. Typical NVOCCs will guarantee a steamship line a certain amount of freight per week or month and purchase the necessary space on a wholesale basis for shipment of cargo to and from a given port. They publish their own tariffs and receive and consolidate cargo of different shippers for transportation to the same port. They issue bills of lading to acknowledge receipt of cargoes for shipment. Unlike NVOCCs, freight forwarders do not publish their own tariff and consolidate small shipments. Forwarders use the services of NVOCCs and facilitate the movement of cargo without operating as carriers. Non-vessel-operating common carriers are often owned by freight forwarders or large transportation companies.

A forwarder also differs from a customs broker in that the latter deals with the clearing of imports through customs, whereas a forwarder facilitates the transportation of exports. The broker is licensed by the Treasury Department; while the forwarder is licensed by the Federal Maritime Commission (FMC).

Licensing Requirements

To be eligible for an ocean freight forwarder's license, the applicant must demonstrate to the FMC that he or she (1) has a minimum of three years' experience in ocean freight forwarding duties in the United States and the necessary character to render such services, and (2) has obtained and filed a valid surety bond with the FMC. A shipper whose primary business is the sale of merchandise can perform forwarding services without a license to move its own shipments. In such a case, the shipper is not entitled to receive compensation from the carrier for its services. A license is not required for an individual employee or unincorporated branch office of a licensed ocean freight forwarder. A common carrier or agent thereof may also perform forwarding services without a license with respect to cargo carried under such carrier's own bill of lading (FMC, 1984).

Other Obligations and Responsibilities

- A description of the freight forwarder as consignee on an inland transport bill of lading (i.e., truck or rail) may subject the forwarder to liability for freight charges to the airport or seaport. This can be avoided by clearly indicating on the forwarder's delivery instructions that the forwarder is acting merely as an agent and does not have any ownership interest in the merchandise.
- The forwarder is liable to the shipper for its own negligence in selecting the carrier, handling documentation, directing cargo, and classifying shipments. The forwarder, for example, must not rely totally on the shipper's instructions with respect to the classification of a shipment. The forwarder must take reasonable measures to ensure that the classification is proper and consistent with the description on the commercial invoice, bill of lading, and other documents.
- In cases in which the forwarder acts as an NVOCC, liability is that of a common carrier for loss or damage to cargo.
- The forwarder's liability is limited to the lesser of $50.00 per shipment or the fee charged for its services. Any claims by the exporter

against the forwarder must be presented within ninety days from the date of exportation.

- Each freight forwarder is required to maintain current and accurate records for five years. The records should include general financial data, types of services, receipts, and expenses.
- Forwarders are prohibited from providing any rebates to shippers or sharing any compensation or forwarding fees with shippers, consignees, or sellers. Non-vessel-operating common carriers can receive compensation from carriers only when they act as mere forwarders, that is, when they do not issue bills of lading or otherwise undertake carriers' responsibilities.

CHAPTER SUMMARY

Documents Frequently Used in Export-Import Transactions

1. Air waybill
2. Bill of exchange
3. Bill of lading
4. Through bill of lading
5. Consular invoice
6. Certificate of origin
7. Inspection certificate
8. Insurance certificate
9. Commercial invoice
10. Dock's receipt
11. Destination control statement
12. Shipper's export declaration
13. Pro forma invoice
14. Export packing list
15. Manifest

Air Transportation

Reasons for the Growth of Airfreight

Growing demand for imports of heavy equipment and services in many developing countries; the need for timely delivery of imports; technological changes; the role of integrators and forwarders

Determinants of Air Cargo Rates

Distance, weight and size of cargo, commodity description, special services

Carriage of Goods by Air

Major international rules:

1. The Warsaw Convention (1929)
2. The Warsaw Convention—Amended (1955)

Ocean Freight

Types of ocean carriers: private fleet, tramps, conference lines

Carriage of Goods by Sea

Major international rules:

1. The Hague Rules (1924)
2. The Hague-Visby Rules (1968)
3. The Hamburg Rules (1978)

All three conventions cover rights and duties of parties to a contract of carriage by sea: Duty of carrier, carrier's liability, period of responsibility, limitation of action, and limits of carrier's liability.

Land Transport

1. *Rail transport:* It handles bulk cargo; absorbs loading, unloading, and other charges.
2. *Trucking:* Compared to rail transport, trucking has the advantage of flexibility, faster service, and lower transportation costs.

Inland Carriage

Inland carriage is the use of an inland carrier to move merchandise from the exporter's warehouse to the sea or airport. Major international rules governing inland carriage:

1. Convention on the Contract for the International Carriage of Goods by Road.
2. Convention Concerning International Carriage by Rail.

Both conventions cover areas such as liability for loss or damage to shipment, delays in delivery, and time limits for bringing action.

Freight Forwarders

A freight forwarder facilitates the movement of cargo to the overseas destination on behalf of shippers and processes the documentation or performs activities related to those developments.

Role and function of a freight forwarder:

1. Advises shipper on the most economical choice of transportation.
2. Books space and arranges for pickup, transportation, and delivery of goods.

Licensing requirements: To be eligible for a license as a freight forwarder, the applicant must demonstrate to the FMC that he or she has (1) a minimum of three years' experience in ocean freight forwarding duties in the United States; (2) the necessary character to render such services; and (3) a valid surety bond filed with the FMC.

REVIEW QUESTIONS

1. What is the difference between a bill of exchange and a bill of lading? Are straight bills of lading negotiable?
2. What is the significance of these documents for importers: certificate of origin, destination control statement, pro forma invoice?
3. What factors are likely to contribute to the growth in air freight in future? Is it a major mode of transportation for cargo?
4. What are the three major types of ocean carriers?
5. What is the carrier's duty under a bill of lading? Discuss the "Himalaya clause."
6. State the major differences between the Hamburg rules and the Hague/Hague-Visby rules on carriage of goods by sea.
7. Discuss the difference between a freight forwarder and NVOCC.
8. BG, a stevedoring company in the employment of Tatek shipping, negligently dropped several containers of soft drinks as it was loading them on the ship from Port Everglades, Florida. Is the container a package under the Carriage of Goods by Sea Act? The contents of the container were described in the bill of lading as 2,300 cases of soft drinks, with each case containing four six-packs. Can the shippers claim from Tatek and/or BG?

CASE 9.1. WHAT CONSTITUTES
A PACKAGE UNDER COGSA?

In 1936, Congress enacted the Carriage of Goods by Sea Act (COGSA) in order to implement the Hague Rules, which the United States signed in 1924. The language in COGSA is almost identical to the Hague Rules except in regard to the carrier's limitation of liability. The Hague Rules limit a carrier's liability to £100 per package or unit, whereas COGSA limits such liability to $500 per package, or in the case of goods not shipped in packages, per customary freight unit. They both indicate that the limitation of carrier's liability applies unless the nature and value of such goods have been declared by the shipper before shipment and inserted in the bill of lading.

Given the absence of a definition for the term "package," courts and scholars in the field have provided different interpretations. It has become a major source of litigation in cargo damage claims.

When a cargo is fully boxed or crated in such a manner that the identity of the cargo is concealed, the cargo is considered a COGSA package regardless of size, shape, or weight. If, however, the cargo has been partially packaged for facilitating transportation, the parties' description of the cargo in the bill of lading is a determinative factor. In a case where a company sought damages from a carrier for the loss of 1,680 television tuners shipped from New York to Rio de Janeiro, the court rejected that each cardboard carton was a package and held that each pallet constituted a package. The complete shipment consisted of nine pallets, each loaded with six cardboard cartons holding forty tuners. The dock receipt, the bill of lading, and other documents all indicated that the shipment consisted of nine packages.

Another case involves a container load of perfumes and cosmetics shipped from France to Florida that mysteriously disappeared while in a marine terminal at Port Everglades, Florida. The perfumes and cosmetics in the missing container were packaged in a total of 2,270 shoebox sized corrugated cardboard cartons, which were then consolidated into forty-two larger units. They were bound together with plastic wrap and packed onto forty-two pallets with two cartons remaining. The insurance company paid the shipper for the loss under a cargo insurance policy and brought a subrogation action against the carrier. The onboard bill of lading described the cargo as four container units. The pro-forma invoice and the revised bill of lading stated forty-two packages plus two cartons. The carrier issued a clean bill of lading with these particulars (forty-four packages). If the bill of lading does not show how many separate packages there are, then each container is generally considered a package.

CASE 9.2. THE CONTAINER REVOLUTION

Until the 1960s, nearly all international cargo was delivered to the dockside in small packages and shipped on break-bulk ships. They came in boxes, crates, barrels, and drums and loaded on board ship, stowed, and at the end of the voyage, unloaded individually. This process was complicated, time-consuming and exposed cargo to damage and theft.

The container revolution involved the introduction of truck-trailer-sized boxes as cargo containers. These standardized containers can be filled with cargo at the farm, factory, or loading depot, sealed and taken by truck, train, or barge to a port where it is put on board a ship. It greatly reduced cargo handling time (it costs much less to load and unload containers by crane than it is to load and unload individual packages). Containers also eliminated costs associated with shore side warehouses to protect conventional cargo from the weather. Export costs relating to crating, packaging, etc., as well as potential loss or damage to cargo, is substantially reduced.

In typical container transportation (1) the shipper puts individual packages or cartons in a container, usually at an inland facility, and (2) the container is moved by rail or truck to a container yard close to a seaport. Once the ship arrives, the container is pulled by a tractor alongside the ship and placed on board the container ship by cranes. Container ships have specially built vertical cells which are designed to firmly hold the containers in place during the voyage. Today over 90 percent of the world trade is moved in containers. Only a handful of commodities are shipped in break-bulk: steel, paper, plywood. Even rubber and cocoa beans, which were largely shipped in break-bulk, are now moved in containers. The container revolution necessitated development of port infrastructure such as dockside cranes, standardized containers, and the designation and building of specific areas for containers, as well as connections to railways and highways.

Questions

1. In Case 9.1, what is the correct number of COGSA packages?
2. Discuss the major benefits of cargo containers.

SECTION IV:
PAYMENT TERMS
AND PROCEDURES

Chapter 10

Exchange Rates
and International Trade

FOREIGN EXCHANGE TRANSACTIONS

An exchange rate is the number of units of a given currency that can be purchased for one unit of another currency. It is a common practice in world currency markets to use the indirect quotation, that is, quoting all exchange rates (except for the British pound) per U.S. dollar. *The Financial Times* foreign exchange data for September 16, 2006, for example, shows the quotation for the Canadian dollar as being 1.1218 per one U.S. dollar. Direct quotation is the expression of the number of U.S. dollars required to buy one unit of foreign currency. The direct U.S. dollar quotation on September 16, 2006, for the Canadian dollar was U.S. $0.89. Although it is common for foreign currency markets around the world to quote rates in U.S. dollars, some traders state the price of other currencies in terms of the dealer's home currency (cross rates), for example, Swiss francs against Japanese yen, Hong Kong dollar against Colombian pesos, and so on (see Table 10.1). Strictly speaking, it is reasonable to state that the rate of the foreign currency against the dollar is a cross rate to dealers in third countries.

The foreign exchange market is a place where foreign currency is purchased and sold. In the same way that the relationship between goods and money in ordinary business transactions is expressed by the price, so the relationship of one currency to another is expressed by the exchange rate. A large proportion of the foreign exchange transactions undertaken each day is between banks in different countries. These transactions are often a result of the wishes of the banks' customers to consummate commercial transactions, that is, payments for imports or receipts for exports. Other reasons for individual companies or governments to enter into the foreign

Export-Import Theory, Practices, and Procedures, Second Edition

TABLE 10.1. Currency Trading, Monday, August 21, 2006

Selected Countries	Indirect Quotation Currency per U.S. $	Cross Rates (per Yen/per Lira)
Canada	1.12	0.00971/0.7710
France	0.78	0.00674/0.5348
Germany	0.78	0.0049/0.3636
United Kingdom	0.53	0.0049/0.3636
Japan	——	——/0.125
U.S.	115.74	0.0084/0.6901

Source: Adapted from CNN Money, 2006.

exchange market as buyers or sellers of foreign currencies include the following:

- Foreign travel and purchase of foreign stocks and bonds; foreign investment; receipt of income such as interest, dividends, royalties, and so on, from abroad; or payment of such income in foreign currency.
- Central banks enter the foreign exchange market and buy or sell foreign currency (in exchange for domestic currency) to stabilize the national currency, that is, to reduce violent fluctuations in exchange rates without destroying the viability and freedom of the foreign exchange market.
- Speculation, that is, purchase of foreign currency at a low rate with the hope to sell it at a profit.

Foreign exchange trading is not limited to one specific location. It takes place wherever such deals are made, for example, in a private office or even at home, far away from the dealing rooms or facilities of companies. Most of these transactions are carried out between commercial banks and their customers as well as among commercial banks themselves, which buy and sell foreign currencies in response to the needs of their clients. For example, a Canadian bank sells Canadian dollars to a French bank in exchange for French francs. This transaction, in effect, allows the Canadian bank the right to draw a check on the French bank for the amount of the deposit denominated in francs. Similarly, it will enable the French bank to draw a check in Canadian dollars for the amount of the deposit (DeRosa, 1991).

Foreign exchange rates are based on the supply and demand for various currencies, which, in turn are derivatives of the fundamental economic factors and technical conditions in the market (Salvatore, 2005). In the United States, for example, the continuous deterioration in the trade deficit in the 1970s, mainly due to increased consumption expenditures on foreign goods, led to an oversupply of dollars in foreign central banks. This in turn resulted in a lower dollar in foreign exchange markets. Besides a country's balance of payments position, factors such as interest rates, growth in the money supply, inflation, and confidence in the government are important determinants of supply and demand for foreign currencies and, hence, the exchange rate. The following are some examples (see also Table 10.2):

- The U.S. dollar depreciated substantially against the Euro and other major currencies over the recent period partly due to interest rate tightening by the European Central Bank, and high U.S. trade and budget deficits. Since the end of 2002, for example, the dollar has lost about half of its value against the Euro. Currency traders buy currencies of countries with high interest rates in order to maximize their investment returns and sell those currencies with low interest rates.
- The Mexican peso has been appreciating in 2006 due to an increase in the inflow of funds resulting from the rise of international oil prices. The increase of foreign investment in the country has also contributed to the rise in value of the peso, thus causing a reduction in its current account deficit and foreign debt.
- The Indonesian currency, the rupiah, has appreciated in value since 2004 due to political stability and steady economic growth.

Exchange rate fluctuations can have a profound effect on international trade. Export-import firms are vulnerable to foreign exchange risks whenever they enter into an obligation to accept or deliver a specified amount of foreign currency at a future point in time. These firms are then faced with a prospect that future changes in foreign currency values could either reduce the amount of their receipts or increase their payments in foreign currency. A U.S. importer of Japanese components, for example, took a $1 million loss when the dollar took an unexpected fall against the yen in 1993, wiping out a significant portion of the company's profits. In some cases, it may also be that such changes will bring about financial benefits. In the previous example, the U.S. importer could have reduced its payments in dollars if the yen had depreciated against the dollar.

The most important types of transactions that contribute to foreign exchange risks in international trade include the following:

- Purchase of goods and services whose prices are stated in foreign currency, that is, payables in foreign currency

- Sales of goods and services whose prices are stated in foreign currency, that is, receivables in foreign currency
- Debt payments to be made or accepted in foreign currency

Most export-import companies do not have the expertise to handle such unanticipated changes in exchange rates. Banks with international trade capabilities and consultants can help assess currency risks and advise companies to take appropriate measures.

The impact of exchange rate fluctuations on export trade can be illustrated by the following example. Since the dollar began to decline in January 2002, many European and Asian exporters to the U.S. market have been faced with the difficult task of balancing the need to increase prices to preserve profit margins and the importance of keeping prices stable to maintain market shares. Wholesale prices for Heineken beer, for example, have only been increased twice by a mere 2.5 percent. Many exporters have been reluctant to increase the prices of their exports to fully offset the decline in the dollar. Some have responded by shifting factories to North America in order to cushion them from currency fluctuations. Prominent examples include the establishment of production facilities by DaimlerChrysler in Alabama, BMW in South Carolina, and so on.

The impact of exchange rate risks is felt more by export-import companies than domestic firms. To the extent that an exporter's inputs are domestic, a strong domestic currency could lead to loss of domestic and foreign markets. Importers also face a loss of domestic markets due to the rise in the price of imports if the domestic currency weakens. In addition, such firms are

TABLE 10.2. Relative Position of Major Currencies, 2002 (percentages)

Currency	Foreign Exchange Trading	International Bank Loans	International Bond Offering	Trade Invoicing	Foreign Exchange Reserves
U.S. dollar	45.20	50.30	48.40	52.00	64.80
Euro	18.80	51.00	44.30	24.80	14.60
Japanese yen	11.40	−7.60	1.20	4.70	4.50
Pound sterling	6.60	4.30	5.20	5.40	4.40
Swiss franc	3.10	0.40	−0.20	n/a	0.70
Others	14.90	1.60	1.10	13.10	11.00

Source: Bank for International Settlements, March, 2002; IMF, IMF Annual Report, 2003.

vulnerable to exchange risks arising from receivables or payables in foreign currency (see International Perspective 10.1 for impact of exchange restrictions).

PROTECTION AGAINST EXCHANGE RATE RISKS

There are several ways in which export-import companies can protect themselves against unanticipated changes in exchange rates. The risk associated with such transactions is that the exchange rate might change between the date when the export contract was made and the date of payment (the settlement date), which is often sixty to ninety days after contract or shipment of the merchandise.

Shifting the Risk to Third Parties

Hedging in Financial Markets

Through various hedging instruments, firms could reduce the adverse impact of foreign currency fluctuations. This allows firms to lock in the

---

INTERNATIONAL PERSPECTIVE 10.1.
Exchange Restrictions

There are only a few countries that impose no restrictions on the use of the foreign exchange market. This means that their currency is fully convertible into foreign currency for all uses: for trade in goods and services, as well as international financial activities. Many Western economies such as Canada, the United States, Japan, the United Kingdom, and Germany, have convertible currencies. Currencies of most developing and former communist nations, however, are either not convertible or legally convertible only at artificial, government-established rates. Such exchange restrictions may be imposed for competitive reasons (keeping a lower value), to promote foreign investment, or to discharge debt payments (maintaining a high value). The most extreme form of exchange restrictions (control) is limitation of the availability of foreign currency to purchase imports. Limits could also be placed on the use of foreign currency for certain transactions, such as imports of luxury goods, to conserve foreign currency. In terms of exports, exchange control rules could require that exports are properly paid for and payment is forthcoming within a reasonable time, that is, proceeds from exports are to be repatriated to the country's bank within a given period of time after shipment.

exchange rate today for receipts or payments in foreign currency that will happen sometime in the future. Current foreign exchange rates are called spot prices; those occurring at some time in the future are referred to as forward prices. If the currency in question is more expensive for forward delivery (for delivery at some future date) than for ordinary spot delivery (i.e., for delivery two business days following the agreed-upon exchange date), it is said to be at a premium. If it is less expensive for forward delivery than spot delivery, it is said to be at a discount.

In Table 10.3, the forward krone is at a premium since the forward krone is more expensive than the spot. The forward Canadian dollar is at a discount because its forward price is cheaper than spot. When viewed from the point of view of the U.S. dollar, it can also be stated that the forward dollar is at a discount in relation to the krone or that the forward U.S. dollar is at a premium in relation to the Canadian dollar.

It is pertinent to underscore some salient points about hedging in foreign exchange markets:

- *Hedging is not always the most appropriate technique to limit foreign exchange risks:* There are fees associated with hedging, and such costs reduce the expected value from a given transaction. Export-import firms should seriously consider hedging when a high proportion of their cash flow is vulnerable to exchange rate fluctuations. This means that firms should determine the acceptable level of risk that they are willing to take. In contrast, firms with a small portion of their total cash exposed to foreign exchange rate movements may be better off playing the law of averages—shortfalls could be eventually offset by windfall gains.
- *Hedging does not protect long-term cash flows:* Hedging does not insulate firms from long-term adjustments in currency values (O'Connor and Bueso, 1990). Thus, it should not be used to cover anticipated changes in currency values. A U.S. importer of German goods would have found it difficult to adequately hedge against the predictable fall of the dollar during the 1973-1980 period. The impact of such action is felt in terms of higher dollar prices paid for imports.
- *Forward market hedges are available in a very limited number of currencies:* Most currencies are not traded in the forward market. However, many countries peg their currency to that of a major industrial country whose currency is traded in the forward market. Many Latin American countries, for example, peg their currencies to the U.S. dollar. This insulates U.S. firms from foreign exchange risk in these countries unless the country changes from the designated (pegged)

official rate. Foreign firms, that is, non–U.S. firms, in these countries can reduce potential risks by buying or selling dollars (in the event of purchases or sales to these countries) forward as the case may be.

Example 1. Suppose the Colombian peso is pegged to the U.S. dollar at $1 = 1,000 pesos. A British firm that is to make payment in pesos for its imports from Colombia, could hedge its position by buying U.S. dollars forward. On the settlement date, pounds will be converted into dollars, which, in turn, could be converted into pesos. This assumes that Colombia does not change the pegged rate during the period.

• *Hedging should not be used for individual transactions:* Since most export-import firms engage in transactions that result in inflows and outflows of foreign currencies, the most appropriate strategy to reduce transaction costs is to hedge the exported net receivable or payable in foreign currency.

Example 2. Suppose a Canadian firm has receivables from two Japanese buyers amounting to five million yen and payables to four Japanese suppliers worth nine million yen. Instead of hedging all six transactions, the Canadian firm should cover only the net short position (i.e., four million yen) in yen. This reduces the transaction cost of exchanging currencies for the firm.

Spot and Forward Market Hedge

As previously noted, a spot transaction is one in which foreign currencies are purchased and sold for immediate delivery, that is, within two business days following the agreed-upon exchange date. The two-day period is intended to allow the respective commercial banks to make the necessary transfer. A forward transaction is a contract that provides for two parties to exchange currencies on a future date at an agreed-upon exchange rate. The forward rate is usually quoted for one month, three months, four months, six months, or one year. Unlike hedging in the spot market, forward market

TABLE 10.3. Hypothetical Exchange Rates, Currency per U.S. Dollar

	Danish Krone	Canadian Dollar
Spot rate	1.8037	1.4257
Thirty-day forward	1.7948	1.4296
Ninety-day forward	1.7887	1.4273

hedging does not require borrowing or tying up a certain amount of money for a period of time. This is because the firm agrees to buy or sell the agreed amount of currency at a determinable future date, and actual delivery does not take place before the stipulated date.

> *Example 1: Spot market hedge.* On September 1, a U.S. importer contracts to buy German machines for a total cost of 600,000 euros. The payment date is December 1. When the contract is signed on September 1, the spot exchange rate is $0.5000 per euro and the December forward rate is $0.5085 per euro. The U.S. importer believes that the euro is going to appreciate in value in relation to the dollar.

The import firm could buy 600,000 euros on the spot market on September 1 for $300,000 and deposit the euros in an interest-bearing account until the payment date. If the firm does not hedge, and the spot exchange rate rises to $0.5128 euro on December 1, the importer will suffer a loss of $7,680, or $(0.5128 - 0.5000) \times 600,000$.

The import firm could also borrow $300,000 and convert at the spot rate for 600,000 euros. The euros could be lent out, put in certificates of deposit, and so forth, until December 1, when payment is to be made to the exporter. The U.S. dollar loan will be paid from the proceeds of resale etc., without any foreign exchange exposure. This is often referred to as credit hedge.

> *Example 2: Forward market hedge.* On September 1, a U.S. exporter contracts to sell U.S. goods for SF (Swiss francs) 250,000. The goods are to be delivered and payment received on December 1. When the contract is signed, the spot exchange rate is $0.6098/SF and the December forward rate is $0.6212/SF. The Swiss franc is expected to depreciate and the December 1 spot exchange rate is likely to fall to $0.5696/SF.

The U.S. exporter has two options: First, it can sell its franc receivable forward now and receive $0.6212 per franc on the settlement date (December). Second, it can wait until December and then sell francs on spot. Clearly, the forward market hedge is preferable, and the U.S. exporter would gain: $(0.6212 - 0.6098) \times 250,000 = \$2,850$. The decision to use the forward market is to be made on an assessment of what the future spot rate is likely to be. It is also important to bear in mind the impact of transaction costs before a firm makes a decision on what action to take. A credit hedge could have been feasible if the spot rate in United States had been higher than the forward rate.

Swap

A swap transaction is a simultaneous purchase and sale of a certain amount of foreign currency for two different value dates. The central feature of this transaction is that the bank arranges the swap as a single transaction, usually between two partners. Swaps are used to move out of one currency and into another for a limited period of time without the exchange risk of an open position.

> *Example.* A U.S. firm sells semiconductor chips to Nippon, a Japanese firm, for sixty million yen, and payment was made upon receipt of shipment on October 1. The U.S. firm has payables to Nippon and other Japanese firms of about sixty million yen for the purchase of merchandise, with payment due on January 1. The spot exchange rate on October 1 is 120 yen per dollar and the January sixty-day forward rate is 125 yen per dollar.
>
> The U.S. firm sells its sixty million yen receipts on the spot market for $500,000 at the price of $1 = 120 yen. Simultaneously, the firm contracts with the same or different bank to purchase sixty million yen in sixty days at the forward price of 125 yen per dollar. In addition to its normal profits on its exports, the U.S. firm has made a profit of 2.5 million yen from its swap transaction. In cases in which the delivery date to the Japanese firms is not certain, the U.S. firm could use a time option that leaves the delivery date open, while locking the exchange rate at a specified rate.

Other Hedging Techniques

Export/import companies can use different techniques in order to avoid foreign exchange risk:

- *Hedging receipts against payables:* An export firm that has receivables in foreign currency (thirty million British pounds) could hedge its receipts against a payable of thirty million pounds to the same or another firm at about the same time. This is achieved with no additional cost and without going through the foreign exchange market. The same method could be used between export-import firms and their branches or other affiliate companies abroad.
- *Acceleration or delay of payments:* If an importer reasonably believes that its domestic currency is likely to depreciate in terms of the currency of its foreign supplier, it would be motivated to accelerate its payments. This could be achieved by buying the requisite foreign currency before it appreciates in value. However, payments could be delayed if the buyer believes that the foreign currency in which payment is to be made is likely to depreciate in value in terms of the domestic currency.

Guarantees and Insurance Coverage

In certain cases, exporters require a guarantee by the importer, a bank, or another agency against the risk of devaluation or exchange controls. Certain types of insurance coverage are also available against exchange controls. In view of its high cost, hedging is a better alternative than insurance.

Shifting the Risk to the Other Party

Invoicing in One's Own Currency

Risks accompany all transactions involving a future remittance or payment in foreign currency. If the payment or receipt for a transaction is in one's own currency, the risk arising from currency fluctuations is shifted to the other party. Suppose a Korean firm negotiated to make payments (ninety days after the contract date) in its domestic currency (won) for its imports of equipment from a Canadian manufacturer. This shifts the foreign currency risk to the exporter, which will have to convert its won receipts into Canadian dollars. Payment in one's own currency not only shifts the risk of devaluation to the other party but also of the risk of imposition of exchange controls by the importing country against convertibility and repatriation of foreign currency.

Invoicing in Foreign Currency

In the event that the agreement stipulates that payment is to be made in foreign currency, it is important for the exporter to require inclusion of a provision that protects the value of its receipts from currency devaluation. In the previous example, the contract could provide for an increase in payment to compensate the Canadian manufacturer/exporter for losses arising from currency fluctuations.

Another method would be to make certain assumptions about possible adverse changes in the exchange rate and add it to the price. If currency changes are likely to result in a 10 percent loss, the price change could be increased by that percentage (see International Perspective 10.2 for an overview of the Euro).

An export contract could also provide for the establishment of an escrow account in a third country's currency (stable currency) from which payments will be made. This protects the exporter from losses due to depreciation of the importer's currency.

INTERNATIONAL PERSPECTIVE 10.2.
The Euro: A brief overview

What is the euro? The euro is a common currency that replaced all the separate currencies of the individual countries of the European Union (EU). On January 1, 1999, the euro became the legal currency of eleven members of the European Union. In 2002, the euro paper currency and coins became the sole legal tender in the twelve participating members of the European Union.

Participating members: Austria, Belgium, Finland, France, Germany, Greece, Ireland, Italy, Luxembourg, the Netherlands, Portugal, and Spain. Denmark, Sweden, and the United Kingdom declined to participate at this stage.

The Convergence Criteria: In order to participate in the single European currency, countries were required to meet certain conditions: inflation rates below 2 to 3 percent, public debt to be no more than 60 percent GDP, and the budget deficit to be less than or equal to 3 percent GDP.

Benefits and Costs: (1) For businesses that are involved in cross-border trade, the euro will eliminate the cost of foreign exchange (hedging expenses, etc.) with regard to all intra-European transactions. There will also be no foreign currency risks in relation to cross-border investments within the EU. (2) European businesses will benefit from low inflation and interest rates which is an important policy of the European Central Bank. (3) Besides eliminating exchange rate uncertainty, the euro allows consumers and businesses to compare costs and prices. This, in turn, puts a downward pressure on prices and eliminates the practice of charging different prices in different markets within Europe. (4) Member states will achieve rapid economic and financial integration. It will also lead to greater economic and budgetary discipline and reduced cost of borrowing in international financial markets. (5) Seigniorage from use of the euro as an international currency. The major costs associated with the euro pertain to the inability of members to pursue independent policies to address specific macroeconomic problems. In a fully integrated economy like the United States, such problems are overcome by labor mobility or fiscal redistribution.

Timetable (1998-2002): (1) 1998: Creation of European Central Bank and commencement of production of euro banknotes and coins. (2) 1999-2001: determination of conversion rates for the euro, establishment and execution of the single monetary policy in euros, commencement of foreign exchange operations, and issuance of public debt in euros. Businesses and customers were given the option to choose to use either the euro or national currency. Increased use of euros for bookkeeping transactions. (3) 2002: Changeover of the economy to euro and circulation of euro banknotes and coins. Withdrawal of national currencies.

CHAPTER SUMMARY

Exchange Rates

An exchange rate is the number of units of a given currency that can be purchased for one unit of another currency.

Reasons for the Existence of the Foreign Exchange Market

1. Foreign travel
2. Purchase of foreign stocks and bonds
3. Foreign investment and other receipts and payments in foreign currency
4. Reduction of currency fluctuations
5. Speculation

REVIEW QUESTIONS

1. Differentiate between spot and forward exchange rate. How can a U.S. import firm use the forward market to protect itself from the adverse effect of exchange rate fluctuations?
2. What does it mean when a currency is trading at a discount to the U.S. dollar in the spot market?
3. Why do export-import firms enter the foreign exchange market?
4. Hedging is not always the most appropriate technique to limit foreign exchange risks. Discuss.
5. If a Canadian exporter accepts payments in foreign currency from buyers in the United States, which party bears the currency fluctuation risk? Explain.
6. The euro has now replaced twelve national currencies. What are the implications of this development to companies exporting to the European Union?
7. Suppose that the spot rate of the U.K. pound today is $2.00 while the six-month forward rate is $2.05. How can a U.S. importer who has to pay 30,000 U.K. pounds in six months hedge his or her foreign exchange risk?
8. In reference to question 7, what happens if the U.S. importer does not hedge and the spot rate of the pound goes up to $2.10?

9. Suppose the spot rate of the yen today is $0.0084 while the three-month forward rate is $0.0076. (1) How can a U.S. exporter who is to receive 350,000 yen in three months hedge his/her foreign exchange risk? (2) What happens if the exporter does not hedge and the spot rate of the yen in three months is $0.0078?
10. Do you think the U.S. dollar will continue to maintain its key currency status? Explain.

CASE 10.1. WILL THE U.S. DOLLAR MAINTAIN ITS KEY CURRENCY STATUS?

The global economy has largely depended on the United States, which absorbs about 20 percent of global exports. Many countries lack sufficient domestic demand to sustain economic growth. They consume limited imports and often depend on exports to the U.S. market. For example, exports to the United States accounts for 35 percent of China's GDP and 25 percent of the combined GDP of Canada and Mexico in 2005. In the face of the mounting U.S. trade deficits (over $800 trillion in 2006), there is likely to be a shift in the mix of global consumption away from the United States. Other developed and rich developing nations will have to boost private consumption and move the world away from excessive dependence on the U.S. market. This also requires addressing structural impediments to import demand in these countries.

The United States has maintained a strong dollar policy because this keeps U.S. inflation low (due to low price of imports) and makes U.S. assets expensive for foreign investors. Countries exchange their exports for dollars which are often invested in U.S. treasuries to shore up the value of their domestic currencies.

Despite rising U.S. trade and budget deficits, the dollar remains the major currency for conducting international trade and investment. For example, 45.2 percent of foreign exchange trading was in dollars compared to 19 percent in euros in 2002. Critical commodities such as oil are denominated in dollars.

A number of factors lead one to believe that the dollar will continue to maintain its key currency status.

- U.S. economic growth has been and will remain significantly stronger than Japan and other major euro-zone countries. Inflation has been tamed due to low cost imports.
- The United States has a large, open credit market, diversified financial institutions, and an independent central bank. Japanese and European

financial institutions lack the breadth and depth of their U.S. counter-parts. Many are beginning to recover after scandals.
- Incentives for investments (rates of return, yields) in the United States are higher than in Japan and Europe.

Questions

1. Why does the U.S. government maintain a strong dollar policy?
2. Do you think the euro will replace the U.S. dollar as a key global currency in the coming decade? Discuss.

Chapter 11

Methods of Payment

The rapid growth and expansion in global trade cannot be sustained without efficient and timely payment arrangements. Nonpayment or delays in payment for imports could tie up limited credit facilities and create liquidity problems for many exporting companies. Advance payments by overseas customers would similarly tie up a buyers' limited resources and do not necessarily guarantee delivery of agreed merchandise. The ideal payment method is one that protects the contending interests of both sellers and buyers.

Exporters often seek to develop foreign markets by using payment arrangements that are less costly to the buyer, such as consignment sales, open accounts, and documentary drafts, whereby the seller is paid by the foreign wholesaler or retailer, only after the goods have been received or sold. It is estimated that approximately 35 to 50 percent of exports from the United States and the United Kingdom are sold on open account and/or consignment (Cheeseright, 1994). This means that the risk of delay in payment or nonpayment could have a crucial effect on cash flow and profits (see Figure 11.1).

Export companies need access to credit reports on a global basis. There is a need to increase the existing database on companies in different parts of the world to ensure that formal reviews on credit decisions are based on current and reliable information. It is also important to consider credit insurance and other safeguards.

CONSIGNMENT SALES

This is a method in which the exporter sends the product to an importer on a deferred payment basis; that is, the importer does not pay for the merchandise until it is sold to a third party. Title to the merchandise passes to the importer only when payment is made to the exporter (Shapiro, 2006).

Export-Import Theory, Practices, and Procedures, Second Edition

Risk to Exporter

Least Risk ◀ - ▶ Highest Risk

Cash in	Confirmed	Irrevocable	Bank	Bank	Consignment
Advance	Irrevocable Letter of Credit	Letter of Credit	Collection (Sight Draft)	Collection (Time Draft)	Sales, Open Account

Highest Cost ◀ - ▶ Least Cost

Cost to Buyer

FIGURE 11.1. Export Payment Terms Risk/Cost Tradeoff

Consignment is rarely used between unrelated parties, for example, independent exporters and importers (Goldsmith, 1989). It is best used in cases involving an increasing demand for a product for which a proportioned stock is required to meet such need (Tuller, 1994). It is also used when a seller wants to test-market new products, or test the market in a new country.

For the exporter, consignment is the least desirable form of selling and receiving payment. The problems associated with this method include the following:

- *Delays in payment:* Buyer bears little or no risk, and payment to seller is delayed until the goods are sold to a third party. This ties up limited credit facilities and often creates liquidity problems for many exporting firms.
- *Risk of nonpayment:* Even though title to the goods does not pass until payment is made, the seller has to acquire possession of merchandise (to sell in the importer's country or ship back to the home country) in the event of nonpayment. This involves litigation in the importer's country, which often is time-consuming and expensive.
- *Cost of returning merchandise:* If there is limited success in selling the product, there is a need to ship it back to the exporter. It is costly to arrange for the return of merchandise that is unsold.
- *Limited sales effort by importers:* Importers may not be highly motivated to sell merchandise on consignment because their money is not tied up in inventory. They are likely to give priority to products in which they have some financial involvement.

In view of these risks, consignment sales should be used with overseas customers that have extremely good credit ratings and are well known to the exporter. They would also be satisfactory when the sale involves an affiliated firm or the seller's own sales representative or dealer (Onkvisit and Shaw, 1997). This method is frequently used by multinational companies to sell goods to their subsidiaries.

A number of issues should be considered before goods are sold on consignment between independent exporters and importers. First, it is important to verify the creditworthiness of foreign importers, including data on how long particular companies take to settle bills. Credit agencies have invested heavily in technology to improve the quantity and quality of information they provide to their clients (Kelley, 1995). Exporters can have instant access to information on overseas customers from such credit agencies. No exporting company should consider itself too small to take advice on credit matters. Bad and overdue debts erode profit margins and can jeopardize the viability of an otherwise successful company.

Information on credit worthiness should also include analysis of commercial or country risk factors such as economic and political stability as well as availability of foreign currency to purchase imports. U.S. banks and their overseas correspondents and some government agencies have credit information on foreign customers.

It is also advisable to consider some form of credit insurance to protect against default by overseas customers. Outstanding debt often makes about 30 percent of an export company's assets, and it is important to take credit insurance to protect these assets. Credit insurance also helps exporters obtain access to a wide range of banking services and an improved rate of borrowing (Kelley, 1995). Financial institutions tend to look more favorably on businesses that are covered and are often prepared to lend more money at better terms. The parties should also agree on who will be responsible for risk insurance on merchandise until it is sold and payment is received by the seller, and who pays for freight charges for returned merchandise.

OPEN ACCOUNT

An open account is a contractual relationship between an exporter and importer in which a trade credit is extended by the former to the latter whereby payment is to be made to the exporter within an agreed period of time. The seller ships the merchandise to the buyer and separately mails the relevant shipping documents. Terms of payment range from 30 days to 120 days after date of shipping invoice or receipt of merchandise, depending on the country (Reynolds, 2003).

As in the case of consignment sales, open account is rarely used in international trade between independent exporters and importers. Exporters are often apprehensive of potential defaults by overseas customers. They lack accurate information or may doubt the reliability of available data on foreign buyers to evaluate and determine their credit worthiness to purchase on open account. Unlike consignment sales, importers are expected to remit payment within a certain agreed-upon period regardless of whether they resold the product to third parties.

Open account is often used to increase sales by assisting foreign distributors to start new, or expand existing, product lines. It could also be used when a seller wants to test-market a new product or try a new market in a different country.

This arrangement gives the buyer/distributor enough time to resell the product to domestic customers and then pay the exporter, while generating business goodwill for future dealings. Many developing nations prohibit purchases on open account and consignment sales because of currency restrictions and lack of control over their balance of payments (Shapiro, 2006).

A major weakness of this method is that the importer could delay payment until merchandise is received, even when the importer is expected to pay within a specified period after shipment. There is also a greater risk of default or nonpayment by the buyer. This makes it difficult to sell the account receivable.

Open-account financing is often used for trade between parent and subsidiary companies. It is also used for sales to well-established customers with good credit ratings. When open-account sales to third parties are contemplated, it is important to verify the integrity of the buyers through a credit investigation. This should also take into account the importing country's political and economic conditions. Sources range from commercial credit agencies, such as Equifax and Dunn and Bradstreet, to chambers of commerce, trade associations, commercial banks, and public agencies, such as the Department of Commerce. It is advisable to insure trade debts to protect the seller against default by the importing company. Another safeguard would be to secure collateral to cover a transaction.

DOCUMENTARY COLLECTION (DOCUMENTARY DRAFT)

The documentary collection or documentary draft is one of the most customary methods of making payments in international trade. To facilitate the transaction, two banks are usually involved, one in the exporter's country and one in the buyer's country. The banks may be independent banks or branches of the same bank.

A draft can be drawn (documents payable) in the currency of the country of payment or in a foreign currency. This method of payment falls between the open account, which favors the buyer, and letter of credit, which protects the exporter. Bank fees are less expensive, usually a specific sum for each service, as opposed to a percentage of the transaction amount, which is used for letters of credit.

A typical documentary collection procedure includes the following steps (see also Figure 11.2):

- After the exporter (drawer) and overseas customer (drawee) agree on the terms of sale, the exporter arranges for shipment and prepares the necessary documents such as invoice, bill of lading, certificate of origin, and draft.
- The exporter forwards the documents to its bank (remitting bank) with instructions.
- The remitting bank then forwards the documents to its overseas correspondent bank (collecting bank) in the importer's country, with the exporter's instruction letter that authorizes release of documents against payment (D/P) or acceptance (D/A) or other terms.
- The collecting bank contacts the importer to effect or accept payment. If the instruction is documents against payment (D/P), the importer pays the collecting bank in exchange for the documents. The collecting bank will then send proceeds to the remitting bank for payment to the seller. If the instructions are documents against acceptance (D/A), the collecting bank will release documents to the overseas customer only upon formal acceptance of the draft. Once accepted, the collecting bank will release the documents to the buyer. On or before maturity, the collecting bank will present the accepted draft for payment. When the buyer pays, the collecting bank will remit the funds in accordance with instructions.

The basic instructions for collection of shipping documents (in addition to those pertaining to release of documents and remittance of funds) include the following:

- Procedures as to how nonpayment or nonacceptance is to be communicated to the remitting bank
- Instructions as to who pays the bank's collection charges
- Listing of documents enclosed
- Name of a party to be contacted in case a problem arises

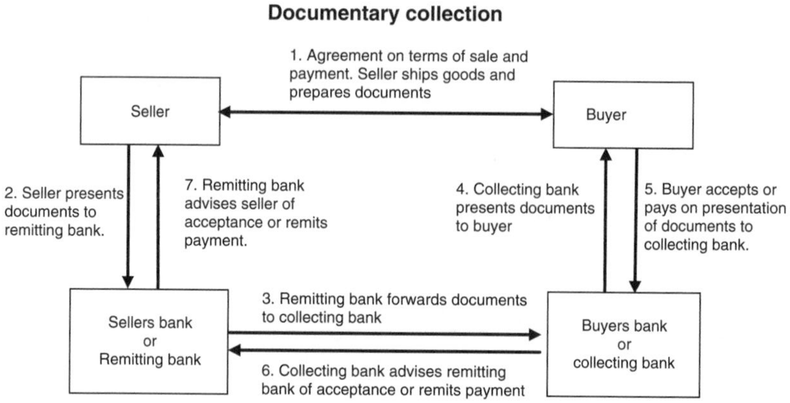

Documentary collection

1. Agreement on terms of sale and payment. Seller ships goods and prepares documents

Seller

Buyer

2. Seller presents documents to remitting bank.

7. Remitting bank advises seller of acceptance or remits payment.

4. Collecting bank presents documents to buyer

5. Buyer accepts or pays on presentation of documents to collecting bank.

Sellers bank or Remitting bank

3. Remitting bank forwards documents to collecting bank

6. Collecting bank advises remitting bank of acceptance or remits payment

Buyers bank or collecting bank

FIGURE 11.2. Documentary Collection

The banking practice relating to documentary draft is standardized by the Uniform Rules for Collections (International Chamber of Commerce [ICC], 1995). The uniform rules apply only when the parties to the contract agree to be governed by those standards. The rules set out the rights and duties of banks and users of documentary collections (Reynolds, 2003).

Documents against Payment

In a typical document against payment (D/P) transaction, the exporter draws a draft on the foreign buyer (drawee) through a foreign bank (collecting bank) that receives the collection documents from the exporter's remitting bank (Wells and Dulat, 1991). In this instance, a sight draft is presented with other documents specified by the buyer or the buyer's country and the collecting bank will provide these documents to the buyer upon payment. This means that the buyer does not receive the documents and thus will not obtain possession of the goods until payment is made to the collecting bank. This method is widely used in foreign trade and often designated as "sight draft, documents against payment" (S/D, D/P).

The original order bill of lading giving title to the goods is made out to the order of the shipper and is endorsed by the latter either in blank or the order of the collecting bank (Maggiori, 1992). This ensures that the seller retains title and control of the shipment until it reaches its destination and payment is made to the collecting bank. When the collecting bank is paid, it endorses the bill of lading and other documents to the buyer. The original bill of lading must be properly endorsed by the buyer and surrendered to the carrier before buyer procures possession of the shipment.

Order bills of lading are not available with air shipments. If the importer's name is on the air waybill (not a negotiable document) as consignee, often nothing more is needed to hand over the merchandise to the buyer (importer) than the latter's identification, and that the importer could obtain the goods without payment. This problem can be resolved by designating a third party, such as a custom broker or, with prior permission, a collecting bank as consignee on the air waybill. The importer's name should be mentioned as the party to be notified for identification of shipment.

In using S/D, D/P, there remains the potential risk of nonpayment by importer. The buyer's ability or willingness to pay may change between the time the goods are shipped and the time the draft is presented for payment (McMahon et al., 1994). It could also be that the policy of the importing country may change (e.g., exchange controls), making it difficult for the importer to make payments. In the event of nonpayment by the buyer, the exporter has the choice of having the merchandise shipped back or selling it to another buyer in the importing country.

Documents against Acceptance

In this method, the exporter allows the overseas customer a certain period of time to effect payment for the shipment. The buyer receives the documents, and thus the title, to the goods in exchange for acceptance of the draft to pay at some determinable future date. A time draft is used to establish the time of payment; that is, that the payment is due within a certain time after the buyer accepts the draft. A date draft, which specifies the date of payment, is sometimes used. When a time draft is used, the customer can potentially delay payment by delaying acceptance of the draft. An exporter can prevent such delays by either using a date draft or tying the payment date to the date on the bill of lading (e.g., thirty days from the date of the bill of lading) or draft. The collecting bank holds the draft to present for payment on the maturity date.

This method offers less security than an S/D, D/P because documents that certify ownership of merchandise are transferred to an overseas customer prior to payment. Even when the customer is willing and able to pay, payment can be prolonged by delaying acceptance of the time draft. This method is quite similar to open-account sales in which the exporter extends a trade credit to an overseas customer in exchange for payment at some determinable future date. One major difference between the two methods is that in the case of documents against acceptance (for which a time or date draft is used), the draft is a negotiable instrument (unlike an account receivable in an open account) that can be sold and easily converted into cash by the exporter before maturity.

A draft drawn on and accepted by a bank is called a banker's acceptance. Once accepted, the draft becomes a primary obligation of the accepting bank to pay at maturity. If the draft is accepted by nonbank entities, such as importers, it is known as a trade acceptance. The greater the credit worthiness of the party accepting the draft, the greater the marketability of the banker's or trade acceptance. They are important tools which can be negotiated or discounted to companies engaged in trade finance and which can serve the financing needs of exporters.

Direct Collection

Exporters can bypass the remitting bank and send documents directly to the foreign collecting bank for payment or acceptance. This reduces bank charges and speeds the collection process. In this case, the collecting bank acts as the exporter's agent for follow-up and collection without the involvement of the remitting bank.

Liability and Responsibility of the Banks

The Uniform Rules for Collections (ICC, 1995) distinguish two types of collection arrangements: clean collections and documentary collections. In the case of clean collections, a draft is presented to the overseas buyer for the purpose of obtaining payment or acceptance without being accompanied by shipping documents. Documentary collections, which is the subject of this chapter, however, involves the presentation of shipping (commercial) and financial documents (draft or promissory note) by the collecting bank to the buyer. In certain cases in which a collection is payable against shipping documents without a draft (invoice is used in lieu of a draft), it is termed cash against documents.

In documentary collections, banks act as agents for collection and assume no responsibility for the consequences arising out of delay or for loss in transit of any messages, letters, or documents (ICC, 1995). They do not question documents submitted for collection and are not responsible for their form and/or content or for the authenticity of any signatures for acceptance. However, they have to act in good faith and exercise reasonable care in execution of the collection order. The bank's major responsibilities include the following:

- *Verification of documents received:* The banks check whether the documents appear to be as listed in the collection order and advises the party in the event of missing documents.
- *Compliance with instructions in the collection order:* The exporter instructs the remitting bank on payment whether the documents shall be handed to a representative in case of need and what to do in the event of nonpayment or nonacceptance of the draft. These instructions are then sent along with other documents by the remitting bank to the collecting bank. The latter is only permitted to act upon these instructions.

In case the buyer refuses to pay, accept the draft, or pay the accepted draft at maturity, exporters often instruct the collecting bank to (1) protest; that is, to present the dishonored draft again, (2) warehouse the merchandise, or (3) send the merchandise back to the exporter. The collecting bank may be requested to contact the exporter's agent for clearance of the merchandise. All charges for carrying out these instructions are borne by the exporter. If the collecting bank releases the documents to the overseas customer contrary to instructions, the bank is liable to the seller; it has to pay the seller and collect from the buyer (see International Perspective 11.1).

The use of documentary collections offers certain advantages. It reduces transaction costs for both parties, helps maintain suitable levels of control for exporters, and speeds up the flow of transactions. The major risk with this method, however, is the buyer being unable or unwilling to pay or accept the draft on presentation. It is thus important to check credit references, consider taking out credit insurance, or secure collateral to cover the transaction.

DOCUMENTARY LETTER OF CREDIT

A letter of credit (L/C) is a document in which a bank or other financial institution assumes liability for payment of the purchase price to the seller on behalf of the buyer. The bank could deal directly or through the intervention of a bank in the seller's country. In all types of letters of credit, the buyer arranges with a bank to provide finance for the exporter in exchange for certain documents. The bank makes its credit available to its client, the buyer in consideration of a security that often includes a pledge of the documents of title to the goods, or placement of funds in advance, or of a pledge to reimburse with a commission (Reynolds, 2003). The essential feature of this

INTERNATIONAL PERSPECTIVE 11.1.
Protesting with Delinquent Overseas Customers

When a foreign buyer refuses to pay a sight collection or to accept a term draft, the collecting bank will advise the exporter and either proceed according to the collection instruction or new instruction from the exporter or its bank.

There are a number of reasons why buyers are unwilling to pay or accept a term draft.

- If the price of goods falls after order, buyers often try to find excuses to refuse the goods.
- The amount invoiced is higher than what was agreed in the contract or that the shipment was made earlier or later than the agreed date.
- The description of the goods is not consistent with what was agreed between the parties.
- Certain documents are missing to clear goods through customs or that import license was not obtained for the goods.

One course of action available to the exporter is to protest (through its bank) the customer's refusal to honor the sales contract (other available options include negotiating the terms, finding a new buyer or shipping the goods back to the exporter). Protest entails contacting a notary public or attorney (in the buyer's country) for the purpose of legally presenting a draft to the importer. It enables the exporter to maintain his or her right of recourse against the overseas buyer. There are a number of limitations to protest actions:

- Protests are not allowed in certain countries. In some countries such as Peru, a supplier must protest within seven days after the maturity date of the draft. This does not provide sufficient time to the exporter to assess the situation.
- Protests can be quite costly in some countries.
- Such actions may damage future business dealings with customers, especially if the exporter was partly responsible for the problem.

method, and its value to an exporter of goods, is that it superimposes upon the credit of the buyer the credit of a bank, often one carrying on business in the seller's country. The letter of credit is a legally enforceable commitment by a bank to pay money upon the performance of certain conditions, stipulated therein, to the seller (exporter or beneficiary) for the account of the buyer (importer or applicant).

A letter of credit (L/C) is considered an export or import L/C depending on the party. The same letter of credit is considered an export L/C by the seller and an import L/C by the buyer. The steps involved in Figure 11.3 are as follows:

1. The Canadian buyer in Montreal contracts with the U.S. seller in New York. The agreement provides for the payment to be financed by means of a confirmed, irrevocable documentary credit for goods delivered CIF, port of Montreal. ~

2. The Canadian buyer applies to its bank (issuing bank), which issues the letter of credit with the U.S. seller as beneficiary.

3. Issuing bank sends the letter of credit to an advising bank in the United States, which also confirms the letter of credit.

4. The advising bank notifies the U.S. seller that a letter of credit has been issued on its behalf (confirmed by the advising bank) and is available on presentation of documents.

5. The U.S. seller scrutinizes the credit. When satisfied that the stipulations in the credit can be met, the U.S. seller will arrange for shipment and prepare the necessary documents, that is, commercial invoice, bill of lading, draft, insurance policy, and certificate of origin. Amendments may be necessary in cases in which the credit improperly describes the merchandise.

6. After shipment of merchandise, the U.S. seller submits relevant documents to the advising/confirming bank for payment. If the documents comply, the advising/confirming bank will pay the seller. (If the L/C provides for acceptance, the bank accepts the draft, signifying its commitment to pay the face value at maturity to the seller or bona fide holder of the draft—acceptance L/C. It is straight L/C if payment is made by the issuing bank or the bank designated in the credit at a determinable future date. If the credit provides for negotiation at any bank, it is negotiable L/C.)

7. The advising/confirming bank sends documents plus settlement instructions to the issuing bank.

8. On inspecting documents for compliance with instructions, the issuing bank reimburses/remits proceeds to the advising/confirming bank.

9. The issuing bank gives documents to the buyer and presents the term draft for acceptance. With a sight draft, the issuing bank will be paid by the buyer on presentation of documents.

10. The buyer arranges for clearance of the merchandise, that is, gives up the bill of lading and takes receipt of goods.

11. The buyer pays the issuing bank on or before the draft maturity date.

Issuing banks often verify receipt of full details of the L/C by the advising bank. This is done by using a private test code arrangement between banks.

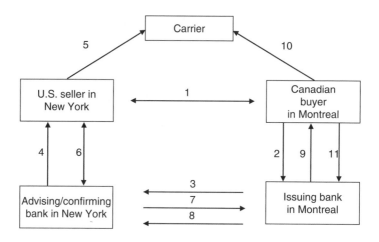

FIGURE 11.3. Documentary Letter of Credit

Credits are opened and forwarded to the advising/confirming bank by mail, telex, or cable. Issuing banks can also open credits by using the SWIFT system (Society for Worldwide Interbank Financial Telecommunications), which allows for faster transmission time. It also allows member banks to use automatic authentication (verification) of messages (Ruggiero, 1991).

The letter of credit consists of four separate and distinct bilateral contracts: (1) a sales contract between the buyer and seller; (2) a credit and reimbursement contract between the buyer and issuing bank, providing for the issuing bank to establish a letter of credit in favor of the seller and for reimbursement by the buyer; (3) a letter of credit contract between the issuing bank and the beneficiary (exporter), in which the bank will pay the seller on presentation of specified documents; and (4) the confirmed advice also signifies a contract between the advising/confirming bank and the seller, in which the bank will pay the seller on presentation of specified documents.

When the letter of credit is revocable, the issuing bank could amend or cancel the credit at any time after issue without consent from, or notice to, the seller. Revocable L/Cs are seldom used in international trade except in cases of trade between parent and subsidiary companies because they do not provide sufficient protection to the seller. Under the Uniform Customs and Practice for Documentary Credits (UCP), letters of credit are deemed irrevocable unless specifically marked revocable (ICC, 1993). Irrevocable credits cannot be amended or cancelled before their expiry date without express consent of all parties to the credit. The terms revocable and irrevocable refer only to the issuing bank. In cases in which sellers do not know of, or have little confidence in, the financial strength of the buyer's country or the issuing bank, they often require a bank in their country to guarantee payment (i.e., confirm the L/C).

There are several advantages of using letters of credit. They accommodate the competing desires of the seller and overseas customer. The seller receives payment on presentation of documents to the bank after shipment of goods, unlike open-account sales or documentary collection. In cases in which the advising bank accepts the L/C for payment at a determinable future date, the seller can discount the L/C before maturity. Buyers also avoid the need to make prepayment or to establish an escrow account. Letters of credit also ensure that payment is not made until the goods are placed in possession of a carrier and that specified documents are presented to that effect (Shapiro, 2006).

One major disadvantage with an L/C for the buyer is that issuing banks often require cash or other collateral before they open an L/C, unless the buyer has a satisfactory credit rating. This could tie up the available credit line. In certain countries, buyers are also required to make a prior deposit before establishing an L/C. Letters of credit are complex transactions between different parties, and the smallest discrepancy between documents could require an amendment of the terms or lead to the invalidation of the credit. This may expose the seller to a risk of delay in payment or nonpayment in certain cases.

A letter of credit is a documentary payment obligation, and banks are required to pay or agree to pay on presentation of appropriate documents specified in the credit. This payment obligation applies even if a seller ships defective or nonexistent goods (empty crates/boxes). The buyer then has to sue for breach of contract. The interests of the buyer can be protected by structuring the L/C to require, as a condition of payment, the following:

- The presentation of a certificate of inspection executed by a third party certifying that the goods shipped conform to the terms of the contract of sale. If the goods are defective or nonconforming to the terms of the contract, the third party will refuse to sign the certificate and the seller will not receive payment. In such cases, it is preferable to use a revocable L/C.
- The presentation of a certificate of inspection executed or countersigned by the buyer. It is preferable to use a revocable L/C to allow the bank to cancel the credit.

- A reciprocal standby L/C issued in favor of the buyer in which the latter could draw on this credit and obtain a return of the purchase price if the seller shipped nonconforming goods (McLaughlin, 1989).

Governing Law

The rights and duties of parties to a letter of credit issued or confirmed in the United States are determined by reference to three different sources:

- *The Uniform Commercial Code (UCC):* The basic law on letter of credit is codified in article 5-101 to 5-117 of the Uniform Commercial Code. This article has been adopted in all states of the Union. However, some states (New York, Missouri, Alabama) have introduced an amendment providing that article 5 will not apply if the letter of credit is subject, in whole or in part, to the Uniform Customs and Practice for Documentary Credits.
- *The Uniform Customs and Practice for Documentary Credits (UCP):* Parties to the letter of credit frequently agree to be governed by the rules of the UCP, which is a result of collaboration between the International Chamber of Commerce, the United Nations, and many international trade banks. The UCP is periodically revised to take into account new developments in international trade and credit (the latest revision was in 1993). The Uniform Commercial Code provision on letters of credit and the UCP complement each other in many areas. Under both the UCC and UCP, the terms of the credit can be altered by agreement of the parties.
- *General principles of law:* In cases in which the UCC or UCP provisions are not sufficient to resolve a dispute, courts apply general principles of law insofar as they do not conflict with the governing law (UCC or UCP) or agreement of the parties.

Role of Banks under Letters of Credit

The buyer's bank issues the letter of credit at the request of the buyer. The details of the credit are normally specified by the buyer. Since the seller wants a local bank available to which the seller can present the letter of credit for payment, an additional bank often becomes involved in the transaction. The second bank usually either "advises" or "confirms" the letter of credit. A bank that advises on the L/C gives notification of the terms and conditions of the credit issued by another bank to the seller. It assumes no liability for paying the letter of credit. Its only obligation is to ensure that the beneficiary (seller) is advised, credit delivered, and to ensure the apparent authenticity of the credit.

An issuing bank may also request a bank to confirm the letter of credit. A confirming bank promises to honor a letter of credit already issued by another bank and becomes directly obligated to the beneficiary (seller), as though it had issued the letter of credit itself. It will pay, accept, or negotiate a letter of credit upon presentation of specific documents that comply with the terms and conditions of the credit. A confirming bank is entitled to reimbursement by the issuing bank, assuming that the latter's instructions have been properly executed. It, however, faces the risk of nonpayment if the issuing bank or the buyer is unable or unwilling to pay the confirming bank, in which case it will be left with title to the goods and obliged to liquidate them to offset its losses.

Both the confirming and issuing banks have an obligation toward the exporter (beneficiary) and the buyer to act in good faith and with reasonable care in examining the documents. The basic rule pertaining to a bank's liability to a beneficiary is that the bank should honor the L/C if the documents presented comply with the terms of the credit. The following circumstances cannot be used by banks as a basis to dishonor (refusal to pay or accept a draft) letters of credit:

- *Dishonor to serve the buyer's interests:* In this case, claims are made by a bank's customer (buyer) that the beneficiary has breached the sales contract or that the underlying agreement has been modified or amended in some way in the face of complying documents. This includes cases of dishonor based on the bank's knowledge or reasonable belief that the goods do not conform to the underlying contract of sale.
- *Dishonor to serve the bank's own interests:* This occurs when the sole reason for dishonor is the bank's belief that it would not obtain reimbursement from its insolvent customer. This involves situations in which the buyer becomes insolvent after the L/C is issued and before the beneficiary's draft is honored.
- *Dishonor after express waiver of a particular discrepancy:* A bank dishonors an L/C after it has expressly agreed to disregard a particular discrepancy.
- *Dishonor without giving the beneficiary an opportunity to correct the discrepancy:* If the issuing bank decides to refuse the documents, it must give notice to that effect, stating the discrepancy without delay, and must also state whether it is holding the documents at the disposal of and returning them to the remitting bank or beneficiary, as the case may be (Arzt, 1991; Rosenblith, 1991).

Banks may properly dishonor a letter of credit in cases of fraud or forgery, even if the documents presented to the beneficiary appear to comply with the terms of credit. This assumes that there are no innocent parties involved in the presentation of the letter of credit to the bank. Banks are subject to two principles in the conduct of their letter-of-credit transactions: the independent principle and the rule of strict compliance.

The Independent Principle

The letter of credit is separate from, and independent of, other contracts relating to the transaction. Each of the four contracts in a letter-of-credit transaction is entirely independent. It is irrelevant to the bank whether the seller/buyer has fully carried out its part of the contract with the buyer/seller. The bank's duty is to establish whether the stipulated documents have been presented in order to pay (accept to pay) the exporter. It is not the bank's duty to ascertain whether the goods mentioned in the documents have been shipped or whether they conform to the terms of the contract. Article 3 of the UCP states:

> Credits by their nature are separate transactions from the sales or other contract(s) on which they may be based and banks are in no way concerned with or bound by such contract(s), even if any reference whatsoever to such contract(s) is included in the credit. (ICC, 1993, p. 11)

The independent principle is subject to a fraud exception. A bank can refuse payment if it has been informed that there has been fraud or forgery in connection with the letter-of-credit transaction and the person presenting the documents is not a holder in due course (as third party who took the draft for value, in good faith, and without knowledge of the fraud). In one case, for example, a buyer notified the issuing bank not to pay the seller under the letter of credit, alleging that the seller had intentionally shipped fifty crates of rubbish in place of fifty crates of bristles. The bank's refusal of payment was accepted by the court as a justifiable reason in view of fraud in the underlying transaction (Ryan, 1990). U.S. courts have held in several cases that banks are justified in dishonoring L/Cs when the documents are forged or fraudulent. The UCP is silent on the question of fraud. Article 15 of the UCP states that banks assume no liability or responsibility for the form, sufficiency, accuracy, genuineness, or legal effect of any documents. Article 9 also states that the obligation to honor an irrevocable L/C exists provided the stipulated documents are presented (ICC, 1993, p. 12). In credit operations, all parties concerned deal in documents and not in the goods to which the documents relate. Thus, when the L/C is governed by the UCP, it appears that the bank must pay, regardless of any underlying fraud. A bank would, however, be liable for the money paid out if it participated in the fraud.

The Rule of Strict Compliance

The general rule is that an exporter cannot compel payment unless it strictly complies with the conditions specified in the credit (Rosenblith, 1991). When conforming documents are presented, the advising bank must pay, the issuing bank must reimburse, and the buyer is obliged to pay the issuing bank. In certain cases, courts have refused to recognize the substantial-compliance argument by banks to recover their payments from buyers (unless it involves minor spelling errors or insignificant additions or abbreviations in drafts) (Rubenstein, 1994). The reason behind the doctrine of strict compliance is that the advising bank is an agent of the issuing bank and the latter is a special agent of the buyer. This means that banks have limited authority and have to bear the commercial risk of the transaction if they act outside the scope of their mandate (Macintosh, 1992; Barnes, 1994). In addition, in times of falling demand, the buyer may be tempted to reject documents that the bank accepted, alleging that they are not in strict compliance with the terms of the credit.

Two assumptions underlie the doctrine of strict compliance:

1. *Linkage of documents:* The documents (bill of lading, draft, invoice, insurance certificate) are linked by an unambiguous reference to the same merchandise.
2. *Description of goods:* The goods must be fully described in the invoice, but the same details are not necessary in all the other documents. What is important is that the documents, when taken together, contain the particulars required under the L/C. This means that the invoice could include more details than the bill of lading as long as the enlarged descriptions are essentially consistent with those contained in the bill of lading (Schmitthoff, 1986).

Discrepancies

Discrepancies occur when documents submitted contain language or terms different from the letter of credit or some other apparent irregularity. Most discrepancies occur because the exporter does not present all the documents required under the letter of credit or because the documents do not strictly conform to the L/C requirements (Reynolds, 2003).

Example

Dushkin Bank issued an irrevocable L/C on behalf of its customer (buyer), John Textiles, Incorporated. It promised to honor a draft of KG Company (exporter) for $250,000, covering shipment of "100 percent acrylic yarn." KG Company presented its draft with a commercial invoice describing the merchandise as "imported acrylic yarns."

Discrepancy: The description of the goods in the invoice does not match that stated in the letter of credit. Dushkin Bank could refuse to honor the draft and return the documents to the exporter.

To receive payment under the credit, the exporter must present documents that are in strict accord with the terms of the letter of credit. It is estimated that over 50 percent of documents presented under L/Cs contain some discrepancy.

There are three types of discrepancies:

- *Accidental discrepancies:* These are discrepancies that can easily be corrected by the exporter (beneficiary) or the issuing bank. Such discrepancies include typographical errors, omission to state the L/C number, errors in arithmetic, and improper endorsement or signature on the draft. Once these discrepancies are corrected (within a reasonable period of time: twenty-one days after shipment of merchandise and before the expiry date of the L/C), the bank will accept the documents and pay the exporter.
- *Minor discrepancies:* These are minor errors in documents that contain the essential particulars required in the L/C and can be corrected by obtaining a written waiver from the buyer. Such errors include failure to legalize documents, nonpresentation of all documents required under the L/C, and discrepancy between the wording on the invoice and the L/C. Once these discrepancies are waived by buyer, the transaction will proceed as anticipated.
- *Major discrepancies:* These are discrepancies that fundamentally affect the essential nature of the L/C. Certain discrepancies cannot be corrected under any circumstances: presentation of documents after the expiry date of the L/C, shipment of merchandise later than the specified date under the L/C, or expiration of the L/C. However, other major discrepancies can be corrected by an amendment of the L/C. Amendments require the approval of the issuing bank, the confirming bank (in the case of a confirmed L/C), and the exporter. Examples of discrepancies that can be amended include presentation of an incorrect

bill of lading, a draft in excess of the amount specified in the credit, and making partial shipments not allowed under the credit.

Discrepancies that can be corrected (accidental, minor, and certain major discrepancies) must be rectified within a reasonable period of time after shipment and before the expiry of the letter of credit. Most letters of credit require that the document be submitted within a reasonable period of time after the date of the bill of lading. If no time is specified, the UCP requires submission of shipping documents to banks within twenty-one days (see International Perspective 11.2 for common discrepancies in letters of credit).

In cases in which the buyer is looking for an excuse to reject the documents (when the price of the product is falling, the product is destroyed on shipment, etc.), the buyer may not accede to a waiver or amendment of the discrepancy or may do so in consideration for a huge discount off the contract price. The buyer could also delay correction, in which case the exporter loses the use of the proceeds for a certain period of time. Besides incurring further bank charges to correct the discrepancy, the seller also faces the risk that the credit will expire before the discrepancies are corrected.

INTERNATIONAL PERSPECTIVE 11.2.
Common Discrepancies in Letters of Credit

Over 80 percent of letters of credit documents are rejected by the bank upon presentation. It is thus important to ensure that errors are avoided or detected, and appropriate corrections made to avoid (nonpayment) delays in payments. Here are some of the common discrepancies:

- Draft is not signed, or it is not consistent with the letter of credit (in terms of the amount, maturity date, etc.) and shows evidence of forgery or alteration.
- Insurance policy is not consistent with the invoice, letter of credit dated after the date of bill of lading or not endorsed.
- Commercial invoice does not conform to description of goods (including quantity, measurements, etc.) in draft or letter of credit and fails to show terms of shipment.
- Bill of lading/air waybills differ from the letter of credit, show evidence of forgery or alteration, or not endorsed. It may also be that onboard notations are not dated or signed and that the bill of lading is incomplete (missing originals).
- Incomplete documentation, description of merchandise not consistent between documents, letter of credit overdrawn/expired, or the draft and documents presented after time called for in the letter of credit.

When the discrepancy stands (the discrepancy cannot be corrected or the buyer refuses to waive or amend the terms of the credit), the seller can still attempt to obtain payment by requesting the bank to obtain authority to pay or send the documents for collection (documentary collection) outside the terms of the L/C. If the buyer refuses to accept the documents, the bank will not pay the seller (exporter) and the exporter has to either find a buyer abroad or have the merchandise returned. If the confirming/issuing bank accepts documents that contain a discrepancy, then it cannot seek reimbursement from its respective customers (issuing bank/buyer, respectively).

When the issuing bank decides to refuse the document, it must notify the party from which it obtained the document (the remitting bank or the exporter) without delay, stating the reasons for the rejection and whether it holds the documents at the disposal of, or is returning them to the presenter (see International Perspective 11.3 for unworkable terms in letters of credit).

CASH IN ADVANCE

This method of payment requires the buyer to pay before shipment is effected. The seller assumes no risk of bad debt and/or delays in payment because advance payment is a precondition to shipment.

INTERNATIONAL PERSPECTIVE 11.3.
Unworkable Terms in Letters of Credit

Compliance with certain national policies: Some Middle Eastern countries require a document certifying that the ship carrying the merchandise destined to them will not make stops at Israeli ports. Complying with such requirements, for example, will violate the antiboycott provisions of U.S. law.

Contradictory/different terms: The requirement of the use of the term FOB (free on board) with an additional statement that freight be prepaid to destination, requiring the beneficiary to submit a certificate providing the origin of each component in an assembled product, (chambers of commerce will only certify local, not foreign, components) and requiring carrier's insurance policy (as opposed to certificate of insurance) will make it difficult for buyers to comply.

Setting unrealistic performance conditions: Different motivations often lead to the setting of shipping dates, expiration dates, or presentation dates for payments that are not realistic and often difficult to comply.

Sellers often require advance payment in cases in which the creditworthiness of the overseas customer is poor or unknown and/or the political/economic conditions of the buyer's country are unstable. Cash in advance is sometimes used between related companies. It is also common to require money in advance for samples.

OTHER LETTERS OF CREDIT

Transferable Letter of Credit

Exporters often use transferable L/C to pay a supplier, while keeping the identity of the supplier and the foreign customer from each other, lest they conduct the next transaction without the exporter. This method is often used when the exporter acts as an agent or intermediary. Under a transferable L/C, the exporter (beneficiary) transfers the rights and certain duties, such as shipment, under the credit to another person, usually its supplier (transferee), who receives payment, provided that the conditions of the original credit are met. The bank requested by the beneficiary to effect the transfer is under no obligation to do so, unless it has expressly consented to it.

It is important to note the following with respect to such letters of credit:

- A credit is transferred only if it is expressly designated as "transferable" by the issuing bank.
- It can be transferred only once. The credit is automatically divisible and can be transferred in fractions, provided that partial shipments are not excluded.
- The name and address of the first beneficiary may be substituted for that of the buyer. This would mask the identity of the true suppliers of the merchandise from the buyer.
- The transferee receives rights under this type of L/C. Such a transfer requires the consent of the buyer and of the issuing bank.
- The supplier might demand that the exporter actually transfer the letter of credit in its entirety, without substitution of invoices. The beneficiary (exporter) will receive a commission independent of the L/C transaction.

Example 1: A Canadian bank opens a transferable credit in the amount of $90,000 in favor of a U.S. exporter in Florida for a shipment of tomatoes. The exporter had located a supplier in Texas and had decided to use $85,000 of the credit to pay the supplier. The exporter asks the advising bank in Florida to effect a transfer in favor of the supplier. The supplier is advised of the transfer by the advising bank. The new credit does not men-tion the amount of the original credit or the name of the foreign buyer but substitutes the name of the exporter (original beneficiary) as the buyer. When the supplier presents conforming documents to the advising bank in Florida, the bank substitutes the exporter's invoice for that of the supplier, pays $85,000 to the supplier, and pays the difference to the exporter. The advising bank forwards the documents to the Canadian bank, which has no knowledge of the transfer for reimbursement.

Transferable L/C is different from assignment of proceeds under the credit. In assignment, the exporter asks the bank holding the L/C to pay either the entire amount or a percentage of the proceeds to a specified third party, usually a supplier. This allows the exporter to make domestic purchases with limited capital by using the overseas buyer's credit. This is done by assigning the proceeds from the buyer's L/C. The beneficiary (exporter) of a letter of credit may assign its rights to the proceeds of the L/C, even if the L/C expressly states that it is nontransferable. Only the beneficiary (not assignee) has rights under the credit, and the overseas buyer, as well as the issuing bank, often has no knowledge of the assignment.

Example 2: A U.S. exporter has a letter of credit for $40,000 from a buyer in Brazil. The exporter had located a supplier within the United States that will sell the product for $25,000. However, the supplier would not release the product for shipment without some down payment or collateral. The exporter (assignor) could assign part of the proceeds ($25,000) from the L/C to the supplier (assignee). The assignee will then provide the merchandise to the exporter, who will arrange shipment. The exporter (assignor) must submit documents that comply with the credit in order for the advising bank to pay the assignee (supplier). The remainder ($15,000) will be paid to the exporter.

Back-to-Back Letter of Credit

This is a letter of credit that is issued on the strength of another letter of credit. Such credits are issued when suppliers or subcontractors demand payment from the exporter before collections are received from the customer. The back-to-back L/C is separate from the original L/C, and the bank that issued the former is obligated to make payment to suppliers regardless of the outcome of the latter. If there is a default on the original L/C, the bank is left with worthless collateral.

Example: A Japanese manufacturer (exporter) of cars has a letter of credit issued for 1,000 cars by a buyer in New York. Payment is to be made ninety days after shipment. However, subcontractors require payment to be made for spare parts purchased in ten days (earlier than the date of payment provided under the L/C). The Japanese exporter presents the buyer's L/C to the advising bank in Tokyo and asks the bank to issue a new L/C to the subcontractor, payable in ten days. The first L/C is used as collateral to issue the second L/C in favor of the subcontractor.

Revolving Letter of Credit

Banks make available letters of credit with a set limit for their customers that allow for a free flow of merchandise until the expiry date of the credit. This avoids the need to open credits for each shipment. The value of the credit allowed can be reinstated automatically or by amendment. If credits designated for use during one period can be carried over to the next period, they are termed as cumulative. They are noncumulative if any unused amount is no longer available.

Example 1: Queen's Bank in Fort Lauderdale opens a revolving line of credit for up to $150,000 in favor of Kegan Enterprises, Incorporated, for the importation of handicrafts. Kegan Enterprises agrees to purchase toys (for $50,000) from Korea and requests Queen's Bank to open an L/C for $50,000 in favor of the seller in South Korea. If the credit provides for automatic reinstatement, $100,000 will be readily available for other purchases. In other cases, Kegan Enterprises will have to wait for approval from the bank, reinstating the credit ($100,000) to use for another shipment.

Example 2: Suppose Queen's Bank opens a letter of credit of up to $15,000 a month for six months in favor of Kegan Enterprises. If the credit states that it is cumulative, $30,000 credit not used during the first two months could still be used during the next four months. If it is noncumulative, the credit not used during the two-month period cannot be carried over for use in the next four months.

Red-Clause Credit

Such credits provide for advance payment to an exporter before presentation of shipping documents. It is intended to provide pre-export financing to an agent or distributor for purchase of the merchandise from a supplier. When financing is conditional on presentation of negotiable warehouse receipts issued in favor of the advising bank, it is termed green-clause credit.

Deferred-Payment Credit

This is a letter of credit whereby the bank undertakes an obligation to pay at a future date stipulated on the credit, provided that the terms and conditions of the credit are met.

Example: Suppose a U.S. buyer agrees to buy lumber valued at $40 million from a Canadian seller. The parties agree to use a deferred-payment credit. In this case, the U.S. buyer asks its bank to open (issue) a letter of credit obligating itself to pay the seller sixty days after the date of the bill of lading. If the documents are as stipulated in the credit, the bank undertakes an obligation to pay the Canadian seller sixty days after the date of the bill of lading. No draft, however, need accompany the documents.

What are the major differences between an acceptance letter of credit and a deferred-payment credit? In the case of acceptance credits, the bank undertakes an obligation to accept drafts drawn on itself provided that stipulated documents are presented. Assume that a Canadian seller and a U.S. buyer agreed to use an acceptance credit payable sixty days after presentation of shipping documents. Once the Canadian seller presents the requisite shipping documents and draft of the advising bank, the bank will stamp the draft "accepted," if it is in strict compliance with the credit. This represents the bank's obligation to pay on the maturity date of the draft. Once accepted by the bank, the draft becomes a negotiable instrument that can be discounted by the accepting bank, enabling the seller to receive payment for the goods in advance of the maturity date of the acceptance. In the case of deferred-payment credits, no draft accompanies the documents. The agreement providing for the Canadian bank to pay the seller sixty days after the date of the bill of lading represents the bank's undertaking of a deferred-payment obligation. In this case, no negotiable draft is generated and there is no way to discount the bank's deferred payment obligation. Any advance payment by the bank to the seller often requires a collateral or security interest in the proceeds of the deferred credit. Such credits developed primarily as a way of avoiding charges and fees associated with acceptance credits.

Standby Letter of Credit

The standby letter of credit is generally used to guarantee that a party will fulfill its obligation under a contract. Such credits are opened to cover the account party's business obligations to the beneficiary. A standby letter of credit is thus a bank's guarantee to the beneficiary that a specific sum of the money will be received by the beneficiary in the event of default or nonperformance by the account party under a sales or service contract (Reynolds, 2003). Similar to the documentary letter of credit, a standby credit is payable against presentation of documents that comply with the terms of the standby credit. The documents required to be presented by the beneficiary often include a sight draft and the beneficiary's written statement of default by the account party.

A major problem with such credits is that payments are often required to be made upon the issuing bank's receipt of a signed statement by the beneficiary that the account party did not perform under the contract and that the credit is currently due and payable. There is a possibility of unfair and capricious calling in of the credit, despite the absence of default or nonperformance by the account party. To protect account parties under a standby credit from such unjustified demand by beneficiaries, the following steps are often recommended:

* Include a clause under the credit requiring that the beneficiary present certification by a third party or court that default has occurred.
* Take out an insurance policy that covers commercial and political risk. This would cover exporters against, inter alia, contract repudiation as well as unfair callings by private entities or governments.
* Take out a surety bond issued by an insurance company (instead of a performance bond issued by a bank) to guarantee performance under the contract. Whereas banks honor a drawing under a standby letter of credit based on the face value of the beneficiary's statement of default, insurance companies verify the validity of the claim before payment. If the claim is unfounded, the insurance company will deny payment. However, if the insured's default is proven, payment is made under the credit and thereafter the company will recover from the insured (Kozolchyk, 1996).

The standby letter of credit is commonly used in the case of contractor bids and performance bonds, advance payments, open account sales, and loan guarantees.

Contractor Bids and Performance Bonds

Bid bonds are issued to a customer to show the seller's real interest and ability to undertake the resulting contract. This is intended to protect buyers from losses incurred in accepting invalid bids. The bid would be legitimately called in if a successful bidder failed to accept the contract.

Example: The Ministry of Defense of the state of Urbania want to buy 400,000 pairs of winter boots for the military. They invite domestic and foreign manufacturers to submit bids. All bidders are also required to submit a bid bond issued by a reputable surety company or a bank. Nunez Shoes, Limited, a U.S. footwear company, is awarded the contract. A few days later, Nunez Shoes writes a letter to the Ministry of Urbania, stating that it cannot carry out the contract because the company does not have enough supplies and an adequate labor force. Based on the contract, the ministry will be entitled to draw under the credit.

Standby credits are also issued to guarantee performance under a sales and service contract. Using the previous example, suppose Nunez Shoes signs the contract to deliver 400,000 winter boots to Urbania. The ministry could require Nunez Shoes to post a performance bond issued by a reputable bank as guarantee that it will live up to the terms of the sales contract. Performance bond credits are issued for a percentage of the total contract value. Suppose Nunez Shoes manages to deliver only 50 percent of the shoes before the expiry of the sales contract. The ministry will then be entitled to draw under the credit on presentation of the necessary documents.

Performance Guarantees against Advance Payments

These are bonds issued to guarantee the return of cash advanced by the customer if the seller does not comply with the terms of the contract.

Example: Using the previous example, suppose Nunez Shoes signs the contract with the Ministry of Urbania to supply the winter boots but requires an advance payment of $40,000. The ministry, in turn, could require Nunez Shoes to post an advance payment bond (a standby L/C with a bank to guarantee the return of money advanced by the ministry in the event of default by the seller). In the event that Nunez Shoes does not deliver the product as agreed under the contract, the ministry would be entitled to call in the credit, that is, to recover its advance payment on presentation of complying documents.

Guarantee against Payments on Open Account

This type of credit protects the seller in the event that the buyer fails to pay or delays payment. The seller asks the buyer to have a standby letter of credit issued in its favor. Suppose payment is to be made within ninety days to the seller under an open account transaction and the buyer fails to pay. The seller could then request payment under the credit against presentation of stipulated documents, such as a sight draft, commercial invoice, and the seller's signed written statement.

Loan Guarantees

Standby credits are often issued by banks when an applicant guarantees repayment of a loan taken by another party. Suppose a subsidiary of Nunez Shoes, in England, borrows 200,000 British pounds from a bank in London.

If the applicant's financial position is not well-known to the bank, the bank could agree to extend the loan, provided the parent company (Nunez Shoes in the United States) guarantees payment. Under this arrangement, Nunez Shoes, United States, would have a standby L/C issued in favor of the bank in London. Upon receiving the credit, the London bank will grant the loan to the subsidiary. If Nunez Shoes, England, defaults in repaying the loan, the bank will draw on the credit. In addition to this situation, standby credits are employed to cover rental payments, customs duties, royalties, and tax shelter transactions.

CHAPTER SUMMARY

Consignment Sales

Exporter sends product to importer on a deferred-payment basis. Importer pays seller upon sale of product to a third party. Exporter retains title to goods until payment.

Open-Account Sales

Exporter ships merchandise to overseas customer on credit. Payment is to be made within an agreed time after receipt of merchandise.

Documentary Draft

This is a service offered by banks to sellers to facilitate payment of a sale of merchandise on an international basis. Under this method, the exporter draws a draft on a buyer after shipment of the merchandise, requesting payment on presentation of documents (documents against payment) or acceptance of the draft to pay at some future determinable date (documents against acceptance).

Banker's (Trade) Acceptance

If a draft is drawn on and accepted by a bank, it is called banker's acceptance. If a draft is accepted by nonbank entities, such as importers, it is trade acceptance.

Role of Banks

1. *Verification of documents:* This is to determine whether the documents appear as listed in the collection order and to advise the party in the event of missing documents.
2. Compliance with instructions in the collection order.
3. Act as agents for collection and assume no responsibility for damages arising out of delay or for the substance and form of documents. However, they have to act in good faith.

Clean Collections

This is a documentary draft presented to buyer for payment of acceptance without being accompanied by shipping documents.

Documentary Collections

This is a documentary draft accompanied by shipping documents.

International Rules Governing Documentary Collections

Uniform Rules for Collections, 1995, International Chamber of Commerce Publication No. 522.

Documentary Letter of Credit (L/C)

This is a document in which a bank or other financial institution assumes liability for payment of the purchase price to exporter on behalf of overseas customer.

Parties to the L/C Contract

1. *Sales contract:* Exporter (beneficiary) and importer (account party).
2. *Credit reimbursement contract:* Importer and issuing bank.
3. *L/C contract:* Opening bank and beneficiary.
4. *Confirmation agreement:* Confirming bank and beneficiary.

International Rules on L/C

The Uniform Customs Practices for Documentary Credits (UCP), 1993 revision, International Chamber of Commerce Publication No. 500.

Role of Banks

1. Banks should act equitably and in good faith.
2. *Independent principle:* Credits are separate transactions from sales or other contracts, and banks are in no way concerned with, or bound by, such contracts. The independent principle is subject to a fraud exception.
3. *Rule of strict compliance:* Exporter cannot compel payment by banks unless the documents presented strictly comply with the terms specified in the credit.

Discrepancies

Accidental Discrepancies

Discrepancies that can easily be corrected by the beneficiary or the issuing bank.

Minor Discrepancies

Discrepancies that can be corrected by a written waiver from the buyer.

Major Discrepancies

Discrepancies that either cannot be corrected or can only be corrected by an amendment to the L/C.

Cash in Advance

A method of payment requiring the buyer to pay before shipment is effected.

Letters of Credit

1. *Irrevocable.* L/Cs that cannot be amended or canceled without the agreement of all parties to the credit, that is, the beneficiary, the buyer, and the issuing bank.
2. *Revocable.* L/Cs that may be amended or canceled by issuing bank without prior notice to the exporter (beneficiary). However, issuing banks must honor drafts duly negotiated by other banks prior to revocation.

3. *Confirmed.* A credit in which another bank, usually the advising bank, confirms its obligation to honor drafts and documents presented by the beneficiary, in accordance with the terms of the credit. This applies only to an irrevocable L/C, as the revocable L/C would become irrevocable if another bank added its confirmation.
4. *Transferable.* L/Cs that permit a beneficiary to transfer the credit to a second beneficiary. Similar to back-to-back L/Cs, but only one credit is issued.
5. *Back-to-back.* A letter of credit that is issued on the strength of another L/C.
6. *Revolving.* An agreement in which the buyer is allowed to replenish the credit after it is drawn down by a seller.
7. *Red-clause credit.* Advances or pre-export financing provided to an agent or distributor for the purchase of merchandise from a supplier. Such advances are made without presentation of documents.
8. *Green-clause credit.* When advances are made on presentation of warehouse receipts.
9. *Deferred-payment credit.* The seller agrees not to present a sight draft until after a specified period following presentation of documents. No draft need accompany the documents. When it is accompanied by a draft, it becomes an acceptance L/C.
10. *Standby.* A credit used to guarantee that a party will fulfill its obligation under a sales or service contract. Types of standby L/Cs: contractor bids and performance bonds, performance guarantees against advance payments, guarantee against payments on open account, and loan guarantee.
11. *Straight.* An L/C that is payable at the issuing bank or at a designated bank nominated in the letter of credit.
12. *Negotiable.* An L/C that can be negotiated at any bank. This means that the issuing bank will reimburse any bank that pays against the documents stipulated in the credit.

REVIEW QUESTIONS

1. Discuss the distribution of risk in the following export payment terms: consignment, time draft.
2. What are the advantages and disadvantages of these payment terms: documentary collections, open account sales, revocable letters of credit?

3. State the different steps involved in a confirmed documentary letter of credit, with payment terms of ninety days sight.
4. Compare and contrast documentary collections and documentary letter of credit.
5. The manager of the letter of credit division of Citibank in Chicago learns that the ship on which a local exporter shipped goods to Yokahama, Japan, was destroyed by fire. He knows that the buyer in Yokahama will never receive the goods. The manager, however, received all the documents required under the letter of credit. Should the manager pay the exporter or withhold payment and notify the overseas customer in Japan?
6. Compare the role and responsibility of banks in documentary collections and letters of credit.
7. What is the independent principle?
8. Discuss the rule of strict compliance.
9. Provide an example of a major discrepancy in letters of credit.
10. Briefly describe the following: transferable L/C, back-to-back L/C, deferred L/C, standby L/C.

CASE 11.1. DISHONORING LETTERS OF CREDIT

In June 2005, JFTC, a Chinese company, agreed to purchase 1,000 metric tons of fertilizers from VA Trading Corporation (VATC) located in Houston, Texas. JFTC obtained a letter of credit from the Bank of China (BC) for the purchase price of $1.2 million. Payment was to be made to VATC after delivery of the merchandise and presentation of requisite documents to the Bank of China in accordance with UCP 500.

The market price of fertilizers had declined significantly and the buyer requested for a concession. VATC refused to reduce the price. VATC presented the documents specified under the letter of credit (after shipping the goods to JFTC) to Texas Commerce Bank (TCB) which would forward the documents to the BC. Although TCB pointed out certain discrepancies between the documents and letter of credit, it did not believe that they would lead to any problems.

The Bank of China notified TCB of the discrepancies and indicated its willingness to contact the buyer (JFTC) about acceptance. JFTC refused to waive the discrepancies and the Bank of China returned the documents to TCB. VATC was not paid for the shipment.

Questions

1. Discuss the various options available to VATC.
2. Do you think the alleged discrepancies between the documents and letter of credit could be adequate grounds for dishonoring the letter of credit?
3. Do you think JFTC or its bank provided adequate notice to VATC according to UCP 500?

CASE 11.2. THE INDEPENDENT PRINCIPLE IN LETTERS OF CREDIT

A bank in New York issued a letter of credit to a beneficiary (seller) in Spain at the request of the buyer covering the shipment of building products. When the seller presented the documents to the bank for payment, the bank declined to pay on the ground that it had no opportunity to test the quality of the products. The letter of credit did not require that a testing certificate from an independent laboratory accompany the documents.

Questions

1. Was the bank justified in withholding payment?
2. Does the buyer or the bank have the right to demand inspection of the quality of the merchandise?
3. What is the importance of the independent principle for this case?

Chapter 12

Countertrade

ORIGINS OF COUNTERTRADE

Countertrade is any commercial arrangement in which sellers or exporters are required to accept in partial or total settlement of their deliveries, a supply of products from the importing country. In essence, it is a nation's (or firm's) use of its purchasing power as a leverage to force a private firm to purchase or market its marginally undesirable goods or exact other concessions in order to finance its imports, or obtain needed hard currency or technology. Although the manner in which the transaction is structured may vary, the distinctive feature of such arrangements is the mandatory performance element that is either required by the importer or the importer's government, or made necessary by competitive considerations (Verzariu, 1985, 1992).

The origins of countertrade can be traced to the ancient times when international trade was based on the free exchange of goods. Barter flourished in Northern Mesopotamia as early as 3000 BC when inhabitants traded in textiles and metals. The Greeks also profited by the exchange of olive oil and wine for grain and metals sometime before 2000 BC (Brinton et al., 1984; Anyane-Ntow and Harvey, 1995). Even with the flourishing of a money economy, barter still continued as a medium of exchange. Present-day countertrade involves more than the use of simple barter. It is a complex transaction that includes the exchange of some currency as well as goods between two or more nations. A countertrade transaction may, for example, specify that the seller be paid in foreign currency on the condition that seller agrees to find markets for specified products from the buyer's country.

The resurgence of countertrade has often been associated with East-West trade. At the start of the 1950s the former communist countries of Eastern Europe faced a chronic shortage of hard (convertible) currency to purchase

Export-Import Theory, Practices, and Procedures, Second Edition

needed imports. In their dealings with Western countries, they insisted that their products be taken in exchange for imports from the latter countries. This practice also proved quite attractive to many developing nations, which also suffer from a shortage of convertible currency. The use of countertrade has steadily increased and is presently estimated to account for approximately 15-20 percent of world trade (Hennart and Anderson, 1993). By the end of 1995, the number of countries using countertrade exceeded 100. Although there may be disagreements concerning the current volume of countertrade, the broad consensus is that countertrade constitutes a significant and rapidly growing portion of world commerce (McVey, 1984; Bost and Yeakel, 1992). A large number of U.S. corporations find it difficult to conduct business with many countries without relying on countertrade. For example, about two-thirds of foreign purchases of American commercial and military jets are paid for with local products instead of cash (Bragg, 1998; Angelidis, Parsa, and Ibrahim, 2004). In response to this growing interest, some U.S. banks have established their own countertrade departments.

> *Example:* PepsiCo traded drink concentrate for Basmati rice in India and for silk and mushrooms in China. The mushrooms are used in PepsiCo's Pizza Hut chain and the silk is dyed, printed, and sold for profit (Welt, 1990).

In the 1980s, countertrade was mainly used as a vehicle for trade finance. It is now used to meet a broad range of business objectives: capital project financing, production sharing, repatriation of profits from countries with hard currency shortages, and competitive bidding on major government procurements (Caves and Marin, 1992; Egan and Shipley, 1996).

Other Examples of Countertrade

- Indonesia negotiated for a power station project with Asea Brown Boveri and for an air traffic control system with Hughes Aircraft. Counterpurchase obligations were to be 100 percent of the FOB values. The firms export, through a trading company, a range of Indonesian products: cocoa to the United States, coal to Japan, and fertilizer to Vietnam and Burma.
- Lockheed Martin agreed to sell F-16 military aircraft to Hungary in exchange for large investment and counterpurchase commitments. The firm agreed to buy $250 million (U.S.) worth of Hungarian goods. It established an office in Budapest to participate in tendering and to procure the country's industrial goods for export.
- Taiwan purchased 60 Mirage 2000-5 from a French aviation company, Dussault. In return, Dussault undertook a joint venture with

Taiwan's aerospace company, Chenfeng, for the production of key aircraft parts and components for local aircraft and export (Anonymous, 1997a,b,c).

BENEFITS OF COUNTERTRADE

Benefits for Buyers

Transfer of Technology

In exchange for a guaranteed supply of raw materials or other scarce resources, a developed nation will provide the capital, equipment, and technology that is needed to develop such resources. Western firms, for example, assisted Saudi Arabia in the development of its refinery and petrochemical industry in exchange for the right to purchase a certain amount of oil over a given period of time.

Alleviating Balance of Payments Difficulties

The debt crisis of the 1980s, coupled with adverse movements in the price of key export commodities, such as coffee or sugar, left many developing countries with severe balance-of-payments difficulties. Countertrade has been used as a way of financing needed imports without depleting limited foreign currency reserves. Some countries have even used it as a way of earning hard currency by promoting the export of their domestic output. Countertrade has thus helped these nations avoid the burden of additional borrowing to finance imports as well as the need to restrict domestic economic activity. After the debt crisis, private lending by commercial banks has virtually dried up and now represents about 5 percent of long-term capital flows to developing nations, compared with 40 percent a decade ago. Countertrade is also used as a method of entering a new market, particularly in product areas that invite strong competition.

Maintenance of Stable Prices for Exports

Countertrade allows commodity exporters to maintain nominal prices for their products even in the face of limited or declining demand. The price of the product that is purchased in exchange could be increased to take into account the inflated price of exports. In this way, an exporter can dispose of its commodities without conceding the real price of the product in a competitive market. In the case of cartels, such as OPEC (Organization of Petroleum Exporting Countries), a member could attract customers for countertrade opportunities without violating price guidelines.

Benefits for Exporters

Increased Sales Opportunities

Countertrade generates additional sales that would not otherwise be possible. It also enables entry into difficult markets.

Access to Sources of Supply

Countertrade provides exporters access to a continuous supply of production components, precious raw materials, or other natural resources in return for sales of manufactured goods or technology.

Flexibility in Prices

Countertrade enables the exporter to adjust the price of a product in exchange for overpriced commodities (see International Perspective 12.1 on organizing for countertrade).

THEORIES ON COUNTERTRADE

A limited number of empirical studies on countertrade have been conducted. The following findings characterize some of the theoretical studies on countertrade practices:

- Countertrade is positively correlated with a country's level of exports. This means that a higher level of international commercial activity is associated with a high level of countertrade (Caves and Marin, 1992; Hennart and Anderson, 1993).
- Countertrade is often used as a substitute for foreign direct investment (FDI). Even though FDI reduces market transaction costs (i.e., by internalizing sources of raw materials and components through vertical integration), multinational companies resort to countertrade as a second-best solution when host countries impose restrictions on inward FDI. Countries engaged in heavy countertrade tend to be those that severely restrict inward FDI. FDI may also be less attracted to politi-

cally risky countries, in spite of their positive attitudes toward foreign investment. Such countries are likely to have a high level of countertrade activity (Hennart, 1990).

- The stricter the level of exchange controls, the higher the level of countertrade activity. This appears to be a response to the restrictions imposed on the acquisition of foreign currency. Some studies also show that a significant percentage of countertrade has little to do with foreign exchange shortages, but rather is intended to reduce high transaction costs that affect the purchase of technology or intermediate products.
- Countertrade is positively correlated with a country's level of indebtedness. Casson and Chukujama (1990) show that countries with higher debt ratios are more strongly engaged in barter. A country's creditworthiness, as measured by a composite of ratings of international banks, is positively correlated with its barter activities (Hennart and Anderson, 1993).

INTERNATIONAL PERSPECTIVE 12.1.
The Mechanics of a Barter Transaction

Suppose a private firm is selling drilling equipment to country A in exchange for ten tons of basmati rice. One method is to use reciprocal performance guarantees such as performance bonds or standby letters of credit. Each party posts a guarantee, and this provides payment to the aggrieved party in the event of failure by the other party to perform its part of the contract (i.e., failure to deliver the goods or delivery of nonconforming goods). However, the fees charged by banks for such guarantees are quite high. Another method is to use an escrow account to secure performance of an obligation by each party. The steps used are as follows:

- The firm opens a documentary letter of credit in favor of country A. In cases where the product is passed to a trading company, the letter of credit is opened by the trading company in favor of the nation.
- Country A delivers the rice to the firm or trading company and title is transferred.
- When the title passes to the firm, funds equal to the value of the rice shipped is transferred by the firm under the letter of credit into an escrow account.
- The firm makes delivery of the drilling equipment simultaneously, or at a later date, to country A and title is transferred to the nation.
- Funds in the escrow account are released to the firm.
- In the event the firm delivers nonconforming goods or fails to deliver the goods, the funds in the escrow account are paid to the nation.

FORMS OF COUNTERTRADE

Countertrade takes a variety of forms (see Figure 12.1). Such transactions can be divided into two broad categories:

- Transactions in which products and/or services are traded in exchange for other products and/or services: these include barter, switch trading, and clearing arrangements.
- Transactions that feature two parallel money-for-goods transactions: these include buy-back, counterpurchase, and offset arrangements.

Exchange of Goods (Services) for Goods (Services)

Barter

A classic barter arrangement involves the direct exchange of goods/ services between two trading parties (see International Perspective 12.2). An exporter from country A to country B is paid by a reciprocal export from country B to country A and no money changes hands. The transaction is governed by a single contract. In view of its limited flexibility, barter accounts for less than 15 percent of countertrade contracts. The major problems with barter relate to the determination of the relative value of the goods traded and the reluctance of banks to finance or guarantee such transactions.

> *Example:* In 1996, Ukraine agreed to barter its agricultural products for 2 million tons of oil from Iran. A Macedonian company agreed to pay 30 percent of the price for the purchase of Russian gas in goods/ services such as medicines, pipes, and construction work.

Switch Trading

This is an arrangement in which a switch trader will buy or market countertraded products for hard currency (Figure 12.2). The switch trader will often demand a sizable fee in the form of a discount on the goods delivered.

> *Example:* A U.S. company exports fertilizer to Pakistan. However, the goods to be counter delivered by Pakistan are of little interest to the U.S. seller. A Romanian company (switch trader) converts the Pakistani goods into cash, pays the U.S. exporter, and retains a commission.

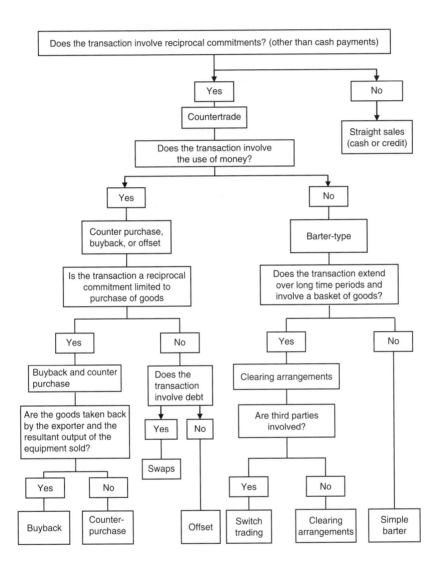

FIGURE 12.1. Classification of Forms of Countertrade *Source:* Figure 12.1 originally appeared in Hennart, J (1990). "Some Empirical Dimensions of Countertrade," *Journal of International Business Studies,* 21(2), p. 245; The Academy of International Business. Reprinted by permission.

INTERNATIONAL PERSPECTIVE 12.2.
Organizing for Countertrade

Once a firm has made a decision to countertrade, it has two organizational options: to use third parties such as consultants and trading houses, or establish a countertrade department within the company. Each approach has its own benefits and disadvantages.

The following is a brief overview of the benefits and costs of establishing a countertrade unit within the firm.

Advantages
- Direct contact with the customer
- Opportunity for learning and flexibility
- Confidentiality and control over the operation

Disadvantages
- Costly and mostly suitable for multinational companies with broad-based product lines.
- Complex and involves corporate planning and coordination of staff.
- Limited expertise; problems with disposing of countertraded goods.

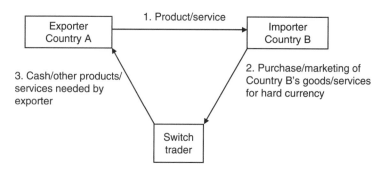

FIGURE 12.2. Switch Trading

Clearing Arrangements

Under these arrangements, two governments agree to purchase a certain volume of each other's goods and/or services over a certain period of time, usually a year. Each country sets up an account in one currency, for example, clearing dollar, pound, or local currency. When a trade imbalance exists, settlement of accounts can be in the form of hard-currency payments for the shortfall, transfer of goods, issuance of a credit against the following year's clearing arrangement, or by switch trading. In switch trading, the creditor country can sell its credit to a switch trader for a discount and receive cash payment. The switch trader will subsequently sell the corresponding goods to third parties (see Figure 12.3).

Example: A Swedish company, Sukab, accumulated a large surplus in its clearing account with Pakistan. Sukab sold its credit to Marubeni, a Japanese company, at a discount and Marubeni in turn liquidated this imbalance by purchasing Pakistani cotton and exporting it to a third county for hard currency (Anonymous, 1996).

Parallel Transactions

Buyback (Compensation Agreement)

In a buyback or compensation transaction, a private firm will sell or license technology or build a plant (with payment in hard currency) and agree to purchase, over a given number of years, a certain proportion of the output produced from the use of the technology or plant. The output is to be purchased in hard currency. However, since the products are closely related, a codependency exists between the trading parties (see Figure 12.4). The

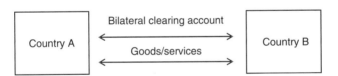

FIGURE 12.3. Clearing Arrangement

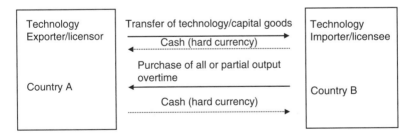

FIGURE 12.4. Buyback

duration of a compensation arrangement could range from a few years to thirty years or longer in cases in which the technology supplier (seller) is dependent upon the buyer's output for itself and its subsidiaries. The arrangement involves two contracts, each paid in hard currency, that is, one for the delivery of technology and equipment and another for the buyback of the resulting output. The two contracts are linked by a protocol that, inter alia, stipulates that the output to be purchased by the technology supplier is to be produced with the technology delivered. Since the agreement entails transfer of proprietary technology, it is quite important to pay special attention to the protection of patents, trademarks, and know-how, as well as to the rights of the technology recipient (importer/buyer) with respect to these industrial property rights.

> *Examples:* A Japanese company exports computer chip processing and design technology to Korea, Singapore, and Taiwan, with a promise to purchase a certain percentage of the output over a given period of time. Levi Strauss transfers its know-how and trademark to a Hungarian firm for the production and sale of its products, with an agreement to purchase and market the output in Western Europe.

Counterpurchase

As in compensation arrangement, counterpurchase consists of two parallel hard currency-for-goods transactions (see Figure 12.5). However, in counterpurchase, a firm sells goods and/or services to an importer, promising to purchase from the latter or other entities in the importing nation goods that are unrelated to the items sold. The duration of such transactions is often short (three to five years), and the commitment usually requires a reciprocal

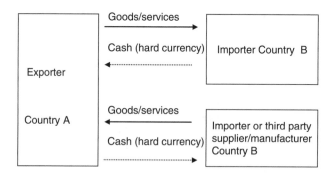

FIGURE 12.5. Counterpurchase

purchase of less than the full value of the original sale. In cases in which the reciprocal purchase involves goods that are of low quality or in excess supply, the firm usually resells them to trading companies at a discount. Since the arrangement is often governed by two separate contracts, financing can be organized in a way that is similar to any other export transaction. In addition to flexibility in financing, the contractual separation also provides for separate provisions with regard to guarantee coverage, maturity of payments, and deliveries. As in compensation agreements, the two contracts are linked by a third contract that ties the purchase and sales contracts together and includes terms such as the ratio between purchases and sales, starting time of both contracts, import-export verification system, and so forth (Welt, 1990; see International Perspective 12.3 on countertrade contracts).

> *Examples:* In 1989, PepsiCo and the former Soviet Union signed a $3 billion deal in which PepsiCo agreed to purchase and market Russian Vodka and ten Soviet-built ocean vessels in return for doubling its Soviet bottling network and nationwide distribution of soft drinks in aluminum and plastic bottles. Rockwell and the Government of Zimbabwe signed a contract in which Rockwell offered to purchase Zimbabwe's ferro chrome and nickel in exchange for its sale of a printing press to Zimbabwe.

Offsets

An offset is a transaction in which an exporter allows the purchaser, generally a foreign government, to "offset" the cost of purchasing its (the exporter's) product (Cole, 1987; see Figure 12.6). Such arrangements are mainly used for defense-related sales, sales of commercial aircraft, or sales of other high-technology products. Offsets are used by many countries as a way to compensate for the huge hard-currency payments resulting from the purchase, as well as to create investment opportunities and employment. Such arrangements became widespread after 1973 when OPEC sharply increased the price of oil and countries were left with limited hard currency to pay for major expenditures (Schaffer, 1989; Egan and Shipley, 1996).

Direct Offsets

These are contractual arrangements often involving goods or services related to the products exported. Direct offsets include coproduction, subcontractor production, investments, and technology transfer.

Coproduction: This is an overseas production arrangement, usually based on a government-to-government agreement that permits a foreign government or producer to acquire the technical information to manufacture

INTERNATIONAL PERSPECTIVE 12.3.
Negotiating Countertrade Contracts: Pointers

Costs: All costs are included into one price. The price also includes the commission payable to dispose of the countertraded goods.

Contract(s): One or separate contracts can be used. Separate contracts are signified by three legal documents: the original sales contract, which is similar to any standard export contract; the subsequent agreement to purchase from the original buyer a certain amount of goods over a given time period and some type of protocol that tie the two contracts together.

Barter contract: Barter usually requires one contract. Key provisions include: (1) description of goods to be sold and countertraded; (2) guarantee of quality; (3) penalty or other arrangements in the event of late delivery, failure to deliver, or delivery of nonconforming goods. This includes bank guarantee or other guarantee in the form of standby letter of credit in the event of default and providing for full payment; and (4) provisions for settlement of disputes.

Buy-backs, counterpurchase, or offsets: Such contracts require the use of one or separate contracts. Key provisions include: (1) the compensation ratio: this establishes the counterpurchase commitment by the original exporter; (2) range of products to be countertraded: parties must agree on the list of products to be purchased; (3) assignment clause: this enables the original seller to transfer its counterpurchase or buyback obligation to a trading house or a barter business club; (4) The penalty clause: this provides for penalties in the event that the original seller fails to fulfill its obligations (i.e., quality specifications and delivery schedules); (5) marketing restrictions: it may be important to secure the right to dispose of the countertraded goods in any market; and (6) provisions on force majeure (delay or default in performance caused by conditions beyond the party's control), applicable law (i.e., the law governing the contract), and dispute settlement.

all or part of an equipment or component originating in the exporting country. It may include a government-to-government production under license. The essential difference between coproduction and licensed production is that the former is normally a joint venture, while the latter does not entail ownership and/or management of the overseas production by the technology supplier. In coproduction, there is usually a government-to-government negotiation, whereas licensed production is based on direct commercial arrangements between the foreign manufacturer and host government or pro-

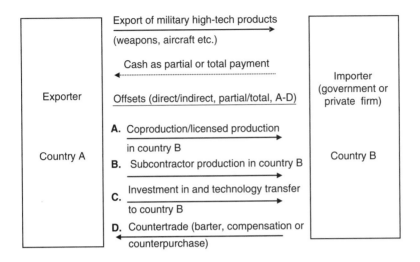

FIGURE 12.6. Offsets

ducer. In most cases, coproduction and licensed production are direct offsets because the resulting output directly fulfills part of the sales obligation.

> *Example:* France purchased AWACS (airborne warning and control system) aircraft from Boeing, based on a coproduction arrangement between the U.S. and French governments. According to the agreement, 80 percent of the contract value was to be offset by the purchase of engines produced through a joint venture between General Electric and a French firm.

Subcontractor production: This is usually a direct commercial arrangement between a manufacturer and an overseas producer (in the host country) for the production of a part or component of the manufacturer's export article to the host country. Such an arrangement does not often involve licensing of technological information.

> *Example:* In 1996, Italy announced plans to purchase four U212 submarines from Germany. The industrial cooperation agreement will give Italian companies substantial subcontracting work in building the submarines and their systems. Indirect offsets (i.e., arrangements involving goods and services unrelated to the exports) will also be utilized as compensation for the predominance of German-supplied subsystems and components.

Overseas investments: These are investments arising from the offset agreement that usually take the form of capital investment to establish or expand a company in the purchasing country.

> *Example:* The Greek government purchased forty F-16s, and as part of the offset, the U.S. supplier firms were required to undertake investment, trade, and technology transfer programs. The U.S. firms agreed to contribute $50 million in capital over a ten-year period.

Technology transfer: Even though technology transfer provisions could be included in coproduction or licensed production arrangements, they are often distinct from both categories. A technology transfer arrangement usually involves the provision of technical assistance and R & D capabilities to the joint venture partner or other firms as part of the offset agreement.

> *Example:* Spain purchases F-18 aircraft from the United States under an offset arrangement that requires the transfer of aerospace and other high technology to Spain, as well as the promotion of Spanish exports and tourism.

Indirect offsets are contractual arrangements in which goods and services unrelated to the exports are acquired from, or produced in, the host (purchasing) country. These include, but are not limited, to certain forms of foreign investment, technology transfer, and countertrade.

> *Example:* As part of the cooperative defense agreement, the Netherlands purchased patriot fire units from Raytheon Corporation of the United States for $305 million. Raytheon agreed to provide $115 million in direct offsets and $120 million in indirect offsets. The latter obligation was to be discharged through the purchase of goods and services in the Netherlands.

Arms sales account for a substantial part of offset transactions, which, in turn makes up for the largest percentage of countertrade deals.

COUNTERTRADE AND THE WTO

The prevalence of countertrade practices has directed the attention of policymakers to its potentially disruptive effects on international trade. Trade experts claim that countertrade represents a significant departure from the principles of free trade and could possibly undermine the delicate multilateral trading system that was carefully crafted since World War II. This movement toward bilateral trading arrangements deprives countries of the benefits of multilateral trade that GATT/WTO negotiated to confer upon members. Private countertrade transactions, however, fall outside the purview of the GATT, which regulates only governmental actions.

In addition, countertrade tends to undermine trade based on comparative advantages and prolongs inefficiency and misallocation of resources. For example, a country may have to purchase from a high-cost/low-quality overseas supplier to fulfill its obligation under the export arrangement. Countertrade also slows down the exchange process and results in higher transaction costs in the form of converting goods into money, warehousing, and discounting to a trader when it cannot use the goods received.

Countertrade is also inconsistent with the national treatment standard, which is embodied in most international and regional trade agreements. The national treatment standard of the GATT/WTO, for example, requires that imported goods be taxed and regulated in the same manner as domestically produced goods. Any commercial transaction that requires the overseas supplier (exporter) to purchase a specified portion of the value of the exports from the purchaser would violate the national treatment standard (Roessler, 1985).

Countertrade constitutes a restriction on imports. The GATT/WTO prohibits restrictions other than duties, taxes, or other charges applied to imports. This means that if import licenses are granted on the condition that the imports are linked to exports, such countertrade practices would constitute a trade restriction prohibited under the general agreement. Without this government restriction, the producer would be able to import any amount of product that efficiency and consumer demand dictated. Such restrictions would be in conformity with the agreement if they are imposed to safeguard a country's balance of payments (external financial position), as well as to protect against a sudden surge in imports of particular products (emergency actions).

COUNTERTRADE AND THE INTERNATIONAL MONETARY FUND

The International Monetary Fund (IMF) imposes a dual regime: on the one hand, it attempts to deter members from restricting international payments and transfers for current international transactions, while, on the other hand, it permits its members to regulate international capital movements as they see fit. Payments for current transactions involve an immediate quid pro quo (i.e., payments in connection with foreign trade, interest, profit, dividend payments, etc.), while capital payments are unilateral (loans, investments, etc.). A governmental measure requiring or stimulating countertrade would constitute an exchange restriction on current transactions if it involved a direct limitation on the availability or use of foreign currency.

GOVERNMENTS' ATTITUDES TOWARD COUNTERTRADE

Consistent with their commitment to a nondiscriminatory trading system, many countries are opposed to government-mandated countertrade because it distorts the free flow of trade and investment. Yet, they do not publicly discourage firms from engaging in countertrade (U.S. ITC, 1985; Office of Management and Budget, 1986).

The U.S. policy on countertrade was developed in 1983 by an interagency working group. The policy does the following:

- It prohibits federal agencies from promoting countertrade in their business or official contracts.
- It adopts a hands-off approach toward those arrangements which do not involve the U.S. government or are pursued by private parties. This means that the U.S. government will not oppose participation of U.S. companies in countertrade deals unless such activity has negative implications on national security.
- It provides no special accommodations for cases involving such transactions. The Export-Import Bank (Ex-Im Bank) will not provide financing support for the countertrade component of a transaction or accept countertrade as security, but the U.S. export component is eligible for all types of Ex-Im Bank support. Any repayment to Ex-Im Bank must be in hard currency and not conditional on the fulfillment of a side contract associated with countertrade.

In view of congressional concern with respect to such practices, the 1998 Trade Act mandated the establishment of an office of barter within the Department of Commerce's International Trade Administration and of an interagency group on countertrade. The Barter and Countertrade Unit established within the Department of Commerce now provides advisory services to firms interested in such transactions, while the interagency group on countertrade reviews and evaluates U.S. policy on countertrade and makes recommendations to the president and Congress.

Some countries have officially instituted mandatory countertrade requirements for any transaction over a certain value. Australia, for example, mandates local content and other investment requirements for all defense purchases valued at U.S.\$5 million and above (Liesch, 1991). Certain countries have passed laws providing for counterpurchase operations and the extension of bank guarantees in the form of performance bonds. Indonesia, for example, established a countertrade division within the Ministry of Trade and has mandated countertrade requirements for any transaction exceeding $500,000 (Verdun, 1985; Liesch, 1991). Other countries may not have an official policy on countertrade or may even be opposed to it due to their position on free trade. However, this opposition often yields to the realities of international trade and competition, and a number of these countries are seen providing tacit approval to such transactions (see International Perspective 12.4 for countertrade with Latin American countries).

CHAPTER SUMMARY

What is countertrade?

Countertrade is any commercial arrangement in which the exporter is required to accept, in partial or total settlement of his or her deliveries, a supply of products from the importing country. Barter could be traced to ancient times. Presently, countertrade is estimated to account for 15 to 20 percent of world trade.

Benefits of countertrade

Benefits for buyers

1. Transfer of technology
2. Alleviation of balance of payments difficulties
3. Market access and maintenance of stable prices

Benefits for exporters

1. Increased sales opportunities
2. Access to sources of supply
3. Flexibility in prices

Theories on countertrade

1. Countertrade is positively correlated with a country's level of exports.
2. Countertrade is partly motivated in order to substitute for FDI.
3. The stricter the level of exchange controls, the higher the level of countertrade activity.

INTERNATIONAL PERSPECTIVE 12.4.
Countertrade with Latin American Countries

A recent study on countertrade with Latin American countries (Angelidis et al., 2004) reports the results of a survey of firms engaged in countertrade transactions. The survey reveals that the following industries account for over 75 percent of transactions: defense (33.3 percent), manufacturing (30.3 percent), and chemicals (27.3 percent). The participants largely employed counterpurchases and offsets.

The survey also provides a detailed analysis of the major reasons for and challenges of countertrading with these countries.

Reasons for countertrade
• Inadequate foreign currency reserves
• A way to gain competitive advantage
• Only way to do business, demanded by customers
• Increases production capacity and helps achieve growth
• Supply of reliable and low cost inputs
• Circumvent protectionist regulations; reduce adverse impact of foreign currency fluctuations
• Release blocked funds
• Increased difficulty of obtaining credit for the buyer
• Availability of expertise in countertrade for buyer or seller

Challenges of countertrade
• Often involves complicated and time-consuming negotiations
• May result in increase in transaction costs, product mismatch, and the purchase of low quality goods
• Problems with disposition of acquired (lack of ready) merchandise, price-setting as well as loss of purchasing flexibility
• Involvement of third parties and the possibility of customers becoming competitors

Forms of countertrade

Exchange of goods/services for goods/services

1. *Barter:* Direct exchange of goods and services between two trading parties.
2. *Switch trading:* An arrangement in which the switch trader will buy or market countertraded goods for hard currency.
3. *Clearing arrangement:* A method in which two governments agree to purchase a certain volume of each other's goods/services over a given period of time. In the event of trade imbalance, settlement could be in

hard currency payments, transfer of goods, issuance of a credit, or use of switch trading.

Parallel transactions

1. *Buyback:* An arrangement in which a private firm will sell or license technology to an overseas customer with an agreement to purchase part of the output produced from the use of such technology. The agreement involves two contracts, both of which are discharged by payment of hard currency.
2. *Counterpurchase:* Two parallel transactions in which a firm exports a product to an overseas buyer with a promise to purchase from the latter or other parties in the country goods not related to the items exported.
3. *Offsets:* A transaction in which an exporter allows the purchaser, usually a foreign government, to reduce the cost of purchasing the exporter's product by coproduction, subcontracting, or investments and transfers of technology.

Offsets

Direct offsets

1. *Coproduction:* Joint venture or licensing arrangements with overseas customer
2. *Subcontractor production:* Arrangement for production in the importing country of parts or components of the export product destined to the latter
3. *Investments and transfer of technology:* Certain offset agreements provide for investments and technology transfer to the importing country

Indirect offsets

Offset arrangements in which goods and services unrelated to the exports are acquired from or produced in the importing country.

Countertrade and the GATT/WTO

Concerns of the GATT/WTO with countertrade:

1. Countertrade represents a significant departure from the principles of free trade based on comparative advantage.
2. Countertrade results in higher transaction costs.

3. Countertrade is inconsistent with the national treatment standard which is embodied in most trade agreements.

Governments' attitude toward countertrade

U.S. government policy toward countertrade:

1. U.S. government prohibits federal agencies from promoting countertrade in their business.
2. Adopts a hands-off approach in relation to private transactions.

Some countries have a countertrade requirement for certain purchases exceeding a given amount. Such transactions are quite common in defense purchases.

REVIEW QUESTIONS

1. What are the major factors accounting for the resurgence of countertrade?
2. What is the benefit of countertrade for exporters?
3. "Countertrade is used as a substitute for FDI." Discuss.
4. What is the difference between switch trading and clearing arrangement?
5. Describe the steps involved in a typical barter transaction.
6. Compare and contrast buyback with counterpurchase arrangement.
7. Discuss direct offsets and its components.
8. What are the challenges of countertrade with Latin American countries?
9. What is the U.S. government attitude toward countertrade?
10. Discuss the concerns of WTO with countertrade.

CASE 12.1. THE BOFORS-INDIA COUNTERTRADE DEAL

Bofors AB is a Swedish company that specializes in the manufacturing and sales of weapon systems such as antiaircraft/antitank guns, artillery, and other ammunition. The Indian government concluded an agreement with Bofors AB for the purchase of 410 FH77B howitzers ($1.3 billion) in 1986. The FH77B howitzer is a powerful, highly mobile artillery system. It has a gun with a range of 30 km and a capability to fire three rounds in 13 seconds. It can be integrated with a 6 3 6 all terrain vehicle.

The agreement provided for the purchase of goods from India amounting to not less than 50 percent of the value of the contract. Given its lack of experience in countertrade, Bofors AB signed a contract with other Swedish and U.S. trading companies to fulfill its countertrade agreement with India. Among these companies, Sukab took the leading role due to its vast experience in international trade and expertise in countertrade. Sukab is owned by over 80 Swedish companies and set up after World War II to promote Swedish exports.

Pursuant to the agreement, Sukab promoted the sale of Indian goods in Sweden through various channels including seminars held by Swedish trade councils and chambers of commerce. It also set up offices in India to provide export training, that is, on the best ways and means of exporting Indian goods to Sweden.

The Indian government had to approve of all the products being exported. Bofors AB was provided with a list of approved products. Certain products were specifically excluded from exports.

The major factor that motivated India to enter into the countertrade arrangement was its lack of sufficient hard currency to pay for the purchase of the howitzers. The countertrade arrangement provided an opportunity to India to generate enough hard currency to fulfill a portion of its commitments. Furthermore, the arrangement allowed India to expand its distribution channels and gain new markets. The countertrade arrangement also allowed Bofors AB to win the contract over other competing firms.

Questions

1. Do you think this to be an ideal trading arrangement for Bofors AB?
2. Would this form of trade arrangement be more beneficial to India than Bofors? Explain.

CASE 12.2. OFFSETS IN U.S. DEFENSE TRADE

U.S. defense contractors entered into 513 offset agreements valued at $55.1 billion during the period 1993-2004. The agreements were signed with forty-one foreign governments for the purchase of U.S. defense weapon systems totaling $77.2 billion. The value of the offset agreements accounted for 71.4 percent of the total value of the related export contracts during the period. Most of these agreements involved sales of aerospace defense systems such as missiles, aircraft engines, and so on.

Offsets and related defense system exports are concentrated among a few purchaser governments. Ten governments (out of a total of 41) accounted for 77.4 percent of the defense system purchases and 75 percent of the offset agreements (1993-2004; see Table 12.1).

European countries accounted for the majority of the U.S. weapon system exports (47 percent) and offset activity (66 percent) followed by Asian countries. They often require a minimum of 90 percent offsets on purchases of U.S. defense systems. The average offset requirement by non-European countries was estimated at 47 percent during 1993-2004. However, it has shown a marked increase over the years. The average offset requirement (by value) demanded by S. Korean firms, for example, increased from 33 percent (1993-1998) to 69 percent (1999-2004).

The increase in offset requirements by purchasing governments is partly motivated by the need to increase domestic employment and sustain domestic defense companies, as well as deflect domestic political concerns about significant public outlays for foreign-made defense systems.

Multipliers are incentives used by purchasing countries to stimulate particular types of offset transactions. Prime contractors, for example, receive added credit toward their obligation above the actual value of the transaction when multipliers are used. A negative multiplier is used to discourage

TABLE 12.1. Top Ten Governments by Export Contracts (1993-2004) (Billion U.S. $)

Country	No. of Agreements	Export Contracts	Offset Agreements
United Kingdom	41	11.89	10.05
Taiwan	39	10.84	2.17
S. Korea	58	8.28	5.13
Greece	48	6.31	7.15
Canada	25	4.42	4.28
Israel	46	4.42	4.28
Saudi Arabia	N/A[a]	4.09	1.43
Poland	N/A	4.09	1.43
Australia	16	3.49	1.60
Turkey	17	2.69	1.25

[a]N/A: Not available.

Source: U.S. Department of Commerce, 2005.

certain types of offsets. It is estimated that about 8.4 percent of European offset transactions had a multiplier greater than one. In the case of negative multipliers, U.S. exporters (contractors) are only credited a portion of the total value of the transaction (see Table 12.2).

A cursory evaluation of the distribution of U.S. offset transactions shows that subcontracts and coproduction (foreign production of goods/services related to the weapon system sold) accounted for 78.3 percent of the value of all direct offset transactions ($10 billion). The purchases category of indirect offsets (foreign production of goods and services) accounted for 62.9 percent of all indirect offset transactions ($12.1 billion) for 1993-2004 (see Table 12.3).

TABLE 12.2. Multipliers by Region and Dollar Values (Billion U.S. $) (1993-2004)

Region	Value of Transactions with Multiplier , 1	Value of Transactions with Multiplier 5 1	Value of Transactions with Multiplier . 1	Total Value
Europe	0.79 (3.7%)	18.79 (88%)	1.80 (8.4%)	21.38
Middle East/Africa	0.05 (1.1%)	4.50 (93.1%)	0.28 (5.8%)	4.83
Asia	0.25 (5%)	4.60 (90%)	50.27 (5.3%)	5.13
N and S. America	0.09 (8%)	1.11 (91%)	0.01 (1.5%)	1.23

Source: U.S. Department of Commerce, 2005.

TABLE 12.3. Offset Transactions by Category, 1993-2004

Category	%
Direct	
Subcontract	62
Coproduction	16.3
Technology transfer	12.1
Training	3.7
Others	5.8
Indirect	
Purchases	62.9
Technology transfer	15.6
Credit transfer	7.4
Others	14.1

Source: U.S. Department of Commerce, 2005.

Questions

1. Does the practice of offsets in defense contracts violate the U.S. official position (as well as its commitment to WTO) on countertrade?
2. Do you think such practices should be extended to commercial products? Discuss.

SECTION V:
FINANCING TECHNIQUES
AND VEHICLES

Chapter 13

Capital Requirements
and Private Sources of Financing

Many small and medium-sized businesses suffer from undercapitalization and/or poor management of financial resources, often during the first few years of operation. Typically, the entrepreneur either overestimates demand for the product or severely underestimates the need for capital resources and organizational skills. Undercapitalization may also be a result of the entrepreneur's aversion to equity financing (fear of loss of control over the business) or the lender's resistance to provide capital due to the entrepreneur's lack of credit history and a comprehensive business plan (Gardner, 1994; Hutchinson, 1995).

Large corporations have an advantage in raising capital compared with small businesses. They have greater bargaining strength with lenders, they can issue securities, and they have greater access to capital markets around the world. However, major changes are taking place in small/medium-sized business financing due to three important factors: technology, globalization, and deregulation. Information technology enables the financial world to operate efficiently, to decentralize while improving control. It also provides businesses seeking capital to choose from a vast range of financial instruments (Grimaud, 1995). Globalization allows businesses to turn increasingly to international markets to raise capital. With a touch of a button, businesses will have access to individual or corporate sources of finance around the world. With deregulation, in many countries, competition in financial products is allowed across all depository institutions. The distinction between investment and commercial banking is quite blurred, and both sectors now compete in the small business financing market.

It is important to properly evaluate how much capital is needed, in what increments, and over what time period. First are the initial capital needs to start the export-import business. Start-up costs are not large if the exporter-importer begins as an agent (without buying for resale) and uses his or her own home as an office. Initial capital needs are for office supplies and equipment—telephone, fax, computer—and a part-time assistant. The business could also be started on a part-time basis until it provides sufficient revenues to cover expenses, including the owner's salary. However, when the business is commenced with the intention of establishing an independent company with products purchased for resale (merchant, distributor, etc.), a lot more capital is needed to prepare a business plan, travel, purchase, and distribute the product, and exhibit in major trade shows. Second, capital is needed to finance growth and for expansion of the business. It is thus critical to anticipate capital needs during the time of growth and expansion as well as during abnormal increases in accounts receivable, inventory levels, and changes in the business cycle.

The capital needs and financing alternatives of an export-import business are determined by its stage of evolution, ownership structure, distribution channel choice, and other pertinent factors. A very small sum of money is often needed to start the business as an agent because no payments are made for merchandise, transportation, or distribution of the product. However, initial capital needs are substantial if a person starts the business as a merchant, distributor, or trading company with products available for resale. This entails payments for transportation, distribution, advertising and promotion, travel, and other expenses.

Capital needs at the start-up stage may be smaller compared to those needed during the growth and expansion period. However, this depends on the degree of expansion and the capital needed to support additional marketing efforts, inventories, and accounts receivable. The ownership structure of an export-import firm tends to have an important influence on financing alternatives and little or no influence on capital needs. Studies on small business financing indicate the following salient features:

- Incorporated companies are more likely to receive equity (and other nondebt) financing than debt financing because lenders perceive the incorporated entity as having a greater incentive to take on risky ventures due to its limited liability (Brewer et al., 1996).
- Younger firms are more likely to obtain equity (nondebt) than debt financing. The probability of receiving debt financing increases with age. This is consistent with standard theories of capital structure, which state that such businesses have little or no track record on which to base financing decisions and are often perceived as risky by lenders.

- Firms with high growth opportunities, a volatile cash flow, and low liquidation value are more likely to finance their business with equity than debt. In firms with high growth opportunities, conflicts are likely between management and shareholders over the direction and pace of growth options, and this reduces the chances of debt financing. However, businesses with a good track record and high liquidation value (with assets that can be easily liquidated) have a greater chance of financing their business with debt rather than equity (Williamson, 1988; Stulz, 1990; Schleifer and Vishny, 1992).

CAPITAL SOURCES FOR EXPORT-IMPORT BUSINESSES

Capital needs to start the business or to finance current operations or expansion can be obtained from different sources. Internal financing should be explored before resorting to external funding sources. This includes using one's own resources for initial capital needs and then retaining more profits in the business or reducing accounts receivables and inventories to meet current obligations and finance growth and expansion. Such reductions in receivables or inventories should be applied carefully so as not to lead to a loss of customers or goodwill, both of which are critical to the viability of the business.

External financing takes different forms and businesses use one or a combination of the following:

- *Debt or equity financing:* Debt financing occurs when an export-import firm borrows money from a lender with a promise to repay (principal and interest) at some predetermined future date. Equity financing involves raising money from private investors in exchange for a percentage of ownership (and sometimes participation in management) of the business. The major disadvantage with equity financing is the owner's potential loss of control over the business.
- *Short-term, intermediate, or long-term financing:* Short-term financing involves a credit period of less than one year, while intermediate financing is credit extended for a period of one to five years. In long-term financing, the credit period ranges between five and twenty years.
- *Investment, inventory, or working capital financing:* Investment financing is money used to start the business (computer, fax machine, telephone, etc.). Inventory capital is money raised to purchase products for resale. Working capital supports current operations such as rent, advertising, supplies, wages, and so on. All three could be financed by debt or equity.

Several sources of funding are available to existing export-import businesses that have established track records. However, financing is quite limited for initial capital needs, and the entrepreneur has to use his or her own resources or borrow from family or friends. It is also important to evaluate funding sources not just in terms of availability (willingness to provide funding) but also in regard to the capital's cost and its effect on business profits, as well as any restrictions imposed by lenders on the operations of the business. Certain loan agreements, for example, prevent the sale of accounts receivable or equipment, or require the representation of lenders in the firm's management. The following is an overview of possible sources of capital for export/import businesses.

Internal Sources

This is the best source of financing for initial capital needs or expansion because there is no interest to be paid back or equity in the business to be surrendered. Start-up businesses have limited chances of obtaining loans so self-funding becomes the only alternative. Internal sources include the following:

- Money in saving accounts, certificates of deposit, and other personal accounts
- Money in stocks, bonds, and money market funds

External Sources

Family and Friends

This is the second-best option for raising capital for an export-import business. The money should be borrowed with a promissory note indicating the date of payment and the amount of principal and interest to be paid. As long as the business pays a market interest rate, it is entitled to a tax deduction and the lender gets the interest income. In the event of failure by the business to repay the loan, the lender may be able to deduct the amount as a short-term capital loss. Such an arrangement protects the lender and also prevents the latter from acquiring equity in the business.

Banks and Other Commercial Lenders

The largest challenge to successful lending is the turnover rate of small businesses. In general, fewer than half of all small businesses survive beyond the third-year mark. However, the survival rate for export-import businesses is generally higher than that of other businesses. Due to the level of risk, banks and other commercial lenders tend to avoid start-up financing without collateral. A 1994 IBM consulting group survey of small businesses revealed that bank credit was the most popular primary source of capital in the United States, followed by internally generated funds. Credit cards were not a significant source of financing. Of the businesses, 58 percent maintained a working capital line of credit, followed by term loans (42 percent). Only 3 percent of the businesses used Small Business Administration (SBA) loans (Anonymous, 1995).

Banks remain the cheapest source of borrowed capital for export-import firms as well as other small businesses. To persuade a bank to provide a loan, it is essential to prepare a business plan that sets clear financial goals, including how the loan will be repaid. Banks always review the ability of the borrower to service the debt, whether sufficient cash is invested in the business, as well as the nature of the collateral that is to be provided as a guarantee for the loan. Bankers always investigate the five Cs in making lending decisions: character (trustworthiness, reliability), capacity (ability and track record in meeting financial obligations), capital (significant equity in the business), collateral (security for the loan), and condition (the effect of overall economic conditions) (Lorenz-Fife, 1997). Even though it is often difficult to obtain a commercial loan for start-up capital, a good business plan and a strong, experienced management team may entice lenders to make a decision in favor of providing the loan. The following are different types of financing.

Asset-based financing. Banks and other commercial lenders provide loans secured by fixed assets, such as land, buildings, and machinery. For example, they will lend up to 80 percent of the value of one's home minus the first mortgage. These are often long-term loans payable over a ten-year period. Business assets, such as accounts receivable, inventories, and personal assets (savings accounts, cars, jewelry, etc.), can be used as collateral for business loans. With accounts receivable and inventories, commercial lenders usually lend up to 50 percent and 80 percent of their respective values. Use of saving accounts as collateral could reduce interest payment on a loan. Suppose the interest on the savings account is 4 percent and the business loan is financed at 12 percent. The actual interest rate that is to be paid is reduced to 8 percent.

Lines of credit. These are short-term loans (for a period of one year) intended for purchases of inventory and payment of operating costs. They may sometimes be secured by collateral such as accounts receivable based on the creditworthiness and reputation of the borrower. A certain amount of money (line of credit) is made available, and interest is often charged on the amount used. Certain lenders do not allow use of such lines of credit until the business's checking account is depleted.

Personal and commercial loans. Owners with good credit standing could obtain personal loans that are backed by the mere signature and guarantee of the borrower. They are short-term loans and subject to relatively high interest rates. Commercial loans are also short-term loans that are often backed by stocks, bonds, and life insurance policies as collateral. The cash value of a life insurance policy can also be borrowed and repaid over a certain period of time.

Credit cards. Credit cards are generally not recommended for capital needs for new or existing export-import businesses because they are one of the costliest forms of business financing. They charge extremely high interest rates and there is no limit on how much credit card issuers can charge for late fees and other penalties (Fraser, 1996). If financing options are limited, credit cards could be used if the probability of the business succeeding is very high (if you have made definite arrangements with foreign buyers, etc). One should shop for the lowest available rates and plan for bank or credit union financing at a later date, if the debt cannot be retired within a short time period, possibly with an account receivable or inventory as collateral. A survey of small and medium-sized businesses by Arthur Anderson and Company in 1994 showed that 29 percent of businesses use credit cards for capital needs (Field, Korn, and Middleton, 1995).

Small Business Administration (SBA)

The SBA has several facilities for lending that can be used by export-import businesses for capital needs at different stages of their growth cycle (see Table 13.1).

Small business investment companies (SBICs). SBICs are private companies funded by the SBA that were established to provide loan (sometimes equity) capital to small businesses. Even though they prefer to finance existing small businesses with a track record, they also consider loans for start-up capital. Members of a minority group could also consider a similar lending agency funded by the SBA that is intended to finance minority start-up or existing businesses.

The SBA guaranteed loan (7(a) loan guarantee program). The guarantee by the SBA permits a lending institution to provide long-term loans to start-up or existing small businesses. Export-import businesses can use the money for their working capital needs, for example, to purchase inventory and help carry a receivable until it is paid, to purchase real estate to house

TABLE 13.1. SBA Funding for Export-Import and Other Small Businesses

Program	Brief Overview
1. The 7(a) Loan Guarantee: Start-up/ expansion/ working capital	Loans made by private lenders are guaranteed up to $2 million, which could cover up to 50 percent of the loan. Funds could be used to buy land and buildings, to expand facilities, to purchase equipment, or for working capital.
2. Certified Development Company (CDC)/ 504 Loan	CDCs are nonprofit economic development agencies, certified by the SBA. The owner is to contribute a minimum of 10 percent equity in the business. The loans are available up to $750,000. Loans can be used to purchase land, for improvement or renovation of facilities, and to purchase machinery or equipment. Project assets are often used as collateral. It cannot be used for working capital. (Up to 40 percent cost of fixed assets.)
3. Small Business Investment Companies (SBICs)	They are licensed by SBA and lend their own capital as well as funds borrowed through the federal government to small businesses, both new and already established. SBICs make either equity investments or long-term loans to companies with growth potential. Investment is not to exceed 20 percent of its private capital in securities or guarantees in any one concern. (Loans for start-up or expansion.)
4. Low Documentation	Designed to increase the availability of funds under $100,000 and to expedite the loan review process. (Loan guarantees for start-up or expansion/working capital.)
5. International Trade Loan	Used for businesses preparing to engage in, or already engaged in, international trade, or for those adversely affected by competition from imports. Used to develop and expand export market or for working capital. Loans are guaranteed up to $2,000,000. (Loan guarantees to expand market/working capital.)
6. Fast track	This was designed to increase capital available to businesses seeking loans up to $250,000. It is currently offered as a pilot with a limited number of lenders. (Loan guarantee for start-up/expansion/working capital.)
7. Export Working Capital	This was designed to provide short-term working capital to exporters. Maximum loan guarantee is $750,000. Loan requests above $833,333 are processed by Ex-Im Bank. (Loan guarantee.)
8. Microloans	These range from $100 to $25,000. Funds available to nonprofit intermediaries, who in turn make loans to small business borrowers. Collateral and personal guarantee are required. Loan maturity may be as long as six years. (Loan for start-up/expansion/working capital.)

the business, and for acquisition of furniture and fixtures. The SBA guarantee is available only after the business has failed to obtain financing on reasonable terms from other private sources. It is considered to be a lender of last resort.

The Certified Development Company. The Certified Development Company (CDC 504) program assists in the development and expansion of small firms and the creation of jobs. This program is designed to provide fixed-asset financing and cannot be used for working capital or inventory, consolidating or repaying debt. (For an overview of SBA loans, see International Perspective 13.1)

Finance Companies

The following are different ways of raising capital from finance companies to start or expand an export-import business.

Loans from insurance companies and pension funds. Life insurance policies can be used as collateral to borrow money for capital needs. Pension funds also provide loans to businesses with attractive growth prospects. Pension funds and insurance company loans are intermediate and long-term

INTERNATIONAL PERSPECTIVE 13.1.
SBA Loans and Their Features

1. **Guaranty Loans:** The loans are made and disbursed by private lenders and guaranteed by SBA up to a certain amount. This means that if the borrower defaults on the loan, SBA will purchase an agreed-upon percentage of the unpaid balance. Direct and participation loans (loans made jointly by SBA and other lenders) are quite few and have even decreased over the years.
2. **Interest Rates:** Unless otherwise stated, maximum rates for guaranteed loans are 2.25 percent above prime for a loan greater than $50,000 with maturity of less than seven years and 2.75 percent above prime for loans from seven to twenty-five years. Rates on loans under $50,000 may be higher.
3. **Guarantee Fee:** Payment of a guarantee fee is required for all guaranteed loans. Loans are to be secured by a collateral and personal guarantee.
4. **Guarantee of Last Resort:** SBA loans are provided as a matter of last resort, that is, when borrowers cannot obtain credit without SBA guarantee. The borrower is expected to have some personal equity to operate the business on a sound financial basis.

credits (five to fifteen years). Banks often introduce such lending agencies to their clients when the funds are needed for longer than the banks' maximum maturity period.

Commercial finance companies. These companies grant short-term loans using accounts receivable, inventories, or equipment as collateral. They can also factor (buy) accounts receivable at a discount and provide the export-import firm the necessary capital for growth and expansion. Factoring is a way of turning a firm's accounts receivable into immediate cash without creating new debt. The factoring company will collect the accounts receivable (A/R), assume credit risks associated with the A/R, conduct investigations on the firm's existing and prospective accounts, as well as do the bookkeeping with respect to the credit. In most cases, a factoring company will advance 50 to 90 percent of the face value of the receivables and later pay the balance less the factor's discount (4 to 7 percent of face value of receivables) once the receivables are collected. An export-import firm could easily factor its receivables so long as it sells to government clients or to major companies that have good credit. The disadvantage with this method is that it is expensive and could absorb a good part of the firm's profits.

Equity Sources

For many export-import businesses, the ability to raise equity finance is quite limited. Although such funding provides the owner with initial capital needs, money for expansion, or working capital, it means some dilution of ownership and control. Finding compatible business partners and shareholders is always difficult. There are three sources for equity funding:

- Family and friends
- *Business angels (invisible venture capitalists):* Business angels provide start-up or expansion capital and are the biggest providers of equity capital for small businesses. They can be found through networking advertisements, newspapers, or the World Wide Web. This segment is estimated to represent about 2,000 individuals or businesses investing between $10 billion to $20 billion each year in over 30,000 businesses (Lorenz-Fife, 1997).
- *Venture capitalists:* Venture capitalists provide equity capital to businesses that are already established and need working or expansion capital. The Small Business Administration (SBA) estimates that 500 venture capital firms are currently investing about $4 billion a year in some 3,000 ventures. They may not be suitable for small export-import firms because (1) their minimum investment is about $50,000

to $100,000; (2) they seldom provide funding for start-up capital because they are interested in companies with a proven track record and market position; and (3) they expect high returns (10 to 15 percent) on their investments over a relatively short period of time.

PRIVATE SOURCES OF EXPORT FINANCING

In many export transactions, the buyer is unable or unwilling to pay for the goods at the time of delivery. This means that the seller has to agree to payment at some future date or that the buyer should seek financing from third parties. The seller may seek financing from the buyer or third parties for purchasing goods from suppliers, to pay for labor, or to arrange for transportation and insurance (preshipment financing). The exporter may also need postshipment financing of the resulting account or accounts receivable or both (Silvester, 1995).

Competitive finance is a crucial element in export strategies, especially for small and medium-sized companies. Exporters should carefully consider the type of financing required, the length of time for repayment, the loan's effect on price and profit, as well as the various risks that may be associated with such financing.

In extending credit to overseas customers, it is important to recognize the following:

1. Normal commercial terms range from 30 to 180 days for sales of consumer goods, industrial materials, and agricultural commodities. Custom-made or high-value capital equipment may warrant longer repayment periods.
2. An allowance may have to be made for longer shipment periods than are found in domestic trade because foreign buyers are often unwilling to have the credit period start before receiving the goods.
3. Customers are usually charged interest on credit periods of a year or longer and seldom on short-term credit of up to 180 days. Even though the provision of favorable financing terms makes a product more competitive, the exporter should carefully assess such financing against considerations of cost and risk of default.

Financing by the Exporter

Open Account

Under this arrangement, an exporter will transfer possession or ownership of the merchandise on a deferred-payment basis (payment deferred for an agreed period of time). This can be done in the case of creditworthy customers who have proven track records. In the case of customers who are not well-known to the exporter, such arrangements should not be undertaken without taking out export credit insurance.

Consignment Sales

Importers do not pay for the merchandise until it is sold to a third party. Exporters could take out an insurance policy to cover them against risk of nonpayment.

Financing by the Overseas Customer

Advance Payment

The buyer is required to pay before shipment is effected. The advance payment may comprise of the entire price or an agreed-upon percentage of the purchase price. An importer may secure the advance payment through a performance guarantee provided by a third party. Export trading or export management companies, for example, often purchase goods on an advance-payment or cash-on-delivery basis, thus eliminating the need for financing. They can also use their vast international networks to help the exporter obtain credit and credit insurance.

Progress Payment

Payments are tied to partial performance of the contract, such as production, partial shipment, and so on. This means that a mix of advance and progress payments meets the financing needs of the exporter.

Financing by Third Parties

Short-Term Methods

Loan secured by a foreign account receivable. An exporter can borrow money from a bank or finance company to meet its short-term working capital needs by using its foreign account receivable as collateral. In most cases, the overseas customer is not notified about the loan. As the customer makes payment to the exporter, the exporter, in turn, repays the loan to the lender. It is also possible to notify the overseas customer about the collateral and instruct the latter to pay bills directly to the lender. This may, however, put to question the financial standing of the exporter in the eyes of the overseas buyer.

An exporter can usually borrow 80 to 85 percent of the face value of its accounts receivable if the receivables are insured and the exporter and overseas customer have good credit ratings.

Most banks are reluctant to lend against receivables that are not insured. The bank's security is effected through assignment of the exporter's foreign accounts receivable. Documentary collections are easier and less expensive to finance than sales on open accounts because the draft in documentary collections is a negotiable instrument (unlike open account sales, which are accompanied by an invoice and transport documents) that can easily be sold or discounted before maturity. Although most lenders are interested in providing a loan against foreign receivables, it is not uncommon to find some that would purchase them with full or limited recourse. In both cases, most banks require insurance. (Once the receivables are sold, the exporter will be able to remove the receivables and the loan from its balance sheet.)

Trade/banker's acceptance. This arises when a draft drawn by the seller is accepted by the overseas customer to pay a certain sum of money on an agreed-upon date. The exporter could obtain a loan using the acceptance as collateral or discount the acceptance to a financial institution for payment. In cases in which the debt is not acknowledged in the form of a draft, the exporter could sell or discount the invoice (invoice acceptance) before maturity. In both cases, the acceptances are usually sold without recourse to the exporter and the latter is relieved from the responsibility of collection.

A draft drawn on, and accepted by, a bank is called a banker's acceptance. Once accepted, the draft becomes a primary obligation of the accepting bank to pay at maturity. This occurs in the case of documents against acceptance (documentary collection or acceptance credit), whereby payment is to be made at a specified date in the future. The bank returns the draft to the seller with an endorsement of its acceptance, guaranteeing payment to the seller (exporter) on the due date. The exporter may then sell the accepted draft at a discount to the bank or any other financial institution. The exporter could also secure a loan using the draft as collateral. The marketability of a banker's or trade acceptance is dependent on the creditworthiness of the party accepting the draft.

Letter of credit. In addition to the acceptance credit discussed previously, the letter of credit could be an important instrument of financing exports:

1. *Transferable letter of credit:* Using this method, the exporter transfers its rights under the credit to another party, usually a supplier, who receives payment. When the supplier presents the necessary documents to the advising bank, the supplier's invoice is replaced with the exporter's invoice for the full value of the original credit. The advising

bank pays the supplier the value of the invoice and will pay the difference to the exporter.

2. *Assignment of proceeds under the letter of credit:* The beneficiary (exporter) may assign either the entire amount or a percentage of the proceeds of the L/C to a specified third party, usually a supplier. This allows the exporter to make purchases with limited capital by using the overseas buyer's credit. It does not require the assent of the buyer or the buyer's bank.

3. *Back-to-back letters of credit:* A letter of credit is issued on the strength of another letter of credit. Such credits are issued when a supplier or subcontractor demands payment from the exporter before collections are received from the customer. The exporter remains obligated to perform under the original credit, and if default occurs, the bank is left holding a worthless collateral.

Factoring. Factoring is a continuous arrangement between a factoring concern and the exporter, whereby the factor purchases export receivables for a somewhat discounted price (usually 2 to 4 percent less than the full value). The amount of the discount depends on a number of factors, including the kind of products involved, the customer, the factoring entity, and the importing country. Factoring enables exporters to offer terms of sale on open account without assuming the credit risk. Importers also prefer factoring because by buying on open account, they forgo costly payment arrangements such as letters of credit. It also frees up their working capital. In the case of importers that have not yet established a track record, banks often will not issue letters of credit and open account sales may be the only available option.

In export factoring, the exporter receives immediate payment and the burden of collection is eliminated. Factors have ties to banks and financial institutions in other countries through networks such as Factors Chain International, which enables them to check the creditworthiness of an overseas customer, to authorize credit, and to assume financial risk.

Increases in global trade and competition have resulted in the search for alternative forms of financing to accommodate the diverse needs of customers. In highly competitive markets, concluding a successful export deal often depends on the seller's ability to obtain trade finance at the most favorable terms for the overseas customer.

International factoring has grown by about 500 percent during the past ten years, amounting to $20 billion in 1994. In the United States, the factoring industry handles about $2 billion in foreign trade (Ioannou, 1995). The export factoring business grew by 14 percent in 1991, compared with a 9 percent increase in domestic factoring (Ring, 1993). It is now available in about forty countries, mostly concentrated in North America, Western Europe, and Asia. Even though export factoring has been traditionally associated with the sale of textiles, apparel, footwear, or carpets, it is now used for a host of diversified products.

A typical export factoring procedure includes the following steps: Upon receipt of an order from an overseas customer, the exporter verifies with the factor, through its overseas affiliate, the customer's credit standing and determines whether the factor is willing to authorize credit and to assume financial risk. If the factor's decision is in favor of authorizing credit to the overseas customer, then the parties follow the procedure described in Figure 13.1.

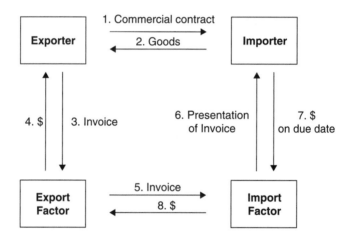

FIGURE 13.1. Export factoring: (1) the exporter and importer enter into a commercial contract and agree on the terms of sale (i.e., open account), (2) the exporter ships the goods to the importer, (3) the exporter submits the invoice to the export factor, (4) the export factor provides (cash in advance) funds to the exporter against receivables until money is collected from the importer. The exporter often receives up to 30 percent of the value of the receivables ahead of time and pay the factor interest on the money received, or the factor pays the exporter, less a commission charge, when receivables are due (or shortly thereafter). The commission often ranges between 1 and 3 percent, (5) the export factor passes the invoice to the import factor for assumption of credit risk, administration, and collection of the receivables, (6) the import factor presents the invoice to the importer for payment on the agreed-upon date, (7) the importer pays the import factor, and (8) the import factor pays the export factor. In cases where the export factor advanced funds up to a certain percentage (e.g., 30 percent) of the exporter's receivables, the remaining portion (70 percent of receivables less interest or other charges) is paid by the export factor to the exporter.

Arrangements with factors are made either with recourse (exporter liable in the event of default by buyer or other problems) or without recourse in which case a larger discount may be required since the exporter is free of liability. (For advantages and disadvantages of this financing method, see Table 13.2.)

Intermediate- and Long-Term Methods

Buyer credit. Some export sales, such as those involving capital equipment, often require financing terms that extend over several years. The importer may obtain credit from a bank or other financial institution to pay the exporter. The seller often cooperates in structuring the financing arrangements to make them suitable to the needs of the buyer.

Forfaiting. Forfaiting is the practice of purchasing deferred debts arising from international sales contracts without recourse to the exporter. The exporter surrenders possession of export receivables (deferred-debt obligation from the importer), which are usually guaranteed by a bank in the importing country, by selling to a forfaiter at a discount in exchange for cash. The

TABLE 13.2. Advantages and Disadvantages of Export Factoring

Advantages	Disadvantages
• Factoring allows immediate payment against receivables and increases working capital.	• Factoring is not available for shipments with value of less than $100,000. It is appropriate for continuous or repetitive transactions (not one-shot deal). Factors often require access to a certain volume of the exporter's yearly sales.
• Factors conduct credit investigations, collect accounts receivable from importer, and provide other bookkeeping services.	• Factors do not work for receivables with maturity of over 180 days.
• Factors assume credit risk in the event of buyer's default or refusal to pay (nonrecourse).	• Factors generally do not work with most developing countries because of their inadequate legal and financial framework.
• Factoring is a good substitute for bank credit when the latter is too restrictive or uneconomical.	• Exporter could be liable for disputes concerning merchandise (quality, condition of goods, etc.) and contract of sale.

deferred debt may be in the form of a promissory note, bill of exchange, trade acceptance, or documentary credit, which are unconditional and easily transferable debt instruments that can be sold on the secondary market.

The origins of forfaiting date back to the 1940s, when Swiss financiers developed new ways of financing sales of West German capital equipment to Eastern Europe. Since Eastern European countries did not have enough hard currency to finance imports, they sought intermediate-term financing from their suppliers. The leading forfait houses are still located in Europe.

In a typical forfaiting transaction, the overseas customer does not have hard currency to finance the sale and requests to purchase on credit, usually payable within one to ten years. The exporter (or exporter's bank) contacts a forfaiter and provides the latter with the details of the proposed transaction with the overseas customer. The forfaiter evaluates the transaction and agrees to finance the deal based on a certain discount rate and other conditions. The exporter then incorporates the discount into the selling price. Discount rates are fixed and based on the London Interbank Offered Rate (LIBOR), on which floating interest rates are based. The forfaiter usually requires a guarantee or aval (letter of assurance) from a bank in the importer's country and often provides the exporter with a list of local banks that are acceptable as guarantors. The guarantee becomes quite important, especially in cases of receivables from developing countries. Once an acceptable guarantor is found, the exporter ships the goods to the buyer and endorses the negotiable instruments in favor of the forfaiter, without recourse. The forfaiter then pays the exporter the discounted proceeds.

Although export factoring and forfaiting appear quite similar, there are certain differences in terms of payment terms, products involved, continuity of transaction, and overall use:

1. Factors are often used to finance consumer goods, whereas forfaiters usually work with capital goods, commodities, and projects.
2. Factors are used for continuous transactions, but forfaiters finance one-time deals.
3. Forfaiters work with receivables from developing countries whenever they obtain an acceptable bank guarantor; factors do not finance trade with most developing countries because of unavailability of credit information, poor credit ratings, or inadequate legal and financial frameworks.
4. Factors generally work with short-term receivables, whereas forfaiters finance receivables with a maturity of over 180 days. (See Table 13.3 for advantages and disadvantages of this financing method.)

TABLE 13.3. Forfaiting

Advantages

1. Forfaiters purchase receivables as a one-shot deal without requiring an ongoing volume of business, as in the case of factoring.
2. Financing can cover 100 percent of the sale. Improves cash flow and reduces transaction cost for the exporter since responsibility for collection is assumed by the forfaiter. Forfaiter also assumes all of the payment risk (i.e., credit risk of the guarantor bank, the interest rate risk as well as the buyer's country risk).

Disadvantages

1. It is not available for short-term financing (less than 180 days). Terms range from one to ten years.
2. Transaction size is usually limited to $250,000 or more.
3. Interest and commitment fees (if advance payment is required by exporter) may be high.
4. Exporter is responsible for quality, condition of goods, delivery, overshipment, and other contract disputes.
5. Exporter is responsible for obtaining a bank guarantee for the buyer.

The following are some examples of forfaiting transactions:

- The Bankers Association for Foreign Trade (BAFT) arranged with a cotton machinery company to sell over $500,000 worth of cotton lint removal machinery payable eleven months from the date on the bill of lading. A Greek commercial bank issued the letter of credit, which called for acceptance drafts. Bankers Trust of New York confirmed the letter of credit, and Midland Bank undertook the forfaiting transaction.
- Morgan Grenfell Trade Finance Limited purchased receivables from U.S. exporters to Peru. The finance company required the guarantee of one of the large Peruvian banks and accepted a repayment period of up to five years.
- Morgen Grenfell also financed the down payment in cash (forfaiting) of the sale of electric turbines to Mexico, which was financed by Ex-Im Bank. The Ex-Im Bank required a 15 percent down payment.
- The Export Development Corporation (EDC) of Canada purchases accounts receivable from Canadian exporters provided the promissory notes issued by the overseas customer are guaranteed by a bank acceptable to the EDC, the transaction complies with the Canadian content requirement, and the promissory note does not exceed 85 percent of the contract price.

Export leasing. This is a financing scheme in which a third party, be it an international leasing entity or a finance firm, purchases and exports capital equipment with a view to leasing it to the importer in another country on an intermediate to long-term basis. This arrangement is suitable for the export of capital goods. The lessor could be located in the exporting or importing country. Whether it is an operating or finance lease, the legal ownership of the asset remains with the lessor and only possession passes to the lessee. Under the operating lease, the lease rentals are not intended to amortize the capital outlay incurred by the lessor when the equipment was purchased. Instead, the capital outlay and profit are intended to be recovered through the re-leasing of the equipment and/or through its residual value on its eventual sale. It is not a method of financing the acquisition of the equipment, but a lease for a specified period. The lease is reflected in the balance sheet of the lessor and not the lessee. Under the finance lease, the lease rentals are intended to amortize the capital costs of acquisition as well as to provide profit. Usually, the lessee chooses the equipment to be leased and bears the cost of maintenance and insurance. The lease is reflected in the balance sheet of the lessee and not the lessor.

For businesses that need new equipment but lack the necessary resources or hard currency to purchase, leasing becomes an attractive option. It requires little or no down payment, and the equipment can be bought at the end of the lease agreement for a nominal price. Lease payments are tax deductible in many countries. Since such payments do not appear as liabilities in the financial statements, they preserve the lessee's financial position and do not reduce its ability to borrow for other reasons. Other advantages of leasing are that (1) one can lease up-to-date equipment that may be too expensive to purchase, and (2) the lessee can always trade in the old equipment in the event of obsolescence and obtain new even before the end of the lease. There are, however, certain disadvantages: (1) it may attract adverse tax consequences in certain countries, and (2) the cost of leasing is often higher than other financing methods.

CHAPTER SUMMARY

Major Changes in Small Business Financing

Technology, globalization, and deregulation.

Determinants of Capital Needs and Financing Alternatives

Stage of evolution, ownership structure, and distribution channels.

Internal Financing

Using one's own resources, retaining more profits in the business, and reducing accounts receivable and inventories.

External Financing

Forms of External Financing

Debt or equity financing; short-term/intermediate/long-term financing; investment, inventory, or working capital financing.

Sources of External Financing

Family and friends, banks (asset-based financing, lines of credit, personal and commercial loans, credit cards), Small Business Administration, finance companies, and equity sources.

Financing by the Exporter

1. *Open account:* Payment is deferred for a specified period of time.
2. *Consignment contract:* Importer pays after merchandise is sold to a third party.

Financing by the Importer

1. *Advance payment:* Payment is before shipment is effected.
2. *Progress payment:* Payment is related to performance.

Financing by Third Parties

Short-Term Methods

1. *Loan secured by a foreign accounts receivable:* Account receivable used as collateral to meet short-term financing needs.
2. *Trade/banker's acceptance:* A draft accepted by the importer is used as collateral to obtain financing.
3. *Letter of credit:* Transferable letter of credit (L/C), assignment of proceeds under an L/C, and a back-to-back L/C used to secure financing.
4. *Factoring:* An arrangement between a factoring concern and exporter whereby the factor purchases export receivables for a discount.

Intermediate- and Long-Term Methods

1. *Buyer credit:* Importer obtains a credit from a bank or financial institution to pay the exporter.
2. *Forfaiting:* Purchase of deferred debts arising from international sales contracts without rcourse to the exporter.
3. *Export leasing:* A firm purchases and exports capital equipment with a view to leasing.

REVIEW QUESTIONS

1. What are the major changes taking place in small and medium-sized business financing?
2. What factors determine capital needs and financing alternatives in export-import trade?
3. State the common external sources of financing for export-import businesses.
4. Describe the following: SBICs, Certifed Development Company, CDC/504 loan program, International trade loan.
5. Discuss the various methods in which a letter of credit can be used to finance exports.
6. What is export factoring? How does it differ from forfaiting?
7. State the typical steps involved in export factoring.
8. What are the disadvantages of factoring?
9. Is venture capital generally suitable for export firms?
10. What is the various loan facilities provided by the SBA to export businesses?

CASE 13.1. TADOO'S SALES TO BELGIUM

Tadoo, Inc. is a chemical company incorporated in the state of Tennessee and engaged in the production and sale of various chemical products used to kill harmful insects or strip leaves from trees. Since the company was established in 1980, it has generated gross sales of over $60 million largely from sales in the United States and west European countries. Its sales agents and distributors are located in over a dozen countries.

In September 2000, the Belgian government advertised for a purchase of $20 million chemical products. The winner of the bid was required to provide financing for a period of two years. Given Tadoo's inability to secure private or public financing for the sale, it decided to contact a forfaiter to explore the possibility of financing the deal. Tadoo provided the forfaiter with important details to establish the viability of the transaction including its delivery date, repayment terms (four semiannual repayments over a two-year period), interest rate (payable by buyer), and a letter of credit instrument to be opened in favor of Tadoo through a Belgian bank.

The forfaiter calculated the expected costs (discount rate, commitment fees, etc.) necessary to sell the receivable and added it to the commercial contract so that Tadoo will be able to receive 100 percent of the required cash value. This helped Tadoo to submit a contract price that will include financing expenses. The forfaiter also examines the structure of the transaction to ensure that it has maximum liquidity. This includes the financing period, country risk, and credit risk. The forfaiter is expected to resell the transaction in the market.

Prior to the submission of the bid, Tadoo entered into a detailed contract with the forfaiter. The contract required Tadoo to sell the receivable to the forfaiter and stated the terms and conditions of the contract. It also provided Tadoo with the option to cancel the contract with no liability in the event that Tadoo fails to win the bid. A month after the submission of the bid, the Belgian government informed Tadoo that it has been awarded the contract.

Tadoo began to manufacture the product and supplied the product to the buyer in special shipping containers in accordance with the terms of the contract. Four bills of exchange were accepted by the Belgian Bank and later endorsed by Tadoo to the forfaiter without recourse and provided to the latter with supporting documentation. The forfaiter received and verified the documents and paid $20 million to Tadoo. Tadoo is required to honor all its contractual commitments pertaining to product support and warranty but the financial risk associated with the bill of exchange maturing over a two-year period had been sold to the forfaiter without recourse.

Questions

1. Would Tadoo encounter problems if it was exporting to a developing country?
2. Is this method more beneficial to Tadoo than other forms of financing?

Chapter 14

Government Export Financing Programs

Exporters prefer to be paid on or before shipment of the goods, whereas buyers want to delay payment until they have sold the merchandise. To expand export sales, many governments offer a wide choice of financing programs. Such assistance increases the exporter's credit line needed for corporate and domestic transactions, neutralizes financing as a factor, and creates a level playing field with competitors in other countries who also benefit from similar financing programs.

Programs are usually categorized as short-term (usually under two years), intermediate-term (usually two to five years), and long-term (usually over five years) financing. Government financing could be in the form of supplier credit or buyer credit. Supplier credits are credits extended to the buyer by the exporter, that is, the exporter arranges for government financing. Such credits also include a direct extension of credit by the exporter, as well as the latter's arrangement of financing from other private sources. Buyer's credits are extended to the buyer by parties other than the exporter. Banks, government agencies, or other private parties (domestic or foreign) could provide buyer credits. This chapter is primarily devoted to supplier or buyer credits that are extended by government agencies.

Government financing generally includes the provision of insurance or guarantees to exporters or lending institutions, as well as the extension of official credit, interest, or subsidies to the exporter or overseas customer. Either of these financing schemes may be combined in a single transaction. Some governments provide a whole range of services, such as guarantees, insurance, credit, etc., while others provide some or all of these services insofar as they are not readily available in the market.

The OECD (Organization for Economic Cooperation and Development) has developed guidelines on export credits for its members. These are intended to provide the institutional framework for an orderly export credit market, thus preventing an export credit race in which exporting countries

Export-Import Theory, Practices, and Procedures, Second Edition

compete on the basis of who provides the most favorable financing terms rather than on the basis of who provides the best-quality product at the lowest price. The guidelines provide for the following:

- A minimum of 15 percent of the contract price to be paid in cash
- Maximum repayment term of eight and a half years, with exceptions for poor countries
- Minimum interest rates for set periods of up to five, eight-and-a-half, and ten years
- Gradual abolition of subsidized interest rates and adjustment of discount rates for aid loans to better reflect market realities
- The establishment of related conditions for certain sectors, including agriculture, that are not covered by the guidelines

EXPORT-IMPORT BANK
OF THE UNITED STATES (EX-IM BANK)

The Ex-Im Bank was created in 1934 and established under its present law in 1945, with the aim of assisting in the financing of U.S. export trade. It was originally established to finance exports to Europe after World War II. Ex-Im Bank's role in promoting U.S. exports is likely to be more significant now than in the past few decades because (1) the U.S. economy is more internationalized and exports constitute a growing share of the GNP, and (2) there has been a substantial increase in the volume of international trade and competition for export markets is quite intense.

Ex-Im Bank is intended to supplement, but not compete with, private capital. It has historically been active in areas in which the private sector has been reluctant to provide export financing. Ex-Im Bank has three main functions: (1) provide guarantees and export credit insurance so that exporters and their bankers give credit to foreign buyers, (2) provide competitive financing to foreign buyers, and (3) negotiate with other countries to reduce the level of subsidy in export credits (Ex-Im Bank, 1997a).

Over the past few years, Ex-Im Bank has focused on a broad range of critical areas, such as provision of greater support to small businesses, export promotion to developing nations, and promoting exports of environmentally beneficial goods and services. It has also been engaged in expanding project finance capabilities as well as in reducing trade subsidies of other governments through bilateral or multilateral negotiations.

In its more than seventy years of operations, the bank has supported more than $455 billion of U.S. exports (2004). It has assisted U.S. exporters to win export sales in many countries and undertakes risks the private sector is unwilling or unable to take. The bank also attempts to neutralize financing provided by foreign governments to their exporters when they are in competition for export sales with U.S. exporters. (See International Perspective 14.1 for criteria for loans and loan guarantees.) However, the bank does require reasonable assurance of repayment for the transactions it authorizes and closely monitors credit and other risks in its portfolio.

Annual authorizations have ranged from $9.2 billion to $13.32 billion over the past five years. The largest share of the bank portfolio involves financing transportation, energy, and construction, with the largest concentration in the aircraft sector (see Tables 14.1 and 14.2). The highest geographic

INTERNATIONAL PERSPECTIVE 14.1.
General Ex-Im Bank Criteria for Loans and Loan Guarantees

Foreign Content Policy: To be eligible for support, items must be shipped from the United States and the foreign content (cost of foreign components incorporated in the item in the United States) must be less than 50 percent of the total cost to produce the item. In the case of U.S. items supplied to a foreign project under long-term program support, Ex-Im Bank support is available even though the U.S. items aggregate less than 50 percent of the total project cost (intermediate-term loans and guarantees).

Repayment Terms: Repayment usually begins about six months after shipment or project completion, and payments of principal and interest must be made semiannually. Applicable payment term for a transaction can be determined by (1) identifying the country group (I or II) in the list where the product is exported, (2) find the standard term that applies to the country group and the contract price of one's transaction, and (3) review the terms in chart II and shorter/longer than standard terms.

Scope of Coverage: Ex-Im Bank's loans, guarantees, and intermediate-term insurance cover 85 percent contract price. The foreign buyer is required to make a 15-percent cash payment. Fees charged are based on the risk assessment of foreign buyer or guarantor, the buyer's country, and term of the credit.

Interest Rates and Shipping: Interest rates and maximum maturity terms are subject to OECD guidelines. The lender sets the rate in guarantee programs while loans are often negotiated at fixed rates. Ex-Im Bank-supported sales of more than $10 million in loans or loan guarantee must be shipped in a vessel of U.S registry unless a waiver has been obtained by the foreign buyer from the U.S. Maritime Administration. This applies in the case of long-term financing programs.

TABLE 14.1. Ex-Im Bank Authorizations, (Million U.S. Dollars) and Top Beneficiaries by Country, 2004

	2004	2000-2003	Country	Exposure[a] (%)	Total
Long-term			Mexico	6.49	10.62
Loans	227.10	534.25	China	4.11	6.72
Guarantees	7,112.10	6,062.60	Turkey	2.96	4.84
Subtotal, long-term	7,339.20	6,596.85	Brazil	2.78	4.55
			Korea	2.68	4.38
Medium-term			Indonesia	2.62	4.28
Loans	0	5.18	U.S.A.	1.88	3.08
Guarantees	540.60	678.95	Saudi Arabia	1.72	2.82
Insurance	911.50	675.25	Venezuela	1.47	2.40
Subtotal, medium-term	1,452.10	1,359.38	Malaysia	1.45	2.37
Short-Term			Total	28.16	46.06
Working capital	880.40	675.25	Total Exposure	61.15	
Insurance	3,649.30	1,994.70			
Subtotal, short-term	4,529.70	2,670.02			
Total-authorization	13321	10626.25			

Source: Ex-Im Bank Annual Report, 2004.

[a]Authorizations 2000-2003 (average); Exposure in billion U.S. dollars.

TABLE 14.2. Ex-Im Bank's Geographic and Industry Exposure, 2004 (Million U.S. Dollars)

Region	2004	Total (%)	Industry	2004	Total (%)
Asia	17,967.50	29.40	Air transportation	23475.00	38.40
Latin America	15,570.30	25.50	Power projects	6577.70	10.80
Europe/Canada	10,840.70	17.70	Oil and gas	6415.50	10.50
Africa/Middle East	9,222.30	15.10	Manufacturing	4309.10	7.00
All others	7,547.40	12.30	Others	20370.90	33.30

Source: Ex-Im Bank Annual Report, 2004.

exposure is in Asia, with over 29 percent of the total. Ex-Im Bank also has enhanced financing available for certain categories of exports: environmentally beneficial goods and services, medical equipment, and transportation security equipment. The bank provides assistance to U.S. exporters of goods and/or services insofar as the exports include a minimum of 50 percent U.S. (local) content and are not military related. Its financing decision is determined, inter alia, upon an assessment of the borrower's capability to repay the loan. There are four major export financing programs provided by Ex-Im Bank (U.S. Department of Commerce, 1990; Reynolds, 2003):

- Working capital loan guarantees for U.S. exporters
- Credit insurance
- Guarantees of commercial loans to foreign buyers
- Direct loans to foreign purchasers.

U.S. government support for the Bank has been the subject of criticism from various groups:

- The environmental community contends that the Bank provides loans and loan guarantees for projects that harm the environment. These groups raise concerns about the harmful effects of Ex-Im Bank-assisted oil drilling and pipeline project in Chad and Cameroon, coal-fired power plant in Indonesia, and the loan guarantees for the sale of nuclear fuel to the Czech Republic.
- It is often stated that the bank's assistance is largely provided to a small number of large U.S. firms such as Boeing, Bechtel, GE, and Halliburton, as well as countries that do not need financial support in the form of loans, loan guarantees, or insurance. In view of the fact that Ex-Im Bank supports about 1 percent of U.S. exports, critics suggest that it has a marginal impact on overall U.S. exports or its trade balance.
- Some of Ex-Im Bank's loans to foreign companies have contributed to harm domestic industries. It is alleged that the $18 million loan to the Chinese Iron and Steel industry, for example, adversely affected the competitiveness of local industries (www.exim.gov).

Working Capital Guarantee Program

The availability of adequate working capital is critical for the maintenance and expansion of a viable export-import business. Banks are often reluctant to make financing available because the businesses either have reached the borrowing limits set by their banks or do not have the necessary collateral. The working capital guarantee program is intended to encourage commercial lenders to make loans for various exports-related activities (see Figure 14.1). Such loans may be used for the purchase of raw materials and finished products for export, to pay for overhead, as well as to cover standby letters of credit, such as bid bonds, performance bonds, or payment guarantees (Ex-Im Bank, 1997b,c).

Exporters may apply to the Ex-Im Bank for a preliminary commitment for a guarantee. The lender also may apply directly for a final authorization. In the case of preliminary commitment, the Ex-Im Bank will outline the general terms and conditions under which it will provide the guarantee to the exporter, and this can be used to approach various lenders to secure the most attractive loan package.

The lender must apply for the final commitment. An exporter may also apply through a lender that has been granted a guarantee by the Ex-Im Bank. Such lenders have been granted preapproved credit authority (delegated authority) to process working capital loans under established criteria without preapproval from Ex-Im Bank. For small business exporters, the Small Business Administration (SBA) can guarantee a working capital loan up to $1.1 million or up to $2.0 million under a coguaranty agreement with the Ex-Im Bank. Guarantees may be approved for a single loan or a revolving line of credit.

The major features of the working capital guarantee program are as follows:

Qualified Exports. Eligible exports must be shipped from the United States and have at least 50 percent U.S. content. If the export has less than 50 percent U.S. content, the bank will only support up to the percentage of the U.S. content. Military items as well as sales to military buyers are generally not eligible.

Guarantee Coverage and Term of the Loan. In the event of default by the exporter, Ex-Im Bank will cover 90 percent of the principal of the loan and interest, up to the date of claim for payment, insofar as the lender has met all the terms and conditions of the guarantee agreement. Guaranteed loans generally have maturities of twelve months and are renewable.

FIGURE 14.1. Working Capital Guarantee Program

Collateral and Borrowing Capacity. Guaranteed loans are to be secured by a collateral. Acceptable collateral may include export-related inventory, export-related accounts receivable, or other assets. Inventory and accounts receivable include goods purchased or sales generated by use of the guaranteed loan. For service companies, costs such as engineering, design, or allocable overhead may be treated as collateral. In the case of letters of credit issued under the guaranteed loan, collateral is required only for 25 percent of the value of the letter of credit.

Exporters can borrow up to 75 percent of their inventory including work-in-process and up to 90 percent of their foreign account receivable thus increasing their borrowing capacity. Table 14.3 illustrates borrowing capacity with and without the working capital facility.

Qualified Exporters and Lenders. Exporters must be domiciled in the United States (regardless of domestic/foreign ownership requirements), show a successful track record of past performance, including an operating history of at least one year, and have a positive net worth. Financial statements must show sufficient strength to accommodate the requested debt.

Any public or private lender may apply under the program. Eligibility is determined on many factors, including the lender's financial condition, knowledge of trade finance, and ability to manage asset-based loans. Lenders may be approved as priority lenders or delegated authority lenders. Approved lenders under the priority lender program submit final commitment

TABLE 14.3. Increased Borrowing Capacity under the Ex-Im Bank Working Capital Guarantee Program

Collateral	Amount	Working Capital Without Ex-Im-Bank		Working Capital With Ex-Im-BankGuarantee	
		Advance Rate (%)	Borrowing Base	Advance Rate (%)	Borrowing Base
Export inventory Supported by an export order					
Raw materials	300,000	20	60,000	75	225,000
Work in process	300,000	0	0	75	225,000
Finished goods	600,000	50	300,000	75	450,000
Foreign Account Receivable (FAC)					
FAC	500,000	0	0	90	450,000
L/C backed account receivable	600,000	70	420,000	90	540,000
Total borrowing base			780,000		1,890,000

Source: Ex-Im Bank Annual Report, 2004.

applications to Ex-Im Bank and receive a decision within ten business days. The lender, prior to submission to Ex-Im Bank, must approve the loan application. However, approved delegated authority lenders are allowed to approve loans and receive a guarantee from Ex-Im Bank without having to submit individual applications for approval.

> *Example:* Integrated Medical Systems of Signal Hill, California, was able to export portable intensive care units to military and civilian buyers in Finland, Saudi Arabia, and China by taking advantage of Ex-Im Bank's $500,000 Working Capital Guarantee. In October, 2004, Ex-Im Bank and the Maritime Administration signed a memorandum of understanding to establish Ex-Im Bank guaranteed working capital loans for U.S. companies involved in shipping, logistics, and other ocean transportation services. Ex-Im Bank agreed to increase its working capital guarantee from 90 to 95 percent (and the minimum threshold for the guaranteed transactions from $10 to $20 million) for U.S. companies that ship on U.S. flag vessels.

Export Credit Insurance Program (ECIP)

The purpose of the ECIP is to promote U.S. sales abroad by protecting exporters against loss in the event of default by a foreign buyer or debt arising from commercial or political risks. The policy also enables exporters to obtain financing more easily because, with prior Ex-Im Bank approval, the proceeds of the policy can be readily assigned to a financial institution as collateral. Ex-Im Bank offers a wide range of policies to accommodate many different insurance needs of exporters and financial institutions (Wells and Dulat, 1996). For example, insurance policies may apply to shipments to one buyer or many buyers, cover short-term (180 days or less) or intermediate-term (generally one to five years) credit, and provide comprehensive coverage for commercial as well as specific or all political risks. There are also policies specifically geared to small businesses that are beginning to export their goods or services (small business policy). Some export credit insurance program (ECIP) highlights include the following:

- *U.S. contents requirements:* To be eligible for support, the products sold must be produced in the United States. For short-term and intermediate-term sales, at least 50 percent of the value of the product must be of U.S. origin (excluding price markup). In the case of service exports, services must be performed by U.S.–based personnel or U.S. personnel temporally assigned in the host country.
- *Restrictions on sales:* ECIP may not be provided for exports destined for military applications (with some exceptions) or to communist nations unless it is determined by the president to be in the U.S. national interest.

- *Insurance policies under ECIP:* (1) export policies (short-term): single-buyer/multi-buyer policy, small business policy; (2) lender policies (short-term): letter of credit policy, financial institution buyer/supplier credit policy; (3) policies for exporters and lenders: documentary and nondocumentary policy.
- *Other policies:* Other policies include leasing policy and foreign dealer policy.

Exporter Policies (Short-Term)

Single-Buyer versus Multibuyer Policy

Single-buyer policies insure short-term, intermediate-term, or combined (i.e., short and medium)-term sales to one buyer (www.exim.gov). The multibuyer policy, however, is intended to provide coverage for short-term export sales to many different buyers. Besides repayment terms, which typically range up to 180 days, the short-term single-buyer and short-term multiple-buyer policies have many similarities (see also Figure 14.2):

1. In both cases, eligible exports usually include consumables, agricultural commodities, raw materials, consumer durables, spare parts, and services. Products must have at least 51 percent U.S. content, including labor but excluding product markup.
2. Eligible exporters are U.S. firms or foreign companies doing business in the United States and foreign corporations controlled by U.S. companies. Buyers must be creditworthy and located in an acceptable country. Only exporters may apply for both types of policies. Coverage does not include confirmed letters of credit, cash in advance, and certain military-related items.
3. The risks covered include commercial and specified political risks. Commercial risks generally include buyers' insolvency or failure to pay when an obligation is due. Political risks include losses caused by war, revolution, cancellation of an export-import license, or inability to transfer money.

FIGURE 14.2. Guarantees

In the case of multibuyer policy, the exporter may choose between two options for coverage of the principal amount of the sale. First, split coverage offsets 100 percent for political losses, combined with 90 percent for commercial losses. Second, equalized coverage counters 95 percent of political and commercial losses. Under either option, commercial loss coverage is increased to 98 percent for approved, bulk agricultural exports and 100 percent for sovereign obligors, that is, entities which offer the full faith and credit of the importing country's government. The single buyer policy covers 90 percent of political and commercial losses. In both cases, the exporter may request preshipment coverage to lock-in coverage conditions for a specified period of time.

Policies for Small Business Exporters

Ex-Im Bank offers a short-term insurance policy (small business insurance policy) that is intended to meet the credit requirements of small, less experienced exporters. The coverage is available for companies with average annual export credit sales of less than $5 million for the two years prior to application and which meet the eligibility requirements for small business. It is quite similar to single- and multibuyer policies in terms of eligible products (U.S. content), credit terms, and scope of coverage (excludes letters of credit and so on), and also provides special incentives for exporters of environmentally related goods and services. Political losses are covered at 100 percent while commercial losses are covered at 95 percent. It has no first loss deductible (www.exim.gov).

Lender Policies (Short-Term)

Bank Letter of Credit Policy

The bank letter of credit policy is intended to encourage banks to support U.S. exports by protecting them against loss on irrevocable letter of credit issued by foreign banks for the purchase of U.S. goods. This policy covers a confirming bank's losses resulting from the failure of a foreign financial institution (the issuing bank) to honor its letter of credit to the insured bank. The policy can only be used with irrevocable letters of credit and for eligible exports. The policy covers against commercial and political risks. Equalized coverage for commercial and political risks or political only coverage is available.

The Financial Institution Buyer Credit Policy

The financial institution buyer credit policy protects financial institutions against losses on short-term direct credit loans or reimbursement loans to foreign entities for importing U.S. goods and services. The direct buyer credit loan is a loan extended to a foreign entity by a financial institution for the importation of U.S. goods and services; while the reimbursement loan is the financial institution's reimbursement of a buyer's payments to U.S. suppliers. The policy covers against commercial and political risks.

The Financial Institution Supplier Credit Policy

This policy is intended to protect lenders financing the export receivables of small businesses on a nonrecourse basis. Policyholders may be given the authority to approve exporters that participate under the policy as well as to approve many of the buyers that exporters elect to finance. Eligible exporters are small businesses with annual export credit sales of less than $5 million (U.S.) for the prior two years (excluding cash-in-advance and confirmed L/C sales).

Policy for Exporters and Lenders (Intermediate-Term)

The intermediate term export credit insurance enables exporters and financial institutions to insure their foreign receivables against political and commercial losses. The policy provides a maximum cover of $10 million (U.S.) with payment terms ranging from one to five years. It supports the sale of U.S. capital equipment, installation, and a complement of spare parts. It can be used for single sales or repetitive transactions.

Other Policies

Financing and Operating Leases

Financing and operating leases are two separate lease policies that are intended to insure both the stream of lease payments and the fair market value of the leased products. The policy covers against political and commercial risks or against political risks only. The major difference between financing and operating lease is that in the case of the former, little residual value remains in the leased product and ownership is transferred to the lessee at the end of the lease, and in the case of an operating lease, a residual value remains at the end of the lease and the lessor repossesses, sells, or otherwise disposes of the product as it sees fit. The title to the leased product, which can be either new or used equipment, must be maintained by the lessor who takes out the insurance policy.

The Foreign Dealer Policy

The foreign dealer policy is designed to provide competitive support for financing U.S. capital goods exports through foreign dealerships. It is useful to small and medium-sized U.S. exporters that need to arrange financing for their overseas dealers. It combines short-term financing of inventory with the option to roll over that financing for a longer term. This policy is presently available to financial institutions.

Guarantees

Ex-Im Bank guarantees provide repayment protection for private-sector loans to creditworthy buyers of U.S. exports (see Figure 14.2). The program covers 100 percent of the commercial and political risks (85 percent of U.S. contract amount). The foreign buyer is required to make at least a 15 percent cash payment. Exports supported under this program are capital equipment, services, and projects, and the loan guarantees are offered for intermediate- and long-term sales. Guarantees of $20 million or less do not require shipment on U.S.–registered vessels. The credit may be for any amount. The guarantee is unconditional and transferable (Reynolds, 2003).

There is also a special coverage or guarantee (credit guarantee facility) extended by Ex-Im Bank to United States or foreign lenders on lines of credit to foreign banks or large foreign buyers. The products supported, as well as the coverage and terms, are identical with the guarantee program discussed previously. The facility can finance small transactions with minimal paperwork. When a financing institution is extending a loan of $10 million or less to a borrower with Ex-Im Bank's guarantee, Ex-Im Bank requires only that a note be issued in favor of the financing institution, meaning that a credit agreement is not often required (see Figures 14.2 and 14.3).

FIGURE 14.3. Credit Guarantee Facility

Example: Ex-Im Bank recently guaranteed a $930 million commercial loan to the Qatar Liquefied Gas Co. to support the export of U.S. goods and services in order to build a natural gas project and related facilities. It also guaranteed a long-term loan extended to Albania for the purchase of U.S. air traffic automation system from Lockheed Martin.

Example: In 2001, The Ex-Im Bank of the United States provided a $32 million medium-term credit guarantee facility to support the sale of $35 million of equipment and services by various U.S. companies to Algerian buyers. Banque Exterieure d'Algerie (BEA) SPA, Algiers, the largest of Algeria's five state-owned commercial banks, is the borrower and primary source of repayment on the transaction. Societe Generale, New York, New York, is the guaranteed lender.

Direct Loans Program

Under this program, Ex-Im Bank provides a fixed-rate loan directly to established creditworthy foreign buyers for the purchase of U.S. capital equipment, projects, and related services. The loan covers up to 85 percent of the U.S. export value. The buyer is required, however, to make a cash payment for the difference, that is, 15 percent of the value. The loan is often used by buyers when the financed portion exceeds $10 million. A loan agreement as well as shipment on U.S. registered vessels is required. The program supports intermediate and long-term sales. Transactions normally range from five to ten years, depending on the export value, the product, the importing country, and terms offered by the competition (see Figure 14.4).

Project Finance Program

This program supports exports of U.S. capital equipment and related services for projects whose repayment depends on project cash flows, as defined in the contract. It is suitable for major U.S. suppliers and sponsors that do not have adequate access to bank or government guarantees. There is no limit on the size of the transaction. Any combination of either direct loans or guarantees for commercial bank loans, with political-risk-only or

FIGURE 14.4. Direct Loan Program

comprehensive coverage, are available. The basic coverage and terms are as follows:

1. The foreign buyer makes a 15 percent cash payment. Direct loan and/or guarantee covers up to 85 percent of the U.S. contract amount.
2. Political-risk-only coverage is available during construction and for postcompletion financing.
3. Repayment terms are subject to OECD guidelines.
4. No coverage is provided for precompletion commercial risks.
5. Approvals are subject to Ex-Im Bank's environmental procedures and guidelines.

Ex-Im Bank also offers financing to foreign purchasers of U.S. commercial aircraft, ships and so on under its direct loan, guarantee and insurance programs.

SMALL BUSINESS ADMINISTRATION

The Small Business Administration (SBA) also provides a few programs for U.S. exporters. To qualify for the programs, applicants must meet the definition of a small business under SBA's size standards and other eligibility requirements (see Table 14.4 for authorization limits). The SBA Act defines an eligible small business as one that is independently owned and operated and not dominant in its field of operation. It has established size standards that define the maximum size of an eligible small business. The following represent general guidelines to determine a small business:

Industry	Maximum size
Retail and Service	$6.0 to $24.5 million in average annual receipts
Construction	$12.0 to $28.5 million in average annual receipts
Agriculture	$0.75 to $6.0 million in average annual receipts
Wholesale	No more than 100 employees
Manufacturing	500 to 1,500 employees

Some of the SBA programs that are intended to promote exports are as follows.

Export Working Capital Program Loans (EWCP)

The EWCP is a combined effort of the SBA and Ex-Im Bank to provide short-term working capital to U.S. exporters. To be processed by the SBA,

TABLE 14.4. Small Business Authorization (Million U.S. $)

	2004	2003
Export credit insurance	1,570.6	1,361.6
Working capital guarantee	620.3	622.3
Guarantees	2,257.3	2,075.2

Source: Eximbank Annual Report, 2004.

loan guarantee requests must be equal to or less than $1.00 million. Loan requests greater than $1 million are processed by the Ex-Im Bank. The applicant must be in business for one year (not necessarily exporting) at the time of application. The agency can guarantee up to 90 percent of loans up to $1 million. If it is combined with an SBA international trade loan, it can guarantee up to $1.25 million for working capital and fixed asset financing. The loan may be used for purchase of inventory, raw material, or for the manufacture of a product. A borrower must give SBA a first security interest equal to 100 percent of the EWCP guaranty amount. Collateral must be located in the United States (Small Business Administration, 2007).

International Trade Loan Program

This program assists small businesses that are already engaged or preparing to engage in international trade and those which are adversely affected by import competition. The SBA can guarantee as much as $1,250,000 in combined working capital (provided under the EWCP), and facilities and equipment loans. The guaranty by SBA for the working capital portion as well as that for fixed assets is limited to $1 million, respectively. The guarantee percentage and amount is similar to the EWCP. Collateral is required and must be located in the United States.

In both programs, the SBA provides loan guarantees only if the exporter is unable to obtain financing from private sources without its support.

SBA Export Express

SBA Export Express is a flexible financing tool available to assist small businesses in developing and expanding export markets. Approved lenders use streamlined and expedited loan review and approval procedures. Small Business Administration provides participating lenders with a payment guarantee up to a maximum loan amount of $250,000. The guarantee on loans of up to $150,000 is 85 percent (75 percent for loans exceeding $150,000 up to a maximum of $250,000). Proceeds can be used for financing export development activities (participation in trade shows, and so on), transaction specific financing for overseas buyers, revolving lines of credit for exports, and acquiring or expanding facilities used in the United States to produce goods or services for export, as well as financing standby letters of credit used as bid or performance bonds in foreign contracts.

OVERSEAS PRIVATE INVESTMENT CORPORATION (OPIC)

The Overseas Private Investment Corporation (OPIC) is a wholly owned U.S. government corporation that supports American private investment in developing nations and emerging market economies. Its programs are presently available for new and expanding businesses in some 140 countries worldwide. The program has generated positive net income for every year of operation since its inception in 1971 and has accumulated reserves of over $2.6 billion. Since 1971, OPIC has supported investments worth nearly $100 billion and generated about $43 billion in U.S. exports. Although OPIC is primarily intended to promote U.S. investment abroad, it has played a significant role in expanding American exports. Projects backed by OPIC in 1996, for example, were estimated to generate $9.6 billion in U.S. exports and create or support about 30,000 jobs. A recent OPIC-supported power project in Indonesia, for example, is expected to purchase more than $1 billion in U.S. equipment and supplies and support more than 3,000 American jobs. OPIC–backed investments in these countries are also likely to depend on a constant supply of U.S. components, supplies, or raw materials. In short, OPIC helps developing nations expand their economies and become viable markets for U.S. goods and services (www.opic.gov).

The Overseas Private Investment Corporation assists American investors through four principal activities designed to promote overseas investment and reduce associated risks:

Financing of Business Through Loans and Loan Guarantees

The Overseas Private Investment Corporation provides intermediate- and long-term project financing through loans and loan guarantees in countries where conventional financial institutions often are reluctant or unable to provide financing. All projects considered for financing must be commercially and financially sound and managed by people with a proven track record of success in the same or related business. The Overseas Private Investment Corporation, for example, carefully reviews whether the project will generate adequate cash flow to pay all operational costs, to service all debt, and provide owners with an adequate return on their investments. The proceeds of OPIC financing may be spent for capital goods and services in the United States, the host country, or other less-developed countries. The following are the major features of the program (www.opic.gov).

Ownership

Projects wholly owned by governments are not eligible. The Overseas Private Investment Corporation finances overseas ventures wholly owned by U.S. companies, or joint ventures in which the U.S. investor has at least 25 percent equity. As a rule, at least 51 percent of the voting shares of the overseas venture must be held by the private sector. Financing is provided in cases in which the government holds majority ownership, insofar as management remains in private hands.

OPIC Participation

The Overseas Private Investment Corporation assists in designing and coordinating the financial plan with other lenders and investors. It usually participates by providing up to 50 percent of the total cost of a new venture. The percentage is often higher in the case of an expansion of an existing business.

Financing and Loan Terms

For projects sponsored by U.S. small businesses or cooperatives, financing is provided through direct loans ranging from $2 to $10 million. Loan guarantees are often used for large-scale projects and range from $10 to $200 million. The guarantees are issued to U.S. financial institutions that are more than 50 percent owned by U.S. citizens, corporations, or partnerships. Foreign corporations that are at least 95 percent U.S. owned are also eligible. Funding sources include commercial banks, pension funds, and insurance companies. The Overseas Private Investment Corporation loans typically provide for a final maturity of five to fifteen years, following a certain grace period during which only interest is payable. For loan guarantees, OPIC charges the borrower a guarantee fee that may include an income-sharing provision (www.opic.gov).

Providing Support to Private Investments

The Overseas Private Investment Corporation provides finance to a number of privately owned and managed investment funds so that these funds extend equity capital to facilitate business formation and expansion. Some funds invest primarily in small companies, whereas others invest in larger projects. Participation in equity ownership ranges from 5 to 40 percent of the company's portfolio. To be eligible for funding, the overseas company must have a significant business connection with the U.S. economy and a positive impact on U.S. employment, the environment, and workers' rights. OPIC-supported investment funds presently operate in Africa, East Asia, South America, and Eastern Europe.

Insuring Investments Against a Broad Range of Political Risks

The Overseas Private Investment Corporation offers many programs to insure investments in developing nations against political risk. The following risks are covered:

1. *Currency inconvertibility:* This is the inability to convert profits, debt services, and other remittances from local currency into U.S. dollars.
2. *Expropriation:* This involves loss of investment due to expropriation, nationalization, or confiscation by the host government.
3. *Political violence:* This relates to loss of assets or income due to war, revolution, civil war, terrorism, and so forth. An investor may purchase a separate policy for loss of business, loss of assets, or both. Coverage is available for new or existing investments. Special insurance programs are available for the following sectors: financial institutions, leases, oil and gas projects, natural resource projects, contractors, and exporters.

The Overseas Private Investment Corporation insurance is available to citizens of the United States, businesses created under U.S. law with majority ownership by U.S. citizens, and foreign companies with a minimum ownership of 95 percent equity by U.S. citizens.

Engaging in Outreach Activities

This is mainly designed to inform the U.S. business community of investment opportunities abroad.

Investments by OPIC clients may take many forms, including equity investments, loans, service contracts, leases, joint ventures, franchises, and other arrangements (www.opic.gov). In the event that the project is foreign owned, OPIC insures the portion of the project (investment) made by the U.S. investor. The Overseas Private Investment Corporation does not participate in projects subject to performance requirements that would substantially undercut U.S. trade benefits from the investment (e.g., local content, maximum import and minimum export requirements imposed by host states).

PRIVATE EXPORT FUNDING CORPORATION

The Private Export Funding Corporation (PEFCO) is a major source of capital for intermediate- and long-term fixed-rate loans for U.S. exports. It acts as a supplemental lender to traditional sources by making loans available for foreign purchasers of U.S. goods and services.

The Private Export Funding Corporation is a private corporation owned by banks and industrial and financial companies. It works closely with Ex-Im Bank. Ex-Im Bank unconditionally guarantees all PEFCO loans. The Private Export Funding Corporation often lends in conjunction with one or more commercial banks and will cover up to 85 percent of the export value. The Private Export Funding Corporation generally does not make loans of less than $1 million, and this makes it suitable for high-cost purchases, such as aircraft, industrial plants, and so on, that require large amounts of money for extended terms. The Private Export Funding Corporation has a program for small business exporters to provide short-term working capital through private lenders or directly to small business exporters as a lender of last resort (www.pefco.com).

U.S. DEPARTMENT OF AGRICULTURE

The U.S. Department of Agriculture (USDA) provides financial support for U.S. agricultural exports through various programs, such as the following:

- GSM-102 program provides credit guarantees for up to three years and will cover 98 percent of the export value and up to 2.8 percent points of interest on the guaranteed value.
- GSM-103 program offers credit guarantees with terms of greater than three but not more than ten years. Both guarantees cover commercial and noncommercial risks.
- Public Law 480 authorizes U.S. government financing of sales of U.S. agricultural products to friendly countries on concessional terms (www.usda.gov).

In addition to government programs, more than a dozen state governments have introduced export financing programs. Some of the programs implemented in California and Illinois have the following essential features: (1) state-funded loan guarantee programs, (2) preshipment and postshipment assistance in the form of loans to lenders and loan guarantees to exporters and their banks, and (3) state agency acting as a delivery agent for Ex-Im Bank programs.

CHAPTER SUMMARY

Ex-Im Bank

Ex-Im Bank is an independent agency of the U.S. government, the purpose of which is to aid in financing and to facilitate trade between the United States and other countries. The bank, which is expected to be self-sustaining (except for the initial capital of $1 billion to start operations), makes loans and guarantees with reasonable assurance of repayment. It complements private sources of finance.

Working Capital Guarantee Program

This enables exporters to meet critical pre-export financing needs, such as inventory build-up or marketing. Ex-Im Bank will guarantee 90 percent of the loan provided by a qualified lender. The guarantee has a maturity of twelve months and is renewable.

Export Credit Insurance Program

It comprises of a wide range of policies to accommodate different insurance needs. Its major features are: U.S. content requirements and restrictions on sales destined for military use and to communist nations.

1. *Short-term single-buyer policies:* These cover a single sale or repetitive sales over a one-year period to a single buyer. They provide coverage against political and commercial risks. They support products such as consumables, raw materials, spare parts, low-cost capital goods, etc.
2. *Short-term multibuyer policies:* These cover short-term export sales to many different buyers against political and commercial risks. Product coverage is the same as for single-buyer.

3. *Small business policy (graduate to short-term multibuyer when annual export credit sales exceed $3 million):* This short-term policy covers small businesses with average annual export credit sales of less than $3 million. It provides coverage against political and commercial risks.
4. *Small business environmental policy:* This short-term policy provides coverage to small businesses that export environmental goods and services against political and commercial risks.
5. *Financial institution buyer credit policy:* This protects financial institutions against losses on short-term direct credit loans or reimbursement loans to foreign buyers of U.S. goods and services.
6. *The bank letter of credit policy:* This provides coverage against the failure of a foreign financial institution (the issuing bank) to honor its letter of credit to the insured bank.
7. *Financing and operating lease policy:* These two separate leases provide coverage against political and/or commercial risks—policies protect lessor against loss of a stream of lease payments and fair market value of the leased product.

Guarantees

The program provides repayment protection for private-sector loans to creditworthy buyers of U.S. goods and services. There is also special coverage for United States or foreign lenders on lines of credit extended to foreign banks or foreign buyers.

Direct Loan Program

This is an intermediate/long-term loan provided to creditworthy foreign buyers for the purchase of U.S. capital goods and services.

Small Business Administration (SBA)

The SBA provides certain programs for small business exporters.

Export Working Capital

This guarantees short-term working capital loans to U.S. small business exporters.

International Trade Loan Program

This guarantees loans to small businesses that are already engaged or plan to engage in international trade as well as those which are adversely affected by import competition.

Overseas Private Investment Corporation (OPIC)

This self-supporting agency of the U.S. government insures U.S. investors against political and commercial risks and provides financing through loans and loan guarantees.

Private Export Funding Corporation (PEFCO)

This private corporation works in conjunction with Ex-Im Bank in the financing of foreign purchases of U.S. goods and services. Loans from PEFCO are guaranteed by Ex-Im Bank.

Department of Agriculture

The USDA provides financial support for export of U.S. agricultural products through GSM-102, GSM-103, and Public Law 480.

State and Local Export Financing Programs

States provide different programs to expand exports: loans, loan guarantees. They also act as delivery agents for Ex-Im Bank programs.

REVIEW QUESTIONS

1. What is the difference between buyer and supplier credit?
2. State the OECD guidelines on export credits.
3. Describe the origins and activities of the Ex-Im Bank.
4. What are some of the criticisms of the Ex-Im Bank?
5. What is the difference between the working capital guarantee program and the direct loans program?
6. What kinds of exports are eligible under the working capital program?
7. Compare and contrast the single-buyer and multiple-buyer policy.
8. Discuss the role of OPIC in promoting U.S. exports.
9. How does PEFCO promote U.S. exports?
10. State some of the programs available to promote U.S. agricultural exports.

CASE 14.1. TRADE FINANCE FOR SMALL
AND MEDIUM-SIZED ENTERPRISES
IN TRANSITION ECONOMIES

Primary and intermediate commodities continue to dominate the composition of exports from the Commonwealth of Independent States (CIS): Armenia, Azerbaijan, Belarus, Georgia, Kazakhstan, Kyrgyzstan, Russia, Moldova, Tajikistan, Turkmenistan, Ukraine, and Uzbekistan. Such exports may not need elaborate long-term financial arrangements unlike the high value-added exports from countries of Central and Eastern Europe.

According to the OECD Consensus Risk Classification of 2001, country risks for export credit are subdivided into seven levels, with one signifying minimal risk and category seven indicating the highest risk. Among the transition economies, the Czech Republic, Hungary, Poland, and Slovenia were ranked at level 2, followed by Latvia and Croatia (level 4), Bulgaria and Lithuania (level 5), and Kazakhstan, Romania, and Russia (level 6). All other transition economies were categorized as very high risk countries at level 7. In many of the countries with high risk perceptions, payment terms are largely based on letters of credits and cash in advance. In Russia, for example, three out of five import shipments require advance payments. For small and medium-sized imports in these countries, the use of letters of credit, cash in advance represents a significant cost, with adverse effect on their competitiveness.

In many of these countries, the banking system is not well developed to handle foreign trade transactions. In 1999, for example, the sum of loans to the private sector was estimated at about 20 percent of GDP compared to that of over 100 percent for Eurozone countries (IMF, 2003).

Adequate trade finance facilities for small and medium-sized enterprises are limited in view of the banks' reluctance to service small companies due to the perception of high risk associated with such financing and the costs of evaluating the creditworthiness of small clients. Trade is often hampered by the limited availability of preshipment working capital financing as well as burdensome collateral requirements. In most of these countries, banks do not provide medium- and long-term trade financing. The average length of commercial credits granted in most countries varies from three to six months. In Russia, for example, commercial loans granted for more than one year accounted for only 18 percent of total commercial loan volume in 2000 (USAID, 2000; Economic Commission for Europe, 2003). The role of leasing in capital investment and trade financing remains quite limited.

In the 1990s, most transition economies introduced export credit insurance and guarantee schemes, and established export credit agencies and state-sponsored Export-Import banks. Besides receiving training and technical advice from the Berne Union (The International Union of Credit and Investment Insurers), many of the more developed members such as Hungary, Poland, and the Czech Republic have become full members of the Berne Union; that is, they have met the benchmarks for membership in terms of trade turnover insured per year and annual premium income. For many of the less developed countries in Central and Eastern Europe, Ex-Im Banks and export credit agencies remain undercapitalized, lack reliable credit information, and face difficulties collecting "problem" loans.

Questions

1. Do many transition economies use letters of credit as an important means of payment for international trade? Discuss.
2. Briefly discuss the role of trade financing in transition economies.

CASE 14.2. EX-IM BANK FINANCING: SELECTED CASES

Bluefield Associates (Working Capital Guarantee and Credit Insurance): Bluefield Associates of Ontario, California, is a small business manufacturer of skin care products. It was founded in 1991 and has approximately fifty employees.

The company has an Ex-Im Bank-guaranteed working capital line of credit from East-West Bank of San Marino, California. It uses the working capital guarantee to enable its lender to lend against foreign accounts receivable and increase its working capital. East-West Bank is an Ex-Im Bank delegated authority lender that can commit Ex-Im Bank's working capital guarantee at the time the loan is processed.

Bluefield Associates also uses Ex-Im Bank's multibuyer export credit insurance to minimize risk and to secure protection against buyer default for either political or commercial reasons. The credit insurance facility can also be used as a financing tool to obtain working capital loans against insured foreign receivables.

The company exports its products to twelve countries in Sub-Saharan Africa and Europe. In the past few years, it has managed to substantially increase its export sales and triple the number of its foreign buyers.

Chief Industries (Medium-Term Insurance): Chief Industries, Inc., of Grand Island, Nebraska, is a diversified manufacturer of fabricated steel for grain handling, grain storage, and other industrial uses. It designs and manufactures a complex line of buildings and grain storage systems. The company has experienced double-digit growth of its export sales over the past few years, ranging in value from $0.5 to $1.5 million (U.S.) per transaction. Growing international sales have enabled the company to expand its workforce.

Ex-Im Bank's medium term insurance in 2004 helped chief industries to arrange commercial bank financing for their foreign buyers. It protects U.S. sales to a single foreign buyer against the risk of default due to political or commercial reasons. The policy covers transactions with a particular buyer for either single or repetitive sales.

The company obtained Ex-Im Bank's medium-term insurance to support sales to private agricultural producers in Mexico. The insured lender was Wells Fargo Bank in El Paso, Texas. The company also benefited from Ex-Im Bank's medium-term insurance to support a $1.1 million (U.S.) sales to a private buyer in Russia.

Input/Output, Inc. (Medium-Term Financing): Input/Output is a seismic-imaging technology company located in Stafford, Texas. It has a workforce of 800 employees worldwide (with about 500 in the United States). In 2004, the company used its Ex-Im Bank's medium-term financing to export over $16 million (U.S.). (Ex-Im Bank's medium-term loan guarantee).

The transaction involved a leasing structure in which Input/Output's equipment was purchased by a Russian leasing company. It was to be leased to companies involved in oil/gas exploration in Siberia and Tartarstan. The borrower was Ural-Siberian Bank (Russia's bank) and the guaranteed lender was American Express in New York. The financing enabled the company to export on three-year repayment terms and to helps the firm compete successfully in these markets.

Question

1. Describe how the previously mentioned programs differ in terms of their product and risk coverage.

SECTION VI:
EXPORT REGULATIONS
AND TAX INCENTIVES

Chapter 15

Regulations and Policies
Affecting Exports

EXPORT LICENSING AND ADMINISTRATION

Governments use export controls for a variety of reasons. Such controls are often intended to achieve certain desired political and economic objectives. The first U.S. export control was introduced in 1775 when Continental Congress outlawed the export of goods to Great Britain. Since then, the United States has restricted exports to certain countries through legislation such as the Embargo Act, Trading with the Enemy Act, The Neutrality Act, and the Export Control Act.

The Export Control Act of 1949 represents the first comprehensive export control program enacted in peacetime. Export controls prior to this time were almost exclusively devoted to the prohibition or curtailment of arms exports (arms embargoes). The 1949 legislation was primarily intended to curtail the export of certain commodities to communist nations during the Cold War era. Export controls were thus allowed for reasons of national security, foreign policy, and short supply. Given America's dominant economic position in the postwar era, it provided leadership in international economic relations and pursued an active foreign policy (Stenger, 1984; Moskowtz, 1996).

In 1969, the often stringent and far-reaching restrictions were curtailed and the new law (Export Administration Act, 1969) attempted to balance the need for export controls with the recognition of the adverse effects of an overly comprehensive export control system on the country's economy. This came at a time when the United States was losing ground to other nations in economic performance, such as balance of trade, exports, and so on. The overvalued dollar and inflation, for example, had adversely affected its

Export-Import Theory, Practices, and Procedures, Second Edition

competitiveness in foreign markets and shrank its trade surplus from $6.8 billion in 1964 to a mere $400 million in 1969. The promotion of exports was considered essential to improving the country's declining trade surplus and overall competitiveness as well as to reducing the growing unemployment. The general trend in 1969 and thereafter has been to ease and/ or strengthen the position of exporters and increase the role of Congress in implementing export control policy. Some examples are as follows:

1. The Equal Export Opportunity Act of 1972 curtailed the use of export controls if the product (that is subject to such restrictions) was available from sources outside the United States in comparable quality and quantity. This was because export controls would be ineffective if certain commodities were available from foreign sources. The 1977 amendment prohibited the president from imposing export controls without providing adequate evidence with regard to its importance to U.S. national security interests. In the event that the president decided to prohibit or control exports, the law required him to negotiate with other countries to eliminate foreign availability.

   The scope of presidential authority to regulate U.S. foreign transactions, including the imposition of export controls, was restricted to wartime only. A statute (the International Emergency Economic Powers Act, 50 U.S. Code 1701 4 seq.) was also passed to regulate presidential powers in the area of export controls during national emergencies. As of 1998, restrictions based on national emergencies have been imposed against Angola, Iraq, Libya, North Korea, Iran, Haiti, and Yugoslavia. In short, the president can impose export controls outside emergency and wartime periods only upon extensive review and consultation with Congress.

2. In 1977, Congress introduced limitations on the power of the executive branch to prohibit or curtail agricultural exports. Any prohibition of such exports was considered ineffective without the approval of Congress by concurrent resolution.

3. The 1979 Export Administration Act (EAA) also emphasized the important contribution of exports to the U.S. economy and acknowledged the necessity of balancing the need for trade and exports and national security interests. The law also gave legal effect to the agreement of the Coordinating Committee for Multilateral Export Controls (COCOM), which was established in 1949 to coordinate export controls of technology to communist countries. It was dissolved in 1994.

4. The 1985 amendments to the Export Administration Act further restricted the power of the president to impose foreign policy controls

that interfere with contracts entered into before the decision to restrict exports, except under very specific circumstances. Congress also established validated licenses for multiple exports, allowing exporters to make successive shipments of the same goods under a single license, waived licensing requirements for certain low-tech goods exports to COCOM nations, and shortened by one-third the time period for issuing licenses for exports to non-COCOM members. In view of certain international incidents, such as the downing of the Korean aircraft by the former Soviet Union, however, the law tightened export controls on the acquisition of critical military goods and technology by the former Soviet Union and its allies.

Export controls were originally intended to be used against former communist countries. However, with the end of the cold war, no longer was there a single, clearly defined adversary, and it became necessary to adjust the system of export controls to take into account the new reality in international relations. An increasingly global economy also presented new challenges for managing export controls. The growing number of global suppliers of high technology and defense-related items, an increased level of global R & D, and the dissemination of dual use technologies, as well as divergent views among Western countries, militated in favor of liberalization of export controls. Prior to September 11, 2001, substantial liberalization of controls had taken place in many areas, such as high performance computers, telecommunication, and so on. Export controls were aimed at, inter alia, restricting a narrow range of transactions that could assist in the development of weapons of mass destruction by certain countries. The control system essentially focused on a small group of critical goods and technology, and on specific end uses and end users, in addition to certain "reckless" nations that must be stopped from acquiring weapons of mass destruction.

Current Developments in Export Controls

Since the events of September 11, 2001, the U.S. government introduced certain restrictions on exports. First, it prohibits the conduct of business with any group whose names appear on the lists of denied persons maintained by the Office of Foreign Assets Control. The list includes terrorists, individuals and/or companies associated with terrorists, or terrorist organizations. Second, a deemed export license is required before foreign nationals engaged in research in the United States (U.S. university campus) receive technology or technical data on the use of export-controlled equipment/materials.

For a deemed license to be required, the information being conveyed would have to both involve controlled equipment (and other materials) and one that is not publicly available. The fundamental research exclusion applies to information in the United States that is broadly shared with the scientific community and not restricted for proprietary reasons or specific national security concerns. Third, there have been efforts to strengthen the multilateral regime on export controls. A focus has been placed on controlling the export of weapons of mass destruction to hostile countries. Since the terrorist attacks of September 11, 2001, many Western governments deny risky exports, while approving legitimate ones more efficiently (Walsh, 2002). (See International Perspective 15.1 for multilateral export controls.)

INTERNATIONAL PERSPECTIVE 15.1.
Multilateral Export Regimes

- **The Australian Group (AG):** The AG was formed in 1984 to harmonize export controls on chemical and biological weapons. It has thirty-four member countries. Its activities serve to support the objectives of the Biological Weapons Convention (BWC) and Chemical Weapons Convention (CWC) by enhancing the effectiveness of national export licensing measures. The group considers export licensing as a vital means of ensuring that legitimate trade in chemicals, biological agents, and related equipment is not adversely affected while facilitating transparency to discourage the sale of such products to parties that could develop a biological and chemical weapons program.
- **Nuclear Suppliers Group (NSG):** The NSG was established in 1992 by a group of nuclear supplier countries (forty-four member countries). It seeks to contribute to the nonproliferation of nuclear weapons through the implementation of guidelines for nuclear and nuclear-related exports.
- **Missile Technology Control Regime (MTCR):** The MTCR was established in 1987 to coordinate national export controls in order to prevent missile proliferation. It has thirty-four member countries. Through a system of export licenses, member countries attempt to control transfers that contribute to delivery systems for weapons of mass destruction.
- **Wassenaar Arrangement (WA):** The WA was founded in 1996 to replace the East-West technology control program under the Coordinating Committee for Multilateral Export Controls (COCOM), which was disbanded in 1994. It is intended to review export controls on conventional arms and sensitive dual goods and technologies. It has thirty-three member countries. The agreement provides for enhanced cooperation between members through information exchange on a regular basis.

U.S. Export Administration Regulations

Administration of Export Controls

The Export Administration Regulations (EAR) are designed to implement the Export Administration Act (EAA) of 1979 and subsequent amendments. The EAR is administered by the U.S. Department of Commerce, Bureau of Industry and Security (BIS). The EAR is not permanent legislation. When it lapsed, presidential executive orders under the Emergency Powers Act directed and authorized the continuation of the EAR. The regulations also implement antiboycott law provisions.

U.S. export controls are primarily imposed for the following reasons (EAR, part 742):

1. *Protect national security:* To restrict the export/re-export of items that would make a significant contribution to the military potential of any other country that would prove detrimental to the national security of the United States. This includes the exports of high performance computers, software, and technology to particular destinations, end users, and end uses.
2. *Further foreign policy goals:* To restrict the export/re-export of goods and technology to further the foreign policy objectives of the United States, that is, human rights, regional stability, and antiterrorism. It is also used to implement unilateral or international sanctions such as those imposed by the United Nations or the Organization of American States.
3. *Preserve scarce natural resources:* To restrict the export of goods, wherever necessary, in order to protect the domestic economy from the excessive drain of scarce resources (crude petroleum, certain inorganic chemicals), and to reduce the serious inflationary impact of foreign demand. Domestically produced crude oil and certain unprocessed timber harvested from federal and state lands are controlled for short supply reasons (EAR, part 754).
4. *Control proliferation:* To prevent the proliferation of weapons of mass destruction, such as nuclear, chemical, and biological weapons, which are often maintained as part of multilateral control arrangements (EAR, part 742.2).

The core of the export control provisions of the EAR concerns exports from the United States. However, the term "exports" has been given broad meaning to include activities other than exports or to apply to transactions outside the United States.

The scope of the EAR covers the following:

- *Exports from the United States:* This also includes the release of technology to a foreign national in the United States through such means as demonstration or oral briefing (deemed export). The return of foreign equipment to its country of origin after repair in the United States, shipments from a U.S. foreign trade zone, and the electronic transmission of nonpublic data that will be received abroad also constitute U.S. exports.
- Re-exports by any party of commodities, software, or technology exported from the United States.
- Foreign products that are direct products of technology exported from the United States.
- *U.S. person activities:* The EAR restricts the involvement of "U.S. persons," that is, U.S. firms or individuals, from exporting foreign-origin items or from providing services that may contribute to the proliferation of weapons of mass destruction. The regulations also restrict technical assistance by U.S. persons with respect to encryption commodities or software (EAR, part 732; see International Perspectives 15.2 and 15.3).

The Bureau of Industry and Security (BIS) is the primary licensing agency for dual use exports. The term "dual use" distinguishes items (i.e., commercial items with military applications) covered by EAR from those covered by the regulations of certain other export licensing agencies, such as the Departments of State and Defense. Although dual use is often employed to refer to the entire scope of the EAR, the EAR also applies to some items that have solely civilian uses. It is also important to note that the export of certain goods is subject to the jurisdiction of other agencies, such as the Food and Drug Administration (drugs and medical devices), the Department of State (defense articles), and the Nuclear Regulatory Commission (nuclear materials).

Commerce Export License

Exports and other activities that are subject to the EAR are under the regulatory jurisdiction of the BIS. They may also be controlled under export-related programs of other agencies. Before proceeding to complete any export transaction, it is important to determine whether a license is required. The modalities of transportation is immaterial in the determination

INTERNATIONAL PERSPECTIVE 15.2.
Do You Need a Commerce Export License?

Even though the majority of U.S. export/re-exports does not require a license (EAR 99), it is important to establish whether a license is required for your exports from the United States. In 2004, The Bureau of Industry and Security (BIS) reviewed 15,534 license applications (995 were deemed exports) covering transactions estimated at $15.3 billion and approved over 84 percent of these applications. The average processing time for a completed license application was thirty-six days (2004) compared to forty-four days (2003).

How do you establish whether you need an export license for your product?

A. *Nature of the product intended for export:* It is important to know whether the item you intend to export has a specific Export Control Classification Number (ECCN). You may require a license if your item is listed on the Commerce Control List (CCL) and the country chart in the regulations states that a license is required to that country.

   If your item falls under the jurisdiction of the Department of Commerce and is not listed on the CCL, it is designated as EAR 99 (low-tech items that do not require a license unless they are destined to an embargoed country or to an end user of concern in support of a prohibited end use).

B. *Ultimate destination, end user, and end use of the product intended for export:* A license is required for virtually all exports to embargoed destinations (Cuba, North Korea, etc). You need to consult the list of embargoed countries by three agencies: Departments of Commerce, State, and Treasury. Certain individuals and organizations are prohibited from receiving U.S. exports, while others may only receive such goods if they have been licensed (including EAR 99). It is important to consult the list of individuals and organizations engaging in activities related to the proliferation of weapons of mass destruction, terrorism and narcotics trafficking, and persons whose export privileges have been revoked by BIS. A license requirement may be based on the end use in a transaction, primarily for proliferation purposes.

of export licenses; that is, an item can be sent by regular mail, hand carried on an airplane, or transmitted via e-mail or during a telephone conversation.

The following steps are important in establishing whether a given export item is subject to a license (Figure 15.1).

Step 1: Is the item (intended for export) subject to EAR? Items subject to the EAR regulations include all items in the United States or abroad (including

INTERNATIONAL PERSPECTIVE 15.3.
General Prohibitions and License Exceptions

General Prohibitions: Export/re-export and conduct subject to EAR which are prohibited without a license or a license exception from BIS.

- Export/re-export of controlled items to listed countries.
- Re-exports and export from abroad of foreign-made items incorporating more than a de minimis amount of controlled U.S. content. For certain countries and commodities, de minimis is defined as re-exports of foreign-made commodity incorporating controlled U.S.–origin commodities valued at 10 percent or less of the total value of the foreign made commodity.
- Re-export and export from abroad of the foreign-produced direct product of U.S. technology and software.
- Engaging in actions prohibited by a denial order, violation of any order, and proceeding with transactions with knowledge that a violation has occurred or is about to occur.
- Export or re-export to prohibited end uses or end users, to embargoed destinations.
- Engaging in actions that support proliferation activities and export/re-export through or transit through specific countries (Albania, North Korea, Russia, etc.) without a license or license exception (EAR, part 736).

License Exceptions (Items that can be exported without a license)

- GBS: Authorizes export/re-exports to country Group B (Western countries).
- LVS: Authorizes limited value shipments (single shipment) to country Group B.
- CIV: Allows exports/re-exports for civil end uses/users to Group D1 countries (except North Korea).
- TSR: Technology/software export/re-exports destined to country Group B.
- GFT: Allows export/re-exports of gift parcels to an individual, or religious or charitable organization located in any country.
- BAG: Authorizes individuals leaving the United States to take to any destination personal baggage, effects, vehicles, and tools of trade.
- TMP: Authorizes various temporary exports/re-exports (EAR, part 740).

those in a U.S. free trade zone), foreign-made items that are direct products of U.S.–origin technology or software (or that incorporate U.S.–origin materials exceeding certain minimum levels), or certain activities of U.S. persons related to the proliferation of weapons of mass destruction (Figure 15.2) and technical assistance with regard to encryption commodities or soft-

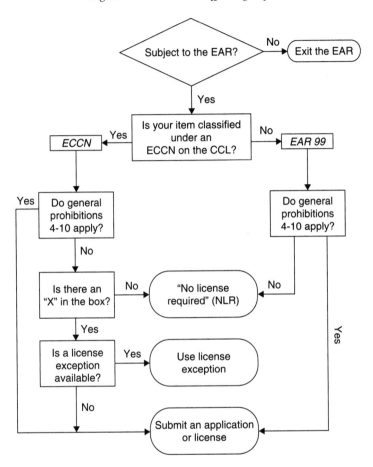

FIGURE 15.1. Steps to Determine Whether a Commerce Export Control License Is Required

ware. It also covers activities of United States or foreign persons prohibited by any order (denied parties). Publicly available technology and software, phonograph records, magazines, and so on, are excluded from the scope of EAR.

If the item is subject to the EAR, it is necessary to classify it under an ECCN (Export Control Classification Number) on the CCL (Commerce

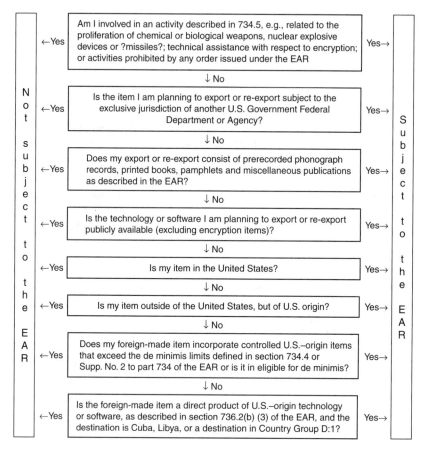

FIGURE 15.2. Steps to Determine Whether a Transaction Is Subject to the EAR

Control List). If it is not subject to EAR, there is no need to comply with the EAR. It may be necessary to comply with the regulations of another agency.

Step 2: Is the item classified under the ECCN on the CCL? Any item controlled by the Department of Commerce has an ECCN. Exporters should classify their product against the CCL. They can also send an export classification request to the Department of Commerce. A request can also be made if an item has been incorrectly classified and/or should be transferred to another agency. Given certain changes that are made with regard to product classifications and the EAR, it is important to monitor for any modifications to your product including eligibility for a license exception to certain destinations. Some companies may opt to use a computerized product/country license determination matrix.

Step 3: Do the general prohibitions (4-10) apply? Whether a product is listed under an ECCN on the CCL or not (EAR 99), it is important to determine if general prohibitions apply, that is, export/re-export to prohibited end uses, users, or to embargoed destinations. The general prohibitions also include engaging in activities prohibited by a denial order or supportive of proliferation activities as well as in-transit shipments through certain destinations.

If an item is not listed under the ECCN on the commerce control list (EAR 99), and general prohibitions do not apply, no license is required. However, if the prohibitions apply (for items listed/not listed on ECCN), an application for a license should be submitted.

Step 4: Are there any controls on the country chart? The commerce country chart allows you to determine the export/re-export requirements for most items listed on the CCL. If an "X" appears in a particular cell, transactions subject to that particular reason for control (national security, antiterrorism, etc.)/destination combination require a license unless a license exception applies. No license is required if there is no "X" indicated in the CCL and the country chart (see sample analysis using the CCL and country chart).

Step 5: Applying for an export license: The Bureau of Industry and Security provides formal classification for a product or service, advisory opinion, or licensing decision upon review of a completed application submitted in writing or electronically. Even though it is the applicant's responsibility to classify the export, the BIS could be requested to provide information on whether the item is subject to the EAR and, if so, its correct ECCN. In addition to the classification requests, potential applicants could also seek advisory opinions on whether a license is required or is likely to be granted for a particular transaction. Such opinions, however, do not bind the BIS from issuing a license in the future (see International Perspective 15.4 for automated services).

Step 6: Destination Control Statement, shipper's export declaration, and record keeping: A destination control statement (DCS) is intended to prevent items licensed for exports from being diverted while in transit or thereafter. A typical DCS reads as follows:

> These commodities, technology, or software were exported from the United States in accordance with the Export Administration Regulations for ultimate destination (name of country). Diversion contrary to U.S. law is prohibited.

A DCS must be entered on all documents covering exports from the United States of items on the CCL and is not required for items classified as

INTERNATIONAL PERSPECTIVE 15.4. Automated Services

AES (Automated Export System): A computerized method for filing shipper's export declarations. It streamlines the export reporting process by reducing the paper work burden on the trade community.

ELAIN (Export License Application and Information Network): A system that allows electronic submission of license applications through private vendors.

ERIC (Electronic Request for Item Classification): A supplementary service to ELAIN that allows exporters to submit commodity classification requests electronically to BIS.

SNAP (Simplified Network Application Process): A method for submitting applications over the internet with a web browser.

STELA (System for Tracking Export License Applications): An automated voice response system that provides applicants with the status of their license and product classification applications. When the application is approved without conditions, STELA allows exporters to ship their goods without the need to wait for a formal letter from BIS.

EAR 99 (unless it is made under license exception BAG or GFT). Destination control statement requirements do not often apply to re-exports. For holders of a special comprehensive license (SCL), use of a DCS does not preclude the consignee from re-exporting to any of the SCL holder's other approved consignees or to other countries for which prior BIS approval has been received. A SCL allows experienced, high volume exporters to export a broad range of items. It was introduced in lieu of special license and allows exportation of all commodities to all destinations (with some exceptions). Another DCS may be required on a case-by-case basis. The DCS must be shown on all copies of the bill of lading, the air waybill, and the commercial invoice (EAR, part 748).

Even though there are few exceptions, submission of a shipper's export declaration (SED) to the U.S. government is generally required under the EAR. Information on the SED, such as value of shipment, quantity, and so on, is also used by the Census Bureau for statistical purposes. The exporter or the authorized forwarding agent submits the SED, which includes information such as criteria under which the item is exported (i.e., license exception, no license required, license number, and expiration date), ECCN, and other relevant information.

The exporter is required to keep records for every export transaction for a period of five years from the date of export. The records to be retained include contracts, invitation to bid, books of account, financial records, restrictive trade practices, and boycott documents or reports (EAR, part 762).

Following is an analysis using the CCL and country chart. In order to determine whether a license is required to export/re-export a particular item to a specific destination it is essential to use the CCL in conjunction with the country chart (EAR, part 774).

To demonstrate the type of thought process needed to complete this procedure, a sample entry and related analysis is provided.

> *Example:* The item destined for export to India is valued at approximately $10,000 and classified under ECCN 2A000a. Based on the item classification, we know that the entire entry is controlled for national security and antiterrorism reasons. The item appears in the Country Chart column and the applicable restrictions are NS Column 2 and AT Column 1. An "X" appears in the NS Column 2 cell for India, but not in the AT Column 1 cell. This means that a license is required unless it qualifies for a license exception or Special Comprehensive License. It may qualify under a license exception (GBS).

Sanctions and Violations

The enforcement of the EAR is the responsibility of the BIS, Office of Export Enforcement (Department of Commerce). The Office of Export Enforcement (OEE) works with various government agencies to deter violations and impose appropriate sanctions. Its major areas of responsibility include preventive enforcement, export enforcement, and prosecution of violators.

Preventive enforcement is intended to stop violations before they occur by conducting prelicense checks to determine diversion risks, reliability of overseas recipients/end users of U.S. commodities/technology, and postshipment verifications. In 2004, BIS's investigations resulted in the criminal convictions of twenty eight individuals and businesses, with $2.9 million in penalties (www.bis.doc.gov). The BIS's Office of Export Enforcement also conducts investigations of potential export control violations. When preventive measures fail, it pursues criminal and administrative sanctions. Violations of the EAR are subject to both criminal and administrative penalties. Fines for export violations can reach up to $1 million (U.S.) per violation in criminal cases, $11,000 per violation in most administrative cases, and $120,000 in cases involving national security issues. In addition, violators may be subject to prison time and denial of export privileges by placing them on the denied persons list.

The EAR also provides certain indicators to help exporters recognize and report a possible violation. It reminds exporters to look for the following in export transactions:

- If one of the parties to the transaction has a name or address that is similar to an entity on the U.S. Department of Commerce's list of denied persons.
- If the transaction has "red flags," that is, (1) the customer or purchasing agent is reluctant to offer information about the end use of the product; (2) the customer is willing to pay cash for a very expensive item (when the terms provide for financing), has little or no business background, and is unfamiliar with the product, or the customer declines routine training installation or other services; (3) the product ordered is incompatible with the technical level of the country and its packaging is inconsistent with the stated method of shipment or destination; and (4) the shipping routes are abnormal for the producer and destination, delivery dates are vague, and a freight forwarding firm is listed as the product's final destination.

ANTIBOYCOTT REGULATIONS

The U.S. antiboycott provisions of the Export Administration Act prohibits U.S. firms from participating in foreign boycotts or embargoes not authorized by the U.S. government. Even though this law was primarily aimed at the Arab boycott against Israel, it prevents U.S. firms from being used to implement foreign policies of other nations that are inconsistent or contrary to U.S. policy. The law requires companies to report boycott-related requests by other nations and imposes a range of sanctions in the event of violations. In September, 2004, for example, St. Jude Medical Export, an Australian subsidiary of a Minnesota-based U.S. exporter, agreed to pay a $30,000 civil penalty to settle charges that it violated the antiboycott provisions of the EAR. The Bureau of Industry and Security charged that the firm violated the EAR by (1) its failure to report its receipt of three requests from the Iraqi government agency to adhere to the rules of the Israeli boycott during the 2000-2001 reporting period, and (2) its agreement to refuse to do business with blacklisted persons.

Scope of Coverage

Who Is Covered by the Laws?

The sources of U.S. antiboycott regulations can be found in the Export Administration Act (EAA) and its implementing regulation, the Export Administration Regulations (EAR), and the Internal Revenue Code. The EAR applies to all "U.S. persons" (individuals and companies located in the United States). It also covers foreign subsidiaries that are controlled by a U.S. company in terms of ownership or management. In such cases, the foreign affiliate will be subject to the antiboycott laws and the U.S. parent will be held responsible for any noncompliance. The regulations cover the activities of individuals or companies relating to the sale purchase or transfer of goods or services within the United States or between the United States and a foreign country. This includes U.S. exports, imports, financing, forwarding and shipping, and certain other transactions that may take place outside the United States. To trigger the application of the antiboycott laws, the activity must involve U.S. Commerce with foreign countries (EAR, part 760).

What do the Laws Prohibit?

Refusals to do business. The law prohibits any U.S. person from refusing to do business (expressly or implicitly) with any person pursuant to a request, agreement, or requirement from a boycotting country. The use of a designated list of persons also constitutes a refusal to do business prohibited under the act.

Discriminatory actions. The statute prohibits any U.S. person from discriminating against an individual (who is a U.S. person) on the basis of race, religion, gender, or national origin. It also prohibits similar action against a U.S. corporation based on the race, religion of the owner, officer, director, or employee. Such prohibitions apply when the action is taken in order to comply with or support an unsanctioned foreign boycott.

Furnishing information to a boycotting country. The statute prohibits furnishing information about any business relationship with or in a boycotted country or with black-listed firms or persons. It also prohibits actual furnishing of, or agreements to furnish, information about the race, religion, sex, or national origin of another U.S. person, or any U.S. person's association with any charitable organization that supports the boycotted country.

Implementing letters of credit with prohibited conditions or requirements. The statute also prohibits any U.S. person from implementing a letter of credit that contains a condition or requirement from a boycotting country.

This includes issuing, honoring, paying, or confirming a letter of credit. The prohibition applies when a beneficiary is a U.S. person and the transaction involves the export of U.S. goods (i.e., shipment of U.S.–origin goods or goods from the United States).

Some exceptions to the prohibitions include the following:

- Compliance with import requirements of a boycotting country
- Compliance with unilateral and specific selections by buyers in a boycotting country
- Compliance with a boycotting country's requirements regarding shipment and transshipment of exports
- Compliance with immigration, passport, visa, employment, and local requirements of a boycotting country

Reporting Requirements

The regulations require U.S. persons to report quarterly to the U.S. Department of Commerce any requests they have received to take any action to comply with, further, or support an unsanctioned foreign boycott. The U.S. Treasury also requires taxpayers to report activities in or with a boycotting country and any requests to participate in a foreign boycott (see International Perspective 15.5).

INTERNATIONAL PERSPECTIVE 15.5.
Requests That Are Not Reportable

- To refrain from shipping on a carrier owned or leased by a particular country or its nationals, or a request to certify to that effect.
- To ship goods via a prescribed route, or refrain from shipping via a prescribed route, or to certify to that effect.
- To supply information regarding the country of origin of goods, the name of the supplier, provider of services, or the destination of exports.
- To comply with the laws of another country other than one that requires compliance with the country's boycott laws.
- To supply information about the exporter or exporter's family for immigration, passport, or employment purposes.
- To supply a certificate by owner/master that the vessel, aircraft, etc., is eligible to enter a particular port pursuant to its laws.
- To supply a certificate from an insurance company stating that the company has an agent or representative in the boycotting country including the name and address of such agent.

Penalties for Noncompliance

The law provides both criminal and civil penalties for violations of the antiboycott statute. On the criminal side, a person who knowingly violates the regulations is subject to a fine of up to $50,000 or five times the value of the exports involved, whichever is greater. It may also include imprisonment of up to five years. In cases in which the violator has knowledge that the items will be used for the benefit of countries or persons to which exports are restricted for national security or foreign policy purposes, the criminal penalty varies. For individuals, a fine may be imposed up to $250,000 and/ or imprisonment of up to ten years. For firms, the penalty for each violation can be $1 million or up to five times the value of the exports involved, whichever is greater. Administrative or civil penalties may include any or all of the following: revocation of export licenses, denial of export privileges, exclusion from practice, and imposition of fines of up to $11,000 per violation, or $100,000 if the violation involves items controlled for national security reasons. The treasury may also deny all or part of the foreign tax benefits.

FOREIGN CORRUPT PRACTICES

The Foreign Corrupt Practices Act (FCPA) of 1977 was enacted as a public response to the Watergate Scandal and the disclosure of corrupt payments by U.S. multinationals to foreign government officials in order to obtain business. The Security Exchange Commission (SEC) investigations revealed that 117 Fortune 500 companies had paid millions of dollars to foreign governments. Substantial payments were made by companies such as Exxon ($56.7 million), Northrop ($30.7 million), and Lockheed Martin ($25 million) to foreign officials (Impert, 1990). The overriding public concern was that this practice could tarnish the reputation of the United States in the world and was not in the best interest of U.S. corporations.

The legislation represents an attempt to enforce morality and ethics in the conduct of international business transactions. The FCPA was enacted as an amendment to the Securities and Exchange Act of 1934. It was later amended in 1988, as part of the Omnibus Trade and Competitiveness Act. In 1998, the FCPA was again amended to implement the OECD convention on combating bribery of foreign public officials in international business transactions (see International Perspective 15.6 for corruption index in certain countries).

The principal objectives of the legislation are:

- To prohibit the bribery of foreign officials by U.S. individuals and corporations to obtain or retain a business and
- To establish standards for maintaining corporate records and internal accounting control objectives.
- The anti-bribery provision applies to all publicly held corporations registered with SEC and all domestic concerns. The 1998 amendments expanded the application of the antibribery provisions to cover "any person" who commits bribery on U.S. territory regardless of whether the accused is a resident or does business in the United States. In addition, individual corporate employees can be prosecuted even if the corporation is found not guilty of violating the FCPA (Gleich and Woodward, 2005). The accounting standards and objectives apply only to SEC registrants or those that are required to file reports with the SEC.

INTERNATIONAL PERSPECTIVE 15.6.
Corruption Perception Index Selected Countries (2005)

Country	Level of Corruption	Country	Level of Corruption
Argentina	2.8	Japan	7.3
Australia	5.8	Kenya	2.1
Brazil	3.7	Mexico	3.5
Canada	8.4	Nigeria	1.9
China	3.2	Pakistan	2.1
Colombia	4.0	Russia	2.4
Costa Rica	4.2	Thailand	3.8
Egypt	3.4	United States	7.6
France	7.5	Uruguay	5.9
India	2.9	Venezuela	2.3
Indonesia	2.2	Zimbabwe	2.6

Source: Adapted from Transparency International, 2005.

Note: The measure is taken out of ten points. It ranges from 10 (squeaky clean) to 0 (highly corrupt).

Scope of Coverage

Who Is Subject to the FCPA?

The act applies to all publicly held corporations registered with the SEC and other domestic concerns. Domestic concerns are broadly defined to include all U.S. citizens and residents as well as any entity whose principal place of business is in the United States or incorporated under the laws of the United States.

A U.S. parent company may be liable for corrupt payments by its foreign subsidiary if the U.S. parent company knew or participated in the subsidiary's corrupt action or took no measures to discourage such payments. The FCPA covers activities of foreign agents and employees of domestic concerns and U.S. nationals living anywhere in the world who have little contact with the United States (Atkinson and Tillen, 2005).

What Is Covered by the FCPA?

The antibribery provision prohibits American businesses from using interstate commerce to pay off foreign officials to obtain or retain a business. Payment to any foreign official to obtain the performance of routine governmental action is explicitly exempted. The 1988 amendments to the FCPA changed the knowledge requirement and the definition of grease payments, added certain defenses to charges of bribery under the statute, increased penalties, and authorized the president to negotiate an international agreement prohibiting bribery.

The knowledge requirement. The 1977 act prohibited any payments while knowing or having reason to know that they would be used to bribe foreign officials. It was believed that a broad application of the "reason to know" standard would put many multinational companies under the risk of liability for the actions of their sales agents who engage in bribery without their approval. Such a standard would also invite unwarranted scrutiny of distributors or sales agents in countries that are considered to be corrupt. Given such legitimate business concerns, the "reason to know" standard was removed from the act and objective criteria established with respect to such conduct. This standard is narrower and holds businesses liable only if they are substantially certain that the illicit payments are to occur or that such a circumstance exists (Hall, 1994).

Exemption of payments for ministerial or clerical duties. The amendment based permissible bribes on the purpose for which payment is made, as opposed to the official position of the recipient. It excludes payments for routine governmental actions from the application of the act.

Additional defenses against charges of bribery. Payments are not considered corrupt if they are lawful under the laws of the foreign country and if they are used to reimburse foreign officials for reasonable expenditures, such as visits to manufacturing facilities, promotion, and so on.

Increased penalties. The maximum fine for a corporation was increased from $1 million to $2 million. For individuals, the maximum fine was also increased from $10,000 to $100,000. Individuals and corporate employees were made criminally liable even when the corporation is not in contravention of the FCPA.

Authorization to negotiate an international agreement. The act authorizes the president to negotiate an international agreement with countries that are members of the OECD to prohibit bribery.

The accounting provisions of the FCPA are intended to prevent companies from escaping detection by maintaining dubious accounts or slush funds. It requires any corporation that has certain classes of shares with the SEC to (1) make and keep accurate books and accounts that fairly reflect the transactions and (2) maintain a system of internal accounting controls in order to prevent the unauthorized use of corporate assets and transactions and to ensure the accuracy of corporate records.

Enforcement and Penalties

Enforcement of the FCPA is the joint responsibility of the SEC and the Department of Justice (DOJ). The DOJ has authority for civil enforcement of violations by domestic concerns with respect to the antibribery provisions. It also has exclusive jurisdiction over criminal prosecution in relation to the accounting as well as antibribery provisions of the statute. The SEC has similar authority for civil enforcement of violations of the antibribery and accounting provisions.

Criminal penalties may reach up to $2 million for public corporations and domestic concerns, and $100,000 and/or a maximum of five years for officers, directors, or employees who commit willful violations of the antibribery provisions. With regard to civil penalties, a maximum of $10,000 may be levied against any company, employee, officer, or director. Injunctive relief is also available to forestall a violation. Violations of the accounting provisions can result in a fine of $2.5 million for companies or up to ten years of imprisonment for individuals.

Since the introduction of the FCPA, several U.S. companies have been investigated for bribing foreign officials to obtain contracts. Over the past few years, some companies were indicted and fined for bribing foreign officials in order to use their influence to secure government contracts. Here are some examples:

- In 1995, Lockheed Martin was indicted for paying an Egyptian legislator $1 million through a consulting firm for helping Lockheed secure the sale of three transport planes. The company agreed to a settlement by paying a $24.8 million penalty (Anonymous, 1995).
- In 1990, Young and Rubicam, a New York-based advertising firm, entered a guilty plea and paid a $500,000 fine for bribing a former official of the Jamaican Ministry of Tourism to secure a contract with the Jamaican Tourist Board (Lipman, 1990).

U.S. companies could seek an advisory opinion from the DOJ on whether a particular transaction would violate the FCPA. Any opinion by the DOJ that sanctions a proposed transaction would create a presumption of legality.

Measures for Compliance with the FCPA

Implementing Due Diligence Procedures

It is advisable to prepare internal procedures to evaluate and select foreign partners and agents. Once an appointment has been made consistent with the internal procedures, a written agreement is needed to govern the relationship between the parties. Such an agreement should generally state that the agent/partner has no authority to bind the exporter and that the agreement is valid insofar as the foreign agent/partner complies with the FCPA and the foreign country's laws. It should also stipulate that the agent/partner is not an employee, officer, or representative of any government agency. The exporter should be promptly notified of any changes in representation.

Seeking an Advisory Opinion from the Government

The DOJ provides an advisory opinion on the legitimacy of a proposed transaction. Other federal agencies also provide an advisory opinion.

Adopting Internal Measures and Controls

Internal procedures should be established to guide employees. Such programs include procedures for reporting and investigations; seeking the opinion of counsel; policies for employees, agents, or joint venture partners; and training programs for officers and employees.

International Efforts to Control Corruption

- The OECD Antibribery Recommendation, 1994
- The OECD Convention on Combating Bribery, 1997
- The ICC Rules of Conduct to Combat Extortion and Bribery, 1977 (revised in 1996)
- Transparency International (TI), which has as its mission to enhance public transparency and accountability in international business transactions and in the administration of public procurement

ANTITRUST LAWS AND TRADE REGULATION

Antitrust laws are intended to enhance efficiency and consumer welfare by proscribing practices that lessen competition or create a monopoly. Such laws also meet the sociopolitical objective of dispersing economic power. Historically, monopolies were often sanctioned in the area of trade and commerce. During the colonial period, for example, private companies such as the East India Company (1600), The Dutch West India Company (1621), and The Hudson Bay Company (1670) received charters from governments that granted them a monopoly of trade. In North America, British merchants were given monopolies over the export and import of goods.

The idea of monopoly rights was soon found unacceptable, as it restricted the rights of individuals from competing freely. In many European countries, it was viewed as incompatible with the competitive integrity of markets and free trade. By 1860, Britain had unilaterally abrogated the rights of commercial monopolies given to particular companies (Johns, 1988). In the United States, there was a call for legislation to control "dangerous conspiracies against the public good" (Shenefield and Stelzer, 1993). The Sherman Act was passed in 1890.

Antitrust laws are often referred to as the Magna Carta of free enterprise because they preserve free competition in domestic and foreign trade as well as minimize government intervention in business affairs.

U.S. Antitrust Regulations

U.S. antitrust laws can be grouped into three categories:

1. *General prohibitions:* The Sherman Act, the Federal Trade Commission (FTC)
2. *Specific prohibitions:* The Clayton Act and amendments
3. *Exemptions*

General Prohibitions

The Sherman Act outlaws certain concerted activity in restraint of trade between two or more parties. The U.S. Supreme Court has developed certain criteria to determine the lawfulness of a given restraint: the per se rule and the rule of reason. The per se rule applies to those restraints of trade which are prohibited regardless of their effect on competition or economic welfare.

Per se violations include price-fixing, division of markets (market sharing) between competitors, and certain boycotts by sellers or buyers (i.e., an agreement between competitors not to deal with a customer or supplier). Restraints that are not categorized as per se violations are subject to the rule of reason; that is, practices are restricted only if they have an adverse effect on competition. This often requires analysis of the competitive structure of the firm, the firm's market share and/or power, and other relevant factors. The Sherman Act also prohibits monopoly abuse and attempts or conspiracies to monopolize trade or commerce with foreign nations. If a firm has a high market share as a result of improved productivity, it is not considered objectionable unless it is obtained through systematic conduct designed to harm competitors.

The FTC proscribes unfair competitive practices even though they do not violate specific provisions of either the Sherman Act or the Clayton Act. It also prohibits unfair or deceptive practices in or affecting foreign commerce. The commission has authority to issue interpretative rules and general statements of policy, rules, and guidelines that define unfair or deceptive business practices.

Specific Prohibitions

The Clayton Act proscribes any acquisition of the stocks or assets of another entity affecting commerce in any part of the United States that results in the creation of a monopoly or a substantial lessening of competition. The Clayton Act is not limited to the acquisition of a competitor. It also prohibits price discrimination between two purchasers without just cause or exclusive dealing in foreign commerce that tends to create a monopoly or lessen competition in the United States. Exclusive dealing (tying) occurs when the seller sells a product only on the condition that the purchaser will not deal in the goods of the seller's competitor.

Exemptions

Certain export activities of U.S. companies are exempt from the reach of U.S. antitrust laws. These exemptions came in the wake of increasing U.S. trade deficits and were intended to encourage U.S. companies to form alliances in order to increase exports overseas. The development of export trading companies (ETCs) was sought to benefit export firms through the creation of economies of scale and diffusion of risk. The following are some of the exemptions in the area of export trade.

The Webb-Pomerene Act. The Webb-Pomerene Act allows U.S. firms to establish export cartels for the sole purpose of marketing their products overseas. This exemption from the antitrust laws allows competing firms to set prices, allocate orders, consolidate freight, or arrange shipments and, until 1982, applied only to merchandise exports. The Export Trading Company Act (ETC) of 1982 extended the application of the Webb-Pomerene Act to services.

Export trade certificate of review. The ETC Act provides a procedure for issuing a certificate of review exempting U.S. applicants from antitrust liability. Under this procedure, applicants disclose their plans for overseas trade with the government and obtain preclearance, that is, obtain the government's approval for their future export activity. The Commerce and Justice Departments issue the certificate to potential exporters after establishing that their conduct or activity does not substantially lessen competition or unreasonably affect prices in the United States. Applicants are exempt from antitrust laws so long as the minimum standards are met under the act. The ETC Act also provides protection to certificate holders against frivolous lawsuits by competitors that are intended to forestall their export activities.

Application of antitrust laws to international business transactions. Title IV of the ETC Act exempts exporting and other international business transactions from the application of the Sherman and FTC Acts unless the export conduct has a direct, substantial, and reasonably foreseeable effect on domestic trade or commerce. Anticompetitive acts directed at exports without effect on domestic commerce of a U.S. person are treated as foreign transactions and out of reach of U.S. antitrust laws. In the absence of this legislation, the antitrust laws would otherwise have extended to any anticompetitive conduct (agreements, conspiracy, etc.), regardless of its effect on U.S. import, export, or domestic commerce. Although this exemption could be used as an alternative to export certification or preclearance, it does not provide the immunity from prosecution that is available under the latter arrangement.

The following are generally considered to be a checklist of practices that businesses should avoid:

1. Discussing prices with competitors
2. Pricing below cost to drive out a competitor or discourage a new entrant
3. Dividing markets with other competitors
4. Compelling dealers to charge a given price
5. Tying the sale of one product to another
6. Charging customers different prices without reasonable justification
7. Terminating a customer without reasonable justification
8. Abusing market power to the disadvantage of consumers and competitors
9. Joining with a competitor to the disadvantage of other competitors
10. Suggesting that a supplier purchase from another division of the subsidiary

It is also important for companies to establish an antitrust compliance program.

Extraterritorial Application of U.S. Antitrust Laws

The U.S. antitrust laws are not limited to transactions that take place within U.S. borders. Overseas transactions with a substantial and foreseeable effect on U.S. commerce are subject to U.S. antitrust laws. Efforts by the United States to exercise its jurisdiction outside its borders have often been frustrated by foreign governments that did not want any infringements of their sovereignty. Some countries have enacted legislation to block the enforcement of U.S. laws within their countries, including any cooperation with respect to submission of evidence and documents. In view of such opposition, the U.S. government has resorted to bilateral antitrust agreements with various countries concerning the extraterritorial application of national antitrust laws. The agreements generally provide for the exchange of information, prior notification of enforcement actions, and consultation on policy matters.

Enforcement and Penalties

The DOJ and the FTC enforce U.S. antitrust laws. Whereas the DOJ can initiate civil or criminal suits against alleged violators, the FTC or states, through the attorney general, are empowered to bring only civil cases. Private parties that have been adversely affected by a violation of antitrust laws can also sue in federal court for an injunction or damages.

Penalties in criminal cases may involve fines up to $100,000 and imprisonment for up to three years for individuals. Corporations may be fined up to $1 million. Civil penalties could also result in hefty fines (see International Perspective 15.7).

INTERNATIONAL PERSPECTIVE 15.7.
Matsushita Co. Ltd. versus Zenith Radio Corporation

Background and facts: In 1974, Zenith filed a suit against a group of Japanese firms, including Matsushita, claiming that they had engaged in predatory pricing (pricing below cost) as part of a collusive plan to drive U.S. firms out of the color television market (CTV). It was alleged that the Japanese producers had agreed to limit the number of U.S. distributors to five and to set minimum prices in the U.S. market. It was also alleged that, notwithstanding the minimum prices, the companies agreed to provide substantial rebates to their U.S. distributors. In Japan, the producers controlled the retail outlets and used their control to fix retail prices, and retail market shares, and to restrict retailers from selling competitive products. It was also found that the Japanese firms never gained more than 45 percent of the U.S. market share and did not raise prices in twenty years. The district court held for Matsushita and other defendants and Zenith appealed. The appellate court reversed the trial court's decision. Matsushita and others appealed to the U.S. Supreme Court.

Decision: The Supreme court reversed the decision of the appellate court. The court stated that Zenith's accusations that Japanese firms were conspiring to drive U.S. industry out of business in order to monopolize the U.S. CTV market not only were untrue but could not have been possibly true. Elaborating on this issue, the court stated:

"If predatory pricing conspiracies are generally unlikely to occur, they are especially so, where, as here, the prospect of attaining monopoly power seems slight. Two decades after their conspiracy is alleged to have commenced, petitioners appear to be far from achieving this goal: the two largest shares of the retail market are held by RCA and the respondent Zenith. The alleged conspiracy's failure to achieve its ends in the two decades of its asserted operation is strong evidence that the conspiracy does not in fact exist. . . . Petitioners had every incentive not to engage in the conduct with which they are charged, for its likely effect would be to generate losses for the petitioners with no corresponding gains."

Source: 106 S. Court 1349 (1986).

INCENTIVES TO PROMOTE EXPORTS

From the 1870s until 1971, U.S. exports typically exceeded U.S. imports, except during World War II. Even during this period, U.S. exports fell below imports because a substantial percentage of the exports was not sold, but provided to allies under the Marshall Plan. All this began to change in the 1970s. The U.S. registered a trade deficit in 1971. The merchandise trade balance showed a \$2.27 billion deficit (1971) in contrast to the previous decades when exports exceeded imports. Some of the contributing factors to this state of affairs included the overvalued dollar and increased government expenditures at home and abroad that often resulted in purchases of foreign products and services. This situation was further exacerbated in 1973 when oil prices sharply increased and worsened the U.S. trade deficit due to large increases in expenditures for imports for petroleum products (Stein and Foss, 1992).

Domestic International Sales Corporation and the GATT

In an effort to remedy the worsening trade imbalance, the government enacted the Revenue Act of 1972. The act created the Domestic International Sales Corporation (DISC) to promote U.S. exports by providing tax incentives that would lower the cost of exporting goods in foreign markets. The legislation was also intended to remove the disadvantage of U.S. companies engaged in export activities through domestic corporations (Chou, 2005).

The DISC statute was also intended to offset the competitive disadvantage faced by U.S. firms in view of the various incentives provided by major trading nations to their export firms. Under the DISC scheme, a U.S. corporation could export its products through a subsidiary (DISC) organized in the United States (a shell corporation) with minimum capital of \$2,500. The DISC was required to engage almost exclusively in export sales. The tax implications of a corporation that elected to be treated as a DISC were as follows:

- Approximately half of DISC's earnings were taxed at the shareholder level regardless of whether they were distributed to shareholders (constructive dividends).
- The remainder of DISC's earnings was not taxable to the shareholder until actually distributed. This allowed for an indefinite deferral of tax. In effect, this amounted to a de facto tax exemption on about half of DISC's earnings because deferred taxes may never become due.

- Deferred taxes became due when distributed to shareholders, when a shareholder disposed of its DISC stock, or the corporation ceased to qualify as a DISC.

The DISC came under increasing attack by U.S. trading partners as an unfair and illegal subsidy to U.S. exporters. In a complaint by the EEC and Canada against the United States, the GATT panel issued a report stating that the DISC scheme conferred a tax benefit to exports and resulted in the price of exports being lower than similar goods for domestic consumption. The panel concluded that the scheme was in violation of the GATT treaty (GATT, 1977). Even though the United States never conceded to the inconsistency of the DISC with the GATT agreement, it nevertheless proceeded to replace the DISC with an alternative scheme that was acceptable to the GATT. (A vestige of the old DISC, the Interest Charge-DISC remains to date.)

The Tax Reform Act of 1984 created the Foreign Sales Corporation (FSC) to promote U.S. exports. Once the FSC is incorporated outside the United States and satisfies other requirements in the statute, its earnings are exempt from U.S. taxation. Although the FSC provides a benefit to U.S. exporters comparable to the DISC, it is permitted under the GATT because the GATT treaty does not require member countries to tax "economic processes" that take place outside their territory (Levin, 2004).

The European Union filed a complaint with the WTO asserting that the FSC regime was an illegal subsidy inconsistent with the GATT treaty (1998). In 1999, the WTO ruled in favor of the EU and called for the elimination of the FSC regime by 2000. In response to the WTO ruling, the United States repealed the FSC and enacted the Extraterritorial Income Exclusion Act (ETI) (2000) which provides U.S. exporters with the same tax benefit as the FSC. It allows U.S. exporters to exclude from federal income tax 15 percent of their net income from the export sale of qualified U.S.–origin goods. Alternatively, exporters of low profit items could exclude 1.2 percent of their gross receipts (not to exceed 30 percent of the net) from the export sale of qualified U.S.–origin goods (not more than 50 percent of the value is attributable to foreign content). The EU again challenged the ETI as an unfair subsidy to U.S. corporations and the WTO dispute settlement body found that it violated the treaty (2001). The ETI was phased out in 2004. The IC-DISC appears to be one of the few remaining tax incentives for U.S. exporters (Clausing, 2005; Gravelle, 2005) (see International Perspective 15.8 for export incentives in agriculture).

INTERNATIONAL PERSPECTIVE 15.8.
Agricultural Export Incentives

- **Market development:** The largest promotional programs are those pertaining to foreign market development and access to foreign markets. The programs allow for reimbursement of expenses incurred in approved activities.

- **Commercial export financing:** Provision of short and intermediate term commercial financing through the Commodity Credit Corporation. A buyer/supplier guarantee program is available for the purchase of U.S. agricultural exports.

- **Concessional sales:** Under Public Law 480, the U.S. government provides food aid under different arrangements (Title I, II and III).

- **Programs to offset the effects of unfair trade practices:** Such programs are intended to expand U.S. agricultural exports and to challenge unfair trade practices through the provision of subsidies and so on.

Interest-Charge Domestic International Sales Corporations (IC-DISCs)

The IC-DISC is a tax deferral vehicle (on the first $10 million U.S. export sales) that can be used by small and medium-sized exporting companies. It provides a 20 percent tax savings for qualifying U.S. exporters in view of the favorable dividend tax rules under the Jobs and Growth Tax Relief Reconciliation Act of 2003 (Loizeau, 2004).

To be eligible for IC-DISC status, corporations must satisfy certain requirements:

1. It must be a U.S. corporation.
2. At least 95 percent of its foreign trading gross receipts for the tax year must be "qualified exports receipts." Qualified export receipts include receipts from sales, leases, or rental of export property (Section 993 (a)). It also includes gross receipts for services related to warranty, repair, transportation of export property, engineering or architectural services from overseas projects, and interest on qualified export assets.
3. The adjusted basis of its qualified export assets must be at least 95 percent of its total assets at the end of the tax year. Qualified export assets include accounts receivable, temporary investments, export property, assets used primarily in connection with the production of qualified export receipts and loans to producers.

4. It has one class of stock with a minimum value (capital) of $2,500.
5. A timely election to be treated as an IC-DISC for the current tax year.
6. Certain personal holding companies, financial, insurance institutions as well as companies that are members of any controlled group of which an FSC is a member are ineligible to be treated as an IC-DISC.

How Does an IC-DISC Work?

Step 1: A U.S. exporter (or shareholder) forms a tax-exempt IC-DISC corporation.

Step 2: The U.S. exporter pays the IC-DISC commission. The allowable commission rate is the greater of either 50 percent export net income or 4 percent of gross export income.

Step 3: The U.S. exporter deducts the commission paid to the IC-DISC from its income taxed at 35 percent. (The IC-DISC pays no U.S. income tax on the commission income.)

Step 4: When the IC-DISC pays dividend to its shareholders, the shareholders pay dividend income tax of 15 percent. (On income at IC-DISC, which is accumulated and untaxed, shareholders are required to pay interest.)

Tax Benefits of IC-DISC

1. *Reduced taxable income:* The U.S. exporter pays an annual tax deductible commission on its export sales to the IC-DISC. This reduces its taxable base at the corporate level by the commission paid to the IC-DISC.
2. *Increased dividend income to shareholders:* The entire commission paid to the IC-DISC can then be distributed as a dividend at the end of taxable year. This payment could be subject to only a 15 percent individual dividend tax rate rather than the corporate tax rate of 35 percent.
3. *Deferral of IC-DISC income from taxation:* The IC-DISC is not subject to tax. However, its U.S. shareholders are subject to tax on deemed dividend distributions from the IC-DISC, which does not include income derived from the first $10 million of the IC-DISC's qualified export receipts each year. Thus, the IC-DISC allows a U.S. shareholder to defer paying tax on income attributable to $10 million of export sales. The U.S. shareholder must, however, pay an interest charge on its IC-DISC earnings (deferred tax liability) until it is distributed (see Table 15.1).

TABLE 15.1. An Example to Illustrate IC-DISC Tax Savings

	Without IC-DISC	With IC-DISC		
		Combined	Exporter	IC-DISC
Foreign trading gross receipts	5,000,000	5,000,000		
Cost of goods sold	3,000,000	3,000,000		
Selling, administrative expenses	1,000,000	1,000,000		
Export net income	1,000,000	1,000,000	1,000,000	
Tax rate	35%			
Tax paid	350,000			
IC-DISC greater of				
4% export gross receipts			200,000	
50% export net income			500,000	
IC-DISC commission			500,000	
IC-DISC commission deduction			500,000	500,000
Tax base after IC-DISC commission			500,000	500,000
Tax base after			35%	15%
Tax paid		250,000	175,000	75,000
Tax saving (net)		350,000 − 250,000 = 100,000		

CHAPTER SUMMARY

Objectives of Export Controls

These include national security, foreign policy, nonproliferation of weapons of mass destruction, and prevention of excessive draining of scarce natural resources.

Export Controls and Major Developments

With the end of the Cold War, controls have been substantially liberalized and simplified. Present controls focus on a small group of critical goods, technology, and countries. However, after the events of September 2001, certain restrictions have been imposed on exports.

Scope of Export Administration Regulations (EAR)

The EAR covers exports, re-exports, foreign products that are made using U.S. technology, and U.S. person activities.

Determining License Requirements

Step 1: Is the (item subject to export) transaction subject to Export Administration Regulations (EAR)?

Step 2: If so, is an export license required based on product characteristics, destination, and use/user, and the general prohibitions?

Step 3: If yes, is there a license exception?

Step 4: If no, apply for a license. If yes, no license required.

Step 5: Whether export is made under a license or not, exporters have to comply with SED/DCS and record-keeping requirements.

Indicators That Help Identify and Report Possible Violations

One of the parties to the transaction is on the list of denied persons or the transaction has red flags.

The U.S. Antiboycott Law

The law prohibits U.S. firms from participating in foreign boycotts not authorized by the U.S. government.

Who Is Covered by the Laws?

Individuals and companies located in the United States, foreign subsidiaries controlled by a U.S. company, and all activities involving U.S. commerce with foreign nations are covered.

What Do the Laws Prohibit?

Prohibitions include refusals to do business, discriminatory actions against a U.S. individual or company in order to support an unsanctioned foreign boycott, furnishing information to a boycotting country, and implementing letters of credit with prohibited conditions.

Exceptions to the Prohibitions

These include compliance with import/shipping and documentary requirements of boycotting country, compliance with shipment/transshipment/

specific carrier or route selection requirements of boycotting country, compliance with immigration/passport/employment, and other local law requirements of boycotting country.

Enforcement and Penalties

Penalties for noncompliance:

1. *Criminal penalties:* Fines and/or imprisonment
2. *Civil penalties:* Revocation of export license, denial of export privileges, imposition of a fine, denial of tax benefits

The Foreign Corrupt Practices Act (FCPA)

Principal objectives behind FCPA: To prohibit bribery of foreign officials by U.S. individuals and corporations to obtain or retain a business; to establish standards for maintaining corporate records and internal accounting control objectives.

Who Is Subject to the FCPA?

1. All U.S. citizens and residents
2. All entities with their principal place of business in the United States or incorporated in the United States.

Enforcement and Penalties

FCPA is enforced by the SEC and the U.S. DOJ.
Criminal penalties: $2 million for corporations and/or a maximum of five years for officers, directors, or employees who commit willful violations of the FCPA.
Civil penalties: Fine of $10,000 against any company, employee, or officer, $2.5 million fine imposed for violating the accounting provisions. Injunctive relief is also available.

Measures for Compliance with the FCPA

These include implementing due diligence procedures, seeking an advisory opinion from the government, and adopting internal measures and controls.

Antitrust Regulation and U.S. Trade

There are three categories of antitrust laws:

1. *General prohibitions:* The Sherman Act, The FTC.
2. *Specific prohibitions:* The Clayton Act. Covers restraints to commerce through mergers, acquisitions, exclusive dealing, and similar arrangements that lessen competition.
3. *Exemptions:* Exemptions from antitrust laws in the area of export trade include the Webb-Pomerene Act, Export Trade Certificate of Review, and Title IV of the ETC Act.

Extraterritorial Application of U.S. Antitrust Laws

Overseas transactions with a substantial and foreseeable effect on U.S. commerce are subject to U.S. antitrust laws.

Enforcement and Penalties

Institutions that enforce U.S. antitrust laws:

1. The DOJ initiates civil or criminal suits against alleged violators.
2. The FTC initiates only civil cases.

Penalties:

1. *Criminal penalties:* Fines up to $100,000 and imprisonment for up to three years (individuals); fines of up to $1 million for corporations.
2. *Civil penalties:* Hefty fines.

Incentives to Promote Exports

Interest-charge DISCs: Under this arrangement, taxes on export sales can be deferred. However, shareholders must pay interest on their proportionate share of the accumulated taxes deferred. Operational rules are similar to pre-1985 DISCs.

REVIEW QUESTIONS

1. State the major U.S. regulations that have a major impact on exports.
2. Discuss current developments in U.S. export controls.

3. What are the major objectives of U.S. export regulations? How do you establish whether a product needs an export license?
4. What types of actions does the U.S. antiboycott law prohibit? What kinds of requests are not reportable?
5. Discuss the knowledge requirement under the FCPA. Provide examples of U.S. companies indicted for bribing foreign officials.
6. Describe some of the international efforts to control corruption.
7. Discuss the major antitrust exemptions in the area of export trade.
8. Discuss the major incentives to promote exporters since 1972.
9. How does the IC-DISC work?
10. Do you think the IC-DISC will be attacked by U.S. trading partners as an unfair subsidy to U.S. exporters? Why/why not?

CASE 15.1. EXPORT TRADE CERTIFICATE OF REVIEW

Joint Export Activities to Reduce Costs and Risks: Export Trade Certificates of Reviews (COR) are issued by the Department of Commerce (with concurrence of the DOJ) and provide antitrust protection for certain specified export activities. Companies holding certificates can work together in the appointment of exclusive agents or distributors, limitations of pricing, or the handling of competitive products. The benefits of COR include the reduction of transportation, warehousing, and marketing costs. It also allows firms to establish joint facilities, set common prices, divide markets and sales territories, bid on large contracts, as well as share space in overseas trade shows. Small and medium-sized companies are able to spread costs and minimize risks in exporting without violating U.S. antitrust legislation. Congress viewed the uncertain application of U.S. laws to export activities as impediments to the growth and expansion of U.S. exports. The certificate provides antitrust preclearance for the specified export activities.

U.S. residents, partnerships, or corporations as well as state and local government entities can apply for COR. Over the past few years, a large number of trade associations have taken advantage of the program for their member firms. If the application meets certification standards, the Commerce Department is required to issue the COR within 90 days of submission. With COR, companies are immune from federal and state antitrust actions. In private antitrust actions, it alters the burden of proof to the advantage of the certificate holder (CH), shortens the statute of limitations covering the CH's conduct, provides for recovery of legal expenses (in cases where the CH prevails), and reduces liability. Since the introduction of the legislation in 1982, COR was challenged in court (1998) by Horizon International only

382 EXPORT-IMPORT THEORY, PRACTICES, AND PROCEDURES

over the certificate issued to another firm. The United States appeals court unanimously upheld the validity of the certificate (COR).

It is important to note that COR will not be granted if the export activity does any of the following:

1. Reduces competition in the United States or results in the substantial restraint of export trade of any U.S. competitor
2. Unreasonably affects prices of the covered product or services in the United States
3. Is carried out with the expectation that the products or services will be re-exported to the United States

Selected Holders of COR

- The Association of Manufacturing Technology (AMT) of McLean, Virginia, represents the interests of American providers of manufacturing machinery and equipment. Founded in 1902, its goal is to promote technological advancements in the design, manufacture, and sale of members' products as well as act as industry advocate on trade matters to governments and trade organizations throughout the world. The AMT received its COR in 1987 with a view to enhancing the trade competitiveness of its members. Recently, its members were able to cooperate in order to win the contract to supply a large Chinese aircraft plant with the requisite machinery to modernize and win Western aircraft parts contracts. Such cooperation would have been difficult without the COR.
- American Film Export Association (AFEA) of Los Angeles, California, is a trade association that provides members with marketing support services, government relations, and statistical data. It received COR in 1987 and has used this opportunity to expand export opportunities for its members. American Film Export Association fosters the exchange of information among its exporting members on foreign market conditions including vital credit data on more than 500 film and television buyers in over 50 countries. It also assists members in reducing delays in product delivery to overseas distributors, provides international model licensing agreements, and administers its arbitration tribunal, which resolves disputes regarding distribution.
- Florida Citrus Exports (FCE) operates as an export joint venture of nine members including grower-owned cooperatives and packing houses. It received COR in 1995 and has been able to assist members to cut export costs and increase export effectiveness. The COR allows mem-

bers to share transportation and market development costs, engage in joint promotional activities, speak with one voice in negotiations with export service providers and foreign buyers, prepare joint bids, assist each other in maintaining quality standards, and spread risks. The coordination of transportation is particularly important in exporting perishable commodities.

Questions

1. What are the benefits of certificates of review to U.S. exporters?
2. A certificate of review is not granted in certain cases. Discuss.

CASE 15.2. ENFORCEMENT OF EXPORT REGULATIONS

Bureau of Industry and Security (BIS): Export Enforcement

Export of national security controlled technology to China: In April 2004, Suntek Microwave, Inc., of Newark, California, pled guilty to charges that (1) it shipped detector log video amplifiers (DLVA), items controlled for national security reasons, to a company controlled by the Chinese government without obtaining the required export license; (2) it failed to obtain export licenses under the "deemed export" provisions of the EAR for Chinese nationals who worked at the company and were trained in DLVA manufacturing technology controlled by the EAR. Bureau of Industry and Security imposed on Suntek a $275,000 administrative penalty (and its former president, $187,000) and issued orders denying them export privileges for twenty years. Both were also subject to criminal penalties (Suntek: $339,000 fine; former president: one year imprisonment).

Export of pulse generators to denied persons in India: In June 2004, BNC Corp of California was sentenced to five years probation and a $300,000 criminal fine for illegally exporting pulse generators to two end users in India that were listed on the BIS entity list for nuclear nonproliferation reasons. BIS also issued a five-year suspended denial of export privileges.

Bureau of Industry and Security (BIS): Antiboycott Compliance

Furnishing prohibited business information to end user in Syria (2004): Invitrogen, Inc., of Rockville, Maryland, furnished its business relationship with Israel when it certified to the end user that the U.S.–origin goods the company sold to Syria were "not of Israeli origin and did not contain any Israeli materials." The antiboycott provisions of the EAR prohibit U.S. persons from complying with certain requirements of unsanctioned foreign boycotts, including providing information about business relationships with Israel and refusing to do business with persons on boycott lists. The EAR also requires that persons report their receipt of certain boycott requests to the Department of Commerce. The company agreed to a $2,000 civil penalty.

Security and Exchange Commission (SEC)/Department of Justice (DOJ): FCPA

Schering-Plough (SP) settles with SEC for its alleged violation of FCPA's accounting provisions (2004): Schering-Plough (SP) of Kenilworth, New Jersey, accepted to settle an SEC investigation into its alleged violations of the FCPA's accounting provisions. The SEC alleged that SP-Poland paid about $76,000 to the Chudow Castle Foundation (CC Foundation) (February 1999 to March 2002) in order to induce the director to influence the purchase of its pharmaceutical products with the health fund. The president of the CC Foundation was also director of the Silesian Health Fund. The SEC alleged that, even though the payments were made to a bona fide charity, they were made with the intention of inducing the foundation's president to use his authority as director of the fund to promote the purchase of SP-Poland's pharmaceutical products. None of the payments made by SP-Poland to the CC Foundation were accurately reflected on the books and records of the parent company. SP's system of internal accounting controls was inadequate to prevent or detect improper payments. SP agreed to pay a $500,000 penalty, and institute adequate internal controls.

ABB Vetco Gray Inc. pleads guilty to foreign bribery charges (2004): ABB Vetco Gray, Inc. (Vetco U.S.), and ABB Vetco Gray UK Ltd. (Vetco U.K.), both subsidiaries of Swiss Co. ABB Ltd. pleaded guilty to two counts of bribery in violation of the FCPA. The two companies paid bribes and other things of value (including automobile, shopping trips, etc.) to Nigerian government officials that evaluate and approve potential bidders for contract work on oil exploration projects in Nigeria, including bidders that seek subcontracts with foreign oil and gas companies. They paid more than $1 million in exchange for obtaining confidential bid information and favorable recommendations from Nigerian government officials in connection with seven oil and gas construction contracts in Nigeria from which the companies expected to realize profits of almost $12 million. The SEC also filed a complaint against the parent company, ABB Ltd. (whose stock is traded in the United States), for alleged violations of antibribery, books and records, and internal control provisions of the FCPA.

Vetco U.S. and Vetco U.K. each agreed to pay criminal fines of $5.25 million. This means that the DOJ will prosecute non–U.S. companies for violations of FCPA in antibribery provisions, even if the conduct leading to the violation took place outside the United States. It appears that the DOJ has to show that the non–U.S. companies conspired/acted with U.S. persons when engaging in the prohibited conduct. ABB Ltd. (parent company) agreed to establish adequate system of internal control, pay civil penalty of $10.5 million and $5.9 million in disgorgement and prejudgement interest.

Questions

1. In the case of Schering-Plough and Vetco Gray, do you think that adequate internal controls would have prevented corruption?
2. Do you think that preventing certain shipments from going to firms controlled by the Chinese government (Suntek case) would achieve the goal of protecting U.S. national security?

SECTION VII:
IMPORT PROCEDURES
AND TECHNIQUES

Chapter 16

Import Regulations, Trade Intermediaries, and Services

IMPORT RESTRICTIONS IN THE UNITED STATES

Tariffs

All goods imported into the United States are subject to duty or duty-free entry, depending on their classification under the applicable tariff schedule and their country of origin. For dutiable products, three different methods are used to levy tariffs:

1. *Ad valorem duty:* The duty levied is a percentage of the value of the imported product. It is the type of duty most often applied. An example would be a 2 percent ad valorem on imports of leather shoes. The duty obligation is proportional to the value of the dutiable cargo and bears no relation to the quantity imported.
2. *Specific duty:* This duty rate is based on the physical unit or weight or other quantity. Such duty applies equally to low- and high-priced goods. To the extent that the same duty rate is applied to similar goods with different import prices, specific duties tend to be more restrictive of low-priced goods. When the price of imports rises, the rate remains unchanged, and, subsequently, the effect of the specific duty declines. Examples would be a $9.00 per ton (wheat) or $2.50 per dozen (fountain pens) charges.
3. *Compound duty:* Compound duty combines both ad valorem and specific duty. An example would be $2.00 per pound and 4 percent ad valorem (chicken imports).

Export-Import Theory, Practices, and Procedures, Second Edition

Most merchandise imported into the United States is dutiable under the most-favored-nation (MFN) rate. The MFN principle is expressed in Article I of the GATT and in a number of bilateral and other treaties. Under this principle, any advantage or favor granted by the United States (a member of the GATT) to any import originating from any other country shall be accorded, unconditionally, to the like product originating from all other GATT/WTO members. If the MFN treatment is provided as a result of a bilateral treaty (MFN treatment for goods from China, not a member of the GATT/WTO), an obligation arises to treat imports from that country as favorably as imports from any other member of the GATT/WTO. Certain communist countries, such as Cuba and North Korea, are not accorded MFN status and thus denied the benefit of the low rates of duty resulting from trade agreements entered into by the United States.

Nontariff Barriers

Even though most goods freely enter the United States, there are some restrictions on the importation of certain articles (see International Perspective 16.1 and Tables 16.1 and 16.2). The rules prohibit or limit the entry of some imports, limit entry to certain ports, restrict routing, storage, or use, or require treatment, labeling, or processing as a condition of release from

---

INTERNATIONAL PERSPECTIVE 16.1. Consumer Products and Import Restrictions in the United States

Products or product categories with no import restrictions
Ceramic tableware, artwork, crafts, gems and gemstones, glass and glass products, household appliances, jewelry and pearls, leather goods that are not from endangered species, metals, musical instruments, optics and optical instruments, paper and paper products, plastics and plastic products, rubber and rubber products, sporting goods, tools, and other utensils.

Products or product categories subject to certain restrictions or requirements
Aerospace products, live animals and animal products, beverages, chemicals, combustibles, cosmetics, drugs and explosives, foods, radioactive and radio frequency devices, used merchandise, vehicles.

Products or product categories that are generally prohibited
Food products grown or produced in disease-ridden regions, products derived from endangered species, products that infringe intellectual property rights, obscene or pornographic materials as well as national treasures.

TABLE 16.1. Import Permits/Other Requirements and Respective Government Agencies

Agricultural commodities	
• Cheese, milk and dairy products, fruits and vegetables, meat and meat products (from sources other than cattle, sheep, swine goats, and horses), plant and plant products	U.S. Department of Agriculture (USDA) and The Food and Drug Administration (FDA)
• Insects, livestock and animals, meat and meat products (from cattle, sheep etc.), plant and plant products, poultry and poultry products, seeds	USDA
Arms, ammunition, and radioactive materials	Department of State and Department of the Treasury
• Arms, ammunition, explosives, and implements of war	
Consumer and electronic products	
• Household appliances such as washers, dryers, air conditioners, refrigerators, heaters, etc.	U.S. Department of Energy
• Flammable fabrics	U.S. Consumer safety Commission
• Electronic products such as microwave ovens, X-ray equipment, TV receivers	FDA
Foods, drugs, cosmetics, and medical devices	
• Foods and cosmetics	FDA
• Biological drugs	FDA
• Biological drugs for animals	USDA
• Narcotic drugs and derivatives	U.S. Department of Justice (USDJ)
• Pesticides and toxic substances	U.S. Customs
Textile, wool, and fur products	Federal Trade Commission
Wildlife and pets	U.S. Department of the Interior
Motor vehicles and boats	U.S. Department of Transportation
Alcoholic beverages	FDA
All bottle jackets made of plant materials	USDA
Administering agency for quotas, tariff quotas on imports	U.S. Customs

Source: U.S. Department of Commerce, 2003

TABLE 16.2. Import Barriers in Selected Countries

Country	Tariffs	Nontariff Barriers
Brazil	Average tariff about 12 percent ad valorem. As member of MERCOSUR, external tariff will range from 0 to 35 percent. High tariffs in certain protected sectors such as autos, textiles, and computers.	Onerous registration requirements for all importers. A variety of customs-related nontariff barriers/requirements for imported food and fees for such imports and medical and pharmaceutical products. Sanitary, photo-sanitary requirements for agricultural imports. Subsidies provided for many export products. Inadequate protection and enforcement of certain intellectual property rights.
Canada	Average tariff is 4 to 6 percent ad valorem. Tariff increases as goods become more processed. High tariffs on agri-food, boats etc. No or low tariffs for U.S. and Mexican products.	Cost of service mark-ups and other barriers to imports of wines and spirits. Import license required for certain commodities. Tariff quotas on dairy products, poultry, eggs, and barley products. Subsidies to agriculture, aircraft; use of sanitary and photo-sanitary measures. Use of tariff quotas, import licenses for certain exports.
Germany	Tariffs range from 4 to 17 percent. Raw materials enter with higher rates.	Regulations that hinder the importation of agricultural and biotechnology products. Restrictions on the entry of beef, poultry, dry pet food, hides and skin. Local buying preferences, restrictive packaging, food and drug trademark laws. Certification for wines.
Japan	Average tariff 2 percent ad valorem. Tariffs high on certain imports such as agricultural products, semi-manufactures, etc.	Slow and cumbersome import clearance procedures, product standards, and testing and certification requirements. Highly regulated, inefficient distribution system. Market access impediments in telecommunications, e-commerce. Inadequate protection and enforcement of certain intellectual property rights.

customs. U.S. nontariff barriers fall into the following categories (U.S. Department of Commerce, 2003):

Prohibited Imports

These imports include certain narcotics and drug paraphernalia (materials used to make or produce drugs); counterfeit articles; products sold in violation of intellectual property rights; obscene, immoral, and seditious matter; and merchandise produced by convicts or forced labor.

Imports Prohibited Without a License

These include arms and ammunition, and products from certain countries such as Cuba, Iran, and North Korea.

Imports Requiring a Permit

Such imports include alcoholic beverages, animal and animal products, plant products, and trademarked articles. For example, all commercial shipments of meat and meat food products offered for entry into the United States are subject to the regulations of the Department of Agriculture and must be inspected by the USDA Inspection Service before release by customs.

Imports with Labeling, Marking, and Other Requirements

Certain imports require special labeling. For example, wool and fur products must be tagged, labeled, or otherwise clearly marked to show the importer's name and other required information. All goods imported must be marked individually with the name of the country of origin in English.

Imports Limited by Absolute Quotas

These imports include dairy products, animal feed, chocolate, some beers and wines, textiles and apparel, cotton, peanuts, sugars, syrups, molasses, cheese, and wheat.

Imports Limited by Tariff Quotas

The tariff rates on these imports are raised after a certain quantity has been imported. This applies to cattle, whole milk, motorcycles, certain kinds of fish, and potatoes. Tariff quotas permit a specified quantity of merchandise

to be entered or withdrawn for consumption at a reduced rate during a specified period. When imported merchandise exceeds a tariff quota, the importer
is not allowed to commingle the merchandise and classification with nonquota class goods.

The Buy-American Act 1933

This act provides for the purchase of goods by the U.S. government (for
use within the country) from domestic sources unless they are not of satisfactory quality, or too expensive, or not available in sufficient quantity. The
procurement regulations allow for the purchase of domestic goods even
though they are more expensive than competing foreign merchandise, insofar as the price differential does not exceed six percent (12 percent in high-
unemployment areas) in favor of domestic goods.

U.S. FREE TRADE AGREEMENTS

One of the prominent exceptions to the MFN principle of nondiscrimination in the treatment of imports is that of free-trade areas and other preferential arrangements. This means that imports from countries with which the
U.S. has free trade or similar arrangements are accorded low- or duty-free
status (see International Perspective 16.2).

The U.S./Israel Free Trade Agreement (FTA, 1985)

The agreement provides for free or low rates of duty for merchandise imports from Israel in so far as the imports meet the rules of origin requirements.
For the preferential tariff rate, the product must be grown, produced, or manufactured in Israel, and imported directly into the United States, and the cost
or value of the materials produced in Israel plus the direct costs of processing operations in Israel must be no less than 35 percent of the import value.

The North American Free Trade Agreement (NAFTA, 1994)

The North American Free Trade Agreement eliminates tariffs on most
goods originating in Canada, Mexico, and the United States over a maximum
transition period of fifteen years (i.e., 2008). For most of Mexico–U.S. trade,
NAFTA eliminated existing duties immediately and/or agreed to phase them
out over a period of five to ten years. On a few sensitive items, the agreement
will phase out tariffs over fifteen years. The NAFTA duty treatment is applicable only to goods wholly produced or obtained in the NAFTA region, that
is, goods produced in the NAFTA region wholly from originating materials.

Imports from eligible countries are subject to tariff exemptions or reductions if:

1. The merchandise is destined to the United States without contingency for diversion at the time of exportation,
2. The cost or value of materials produced in the beneficiary country and/or the direct cost of processing performed is no less than 35 percent of the appraised value of the goods, and
3. The United Nations (United Nations Conference on Trade and Development) certificate of origin is prepared and signed by the exporter and filed with the entry of the goods.

There are two important limitations to the application of the GSP. First, the president is required to suspend GSP eligibility on imports of specific article from a particular country when the latter supplied more than $25 million in value of the article during the previous calendar year or over 50 percent of the value of U.S. imports. Since the $25 million limitation was based on the GDP of 1974, appropriate adjustments are made in light of the GDP for the current year. Such limitations do not apply to an eligible least-developed country. Second, the provision of GSP is restricted for the more advanced developing nations. For example, many products from countries such as Israel, Korea, Singapore, and Taiwan were graduated from GSP duty-free treatment.

The Caribbean Basin Initiative (CBI)

The CBI is a program intended to provide duty-free entry of goods from designated Caribbean and Central American nations to the United States. The program was implemented in 1984 and has no expiration date. For CBI duty-free treatment, the merchandise must be wholly produced or substantially transformed in the beneficiary country, be destined to the United States without contingency for diversion at the time of exportation, and meet the 35 percent value-added requirement similar to the GSP scheme. Value attributable to Puerto Rico, the U.S. Virgin Islands, and the U.S. customs territory may be counted toward the 35 percent value-added requirement. In the latter case, the attributable value is counted only up to a maximum of 15 percent of the appraised value of the imported article.

The United States–Caribbean Basin Trade Partnership Act (CBTPA, 2000) expands the trade benefits currently available to Caribbean and Central American countries under the CBI. Except for textile and apparel articles, the CBTPA allows tariff treatment similar to NAFTA for goods excluded from the CBI program (watches, footwear, petroleum products, etc.). Apparel articles assembled in one or more CBTPA beneficiary countries from U.S. or regional fabric or yarn are eligible for duty/quota-free treatment when they enter the United States.

The trade benefits under CBTPA are expected to end in 2008 or the date on which a free trade agreement is concluded between the U.S. and beneficiary countries.

The Andean Trade Preference (ATP)

This program was enacted in 1991 in order to provide duty-free treatment for imports of merchandise from designated beneficiary countries (Bolivia, Colombia, Ecuador, and Peru) to the United States. The eligibility requirements are similar to the CBI. It expired in 2001 and was renewed as part of the Trade Act of 2002. The new program "The Andean Trade Promotion and Drug Eradication Act" provides the same benefits as the ATP. It, however, extends the program by 700 additional products.

A similar arrangement was also made with Marshall Islands and the Federated States of Micronesia in 1989 and has no expiration date.

The African Growth and Opportunity Act (AGOA, 2000)

The AGOA was signed into law in May 2000. It is intended to offer beneficiary countries from sub-Saharan Africa duty-free treatment on more than 1,800 items that are exported to the United States. This is in addition to the standard GSP list of approximately 4,600 items. The program also provides duty and quota exemptions on their exports of textile and apparel products to the U.S. market.

The AGOA benefits are extended to countries that are GSP eligible under the existing criteria. Beneficiary countries are also exempted from competitive need limitations, that is, preferential treatment is not suspended if a country is competitive in the production of the item.

As of January 2005, thirty-seven of the forty-eight sub-Saharan countries were designated as AGOA beneficiaries. The AGOA was amended in 2002 and 2004. The latest revision (AGOA III of 2004) extends preferential treatment for beneficiary countries until 2015.

TRADE INTERMEDIARIES AND SERVICES

Customs Brokers

Customs brokers are persons who act as agents for importers for activities involving transactions with the customs service concerning (1) the entry and admissibility of merchandise, (2) its classification and valuation, and (3) the payment of duties and other charges assessed by customs or the refund or drawback thereof. A customs broker could be an individual, partnership, or corporation licensed by the U.S. Department of the Treasury. Finding an honest and knowledgeable broker is crucial to the success of an import firm (see International Perspective 16.3).

Dishonest brokers have, for example, been known to make incorrect entries at higher rates of duty and to bill the importer and later seek and pocket the refund. Brokers' failure to make timely filing can be costly to the importer (Serko, 1985).

Duties and Responsibilities of Customs Brokers

Record of transactions. Customs brokers are required to keep a correct and itemized record of all financial transactions and supporting papers for at least five years after the date of entry. Such books and papers must be available for inspection by officials of the Treasury Department. Brokers are required to make a status report of their continuing activity with customs. A triennial status report and fee must be addressed to the director of the port through which the license was delivered to the licensee.

Responsible supervision. Licensed brokers must exercise responsible supervision and control over the transaction of the customs business. A broker must provide written notification to customs within thirty days after terminating any employee hired for more then thirty consecutive days.

Diligence in correspondence and paying monies. Each licensed broker is required to exercise due diligence in making financial statements, in answering correspondence, and in preparing and filing records of all customs transactions. Payments of duties and other charges to the government are to

---

INTERNATIONAL PERSPECTIVE 16.3. Criteria for Selecting the Right Customs Broker or Freight Forwarder

- Competitive rate
- Knowledge of the product
- Reputation/integrity
- Service and flexibility
- IT capability
- Account management, financial stability
- Networking capability

be made on or before the date that payments are due. Any payment received by a broker from a client after the due date is to be transmitted to the government within five working days from receipt by the broker. A written statement should be made by the broker (to the client) accounting for funds received for the client from the government, as well as those received from the client when no payment has been made or received from a client in excess of charges properly payable within sixty days after receipt.

Improper conduct. The regulations prohibit the filing of false information, the procurement of information from government records to which access is not granted, the acceptance of excessive fees from attorneys, or the misuse of a license or permit. The licensee of a broker that is a corporation/ association can be revoked if it fails for 120 continuous days to have at least one officer who holds a valid broker license.

License Requirements

To obtain a customs broker license, an individual must be (1) a citizen of the United States (but not an officer or employee of the United States), (2) at least twenty-one years of age, (3) of good moral character, and (4) able to pass an examination to determine that he or she has sufficient knowledge of customs and related laws.

To obtain a broker's license, a partnership or corporation must have one member who is a licensed broker and must establish that the customs transactions are performed by a licensed member or a qualified employee under the supervision and control of the licensed member. Disciplinary action for infractions, such as making false or misleading statements in an application for a license, conviction after filing of a license application, violation of any law enforced by the customs service, and so on, could result in a monetary penalty as well as the revocation or suspension of a license or permit.

A license is not required to transact customs business by the exporter or importer on his or her own account. This also extends to authorized employees or officers of the exporter/importer or customs broker. A license is also not required by a person transacting business in connection with the entry or clearance of vessels or by any carriers bringing merchandise to port. A broker who intends to conduct customs business at a port within another district for which he or she does not have a permit must submit an application for a permit to the director of the relevant port.

Free-Trade Zones

Free-trade or foreign trade zones (FTZ) are areas usually located in or near customs ports of entry and legally outside the customs territory of the United

States. Foreign goods brought into these zones may be stored, broken up, sorted, or otherwise manipulated or manufactured. While conducting these operations, duty payments are delayed until products officially enter into the customs territory.

Merchandise may be admitted into an FTZ upon issuance of a permit by the district director, unless the merchandise is brought in solely for manipulation after entry, is transiting the FTZ (for which a permit is granted), or is domestic merchandise.

The FTZs are operated as public utilities under the supervision of the Foreign Trade Zones Board, which is authorized to grant the privilege of establishing a zone. Regulations are issued by the board covering the establishment and operation of FTZs. The board, which is composed of the Secretary of Commerce (chairperson), the Secretary of the Treasury, and the Secretary of the Army, evaluates applications by public and private corporations for a zone based on the following criteria: the need for zone services in the area, suitability of the site and facilities, justification in support of a zone, extent of state and local government support, views of persons or firms to be affected, as well as regulatory policy and other applicable economic criteria. The board also accepts applications for subzones, that is, special-purpose zones established as adjuncts to a zone for a limited purpose. Such zones are single-user facilities, usually accommodating the manufacturing operations of an individual firm at its plant. Every port of entry is entitled to at least one FTZ (Rossides, 1986; U.S. Department of Commerce, 1998, 2003).

Economic Advantages

- Merchandise admitted into the zone is not subject to customs duty until it is admitted into the customs territory. There is no time limit as to the storage or handling of the merchandise within the zone.
- Businesses can import a product subject to a high rate of duty and manipulate and manufacture it into a final product that is classified under a lower rate of duty when imported into the customs territory. Importers can also bring in products for display to wholesalers or items restricted under a quota until the next quota period. A quota item may also be transformed in an FTZ into an item that can be freely imported without quota restrictions.
- The importer can establish the duty of foreign merchandise when entered into a zone by applying for a "privileged status." Under this scheme, only the duty previously fixed is payable upon entry of the merchandise into the customs territory at a later date even though its

conditions may have changed or resulted in an article subject to a higher rate of duty.

- Duties are paid only on the actual quantity of such foreign goods incorporated in merchandise transferred from a zone of entry into the customs territory. This means that allowances are made for any unrecoverable waste resulting from manufacture or manipulation, thereby limiting the duty to articles actually entered. Savings in duties and taxes may thus result from moisture taken out or dirt removed, and so on. Savings in shipping and taxes may also be possible from shipping unassembled parts into a zone for assembly.
- Merchandise may be remarked or reconditioned to conform to certain requirements for entry into the customs territory.

The popularity of FTZs has grown not only in the United States but also in different parts of the world. By 1998, the number of such zones in the Unites States exceeded 200. Similar growth in the number of FTZs is observed in Africa, Asia, and Eastern Europe. A substantial part of the merchandise (over 80 percent) entered under FTZs in the United States is imported into the United States for domestic consumption, while the rest is exported to foreign markets.

Bonded Warehouses

Bonded warehouses are secured, U.S. customs approved warehouse facilities in which imported goods are stored or manipulated without paying duty until the goods are removed and entered for consumption. Duty is not payable when goods under bond are exported, destroyed under customs supervision, or withdrawn as supplies for vessel or aircraft. Merchandise may be kept in the warehouse for up to five years from the date of importation. The advantages of a bonded warehouse are quite similar to those of FTZs.

Any person desiring to establish a bonded warehouse must submit an application to the district director where such facility is located. On approval of the application, a bond is executed to protect the duty liability. Customs regulations provide for different types of bonded warehouses.

The major differences between a bonded warehouse and an FTZ are as follows: (1) costs for the use of bonded warehouses are generally less than for FTZs, (2) bonded warehouses may be established on a user's facilities and with a limited degree of difficulty as compared with FTZs, and (3) the permitted types of manipulation are more limited in the case of a bonded warehouse than for an FTZ. For example, goods may be stored or otherwise manipulated in a bonded warehouse as long as the process does not involve manufacturing. The assembly of watch heads by combined domestic and foreign components is a manufacture (not a manipulation) prohibited under customs regulations. However, the repackaging of spare watch parts is a manipulation that is allowable.

CHAPTER SUMMARY

Tariffs and Nontariff Barriers as Import Restrictions

Methods of Levying Tariffs

1. *Ad valorem:* Duty based on value of the imported product
2. *Specific:* Duty based on quantity or volume
3. *Compound:* Duty that combines both ad valorem and specific

Nontariff Barriers

Nontariff barriers include quotas, tariff quotas, labeling requirements, licensing requirements, prohibiting the entry of certain imports, and requirements to purchase domestically produced goods.

Preferential Trading Arrangements

NAFTA, U.S./Israel FTA, U.S./Australia FTA, the Caribbean Basin Initiative, Andean Trade Preference, the Generalized System of Preferences, AGOA.

Trade Intermediaries and Services

Customs brokers, free-trade zones, and bonded warehouses.

Customs Brokers

Customs brokers act as agents for importers with regard to (1) the entry and admissibility of merchandise, (2) its classification and valuation, and (3) the payment of duties and other charges assessed by customs or the refund or drawback thereof.

Free-Trade Zones

Free-trade zones are certain designated areas, usually located in or near a customs port of duty, where merchandise admitted is not subject to a tariff until it is entered into the customs territory. Foreign goods brought into an FTZ may be stored, or otherwise manipulated or manufactured. The FTZs are legally considered to be outside the customs territory of a country.

Bonded Warehouses

Bonded warehouses are secured, government-approved warehouse facilities in which imported goods are stored or manipulated without payment of duty until they are removed and entered for consumption.

REVIEW QUESTIONS

1. What are the different ways in which tariffs are levied in the United States?
2. What are the various types of nontariff barriers imposed in the United States?
3. What is the difference between "imports requiring a permit" and "imports prohibited with out a license"? Provide examples.
4. Does the U.S.–Israeli agreement eliminate all trade barriers between the two countries?
5. Discuss the U.S. GSP and conditions for eligibility.
6. Does AGOA allow free trade in textiles and apparel?
7. What is the difference between a customs broker and freight forwarder?
8. Discuss the duties and responsibilities of a customs broker.
9. What is a free trade zone? How does it differ from a bonded warehouse?
10. Discuss some of the economic advantages of free trade zones.

Minicase 16.1

John Tavis, a licensed broker and owner of Rider Logistics, obtains a power of attorney (POA) from a new client, Heather Mathis, owner of Global Imports (importer), on February 3, 2006. Tavis does not possess a national permit; however, he is permitted to practice in the districts of Laredo and Dallas (see 19CFR 127.1, 171 appendix A, HTS: XXII:13).

CUSTOMS POWER OF ATTORNEY

KNOW ALL MEN BY THESE PRESENTS: That Global Imports doing business *as a partnership under the laws of the State of Texas* residing or having a place of business at *2093 Nova Road, DALLAS, TEXAS* hereby constitutes and appoints *John Tavis dba RIDER LOGISTICS and it's authorized employees* , which may act through any of it's licensed officers or employees duly authorized to sign documents by power of attorney as a true and lawful agent and attorney of the grantor named above for and in the name, place, and stead of said grantor from this date and in *ALL Customs Ports* and in no other name, to make, endorse, sign, declare, or swear to any entry, withdrawal, declaration, certificate, bill of lading, carnet, or other document required by law or regulation in connection with the importation, transportation, or exportation of any merchandise shipped or consigned by or to said grantor; to perform any act or condition which may be required by law or regulation in connection with such merchandise; to receive any merchandise deliverable to said grantor.

To authorize other Customs Brokers duly licensed within the territory to act as grantor's agent; to receive, endorse and collect checks issued for Customs duty refunds in grantor's name drawn on the Treasurer of the United States; if the grantor is a non-resident of the United States, to accept service of process on behalf of the grantor;

. . .

This power of attorney is to remain in full force and effect until revocation in writing is duly given to and received by grantee (if the donor of this power of attorney is a partnership, the said power shall in no case have any force or effect in the United States after the expiration 2 years from the dates of its execution);

IN WITNESS WHEREOF: the said GLOBAL IMPORTS has caused these presents to be sealed and signed:

(Signature) (Signed) HEATHER MATHIS (Print Name) HEATHER MATHIS

(Capacity) PARTNER Date: FEBRUARY 3, 2006

Witness: (if required) ALAN SCHULMAN (PARTNER) (Signature) (Signed) ALAN SCHULMAN

If you are the importer of record, payment to the broker will not relieve you of liability for Customs Charges (duties, taxes, or other debts owed Customs) in the event the charges are not paid by the broker. Therefore, if you pay by check, Customs charges may be paid with a separate check payable to U.S. Customs which shall be delivered to Customs by the broker. Importers who wish to utilize this procedure must contact our office in advance to arrange timely receipt of duty checks.

1. What is the expiration date of POA? Unless revoked earlier, for how long is the broker supposed to retain the POA for recordkeeping purposes?
2. Is a POA required when John Tavis, the broker, is acting as the importer of record?
3. Global Imports requests its supplier in Malaysia to ship directly to its client in New York. Can John Tavis issue a POA on behalf of Global Imports to another broker (which is permitted in the Port of New York) to allow the latter to clear goods on behalf of Global Imports?
4. Global Imports does not have an importer of record number. Which CBP form should the broker prepare and file to obtain this number?

CASE 16.1. TAX DEDUCTION FOR PROCESSING IN MAQUILAS: MERE ASSEMBLY OR FABRICATION

U.S. Customs regulations provide for deduction of the costs of U.S. components or materials assembled abroad upon importation into the United States. In order to qualify for this exemption from duty assessment, the components must be exported in a condition ready for assembly without fabrication, and not lost their physical identity by change in form or shape. U.S Customs also requires that the components not be advanced in value abroad except by mere assembly or operations incidental to the assembly process such as cleaning, lubricating, and painting. This has largely facilitated the establishment of maquilas (in bond plants) along the U.S.–Mexico border in order to assemble U.S. components for re-export to the United States.

ABC Corporation of Phoenix, Arizona, attempted to take advantage of this opportunity by shipping U.S. components to Mexico for assembly and re-export. The company shipped straight steel strips from Tuscon, Arizona, to neighboring Nogales, Mexico, for use in luggage, which was later imported into the United States. U.S. customs denied a deduction from the value of the luggage for the cost of steel strips, stating that shaping the steel strips before placing them within the luggage constituted a further fabrication and not mere assembly; that is, the bending process was not incidental to assembly of a component exported from the United States. ABC Corporation does not believe that the denial by U.S. Customs was justified.

Questions

1. Do you agree with U.S. Customs?
2. What is your advice to ABC Corp?

Chapter 17

Selecting Import Products
and Suppliers

TYPES OF PRODUCTS FOR IMPORTATION

One of the most important import decisions is the selection of the proper product that serves the market need. In the absence of the latter, one is left with a warehouse full of merchandise with no one interested in buying it. Nevertheless, importing can become a successful and profitable venture so long as sufficient effort and time is invested in selecting the right product for the target market.

How does one find the right product to import? The following are different types of products to consider.

Unique Products

Products that are unique and different can be appealing to customers because they are a welcome change from the standardized and identical products sold in the domestic market. The fact that a product is imported and different is in itself sufficient for many people to purchase the item. However, some studies indicate product uniqueness in terms of cultural appeal to be a relatively less important variable in the purchasing decision of import managers (Ghymn, 1983).

Less Expensive Products

It is quite common to find imports that perform identically to the competitor's product but can be sold at a much lower price. As customers quickly switch allegiance to buy the imported item, it is quite possible to capture a substantial share of the domestic market.

Export-Import Theory, Practices, and Procedures, Second Edition

For firms selling in mature markets where there is little or no product differentiation, cost reduction provides a competitive advantage (Shippen, 1999). For consumer goods, the provision of quality products at lower prices is quite important in increasing a firm's market share. In the apparel sector, for example, imports presently accounted for over a half of total U.S. market share in 2006, mainly due to their cost advantage.

Availability

Keeping abreast of market trends often helps identify products that are in great demand. For example, increases in the immigrant population from Asia and Latin America have encouraged growth in the import of more and greater variety of spices. The United States imported an annual average of 530 million pounds of spices in 1990 to 1994 compared with 362 million pounds in 1980 to 1984 (Buzzanell and Lipton, 1995). In such cases where there is a continuous increase in demand for the product, imports become a major source of domestic supply because the product is either not produced in the country or not produced in sufficient quantities to satisfy the growing demand. The major reason for global sourcing in the chemical industry, for example, is the unavailability of needed products in the U.S. market.

Products of Better Quality

Many products manufactured abroad are of better quality than those produced domestically. German machine tools, Japanese cars, and French perfumes have proven market demand because of high quality. In some cases, certain designs could best be manufactured overseas. Identifying a quality product has the potential to increase profits.

Today's consumers tend to be quality/brand name conscious and are more willing to pay a higher price for good quality products. The provision of quality service is often as important as the quality of the goods imported. Importers have often managed to offset the disadvantage in the provision of quality service through efficient use of computer technologies such as quick response, just-in-time, and warehouse management systems.

Any one of these types of products can be carefully selected based on one's background and expertise. Someone who likes gardening can import gardening utensils, decorations, and so on, while the computer technician could find imports of items such as peripherals and software enjoyable and easy to handle (see International Perspective 17.1).

INTERNATIONAL PERSPECTIVE 17.1.
Quality Control for Imports

Ensuring quality is the best means of winning consumer confidence and sales. Many manufacturing firms find that they must meet new and different standards criteria (national, corporate, regional, or international) to compete in the global marketplace. Even though the majority of industrial standards are voluntary, there are mandatory government imposed standards in the fields of health and safety, food and drugs, and the environment. In many European countries, consumers often base their purchasing decision on proof of certification for the product or service. European community directives also mandate that companies meet certain product certification standards in order to sell in the European Union.

In the area of imports, quality standards provide a basis for assessing quality of products and services. Suppliers are provided a guide as to the quality of product to be manufactured, while buyers are provided with the confidence that the goods are safe and meet high quality standards. It is important to establish quality testing and inspection procedures, and in the case of large orders, the importer could appoint a quality inspector at the supplier's location to assess and advise the supplier on quality. Acceptance and payment on a letter of credit can be made conditional on receipt of a satisfactory inspection certificate.

An example of a quality control program for imports is the one jointly created by Chrysler, GM, and Ford (the QS-9000). The QS-9000 employs the ISO-9000 international quality assurance standard coupled with industry-specific criteria. The program mandates the use of QS-9000 quality standard by suppliers around the world. It requires organizations to implement continuous performance improvements with regard to quality (ISO-9000) and environmental management (ISO-14000). This is intended to ensure that products or services satisfy the customer's quality requirements and comply with any regulations applicable to those products or services.

FINDING THE PRODUCT

Any one or a combination of the following can be used in order to find, assess, and select the right product for importation.

Domestic Market Research

Primary market research can be conducted by a consulting firm to identify the best line of products for the domestic market. A variety of statistical sources provide data on projected total demand for certain products. Trade flows can also be examined to gather information on domestic demand and growth trends for various products. Some secondary sources also provide important market information, such as domestic market overviews, market share data, and opinions of industry experts. Such secondary market research studies and surveys can be purchased for a fraction of the cost of primary research. Online data can also provide industry and product information.

Trade Publications

Trade publications such as *Trade Channel, Asian Sources,* and *General Merchandise* provide business and trade opportunities in various countries. They include various advertisements of products and services available for import from all parts of the world (Weiss, 1987; Nelson, 2000). Certain banks with international departments often publish newsletters with offers to buy and sell. The prospective importer can also use electronic bulletin boards of the world trade centers to find out what products are available for import.

Foreign Travel

Whenever one visits a foreign country, it is important to look for products that may have a market at home. If a good product is obtained, it would create a profitable business opportunity. One could find new and exciting products that are not currently imported in the public markets, bazaars, or gift stores. Once a good product is identified, a few samples can be purchased. The manufacturer's address can be obtained from the country's trade department or from local vendors, usually for a small referral fee. If one does not travel overseas, it is always possible to ask friends or agents abroad for product information.

Trade Fairs and Shows

One way of finding a product is to attend trade fairs and trade shows. Many exporters find such shows to be an effective means of promoting their products. It is estimated that almost 2,000 trade shows take place in over seventy countries every year. Trade shows represent an entry point into export markets worldwide. Importers will have an opportunity to consider a variety of potential products to buy, to establish personal contacts, identify new prospects, or gather competitive information. Many exporters introduce their products to the foreign market with the hope of writing orders at the show or of finding suitable distributors or manufacturers' agents who will handle their products in overseas markets. Major shows in the United States are published in the *Exhibits Guide*. The Department of Commerce publishes information on upcoming trade fairs and trade shows in the United States and abroad. There are also online sources on various shows and exhibitions in certain product areas to be held in various parts of the world. A recent online announcement, for example, invites buyers and sellers of furniture to the international furniture fair in Copenhagen, Denmark, where major dealers from around the globe are expected to exhibit their furniture.

Foreign Countries' Trade Offices

Most countries have export promotion offices abroad. A trade promotion office provides important information on a country's major export products or services, suppliers, and other helpful contacts. In the absence of a trade promotion office for a nearby country, the embassy could be a good source of information on potential products to import.

Regardless of the method used to find the potential product to import, it is advisable to buy a sample or a small order to determine whether there are any prohibitions or restrictions to entry and whether the product can be sold at a competitive price. The sample can be inspected by a customs broker to establish whether the product can be freely entered and, if allowed entry, the applicable duty rate. The sample could also be shown to a freight forwarder to obtain an estimate of the shipping and insurance cost in order to calculate the price at which the merchandise will be sold. It is important to realistically evaluate the price in terms of competing products in the market. When calculating the total cost plus a decent profit margin, if the price is much higher than a competing product in the market, it may be necessary to go back to the drawing board and try another product.

Suppose the product is not subject to prohibitions or restrictions and can be sold at a competitive price; the next step is to presell the product to likely buyers. This will determine whether people will buy the product and how much they are willing to pay for it. This can be done by the potential importer or salespeople. The process of supplier selection and negotiation to purchase the first shipment should be done only after making an assessment of how much one can realistically sell.

WHAT DETERMINES IMPORT VOLUME?

Much of the literature on imports underlines the importance of high per capita incomes and population size in determining import levels. All other things being equal, countries with higher per capita incomes will be able to import more per person than countries with lower levels (Lutz, 1994). Larger countries (in terms of population) import fewer manufactured goods on a per capita basis because they tend to have a diversified industrial base, as investment will be attracted to these countries to take advantage of their big markets. This view can be exemplified by the case of the United States and Japan, both of which have low import propensities compared to countries such as Belgium or the Netherlands. Economic theory also suggests that import levels are affected by other factors, such as the price of imports denominated in foreign currency, the exchange rate, as well as the price of domestic goods relative to imports (Warner and Kreinin, 1983; Deyak, Sawyer, and Sprinkle, 1993). While relative prices have a predictable and systematic impact on imports, price elasticities tend to be low, in most instances well below unity. This suggests that large relative price swings are required to have an appreciable impact on trade patterns (Reinhart, 1995). For developing countries, however, determinants of import demand include government restrictions on imports and availability of foreign exchange (Sarmad, 1989). The study by Sarmad (1989) examining the factors influencing import demand in Pakistan from 1959 to 1986 found that the policy of devaluation or raising tariffs was not significant in reducing imports except in the case of imports of machinery and transport equipment. In countries with successful import-substitution strategies, the impact of relative prices and tariffs tends to decline in terms of their influence on import demand. Import substitution is a policy that taxes and restricts imports to protect and subsidize domestic industries. This policy, which paradoxically led to more import dependence (e.g., for purchases of raw materials, components, etc.), was a popular economic strategy among some developing nations (Lindert and Pugel, 1996).

SELECTING THE SUPPLIER

The product selected for importation may be manufactured by several firms in different countries or within the same country. The next important step is to assess and select the right supplier based on a number of critical factors, such as quality, delivery time and supplier reliability, transportation cost, import duty implications, protection of intellectual property rights, and ability to meet standard requirements.

A study conducted in 1983 on the decision process of U.S. purchasing agents suggests timely delivery, product brand name, and style as important factors that determine purchasing decisions (Ghymn, 1983). A major concern in the minds of many U.S. importers is the quality of the imported product. In today's marketplace, where many firms are competing for the buyer's attention, it is the customer who defines quality in terms of his or her needs. To be successful, an importer should select a supplier who can deliver a product that satisfies consumer needs, has minimum defects, and is priced competitively. Also adding to the importance of quality and the local market appeal of the product is the availability of core supplier benefits, such as warranties, timely delivery, favorable transportation terms, and after-sales service and reliability. Low-cost suppliers can also be identified based on their proximity to raw materials, labor costs, current exchange rates, or transportation costs.

Import duties could be eliminated or substantially reduced by selecting suppliers located in countries that participate in a preferential trade arrangement. In the United States, for example, most products imported from Canada, Mexico (NAFTA), Caribbean countries (CBI), Israel (FTA), and countries eligible for GSP benefits are subject to duty-free treatment. For example, ceramic tile imported from Italy is subject to a 13.5 percent duty, whereas an identical tile coming from Israel would cost the importer only 4.3 percent duty. To qualify for such favorable treatment, it is necessary to mark the country of origin of the import.

Selection of the supplier should also be based on the integrity of the product. Integrity of the product includes the assumption that the import does not violate any intellectual property rights registered in the country, such as patent, trademark, design, or copyright, and that it meets certain regulatory requirements, such as product compliance with the various import laws relating to marking, labeling, inspections, and safety. There has been a rise in the production and sale of counterfeit and pirated goods in many parts of the world. Industry experts, for example, estimate lost sales from unauthorized use of U.S. intellectual property rights at $60 billion annually. It is also important to select suppliers that use certain product safety standards. For example, food service ceramics must be tested for lead, and toys must meet labeling and safety standards (see International Perspective 17.2).

A potential importer should be aware of any foreign laws that might affect purchase, such as export restrictions or quotas. The importer also needs to ascertain whether the supplier has already appointed other distributors or sales agents in the territory and whether the distribution channels available are acceptable in terms of overall profitability and risk. For example, an agent is likely to realize limited profits if the supplier has a distributor in the market (see International Perspective 17.3 for a typical import transaction).

Once a small number of potential suppliers are identified, a personal visit can be made to perform the necessary evaluation and selection of the right supplier. Final selection will be made based on factors such as (1) international knowledge and experience of supplier, (2) supplier's willingness to

INTERNATIONAL PERSPECTIVE 17.2.
Major Factors in International Supplier Selection

- *Quality assurance:* Certification of potential suppliers for strict quality assurance, technical capability to prevent quality failures, and overall commitment to quality assurance.
- *Financial conditions:* Low cost supplier (purchase price, transportation cost, documentation, etc.), provision of favorable payment terms (open account sales), freight terms such as FOB, CIF.
- *Service performance:* Supplier's commitment and capability for timely delivery of services and technical assistance.
- *Perceived risks:* Political and economic risks such as political instability, currency inconvertibility, and unstable exchange rates.
- *Buyer-supplier relationships:* Financial stability, negotiation flexibility of supplier.
- *Trade restrictions:* Tariff and non-tariff barriers, countertrade requirements by supplier or country.
- *Cultural and communication barriers:* Language, business customs, ethical standards, communication barriers, electronic data exchange capability.

devote sufficient time to develop the market, (3) supplier's willingness to provide necessary training, and (4) provision of certain market exclusivity and acceptable payment arrangement. It is also important to obtain a credit report of the supplier. Such evaluation is critical regardless of the marketing channels adopted by the importer.

INTERNATIONAL SOURCING

The outsourcing of products and services to external suppliers continues to expand, as firms search for ways to lower costs while improving their products to remain competitive. By the end of 1998, it is estimated that U.S. companies have spent more than $100 billion on outsourcing. Outsourcing is commonly used by firms in the areas of communications, computers, and semiconductors Firms that outsource often realize cost savings and an increase in capacity and quality. In spite of its fast growth, outsourcing is frequently perceived to be poorly controlled, high in cost, and a drain on quality

INTERNATIONAL PERSPECTIVE 17.3.
A Typical Import Transaction

Step 1: Once a product is selected (see section on selecting products), the importer writes to overseas suppliers to send price lists and product catalogues.

Step 2: Upon receipt of the price lists and catalogues, the importer then shows the catalogues to potential customers without disclosing the supplier's name and address.

Step 3: If there is a favorable response from potential customers, the importer contacts the overseas supplier to request product samples and pays for shipment by air. In the meantime, importer checks with Customs for the applicable duty and other import requirements for the product.

Step 4: If the product sample received is found acceptable by the importer, the importer then orders a trial shipment by air and makes an advance payment to the supplier. The importer should communicate domestic marking, labeling, and other requirements to the overseas supplier. Supplier's credit references can be obtained from the supplier, banks, and the U.S. Department of Commerce. Potential customers are approached to place orders for the product.

Step 5: As the goods arrive at the airport, the importer arranges with a customs broker to clear customs. The importer sets the selling price.

Step 6: If the trial shipment sells easily, the importer orders large shipments by sea freight and prepares a formal price list and product catalogue.

and service performance (for advantages and disadvantages, see International Perspective 17.4).

A firm can undertake outsourcing under various arrangements.

Wholly Owned Subsidiary

A firm may move production of parts or components to an affiliate established in a low cost location abroad. The firm will then import the output as it is needed. For example, Sony outsources production of parts to its manufacturing plants located in China and other low cost locations around the world.

Overseas Joint Ventures

A firm can import supplies made under a joint venture arrangement. For example, Fujitsu imports parts for its DRAMs production from its joint

INTERNATIONAL PERSPECTIVE 17.4.
Advantages and Disadvantages of Outsourcing

Advantages	Disadvantages
1. Lower price	1. Difficulty in evaluating and selecting qualified suppliers
2. Higher-quality products (qualified suppliers)	2. Potential problems with quality and delivery time
3. Supply of products not available domestically	3. Political and labor problems
4. Advanced technology available from foreign sources	4. Paperwork and extra documentation as well as added costs such as freight, insurance import duties, cost of letter of credit, travel, marking, etc.
5. Satisfy countertrade obligations	5. Currency fluctuations and payment problems
6. Improve international competitiveness	6. Harder to quickly respond to market changes

venture partner in Taiwan. Mitsubishi Electric and Toshiba have also contracted DRAM manufacturing to Taiwanese partners.

In-Bond Plant Contractor

A firm sends raw materials and components to be processed or assembled in a low cost location by an independent contractor. No customs duty is imposed by the country where the goods are assembled (temporarily imported under bond) and when the products are re-exported to the home country, import duties are imposed only on the value added abroad. The most popular is the maquiladora, which allows U.S. or other foreign companies to combine their technology with low cost labor in Mexico. The raw materials or components imported in bond and duty free are processed or assembled for eventual re-export. The maquiladora can also be established as a wholly owned operation of the foreign firm.

Contract Manufacturing

A company enters into a contract with a foreign supplier to import a given quantity of products according to specifications. The supplier manages the day-to-day operation of the production process and allows the importer to focus on other core activities. The contract will provide for assurance of quality and quality control. Nortel, a Canadian-based manufacturer of communications equipment, outsources nearly $1 billion worth of components to contract manufacturers abroad. Cisco uses contract manufacturers to reduce production cost and focus on research and development. Its products are mostly made by global manufacturers such as Flextronics and Jabil.

PRICING THE IMPORTED PRODUCT

Knowledge of the price structure for imported goods makes it possible to determine the appropriate price to be charged for the merchandise. The following price structure in Table 17.1 could be used as a general guide.

IMPORT MARKETING CHANNELS

One of the fundamental decisions for foreign suppliers is whether to sell their products direct or through intermediaries. Relying on an intermediary relieves the producer of international marketing activities. However, the producer forgoes part of the export profit and does not obtain firsthand information on the market, and this, in turn, may reduce the firm's product adaptation capacity.

Two of the important developments in marketing channels have been the involvement of large retail groups in direct importation, and subcontracting of production abroad by major manufacturing companies. In this age of intense competition, firms that manufacture standardized products can no longer rely on firm-specific advantages arising solely from technology. They should focus on ways of minimizing costs by manufacturing certain components (or subcontracting such production) in low cost countries (see International Perspective 17.5).

Direct Channel of Distribution

If a direct channel is adopted, the foreign producer exports through its subsidiary, joint venture representative serving as importer, distributor, and/or wholesaler. It also includes imports manufactured under a subcontracting arrangement.

TABLE 17.1. Landed-Cost Survey, DM Import Company, Davie, FL

Supplier: V. Maundo, Nairobi, Kenya; Quantity: 150 Makonde carvings	
Gross sales price	**3,500.00**
Less cash discount (15%)	525.00
Net sales price	2,975.00
Landed cost	
Purchase price	2,975.00
Packing	—
Inland freight	—
Duty (2975 – insurance ($50) + freight (800)) = 7% (2,125.70)	148.75
Brokerage and banking charges	160.00
Custom bond fee	50.00
Merchandise processing fee	8.00
Harbor maintenance fee	2.00
Total landed cost (CIF, Miami) Expenses	**3,343.75**
Advertising	—
Repacking	15.00
Interest	10.00
ABI (Automatic broker interface fee)	10.00
Total landed costs and expense	**3,378.75**
Unit cost	$22.52 per item
Suggested selling price	$45.00
Net Profit	6,750 ($45 3 150) – 3,378.75 (22.52 3 150) = $3,371.25

Note: Markup is generally 60 to 100 percent for consumer items; 20 to 30 percent for industrial goods; 250 to 300 percent for mail order items.

Indirect Channel of Distribution

This entails exporting the product to an intermediary, usually an import distributor, who serves as channel leader on behalf of the foreign manufacturer. It also includes a commission agent or an import merchant.

In short, a product can be imported by a firm wholly or partly owned by the foreign producer or by independent distributors or agents. Depending on the channel structure, imported merchandise is sold through various outlets: it may be sold to a wholesaler, retailer, or directly to the consumer. Whole-

INTERNATIONAL PERSPECTIVE 17.5.
The Ten Most Common Mistakes of Potential Importers

1. Failure to develop sufficient knowledge of the import process before starting the business including import regulations.
2. Insufficient knowledge of the product to be imported.
3. Insufficient knowledge of the costs involved in obtaining, importing and marketing a product.
4. Neglecting to seek quality products at lowest possible price.
5. Failure to maintain a good working relationship with suppliers, banks, customs brokers and other intermediaries.
6. Inability to develop an appropriate price structure.
7. Insufficient knowledge of the market.
8. Insufficient working capital.
9. Unwillingness to modify products to meet regulations or consumer preferences.
10. Failure to invest sufficient time and effort to develop the business.

saling may bring in less money per item than retail, but it has the advantage of faster inventory turnover, less sales effort, and lower warehousing costs. However, since the wholesaler's sales effort is often spread among dozens of other products, a product may not be given individual attention. A product can be sold directly to retailers such as supermarkets, convenience stores, and specialty or discount stores. The importer could also set up his or her own store and sell the merchandise directly to the consumer. Several importers also sell at the various swap shops and flea markets around the country. Over the past few years, there has been an increase in the use of mail order or direct response television/radio. Even though this approach can be very expensive, it allows the importer to reach millions of consumers in a very short time and possibly make a substantial number of sales very quickly if the product is successful.

FINANCING IMPORTS

Imports can be financed by using methods such as documentary collection, letters of credit, transferable letter of credit, or back-to-back letter of credit. Read the section dealing with the various types of letters of credit.

CHAPTER SUMMARY

Type of Products to Consider for Importation

Products that are unique, are less expensive, have proven market demand, and are of better quality.

Means of Finding, Assessing, and Selecting the Product

1. *Domestic market research:* using primary or secondary market research
2. *Trade publications:* Advertisements in various trade publications, international bank newspapers, and electronic bulletin boards
3. *Foreign travel:* Identifying promising import products during visits abroad
4. *Trade fairs and shows:* Import products found by attending various trade shows and trade fairs domestically and abroad
5. *Trade offices:* Seeking information from trade promotion offices and embassies of various countries on their major export products, as well as from other helpful contacts

Other Steps Before Selecting the Product and Supplier

1. Purchase a sample of the promising item.
2. Request inspection by customs to determine if there are any restrictions to entry of the product and establish the applicable duty.
3. Check with a freight forwarder about shipping and insurance cost.
4. Estimate the price and determine whether the product can be sold at a competitive price.

Determinants of Import Volume

1. High per capita income
2. Population size
3. Price of imports denominated in foreign currency
4. Exchange rates
5. Price of domestic goods relative to imports
6. Price elasticity
7. Government restrictions, availability of foreign exchange

Selecting the Supplier: Important Considerations

1. Product quality, brand name
2. Market appeal, minimum defects
3. Other supplier benefits: Timely delivery, warranties, after-sales service, reliability
4. Protection of intellectual property rights

Import Marketing Channels

1. Direct
2. Indirect

Financing Imports

1. Open account
2. Consignment
3. Documentary collection
4. Letter of credit

REVIEW QUESTIONS

1. What types of products should be seriously considered for importation?
2. What is contract manufacturing?
3. State some of the factors that determine import volume.
4. Explain the major steps involved in a typical import transaction.
5. What are some of the advantages of outsourcing?

CASE 17.1. THE ATA CARNET: UNLOCKING CUSTOMS FOR TEMPORARY ENTRY OF GOODS

The ATA Carnet is an international customs document used by travelers to temporarily import certain goods without paying tariffs or going through customs formalities. The term "ATA" stands for the French words "admission temporaire." It is created by an international convention to promote world trade and can be used in more than ninety countries. Major trading nations such as EU member countries, Australia, Bulgaria, Canada, China, Czech Republic, Hong Kong, Hungary, India, Israel, Japan, Malaysia, New

Zealand, South Africa, Thailand, and the United States all accept ATA carnets. The United States acceded to the ATA Carnet convention in 1986.

In the United States, carnets are issued/ guaranteed by the U.S. Council for International Business (USCIB). The USCIB is liable for the payment of liquidated damages to customs in the event that the carnet holder fails to comply with customs regulations. The carnet is valid for one year from the date of issuance.

There are a number of benefits that can be derived by importers from using the ATA Carnet: (1) avoidance of complicated customs procedures. The ATA Carnet allows the importer to use a single document for clearing goods through customs in several countries. It also allows for unlimited exits from and entries into the U.S. and participating foreign countries during the one-year period of validity, (2) the importer will not be required to pay customs duty or post a temporary import bond.

ATA Carnets cover virtually all goods except food and agricultural products (consumables), disposable, and hazardous items. Merchandise intended for sale or resale must be entered as a regular customs entry. The ATA guaranteeing association (USCIB in the case of the U.S.) requires a security deposit (about 40 percent of the value of goods) to cover any customs claim that might arise from a misused carnet. The deposit is returned upon the cancellation of the carnet. Application for a carnet is made online at www .merchandisepassport.org).

In the case of certain countries that do not accept ATA carnets, companies can apply for a temporary import bond (TIB), a document that can be purchased from a customs broker at the time of entry. The TIB deposits and payments are made in the importing country each time a product is imported.

> *Example:* Harley-Davidson moved its classic bikes, motorcycle parts, and artifacts to ten cities around the world including Barcelona, Hamburg, Toronto, Sydney, and Tokyo, and back to its headquarters in Milwaukee, Wisconsin, in 2002-2003 using the ATA Carnet. The tour intended to celebrate the 100th anniversary of the company was made easier by the carnet which eliminated the need to pay duties and taxes, as well as reduced the delays and costs of physically crossing international borders.

Questions

1. Identify a company in a specific sector and determine how it can take advantage of the ATA carnet system.
2. Are there any disadvantages in using the ATA Carnet?

CASE 17.2. MAYTAG'S TRIAD STRATEGY

Firm strategy plays an important part in determining the competitiveness of an industry in a global market. As governments embrace trade liberalization, local industries have become increasingly exposed to fierce competition from a growing array of international suppliers. Domestic producers of bulk appliances like dishwashers and refrigerators were largely insulated from foreign competition because of their size, which makes them expensive to ship across the ocean. However, low labor and production costs, added to declining transportation costs, has enabled many Asian appliance makers such as China's Haier Group and South Korea's LG Electronics to increase their U.S. market share. They are also opening plants in Mexico and neighboring countries to save on shipping.

Maytag had to adjust to the new competition through global sourcing and collaborative supply chain networks. In the case of dishwashers, its triad strategy entails sourcing the motors from suppliers in China, producing wire harnesses in Mexico, and assembling the parts in Jackson, Tennessee.

Dispensing certain activities across the transnational value chain to lower costs and gain competitive advantage is considered a successful global business strategy. This approach allows U.S. companies to share the risk with suppliers and to choose foreign companies with the best product lines or services.

Maytag selected certain suppliers (of motors for dishwashers) from China largely due to their low prices. However, it decided to make the wire harness in Mexico because they tend to be different in each model and because sudden shifts in demand requires proximity to the market.

Questions

1. Would you advise Maytag to produce motors for the dishwashers in Mexico in view of the latter's proximity to the U.S. market?
2. Would you advise Maytag to lobby the government for higher tariffs on imports of motors and/or wire harnesses in order to produce them in the United States for the domestic and export market?

Chapter 18

The Entry Process for Imports

All goods entering the United States are subject to certain customs procedures regardless of their value or dutiable status. Duties accrue upon the imported merchandise on arrival of the vessel within the customs port (or on arrival of the merchandise within U.S. Customs territory for other means of transport). The making of an entry is generally required within five working days after arrival of the importing vessel or aircraft. "Entry" is the act of filing the necessary documentation with the customs officer to secure the release of imported merchandise. If entry is not made within fifteen calendar days (after arrival of the goods), the goods are placed in a warehouse at the risk and expense of the importer. They may be sold at public auction if entry is not made within six months from the date of importation. Goods subject to depreciation (perishables) and explosive substances may be sold earlier (see International Perspective 18.1).

Goods may be entered by the owner, purchaser, his authorized regular employee, or by a licensed customs broker. When the goods are consigned to "order," the bill of lading, properly endorsed by the consignee, may serve as evidence of a right to make entry. An air waybill may be used for merchandise arriving by air. A nonresident consignee has the right to make entry but any bond taken in connection with the entry shall have a resident corporate surety (in the case of a carnet, a resident guaranteeing association). A foreign corporation in whose name a product is entered must have a resident agent at the place where the port of entry is located. In most cases, entry is made by a person (firm) certified by the carrier bringing the goods to the port of entry. The person (firm) entering the goods is considered the "owner" for customs purposes. The carrier issues a "carrier's certificate" stating that the consignee named in the document is the owner or consignee of the goods. In certain cases, entry may be made by means of a duplicate bill of lading or a shipping receipt (in the latter case, entry must be made by actual consignee

Export-Import Theory, Practices, and Procedures, Second Edition

INTERNATIONAL PERSPECTIVE 18.1.
Avoiding Errors in Invoicing

Any inaccurate or misleading representation or omission of required information in an invoice presented to customs pertaining to an entry may result in delays in release of merchandise or claims against the importer (unless he or she can establish due diligence). The invoice should reflect the real nature of the transaction. All invoices must include the following information:

- Description of port of entry and detailed description of merchandise, that is, grade, quality, quantity, marks, and numbers (for product and/or packages as the case may be) under which the product is sold.
- Description of the name of actual seller, importer, place, and date of sale. It should also include the purchase price in the currency of sale. In the event that the product is shipped other than in pursuance of a purchase agreement, the invoice must state the value which the owner or shipper would have received in the ordinary course of trade.
- All charges included in the invoice price including commissions, insurance etc. As well as any rebates or drawbacks allowed upon exportation of the merchandise. It should also state the value of any materials supplied by the importer.
- Any discounts as well as charges incurred by seller or consignee to deliver the merchandise to buyer and not just the FOB price.

or duly authorized agent). Where the goods are not imported by a common carrier, entry is made by importer who possesses the goods at the time of arrival (see International Perspective 18.2).

The importer or agent pays the estimated duty at the time of making entry even though customs has not yet liquidated the entry (i.e., final assessment of duty has not been made). Imported goods are not legally entered until after the shipment has arrived within the port of entry, delivery of merchandise has been authorized by customs, and estimated duties have been paid. It is the responsibility of the importer to arrange for examination and release of the goods. The required documentation can now be transmitted electronically to customs. U.S. Customs is in the process of moving toward a new paperless system in which importers can file their entries from a single location and clear shipments in hours instead of days.

U.S. Customs and Border Protection (CBP) processed twenty-nine million trade entries and collected about $31.4 billion in tariffs, taxes, and user fees in 2005. Additional revenues accrue from confiscations of cash allegedly

INTERNATIONAL PERSPECTIVE 18.2. Types of Entry

Entry for Consumption: This is the most common type of entry. Merchandise that is not held for examination is released under bond. Even in cases where examination is required (e.g., to determine value, dutiable status, proper markings, or whether shipment contains prohibited articles), certain packages are designated for examination and the rest of the shipment is released under bond.

Entry for Warehouse: Imported goods may be placed in a customs bonded warehouse and payment of duties is deferred until the goods are removed for consumption. No duty is payable if they are re-exported or destroyed under customs supervision. Goods may be manipulated, sorted, or repackaged in the bonded warehouse for eventual consumption or export. In this case, the duty payable is for the manipulated or new product at the time of withdrawal. Goods may remain in a bonded warehouse up to five years from the date of importation.

Entry for Transportation in Bond: Merchandise may be entered for transportation in bond without appraisement to any other port of entry designated by the importer. Only an entry for consumption is accepted if more than a year has elapsed since the date of original importation Customs Form 7512.

Informal Entry: Under this category are commercial entries valued at under $2,000 and household and personal effects, and tools of trade. It does not require the same formalities as consumption entry and is also liquidated at entry.

Mail Entry: Merchandise that is imported by mail. No entry is required on duty-free merchandise not exceeding $2,000 in value. There is also no need to clear shipments for imports of under $2,000 (e.g., parcel delivered by letter carrier). For merchandise whose value exceeds $2,000, formal entry (consumption entry) is required. For mail entry of certain products such as furs, leather, footwear, the limit is $250.

Temporary Importation Under Bond: Certain types of goods that are not imported for sale (or sale on approval) are admitted without payment of duty, under bond, for exportation within one year (could be extended up to three years upon application to the port director) from the date of importation. This generally includes merchandise imported for repair, articles used as models, samples, animals and poultry imported for breeding, etc. The ATA Carnet can be used for this purpose.

Drawback Entry: A refund of 99 percent of all customs duties is allowed under certain conditions: (1) if the imported material is exported in the same condition as when imported or when destroyed under customs supervision within three years of the date of importation, or (2) if the imported merchandise is used in the manufacturing process and exported within five years from the date of importation.

involved in money laundering, penalties for violations of import quotas, and so forth (Bovard, 1998). In addition to the U.S. Customs Service, importers should contact other agencies when questions regarding particular commodities arise. Questions with respect to imports of products regulated by the Food and Drug Administration (FDA), for example, should be forwarded to the nearest FDA district office. Similarly, the respective federal agencies should be consulted whenever an imported product is subject to their regulatory regimes.

THE ENTRY PROCESS

Filing Entry Papers

The entry process requires filing the necessary documents to enable customs to determine whether the merchandise may be released from its custody, as well as for duty assessment and statistical purposes. Both of these processes can be accomplished electronically via the Automatic Broker Interface program. What are entry documents? Entry documents generally consist of (1) an entry manifest (Form 7533) or application and special permit for immediate delivery (Form 3461), (2) a commercial invoice (or pro forma invoice when the commercial invoice cannot be produced), (3) a bill of lading, air waybill, or other evidence of right to make entry, (4) a packing list, if appropriate, and (5) other documents necessary to determine the admissibility of the merchandise. This may include information to determine whether the imported merchandise bears an infringing trademark. If the goods are to be released from customs on entry documents, an entry summary for consumption must be filed. An entry summary includes the entry package returned that allows for release of merchandise and other forms (Form 7501).

Release of Merchandise and Deposit of Estimated Duty

Once the complete entry is made by filing with customs (i.e., the declared value, classification, and rate of duty applicable to the merchandise as well as an entry summary for consumption), the product is released by customs and the estimated duty deposited. A bond must be posted before filing the entry summary to guarantee payment of duties or taxes upon the final assessment of duties or other fees by customs (liquidation of entry). Bonds are required for almost all formal entries, and may be required for some informal entries and temporary importation under bond entries. There are also bonds covering the activities of warehouse proprietors, carriers etc.

If goods are to be released upon entry, an entry summary for consumption must be filed and estimated duties deposited at the port of entry within ten working days of the goods' entry. Immediate release of a shipment can be obtained through a special permit (Form 3461) prior to arrival of the goods. Carriers participating in the Automated Manifest System can receive conditional release authorizations after leaving the foreign country and up to five days before landing in the United States. Upon approval by customs, shipments are released expeditiously after arrival of the merchandise. However, entry summary must be filed and estimated duties deposited within ten working days after release. Immediate delivery release is allowed for certain types of goods: articles for a trade fair, shipment consigned to agency of U.S. government, tariff quota merchandise (in some cases, merchandise under absolute quota), or merchandise arriving from Canada or Mexico (when approved by bond director and bond is on file). In cases where articles subject to different rates of duty are packed together, the commingled articles shall be subject to the highest rate of duty applicable to any part of the commingled lot. However, the consignee or agent can segregate the merchandise to allow customs to ascertain the appropriate duty (within thirty days after notice by customs of such commingling).

A bond is different from a carnet because the latter serves as a customs entry document and as a customs bond. Carnets are ordinarily acceptable without posting further security. Institutions that issue carnets or guarantee the payment obligation under carnets must be approved by customs. In cases where a carnet is not used, a bond is usually required to secure a customs transaction. A single entry bond application is made by the importer or designated person to secure the entry of a single customs transaction, while a continuous bond application is made for multiple transactions. Such application is made to the port director. A single entry bond is generally for the value of the merchandise plus duties, taxes, and fees. Customs bonds (usually 10 percent of the duties, taxes, and fees paid by the importer during the previous thirteen months) are valid until canceled either by the importer or surety. In lieu of a bond, an importer may pledge cash, savings bonds, or treasury notes. Bonds and/or cash are held until one year after an importation is liquidated (or in the case of transportation under bond, the importer demonstrates that the merchandise was either exported or destroyed properly). Customs bonds can be terminated by sending a letter to the port where the bond was originally registered and takes effect ten days after the request is received (sureties are required to send a request to customs and principal and this takes effect thirty days after receipt).

Bonds may be secured through a resident U.S. surety company, a resident and citizen of the United States, or in the form of cash or other government obligations. The list of corporations authorized to act as sureties on bonds and the limits of their bonds is published by the Treasury Department. If individuals sign as sureties, customs often requires two sureties on a bond to protect the revenue and ensure compliance with the regulations. There are also other requirements that individuals have to meet in to act as sureties: U.S. residency and citizenship, evidence of solvency and financial responsibility, and ownership of property that could be used as security within the limits of the port where the contract of suretyship is approved. The current market value of the property, less any debts, and so on, must be equal to or greater than the amount of the bond. In the event of default by the importer, the surety and importer are liable to pay liquidated damages to customs (Serko, 1985) (see Table 18.1).

Liquidation, Protests, and Petitions

Liquidation is the final ascertainment of the duties and drawback accruing on an entry by customs. Liquidation is required for all entries of imported merchandise except the following: temporary importation bond entry, trans-

TABLE 18.1. Bond Requirements by U.S. Customs and Border Protection (CBP)

Type of Bond	Bond Requirements
Single Transaction Bond	
Basic single entry (for general goods)	Value + duty
Quota or visa entries	3 3 value
Temporary importation	2 3 value
Goods unconditionally free of duties	10 percent of value
Autos	3 3 value
Antidumping/countervailing duties	Established by CBP
Continuous Bond	
Basic entries	10 percent of annual estimated duties for the next calendar year and rounded up to the next 10,000 it shall not be less than $50,000
Goods conditionally free of duties	10 percent of duty applicable if the merchandise were dutiable
Goods unconditionally free of duties	0.5 percent 3 annual estimated import value

portation in bond, and imports that are subject to immediate exportation. The liquidation procedure involves determination of the value of imports, ascertainment of their classification and applicable rate of duty, as well as computation of the final amount of duty to be paid. Customs will then establish whether any additional (excess) duty has to be paid (refunded) to the importer, as the case may be, and notify such liquidation to the importer, consignee, or agent by posting a public notice. A formal entry is liquidated when an entry appears on the bulletin notice of liquidation posted in customs.

It is also important to note the following:

- *Limitation on liquidation.* If imported merchandise is not liquidated within one year from the date of entry, it is considered liquidated at the rate and amount of duty stated at the time of entry.
- *Voluntary reliquidation by customs.* Customs could reliquidate any entry within ninety days from the date of notice of the original liquidation.
- *Liquidation for informal, mail, and baggage entries.* The effective date of liquidation for such entries is the date of payment of estimated duties upon entry of merchandise or the date of release by customs under free duty or permit for immediate delivery (Rossides, 1986).

Conversion of Currency

The date of exportation of the goods is the date used to determine the applicable rate of exchange for customs purposes. Liquidation is not final until any protest that has been filed against it has been decided. If an importer disagrees with the liquidation of an entry, a protest may be filed in writing within ninety days after the date of notice of liquidation. The protest could be with respect to any one or more of the following: the appraised value of the merchandise, classification, duties, and other charges, the exclusion of a product from entry, or the refusal to reliquidate an entry. If a protest is denied by the district director, the importer can appeal to the Court of International Trade. The parties have a right to further appeal to the Court of Appeals for the Federal Circuit and from there to the highest court in the country, the Supreme Court of the United States. An importer can also request for further review of the protest other than that provided by the district director. If the protest is denied by the latter, the matter is forwarded for review by the regional commissioner.

Any interested party could file a petition with the secretary of the treasury if the individual/group believes that the appraised value, classification, or rate of duty for an imported merchandise is not correct. The term interested party includes manufacturers, producers, wholesalers, or trade unions in the United States.

THE HARMONIZED TARIFF SCHEDULE
OF THE UNITED STATES

In 1988, the Harmonized Tariff Schedule of the United States (HTSUS) was adopted. This was a commodity description and coding system that is predominantly used by other nations. The Harmonized System was developed under the auspices of the Customs Cooperation Council, with the active participation of governments and private organizations. The major benefits of adopting the Harmonized System are as follows:

- The HTSUS will be in line with the tariff determination procedures of most countries of the world.
- It facilitates the shipment and documentation of merchandise into the United States and creates a uniform and familiar system for U.S. exporters shipping to other countries.
- Such uniformity in classification and coding across countries simplifies the conduct of international trade negotiations and increases the accuracy of international trade statistics.

The HTSUS classifies goods according to their "essential character" or, in the case of apparel, on the basis of the fiber of chief weight. It is a detailed classification system containing approximately 5,000 headings and subheadings organized into ninety-six chapters and twenty sections (see Table 18.2).

Goods imported are subject to duty or duty free status in accordance with their classification under the HTSUS. Duty free status, for example, is available under certain conditional exemptions provided in column 1 of the tariff schedule. Column 2 is intended for countries that do not qualify for the most-favored-nation (MFN) duty rate, and imports under this category are subject to the highest rate. In cases in which the correct classification is not certain or the product falls under more than one classification, it is important to resort to the body of interpretative rules provided under the HTSUS or to seek a binding tariff classification ruling from customs which can be relied on before placing or accepting orders. Although the average tariff rate in the United States is now around 5 percent, some imports are subject to high tariffs: watch parts (151.2 percent), some shoe imports (67 percent). In certain cases, it is also possible for customs to reverse its classification even after the product has been imported and used. The customs service reversed its decision on imports of muffin mix toppings in 1996 and informed the importer to pay $750,000 penalty for violating the U.S. sugar quota (the decision was, however, reversed for the second time). In another case, imports of large antique red telephone booths were blocked on the grounds that the

TABLE 18.2. Harmonized Tariff Schedule of the U.S

Heading/ Sub- heading	Stat. Suffix	Article Description	Units of Quantity	Rates of Duty/ General	Special	2
4902		Newspapers, journals and periodicals, whether or not illustrated or containing advertised material: Appearing at least four times a week				
4902.10.00	00		Kg	free	free	free
4902.90		Other: Newspaper supplements				
4902.90.10	00	Printed by a granure process	No	1.6%	Free (A, CA, E, IL, 5, MX)	25%
4902.90.20	20	Other: Newspapers appearing less than four times a week	Kg	free		
	40	Other business and professional journals and periodicals	No			
	60	Other (including single issues tied together for shipping purposes	No			

Note: CA = Canada (import from Canada), A = GSP countries, MX = Mexico, E = Caribbean Basin countries, IL = Israel, J = Andean Preference Pact.

product was actually a steel product restricted by import quotas (Bovard, 1998). Thus, one cannot overemphasize the importance of obtaining expert opinion, seeking an advance ruling by customs, or establishing reliable procedures on the correct description and classification of a given merchandise before importation (see International Perspective 18.3 for automated services).

CUSTOMS VALUATION

In 1979, the United States adopted the customs valuation system that was the result of the Tokyo Round negotiations of the GATT. Valuation of

INTERNATIONAL PERSPECTIVE 18.3. Automated Services in the United States to Facilitate International Trade

- **Automated Broker Interface (ABI):** The Automated Broker Interface is a component of the U.S. Customs Service's Automated Commercial System that permits participants to electronically file required import data with customs. ABI participants include brokers, importers, carriers, port authorities, or independent service centers. Presently, over 96 percent of all entries are filed through ABI, which speeds up the release of merchandise. Entry summaries are electronically transmitted, validated, confirmed, corrected, and paid. Participants are also informed of current information. Participants can request quota status, visa requirements, entry, or entry summary status. It allows filers to pay for multiple entries with one payment transaction.

- **Automated Clearing House (ACH):** The Customs Automated Clearing House is an electronic payment option that allows participants to pay customs fees, duties, and taxes electronically. Participants' banks must belong to the National Clearinghouse Association. The accuracy and speed of ACH results in a higher volume of transactions.

- **Automated Export System (AES):** The Automated Export System is a joint undertaking between the Bureau of Export Administration, U.S. Customs, and other federal agencies intended to assure compliance with U.S. export regulations and improve trade statistics. Its objective also includes introduction of a paperless reporting system for export information by 2002.

- **Automated Information Systems Security policy (AIS):** This policy provides guidance for the protection of AIS resources by establishing uniform policies and procedures for the customs AIS Security program. It provides security for information that is collected, processed, stored, or transmitted.

- **Automated Manifest System (AMS):** This is a cargo inventory control and release notification system. This interfaces with other systems such as ABI to allow for faster identification and release of low risk shipments. It speeds the flow of cargo and entry processing and provides participants with electronic authorization of cargo release prior to arrival. It also facilitates the intermodal movement and delivery of cargo.

- **AMS paperless master in-bond participants:** This program is designed to take advantage of the detailed information available within the AMS to control the movement and disposition of master in-bond shipments from the custody of the ocean carrier at the port of unlading to the same carrier's custody at the port of destination. AMS tracks and records such merchandise.

- **Cargo Selectivity:** This system is used to sort high risk cargo from low risk cargo and to determine the type of examination required. It accepts data transmitted through ABI and compares it against established criteria.

a product is important because most imported products are subject to tariffs based on the percentage of the value of the import (ad valorem rate). It also helps countries to maintain accurate and comparable records of their international trade transactions.

Imported merchandise is appraised on the basis, and in the order, of the following:

1. Transaction value
2. Deductive value
3. Computed value

The Transaction Value

Transaction value is the invoice price of the goods as they enter the United States. In determining transaction value, the price actually paid or payable will be considered without regard to its method of derivation. The value includes various costs that enhance the good's value to the importer, such as packing costs, sales commissions, and royalties. It also includes any direct or indirect items provided by the buyer free of charge or at a reduced cost for use in the production or sale of merchandise for export to the United States. In short, the transaction value is the price actually paid or payable for imported merchandise, excluding international freight, insurance, and other CIF charges. Transaction value cannot be used in the following situations:

- In cases in which the transaction value cannot be determined (proceeds of subsequent sales, etc.), or is not acceptable (related-party transactions)
- In cases involving restrictions on the sale or use of the product

Example 1

A foreign shipper sold merchandise at $1,500 to a U.S. buyer. The seller subsequently increased the price to $1,650. The invoice price is $1,500.00 because that was the price agreed to and actually paid by the importer. The merchandise should be appraised at $1,500 because the latter was the price actually paid by the buyer—the transaction value.

Example 2

DM, Incorporated, a firm located in Miami, Florida, purchased 10,000 barrels of crude oil from a Venezuelan oil company, Soto, Incorporated, for $250,000. The price consists of $200,000 for the oil and $50,000 for ocean freight and insurance. Soto would have charged $210,000 for the oil. However, since it owes DM $10,000, Soto charged DM only $200,000 for the oil. The transaction value is $210,000, that is, the sum of $200,000 1 $10,000, excluding CIF charges of $50,000 for ocean freight and insurance.

If the transaction value cannot be determined, the transaction value of identical merchandise or, in the absence of that, the transaction value of similar merchandise (commercially interchangeable), will be used. The transaction value of identical and similar merchandise (ISM) will be used under the following circumstances:

- The products (ISM) must have been sold for export to the United States at or about the same time as the merchandise being appraised.
- Value must be based on sales of ISM at the same commercial level and substantially the same quantity as the sale of the merchandise being appraised.
- The ISM must be produced in the same country and by the same person (if not available, by a different person) as the merchandise being appraised.
- In cases involving two or more transaction values for ISM, the lowest value will be used as the appraised value of the imported merchandise.

Deductive Value

This method is used when the transaction value cannot be determined, such as sales between related parties. However, if the importer designates computed value as the preferred method of appraisement, the latter can be used as the next basis of determining value. Deductive value is essentially the resale price of an imported product, with deductions for commissions, profit, and general expenses, transportation and insurance costs (from the country of export to the United States), import duties and taxes, and any cost of further processing after importation. The deductive value is generally calculated by starting with the unit price and making additions to (such as packing costs), and deductions from, that price (see International Perspective 18.4).

Example 1

Merchandise is sold to an unrelated person from a price list which provides favorable unit prices for purchases in larger quantities:

Total Quantity Sold	Unit Price ($)
65	90.00
50	95.00
60	100.00
25	105.00

INTERNATIONAL PERSPECTIVE 18.4.
Unit Price in Deductive Value

One of three prices is used based on time and condition of sale:

- If the merchandise is sold in the condition as imported at or about the date of importation of the merchandise being appraised, the unit price used is the one at which the greatest quantity of the product is sold.
- If the merchandise is sold in the condition as imported, but not sold at or about the date of importation of the merchandise being appraised, the unit price used is the one at which the greatest quantity of the merchandise is sold before the ninetieth day after the date of importation.
- If the merchandise is not sold in the condition as imported and not sold before the close of the ninetieth day after the date of importation of the merchandise being appraised, the unit price used is the one at which the greatest quantity (after processing) is sold before the eightieth day after the date of importation. An amount equal to the value of the further processing is deducted from the unit price in arriving at the deductive value. This method cannot be used if the further processing destroys the identity of the merchandise.

In this example, the unit price used in determining deductive value is $90.00 since the greatest quantity is sold at that price.

Example 2

A foreign parent company sells parts to its U.S. subsidiary in Texas. The product is not sold to unrelated parties and there is no similar or identical merchandise from the country of production. The U.S. subsidiary further processes the product and sells to an unrelated buyer in Florida within 180 days after importation.

In this example, the merchandise should be appraised under deductive value, with allowances for profit and general expenses, freight and insurance, duties and taxes, and the cost of processing.

Computed Value

The computed value starts with the costs of the materials, labor, and overhead in producing the imported goods. Customs then adds profits and general expenses incurred by the producer (based on average estimates for similar goods in the same country) as well as the prorated value of any materials supplied by the buyer free of charge or at reduced price and packing costs (U.S. Department of Commerce, 2003).

Example

Suppose under the previous Example 2, the U.S. importer requested the shipment to be appraised under computed value. The merchandise is appraised using the company's profit and general expenses if not inconsistent with sales of merchandise of the same class or kind.

If none of the previous methods can be used to appraise the imported merchandise, the customs value is based on a value derived from one of these methods, reasonably adjusted or administered flexibly. If an identical or similar product, for example, is not available in the exporting country, customs could appraise an identical or similar product from a third country to determine value.

RULES OF ORIGIN
AND OTHER MARKING REQUIREMENTS

Imported articles are to be marked with the name of the country of origin to indicate to the ultimate purchaser the name of the country in which the product was manufactured. The ultimate purchaser is generally the last person in the United States who will receive the article in the form in which it was imported.

Country-of-origin determination is important because imports are subject to selective tariffs and nontariff barriers depending on the origin of the merchandise. Country-of-origin is the country of manufacture, production, or growth of an article. Most imports, such as those from Canada and Mexico, enter duty free, whereas those from some other nations are subject to a higher tariff, a quota, or even an import ban (e.g., Cuba and North Korea). Customs uses the "substantial transformation test" to determine the country of origin of a product that is made up of components or materials from several different countries. The country of origin is determined to be the one where the product was substantially transformed into its current state (Buonafina and Haar, 1989).

Markings must be legible and located in a conspicuous place where they can be seen with a casual eye in the handling of the merchandise. They should be capable of remaining permanently on the article during transportation or handling. In the case of certain articles for which marking is not required, such as artworks, lumber, sugar, and so forth, their containers must be marked to indicate the English name of the country of origin. There are also special marking requirements for certain articles such as watches, surgical instruments, knives, razors, steel, pipes, and vacuum containers. However, marking is not required for imports not intended for sale (personal use items), products used for further processing, or crude substances, or for items that are incapable of being marked or cannot be marked without injury or prohibitive expense. Other articles not required to be marked with the country of origin include articles valued at no more than $200 that are passed without the filing of a customs entry, articles brought into a foreign trade zone or a bonded warehouse for immediate exportation, and certain coffee, tea, and spice products, etc. Notwithstanding the exemption, the containers must be marked to show the country of origin of such articles (19 CFR 1304).

CHAPTER SUMMARY

Entry of Imports

Entry is the act of filing the necessary documentation with customs to secure release of imported merchandise.

Accrual of Duties on Imports

1. *On arrival of the vessel:* Upon arrival of vessel within the U.S. Customs territory
2. *Arrival of merchandise:* Upon arrival of merchandise within the U.S. Customs territory (for other means of transport)

Who May Enter the Goods

Owner, purchaser, authorized regular employee, or a licensed customs broker

Documentation Required to Enter Merchandise

Entry manifest, commercial invoice, pro forma invoice, packing list, and other necessary documents

Release of Merchandise

After complete entry is made, product is released by customs and estimated duty paid. A bond must be posted to guarantee payment of duty upon final assessment of duty. A bond may be secured through a resident surety company, resident, citizen, or posted in the form of cash or other government obligations.

Liquidation and Protests

1. *Liquidation:* This involves the final ascertainment of the duties and drawback accruing on an entry by customs.
2. *Protests:* If an importer disagrees with the liquidation of an entry, it is possible to file a protest in writing with the district director within ninety days after notice of liquidation. The decision can be appealed to the Court of International Trade, the Court of Appeals for the Federal circuit, and the Supreme Court of the United States.

Harmonized Tariff Schedule of the United States (HTSUS)

HTSUS is a commodity description and coding system that is used by many countries. It classifies goods according to their essential character.

Customs Valuation

Imported merchandise is appraised on the basis and in order of the following:

1. *The transaction value:* Invoice value of the goods as they enter customs
2. *The deductive value:* Resale price of imported merchandise with deductions for profit and general expenses
3. *The computed value:* Cost of materials, labor, and overhead in producing the imported product, plus profits and general expenses incurred by the producer and value of any items supplied by buyer

Rules of Origin and Other Marking Requirements

Marking requirements: Every imported article must be legibly marked with the English name of the country of origin unless otherwise indicated.

REVIEW QUESTIONS

1. When do duties accrue on imported merchandise?
2. What is entry of goods? Who may enter the goods?
3. Explain the difference between single entry bond and a continuous entry bond.
4. What happens to merchandise that is not liquidated within one year from the date of entry?
5. Discuss the advantages of HTSUS.
6. Briefly describe computed value.
7. Why do importing countries require certificates of origin?
8. Describe some of the automated services at U.S. Customs.
9. What is liquidation of entry?
10. Transaction value cannot be used in certain circumstances. Discuss.

Minicase 18.1

A U.S. makeup retailer imports lipstick from an unrelated Mexican company that uses the materials and incurs costs for materials in the assembly of one tube of lipstick, as indicated in the following list. In Mexico, the company assembles the materials into a finished product (a tube of lipstick packaged for retail sale). Upon the importation, the retailer, who is also the importer of record, intends to sell the lipstick for "cost 1 20%."

Part No.	Description	Cost ($)	Country-of-Origin (PN)
1.	Plastic tube base	0.05	Mexico
2.	Plastic tube cover	0.05	Mexico
3.	Plastic swivel base	0.05	Canada
4.	Metal shell	0.05	China
5.	Metal collar	0.05	China
6.	Small round mirror that attaches to bottom of PN 1	0.05	United States
7.	Lipstick mass	0.55	France
8.	Packaging material	0.10	United States

1. What is the per unit entered value?
2. What is the country-of-origin for the retail package?

Minicase 18.2

COMMERCIAL INVOICE

DONGA MICHAEL INC.

Shipper/Exporter Donga Michael Inc. 570, Freedom Road, Taeu Seoul, Korea	**No. and Date of Invoice** US0001E Wednesday, November 15, 2006
For Account and Risk of Messers Tom Salves Stores 23 Furn Rd. Ft. Lauderdale, Fl. 45682	**No. and Date of L/C**
Notify Party	**L/C Issuing Bank**

Port of Lading Kimpo, Korea	**Final Destination** Seattle, WA	**Remarks** P/O No.: IWUVU1
Carrier Aircraft United Parcel Service	**Departure on or about** November 18, 2006	*Marks and Numbers of Pkgs.*

Description of Goods	**Quantity**	**Unit Price (U.S. $)**	**Amount (U.S. $)**
1. Country of Origin: Korea Men's 100% Cotton Knit Polo Shirt Stitch count of 12 stitches per 2 cm in each direction PN: POKNSHRT	1,000pcs	1.50	1,500
2. Country of Origin: Japan Women's Cotton Knit Black Bras Containing Lace PN: AB40ZYI	1,200pcs	2.00	2,400
(2%, Net 15 Days)	**TOTAL 2,200 pcs**		**3,900**

Master Bill: 001-63324833
House Bill: UPS56676406
Estimated Entry Date 11/19/06

1. What is the entered value at customs in Seattle? What is the port code?
2. In June 2006, the Department of Commerce published a countervailing duty order on women's undergarments from Japan (20 percent). It is to be effective from the first of June 2006. What amount is due for this shipment?

Minicase 18.3

1. What is the transaction value of a shipment invoiced at $100,000 if the terms of sale are delivered duty paid (DDP), the ocean freight paid is $6,000, the insurance paid is $850, the duty rate is 6.5 percent, and harbor maintenance fee and merchandise processing fee are paid at 0.125 and 0.21 percent respectively?
2. Calculate the appraised value for a shipment of 10,000 computer monitors with a unit value of $75 CIF, Los Angeles?
   The seller received the cathode ray tubes used in the manufacture of these computer monitors free of charge from a third party that was satisfying a debt owed to the seller of the finished computer monitors.
   The cathode ray tubes, including transportation and insurance, would have cost $25 each.
   There is no through bill of lading associated with this entry.
   Foreign inland freight is $1 each.
   Ocean freight is $2.50 each.
   Marine insurance is $0.50 each.
3. What is the dutiable value for the following transaction? The terms of sale are delivered, duty and fees paid, Chicago. The commercial invoice appears as follows:

```
12,000 dozen baseball caps, @ $30 per dozen  ....... $360,000
International freight charges  ....................    $2,500
International insurance  .......................       $800
Brokerage charges  ............................       $150
Total DDP Price  ..............................  $363,450
```

The caps are classified 6505.90.8090 @ $0.187 per kg. 1 6.8 percent. The net weight of the shipment is 8,000 kg. The actual ocean freight charges were $2,800. Transaction Value is the appropriate basis of appraisement.
4. ———— Is the price actually paid or payable for imported merchandise when sold for exportation to the United States?

CASE 18.1. DEEMED LIQUIDATION BY CUSTOMS

Koyo Corporation of USA (Koyo) imported roller and ball bearings for resale in the United States. At the time of entry, antidumping duty orders issued by Department of Commerce were in effect. The orders required duty deposits to cover estimated antidumping duties between 48 and 74 percent ad valorem. Liquidation of the entries was suspended due to the ensuing litigation. The importers (Koyo) were successful and the rates were substantially lowered.

In view of the successful outcome for Koyo in the litigation, Department of Commerce issued instructions to U.S. Customs to liquidate the entries at lower rates. Customs did not comply with Department of Commerce's instructions. When Koyo contacted customs (one year later) about the liquidation of its entries, customs found these entries to have been "deemed liquidated" at the original higher antidumping duty rate.

Koyo took the case to the U.S. Court of International Trade (CIT) protesting the liquidations (after its initial protest was denied by customs). The issue is whether the deemed liquidations claimed by customs were justified under existing rules. The requirements for deemed liquidation following antidumping proceedings are that: (1) the suspension of liquidation that was in place must have been removed; (2) customs must have received notice of the removal of the suspension; and (3) customs must not liquidate the entry at issue within six months of receiving such notice.

The "deemed liquidation" provision was added to the U.S.Customs law in 1978 to place a limit on the period within which importers would be subject to the prospect of liability for a customs entry and to terminate the government's cause of action for the entry in question.

The court stated that Congress intended to encourage prompt liquidation and did not intend customs not to obey its instructions and thereby retain funds to which it no longer had valid claim. It ordered customs to re-liquidate the entries at the appropriate duty rates, as instructed by Department of Commerce, and refund the duties owed with interest to Koyo (2004 U.S. App; Fed. Circ, 2004).

Questions

1. Do you agree with the decision on prompt liquidation?
2. Conduct Internet research to examine the reasons why Congress introduced the provision on "deemed liquidation."

CASE 18.2. PRODUCT CLASSIFICATION

Better Home Plastics Corp. (BHP) imported shower curtain sets which consisted of an outer textile curtain, inner plastic magnetic liner, and plastic hooks. While the textile curtain is semi-transparent and decorative, the inner liner also matches the curtain and adds to the set's decorative appearance. The sets are sold to retailers at prices ranging from $5.00 to $6.00.

U.S. Customs classified the merchandise under HTSUS 6303.92.0000 at a rate of duty of 12.8 percent ad valorem. BHP protested that classification stating that the merchandise should have been classified under HTSUS 3924.90.1010 (by the set's inner plastic liner) with a prescribed duty of 3.36 percent ad valorem. According to the General Rules of Interpretation, when goods are classifiable under two or more headings such as textile curtain and inner plastic liner, customs must classify the merchandise based on the heading which provides the most specific description (rule of relative specificity). This rule may not apply in cases where both headings are regarded as equally specific and that each refer only to part of the items within the set.

In cases where the rule of relative specificity does not apply, merchandise can be classified by the component that gives their essential character (the essential character test).

BHP contends that the essential character test must be applied to classify the merchandise on the basis of its inner plastic liner while customs believes that the essential character of the product is embodied in the textile curtain because (1) the liner is used for a short time when someone uses the shower while the curtain is employed throughout the day, (2) consumers buy the product because of the decorative function of the outer curtain rather than the inner plastic liner, and (3) the plastic liner is usually replaceable at one-quarter to one-third the price of the set.

Questions

1. Do you agree with the position of BHP? Why/why not?
2. What is the essential character test?

Chapter 19

Import Relief to Domestic Industry

The U.S. trade policy is based on combating unfairly traded imports. There are regulations in place to provide relief to domestic producers that are adversely affected by imports that benefit from government subsidies in home countries or are dumped at low prices in the U.S. market.

ANTIDUMPING AND COUNTERVAILING DUTIES

U.S. antidumping and countervailing duty laws have been subject to several changes over the years; the most recent amendments were to implement the Uruguay Round Agreements of the GATT. An important effect of the agreement is that it has reduced the discretion previously available to the administrating authorities by imposing strict statutory time limits. In the case of an antidumping or countervailing duty petition, for example, domestic authorities are required to make an initial determination within twenty days after the petition is filed. Similar time limits are imposed on the determination of injury. The U.S. Court of International Trade has taken the position that the WTO panel rulings do not have a binding effect (merely persuasive) on U.S. court decisions on such matters (Folsom, Gordon, and Spinogle, 2005).

Antidumping or countervailing duties are statutory remedy that cannot be vetoed by the president except by negotiation of an international trade agreement. Such an agreement may, for example, take the form of voluntary export restraints to restrain the flow of the offending goods to the U.S. market.

It is important to describe the terms that are often used in the analysis of unfair trade practices, that is, dumping, subsidies, and material injury. Dumping is defined as selling a product in the United States at a price that is lower than the price for which it is sold in the home market in the ordinary course of trade (certain adjustments are made for differences in the merchandise, quantity purchased, or circumstances of sale). In the absence of sales or sufficient sales of the like product in the domestic market of the exporting country, dumping may be measured by comparison (1) with a comparable price of a like product sold in a third country, or (2) with the cost of production in the country of origin plus a reasonable amount for administrative, selling, and other costs and for profits (constructed value). Selection of a third country is often based on the similarity of merchandise to the one exported in the United States, volume of sales (country with largest volume of sales), and similarity of market in terms of organization and development to that of the United States. In calculating constructed value, transactions with related parties that do not fairly reflect the usual market price, as well as sales that are made at less than the cost of production, are disregarded. In cases in which the economy of the home market is state-controlled and does not reflect the market value of the product, foreign market value can be determined based on, in order of preference, (1) the price at which such or similar merchandise produced in a non-state-controlled economy is sold either for consumption in that country or another country, including the United States, or (2) the constructed value of such and similar merchandise in a non-state-controlled economy country. Where the price comparison requires a conversion of currencies, such conversion is made using the rate of exchange on the date of sale.

A major problem with the application of such methods is that the surrogate market economy country selected for comparison may be inappropriate (in terms of its level of economic development) or that its producers may not be willing to furnish the information necessary to determine constructed value (Czako, Human, and Miranda, 2003).

There is no agreed-upon definition of subsidies anywhere in the GATT or domestic law. However, it is reasonable to infer from the list of practices that are considered as subsidies that a subsidy is a preferential benefit given by the government to domestic producers. The benefit could be in the form of income or price support of any direct or indirect financial contributions (e.g., grants, loans, tax credits, loan guarantees, etc.; see International Perspective 19.1).

Export subsidies are benefits intended to increase exports; domestic subsidies are granted on a product regardless of whether it is exported or consumed at home. Governments provide domestic subsidies to achieve certain socioeconomic goals, such as optimum employment or location of industries in depressed regions, which could not be attained by the sole efforts of the private sector. Although domestic subsidies may increase the subsidizing country's trade flow, they do not attract international condemnation as export subsidies.

INTERNATIONAL PERSPECTIVE 19.1.
Antidumping Duties and Fair Trade

Antidumping duties are generally intended to prevent predatory pricing by foreign firms. By setting low prices in export markets, they drive domestic producers out of business. Once these firms have gained a controlling interest of the export market, they increase their price to recover their losses. Such economic theory behind antidumping rules is questionable because:

- Such actions are unlikely to escape the attention of governments in importing countries.
- Any subsequent increases in prices are likely to invite other exporters to enter the market thus nullifying the firm's potential gains from market power. Thus, if firms are not certain about future gains from market power, they are not likely to take losses on their export sales.
- Setting different prices in different markets is not inconsistent with normal business practice, especially in imperfect competitive markets.

Existing regulations to establish dumping often lead to unfair and arbitrary outcomes since the standard set to evaluate import price and injury are difficult to meet due to variations in accounting methods, difficulty in collecting price information, lack of transparency in decision-making process, etc. Furthermore, the low burden of proof to establish material harm to domestic producers often leads to acceptance of bogus claims. In the United States, for example, only 17 percent of dumping claims were rejected by the authorities between 1980 and 1997.

For domestic industries which have the support of unions and politicians, even threatening to bring cases often leads foreign exporters to agree to a settlement rather than risk broader trade tension. Many exporters agree to voluntary export restraints. Such agreements, if conducted with consultations of domestic industry, would amount to antitrust violation in many countries.

A study by the ITC indicates that the removal of outstanding antidumping (AD) and countervailing duty (CVD) orders results in a welfare gain. While domestic companies and their workers receiving AD/CVD protection earned $658 million more profits and wages, terminating this protection would have increased overall American business profits and wages by $1.85 billion in industries that were not receiving such protection (USITC, 1995). The economic effects of AD/CVD orders are ranked third behind the Multifiber Arrangement restrictions and the Jones Act maritime restrictions in their net costs to the economy.

It is important to review the rules with respect to permitted or actionable subsidies. If an actionable subsidy is found in a country that is a signatory to the GATT Subsidies Code and that subsidy causes injury to a domestic industry, a countervailing duty is imposed on the subsidized imported product. Proof of injury is not required if the subsidized import comes from a country that is not party to the Subsidies Code or similar agreement. A countervailing duty is imposed to offset the subsidy, that is, equal to the net amount of the subsidy (Trebilcock and Howse, 2005).

Actionable Subsidies

These are subsidies conferred upon a producer to encourage exports (export subsidy) or to promote the use of domestic goods (import-substitution subsidies). They are considered to be industry specific, as opposed to noncountervailable (nonactionable) subsidies that are broadly available and widely used throughout the economy. National programs of subsidies that are designed to specifically assist selected national regions are now considered actionable and subject to retaliation. In all these cases, the benefits obtained are not countervailable if they cannot be calculated in monetary terms. Actionable subsidies include domestic subsidies bestowed on input products used in the production of an imported item (upstream subsidies). However, the input subsidy must be provided in the country of manufacture of the imported product for the application of trade remedy. Countervailable subsides that are small (*de minimis* subsidies), that is, less than 0.5 percent or 2 to 3 percent for developing nations, are disregarded. The Department of Commerce does not make an affirmative countervailing duty determination in such cases.

Nonactionable Subsidies

Nonspecific Subsidies

The determination of whether a subsidy is specific is based on a number of factors, such as the number or proportion of particular industries using the subsidy program as well as the manner in which authorities exercise discretion in providing the subsidy.

Subsidies for Industrial/Research and Competitive Development

These include assistance for research activities conducted by firms or by higher education establishments if such subsidies cover (1) not more than

75 percent of the costs of industrial research or (2) not more than 50 percent of the costs of precompetitive development activity (e.g., translation of industrial research findings into a blueprint or plan for new or improved products or processes).

Subsidies to Entities in Disadvantaged Regions

These subsidies should be part of a general framework of regional development and they are not provided specifically to an enterprise or industry.

Environmental Subsidies

An environmental subsidy is a nonrecurring subsidy for the adaptation of existing facilities (up to 20 percent of the cost) to new environmental requirements.

> *Example 1.* An Italian firm sells a pair of leather shoes manufactured in Milan for $250 in Italy. The same pair of shoes when exported is sold for $150 in the U.S. market. There is no evidence that the firm obtained any financial help from the Italian government. This is a case of dumping.

> *Example 2.* A Colombian firm obtained a low interest loan from a government-owned bank to buy chemical imports that are used for the production of textiles that are exported to the United States. The price of linen textiles (1 foot) is $20 in Colombia, whereas the same type of textile is sold at $12 a foot in New York. This involves upstream subsidies and dumping.

Proof of Injury and Remedies

In both antidumping and countervailing duty investigations, it is important to establish causation: material injury, threat of material injury, or retardation of a U.S. industry producing similar products because of the importation of subsidized and dumped products. Imports do not have to be the sole or even major cause of injury. "Like products" are defined as products which are the same or in the absence of such, "most similar in characteristics and uses" to the foreign product under investigation. In one case, for example, the U.S. International Trade Commission (ITC) defined the U.S. industry as canned mushrooms (not similar to fresh mushrooms). This narrow definition gives the exporter a much larger U.S. market share thus supporting a preliminary injury determination (USITC, 1996a).

Typically, the USITC considers the collective impact of all imports of a product from a given country in arriving at its injury determination. However, in countervailing duty investigations, there is no injury determination for imports from countries that are not signatories of the Subsidies Code or an equivalent arrangement with the United States, unless the goods are entered duty free.

In determining whether there is injury to a U.S. industry, the ITC will consider import volumes, price effects, and impact on domestic producers of like products, as well as all other relevant economic factors that have a bearing on the domestic industry. Domestic industry impact analysis considers the effect of allegedly dumped imports on the development and production of efforts of the domestic industry, employment, and utilization of plant capacity in the relevant industry. For example, threat of material injury can be found if lost sales indicate a threat to future sales, production, and profit. Price undercutting is not a per se basis for a finding of injury if the demand for the product is not price sensitive. Lost sales to the domestic industry have traditionally served as an important element of injury (Czako, Human, and Miranda, 2003). Injury may be shown even in cases involving an improvement in the condition of the industry or a decrease in import volume. Determination of threat of material injury by ITC is made on the basis of evidence that the threat is real and the actual injury imminent, and not based on "mere conjectures and suppositions" (19 U.S. Code 1677).

Once it is established that foreign merchandise is being sold in the United States at less than fair market value and injury to domestic industry is established, an antidumping duty is imposed on the product, that is, an amount by which the foreign market value exceeds the United States price of the merchandise. The causation factor can be satisfied if the dumped or subsidized imports contribute even minimally to injury of domestic industry. A correlation between dumped/subsidized imports and alleged injury is not required for an affirmative injury determination.

The cumulation doctrine is also allowed in determining material injury in dumping or subsidy cases. This means that the effect of dumped and/or subsidized imports from two or more countries of like products (that compete with each other and with domestic products) can be assessed to determine injury to domestic industry. This encourages petitioners to name as many countries as possible. Similarly, if a subsidy is shown to exist and material injury or threat thereof to U.S. industry is found, then a duty equal to the subsidy (countervailing duty) is imposed. In the case of agricultural products, injury could still be established even though the prevailing market price is at or above the minimum support price. This is intended to ensure that injury analysis is not distorted by the beneficial effects of government assistance programs (Trebilcock and Howse, 2005).

ANTIDUMPING AND COUNTERVAILING DUTY PROCEEDINGS

Antidumping (AD) and countervailing duty (CVD) investigations are conducted either on the basis of a petition filed with the Department of Commerce (Commerce) through the International Trade Administration (ITA) and the International Trade Commission (ITC) on behalf of a domestic industry or by Commerce upon its own initiative. In the latter case, Commerce must notify the ITC. In a countervailing duty investigation, the ITC plays an active role only when the foreign government conferring the subsidies has entered a trade agreement such as the Subsidies Code or a similar arrangement with the United States (USITC, 1996a). The procedural steps of a typical investigation are as follows (see Table 19.1):

Initiation of Investigation by Commerce

Once a petition is filed or an investigation started at the initiative of Commerce, ITC begins to investigate material injury, or threat of material injury, etc. to the domestic industry. In the case of a petition, Commerce determines within twenty days whether to initiate or terminate the investigation based on whether the petition adequately alleges material injury or threat thereof with

TABLE 19.1. Antidumping and Countervailing Duty Investigations

Day	Event
0	Petition filed
20	Decision on initiation
45	Preliminary injury determination by ITC[a]
AD: 160	Preliminary determination by ITA
CVD: 85	Preliminary determination by ITA
AD: 235	Final determination by ITA[a]
CVD: 160	Final determination by ITA[a]
AD: 280	Final injury determination by ITC
CVD: 205	Final injury determination by ITC[a]
AD: 287	Publication of order
CVD: 211	Publication of order

Note: AD = Antidumping duty; CVD = Countervailing duty.

[a]If the determination is negative, the investigation is terminated.

sufficient information supporting the allegations, and whether the petition has been filed by or on behalf of the industry (domestic producers or workers supporting the petition must account for at least 25 percent of total production and more than 50 percent of production of those supporting or opposing the petition). In the event that the 50 percent requirement is not met, Commerce must poll the industry or rely on other information to determine if the required level of support for the petition exists. In order to establish a standing to file a petition on behalf of an industry, it is common practice for various producers to file as copetitioners or as copetitioners with unions or trade associations, or for petitioners to secure letters or support from nonpetitioning members of the domestic industry, unions, or trade associations.

If Commerce determines to initiate an investigation, it will begin to establish whether there is a subsidy or dumping in the U.S. market and the commission continues its investigation on injury to domestic industry.

Preliminary Phase of ITC's Investigation

Within forty-five days after a petition is filed or an investigation is begun by Commerce, the ITC makes its preliminary determination, that is, whether there is a reasonable indication of injury to domestic industry. If the determination is negative, or the imports subject to the investigation are negligible, the proceedings terminate.

Preliminary Phase of Commerce's Investigation

If the ITC's determination is affirmative, Commerce makes its preliminary determination based on the information available at the time whether there is a reasonable basis to believe or suspect that a countervailable subsidy or sales at less than fair market value exists.

If Commerce finds a reasonable basis, it estimates the dumping or subsidy margin within 140 and 65 days, respectively, of initiating an investigation. However, such deadlines can be extended if the petitioner requests or the case is extraordinarily complicated.

If Commerce's preliminary determination is affirmative, Commerce (1) suspends liquidation of the investigated merchandise subsequently entered into the United States or withdrawn from warehouse, (2) requires bonds or cash deposits to be posted for each entry of the merchandise in an amount equal to the estimated net subsidy or dumping margin, and (3) continues the investigation. In addition, the ITC institutes a final investigation concerning injury, threat, or retardation. If Commerce's preliminary determination is negative, Commerce's investigation simply continues (USITC, 1996b).

Final Phase of Commerce's Investigation

Within seventy-five days after its preliminary determination, Commerce makes a final determination as to whether a subsidy is being provided or sales at less than fair value are being made. If the final determination is negative, the proceedings end and any suspension of liquidation is terminated, bonds or other security are released, and deposits are refunded. Any party to the proceedings can request for a hearing before final determination by Commerce. If the final determination by Commerce is affirmative, the ITC will then make its determination on injury.

Final Phase of ITC's Investigation

The ITC makes its final determination with respect to material injury, threat thereof, or retardation of domestic industry because of sales at less than market value or subsidies. The investigations must be completed within 120 days after Commerce's affirmative preliminary determination (if Commerce's preliminary determination is affirmative) or within seventy-five days after Commerce's affirmative final determination (if Commerce's preliminary determination is negative).

Issuance of an Order

If the final determination of the ITC is affirmative, Commerce issues an antidumping or countervailing duty order, usually within a week of ITC's determination. The order requires the deposit of estimated antidumping (AD) or countervailing duties (CVD) at the same time as other estimated customs duties pending calculation of the final AD or CVD. If the final determination by the ITC is negative, no AD or CVD is imposed, and any suspension of liquidation is terminated, bonds released, and deposits are refunded (USITC, 1996a). If the petitioner alleges in an investigation the existence of critical circumstance, that is, massive entry of subsidized imports or imports sold at less than fair value in a relatively short period, Commerce's final determination, if affirmative, will include a retroactive suspension of liquidation for all unliquidated entries of merchandise entered into the United States, including those withdrawn from warehouse.

Suspension of Investigation

An investigation can be suspended prior to a final determination by Commerce if the parties (exporting or subsidizing government) involved agree to cease exports or eliminate the dumping margin or subsidy within a few months after suspension of the investigation. At the same time as it suspends a proceeding, Commerce must issue an affirmative preliminary determination. Suspensions are reviewed by the ITC to ensure the injurious effect of imports is eliminated by the agreement. If the ITC determines that the injurious effect is not eliminated, the investigation, if not yet completed, will resume.

Appeal of Determinations

Any interested party adversely affected by a determination by Commerce or ITC may appeal to the U.S. Court of International Trade. In the case of NAFTA members, an interested party may appeal for a review by a binational panel set up under the agreement (see Tables 19.2 and 19.3).

OTHER TRADE REMEDIES

Unfair Trade Practices in Import Trade

The ITC is authorized, upon the filing of a complaint or on its own initiative, to investigate alleged violations of section 337 and to determine whether such violations exist. Section 337 of the Tariff Act of 1930 prohibits (1) the

TABLE 19.2. Disposition of U.S. AD and CVD Investigations, 1998-2004

	Antidumping Duty (%)	Countervailing Duty (%)
Terminated before preliminary commission (ITC) determination	60 (5)	54 (12)
Preliminary ITC determinations		
Affirmative	836 (82)	261 (75)
Negative	188 (18)	89 (25)
Terminated after affirmative preliminary determination by ITC (before final determination)	153 (14)	88 (19)
Final ITC determinations		
Affirmative	461 (67)	118 (52)
Negative	230 (33)	108 (48)

Source: International Trade Commission, 2005.

TABLE 19.3. Top Ten Countries Cited, 1980-2004

Antidumping Cases (%)		Countervailing Duty Cases (%)	
U.K.	3.4	India	3.8
France	3.7	Belgium	4.6
Italy	4.3	U.K.	4.9
Brazil	4.5	Spain	5.1
Canada	4.6	Korea	5.8
Taiwan	5.6	Germany	6.0
Germany	6.0	Canada	6.9
Korea	6.2	Italy	8.2
China	9.5	France	8.2
Japan	10.2	Brazil	10.6
Others	41.9	Others	36.1

Source: International Trade Commission, 2005.

importation of articles that violate a valid and enforceable U.S. patent, trademark, copyright, and so on, for which an industry exists or is in the process of being established in the United States and (2) unfair methods of competition by the importer or consignee that could adversely affect a U.S. industry (19 U.S. Code S.1337). International Trade Commission's investigations also include gray-market imports (i.e., products manufactured abroad by the owner or under license that are imported by unauthorized sources into the United States). The strict definition of gray-market goods is: products that are authorized by the owner of production rights to be made and sold in one market are diverted and sold in another, often unauthorized, market. The problem with such goods in import trade is that they are often purchased at discounted prices abroad and imported into the United States, taking away the market from authorized dealers.

A large percentage of Section 337 cases involve patent infringement; others pertain to violation of other forms of intellectual property. Such actions can also be raised with the U.S. Patent and Trademark Office. The remedies for such violations include the following:

1. A general or limited exclusion order that directs customs to deny entry of certain goods
2. A cease and desist order that enjoins a person from further violation of Section 337

These remedies may be ordered by the ITC in the case of imports infringing upon U.S. intellectual property rights without finding injury. Determinations by ITC may be appealed to the U.S. Court of Appeal for the Federal Circuit (see International Perspective 19.2).

Market Disruption by Imports from Communist Nations

The ITC conducts investigations to establish whether imports of products made in a communist country are causing market disruption to a domestically produced article (19 U.S. Code S.2436). "Market disruption" is defined as a rapid increase in imports that causes material injury or threat thereof to a domestic industry producing a product similar to, or in direct competition with, the imported article. Such investigations may be requested by the president, the U.S. Trade Representative (USTR), Congress, or any interested party. The president may order remedial action in the form of imposition of duties, quotas, and so forth, after receiving the recommendation of the ITC.

Unjustified Foreign Trade Practices

Section 301 of the Trade Act of 1974 was introduced in order to seek open access to U.S. exports in foreign markets. It is directed at foreign government practices that restrict U.S. exports or artificially direct goods or services to the United States. It is applicable to the export of goods and services, investment practices, and intellectual property rights. Under Super 301 Clause of the 1988 Trade Act (renewed in 1994), the U.S. Trade Representative (USTR) is required to examine annually unreasonable or discriminatory restrictions on U.S. exports and then prepare a list of foreign trade practices of foreign countries. If the offending practice remains in place one year after unsuccessful negotiation, punitive tariffs can be imposed equal to the estimated value of lost sales by U.S. firms. Super 301 negotiations have been conducted with many countries, including China and Japan.

Special 301 is another version of Super 301 applicable to intellectual property rights. Priority countries (countries that do not provide adequate protection for intellectual property rights) are identified for bilateral negotiations. A Special 301 investigation is similar to an investigation initiated in response to an industry Section 301 petition. Trade sanctions for noncompliance could be imposed in the event that the country declines bilateral consultations or fails to implement an agreement to open its market or provide adequate protection for U.S. intellectual property rights.

INTERNATIONAL PERSPECTIVE 19.2.
The Semiconductor Industry

The semiconductor industry has been a target of industrial policy in many countries. In the United States, the government paid a large share of R & D expenditures since the 1950s. In Japan, the industry was protected by high tariffs, restrictive quotas, and approval of licensing arrangements. Even after the abolition of formal barriers in the 1970s, the Japanese government provided R & D support, preferential procurement policies etc. In Europe, stiff tariff rates on imports were used to protect domestic firms.

The Semiconductor Accord: The first agreement (1986) between the United States and Japan focused on improving market share, access to the Japanese market, and on terminating unfair trade practices such as dumping by Japanese companies. The Reagan administration applied some $165 million in retaliatory duties on Japanese imports in 1987. The Japanese were compelled to raise prices for their semiconductors sold in the United States in order to avoid the imposition of special tariffs and duties resulting from U.S. antidumping investigations.

The agreement resulted in a rise in U.S. foreign market share (U.S. market share in Japan had grown from 9 to 14 percent in 1991). The price of Japanese chips sold in the United States increased by over 30 percent. The agreement was extended in 1991 endorsing the desirability of increasing the foreign market share in Japan by more than 20 percent by the end of 1992. It also paved the way for U.S. and Japanese firms to enter into joint ventures.

As the 1991 agreement expired in 1996, the two governments announced new industry and government agreements on semiconductors. The key provisions of the new agreement include the continuation of existing cooperative activities between users and suppliers as well as new cooperative activities among suppliers from the two countries. These activities include international standards, designs and environmental data (imports, exports, market size, market growth, openness of market etc.). U.S. and Japanese industries will collect and submit data to their respective governments for review in bilateral consultations. The semiconductor industry in Japan has reached the same profit level as that of the United States, as both are focused on capital expenditures.

Problems with Managed Trade: The major shortcomings with such arrangements are that it is arbitrary and once established, becomes institutionalized and perpetuated. It may also distort competition in the semiconductor industry with adverse effects on users such as the computer industry.

Example 1

Between 1980 and 2004, the U.S. government has placed several sanctions on Chinese imports due to dumping practices. Although China claims to place stringent laws to prevent such practices in view of its membership in the WTO, the country has yet to enforce such regulations. The Department of Commerce recently placed over 90 percent antidumping tariff on a range of products from China. Currently, continuous negotiations are taking place between the United States and China to correct its dumping practices.

Example 2

In 2005, the following countries were identified for their trade policies and practices that have the greatest adverse effect on U.S. products:

1. *China:* Piracy of U.S. intellectual property rights, export of infringing goods (illegal production and export of CD, video, CD-ROM, etc., priority foreign country).
2. *Argentina, Brazil, Egypt, India, Indonesia, Israel, Lebanon, Pakistan, Philippines, Russia, Turkey, and Venezuela:* Lack of adequate and effective protection of intellectual property rights and market access (countries under a priority watch list).
3. *Bahamas, European Union, Poland, Taiwan, and Korea:* Monitored to ensure the implementation of agreements on intellectual property and market access (countries under a watch list) (USTR, 2004, 2005; U.S. Department of State, 2005).

Import Interference with Agricultural Programs

The ITC conducts investigations at the direction of the president to determine whether imports interfere with or render ineffective any program of the Department of Agriculture. The ITC makes its findings and recommendations to the president, who may take appropriate remedial action, including the imposition of a fee or quota on the imports in question. However, fees or quotas may not be imposed on imports from nations that are members of the WTO (USITC, 1997).

Trade Adjustment Assistance

For companies and workers adversely affected by fairly traded imports, trade adjustment assistance is provided in the form of retraining or relocation assistance for workers or certain forms of technical and financial assistance to companies. The Department of Labor (adjustment assistance for workers) or Commerce (adjustment assistance for firms) makes an affirmative determination insofar as imports constitute an important contributing factor to declines in production and sales as well as loss of jobs in the affected industries. Such assistance could be pursued before or in tandem with escape clause proceedings.

The Escape Clause

Under Section 201 of the U.S. Trade Act, 1974, the ITC assesses whether U.S. industries are being seriously injured by fairly traded imports and can recommend to the president that relief be provided to those industries to facilitate positive adjustment to import competition. Relief could take the form of increased tariffs or quotas on imports and/or adjustment assistance for the domestic industry. Such relief is temporary and may be provided for up to five years, with one possible extension of not more than three years. Such actions can be appealed to the U.S. Court of International Trade, then to the Court of Appeals for the Federal Circuit, and from there to the U.S. Supreme Court.

Import Relief Based on National Security

The Tariff Act (19 U.S. Code S.1862) gives the president discretion to restrict imports that threaten national security. The Department of Commerce makes findings and recommendations to the president who may order the imposition of a quota, fee, tariff, or other remedies. Although such remedies are rarely invoked, they could conceivably be used by companies in some strategic sectors. Such remedies are available only if it is established that a strategically important industry is adversely affected by imports and that supplies may not be available during a crisis either from domestic or foreign sources.

CHAPTER SUMMARY

Dumping and Subsidies

Dumping is the selling of a product in a foreign market at a price that is lower than the price for which it is sold in the home market.

Subsidies are any benefit given by the government to domestic producers.

Domestic subsidies are provided to achieve certain socioeconomic goals, such as optimum employment.

Export subsidies are intended to promote exports.

Proof of Injury and Remedies

In both cases, remedies are subject to proof of injury of subsidized or dumped imports. Injury is generally established by considering import volumes, lost sales, and impact on domestic producers of similar products.

Antidumping and Countervailing Duty Proceedings

1. Initiation of investigation by Commerce
2. Preliminary phase of ITC investigation
3. Preliminary phase of Commerce investigation
4. Final phase of investigation by Commerce
5. Final phase of investigation by ITC

Other Categories of Trade Remedies

1. Unfair trade practices, S. 337
2. Market disruption by imports from communist countries
3. Unjustified foreign trade practice, S. 301
4. Import interference with agricultural programs
5. Trade adjustment assistance
6. The escape clause

REVIEW QUESTIONS

1. What is the difference between dumping and subsidies?
2. State the types of nonactionable subsidies.
3. What is to be established in every subsidy and dumping investigation?
4. Briefly describe the preliminary phase of an ITC investigation.
5. Describe the procedural steps in a typical antidumping or countervailing duty investigation.
6. What is market disruption?
7. Explain the escape clause. Can it be applied at any time to protect domestic industry?
8. Describe Special 301. Is it the same as Super 301 of the U.S. Trade Act?

CASE 19.1. SIMILAR PRODUCTS AND DUMPING

A Chilean salmon exporter was accused of dumping salmon in the U.S. market at less than fair value. An antidumping petition was filed in 1997 by the Coalition for Fair Atlantic Salmon Trade. The U.S. Department of Commerce (ITA) initiated an antidumping duty investigation to determine whether Chilean exporters of Atlantic, fresh, farmed salmon were selling in the United States at less than fair market value to the detriment of U.S. industry. The purpose of the investigation was to determine whether dumping duties should be imposed on the subject merchandise when imported into the United States.

ITA conducted an investigation in order to compare the price of the salmon sold in the United States with its "normal value" in Chile (home market). Since the product is not sold in the home market, ITA based normal value on the price of the salmon sold in Japan. The exporter sold "premium" grade salmon in the United States while it sold "premium" and "super premium" grades in Japan. ITA found that (1) salmon industries do not recognize any grade higher than premium grade and all salmon in this range are graded equally; (2) salmon graded as "super premium" are in fact premium grade and comparable in the market place. ITA recognized that the exporter reported higher prices for sales of super-premium grade salmon to Japan (sales of premium salmon to Japan covered a few moths and involved relatively small quantities, thus insufficient to evaluate price differences). The practical consequences of ITA's decision to classify the two grades of salmon (super-premium and premium) as identical in physical characteristics was to impose a dumping margin of 2.23 percent on the Chilean exports of premium salmon in the United States.

Questions

1. Are the products sold in Japan and the United States identical for duty analysis?
2. Based on the information, do you think dumping has occurred in the United States?

Chapter 20

Intellectual Property Rights

Intellectual property rights (IPRs) are associated with patents, trademarks, copyrights, trade secrets, and other protective devices granted by the state to facilitate industrial innovation and artistic creation (Wolfhard, 1991). The grant of exclusive property rights provides owners with personal incentives to make the most productive use of their assets and facilitates transfer by making possible a high degree of exchange. Intellectual property rights are one form of exclusive rights conferred by the state to promote science and technology. The issue of intellectual property has received wider attention compared to other property rights for the following reasons:

- The volume of trade in goods protected by IPRs is becoming increasingly significant as more countries produce and consume products that result from creative activity and innovation (Gadbaw and Richards, 1988).
- The globalization of markets has created opportunities for the production and/or sale of unauthorized copies to supply the newly generated demand. In the first quarter of 2005, over $1.1 billion (U.S.) of counterfeit goods were seized worldwide. Over $500 billion (U.S.) of such goods are seized every year. Copyright piracy amounted to about $500 million (U.S.) in India and $2.5 billion (U.S.) in China in 2004. In China alone, it is estimated that there are about eighty-three manufacturing plants with 765 production lines that specialize in the production of pirated goods (Bird, 2006; Linek and Iwanicki, 2006).

WHAT ARE IPRs?

Intellectual property rights are exclusive rights given to persons over the use of their creation for a given period of time. Such rights are customarily divided into various areas, as detailed in the following material.

Export-Import Theory, Practices, and Procedures, Second Edition

Patents

A patent is a proprietary right granted by the government to inventors (and other persons deriving their rights from the inventor) for a fixed period of years to exclude other persons from manufacturing, using, or selling a patented product or from utilizing a patented method or process. At the expiration of the time for which the privilege is granted, the patented invention is available to the general public, or falls into public domain.

Patents may be granted for new and useful products as well as processes for the manufacture (or methods of use) of new or existing products. The basis for patent protection is promotion of innovative activity, dissemination of technical knowledge, and facilitation of transfer of technology. Even though patents are granted as a recognition of the concept of a natural right in inventions, they provide an incentive for the encouragement of inventions and the promotion of economic development. With the monopoly grant, the patent owner can divulge the invention to the public and still retain exclusive use of it for the period of the patent. At the end of the monopoly period, the patent becomes available for the unrestricted use of the public. Patent protection also encourages transfer of technology through direct investment or licensing. In the United States, patents are valid for a period of twenty years from the filing date. Patent violations are generally referred to as patent infringement or piracy.

Trademarks

A trademark is a word, name, symbol, or device, or any combination of these, used by a manufacturer or seller of goods to identify and distinguish the particular manufacturer's/seller's goods from goods made or sold by others (Ladas, 1975). In general, trademarks perform three functions:

1. Identify one seller's goods and distinguish them from goods sold by others
2. Signify that all goods bearing the trademark come from a single source and are of an equal level of quality
3. Serve as a primary instrument in advertising and selling the goods

An important part of the advertising effort is to develop goodwill. Trademark rights can be acquired by registration or use (reputation). Registered marks are renewable. Once a trader acquires a reputation in respect of a mark, that is, an unregistered mark, it becomes part of that trader's goodwill and is protectable as a registered mark. Violation of trademarks consists of counterfeiting and other forms of infringement, such as advertising, sales, or distribution of goods bearing a similar mark (to that of the owner) that results in deception or confusion. Counterfeiting is the unauthorized use of a mark. In the United States, trademarks are valid for ten years from the date of registration.

Trade Secrets

A trade secret involves a formula, method, or technique that derives independent economic value from not being generally known or available to other persons who can obtain economic value from its disclosure or use (Kinter and Lahr, 1983). The historical roots of trade secrets protection can be traced to ancient China, where death by torture was prescribed for revealing the secret of silk-making to outsiders, and to ancient Rome, where enticing a competitor's servant to disclose business secrets was a punishable offense. In England, the movement of artisans to other countries was prohibited by a series of statutes aimed at preventing knowledge of British processes from reaching possible competitors in Europe and America, and employers sued would-be emigrants and those who tried to seduce them (Ashton, 1988). Violation of trade secrets includes acquisition of a trade secret by improper means or disclosure without the consent of the owner.

In most developed nations, however, protection is afforded through laws pertaining to contracts, criminal law, or torts, such as breach of confidence (Seyoum, 1993; Hannah, 2006). Protection of trade secrets does not expire after a set period of time, as in the case of other IPRs. The owner, in effect, has perpetual monopoly on the innovation. A large part of technology being developed now, perhaps with the exceptions of pharmaceuticals and specialty chemicals, does not get patented. Many high-technology innovations, such as aircraft and automobiles, and most low-technology innovations, such as detergents or food products, are not patented (Williams, 1983). In some countries, a formula might be patentable, while methods of production based on personal skills are not patentable. Patent protection also ends at some point, even if one is able to obtain and keep the patent. Thus, companies prefer to maintain new innovations as trade secrets and protect their technology by contract rather than by patent.

Copyrights

A copyright is a form of protection granted to authors of original works, including literary, dramatic, musical, artistic, and certain other intellectual works. The owner of the copyright has the exclusive right to reproduce, distribute, sell, or transfer the copyrighted work to other persons. In the United

States, copyrights are protected for a minimum period of fifty years after the death of the author. The core copyright industries (i.e., business and entertainment software) are second only to motor vehicles and automotive parts in terms of estimated sales and exports ($53.25 billion of exports in 1995) and also have grown twice as fast as the rest of the U.S. economy.

IPRs AND INTERNATIONAL TRADE

An important feature of IPRs is their exclusiveness and territorial dimension. This means that a patent holder or licensee is the person solely entitled to manufacture and market the patented product within a given territory of the state in which the patent is granted. The exclusive and territorial character of such rights is capable of creating obstacles to both the free movement of goods and competition. For example, a patent or trademark owner in country A may be entitled to block the importation of a product legally manufactured in country B by its own licensee or subsidiary. Although such restrictive use of IPRs interferes with free trade, the grant of monopoly rights is considered an acceptable trade-off to encourage research and the diffusion of new knowledge and technology. In short, free trade between countries as a result of an agreement such as North American Free Trade agreement (NAFTA), EEC, or World Trade Organization (WTO) does not preclude prohibitions or restrictions on imports, exports, or goods in transit justified on the grounds of the protection of IPRs.

A number of issues pertaining to IPRs have important implications to the conduct and growth of international trade. They are as follows.

The Growth of Trade in Counterfeit Goods

The globalization of markets, the increased demand for new products, and the nearly prohibitive R & D costs to develop such products have created incentives for the unauthorized use of IPRs. For example, counterfeiting (false labeling for sale in export markets) has spread from strong brand-name consumer goods to a variety of consumer and industrial goods. Related violations include copyright, patent infringement, and unfair competition. The International Intellectual Property Alliance estimates that over half of all compact disks and about 70 percent of all video games sold in Brazil are pirated (www.iipa.com).

Lack of Adequate Protection for IPRs in Many Countries

An important contributing factor to trade in counterfeit/pirated goods is the lack of adequate protection and effective enforcement of IPRs in many countries. Furthermore, some new technologies do not fit within any of the existing types of intellectual property. In many developing countries, the protection of computer software, biotechnology, and semiconductor chips remains unclear. For example, copyright piracy exceeded over $1.7 billion (U.S.) in Russia alone in 2004. Even though Russia has laws on IPRs, there is limited enforcement by local authorities. Jail sentences for piracy are rare and authorities do not conduct surprise inspections or seize/confiscate equipment (Bird, 2006).

Piracy of IPRs as a Trade Barrier

Given the fact that counterfeit/pirated goods displace those of legitimate producers, such action distorts international trade and has the long-term effect of reducing trade in technology-intensive goods. Piracy leads to the misallocation of resources by diverting trade from legitimate producers to pirates. Trade experts believe that elimination of piracy abroad of U.S. intellectual property could easily wipe out a majority of the U.S. trade deficit.

PROTECTION OF IPRs

Protection under Domestic Laws

Most countries have domestic laws to protect IPRs (for example, see International Perspective 20.1). In the United States, Section 337 of the Tariff Act of 1930 authorizes the International Trade Commission (ITC) to institute an investigation into the importation of articles that may infringe on U.S patents, trademarks, or copyrights. If the ITC determines that a violation exists, the U.S. Customs Service is then charged to enforce an exclusive order, that is, to stop the article from entering the United States or, upon a subsequent violation, the property may be seized and forfeited to the U.S. government. Since 1972, 505 individual cases of alleged IPR violations have been filed against non–U.S. firms in forty countries. Over 70 percent of these section 337 cases were decided in favor of the complainant (Chiang, 2004). Unlike antidumping and countervailing cases where domestic injury must be proved, the U.S. Department of Commerce does not play a role in such cases.

Section 301 of the 1974 U.S. Trade Act contains significant measures to ensure trade compliance. It allows the United States to apply trade sanctions on countries that impose an unjustifiable burden on or restrict U.S. commerce. These include but are not limited to denial of fair and equitable market

INTERNATIONAL PERSPECTIVE 20.1.
Some Red Flags for IPRs

- Importer is known to buy infringing goods and has a history of enforcement actions for IPR violations
- Merchandise is shipped in small quantities on informal entries
- Merchandise is imported from sources (countries and/or vendors) with IPR problems
- Company documents show IPR identifier but the company does not have a license agreement with the owner of IPR
- Invoices with no model or catalog numbers and merchandise without lot numbers, factory codes, expiration dates, or dates of manufacture
- Payment term is COD rather than letter of credit
- Shipment is under-insured
- Vague or unusual shipment terms, unusually high or low value for the merchandise

opportunities such as denial of most-favored nation treatment (MFN) to U.S. goods and services, lack of adequate and effective protection of IPRs (including those that are members of TRIPs), export targeting, and denial of workers' rights. A Section-301 investigation may be commenced by the U.S. Trade Representative's Office (USTR) or any interested party that files a petition with the USTR. The USTR must conclude its investigation within a certain period after initiation of an investigation. It may authorize retaliatory action against the foreign country (see International Perspective 20.2).

Special 301 focuses on unfair IPR practices. The Special 301 Provision of the 1988 Omnibus Trade and Competitiveness Act requires the USTR to identify (by April 30 of each year) countries that fail to provide adequate protection and enforcement for IPRs or deny fair and equitable market access to persons that rely on IPR protection. The USTR classifies countries that fail to provide adequate protection or enforcement into the following three categories.

Priority Foreign Countries

A country may be designated as a priority foreign country if:

- Its policies or practices have the greatest adverse impact (actual or potential) on the relevant U.S. products
- It is not engaged in good faith negotiations to address these problems

INTERNATIONAL PERSPECTIVE 20.2.
Protection and Enforcement of IPRs: Selected Countries

Argentina: The National Intellectual Property Institute (INPI) has begun to approve patents for pharmaceutical products. The service has been extremely slow for issuing patents to products with commercial value. The copyright laws in Argentina generally provide adequate protection, mostly due to the government's ratification of the World Intellectual Property Organization Copyright Treaty. However, this is not enough as recorded music, videos, books, and computer software products continue to be pirated. Currently, the country is under the Special 301 Priority Watch List due to its lack of enforcement of IPRs.

India: India is working to provide product patent protection to drugs, food, agricultural, and chemical substances. The government passed a patent protection ordinance in 2004, which has proved to be a successful measure. India has passed a copyright law in 2000, yet the broadly defined amendments in the Indian Copyright Act allow for increased piracy of films, popular fiction works, cable television shows, and certain textbooks. The United States has placed India on their Special 301 Priority Watch List.

Japan: There is inadequate protection for trademarks and trade secrets. Software piracy is widespread and the narrow interpretation of patents by domestic courts has allowed local competitors to conduct activity that violates the rights of legitimate patent owners. In order for enforcement to take place on copyrighted and patented products, all trademarks must be registered. Any delays in the registration process makes enforcement difficult and open the door to piracy.

China: Inadequate protection and enforcement of IPRs has led to widespread sale of counterfeit/pirated goods. China continues to take measures to provide for adequate protection and enforcement of IPRs. The United States has placed China on their Special 301 Priority Watch List. Despite efforts to protect IPRs, there is a lack of coordination and effort among China's government, agencies, and ministries. There are also problems with local protection of pirates, lack of training, and high corruption.

Source: U.S. Trade Representative (USTR), 2006.

U.S. Customs has the authority to exclude the importation of imports that violate IPRs. Intellectual property rights (patents, trademarks, etc.) subject to protection have to be registered with the U.S. Patent and Trademark Office. Customs monitors imports to prevent the importation of violating articles based on the IPR owner's request or on the Customs' initiative. Customs regulations establish the authority for trademarks, trade names, and copyright to be recorded with Customs; to seize counterfeit articles that violate IPRs; and to restrict the importation of gray market imports. The port director has the authority to demand the redelivery of violating articles and to claim liquidated damages in the event of failure to redeliver the goods. Customs also monitors importations of articles (for a fee) on a nationwide basis and reports to the patent holder the names and addresses of importers of infringing goods.

U.S. Trade Representative is required to initiate a Section 301 investigation within thirty days after identification of a priority foreign country. If negotiations are not successful within six to nine months, the USTR may retaliate against the exports of the country by withdrawing trade agreement concessions and imposing duties or other restrictions on imports. In 2006, no country was identified under this category.

Priority Watch List

In this category are countries whose protection and enforcement of IPRs warrants close monitoring and resolution. The 2006 list of countries under this category includes Argentina, Brazil, China, Egypt, India, and Russia.

Watch List

This category includes a list of countries that warrant special attention because they maintain certain practices or barriers to market access for intellectual property products that are of particular concern. The 2006 list includes Bahamas, Belarus, Bolivia, Bulgaria, Canada, and Chile.

The 2006 review emphasized a number of critical issues: proper and timely implementation of the WTO TRIPs agreement; cracking down on pirated production of optical media such as CDs, VCDs, and CD-ROMs in a number of countries including China, India, and Russia. These include physical and virtual marketplaces for pirated goods (the USTR has begun to implement the Administration's strategy of targeting organized piracy) and ensuring that government ministries only use authorized software. The U.S. government also uses different mechanisms to advance the protection of IPRs: negotiation of free trade agreements and withdrawal of trade preferences such as the general scheme of preference (GSP) if beneficiaries do not provide adequate protection to IPRs (USTR, 2006).

It is important to note that a Special 301 investigation is similar to an investigation initiated in response to an industry Section 301 petition (unfair foreign trade practices), except that the maximum time for the latter is shorter (in cases involving violation of TRIPs) than other Section 301 investigations.

Special 301 is potentially an effective tool to protect U.S. IPRs abroad because it allows the administration to use a variety of trade sanctions (e.g., removal of GSP or MFN status) against a priority foreign country. However, its implementation has been sporadic and inconsistent over the years. For example, certain countries with gross violations of IPRs are not added under the priority country list and in some cases, when identified, sanctions are not imposed. Russia was classified under the "Watch List" category for many years in spite of its rampant black markets in videocassettes, films, music, and so forth. India was classified under the "Priority Foreign Country" category several times; however, no sanctions were imposed even though there was no resolution of the problem through bilateral negotiations.

INTERNATIONAL/REGIONAL PROTECTION

The Paris Convention

The Paris Convention is used in connection with two separate treaties: (1) international protection of industrial property and (2) international copyright protection (the Universal Copyright Convention). The Paris Convention for the protection of industrial property was concluded in 1883 and has gone through various revisions. It applies to industrial property in the widest sense, including patents, trademarks, trade names, and so on. The treaty sets forth three fundamental rules:

1. *National treatment:* The principle of national treatment provides that nationals of any signatory nation shall enjoy in all other countries of the Union the advantages that each nation's laws grant to its own nationals.
2. *Right of priority:* The right of priority enables any resident or national of a member country to apply for protection in any other member state of the convention within a certain period of time (twelve months for patents and six months for trademarks and industrial designs) after filing the first application in one of the member states to the treaty. These later applications will then be regarded as if they had been filed on the same day as the first application. A major advantage of this is that applicants wishing protection in multiple countries need not file all applications at the same time but have six to twelve months from the first application to decide in which countries to apply for protection.
3. *Minimum standards:* The convention lays down minimum standards common to all member countries.

The Universal Copyright Convention

The convention (1952, revised in 1971) establishes the national treatment standard and minimum rules common to all member countries. It also allows countries to set formalities or conditions for the acquisition or enjoyment of copyright in respect to works first published in its country or works of its nationals wherever published.

The Paris Convention is administered by the World Intellectual Property Organization (WIPO), whose mission is to promote the protection of intellectual property throughout the world. World Intellectual Property Organization membership includes more than 130 countries.

The Patent Cooperation Treaty

The Patent Cooperation Treaty (PCT) allows for a single application and a worldwide search for novelty in all member countries; that is, a search is made in one of the designated offices based on a single application without the need to file applications in all other member states. The application with the search report will be forwarded to the countries where the applicant seeks patent protection. Although such a system eliminates duplication of filing and patent examination in each patent office of a member country, each country retains full jurisdiction to grant or refuse a patent in accordance with its own domestic legislation. The PCT has been signed by 133 countries and regional patent systems such as the European Patent Office (EPO) and the African Regional Industrial Property Organization (ARIPO).

Trade-Related Aspects of IPRs (TRIPS)

The developed countries criticize the intellectual property conventions administered by WIPO because their minimum standards are considered insufficient and they contain no provisions for dispute settlement. Member states retain broad discretion in granting IPRs. Existing multilateral treaties failed to protect the most basic rights: certain fields of patentable technologies such as pharmaceuticals, biotechnology, agricultural chemicals, and copyrightable documents such as education materials, have been excluded from protection in many countries. Some countries limit patentability to the process (not the product), and/or limit the duration of patent protection.

They contend that the deficiencies in the protection of IPRs distort international trade and reduce the value of concessions negotiated in various rounds of trade negotiations. The Intellectual Property Committee (IPC), a cross-industry organization of large multinational corporations, notes that:

> Inadequate international protection of intellectual property has become a major cause of distortions in the international trading system—and that it is both appropriate and necessary for intellectual property issues to be dealt with under international trade rules. (Gad, 2003, p. 676)

Subsequent negotiations led to the adoption of the Uruguay Round Agreement on Trade-Related Aspects of Intellectual Property Rights (TRIPS) in 1994. The agreement established multilateral obligations for the protection and enforcement of the IPRs and provided a dispute settlement mechanism under the WTO.

The TRIPS agreement covers almost all forms of intellectual property including patents, trade and service marks, industrial designs, trade secrets, and layout designs of integrated circuits.

The three fundamental features of the agreement are:

1. *Standards:* The agreement sets out minimum standards of protection to be provided by each member country. It provides broader protections for intellectual property rights by granting the MFN treatment for all signatories. It also requires members to comply with existing agreements such as the Paris Convention and the Berne Convention for the protection of literary and artistic works. It further supplements additional obligations on matters where the pre-existing conventions are silent or inadequate.
2. *Enforcement:* The TRIPS agreement lays down domestic procedures and remedies for the enforcement of IPRs.
3. *Dispute settlement:* The agreement makes disputes between WTO members subject to the WTO's dispute settlement procedures. It also authorizes trade sanctions against noncompliant nations.

Regional Conventions

The major regional agreement in the area of IPRs is the European Patent Convention (1973), which under a single application may result in the grant of a European patent valid in all member countries. It is a centralized patent granting system administered by the EPO in Munich, Germany, on behalf of member countries. A similar regional organization is the ARIPO, located in Harare, Zimbabwe. It was established in 1976 to grant regional patents having effect in all designated member countries.

CHAPTER SUMMARY

IPRs

Intellectual property rights are associated with patents, trademarks, copyrights, trade secrets, and other protective devices granted by the state to facilitate industrial innovation and artistic creation.

Major Issues Pertaining to IPRs and International Trade

1. The growth of trade in counterfeit goods.
2. Lack of adequate protection and enforcement of IPRs in many countries.
3. The long-term effect of piracy on trade in technology-intensive goods.

U.S. Classification of Countries That Do Not Provide Adequate Protection of IPRs

1. Priority foreign countries: Countries that do not provide adequate protection to IPRs and whose policies have the greatest adverse impact on U.S. commerce.
2. Priority watch list: Countries that warrant close monitoring and resolution.
3. Watch list: Countries that warrant the special attention.

Regional/International Protection

International Protection

The Paris Convention, the Universal Copyright Convention, the PCT, trade-related aspects of IPRs (the TRIPS) agreement.

Regional Protection

The European Patent Office, the ARIPO.

REVIEW QUESTIONS

1. What is the importance of IPRs to international trade?
2. What are patents? What are the advantages of providing an exclusive (monopoly) right to patent holders?

3. What is the importance of trademarks?
4. Discuss some of the reasons why some inventions are not patented.
5. Explain why piracy of IPRs is a trade barrier.
6. Discuss the level of protection and enforcement of IPRs in Japan and China.
7. What is the right of priority under the Paris Convention?
8. What are the three fundamental principles of the TRIPS agreement?

CASE 20.1. PATENTS AND ACCESS TO LIFESAVING DRUGS

Under the Uruguay Round Agreement (1995), the jurisdiction of WTO was extended toward the protection of IPRs. The agreement covers a wide range of subjects including patents, copyrights, and trade secrets. It allows trade sanctions against countries that fail to abide by the agreement. As regards the protection of pharmaceutical products, the agreement (Trade-Related Aspects of IPRs or TRIPS) attempts to strike a balance between the short-term benefits of proving lifesaving drugs and the long-term objective of encouraging technological innovation. TRIPS imposes the following obligations on member countries: (1) protection of product or process patents for at least twenty years from the date the patent application was filed; (2) nondiscrimination: members cannot discriminate between different fields of technology, places of invention, and whether the products are imported or locally produced; (3) compulsory licensing: governments are allowed to license someone to produce the patent product or process without the consent of the patent owner. A number of conditions must be met: a license must have been attempted unsuccessfully from the owner under reasonable terms (unless there is a national emergency), payment of adequate remuneration, nonexclusion of license.

Many developing countries were concerned with the potential implications of TRIPS for protecting public health. This issue gained world attention when a number of South African drug companies challenged the legality of the newly enacted legislation which allowed for compulsory licensing of patented pharmaceuticals. The U.S. government also threatened to issue a compulsory license order against Bayer AG unless the company made significant quantities of capsules available (at a lower price) to victims of anthrax. Member countries agreed to interpret the TRIPS agreement in a way that supports public health by promoting access to existing drugs and the creation of new medicines. They also agreed to extend exemptions on pharmaceutical patent protection for least developed countries until 2016.

The TRIPS agreement states that compulsory licensing can only be used to supply the domestic market. This means that (1) countries that produce under compulsory license would be unable to export the drug, and (2) countries that do not have the manufacturing capability could not import it for domestic consumption. In August 2003, WTO members agreed to make it possible for countries to import cheaper generics made under compulsory licenses if they are unable to manufacture the medicines themselves.

Questions

1. Does TRIPS balance the interests of drugs companies with that of consumers in developing countries?
2. What are your suggestions that are acceptable to both parties?

Appendix A

Trading Opportunities
in Selected Countries

A.1. TRADING OPPORTUNITIES IN AFRICA
AND THE MIDDLE EAST

Egypt

Country Profile

Population: 77,505,756
Exports: Goods (FOB): $14.33 billion; Services: $6.3 billion
Major Exports: Crude oil and petroleum products, cotton yarn, raw cotton, textiles, metal products
Imports: Goods (FOB): $24.1 billion; Services: $7.6 billion
Major Imports: Machinery and equipment, foods, fertilizers, wood products, durable consumer goods, capital goods
Trade as Percentage of GDP: Exports: 25.5 percent, Imports: 27.7 percent
Major Trading Partners: United States, Germany, Italy.
Currency and Exchange Rate: Egyptian pounds per U.S. dollar—5.78
GDP: $337.9 billion
GDP per capita: $4,400
External Debt: $28.95 billion

Import Policies

- *Entry of goods:* Most commodities can be imported without a license except those that require import licenses (i.e., poultry and poultry parts). There are regulations governing the marketing and labeling of imports.

Export-Import Theory, Practices, and Procedures, Second Edition

- *Tariffs and taxes:* Tariff rates range from 5 to 40 percent on generally imported goods, where the average tariff rate is 27.5 percent. Luxury goods (i.e., automobiles, tobacco, alcoholic drinks, and clothing) are subject to tariff spikes. Tariffs on textiles are over 50 percent. Overall, there has been a 10 percent reduction of tariffs on general imported goods by from 50 to 40 percent.
- *Nontariff barriers:* NTBs included in (1) ad valorem duty on canned peaches, chocolate, confections, and dairy products (2) Inspection for quality control, arbitrary testing procedures that discriminate against foreign products.
- *Intellectual property rights protection (IPRs):* There is inadequate protection and enforcement of IPRs in Egypt. Allegations of trademark infringement, copyright piracy, inadequate patent term, broad compulsory licensing provisions are major trade barriers in trade in technology-intensive products.
- *Documentation requirements:* Required documents are commercial invoice, pro forma invoice, bill of lading/air waybill, packing list, certificate of origin, insurance certificate, consular/customs invoice, sanitary certificate, radiation certificate (agricultural imports).
- *Marketing and distribution:* Agents and distributors generally handle imports. Large retailers import directly from foreign manufacturers.

Best Export Prospects (Exports to Egypt)

- *Agricultural products:* Wheat, corn, soybean meal, beef and veal, cotton, vegetable oils
- *Industrial products:* Agricultural equipment, biotechnology, computers and parts, construction equipment, machine tools, airport and ground support equipment, seafood, oil and gas, medical equipment, water resources equipment, school and office supplies, printing equipment
- *Services:* Travel and tourism, franchising, computer services, architectural, construction and engineering services

Promising Imports from Egypt: Cotton, beans, onions, rice, textiles and clothing, manufactured goods, petroleum and petroleum products, metal products

Israel

Country Profile

Population: 6,276,883
Exports: Goods (FOB): $40.14 billion; Services: $17.7 billion

Major Exports: Machinery, cut diamonds, software, chemicals, textiles and clothing

Imports: Goods (FOB): $40.14 billion; Services: $13.7 billion

Major Imports: Raw materials, military equipment, investment goods, rough diamonds, and oil

Trade as Percentage of GDP: Exports: 46 percent; Imports: 51 percent.

Major Trading Partners: United States, Belgium, Hong Kong, Germany, Switzerland, United Kingdom

Currency and Exchange Rate: New Israeli shekels per U.S. dollar—4.46

GDP: $139.2 billion

GDP per capita: $22,200

External Debt: $73.87 billion

Import Policies

- *Entry of goods:* Israel has import licensing requirements on many food and agricultural products. Under the United States-Israel Free Trade Agreement, all duties on U.S. exports to Israel were eliminated in 1995. Israel has strict marking and labeling requirements and thus it is important for exporters to consult with the Israeli importer prior to shipment of merchandise.
- *Tariff and taxes:* For countries with which Israel does not have a free trade agreement, tariffs range from 0.5 to more than 95 percent of CIF value. Purchase taxes are also imposed on certain luxury and consumer items, such as alcohol, cigarettes, automobiles, color televisions, etc., as well as tariff rate quotas on imported wines.
- *Nontariff barriers:* Certain imports such as certain agricultural products or other substances are prohibited on grounds of national security and human, animal, or plant health. Textile products such as used clothing are restricted and those with second fabrics are banned. Many products are subject to mandatory standards designed to favor domestic products over imports. There are strict regulations on imported meat and meat products.
- *Intellectual property rights protection:* Israel has made the necessary changes to comply with its commitments to the GATT/WTO TRIPS obligations. Cable television, video, and software piracy remains widespread in Israel, as well as trademark infringements in textiles.
- *Documentation requirements:* Required documents are commercial invoice, pro forma invoice, bill of lading/air waybill, packing list, certificate of origin, insurance certificate, sanitary certificate, health certificate (cattle), photo-sanitary certificate (plants and plant products),

special certificate (liquors), registration requirements (drugs), kosher certificate (food products).
- *Marketing and distribution:* Most exports to Israel are handled through local representatives and distributors.

Best Export Prospects

- *Agricultural products:* Wheat, feed grains, dried fruits, tree nuts, beef
- *Industrial products:* Computer parts and software, electronic components, hotel furnishing, hotel fixtures and equipment, machine tools, medical equipment and supplies, pollution control equipment, trucks, trailers, buses
- *Services:* Franchising, information services

Promising Imports from Israel: Dairy products, fruits and vegetables, machinery and equipment, metals, polished diamonds, textiles and clothing, high-tech equipment, chemical and oil products

Nigeria

Country Profile

Population: 128,771,988
Exports: Goods (FOB): $48.1 billion; Services: $4.2 billion
Major Exports: Petroleum, cocoa, rubber
Imports: Goods (FOB): $17.3 billion; Services: $7.3 billion
Major Imports: Machinery and transport, chemicals, food and live animals
Trade as Percentage of GDP: Exports: 53 percent; Imports: 35 percent
Major Trading Partners: United States, Brazil, Spain, China, Netherlands, France, Germany, Italy
Currency and Exchange Rate: Nairas per U.S. dollar—132.59
GDP: $132.1 billion
GDP per capita: $1,000
External Debt: $37.49 billion

Import Policies

- *Entry of goods:* Importers are required to open an irrevocable letter of credit after receipt of an approved revised "form M" processed through their banks. All items entering the country must be labeled in metric terms exclusively. Entries of goods through Nigerian ports are faced with time-consuming inspections and high costs.

- *Tariffs and taxes:* Imports are subject to tariffs ranging from 2.5 (raw materials) to 60 percent (largely plastic and aluminum). Tariffs are eliminated on certain items such as some machinery, tools, tractors, water treatment chemicals, plant, and equipment imported by industrial establishments using gas in the manufacturing process.
- *Nontariff barriers:* Nontariff barriers to trade include: (1) export subsidies and various incentive programs, (2) tendering procedures are nontransparent and often claimed to use the patronage system, (3) ban on items such as pork, pork products, beef, beef products, biscuits, fresh fruit, and several others (are as recent as 2004).
- *Intellectual property rights protection:* Even though there are laws to protect IPRs in Nigeria, enforcement remains quite weak. Nigeria is considered Africa's largest market for pirated goods from third countries. Trademark infringement and piracy of patents (especially pharmaceuticals), sound recordings, and tapes is claimed to be a major problem.
- *Documentation requirements:* Required documents are commercial invoice, pro forma invoice, bill of lading/air waybill, packing list, certificate of origin, insurance certificate, sanitary certificate, disinfection certificate, certificate of analysis.
- *Marketing and sales:* Products are generally exported to Nigeria through local agents and distributors. Machinery and equipment is sometimes purchased directly from overseas manufacturers mainly to avoid delays of the distribution system.

Best Export Prospects

- *Agricultural products:* Wheat, rice, wines and spirits, dairy products
- *Industrial products:* Auto-parts, computers, parts and software, cosmetics, medical equipment, oil and gas machinery, telecommunications equipment

Promising Imports from Nigeria: Cocoa, oil, rubber

South Africa[1]

Country Profile

Population: 44,344,136
Exports: Goods (FOB): $55.3 billion; Services: $11.2 billion
Major Exports: Gold, minerals and metals, food and chemicals

Total Imports: Goods (fob): $56.5 billion; Services: $12.2 billion
Major Imports: Machinery, transport equipment, chemicals
Trade as Percentage of GDP: Exports: 28.2 percent; Imports: 26.4 percent GDP
Major Trading Partners: United States, Germany, Japan, United Kingdom, China, France, Iran, Saudi Arabia
Currency and Exchange Rate: Rand per U.S. dollar—6.19
GDP: $527.4 billion
GDP per capita: $11,900

Import Policies

- *Entry of goods:* Import permits are required only for certain products, such as agricultural, fishery, etc., products. South Africa is part of a customs union (SACU) where products by non-SACU countries are able to move within the four countries (Botswana, Namibia, Lesotho, and Swaziland) with a tariff of 20 percent.
- *Tariff and taxes:* Domestic industries are protected by high tariffs ranging from 3 to 23 percent. Import surcharge is also levied on luxury consumer goods, specifically to textiles and apparel items. Certain items are subject to ad valorem rates.
- *Nontariff barriers:* Import licenses are required for certain products and can be obtained from officials within the Departments of Agriculture, Water Affairs, Sea and Fisheries, Trade and Industry, and Energy Affairs.
- *Intellectual property rights:* Even though there are laws to protect IPRs in South Africa, enforcement remains quite weak. DVDs, video, and software piracy remains widespread in South Africa.
- *Documentation requirements:* Required documents are commercial invoice, pro forma invoice, bill of lading/air waybill, packing list, certificate of origin, health certificate, photo-sanitary certificate, permits for agricultural products.
- *Marketing and distribution:* Import distribution and sale is usually handled by an agent or distributor, selling through established wholesalers or dealers. Certain exports are also distributed through branches or subsidiaries.

Best Export Prospects

- *Agricultural products:* Pet food, seeds, meat, and poultry, wood and wood products

- *Industrial products:* Computers, parts and software, industrial chemicals, security and safety equipment, telecommunications equipment, textile machinery and equipment, drugs
- *Services:* Tourism, healthcare, education and training, franchising

Promising Imports from South Africa: Agricultural products, coal, gold, minerals, and metals.

Zimbabwe[2]

Country Profile

Population: 12,746,990
Exports: Goods (FOB): $1.644 billion; Services: $1.4 billion
Major Exports: Tobacco, gold, ferroalloys, and cotton
Imports: Goods (FOB): $2.059 billion; Services: $0.8 billion
Major Imports: Transport equipment and machinery, chemicals, manufactured goods, petroleum products
Trade as Percentage of GDP: Exports: 43 percent; Imports: 53 percent
Major Trading Partners: South Africa, United Kingdom, Germany, Japan, United States, European Union, Zambia, and China
Currency and Exchange Rate: Zimbabwean dollars per U.S. dollar—15,190.8
GDP: $23.98 billion
GDP per capita: $1,900
External Debt: $5.17 billion

Import Policies

- *Entry of goods:* It is difficult to import products into Zimbabwe since the country places exceptionally high tariffs, quotas, or bans on certain products.
- *Tariff and taxes:* High duties on luxury items such as furniture, bicycles, electronic goods, shoes, carpets, building materials, and motor vehicles, most often 95 percent tariff. Tariffs on manufactured goods range from 22.5 to 80 percent.
- *Nontariff barriers:* NTBs exist in agricultural and mining; include quotas on certain products.
- *Intellectual property rights:* IPRs exist in Zimbabwe but there is a lack of adequate enforcement. Videocassette, audio, and software piracy is widespread.

- *Documentation requirements:* Required documents are commercial invoice, pro forma invoice, bill of lading/air waybill, packing list, certificate of origin, photo-sanitary certificate.
- *Marketing and Distribution:* Marketing and distribution is handled by local agents and distributors.

Best Export Prospects

- *Agricultural products:* Cotton, sugar, beef
- *Industrial products:* Mining, telecommunications and power generation equipment, textile machinery, and transportation equipment
- *Services:* Engineering services, franchising

Promising Imports from Zimbabwe: Gold, tobacco, tea, cotton, and certain manufactured goods

A.2. TRADING OPPORTUNITIES IN THE AMERICAS

Argentina

Country Profile

> *Population:* 39,537,943
> *Exports:* Goods (FOB): $40 billion; Services: $6.2 billion
> *Major Exports:* Edible oils, feeds, motor vehicles
> *Imports:* Goods (FOB): $28.8 billion; Services: $7.6 billion
> *Major Imports:* Machinery, vehicles and transport products, chemicals, plastic
> *Trade as Percentage of GDP:* Exports: 24.0 percent; Imports: 19.0 percent.
> *Major Trading Partners:* United States, Brazil, Germany, China, Chile, Spain
> *Currency and Exchange Rate:* Argentine pesos per U.S. dollar—2.88
> *GDP:* $537.2 billion
> *GDP per capita:* $13,600
> *External Debt:* $119 billion

Import Policies

- *Entry of goods:* Argentina does impose burdensome country of origin requirements, including import licensing on certain commodities. Import licenses are still required for footwear, toys, and textiles (import licensing affects one-fifth of the nation's imports). Regulations cover the marketing and labeling of import goods and their containers.

- *Tariff and taxes:* The average tariff rate is less than 11 percent. Tariffs range from 0 to 0.5 percent on imports of capital goods and raw materials. Tariff on textiles and apparels average at 21.5 percent and can range up to 35 percent.
- *Nontariff barriers:* (1) Imports of pharmaceuticals, foodstuffs, and defense materials require a prior approval of the appropriate government agency, (2) lack of IPRs protection for certain products, such as pharmaceuticals, and inadequate enforcement to combat copyright infringement, such as video piracy.
- *Documentation requirements:* Required documents are commercial invoice, pro-forma invoice, bill of lading or airway bill, packing list, insurance certificate, price list, and sanitary and health certificates if applicable.
- *Marketing and distribution:* Imports can be handled through branches, import houses (import merchants), or local representatives. Government agencies and local manufacturing firms make direct imports.

Best Export Prospects

- *Agricultural products:* Seeds, pet food, fruits and vegetables, cereals, and dairy products
- *Industrial products:* Apparel, auto parts, computers, parts and software, construction and building materials, electrical power equipment, food processing and packaging equipment, telecommunications equipment, oil and gas, medical equipment, pollution control equipment
- *Services:* Travel and tourism, franchising

Promising Imports from Argentina: Oil and oilseeds, wheat, meat, leather, fruits and vegetables, minerals, wood and wood products, fish.

Brazil

Country Profile

Population: 186,112,794
Exports: Goods (FOB): $115.1 billion; Services: $16.1 billion
Major Exports: Iron ore, soybean bran, orange juice, footwear
Imports: Goods (FOB): $78.02 billion; Services: $24.2 billion
Major Imports: Capital goods, chemical products, oil, electricity
Trade as Percentage of GDP: Exports: 17 percent; Imports: 12 percent

Major Trading Partners: European Union, Latin America, United States
Currency and Exchange Rate: reals per U.S. dollar—2.49
GDP: $1.58 trillion
GDP per capita: $8,500
External Debt: $211.4 billion

Import Policies

- *Entry of goods:* Import license is required for most products. Shipping marks, port of destination, and package number (when required) are to be prominently displayed on the package. Product labeling should be written in Portuguese.
- *Tariff and taxes:* The common external tariff (MERCOSUR) ranges between 0 and 22 percent except for certain products such as computers, capital goods, shoes, and consumer electronics. The average tariff for most import is about 11.5 percent. Brazil also has a number of additional taxes and fees on imports including syndicate and brokerage fees. A 60 percent flat fee is applied to all manufactured retail goods imported by individuals.
- *Nontariff barriers:* (1) restrictions on entry of certain agricultural products due to sanitary and photo-sanitary measures; (2) "Buy-national" policies that favor domestic producers; (3) subsidies to encourage production for export and the use of Brazilian inputs in exported products; (4) inadequate protection and enforcement of certain IPRs.
- *Documentation requirements:* Required documents are commercial invoice, pro forma invoice, bill of lading/air waybill, packing list, certificate of origin, insurance certificate, sanitary certificate, health certificate, inspection certificate.
- *Marketing and distribution:* Marketing and distribution is often handled through agents and distributions.

Best Export Prospects

- *Agricultural products:* Poultry products, pet food, cheese products, beer
- *Industrial products:* Agricultural equipment, apparel, computer hardware, parts and software, cosmetics, machine tools, medical equipment and supplies, telecommunication and transportation equipment
- *Services:* Travel and tourism, computer services

Promising Imports from Brazil: Sugar, textiles, tobacco, rubber, oil and petroleum products, fish, footwear, cocoa, coffee

Canada

Country Profile

Population: 32,805,041
Exports: Goods (FOB): $374.3 billion; Services: $53.6 billion
Major Exports: Timber, automobile products, machinery, petroleum
Imports: Goods (FOB): $320.5 Services: $65.0 billion
Major Imports: Machinery and equipment, petroleum, chemicals and automobiles
Trade as Percentage of GDP: Exports: 40.7 percent; Imports: 39.6 percent
Major Trading Partners: United States, Japan, United Kingdom, Germany, Mexico, China
Currency and Exchange Rate: Canadian dollars per U.S. dollar—1.21
GDP: $1.077 trillion
GDP per capita: $32,800
External Debt: $600.7 billion

Import Policies

- *Entry of goods:* Most imports from NAFTA countries are not subject to restrictions. However an import permit is required for textiles and clothing, agricultural, steel, and other products. Labeling is required on all consumer goods indicating the product, quantity, and dealer's name and address. All mandatory information such as product identity and quantity should be written in English and French.
- *Tariff and taxes:* All tariffs between Canada and United States were eliminated by January 1, 1998. For non-NAFTA exporters, the average tariff rate ranges from 0 to 25 percent. Rates are low on raw materials imports and the duty increases as the product is highly processed. The Good and Services Tax (GST) is 7 percent on most imported goods. Certain goods and services such as basic groceries, prescribed drugs, educational and dental services are exempt from GST.
- *Nontariff barriers:* (1) Certain imports are prohibited (some game birds, certain commodities); (2) restrictions apply on the importation of food products, clothing, drugs, firearms; (3) tariff quota rates are applied to certain products such as dairy products, poultry, and eggs.
- *Documentation requirements:* Required documents are commercial invoice, pro forma invoice, bill of lading, packing list, certificate of origin, insurance certificate, sanitary certificate, photo-sanitary certificate.

- *Marketing and distribution:* Imports are marketed and sold through wholesalers, distributions, or manufacturers' sales subsidiaries, or agents. Department stores and other large Canadian buyers purchase through agents located abroad.

Best Export Prospects

- *Agricultural products:* Fruits and vegetables, candy and confectionery.
- *Industrial products:* Auto parts, building products, computers, parts and software, electronic components, medical equipment, telecommunications equipment, mining equipment
- *Services:* Travel and tourism, franchising

Promising Imports from Canada: Wheat, wood pulp, minerals, fish, lumber, textiles and clothing, cereals, auto and auto parts, natural g as

Chile

Country Profile

>*Population:* 15,980,912
>*Exports:* Goods (FOB): $40.6 billion; Services: $7.2 billion
>*Major Exports:* Copper, other metals and minerals, wood products, fish and fishmeal, fruits
>*Imports:* Goods (FOB): $30.09 billion; Services: $7.8 billion
>*Major Imports:* Consumer goods, chemicals, motor vehicles, and fuels
>*Trade as Percentage of GDP:* Exports: 38.0 percent; Imports: 31.0 percent
>*Major Trading Partners:* Asia, European Union, Latin America, United States
>*Currency and Exchange Rate:* Chilean pesos per U.S. dollar—511.45
>*GDP:* $180.6 billion
>*GDP per capita:* $11,300
>*External Debt:* $44.8 billion

Import Policies

- *Entry of goods:* Licensing is used as a means of gathering statistical information and not to control imports. Imports must be marked with country of origin. Packaged goods must be labeled to show quantity, ingredients, and other important features.
- *Tariff and taxes:* Average tariff is about 6 percent on most imports. VAT is 18 percent (all imports) and luxury tax is imposed on certain

products such as jewels, mineral water, automobiles etc. Imported sugar is subject to tariff rate of 98 percent. An ad valorem of 27 percent is applied to all imported liquors.

- *Nontariff barriers:* (1) Export promotion measures are used to assist nontraditional exports, (2) a price band system is established for wheat, vegetable oils and sugar designed to maintain domestic prices for these commodities, (3) there are animal health and photo-sanitary requirements that unduly restrict some imports, (4) shortcomings exist in the protection of patents (no protection for plant and animal varieties), copyrights (lack of protection for computer software), and trademarks (a novelty requirement).
- *Documentation requirements:* Required documents are commercial invoice, pro forma invoice, packing list, bill of lading/air waybill, certificate of origin, sanitary certificate, photo-sanitary certificate, veterinary certificate, certificate of analysis.
- *Marketing and distribution:* Imports are sold through local agents, distributors, or wholesalers.

Best Export Prospects

- *Agricultural products:* Grains, fruits and vegetables, raw cotton, pet foods
- *Industrial products:* Air conditioning and refrigeration, building construction materials, computers, computer parts and software, railroad, security and telecommunications equipment, medical and pollution control equipment, mining, food processing equipment

Promising imports from Chile: Chemicals, copper, iron ore, gold, silver, fruits and vegetables, transportation equipment

Colombia

Country Profile

Population: 42,954,279
Exports: Goods (FOB): $23.06 billion; Services: $2.7 billion
Major Exports: Petroleum, coffee, coal, bananas, flowers
Imports: Goods (FOB): $20.42 billion; Services: $4.8 billion
Major Imports: Industrial equipment, transportation equipment, consumer goods, chemicals
Trade as Percentage of GDP: Exports: 19.1 percent; Imports: 21.2 percent
Major Trading Partners: United States, Mexico, Venezuela
Currency and Exchange Rate: 2,324.08 pesos per U.S. dollar

GDP: $303.1 billion
GDP per capita: $7,100
External Debt: $37.06 billion

Import Policies

- *Entry of goods:* Import licenses are issued for a given period of time and may be extended for one period only. Most imports can be freely imported into the country and their importation is automatically approved upon presentation of an application. Import licenses are, however, required for about 2 percent of products, such as weapons and certain chemicals that may be used in refining cocaine. Used articles (used cars, tires, and clothing) are prohibited from importation. Marking or labeling is only required for food and pharmaceutical products.
- *Tariff and taxes:* Colombia, Venezuela, and Ecuador implemented the Andean Pact common external tariff (CET) which took effect on February 1, 1995. The CET has a four-tier structure, with duty levels of 5, 10, 15, and 20 percent for most products. Average tariff rate ranges between 11 and 13.5 percent. A duty of 5 percent is levied on raw materials, 10 to 15 percent on intermediate and capital goods, and 20 percent on most consumer goods imports. Imports are also subject to a 16 percent VAT.
- *Nontariff barriers:* (1) Import licenses are required for most agricultural products, (2) Exporters also claim of inconsistencies in the application and enforcement of technical standards for certain products, (3) Export subsidies are provided to promote the export of certain products, (4) There is inadequate protection and enforcement of IPRs.
- *Documentation requirements:* Required documents are commercial invoice, pro forma invoice, bill of lading/air waybill, packing list, certificate of origin, insurance certificate, import registration, import declaration, sanitary certificate, photo-sanitary certificate, certificate of purity.
- *Marketing and Distribution:* Imports are usually handled through a local agent or distributor. Large Colombian firms also deal directly with overseas supplies.

Best Export Prospects

- *Agricultural products:* Corn, cotton, wheat, soybean, and processed foods
- *Industrial products:* Air-conditioning and refrigeration equipment, apparel, auto parts, business equipment, computers and parts, construction, mining and metal working equipment, medical equipment
- *Services:* Franchising

Promising Imports from Colombia: Coffee, flowers, vehicles, chemicals, electrical machinery

Mexico

Country Profile

Population: 106,202,903
Exports: Goods (FOB): $213.7 billion; Services: $16.1 billion
Major Exports: Crude oil, oil products, coffee, silver, engines, cotton
Imports: Goods (FOB): $223.7 billion; Services: $21.4 billion
Major Imports: Metal manufactured goods, agricultural machinery, electrical equipment
Trade as Percentage of GDP: Exports: 30.1 percent; Imports: 32.2 percent
Major Trading Partners: United States, Canada, Japan
Currency and Exchange Rate: Mexican pesos per U.S. dollar—10.97
GDP: $1.066 trillion
GDP per capita: $10,000
External Debt: $174.3 billion

Import Policies

- *Entry of goods:* Under NAFTA, Mexico has abolished licensing requirements for goods from member countries. Exporters to Mexico should consult with importers to determine marking and labeling requirements with respect to their products.
- *Tariff and taxes:* Under NAFTA, Mexico has eliminated tariffs on all industrial and most agricultural products from Canada and United States. The remaining tariffs and nontariff barriers on certain agricultural items are to be phased out by 2008. Average duty on NAFTA-qualifying goods is less than 1 percent.
- *Intellectual property rights protection:* Enforcement of IPRs remains weak in spite of the existence of adequate laws to protect such rights in Mexico.
- *Documentation requirements:* Required documents are commercial invoice, pro forma invoice, bill of lading/air waybill, packing list, shipping documents, certificate of origin, sanitary certificate, photosanitary certificate, health certificate.
- *Marketing and distribution:* Main channels for imports in Mexico are local manufacturers and other large buyers, distributors, sales agents, branches, or subsidiaries of foreign manufacturers.

Best Export Prospects

- *Agricultural products:* Corn, oilseed, beans, meat, livestock, wheat
- *Industrial products:* Auto parts and maintenance equipment, building products, electronic components, pollution control equipment, telecommunications equipment, security equipment
- *Services:* Travel and tourism, management consulting, franchising

Promising imports from Mexico: Art and handicrafts, computer products, furniture and wood products, television sets, autos and auto parts, office machines and parts

Venezuela

Country Profile

Population: 25,375,281
Exports: Goods (FOB): $52.73 billion; Services: $1.3 billion
Major Exports: Petroleum, bauxite, aluminum, steel, chemicals, agricultural products, basic manufactured goods
Imports: Goods (FOB): $24.63 billion (2005 est.); Services: $5.4 billion
Major Imports: Raw materials, construction materials, machinery and transport equipment
Trade as Percentage of GDP: Exports: 41 percent; Imports: 21 percent.
Major Trading Partners: Brazil, the Netherlands, United States, Colombia, Argentina
Currency and Exchange Rate: Bolivares per U.S. dollar—2,090.75
GDP: $161.7 billion
GDP per capita: $6,400
External Debt: $39.79 billion

Import Policies

- *Entry of goods:* Import licenses have been generally eliminated except for a small number of products such as weapons and explosives. Import certificates are, however, required for certain products subject to photo-sanitary certificate such as grains, seeds, and plants. Certain imports of pharmaceuticals and cosmetics require registration with the Ministry of Health.
- *Tariff and taxes:* Bolivia has a three-tariff structure for imported goods: Capital goods for industrial development are at 0 percent,

nonessential capital goods at 5 percent, and everything else is subject to a 10 percent duty.

- *Nontariff barriers:* (1) Andean Pact CET rates for agricultural imports are adjusted between the reference prices and the established floor and ceiling prices; (2) enforcement of IPRs remains inadequate.
- *Documentation requirements:* Required documents are commercial invoice, bill of lading/air waybill, packing list, certificate of origin, insurance certificate, import license, sanitary certificate, health certificate, photo-sanitary certificate.
- *Marketing and distribution:* Imports are generally handled through local agents, wholesalers, or distributors.

Best Export Prospects

- *Agricultural products:* Corn, soybeans, wheat
- *Industrial products:* Autos and auto parts, computers, computer parts and software, medical equipment, oil and gas, mining and pollution control equipment, telecommunications equipment, pumps and accessories, security and safety equipment
- *Services:* Franchising, telecommunication services, computer services

Promising Imports from Venezuela: Bauxite, coal, natural gas and petroleum, iron ore

A.3. TRADING OPPORTUNITIES IN ASIA

Australia

Country Profile

Population: 20,090,437
Exports: Goods (FOB): $103 billion; Services: $28.4 billion,
Major Exports: Coal, gold, meat, and wool
Imports: Goods (FOB): $119.6 billion; Services: $29.4 billion
Major Imports: Machinery and transportation equipment, computers and office machines, telecommunication equipment and parts
Trade as Percentage of GDP: Exports: 19.4 percent; Imports: 27.2 percent
Major Trading Partners: ASEAN, United States, Japan, China
Currency and Exchange Rate: Australian dollars per U.S. dollar—1.31
GDP: $642.7 billion
GDP per capita: $32,000
External Debt: $509.6 billion

Import Policies

- *Entry of goods:* Exporters to Australia should comply with federal and state labeling regulations. It is necessary to modify products that have been packaged and labeled overseas.
- *Tariffs and taxes:* Australian duties on manufactured goods currently average 3 percent except for textiles, clothing, footwear, and certain automotive products (about 15 percent). More than 99 percent of tariff rates applied on an ad valorem basis. The high tariffs on these products are to be phased out in stages. Certain categories of goods are subject to tax, for example, household goods (12 percent) and luxury goods (32 percent).
- *Nontariff barriers:* Products that are considered to pose a potential public danger (drugs, steroids, and weapons), as well as food, plants, and animals, are restricted or quarantined due to photo-sanitary concerns. Australia still has in place some standards that restrict product entry. Government procurement policy lacks transparency and tends to favor local companies. Export subsidies are provided to manufacturers of autos and components.
- *Intellectual property rights protection:* There is inadequate protection for test data. "New chemical entities" are protected for five years from the date of registration of the originator products. Parallel importation of books and sound recordings is allowed under certain circumstances.
- *Documentation requirements:* Required documents are commercial invoice, pro-forma invoice, bill of lading/air waybill, packing list, certificate of origin, insurance certificate, photo-sanitary certificate, health certificate (meat and poultry).
- *Marketing and distribution:* Imports are generally sold through local sales agents, distributors, and licensees.

Best Export Prospects

- *Agricultural products:* consumer ready foods, fruits and vegetable juices, canned salmon
- *Industrial goods:* Agricultural machinery, aircraft parts, computer products, electrical, medical, mining and telecommunications equipment, textiles, vehicles and parts, pollution control equipment
- *Services:* Health care services

Promising Imports from Australia: Fish, wheat, meat products, cement and chemicals, processed foods, and wool

China

Country Profile

Population: 1,306,313,812
Exports: Goods (FOB): $762 billion; Services: $74.4 billion
Major Exports: Machinery and equipment, textile and clothing
Imports: Goods (FOB): $628 billion; Services: $84.0 billion
Major Imports: Machinery and equipment, textiles, plastics, iron and steel
Trade as Percentage of GDP: Exports: 40.2 percent; Imports: 39.2 percent
Major Trading Partners: United States, Hong Kong, Japan, South Korea, Taiwan, Germany
Currency and Exchange Rate: Yuan per U.S. dollar—8.19
GDP: $8.158 trillion
GDP per capita: $6,200
External Debt: $242 billion

Import Policies

- *Entry of goods:* China has reduced tariffs, importing licenses, and quotas on almost all major imports. All products sold in China must be marked and certain imported commodities must be inspected and certified to be in compliance with compulsory national standards. Food labeling standards were recently implemented.
- *Tariffs and taxes:* Tariff rates were lowered to an average rate of 12 percent on over 5,000 items. Duties on automobiles have been reduced to 25 percent. A VAT range from 13 to 17 percent is imposed on imported items. Tariff rate quotas are imposed on wheat, corn, rice, soy oil, cotton, barley, sugar, and vegetable oils, and range from 1 to 9 percent.
- *Nontariff barriers:* Existing nontariff barriers include direct subsidies on all exports, lack of transparency of tendering procedures, difficulty of determining the appropriate standard for imports, photo-sanitary and veterinary import quarantine standards that are overly strict and unevenly applied, and restrictions on the type of entities that engage in trade. Quotas are imposed on certain vehicles, motorcycles, watches, machine tools, oil, and rubber.
- *Intellectual property rights protection:* Major steps have recently been undertaken to protect and enforce IPRs in China.
- *Documentation requirements:* Required documents are commercial invoice, pro-forma invoice, bill of lading/air waybill, packing list, certificate of origin, insurance certificates, and sanitary certificates

- *Marketing and distribution:* Companies that handle export/import trade must be approved by the central government. Importation is generally made through local sales agents, international trading companies, or Chinese firms with regional or national networks. Various sales techniques are used such as advertisement, direct mass mailing to end users, trade fairs, and exhibitions.

Best Export Prospects

- *Agricultural products:* Corn, wheat, barley, fruits and vegetables, soybeans, meat and pork
- *Industrial products:* Agricultural and industrial chemicals and machinery, aircraft and parts, biotechnology, building products, computer parts and software, electronic components, machine tools, mining equipment, pharmaceuticals and veterinary medications, pollution control, security and safety as well as telecommunications equipment
- *Services:* Leasing services, oil field machinery services

Promising Imports from China: Textiles and clothing, toys, clocks, watches, bicycles, canned fruits and vegetables, consumer electronics, machine parts, paper products, metals and minerals, pharmaceuticals, and footwear

India

Country Profile

Population: 1,080,264,388
Exports: Goods (FOB): $104 billion; Services: $44.2 billion
Major Exports: Clothing, gems, jewelry, engineering goods, chemicals,
Imports: Goods (FOB): $149 billion; Services: $25 billion
Major Imports: Petroleum, machinery, gems, fertilizer
Trade as Percentage of GDP: Exports: 15.3 percent; Imports: 17.2 percent
Major Trading Partners: United States, Germany, China, United Arab Emirates, United Kingdom
Currency and Exchange Rate: Indian rupees per U.S. dollar—43.6
GDP: $3.678 trillion
GDP per capita: $3,400
External Debt: $119.7 billion

Import Policies

- *Entry of goods:* India's import policy is administered by means of a negative list. The negative list is divided into three categories: (1) banned or prohibited items (fat, oils of animal origin, tallow, etc.); (2) restricted items which require an import license including all consumer goods (livestock products, etc.); and (3) items that can be imported only by government trading companies and subject to cabinet approval regarding time and quantity. Importation of capital goods has been liberalized.
- *Tariff and taxes:* In spite of some liberalization of imports of capital goods and semi-manufactured inputs, overall tariff rates remain quite high. Average tariff rates are about 29 percent. Most agricultural products face trade barriers, which severely restrict or in the case of processed foods, prohibit their import. Agricultural goods face tariff rates between 100 and 300 percent. Consumer goods are similarly restricted. Even though India has undertaken commitments to reduce tariffs under the Uruguay Round, tariffs on imported industrialized goods are 68 percent.
- *Nontariff barriers:* Quotas, cumbersome customs procedures (misclassification of imports, incorrect valuation of goods for duty assessment, corruption), nontransparent and discriminatory government procurement practices and procedures, and export subsidies to domestic industries are some of the nontariff barriers in India. Import licenses are also required on most consumer goods, including motorcycles.
- *Intellectual property rights protection:* Protection and enforcement of trademarks, patents, and copyrights remains weak. No protection is available for service marks. As a member of WTO, India has declared its intention to implement its international obligations under TRIPs.
- *Documentation requirements:* Required documents are commercial invoice, pro-forma invoice, bill of lading/air waybill, packing list, certificate of origin, insurance certificate, health certificate, sanitary certificate, plant certificate.
- *Marketing and sales:* Foreign firms are not allowed to set up Indian branches or subsidiaries. Foreign exchange regulations require that an Indian firm be employed as an agent. Products can also be imported and marketed through a distributor.

Best Export Prospects

- *Agricultural products:* Corn, vegetable oil, cotton, nuts, cashew, wood products, intermediate food products

- *Industrial products:* Aircraft parts, book publishing, aviation equipment, computers, parts and software, industrial chemicals, iron and steel plant equipment, minerals and mineral processing equipment, oil and gas equipment, plastic materials, telecommunication equipment.
- *Services:* Telecommunications, aviation

Promising Imports from India: Carpets, cotton apparel and other textile products, crude oil, diamonds, jewelry and precious metals, fish, fruits and vegetables, handicrafts, leather, tea, tobacco, wood and wood products

Indonesia

Country Profile

Population: 241,973,879
Exports: Goods (FOB): $86.2 billion; Services: $13.0 billion
Major Exports: Textiles, garments, gas, plywood, rubber
Imports: Goods (FOB): $64.0 billion; Services: $24.0 billion
Major Imports: Manufactured goods, chemicals, foodstuffs, fuels
Trade as Percentage of GDP: Exports: 31.3 percent; Imports: 26.5 percent
Major Trading Partners: Japan, United States, Singapore, South Korea
Currency and Exchange Rate: Indonesian rupiahs per U.S. dollar—9,739.35
GDP: $899 billion
GDP per capita: $3,700
External Debt: $140.6 billion

Import Policies

- *Entry of goods:* The Indonesian government places a de facto tariff on all imported products of meat and poultry. Import licenses are required for lubricants, agricultural products, explosives, and certain dangerous chemical compounds. Importers of food and drug-related products must be registered with the Department of Health.
- *Tariff and taxes:* Average tariff is about 7.3 percent and are generally on ad valorem basis. There are exemptions for imports by approved investments or for imports used to produce export goods. A VAT (10 percent) is imposed on the sale of all domestic and imported goods. A luxury tax of 35 percent is also levied on certain products.

- *Nontariff barriers:* Many major food imports (wheat, rice, sugar, soybeans, etc.) are subject to quantitative restrictions. A substantial number of these barriers have been removed in 2005 under Indonesia's commitments to the Uruguay Round. Certain imports of printed material are prohibited. There are de facto quantitative restrictions on imports of meat and poultry.
- *Documentation requirements:* Required documents are commercial invoice, pro-forma invoice, certificate of origin, bill of lading/air waybill, insurance certificate.
- *Intellectual property rights protection:* Indonesia does not provide adequate protection for patents, trademarks, copyrights, trade secrets, industrial designs, and integrated circuit layout designs.
- *Marketing and distribution:* Distribution must be handled through a company owned by a local representative or distributor.

Best Export Prospects

- *Agricultural products:* Cotton, wheat, corn, soybeans, vegetable oils.
- *Industrial products:* Building products, computers, parts, software, construction equipment, electrical power systems, medical equipment, telecommunications, food processing and packaging, pollution control equipment, and pulp and paper industry equipment.
- *Services:* Franchising, tourism, architectural, construction and engineering services.

Promising Imports from Indonesia: Coffee, rubber, spices, minerals (coal, bauxite, gold, nickel, silver), chemicals, electronic goods, furniture, footwear, textiles, wood and wood products.

Japan

Country Profile

Population: 127,417,244
Exports: Goods (FOB): $550.5 billion; Services: $110.2 billion
Major Exports: Semiconductors, office machinery, chemicals, motor vehicles
Imports: Goods (FOB): $451.1 billion; Services: $134.3 billion
Major Imports: Fuels, foodstuffs, chemicals, textiles, office machinery
Trade as Percentage of GDP: Exports: 12.2 percent; Imports: 9.05 percent
Major Trading Partners: Southeast Asia, United States, Australia
Currency and Exchange Rate: yen per U.S. dollar—109

GDP: $3.867 trillion
GDP per capita: $30,400
External Debt: $1.545 trillion

Import Policies

- *Entry of goods:* Most goods do not require an import license. Rice, wheat, and flour are among the few remaining products subject to import quotas. For most products, there is no requirement for country of origin labeling. However, labeling is required in four product categories: textiles, electrical appliances, plastic products, and household consumer goods. In general, most labeling laws are not required at the customs clearance stage but at the point of sale.
- *Tariff and taxes:* Average tariff on industrial products is 2 percent. A consumption tax (general excise tax) is levied on all goods sold in Japan. However, high tariffs exist among a number of food products, including beef, citrus, dairy, and other processed foods, such as processed cheese; most tariffs range from 30 to 40 percent (tariffs are placed to protect the domestic markets).
- *Nontariff barriers:* Existing nontariff barriers to trade include (1) import quotas on certain farm products, fishery products, and processed foods, (2) restrictions on certain agricultural and meat products, (3) highly regulated and inefficient distribution system. The Japanese government has banned imports of fresh potatoes from the United States to prevent the introduction of potato warts and golden nematode.
- *Intellectual property rights protection:* Problematic patent practices, inadequate protection of trademarks and trade secrets, and high levels of end-use software piracy are some of the problems in the protection of IPRs in Japan.
- *Documentation requirements:* Required documents are commercial invoice, bill of lading/air waybill, packing list, certificate of origin, insurance certificate, health certificate (textiles and clothing of wool), photosanitary certificate (plants and animals), inspection certificate, and food import permit.
- *Marketing and distribution:* Most imports and exports are handled by large trading companies with strong ties to Japanese manufacturers. Local agents can be appointed to handle marketing and sales.

Best Export Prospects

- *Agricultural products:* Fresh vegetables, beef, pork, cereals
- *Industrial products:* Air conditioning and refrigeration equipment, building materials, apparel, auto parts and accessories, computer

parts and software, furniture, pet food and supplies, medical equipment, electronic components, telecommunications and pollution control equipment
- *Services:* Travel and tourism, architectural, construction, and engineering services

Promising imports from Japan: Electronic products, auto and auto parts, computer hardware, cameras, office machines, machine tools and optical goods, photographic equipment, watches and clocks, craft, and antiques

A.4. TRADING OPPORTUNITIES IN EASTERN EUROPE

The Czech Republic

Country Profile

> *Population:* 10,241,138
> *Exports:* Goods (FOB): $78.37 billion; Services: $10.8 billion
> *Major Exports:* Manufactured goods, machinery and equipment, chemicals
> *Imports:* Goods (FOB): $76.59 billion; Services: $10.2 billion
> *Major Imports:* Machinery transport equipment, manufactured goods, chemicals
> *Trade as Percentage of GDP:* Exports: 72 percent; Imports: 69 percent
> *Major Trading Partners:* Germany, Slovakia, Austria
> *Currency and Exchange Rate:* Koruny per U.S. dollar—23.72
> *GDP:* $184.9 billion
> *GDP per capita:* $18,100
> *External Debt:* $43.2 billion

Import Policies

- *Entry of goods:* Most goods and services are not subject to import licensing requirements. All consumer products must include labeling information in the Czech language. The Czech Republic has become a member of the European Union and applies its trade policy.
- *Tariff structure:* Average tariff ranges between 4.3 and 5 percent. However, for certain agricultural imports, rates are high (average rate of 13.4 percent).
- *Nontariff barriers:* Import licenses are required on sugar, coal, explosives, and firearms. The Czech Republic is an associate member of the European Union and as such is in the process of harmonizing its

standards based on European and international norms. Foreign investments, specifically in services, remain restricted.

- *Protection of intellectual property rights:* IPRs are generally adequately protected in the Czech Republic.
- *Documentation requirements:* Required documents are commercial invoice, pro forma invoice, bill of lading, air waybill, packing list, certificate of origin, insurance certificate, health certificate, photo-sanitary certificate.
- *Marketing and Distribution channels:* Foreign products are generally sold through agents and distributors. Selling techniques include advertisement through various media, door-to-door sales, and trade fairs and shows.

Best Export Prospects

- *Agricultural products:* Soybean meals, rice, raw cotton, tobacco and tobacco products
- *Industrial products:* Aircraft parts, building materials, electrical power systems, food processing and packaging equipment, medical, telecommunications, and pollution control equipment
- *Services:* Franchising, information services

Promising Imports from the Czech Republic: Cement, chemicals, fuel, machinery and transport equipment, manufactured goods, metals, minerals, timber.

Hungary

Country Profile

Population: 10,006,835
Exports: Goods (FOB): $61.75 billion; Services: $12.3 billion
Major Exports: Machinery and equipment, agricultural and food products and other manufactured goods
Imports: Goods (FOB): $64.83 billion (2005 est.); Services: $11.8 billion
Major Imports: Fuels and electricity, food and agriculture, machinery and equipment, raw materials
Trade as Percentage of GDP: Exports: 66 percent; Imports: 69 percent
Major Trading Partners: Germany, Austria, France, Russia, Italy
Currency and Exchange Rate: Forints per U.S. dollar—196.83
GDP: $159 billion
GDP per capita: $15,900
External Debt: $76.23 billion

Import Policies

- *Entry of goods:* Over 96 percent of products can be imported without an import license. There has been a significant decrease on tariffs, especially imported goods.
- *Tariff and taxes:* Average import duties have been reduced to 7 percent over the past four years. There are special luxury tariffs on imports of automobiles and certain other products. Tariff-rate quotas are required on agricultural products.
- *Nontariff barriers:* Agricultural export subsidies regulations on imports of breeding animals, and for non-WTO consumer goods such as footwear, apparel, dry goods, and fish.
- *Intellectual property rights protection:* There is a lack of adequate protection for IPRs, but enforcement is weak. Piracy has become a common problem; the performance rate of piracy is 50 percent among the public.
- *Documentation requirements:* Required documents are commercial invoice, bill of lading, air waybill, packing list, certificate of origin, insurance certificate, photo-sanitary certificate (plant and plant products), veterinary certificate, registration and approval (pharmaceuticals).
- *Marketing and distribution:* Imports are generally sold through branches, sales agents, or distributors. Exhibitions, printed advertising, and trade fairs are popular selling techniques in Hungary.

Best Export Prospects

- *Agricultural products:* Poultry breeding stock, bovine semen, soybean meal, planting seed
- *Industrial Products:* Computers and computer products, automotive parts and equipment, cosmetics, films, videos and other recreation, pharmaceuticals, oil and gas field machinery, telecommunication products, processed foods, and raw materials
- *Services:* Travel and tourism, franchising

Promising Imports from Hungary: Ceramics and glassware, clothing and footwear, household consumer products, chemicals and pharmaceuticals, automotive parts and vehicles, medical instruments

Poland

Country Profile

Population: 38,635,144
Exports: Goods (FOB): $96.4 billion; Services: $16.3 billion
Major Exports: Manufactured goods, chemicals, machinery and equipments, food and live animals
Imports: Goods (FOB): $99.2 billion; Services: 14.3 billion
Major Imports: Manufactured goods, chemicals, machinery and equipment, and mineral fuels
Trade as Percentage of GDP: Exports: 22.6 percent; Imports: 27.3 percent
Major Trading Partners: Germany, Russia, Italy
Currency and Exchange Rate: Zlotych per U.S. dollar—3.19
GDP: $489.3 billion
GDP per capita: $12,700
External Debt: $123.4 billion

Import Policies

- *Entry of goods:* Most goods entering Poland do not require a license. However, a license is necessary for police and military products, radioactive elements, weapons, alcoholic beverages, and certain foods. Labeling and packaging requirements vary depending on the product. Consumer goods require a product description in Polish on or inside the package. Packaging should clearly indicate the country of manufacture.
- *Tariff and taxes:* Poland, a member of the European Union, applies the common external tariff (CXT) on most imported goods toward all non–EU members. For some luxury and strategic products (alcohol, cosmetics, cigarettes, video cameras, passenger cars, gasoline, and oil) excise tax is also applied.
- *Nontariff barriers:* Export subsidies to state-owned enterprises, product certification and approval procedures that are not in line with international standards, and domestic content requirements for goods purchased by the government are some of the nontariff barriers in Poland. Import quotas apply to some agricultural products. Certificates are required for red meat and poultry products.
- *Intellectual property rights protection:* Although adequate laws exist for the protection of IPRs, enforcement remains weak and has allowed for a certain degree of trademark and copyright infringement. Indus-

try associations estimate that 1996 levels of piracy in Poland were 43 percent in sound recordings and 54 percent in business software.
- *Documentation requirements:* Required documents are commercial invoice, proforma invoice, bill of lading, air waybill, packing list, insurance certificate, sanitary certificate (animal and animal products), photo-sanitary certificate (plants), safety certificate (for certain products).
- *Marketing and distribution:* There are state agencies that accept foreign representation. Imports are also handled through branch offices or distributors. Selling techniques include advertising through newspapers, direct mail publicity, trade fairs and shows.

Best Export Prospects

- *Agricultural products:* Corn, wheat, poultry, meat, beef cattle, forest products
- *Industrial products:* Computers and parts, building products, medical equipment, telecommunications, sporting goods, and recreational equipment
- *Services:* Computer services

Promising Imports from Poland: Agricultural tractors, hams, lamps, berry juices

The Russian Republic

Country Profile

Population: 143,420,309
Exports: Goods (FOB): $245 billion; Services: $24.6 billion
Major Exports: Petroleum, petroleum products, natural gas, wood and wood products, coal, metals, chemicals
Imports: Goods (FOB): $125 billion; Services: $39.4 billion
Trade as Percentage of GDP: Exports: 25.6 percent; Imports: 18.8 percent
Major Imports: Machinery and equipment, consumer goods, medicines, meat, grain, sugar, semi-finished metal products
Major Trading Partners: Germany, Netherlands, Ukraine
Currency and Exchange Rate: Russian rubles per U.S. dollar—28.17
GDP: $1.535 trillion
GDP per capita: $10,700
External Debt: $230.3 billion

Import Policies

- *Entry of goods:* Import licenses are required for importation of various goods including alcohol, vodka, weapons, metals, etc. Products are to be labeled in Russian language. New labeling regulations for food and other consumer imports were recently enacted.
- *Tariffs and taxes:* Average tariffs range from 5 to 30 percent. Tariffs are higher on alcoholic drinks and certain other products. Excise tax applies to a number of luxury goods and varies from 20 to 570 percent. The VAT rate is 18 percent with the exception of food and children's items (10 percent).
- *Nontariff barriers:* Nontariff barriers include export subsidies for manufactured goods, lack of uniform procedures for purchases by government agencies which favors Russian suppliers, costly procedures, and arbitrary certification requirements. Quotas are placed on poultry and tariff rates on pork and beef products. Import licenses are required on goods including televisions, sugar, sporting weapons, self-defense articles, explosives, radio active materials, military equipment, alloys, and stones.
- *Documentation requirements:* Required documents are commercial invoice, bill of lading, air waybill, packing list, certificate of origin, veterinary certificate, safety certificate.
- *Intellectual property protection:* Even though laws exist to protect IPRs, enforcement has been limited. There is extensive piracy of video cassettes, films, music, recordings, books, and computer software.
- *Marketing and distribution:* Import products are marketed through distributors, sales agents, or branch offices. Various media such as television, radio, print, and billboards are used for advertising consumer goods. Exporters to Russia use exhibitions to introduce and market their product.

Best Export Prospects

- *Agricultural and food products:* Apples, poultry, red meats, wine and beer
- *Industrial products:* Machinery and equipment, chemicals, cosmetics, pharmaceuticals, furniture, paper products

Promising Imports from Russia: Petroleum and petroleum products, natural gas, metals, chemicals, natural resources, military products

A.5. TRADING OPPORTUNITIES
IN THE EUROPEAN UNION[3] (E.U.)

Denmark

Country Profile

Population: 5,432,335
Total Export: Goods (FOB): $84.95 billion; Services $42.4 billion
Major Export: Machinery and instruments, meat and meat products, fuels, dairy products
Imports: Goods (FOB): $74.69 billion; Services $37.86 billion
Major Imports: Machinery and equipment, petroleum, chemicals, grain and foodstuffs
Trade as Percentage of GDP: Exports: 49 percent; Imports: 44 percent.
Major Trading Partners: Germany, Netherlands, United Kingdom, Sweden, Japan
Currency and Exchange Rate: Danish kroner per U.S. dollar—5.93
GDP: $182.1 billion
GDP per capita: $33,500
External Debt: $352.9 billion

Import Policies

- *Entry of goods:* Denmark relies on several of the European Union's policies and regulations on imported goods. Most beef products bred on hormones are prohibited, especially from non–EU members. Imports on farm products must follow regulations in accordance with Common Agricultural Policy (CAP).
- *Tariff structure:* Non–EU imports of manufactured goods are subject to rates between 4.2 and 17.3 percent ad valorem, while raw materials enter with higher tariff rates. Most agricultural imports from non–EU countries are covered by the CAP, that is, subject to variable levies.
- *Nontariff barriers (NTBs):* EU imports restrictions apply on imports, including the prohibition of beef cattle bred on hormones. Textiles and clothing enter with a quota system.
- *Intellectual property rights protection:* There is adequate protection for IPRs in Denmark.
- *Documentation requirements:* Required documents are commercial invoice, pro-forma invoice, bill of lading/air waybill, packing list, certificate of origin, sanitary certificate for certain food products.

- *Marketing and distribution channels:* Methods of distribution vary from product to product. Capital goods, commodities, and industrial raw materials are handled by non-stock sales agents. High tech and specialized products are handled by stocking distributors and consumer goods are handled by importing agents and distributors.

Best Export Prospects

- *Agricultural products:* Nuts, cereals, turkey meat, sweet corn, wines, dog and cat food, and forest products
- *Industrial products:* Computers and peripherals, computer software, electrical power systems, medical equipment, oil and gas, pollution control and telecommunication equipment, automotive and aircraft parts, apparel, building products, sporting goods equipment
- *Services:* Architectural, construction and engineering services, travel and tourism services

Promising Imports from Denmark: Meat and dairy products, chemicals, fish, industrial machinery and equipment

France

Country Profile

Population: 60,656,178
Exports: Goods (FOB): $443.4 billion; Services: $116.0 billion
Major Exports: Machinery and transport equipment, chemicals, foodstuffs, agricultural products, iron and steel products
Imports: Goods (FOB): $473.3 billion; Services: $106.0 billion
Trade as Percentage of GDP: Exports: 26 percent; Imports: 27 percent
Major Imports: Crude petroleum, machinery and equipment, vehicles, aircraft, chemicals, iron and steel products
Major Trading Partners: European Union, United States
Currency Exchange Rate: Euros per U.S. dollar—0.79697
GDP: $1.816 trillion
GDP per capita: $29,900
External Debt: $2.826 trillion

Import Policies

- *Entry of goods:* No import licenses are required except for certain agricultural products and commodities subject to state trading. Goods that originate from countries not eligible for such liberalized treatment require individual licenses, normally valid for six months. Exporters to France must comply with EU and French labeling laws. Labels must be written in French and generally state the product, brand name/trademark, composition and usage instructions, name of manufacturer, and price. Mark of origin is also required on all imports.

- *Tariff structure:* France relies on several of the European Union's policies and regulations on imported goods. Most beef products bred on hormones are prohibited, especially from non–EU members. Imports on farm products must follow regulations in accordance with Common Agricultural Policy (CAP).
- *Nontariff barriers (NTBs):* Non–EU imports of manufactured goods are subject to rates between 4.2 and 17.3 percent ad valorem, while raw materials enter with higher tariff rates. Most agricultural imports from non–EU countries are covered by the CAP, that is, subject to variable levies.
- *Intellectual property rights protection:* Intellectual property protection is generally adequate.
- *Documentation requirements:* Required documents are commercial invoice, pro-forma invoice, bill of lading/air waybill, packing list, certificate of origin. For certain imports, sanitary and health certificate, photo-sanitary certificate (certain plants), or certificate of compliance (machinery) are required.
- *Marketing and distribution channels:* Sales agents, branches, and subsidiaries are often used to import into France. Distributors also import foreign goods for resale.

Best Export Prospects

- *Agricultural products:* Fish and seafood, wood, beverages, fresh and dried fruits, fruits and vegetables
- *Industrial products:* Agriculture and food products, agricultural machinery, autos and light trucks, automotive parts and service equipment, avionics and ground support equipment, computers, peripherals and software, electrical power systems, electronic components, films and videos, medical and scientific instruments, pollution control equipment, security and safety equipment, telecommunications equipment
- *Services:* Travel and tourism, insurance, employment services

Promising Imports from France: Machinery and equipment, agricultural products, chemicals, and foodstuff

Germany

Country Profile

Population: 82,431,390
Exports: Goods (FOB): $973 billion; Services: $155 billion
Major Exports: Machinery, vehicles, chemicals
Imports: Goods (FOB): $783 billion; Services: $203.0 billion
Major Imports: Machinery, vehicles, chemicals, foodstuffs
Trade as Percentage of GDP: Exports: 40 percent; Imports: 35 percent
Major Trading Partners: France, Netherlands, United States, United Kingdom
Currency and Exchange Rate: Euros per U.S. dollar—0.79697
GDP: 2.446 trillion
GDP per capita: $29,700
External Debt: $3.626 trillion

Import Policies

- *Entry of goods:* Germany relies on several of the European Union's policies and regulations on imported goods. Most beef products bred on hormones are prohibited, especially from non–EU members. Imports on farm products must follow regulations in accordance with Common Agricultural Policy (CAP).
- *Tariff structure:* Non–EU imports of manufactured goods are subject to rates between 4.2 and 17.3 percent ad valorem, while raw materials enter with higher tariff rates. Most agricultural imports from non-EU countries are covered by the CAP, that is, subject to variable levies.
- *Nontariff barriers:* EU imports restrictions apply on imports, including the prohibition of beef cattle bred on hormones. Textiles and clothing enter with a quota system.
- *Intellectual property rights protection:* IPRs are generally well protected in Germany. However, the level of software piracy continues to be a source of concern.
- *Documentation requirements:* Required documents are commercial invoice, bill of lading/air waybill, packing list, certificate of origin, sanitary certificate.
- *Marketing and distribution channels:* Trade fairs are important tools for introducing new products and/or companies to the German market. Most imports to Germany move through import regional houses, wholesalers, and distributors. Direct sales are also common for ma-

chinery and equipment. Multinationals use branch offices (subsidiaries) to sell their products.

Best Export Prospects

- *Agricultural products:* Catfish, citrus, fats and oils, lumber products, pet food and supplies, beef, wine/beer
- *Industrial products:* Auto-parts, computers, peripherals and software, electronic components, drugs and chemicals, medical equipment, telecommunications, and scientific instruments
- *Services:* Computer services, franchising, information services

Promising Imports from Germany: Machine, machine tools, chemicals, iron and steel products

Ireland

Country Profile

Population: 4,015,676
Exports: Goods (FOB): $102 billion; Services: $57.0 billion
Major Exports: Chemicals, computers, industrial machinery
Imports: Goods (FOB): $65.47 billion; Services: $69.6 billion
Major Imports: Data processing equipment, chemicals, petroleum and petroleum products
Trade as Percentage of GDP: Exports: 96 percent; Imports: 79 percent
Major Trading Partners: United Kingdom, Germany, France, United States
Currency and Exchange Rate: Euros per U.S. dollar—0.79697
GDP: $136.9 billion
GDP per capita: $34,100
External Debt: $1.049 trillion

Import Policies

- *Entry of goods:* Ireland relies on several of the European Union's policies and regulations on imported goods. Most beef products bred on hormones are prohibited, especially from non–EU members. Imports on farm products must follow regulations in accordance with Common Agricultural Policy (CAP). All importers must fill in an intrastate declaration form before entering goods into Ireland (used to distinguish the country of origin of products based on EU states or non–EU states). Ireland is the most favored nation for DFI (ranks first in the world); the country encourages investment from overseas.

- *Tariff structure:* Duty rates on non–EU exports of manufactured goods ranges from 4.2 to 17.3 percent ad valorem (CIF value) and raw materials enter with higher tariffs.
- *Nontariff barriers:* EU imports restrictions apply on imports, including the prohibition of beef cattle bred on hormones. Textiles and clothing enter with a quota system.
- *Intellectual property rights protection:* Generally, adequate protection exists for protection of IPRs.
- *Documentation requirements:* Required documents are commercial invoice, bills of lading/air waybill, packing list, certificate of origin, photo-sanitary certification.
- *Marketing and distribution channels:* Agents, distributors, and representatives are used to import products into Ireland. Retail channels also import a variety of food products.

Best Export Prospects

- *Agricultural products:* Pears, wine, corn gluten feed
- *Industrial products:* Air conditioning and refrigeration equipment, building products, computers, peripherals and software, construction equipment, drug and pharmaceutical, electrical power systems, electronic components, industrial chemicals, medical and telecommunications equipment
- *Services:* Travels and tourism, computer services

Promising Imports from Ireland: Data processing equipment, chemicals, animal and animal products

Italy

Country Profile

Population: 58,103,033
Exports: Goods (FOB): $371.9 billion; Services: $90.0 billion
Major Exports: Engineering products, textiles and clothing, production machinery, motor vehicles
Imports: Goods (FOB): $369.2 billion; Services: $90.6 billion
Major Imports: Engineering products, chemicals, transport equipment, motor vehicles
Trade as Percentage of GDP: Exports: 26 percent; Imports: 27 percent
Major Trading Partners: EU members, United States
Currency and Exchange Rate: Euros per U.S. dollar—0.79697

GDP: $1.645 trillion
GDP per capita: $28,300
External Debt: $1.682 trillion

Import Policies

- *Entry of goods:* Italy relies on several of the European Union's policies and regulations on imported goods. Most beef products bred on hormones are prohibited, especially from non–EU members. Imports on farm products must follow regulations in accordance with Common Agricultural Policy (CAP).
- *Tariff structure:* Italy applies the EU tariffs. Tariffs on imports of non–EU manufactured goods generally range from 4.2 to 17.3 percent. Most raw materials enter with higher tariffs.
- *Nontariff barriers:* EU imports restrictions apply on imports, including the prohibition of beef cattle bred on hormones. Textiles and clothing enter with a quota system.
- *Intellectual property rights protection:* There are problems with respect to piracy of computer software, film, video, and musical recording and adequate penalties to deter such activity do not exist.
- *Documentation requirements:* Required documents are commercial invoice, pro-forma invoice, bill of lading/air waybill, packing list, certificate of origin, health certificate (cattle, horses and other animals, fish and fish products) and photo-sanitary certificate (plants).
- *Marketing and distribution channels:* Distributors transport consumer goods, the largest distributor being Coop Italia. Local agents who know the market generally handle promotion.

Best Export Prospects

- *Agricultural products:* Logs and wood products, oilseeds, cattle and swine, nuts, grain and feed
- *Industrial products:* Aircraft and parts, computers, parts and software, electric power systems, chemicals, pollution control and telecommunication equipment
- *Services:* Computer services, franchising, insurance

Promising Imports from Italy: Textiles and apparel, leather, glassware, food and agricultural products, chemical products, olive oil, precious metals, ceramic goods

The Netherlands

Country Profile

Population: 16,407,491
Exports: Goods (FOB): $365.1 billion; Services: $80.1 billion
Major Exports: Machinery and equipment, chemicals, fuels, food, and tobacco
Imports: Goods (FOB): $326.6 billion; Services: $73.3 billion
Major Imports: Machinery and transport equipment, chemicals, food-stuffs, fuels, clothing
Trade as Percentage of GDP: Exports: 71 percent; Imports: 63 percent
Major Trading Partners: Germany, Belgium, Luxembourg, United Kingdom, United States
Currency and Exchange Rate: Euros per U.S. dollar—0.79697
GDP: $500 billion
GDP per capita: $30,500
External Debt: $1.645 trillion

Import Policies

- *Entry of goods:* The Netherlands relies on several of the EU's policies and regulations on imported goods. Most beef products bred on hormones are prohibited, especially from non–EU members. Imports on farm products must follow regulations in accordance with Common Agricultural Policy (CAP).
- *Tariff structure:* Import tariffs on manufactured goods from non–EU countries range from 4.2 to 17.3 percent of CIF value. Most raw materials enter with higher tariffs.
- *Nontariff barriers:* EU imports restrictions apply on imports, including the prohibition of beef cattle bred on hormones. Textiles and clothing enter with a quota system.
- *Intellectual property rights protection:* IPR's protection is generally adequate.
- *Documentation requirements:* Required documents are commercial invoice, pro forma invoice, bill of lading/air waybill, packing list, certificate of origin, health certificate, and photo-sanitary certificate.
- *Marketing and distribution channels:* Products can be exported through a variety of experienced importers, agents, and distributors. Certain consumer goods are imported directly by wholesalers and retailers.

Best Export Prospects

- *Agricultural products:* Grapefruits, tobacco, wines, honey, pecans
- *Industrial products:* Apparel, auto parts, building products, computers, parts and software, electronic components, laboratory and scientific instruments, medical, pollution control, security as well as telecommunications equipment
- *Services:* Telecommunications services, franchising

Promising Imports from The Netherlands: Agricultural products, beer, chemicals, petroleum products, office machines

The United Kingdom

Country Profile

Population: 60,441,457
Exports: Goods (FOB): $384 billion; Services: $203.0 billion
Major Exports: Fuel and chemicals, manufactured goods, food products and beverages, tobacco
Imports: Goods (FOB): $509 billion; Services: $160.0 billion
Major Imports: Machinery and equipment, fuel, foods, manufactured goods
Trade as Percentage of GDP: Exports: 26 percent; Imports: 30 percent
Major Trading Partners: European Union, China, United States
Currency and Exchange Rate: British pounds per U.S. dollar—0.54
GDP: $1.867 trillion
GDP per capita: $30,900
External Debt: $7.107 trillion

Import Policies

- *Entry of goods:* The United Kingdom relies on several of the EU's policies and regulations on imported goods. Most beef products bred on hormones are prohibited, especially from non–EU members. Imports on farm products must follow regulations in accordance with Common Agricultural Policy (CAP). All importers must fill in an intrastate declaration form before entering goods into the United Kingdom (used to distinguish the country of origin of products based on EU states or non–EU states).

- *Tariff structure:* Import tariffs on manufactured goods from non–EU countries range from 4.2 to 17.3 percent of CIF value. Most raw materials enter with higher tariffs.
- *Intellectual property rights protection:* Protection of IPRs is generally adequate.
- *Documentation requirements:* Commercial invoice, bill of lading/air waybill, packing list, certificate of origin, sanitary certificate.
- *Marketing and distribution:* The distribution of foods is carried out by specialized branches, departmental stores, and cooperatives. Large retail outlets purchase products directly from the foreign manufacturer.

Best Export Prospects

- *Agricultural products:* Forest products, seafood, beer, wine, nuts, pet food
- *Industrial products:* Aircraft and parts, apparel, building products, computers, parts and software, drugs and pharmaceuticals, medical equipment, defense equipment
- *Services:* Tourism, franchising

Promising Imports from the United Kingdom: Textile and apparel, fruits and vegetables, medical equipment, cereals, machinery

NOTES

1. Import policies for South Africa and E.U. countries: The information has been obtained by http://www.fita.org/countries/
2. Information on import policies of Zimbabwe has been obtained from http://www.buyusainfo.net/docs/x_3713085.pdf; http://www.heritage.org/research/features/index
3. Data are for 2005 or latest available year. Data for export/imports is in current U.S. dollars.

BIBLIOGRAPHY

Central Intelligence Agency (2006). *The World Factbook.* Retrieved from http://www.cia.gov/cia/publications/factbook/index.html
The Federation of International Trade Associations (2006). *Country Profiles and Resources.* Retrieved from http://www.fita.org/countries/

Office of the United States Trade Representative (2004). *Foreign Trade Barriers.* Retrieved from http://www.ustr.gov/Document_Library/Reports_Publications/ 2004/2004_National_Trade_Estimate/2004_NTE_Report/Section_Index.html

The Heritage Foundation/Wall Street Journal (2006). *Index of Economic Freedom.* Retrieved from http://www.heritage.org/research/features/index/

U.S. Department of State (2004). *Doing Business in Zimbabwe: A Country Commercial Guide for U.S. Companies.* Retrieved from http://www.buyusainfo.net/ docs/x_3713085.pdf

Wright, J.W. (2006). *The New York Times Almanac: The Almanac of Record.* New York: The New York Times Company.

Appendix B

Importing into the United States

IMPORTANT QUESTIONS

Section 1: Entry of Goods

1. Do I need a license to import goods into the United States?
2. What products are prohibited from importation?
3. What factor should be considered before importation?
4. What are the specific requirements of a commercial invoice when clearing goods from customs?
5. What do you consider before importing goods through mail?
6. What is consumption entry?
7. What is a formal entry and how do I file it?
8. What is general order merchandise?
9. Is Puerto Rico considered part of the customs territory of the United States?
10. Do the following items require an entry during importation?
    i. Articles exported from space within the purview of the Tariff Act of 1930
    ii. Domestic animals driven across a neighboring country by owner for temporary pasturage and brought back within thirty days
    iii. Exported articles that are undeliverable (within forty-five days) and that are within the custody of the carrier or foreign customs service
    iv. Personal goods purchased while overseas
11. What are some of the eligibility requirements for participation in the ABI program?
12. What is required of importers who are habitually late in paying bills to U.S. Customs?
13. Are there taxes or fees required to import goods into the United States other than customs duties?

Export-Import Theory, Practices, and Procedures, Second Edition

14. Can a foreign company export to the United States without an importer of record in the United States?
15. If goods arrive to the port of Miami, can they be cleared at the port of Dallas (if the importer requires it)?

Section 2: Customs Bonds

1. When is a customs bond required?
2. How do you obtain a customs bond?
3. What are the two types of bonds?
4. What are some of the ways in which a bond to ensure the exportation of merchandise may be cancelled?
5. Can a bond rider be used to terminate the bond?
6. What charges are supposed to be paid first on merchandise remaining in a bonded warehouse beyond the specified time?
7. What type of bond is used to indemnify the United States for detention of copyrighted material?

Section 3: Quotas, Marking Requirements, and Trade Agreements

1. What is the difference between absolute and tariff quota?
2. Do most goods from NAFTA countries enter duty free into the United States?
3. What countries are not eligible to normal trade relations (NTR) or most-favored-nation (MFN) duty rates?
4. What is a nonqualifying operation under NAFTA?
5. What happens to imports that are not properly marked?
6. A shipment of beef valued at $5,000.00 is subject to a tariff quota. At the time of importation, a high tariff rate is in effect but a lower rate is soon expected. How can an importer take advantage of the lower rate?
7. When imported merchandise exceeds a tariff quota, the importer may not commingle the merchandise and classification with nonquota class goods. True or false?
8. What is the rate of duty on imports from GSP eligible countries?
9. A claim for preferential treatment under NAFTA may be filed within one year from the date of importation of the goods. True or false?
10. What is origin criteria for textiles and apparel products under NAFTA?

Section 4: Value

1. What is value and what value is used for customs purposes?
2. What are the secondary bases of value if the transaction value cannot be used?

3. In establishing transaction value, what is to be included in the price?
4. What is an assist?
5. What should be excluded from transaction value?
6. A U.S. produce wholesaler imports avocados from Mexico on consignment. A few days after importation, the wholesaler sells the avocados (for $0.25 per avocado) to retailers and receives a 2 percent commission from Mexican sellers. Customs has sufficient information to appraise the merchandise. What is the basis of appraisement for the merchandise?
7. The manufacturer received from the importer, free of charge, design work produced in the United States and 5,000 U.S. originating modules to be incorporated into the production of 5,000 computer monitors. The costs are as follows: cost of acquiring design work: $10,000; cost of transportation to place of production: $100.00; cost of acquiring modules: $75 each; cost of transportation of modules: $5,250.00. What is the transaction value of the shipment of the monitors with a per-unit price of $50 FOB?
8. What is "identical merchandise"?

Section 5: Broker Compliance and Other Areas

1. Is a power of attorney required when a broker is acting as the importer of record?
2. When is a multiple country declaration required?
3. What rate of currency exchange should be used when foreign currency is converted?
4. i. What are the penalties for conducting customs business without a license?
   ii. What are the penalties against any broker who continuously makes the same errors on a particular type of entry, and
   iii. What are the penalties against any broker who does not have a working knowledge of customs operation to render valuable service?
5. What information should be on a bill of lading?
6. Is the commercial invoice required at the time of shipment?
7. How does the duty drawback claim work?
8. Are there laws governing labeling requirements for certain products?
9. Does an importer who sells merchandise to another company that exports it qualify for a duty drawback?
10. Under the following conditions, does the firm indicated qualify for a rejected merchandise drawback claim?

    i. A Miami firm imports 200 pounds of shrimp for its national network of seafood restaurants. When it opened the boxes, it found that it was 200 pounds of pork.

    ii. An importer of oranges finds thirty crates of unordered vegetables.

    iii. A company in New York imports twenty cases of Argentine wine. There was a strike at the port and the wine was not unloaded for a few days. When the importer picked up the wines, they were frozen.

ANSWERS

Section 1: Entry of Goods

1. *Do I need a license to import goods into the United States?* No. However, for certain items such as food products, plant, animal and dairy products, prescription medications, etc., you may require a license or permit from various government agencies.
2. *What products are prohibited from importation?* Certain narcotics, drug paraphernalia, counterfeit articles, obscene and immoral articles, as well as merchandise produced by convicts or through forced labor.
3. *What factor should be considered before importation?* It is important to verify whether an item is subject to quotas and other restrictions or permits, reduced rates of duty, marking of country of origin as well as exclusive rights due to ownership of intellectual property rights by certain companies.
4. *What are the specific requirements of a commercial invoice when clearing goods from customs?* Description of the item, quantity, value (in foreign currency and U.S. dollars), country of origin, place of purchase, name and address of seller, and consignee.
5. *What do you consider before importing goods through mail?* Whether the item be legally sent through the U.S. Postal Service, whether the value is less than $2,000.00 (since items valued at over $2,000.00 require a formal entry), whether the item is subject to restrictions.
6. *What is consumption entry?* This is the most common type of entry and imported goods are intended for use in the United States or directly go into the commerce of the United States without any time or use restrictions. It may be formal or informal.
7. *What is a formal entry and how do I file it?* A formal entry is used for merchandise valued at over $2,000 and is supported by a surety bond to ensure payment of duties and compliance with customs regulations. The major difference between formal and informal entries is the

bond requirement and liquidation process. As regards filing a formal entry, (1) identify the port of entry, relevant product classification, and tariff rate; (2) find out if the products are subject to any special requirements (or if there are any special forms that apply) such as quota, visa, FDA, NAFTA, or GSP; (3) ask the limit of liability for a customs bond. No more than a week before the expected arrival of the merchandise at the port or no later than ten days after arrival, fill out the appropriate forms (Form 5106,7501 etc.), purchase a customs bond and submit to customs along with invoice, packing list, shipping documents, and a cheque. After processing, the merchandise may be subject for release or examination before release. The entry will be liquidated one year after release of merchandise. Until then, the bond or cash will be held as surety.

8. *What is general order merchandise?* Merchandise shall be considered general order merchandise when it is taken into the custody of the port director and deposited in the public stores or a general order warehouse at the risk and expense of the consignee for any of the following reasons: entry is not made within the time provided by customs regulations, entry is incomplete due to failure to pay the estimated duties, entry cannot be made for want of proper documents or other reasons, merchandise is not correctly invoiced. The general order expires six months from the date of importation. Such merchandise may be exported without examination or appraisement if the merchandise is delivered to the exporting carrier within six months from the date of importation. This merchandise may be entered within six months from date of importation for immediate transportation to any port of entry designated by the consignee. After six months from the date of importation, entry for immediate transportation is allowed.

9. *Is Puerto Rico considered part of the customs territory of the United States?* Yes

10. *Do the following items require an entry during importation?*
    i. *Articles exported from space within the purview of the Tariff Act of 1930.* No
    ii. *Domestic animals driven across a neighboring country by owner for temporary pasturage and brought back after thirty days.* Yes
    iii. *Exported articles that are undeliverable (within forty-five days) and that are within the custody of the carrier or foreign customs service.* No
    iv. *Personal goods purchased while overseas.* Yes. Entries must be filed on a timely basis to avoid paying fees to the carrier and the bonded warehouse. Personal importations are generally cleared informally, that is, no bond is required. No duty is assessed if the goods

are valued at less than $200. If the goods are valued at more than $200, a duty as well as a processing fee will be assessed. Imports that require a permit from other government agencies are subject to a formal entry and the posting of a customs bond.

11. *What are some of the eligibility requirements for participation in the ABI program?* The basic eligibility requirements for participation are: the ability to demonstrate a reputable background and the basic skills for performing entry services; the ability to make a commitment for sending not less than 90 percent of entry/entry summary volume electronically; the ability to satisfactorily complete all of the qualification testing phases as outlined in the program; the ability to maintain operational standards for data quantity and quality; the ability to maintain timely updates.

12. *What is required of importers who are habitually late in paying bills to U.S. Customs?* The port director notifies the importer to file the entry summary with duties attached before release of merchandise.

13. *Are there taxes or fees required to import goods into the United States other than customs duties?* Yes. Here are some of them:
    i. Federal excise tax: importation of alcoholic beverages and tobacco.
    ii. Merchandise processing fee (MPF): Ad valorem fee of 0.21 percent for formal entries (minimum of $25.00 and maximum of $485.00). It is based on value of merchandise being imported, not including duty, freight, and insurance. For informal entries, it ranges from $5.00 to $9.00 per shipment.
    iii. Harbor maintenance fee (HMF): This is for merchandise transported by ship and is 0.125 percent of the value of the cargo. Goods arriving by ship are subject to both MPF and HMF.

14. *Can a foreign company export to the United States without an importer of record in the United States?* Yes. A resident agent, such as a broker in the state where the port of entry is located can enter goods on behalf of the corporation.

15. *If goods arrive to the port of Miami, can they be cleared at the port of Dallas (if the importer requires it)?* In general, entry must be filed at the first port of arrival. To clear goods in Dallas, however, an immediate transportation entry (IT) must be filed by a broker, carrier, or importer (i.e., bonded with customs). In Dallas, a consumption or warehouse entry must be filed for clearance from customs.

Section 2: Customs Bonds

1. *When is a customs bond required?* A customs bond is required for imported merchandise valued at over $2,000.00; goods subject to quota

or visa restrictions, or other government requirements; transportation of cargo or passengers to the United States or domestic transportation of imported cargo from one state to another; bonded warehouse facilities for imported or exported goods.

2. *How do you obtain a customs bond?* Customs bonds are obtained through a surety licensed by the Treasury department. The list of licensed sureties is available online.

3. *What are the two major types of customs bonds?* Continuous entry bonds applications are made for multiple transactions while single entry bonds are used to secure the entry of a single customs transaction. Continuous bonds are 10 percent of duties paid for the previous year. Single entry bonds (SEB) are generally in an amount not less than the total entered value plus any taxes and duties. The minimum amount for SEBs is $100.00.

4. *What are some of the ways in which a bond to ensure the exportation of merchandise may be cancelled?* Listing of the merchandise on the outward manifest, inspector's certificate of lading, record of clearance of the vessel, production of a foreign landing certificate (when required by the port director).

5. *Can a bond rider be used to terminate the bond?* No. To be valid, a bond rider must be signed, sealed, witnessed, executed, and filed at the port of approval.

6. *What charges are supposed to be paid first on merchandise remaining in a bonded warehouse beyond the specified time?* Internal revenue taxes.

7. *What type of bond is used to indemnify the United States for detention of copyrighted material?* A single entry bond.

Section 3: Quotas, Marking Requirements, and Trade Agreements

1. *What is the difference between absolute and tariff quota?* When absolute quotas are filled, further entries are prohibited during the remainder of the quota period. While some quotas are allocated to specific foreign countries, others are global. If the quota is exceeded by quota entries, the commodity is released on a pro rata basis. Tariff quotas allow a certain amount of a commodity to be entered at a reduced tariff during the quota period. Quantities entered in excess of the quota for the period are subject to higher duty rates.

2. *Do most goods from NAFTA countries enter duty free into the United States?* Yes. However, proof of certificate of origin and/or country of origin marking on the goods is required. The manufacturer or seller of the goods should provide the importer with such document.

3. *What countries are not eligible to normal trade relations (NTR) or most-favored-nation (MFN) duty rates?* Cuba and North Korea.
4. *What is a nonqualifying operation under NAFTA?* Dismantling.
5. *What happens to imports that are not properly marked?* The goods are seized or penalty issued.
6. *A shipment of beef valued at $5,000.00 is subject to a tariff quota. At the time of importation, a high tariff rate is in effect but a lower rate is soon expected. How can an importer take advantage of the lower rate?* A warehouse entry (type 21) can be filed and when the lower rate is effective, the merchandise can be withdrawn (type 32) and low duty paid.
7. *When imported merchandise exceeds a tariff quota, the importer may not commingle the merchandise and classification with nonquota class goods.* True.
8. *What is the rate of duty on imports from GSP eligible countries?* Zero.
9. *A claim for preferential treatment under NAFTA may be filed within one year from the date of importation of the goods.* True.
10. *What is origin criteria for textiles and apparel products under NAFTA?* To be eligible for duty-free treatment, the yard forward-rule states that the yarn used to form the fabric must originate in a NAFTA country.

Section 4: Value

1. *What is value and what value is used for customs purposes?* Value is the price paid or payable for goods. It includes selling commissions, assists, royalties, packing, and proceeds. Duty is assessed on the price paid and does not include freight and insurance charges.
2. *What are the secondary bases of value if the transaction value cannot be used?* The secondary bases of value, in order of precedence are: transaction value of identical merchandise, transaction value of similar merchandise, deductive value, computed value.
3. *In establishing transaction value, what is to be included in the price?* The packing costs incurred by the buyer; any selling commission incurred by the buyer; the value of any assist; any royalty or license fee that the buyer is required to pay as a condition of the sale; and the proceeds, accruing to the seller, of any subsequent resale, disposal, or use of the imported merchandise.
4. *What is an assist?* Items that the buyer of imported merchandise provides directly or indirectly, free of charge or a reduced cost, for use in the production or sale of merchandise for export to the United States

(tools, dies, molds, engineering, development, artwork, design work etc.)

5. *What should be excluded from transaction value?* The cost, charges etc. for transportation or insurance relating to the shipment of the goods to the United States; costs incurred for constructing, assembling etc. or transportation of the goods after importation; and tariffs and taxes for which the seller is ordinarily liable.

6. *A U.S. produce wholesaler imports avocados from Mexico on consignment. A few days after importation, the wholesaler sells the avocados (for $0.25 per avocado) to retailers and receives a 2 percent commission from Mexican sellers. Customs has sufficient information to appraise the merchandise. What is the basis of appraisement for the merchandise?* Deductive value.

7. *The manufacturer received from the importer, free of charge, design work produced in the United States and 5,000 U.S. originating modules to be incorporated in the production of 5,000 computer monitors. The costs are as follows: cost of acquiring design work: $10,000; cost of transportation to place of production: $100.00; cost of acquiring modules: $75 each; cost of transportation of modules: $5,250.00. What is the transaction value of the shipment of the monitors with a per-unit price of $50 FOB?* Answer: $630,250.

8. *What is "identical merchandise"?* Identical in all respects to the merchandise being appraised; produced in the same country as the merchandise being appraised; or produced by the same person as the merchandise being appraised.

Section 5: Broker Compliance and Other Areas

1. *Is a power of attorney required when a broker is acting as the importer of record?* No. A CBP power of attorney executed by a partnership is valid for two years.

2. *When is a multiple country declaration required?* Multiple country declaration is required for merchandise that has been subject to manufacturing processes in more than one country.

3. *What rate of currency exchange should be used when foreign currency is converted?* The rate of exchange in effect on the date of exportation.

4. i. *What are the penalties for conducting customs business without a license?* $10,000 for any one incident.

   ii. *What are the penalties against any broker who continuously makes the same errors on a particular type of entry?* $1,000.00

iii. *What are the penalties against a broker who does not have a working knowledge of customs operation to render valuable service?* $5,000.00

5. *What information should be on a bill of lading?* Receipt of the goods, contract of carriage, and commitment to deliver the goods at the designated port of destination to the holder of the bill of lading.

6. *Is the commercial invoice required at the time of shipment?* No. It is required at the time of entry.

7. *How does the duty drawback claim work?* Importers can get a refund of duty paid on imports when they are exported or destroyed. Proof of duty payment, export (bill of sale or air waybill) or destruction (witnessed by customs officer) is required. A drawback claim must be made within three years after the date of exportation. A post-importation NAFTA duty refund claim may be filed within one year after the date of importation of the goods.

8. *Are there laws governing labeling requirements for certain products?* Yes. Most textile, wool, and fur products, for example, must have a label or tag disclosing the fiber or fur content, importer, distributor, seller, country of origin, etc.

9. *Does an importer who sells merchandise to another company that exports it qualify for a duty drawback?* No.

10. *Under the following conditions, does the firm qualify for a rejected merchandise drawback claim?*
    i. *A Miami firm imports 200 pounds of shrimp for its national network of seafood restaurants. When it opened the boxes, it found that it was 200 pounds of pork.* Yes.
    ii. *An importer of oranges finds thirty crates of unordered vegetables.* Yes.
    iii. *A company in New York imports twenty cases of Argentine wine. There was a strike at the port and the wine was not unloaded for a few days. When the importer picked up the wines, they were frozen.* No.

Appendix C

Trade Profiles of Selected Nations (2004) (Million U.S. Dollars)

	Merchandise Trade		Services Trade		Trade (% of GDP)	
	Exports	**Imports**	**Exports**	**Imports**	**Exports**	**Imports**
Developed Countries						
Australia	86,423	109,376	24,774	25,613	18	21
Austria	117,417	117,765	48,297	46,195	54	46
Belgium	306,509	285,450	50,459	48,234	84	81
Canada	316,547	279,779	46,370	56,571	38	34
Denmark	76,821	68,191	36,304	33,401	44	38
Finland	61,334	50,824	9,792	12,129	37	32
France	448,714	465,454	109,518	96,452	26	26
Germany	912,261	716,929	133,856	191,706	38	33
Greece	15,198	52,577	32,986	13,560	21	30
Ireland	104,281	60,651	52,158	64,461	80	65
Italy	349,153	351,034	82,484	80,412	27	26
Japan	565,807	454,543	94,933	134,013	12	10
Netherlands	358,187	319,330	71,784	68,564	65	60
New Zealand	20,373	23,201	7,753	6,806	29	29
Norway	81,752	48,082	25,893	23,988	44	30
Spain	178,607	249,308	84,105	57,016	26	29
Sweden	122,537	99,324	38,320	32,908	46	38

Export-Import Theory, Practices, and Procedures, Second Edition

Appendix C *(continued)*

	Merchandise Trade		Services Trade		Trade (% of GDP)	
	Exports	**Imports**	**Exports**	**Imports**	**Exports**	**Imports**
Switzerland	118,527	111,603	41,544	23,653	44	37
UK	346,863	463,467	179,649	140,060	25	28
USA	818,775	1,525,516	321,837	263,598	10	14
High-Income Countries						
Chile	32,025	24,871	5,872	6,401	36	30
Korea	1,380	2,540	41,882	49,928	44	40
Kuwait	28,729	12,005	2,067	6,135	60	33
Malaysia	126,503	105,287	13,459	17,323	121	100
Mauritius	2,004	2,778	1,449	1,005	56	56
Saudi Arabia	126,230	44,576	5,852	11,057	53	25
Singapore	179,547	163,854	41,077	40,470	230	203
Taiwan	593,329	561,230	62,056	71,602	34	31
Trinidad and Tobago	6,349	4,894	672	335	60	48
Middle-Income Countries						
Argentina	34,453	22,320	5,065	6,596	25	18
Bostwana	3,467	3,340	647	652	40	32
Brazil	96,475	65,921	11,615	16,111	18	13
China	265,670	272,893	54,175	30,016	193	184
Colombia	16,224	16,746	2,179	3,987	21	22
Costa Rica	6,297	8,268	2,206	1,293	47	49
Egypt	7,682	12,831	14,046	7,470	29	29
Indonesia	72,330	54,895	17,331	28,265	31	27
Jamaica	1,390	3,772	2,262	1,677	41	58
Mexico	189,083	206,423	13,931	19,250	30	32
Peru	12,547	10,101	1,795	2,628	21	18
Philippines	39,689	42,345	4,101	5,081	52	51
Thailand	97,414	95,353	18,932	22,948	71	66
Turkey	63,121	97,540	23,806	10,229	29	35
Uruguay	2,950	3,114	959	649	30	28
Venezuela	34,210	14,995	1,008	4,271	36	20

Appendix C *(continued)*

	Merchandise Trade		Services Trade		Trade (% of GDP)	
	Exports	Imports	Exports	Imports	Exports	Imports
Low-Income Countries						
Bangladesh	8,150	12,026	420	1,835	16	21
Ethiopia	639	3,080	799	938	19	40
Ghana	2,580	4,320	684	881	35	54
India	75,595	97,339	39,638	40,950	19	23
Kenya	2,693	4,553	1,150	675	26	32
Nigeria	23,657	11,096	3,336	4,969	55	37
Pakistan	13,379	17,949	1,697	5,089	16	15
Tanzania	1,338	2,490	845	963	19	29
Uganda	635	1,491	436	679	14	28
Vietnam	25,625	31,091	2,498	3,698	66	74
Zambia	1,576	2,143	N/A	N/A	20	27
Zimbabwe	1,520	2,550	N/A	N/A	36	44

N/A: Data not available.

Source: Adapted from World Bank (2006). *World Development Indicators.* Washington, DC: The International Bank for Reconstruction and Development/ The World Bank, pp. 206-224.

Appendix D

Average Tariff Rates
of Selected Countries (2002-2004)

Country	Year	Primary Products (%)	Manufactured Products (%)
Algeria	2003	10.5	12.5
Argentina	2004	2.5	7.0
Australia	2004	0.7	4.4
Belgium	2003	0.9	1.4
Brazil	2004	2.0	10.2
Cameroon	2002	19.1	14.2
Canada	2003	0.4	1.0
Chile	2004	1.9	4.4
China	2004	5.6	6.0
Colombia	2004	9.9	9.4
Czech Republic	2003	4.1	4.3
Denmark	2003	0.9	1.4
Egypt	2002	7.7	16.7
France	2003	0.9	1.4
Ghana	2004	27.3	9.6
Hungary	2002	6.7	8.0
India	2004	36.9	25.3
Indoneisa	2003	3.1	5.8
Israel[a]	1993	2.5	4.3
Japan	2004	3.9	1.6
Korea (South)	2002	19.0	5.0

Export-Import Theory, Practices, and Procedures, Second Edition

Appendix D *(continued)*

Country	Year	Primary Products (%)	Manufactured Products (%)
Malaysia	2003	2.1	4.6
Mexico	2004	20.3	12.8
New Zealand	2004	0.5	3.5
Nigeria	2002	20.6	15.5
Norway	2003	1.4	0.2
Peru	2004	9.7	8.4
Philippines	2003	5.0	2.0
Poland	2003	3.7	1.2
Saudi Arabia	2004	10.5	6.6
Singapore	2003	0.0	0.0
Thailand	2003	4.4	9.3
Uganda	2004	5.7	5.3
USA	2004	1.1	1.9
Zambia	2003	9.8	9.2

[a]Data is for 1993.

Source: Adapted from the World Bank (2005). *World Development Indicators.* Washington, DC: The International Bank for Reconstruction and Development/ The World Bank. Available at: http://devdata.worldbank.org/wdi2005/cover .htm.

Appendix E

Ex-Im Bank Programs

Program	Eligible Products/ Services	Description	Eligible Applicants	Other Features
Working Capital				
	All products; services for exports must be performed by U.S.–based personnel	• *Product Description:* Loan guarantee if all products contain 50% U.S. materials. If the products contain less than 50% U.S. materials then Ex-Im Bank will pay only for the U.S. content • *Size:* There is no size limit • *Coverage:* Ex-Im Bank guarantees a 90% bank loan (including interest and principal) • *Repayment:* Repayment varies between one and three years • *Financing Characteristics:* For small/large financing needs all criteria must be met	Exporters who are located in the United States with a one year operating history and they must have a positive net worth	Military or defense products are not eligible. Sales to military buyers are not permitted (unless certain exceptions are applied)
Export Credit Insurance				
1.1 Small Business Export Credit	All products; services for exports must be performed	• *Product Description:* Insurance policy applies to products that contain	A parent company must be a small	Excluded from coverage: confirmed

Export-Import Theory, Practices, and Procedures, Second Edition

Appendix E *(continued)*

Program	Eligible Products/ Services	Description	Eligible Applicants	Other Features
Insurance Policy	by U.S.–based personnel. Products and services must belong to small businesses	51% U.S. materials (including labor). Shipments are also insured on credit terms • *Size:* No size limit on products • *Coverage:* 95% coverage for commercial losses due to insolvency; 100% for political losses; no first loss deductible • *Repayment:* Repayment options are determined by the Ex-Im Bank's financial institution • *Financing Characteristics:* Premium is paid monthly or according to the rate schedule (which depends on the credit term extended and buyer type)	business (defined by the Small Business Administration SBA); have export credit sales (not exceeding $5 million (U.S.); have a one year positive net worth	letters of credit, cash-in-advance sales, and certain military and defense items
1.2 Multibuyer Export Credit Insurance	U.S. goods and services	• *Product Description:* Insurance policy applies to products that contain 51% U.S. materials (including labor). Shipments are also insured on credit terms • *Size:* No size limit on products • *Coverage:* Two types of coverage: (1) Split Coverage: covers less than 90% of commercial losses and less than	Exporters of U.S. goods and services	Excluded from coverage: confirmed letters of credit, cash-in-advance sales, and certain military and defense items

Appendix E *(continued)*

Program	Eligible Products/ Services	Description	Eligible Applicants	Other Features
		100% of political losses (a first loss deductible applied to commercial losses only); (2) Equalized Coverage: covers less than 95% for both commercial and political losses (a first loss deductible is applied to any loss) • *Repayment:* Repayment is done within 180 days or 360 days (for exceptions) • *Financing Characteristics:* Premium is paid monthly or according to the rate schedule (which depends on the credit term extended and buyer type)		
1.3 Short-Term Single-Buyer Export Credit Insurance	U.S. goods and services	• *Product Description:* Insurance policy applies to products that contain 51% U.S. materials (including labor). Shipments (for one buyer) are also insured on credit terms • *Size:* No size limit on products • *Coverage:* Policy covers losses due to commercial and political reasons (the coverage varies with each policy); no first loss deductible	Exporters of U.S. goods and services	Excluded from coverage: confirmed letters of credit, cash-in-advance sales, and certain military and defense items

Appendix E *(continued)*

Program	Eligible Products/ Services	Description	Eligible Applicants	Other Features
		• *Repayment:* Repayment terms up to 180 days (depending on product/service) and 360 days for exceptional products • *Financing Characteristics:* A full nonrefundable premium must be paid up front		
1.4 Leasing Policies	U.S. new or used equipment and related services	• *Product Description:* Leasing coverage applied to new or used equipment and related services; no more than 15% of non– U.S. materials allowed for use in the development of the product. Both policies cover single transactions • *Size:* Ex-Im Bank decides which policy to issue depending on the applicant's size of equipment and its related services; no size limit of product • *Coverage:* Two types of coverage: (1) Operating Lease Policy: coverage for stream of payments provided for a maximum of 100% (sovereign leases) and 90% (for all others); (2) Financing Lease Policy: 100% of each lease	Leasing company, manufacturer, bank, trust, partnership, or other entity foreign or domestic	All transactions must be subject to leasing agreements in order to receive financial help

Appendix E *(continued)*

Program	Eligible Products/ Services	Description	Eligible Applicants	Other Features
		payment (if lessee defaults on payments)		
		• *Repayment:* Periodic payments are due depending on the leasing policy used.		
		• *Financing Characteristics:* Premium is to be paid upon a specified stream of payments (premiums may vary per single transaction due to the variations in policies)		
1.5 Financial Institution Buyer Credit Export Insurance	U.S. manufactured goods	• *Product Description:* A financial institution may extend a loan to any foreign entity that imports U.S. goods and services. Products must be 51% U.S. content • *Size:* No size limit on products • *Coverage:* Policies cover losses due to political events; cancellation of imports/exports licenses after shipments and foreign exchange convertibility (i.e., insolvency); and commercial losses (details on coverage vary among policies) • *Repayment:* Repayments must be made within ninety days of receiving financial aid or at the	U.S. exporters	Certain defense products are not eligible. The policy issued depends on one of two formats: a documentary policy for buyer credits (for non-small business suppliers) or for suppliers of small businesses

Appendix E *(continued)*

Program	Eligible Products/ Services	Description	Eligible Applicants	Other Features
		end of the policy period • *Financing Characteristics:* A premium of $100 must be paid per invoice or paid on the total principal volume		
1.6 Financial Institution Supplier Credit Multibuyer Insurance Policy (FISC)	U.S. goods and services	• *Product Description:* Products must be 51% U.S. content • *Size:* No size limit on products • *Coverage:* Coverage policies vary between a nondocumentary policy and a documentary policy. Both types do cover shipping, insurance, and financial interest • *Repayment:* Repayments must be made within ninety days of receiving financial aid or at the end of the policy period • *Financing Characteristics:* A premium of $100 must be paid per invoice or paid on the total principal volume	Small businesses (as defined by SBA)	
1.7 Letter of Credit Insurance for Banks	Goods produced and shipped from the USA	• *Product Description:* Products must be 51% U.S. content • *Size:* No size limit on products • *Coverage:* Policy covers against any political or	Insurance policy is issued to any bank doing business in the United States	Military defense products are ineligible to receive this policy

Appendix E *(continued)*

Program	Eligible Products/ Services	Description	Eligible Applicants	Other Features
		commercial losses, cancellation of imports/exports licenses after shipments and foreign exchange convertibility (i.e., insolvency) • *Repayment:* Payments are to be made within thirty days of a default • *Financing Characteristics:* A minimal premium of $2,000 is collected for each one year policy (collected upon issuance of the policy)		
1.8 Medium-Term Export Credit Insurance	U.S. goods (including capital equipment, its installation and spare parts)	• *Product Description:* Products must be 51% U.S. content • *Size:* No size limit on products • *Coverage:* Policy covered in either a documentary or nondocumentary format. The policies cover against any political or commercial losses; with a maximum coverage of $10 million under the medium-term policies. Coverage on sales transactions (single and repetitive sales) varies from one to five years (except after seven years)	Eligible applicants include financial institutions (i.e., banks); persons other than exporters or suppliers are not eligible	

Appendix E *(continued)*

Program	Eligible Products/ Services	Description	Eligible Applicants	Other Features
		• *Repayment:* Payments depend upon the total value of sales and the unit value of capital goods • *Financing Characteristics:* Premiums are to be paid on the fifteenth of every month		
1.9 Foreign Dealer Insurance Policy	U.S. goods	• *Product Description:* Products must be U.S. made capital goods (i.e., machinery and equipment) • *Size:* No size limit on products • *Coverage:* Policies on the sale and resale of products • *Repayment:* Payments depend upon the total value of sales and the unit value of capital goods • *Financing Characteristics:* Ex-Im Bank normally covers 100% of the principal and interest on a certain portion. Refinancing is available for products that are resold. Separate premiums are charged based on coverage and refinancing	Small, medium, and large U.S. manufactures that distribute products through foreign dealerships	The "floor plan/rollover" is a feature that is provided within the policy. The feature is designed to cover short-term financing of inventory for resale purposes (in order to finance for a longer term period)

Appendix E *(continued)*

Program	Eligible Products/ Services	Description	Eligible Applicants	Other Features
Loan Guarantee				
1.1 Medium- and Long-Term Financing Guarantees	U.S. goods (including refurbished equipment and software)	• *Product Description:* Products must be made and shipped from the USA • *Size:* No size limit on products • *Coverage:* Ex-Im Bank normally covers 100% of the principal and accrued interest on any amount. Losses due to commercial and political events will be 100% covered • *Repayment:* Repayment terms depend on the borrower's financial condition • *Financing Characteristics:* Flexible financing options are available, including medium-term and long-term financing	International buyers who need financing help (i.e., loans) with U.S. capital equipment and service purchases	Military or defense products are not eligible (unless certain exceptions are applied)
1.2 Project and Structured Finance	U.S. company projects	• *Product Description:* U.S. company projects (especially in foreign markets) • *Size:* No size limit on products • *Coverage:* Coverage varies on the variety of projects based on one of the two types of projects (project and structure finance). There is no price or dollar limit on provided coverage	U.S. exporters and their international customers	The financing policy was created to protect U.S. companies and shareholder interests

Appendix E *(continued)*

Program	Eligible Products/ Services	Description	Eligible Applicants	Other Features
		• Repayment: Ex-Im Bank looks toward future cash flows (from projects) as a form of repayment • *Financing Characteristics:* Financing options are flexible		
1.3 Transportation				
1.3A Aircraft Exports	U.S. manufactured aviation products	• *Product Description:* New and used U.S. manufactured commercial and general aviation aircrafts (i.e., helicopters) • *Size:* No size limit on products • *Coverage:* Coverage varies with the age, size, and new/used status of the aircrafts • *Repayment:* Repayment varies with the age and size of each aircraft • *Financing Characteristics:* Financing options are flexible based on the age and size of aircrafts and whether the aircrafts are new or used	Foreign buyers of U.S. aircraft and transp- ortation products	The Ex-Im Bank cannot finance the export of military aircrafts or the export of civilian aircraft to any foreign military units (unless limited exceptions apply)
1.3B Railroad Exports	U.S. manufactured railroad products	• *Product Description:* New and used U.S. manufactured commercial and general railroad equipment • *Size:* No size limit on products	Foreign buyers of U.S. railroad equipment	Ex-Im Bank is able to support the export of U.S. railroad "infra- structure" equipment (i.e., tracks, switching

Appendix E *(continued)*

Program	Eligible Products/ Services	Description	Eligible Applicants	Other Features
		• *Coverage:* Coverage ranges from 85 to 100% of the equipment • *Repayment:* Repayment depends on the status of the railroad equipment (new/used) • *Financing Characteristics:* Financing options are flexible based the status of the railroad equipment (new/used) Repayment on most equipment must be every six months		and signaling equipment)
1.3C Ship Exports	U.S. manufactured ships	• *Product Description:* New and used U.S. manufactured ships • *Size:* No size limit on products • *Coverage:* Coverage ranges from 85 to 100% of the equipment • *Repayment:* Repayment varies from 5-10 years depending on the status of country category. Repayment must be every six months • *Financing Characteristics:* Financing options are flexible based on the risk profile of the transaction	Foreign buyers of U.S. manufactured ships	U.S. government provides its support of the export of ships through its Overseas Private Investment Corporation (OPIC) and Maritime Administration (MARAD)

Appendix E *(continued)*

Program	Eligible Products/ Services	Description	Eligible Applicants	Other Features
1.3D Finance Lease Structure	U.S. manufactured aircrafts	• *Product Description:* U.S. manufactured aircrafts	Special Purpose Company (SPC) also	
		• *Size:* No size limit on products • *Coverage:* Coverage (provided in terms of a loan) provided up to 85% maximum for an airline's purchase price • *Repayment:* There is no set time limit on the repayment of loans • *Financing Characteristics:* Financing depends on the how often the lease payments are made (may vary per airline leasing options)	referred to as the borrower or SPC "lessor"	
1.4 Credit Guarantee Facility Program	U.S. capital goods and related services	• *Product Description:* U.S. capital goods and related services • *Size:* No size limit on products • *Coverage:* 100% coverage is provided for principal and interest for up to 85% of the export value of the product (with either floating or fixed rates) • *Repayment:* Payments must be repaid between two and five years	U.S. exporters	The program includes the lines of credit between a foreign bank and a bank in the United States

Appendix E *(continued)*

Program	Eligible Products/ Services	Description	Eligible Applicants	Other Features
		• *Financing Characteristics:* U.S. exposure fees are financed. Finance options are based on the time available for repayments		
1.5 Foreign Currency Guarantee (FCG)	U.S. goods and related services	• *Product Description:* U.S. goods and related services • *Size:* No size limit on products • *Coverage:* 100% coverage is provided (including principal and interest); the coverage is provided in U.S. dollars and other foreign currencies (measured in U.S. dollars) • *Repayment:* Payments must be made in full • *Financing Characteristics:* U.S. risk based exposure fees are financed	Buyers of U.S. goods and related services	FCG was established to safeguard U.S. exporting firms from currency exchange/ fluctuation risks. In order to minimize this risk, the Ex-Im Bank estimates the average exchange rate of a certain currency and authorizes foreign transactions on that basis
Finance Lease Guarantees	U.S. capital goods and services	• *Product Description:* U.S. capital goods (i.e., equipment) and services • *Size:* No size limit on products • *Coverage:* 100% coverage on commercial and political risks • *Repayment:* Repayment within five years, with 15% made in cash • *Financing Characteristics:* Flexible financing options are available	International lessees (international buyers of U.S. goods) both in the private and public sectors	Military or defense items are not eligible (including transactions involving military lessees)

Appendix E *(continued)*

Program	Eligible Products/ Services	Description	Eligible Applicants	Other Features
Direct Loan	U.S. capital equipment and services	• *Product Description:* U.S. capital equipment and services. Goods must be shipped from the United States	International buyers both in the private and public sectors	
		• *Size:* No size limit on products • *Coverage:* 100% coverage is provided for principal and interest for up to 85% of the export value of the product • *Repayment:* Repayment in excess of seven years, with 15% made in cash • *Financing Characteristics:* Goods that are eligible for financing must meet Ex-Im Bank's foreign content requirements		
Special Incentives				The Ex-Im Bank now offers U.S. exporters to export their products and services in Africa (as well as offer incentives, coverage, etc. to help manage risk when working in Africa)

Appendix E *(continued)*

Program	Eligible Products/ Services	Description	Eligible Applicants	Other Features
1.1 Small Business Initiative	U.S. goods	• *Product Description:* U.S. goods • *Size:* No size limit on products • *Coverage:* Policy covers against any commercial or political losses (for both single and multibuyer insurance policies). Coverage includes the protection of an exporter due to nonpayments by its foreign buyers • *Repayment:* Repayment of the short-term insurance varies according to policy • *Financing Characteristics:* Premium rates vary according to the insured policy	U.S. exporters of small businesses (as defined by the SBA)	The purpose of this policy is to increase sales in new markets for small U.S. business exporters
1.2 Environmental Exports Program	U.S. goods and services	• *Product Description:* U.S. goods and services that are beneficial to the environment (i.e., instruments to measure air/water quality, effluent pollution control equipment, etc.) • *Size:* No size limit on products • *Coverage:* 100% coverage is provided for political risks (no deductibles) and 95% coverage against commercial losses	U.S. exporters of environmentally beneficial goods and services; U.S. exporters who participate in international environmental projects	U.S. exporters are provided a working capital guarantee to help purchase raw materials and other overhead costs. The exporters are also provided with a short-term insurance policy (multibuyer or single buyer policy)

Appendix E *(continued)*

Program	Eligible Products/ Services	Description	Eligible Applicants	Other Features
		• *Repayment:* Repayment varies between 8.5 and 15 years; depending on the exported products and the country the products are exported		
		• *Financing Characteristics:* An annual premium of $500		
1.3 Medical Equipment Initiative (MEI)	U.S. made medical equipment	• *Product Description:* U.S. made medical equipment • *Size:* No size limit on products • *Coverage:* Political and commercial risks are covered • *Repayment:* Repayment within seven years • *Financing Characteristics:* Financing flexibility and varies according to buyer and the product	U.S. exporters	
1.4 Transportation Security Exports Program (T-SEP)	U.S. made products and services	• *Product Description:* U.S. made security products and services (i.e., machinery, equipment, security systems, etc.); exports that fall into two categories: transportation security exports and exports related to foreign transportation security projects	U.S. exporters	

Appendix E *(continued)*

Program	Eligible Products/ Services	Description	Eligible Applicants	Other Features
		• *Size:* No size limit on products • *Coverage:* Political and commercial risks are covered. Coverage also varies if the policies are medium- or long-term • *Repayment:* Repayment varies according to product category and policy • *Financing Characteristics:* Financing varies according to product/service		
Ex-Im Bank Policies				For further information regarding the updated revisions on the Ex-Im Bank's Charter see www.exim.gov
1.1 Foreign Content for Medium- and Long-Term Exports	U.S. goods and services	• *Product Description:* U.S. U.S. made goods and services (all products must be shipped from the United States) • *Size:* No size limit on products • *Coverage:* A local cost policy (EBD-M-05) determines coverage regarding medium- and long-term exports	U.S. exporters	Only the value of U.S. content in any product is supported by Ex-Im Bank

Appendix E *(continued)*

Program	Eligible Products/ Services	Description	Eligible Applicants	Other Features
		• *Repayment:* A local cost policy (EBD-M-05) determines repayment options • *Financing Characteristics:* A local cost policy (EBD-M-05) determines any applicable financing characteristics		
1.2 Local Cost Policy	U.S. manufactured goods and services	• *Product Description:* U.S. manufactured goods and services (i.e., U.S. security related products) • *Size:* No size limit on products • *Coverage:* A local cost policy determines coverage (i.e., coverage may include environmental exports, medical equipment exports, etc.) • *Repayment:* A local cost policy determines repayment options depending on whether the policy is long-term or medium-term • *Financing Characteristics:* A local cost policy determines any applicable financing characteristics, depending on whether the policy is long-term or medium-term	U.S. exporters of foreign projects	U.S. exporters may open subsidiaries in foreign countries, managed by locals but all equipment used must be from the United States

Appendix E *(continued)*

Program	Eligible Products/ Services	Description	Eligible Applicants	Other Features
1.3 Shipping Requirements: by Maritime Administration (MARAD)	U.S. made products	• *Product Description:* U.S. made products (and must be carried by U.S. vessels to foreign countries) • *Size:* No size limit on products • *Coverage:* Coverage includes guarantees in excess of $20 million dollars (U.S.) • *Repayment:* A repayment period in excess of seven years • *Financing Characteristics:* Any applicable financing characteristics are in excess of seven years	U.S. exporters	If U.S. vessels are not available (for a variety of reasons) for transportation of goods, then waivers may be obtained for goods to be shipped on non–U.S. vessels
1.4 Co-Financing "One-Stop Shop"	U.S. goods and services	• *Product Description:* U.S. goods and services (must be carried by U.S. vessels to foreign countries) • *Size:* No size limit on products • *Coverage:* Ex-Im Bank will provide its standard coverage on all transactions • *Repayment:* Repayment options vary according to each individual seller • *Financing Characteristics:* Financing characteristics vary with each seller	U.S. exporters	The country with the most export credit agencies (ECAs) leads ECA; and in this case, the United States has the highest amount of export credit agencies, therefore, the lead ECA is the Ex-Im Bank

Appendix E *(continued)*

Program	Eligible Products/ Services	Description	Eligible Applicants	Other Features
1.5 Military Policy	U.S. items for civilian use only, including small craft equipment (marine vessels, small aircrafts), are not considered defense articles (even if sold to military personnel)	• *Product Description:* U.S. items for "dual use" purposes (military and commercial/civilian usage); all nonlethal items (to be used for civilian activities only). Items also include small crafts needed for border patrol, drug interdiction, and natural resources • *Size:* No size limit on products • *Coverage:* Coverage varies according to seller • *Repayment:* Repayment options vary according to seller • *Financing Characteristics:* Financing characteristics vary to seller	U.S. exporters	Military or defense items are not eligible for exports (only if the products are sold to a foreign military organization or designed primarily for military usage. Products include humanitarian items (i.e., lifesaving, rescue, or medical equipment) are considered defense items
1.6 Nuclear Procedures and Guidelines	U.S. goods and services associated with exports to nuclear facilities (i.e., power plants, nuclear research reactors, and other related events/items; that are also beneficial to the environment)	• *Product Description:* U.S. goods and services associated with exports to nuclear facilities (i.e., power plants, nuclear research reactors, and other related events/items; that are also beneficial to the environment) • *Size:* No size limit on products • *Coverage:* Coverage varies according to long-term,	U.S. exporters	Each product, depending on its nucleic characteristics and its relations to the environment falls in one of several "Category N"

Appendix E *(continued)*

Program	Eligible Products/ Services	Description	Eligible Applicants	Other Features
		medium-term loans, guarantees, insurance policies, and the applicable categories of the exports • *Repayment:* Repayment varies according to long-term, medium-term loans, guarantees, insurance policies, and the applicable categories of the exports • *Financing Characteristics:* Financing characteristics vary according to long-term, medium-term loans, guarantees, insurance policies, and the applicable categories of the exports		
1.7 Ex-Im Bank and the Environment	U.S. goods and services (must environmental friendly)	• *Product Description:* U.S. goods and services (must be environmental friendly) • *Size:* No size limit on products • *Coverage:* Coverage varies according to categories (Category A or B) that are applicable to the exporting products and services	U.S. exporters (including U.S. exporters who participate in foreign environmentally beneficial programs)	The Environmental policy includes several elements, guidelines, and procedures (including exporting programs; illustrative list of sensitive sectors and areas; environmental impact assessment reports, etc.)

Appendix E *(continued)*

Program	Eligible Products/ Services	Description	Eligible Applicants	Other Features
		• *Repayment:* Repayment options vary according to categories (Category A or B) that are applicable to the exporting products and services • *Financing Characteristics:* Financing characteristics varies according to categories (CategoryA or B) that are applicable to the exporting products and services		
1.8 Used and Refur- bished Equipment	U.S. manufactured goods (i.e., equipment)	• *Product Description:* U.S. manufactured goods (i.e., equipment) that have been used (in the United States only) for a minimum of one year • *Size:* No size limit on products • *Coverage:* Coverage varies according to cost of the refurbishment of the goods that are to be exported. The original financing of the product must be paid in full before the refurbishment process is applicable for coverage • *Repayment:* Repayment options vary according to	U.S. exporters	

Appendix E *(continued)*

Program	Eligible Products/ Services	Description	Eligible Applicants	Other Features
		the contract value of the equipment (up to the remaining useful life of the equipment) • *Financing Characteristics:* Financing characteristics varies according to the contracts		
1.9 Tied Aid	U.S. exporters	Tied Aid Credit program includes information about the different types of aid packages that are available for U.S. exporters. Ex-Im Bank also issues reports regarding the program's success (how the projects helped increase sales of different U.S. exporting firms, etc.)		

Source: U.S. Export-Import Bank (Ex-Im Bank) of the United States.

Appendix F

Sample Export Business Plan: Donga Michael Export Company

EXECUTIVE SUMMARY

Donga Michael is a newly created export company located in Fort Lauderdale, Florida. The company started its operation in September 2005. It exports computers and parts to the Republic of South Africa. Trade in computers between the United States and South Africa has been growing at a faster rate since the end of apartheid. The company intends to supply high-quality computers to the business sector and later to schools and universities.

South Africa is the largest computer market for the United States in sub-Saharan Africa. Every year, it imports computer peripherals and accessories worth over $60 million. With the end of apartheid and the lifting of sanctions, South Africa is open for trade and investment. The development of a black professional and business class and the building of infrastructure facilities to enable all South Africans to participate in the economic life of the country provide enormous business opportunities for U.S. exporters of information technology. Even though there is strong price competition in the computer sector, Donga Michael will focus on the upper end of the consumer market. Donga Michael's competitive advantages over existing companies include a coordinated marketing program, prompt delivery and services, as well as a professional image and expertise in the North American market.

President and founder George Hunat brings a wealth of experience to the firm. Vice President Alice Munroe also has extensive marketing experience. The estimated required investment is $200,000. Mr. Hunat will invest $40,000 of his own personal funds in the business. Ms. Munroe will invest $35,000, while $80,000 will be borrowed from a local bank. The balance of $45,000 is solicited from a venture capitalist who will acquire 37.5 percent of the corporation stock.

Export-Import Theory, Practices, and Procedures, Second Edition

The company intends to become a major player in the South African market in the next five years capturing about 20 percent of the computer market. After this objective is realized, the company intends to explore export opportunities in Zimbabwe, Zambia, and Kenya.

GENERAL INDUSTRY AND COMPANY

The South African computer market is valued at over $1 billion and is changing its focus from mainframes to personal computers (PCs) and PC-based networks. The increasing processing power coupled with decreasing prices for personal computers is also boosting demand for laptop computers and peripheral equipment, including printers and storage devices. Opportunities exist for sales of computers, peripherals, and accessories as South African manufacturing and service companies seek to become more competitive in the domestic and global marketplaces. Presently, about four U.S. companies sell computer hardware to the South African market. Local manufacture of PCs remains negligible, and there is an increasing demand for established computer brand-name products. Donga Michael intends to bring such products into the market at competitive prices to help regain the market share lost during the sanctions period. With closer economic relations between South Africa and other African countries, the South African market will become the beachhead from which exports could be made to neighboring states, such as Zimbabwe, Zambia, Kenya, Tanzania, and Uganda. An encouraging development pertaining to the industry is the revision of U.S. controls on computer exports in 1995. The new regulations eliminate or significantly ease controls on computer exports to most countries of the world, except those which are designated as terrorist states. There are no U.S. restrictions on computer products and accessories that Donga Michael plans to export to South Africa. A problem that plagues the industry in the short term, however, is the shortage of trained manpower to manage the complex and interconnected networks proliferating everywhere.

Donga Michael is a newly created export firm that is incorporated as a Chapter S corporation in the state of Florida. The company will market digital ABD machines with central processing input-output units, parts and accessories, laptop and notebook computers, networking software, and software for computer-aided design and electronic design automation. The products need not be adapted for the South African market except for the different voltages (i.e., 100 V). George Hunat and Alice Munroe comprise the two partners of the firm and also manage the company as president and vice president, respectively.

TARGET MARKET

South Africa has a gross domestic output of $240 billion and a per capita income of $3,700 (as of 2005) and remains the largest economy in sub-Saharan Africa. It possesses a modern infrastructure, supporting an efficient distribution of goods to major urban centers throughout the region and well-developed financial, legal, and communications sectors. Its economic growth has been in the range of 3 to 3.5 percent over the past five years. However, with favorable economic conditions and a stable political climate, it is likely to register higher rates of growth, estimated at 5 to 10 percent in the next few years and beyond. This is critical to offset high unemployment rates. Present efforts to revamp the educational system, boost economic productivity, and provide access to basic services to all South Africans present opportunities for U.S. companies to export computers and other information technology.

Total U.S. exports to South Africa in 2006 amounted to $3.6 billion. The South African information technology market is the twentieth largest in the world and constitutes one of the top ten emerging markets that are being targeted by international computer companies. The base of installed personal computers is slightly over 950,000, and indications are that 84 percent of the top information technology users are investing in client-server systems. Information and communications technology spending is likely to grow from $13 to $18 billion in the next few years. The U.S. market share for computer peripherals was estimated at about 30 percent in 2003, amounting to about $45 million. A couple of reasons account for the continual expansion of the market for computer peripherals and accessories include the following:

1. Because the country ended its isolation and instituted a democratic political system for all South Africans, there is a significant inflow of foreign investment. For example, between 2001 and 2004, about 200 companies set up factories or offices in South Africa. This creates business opportunities for exports of computers and information technology.
2. The black middle class has experienced faster growth since the end of the apartheid system. Hence, this emerging professional and business class will soon be a big consumer market.

In terms of market access, there are no restrictions or quotas on computer peripheral imports to South Africa. These imports are, however, subject to a 10 percent ad valorem tariff and a 14 percent value-added tax. There are no nontariff barriers such as prior deposits or foreign exchange restrictions (see Table F.1).

TABLE F.1. U.S. Exports/Imports to South Africa (Exports/Imports of Electronic Products in 1,000 of Dollars)

Year	2003	2004	2005
Value of U.S. Exports	398,843	474,776	531,069
Value of U.S. Imports	41,869	47,434	56,172

Source: U.S. International Trade Commission (2006). Washington, DC: U.S. Government Printing Office, p. 15.

There is fierce competition in the South African market. Acer Africa is the top PC assembler and distributor, followed by Mustek electronics and IBM. Third-country suppliers from the Far East, Britain, France, Germany, and Italy are also present. Donga Michael should focus on the upper end of the consumer market for use by the business sector. In spite of the relatively high prices compared to the competition, discerning firms know the value of quality products and would be favorably disposed to buying U.S. made computers and parts. U.S.–branded peripherals have high status in South Africa.

MARKETING PLAN AND SALES STRATEGY

Donga Michael, Inc., intends to target the middle- to upper-level business firms that are in the process of using computers for various office functions, such as finance and accounting, word processing, electronic communication, and presentation. It should later begin to focus on high schools, universities, and research centers by entering into a supply agreement with the government. The company can establish retail outlets in major cities, and since it represents a well-known brand, it can have a marketing advantage.

Donga Michael can also promote sales by participating in computer trade exhibitions, advertising, and carefully managed public relations programs, such as sponsorship of special events, charitable donations to social causes, and so on.

MANAGEMENT AND ORGANIZATION

The company is managed by George Hunat, founder and president, and Alice Munroe, vice president and director of sales and marketing. George

Hunat has an MSc in computer engineering from Emory University in Atlanta, Georgia. Since graduation in 1985, he has worked as director of logistics for a multinational firm in San Diego, California (1985-1989), and later joined a successful computer export firm in Silicon Valley, California, as export manager (1989-1997). He has extensive experience in computer sales, marketing, and logistics operations. Alice Munroe received a BA in computer systems from Texas A&M in 1987 and has since worked as a marketing manager for a communications firm in New York.

Donga Michael will employ six people and a clerk. The employees will be trained to handle distribution, storage, transportation, and marketing of Donga Michael's computer products. Two of the trainees will be sent to South Africa to handle marketing and distribution. They will also recruit and train South African employees who will handle the retail outlets in major urban centers. For the first few years, the retail outlets will be located in Johannesburg, Pretoria, and Cape Town (see Table F.2).

The employees and clerk will be paid hourly at $8.00 and $6.00 per hour, respectively. The capital structure and salary level are shown in Table F.2. Future increases in salary will be based on sales performance.

LONG-TERM DEVELOPMENT PLAN

Donga Michael plans to show steady progress over the next five years, becoming one of the largest retailers of computers and parts in South Africa. It plans to capture 20 percent of the market by the year 2008.

The marketing staff will be increased as more sales are generated. Additional sales distribution outlets will be established in other urban areas. After five years, the company plans to expand to Zimbabwe, Zambia, and Kenya. Additional bank financing will be secured to finance the expansion (for financial plan and balance sheet, see Tables F.3 and F.4).

TABLE F.2. Ownership Structure

Partners	Capital	Ownership Share (%)	Salary ($/month)
George Hunat	$40,000 (20%)	33.33	3,500
Alice Munroe	$35,000 (17.5%)	29.16	3,000
Bank Loan	$80,000 (40%)	–	
Venture Capital	$45,000 (22.5%)	37.50	

TABLE F.3. Financial Plan: Donga Michael Export Company Forecasted Income Statements for the Ending Year

	2005 ($)	2006 ($)	2007 ($)	2008 ($)
Sales	120,000	1,120,000	3,980,000	5,200,000
Less cost of goods sold	30,000	350,000	600,000	1,350,000
Commission	10,000	120,000	200,000	420,000
Delivery	32,000	60,000	98,000	150,000
Total variable expenses	**72,000**	**530,000**	**898,000**	**1,920,000**
Less fixed expenses				
Rent	10,000	10,000	10,000	10,000
Advertising	15,000	22,000	25,000	60,000
Travel	20,000	25,000	27,000	20,000
Utilities	7,000	7,500	7,700	8,000
Wages	25,000	38,000	45,000	45,000
Misc.	15,000	18,000	22,000	25,000
Total fixed expenses	**92,000**	**120,500**	**136,700**	**168,000**
Net income	**(44,000)**	**469,500**	**2,945,300**	**3,112,000**

TABLE F.4. Forecasted Balance Sheet for the Ending Year

	2005 ($)	2006 ($)	2007 ($)	2008 ($)
Assets				
Cash	40,000	165,000	600,000	750,000
Accounts receivable	420,000	500,000	700,000	850,000
Inventory	100,000	150,000	160,000	220,000
Other	320,000	400,000	500,000	650,000
Less depreciation	15,000	25,000	30,000	45,000
Total assets	**865,000**	**1,190,000**	**1,930,000**	**2,425,000**
Liabilities				
Accounts payable	150,000	220,000	230,000	150,000
Long-term debt	80,000	50,000	40,000	22,000
Retailed earnings	–	220,000	200,000	400,000
Total liabilities and capital	**230,000**	**490,000**	**470,000**	**572,000**

Appendix G

Sample Import Business Plan: Otoro Import Company

EXECUTIVE SUMMARY

Otoro Imports is a spice importing and marketing corporation established in June 2004. It is located in Los Angeles, California, and specializes in the importation and marketing of high-quality spices at competitive prices. The company also provides certain programs to educate and inform distributors, retailers, and consumers about the use and health benefits of spices.

The United States is the world's largest spice importer and consumer. With the increased ethnic diversity of the population, strong U.S. dollar, and limited domestic production, there is greater demand for and affordability of such foods. The industry is dominated by a small number of companies. Otoro intends to import three types of spices: black and white pepper, paprika, and cinnamon, products showing fast growth in domestic demand.

The management team includes Davie Lee, president, and Howard Tzu, vice president. They both have extensive experience in the spice industry. The company has hired four full-time employees and a clerk. It will hire additional employees as the need arises. The company will market the imports through its retail outlets in California, Florida, and New York, and through outside distributors in other states. Its future plan includes expansion to Canada and Mexico and maintaining a substantial presence in the U.S. market, probably controlling approximately 25 percent of the market by 2010.

GENERAL DESCRIPTION OF INDUSTRY AND COMPANY

Otoro Imports intends to import spices from various countries for sale and distribution in the United States. Besides the importation and marketing of

Export-Import Theory, Practices, and Procedures, Second Edition

high-quality spices, Otoro intends to provide education programs to its distributors and retailers about the various types of spices, their uses, and their health benefits. As sales volume increases, the company also plans to hold free public seminars to inform and educate the North American consumer about the benefits and usage of various spices. The company aims to be known as the premier spice importing and marketing firm in North America. Its development goals are for steady expansion, with profitability by the second year.

The United States is the world's largest spice importer and consumer. Per capita consumption totaled 3.5 pounds in 2002 and it is likely to grow in the next few years. A number of factors contribute to the growing demand for spices in the United States. First, the growth of ethnic populations has caused a surge in the use of the spices common to different cultures. According to the U.S. census, the Asian and Hispanic populations grew by 4.0 and 8.5 million, respectively, between 1995 and 2005. Second, ethnic foods have become increasingly popular in the United States. Today it is rare to see a typical shopping center without an ethnic restaurant. There is also a trend toward the use of spices to compensate for less salt and lower fat levels in foods.

The industry is dominated by a small number of companies that process and market imported or domestically-produced spices. For example, McCormick/Schilling accounts for about 37 percent of the U.S. retail market. Given the trend toward mergers in most sectors, there is a possibility of mergers and acquisitions in the spice industry resulting in fewer, larger firms.

Otoro intends to import high-quality spices at competitive prices. It ensures importation of top-quality spices by maintaining constant communication with foreign producers and stationing a quality control specialist at most export locations to determine and advise on quality before importation into the United States. Importation from Indonesia, India, and China of seven of the most popular spices in the United States (vanilla beans, black and white pepper, capsicums, sesame seed, cinnamon, mustard, and oregano) is planned over the next five years because of their comparative advantages in climate, soil, and labor costs.

The seven products to be imported make up about 75 percent of U.S. spice imports (see Table G.1). The import of spices increased from 292,074 tons in 2004 to 310,874 tons in 2005. There has been a 20 percent increase in spice imports since 2000. Otoro will import three products during the first two years: black and white pepper, paprika, and cinnamon.

Presently, there are no restrictions on the importation of spices into the United States. However, food safety regulations require the treatment of spices to kill insects and microorganisms that thrive under tropical conditions.

TABLE G.1. U.S. Spice Imports

Product	Brief Profile
Vanilla Beans	Imports average over $62 million a year. Major suppliers include Comorus, Madagascar, and the Pacific Islands. Mainly used for ice cream
Black and White Pepper	Imports average over $55 million a year for black pepper and about $12 million for white pepper. Major suppliers are Brazil, India, and Indonesia. Used as seasonings for food
Capsicum and Paprika Peppers	Capsicum peppers are mainly imported from China, India, Mexico, and Palestine. Paprika is imported from Hungary, Morocco, and Spain. Total imports amount to over $62 million a year
Mustard Seed	Import value averages at $138 million a year. There is some domestic production. Most imports come from Canada
Cassia and Cinnamon	Widely used for doughnuts. Most imports come from Indonesia. Import value averages at about $30 million a year
Oregano	Mostly used for pizza. Imported from Mexico and Turkey. Annual imports average about $14 million a year
Sesame Seed	Used in the fast-food sector. Imported from Guatemala, El Salvador, and Mexico. Import value averages about $45 million a year

Otoro will market the imported spices through its retail outlets in California, New York, and Florida. In other states, the product will be marketed through distributors.

TARGET MARKET

Otoro intends to operate retail outlets in major metropolitan centers of California (Los Angeles, San Diego, and San Jose), Florida (Jacksonville, Miami, and Tampa), and New York (New York City, Buffalo, and Rochester). In other states, the products will be marketed through distributors. The major customers include restaurants, fast-food chains, and individual consumers.

Imports have played an important role in the American diet by providing needed spices through out the year and by moderating retail prices during times of shortages or other disruptions in domestic production. The United States produces a limited supply of spices—garlic, onions, mustard, ginger, and capsicum pepper—and its average annual exports are estimated at $89 million. However, the U.S. import share of total domestic consumption stands at about 92 percent (as of 1998), and thus, there is heavy reliance on foreign suppliers. The volume of spice imports grew by about 45 percent in the past decade to an average of 560 million pounds in 2001. The major suppliers include Canada, China, India, Indonesia, and Mexico. India supplied the largest share, at 34 percent in 1996 through 2004.

A number of factors contribute to steady growth and expansion of spice imports in the United States:

- Given the current per capita consumption, total domestic use of spices is likely to increase by over $300 million over the next few years.
- The increased ethnic diversity of the U.S. population will lead to more consumption of spices.
- Because domestic production of spices is limited in volume and variety, the United States will continue to import over 90 percent of its domestic spice needs.
- The increased value of the U.S. dollar in relation to the currencies of our major exporters, such as Indonesia, as well as low U.S. tariffs for spice imports, is likely to increase the availability and affordability of such foods.
- Foreign producers have increasingly adopted new production technologies to meet the necessary safety and quality standards of U.S. consumers and have also enhanced the popularity of imported spices.

There is strong competition from established companies in the industry that sell natural as well as artificial substitutes. However, Otoro's competitive advantage will be in the supply of high-quality spices at competitive prices. Furthermore, current and future needs cannot be met by the existing competition, and Otoro wants to position itself as an important supplier of black and white pepper, paprika, and cinnamon. Industry sources also indicate that these three products will constitute the fastest growing spice import groups in the U.S. market.

MARKETING PLAN AND SALES STRATEGY

Otoro will invest sufficient resources to achieve improvements in quality and reliability. It is important to find a suitable manner of presentation (e.g., bags, baskets, tins, etc.) that is timesaving and attractive to customers. The product will be marketed at a low price to be competitive in the market. Promotion includes participation in food shows and advertising.

MANAGEMENT AND ORGANIZATION

The company is managed by its founder, David Lee (president), and Howard Tzu (vice president). They both worked as managers for a reputable spice trading firm in Las Vegas, Nevada. Four people will be hired during the first phase of operation to clear imports from customs, transport the goods, and warehouse the shipment. The employees and a clerk will be paid $10.00 and $7.00 per hour, respectively. The capital structure and salary level (see Table G.2 for capital and ownership structure) are as follows:

LONG-TERM DEVELOPMENT PLAN

Otoro intends to be a major retailer and distributor of natural spices, capturing about 25 percent of the U.S. market by 2005. In the next five years, expansion plans will be focused on Canada and Mexico. Additional borrowing may be required to finance expansion (see Tables G.3 and G.4).

TABLE G.2. Ownership Structure

Partners	Capital ($)	Ownership Share (%)	Salary ($/month)
David Lee	350,000	58.33	4,000
Howard Tzu	250,000	41.67	3,000
Bank loan	150,000	—	—

TABLE G.3. Otoro Imports: Projected Income Statement

	Year 1 ($)	Year 2 ($)	Year 3 ($)
Total net sales	450,000	800,000	1,500,000
Cost of goods sold	150,000	350,000	650,000
Gross profit	**300,000**	**450,000**	**850,000**
Expenses			
Utilities	35,000	40,000	60,000
Postage	2,000	3,000	4,500
Warehouse	86,000	100,000	250,000
Transportation	40,000	55,000	100,000
Rent	85,000	85,000	85,000
Miscellaneous	60,000	75,000	100,000
Total expenses	**308,000**	**358,000**	**599,500**
Net profit (loss) before taxes	**(8,000)**	**92,000**	**250,500**

TABLE G.4. Start-Up Expenses for the First Six Months

Items	Range ($)
Supplies	1,000-2,000
Insurance	400-600
Rent	2,000-2,500
Utilities	400-600
Insurance	500-700
Furniture, etc.	3,000-5,000
Licenses/taxes	500-200
Advertising	3,000-4,000
Professional services	5,000-8,000
Salaries	200,000-240,000
Inventory	350,000-500,000
Operating capital	5,000-8,000
Total start-up expenses	**570,800-771,600**

Appendix H

Export Sales Contract (Basic Clauses)

PRICES

A. Prices include the following costs:
  i. Seller's usual inspection and factory tests
  ii. Seller's usual packing (or containerizing if applicable) for export
  iii. Freight by Seller's usual means to alongside vessel at the point of export designated by Seller (but not the cost of insurance or charges for pier handling, marshaling, lighterage, and heavy lifts). Insurance to cover the inland shipment shall be arranged by Seller at Buyer's expense if Seller is arranging for the export shipment pursuant to Article 3 of this contract.
B. Unless otherwise stated, prices are quoted in Canadian funds.

TAXES, DUTIES, AND EXCHANGE RATES

A. Prices quoted include all applicable Canadian taxes except for sales, use, excise, value-added, and similar taxes. If sales, use, excise, value-added, or similar taxes are levied against the Seller, the Buyer shall reimburse the Seller upon presentation of invoices therefor. However, where a refund of such taxes may be applied for, the Seller, if promptly furnished by the Buyer with evidence of exportation, will apply for a refund. If the Buyer has reimbursed the Seller, the Buyer shall be credited with the refund.
B. Prices quoted do not include Canadian import duties. All rights in drawback of customs duties paid by the Seller belong to and shall remain in the Seller. At the Seller's request, the Buyer shall provide documents and assistance necessary to process the Seller's drawback claims, failing which, the Buyer shall reimburse the Seller for such import duties. Such reimbursement shall be payable upon presentation of Seller's invoice therefor.

Export-Import Theory, Practices, and Procedures, Second Edition

C. Prices quoted herein are based upon the prevailing rates for taxes and freight at the date of the proposal and, with respect to the purchase price of goods to be bought by the Seller in foreign countries, on duty and exchange rates current at the date of the proposal. Any increase or decrease in these rates or the imposition of any new duties or taxes between the date of the proposal and the date of payment by the Seller will be paid by the Buyer, upon presentation of Seller's invoices therefore, or will be credited to the Buyer.

D. Any taxes, duties, fees, charges, or assessments of any nature levied by any governmental authority other than of Canada in connection with this contract, whether levied against the Buyer, against the Seller or its employees, or against any of the Seller's subcontractors or their employees shall be for the Buyer's account and shall be paid directly by the Buyer to the governmental authority concerned. If the Seller, its subcontractors, or the employees of either are required to pay any such taxes, duties, fees, charges, or assessments in the first instance or as a result of the Buyer's failure to comply with any applicable laws or regulations governing the payment of such levies by the Buyer, the amount of any such payment so made shall be reimbursed by Buyer, payable upon presentation of Seller's invoice therefor.

PAYMENT

A. Payment shall be made in Canadian dollars at Toronto, Canada, as follows:
   i. On all orders of ten thousand dollars ($10,000) or less, payment in full shall be made simultaneously with the giving of the order.
   ii. On orders of over ten thousand dollars ($10,000), payment shall be made through a Letter of Credit to be established by the Buyer at its expense (including any bank confirmation charges). All Letters of Credit shall be in favor of and acceptable to the Seller, shall be maintained in sufficient amounts and for the period necessary to meet all payment obligations, shall be irrevocable and issued or confirmed by a Canadian chartered bank in Toronto within fifteen days after the date of this contract, shall permit partial deliveries, and shall provide for pro rata payments, payable upon presentation of Seller's invoices and Seller's certificate of delivery FOB factory or of delivery into storage with cause therefor.

B. If the Buyer fails to fulfill any payment obligation, the Seller may suspend performance (and any costs incurred by the Seller as a result thereof shall be paid by the Buyer, payable upon presentation of invoices therefor) or may complete performance if Seller deems it reasonable to do so. Seller shall be entitled to an extension of time for performance of its obligations equaling the period of Buyer's nonfulfilment, whether or not the Seller elects to suspend performance. If such nonfulfilment is not rectified by the Buyer promptly upon notice thereof, the Seller may, in addition to its other rights, terminate this contract, and the Buyer shall pay to the Seller its charges for termination, payable upon presentation of Seller's invoice therefor and determined according to the Termination Charges clause (Clause 6).

DELIVERY, TITLE, AND RISK OF LOSS

A. Except as stated in paragraph C below, Seller shall deliver the goods FOB factory. Partial delivery shall be allowed. Any delivery dates given are approximate and are based upon prompt receipt by Seller of all information necessary to permit Seller to proceed with work without interruption.
B. Title and risk of loss and damage shall pass to the Buyer on delivery.
C. If the goods or any part thereof cannot be delivered when ready due to any cause referred to in the EXCUSABLE DELAY clause, the Seller may place such goods into storage (which may be at the place of manufacture). In such event:
   i. Seller's delivery obligations shall be deemed fulfilled and title and risk of loss and damage shall pass to Buyer,
   ii. Any amounts payable to the Seller on delivery shall be payable upon presentation of Seller's invoices and its certification as to such cause, and
   iii. All expenses incurred by the Seller, including, but not limited to, all expenses of preparation and shipment into storage, handling, storage, inspection, preservation, and insurance shall be for Buyer's account and shall be payable upon Seller's presentation of invoices therefor.

EXCUSABLE DELAY

A. The Seller shall not be in breach of any of its obligations under this contract where failure to perform or delay in performing any obligation is due, wholly or in part, to:
   i. a cause beyond its reasonable control;
   ii. an act of God, an act or omission of the Buyer or of any governmental authority (de jure or de facto), wars (declared or undeclared),

       governmental priorities, port congestion, riots, revolutions, strikes or other labor disputes, fire, flood, sabotage, nuclear incidents, earthquake, storm, epidemic; or

iii. inability due to a cause beyond the Seller's reasonable control to obtain necessary or proper labor, materials, components, facilities, energy, fuel, transportation, governmental authorizations or instructions, material or information required from the Buyer. The foregoing shall apply even though any such cause exists at the time of the order or occurs after the Seller's performance of its obligations is delayed by another cause.

B. The Seller will notify the Buyer of any failure to perform or delay in performing due to a cause set out in paragraph A and shall specify, as soon as practicable, when the obligation will be performed. Subject to paragraph C, the time for performing the obligation shall be extended for the period lost due to such a cause.

C. Where the period lost is at least sixty days and the parties have not agreed upon a revised basis for performing the obligation, including the adjustment of the prices, then, either party may, upon thirty days' written notice, terminate this contract, whereupon the Buyer shall pay to the Seller termination charges determined in accordance with the Termination Charges clause (Clause 6).

TERMINATION CHARGES

A. In the event that this contract is terminated by the Seller pursuant to any of its terms, the termination charges payable by the Buyer shall be calculated as follows:

    i material, labor, and indirect expenses committed or incurred to date of termination;

    ii. all costs incurred in the execution of the termination;

    iii. reasonable profit on (i) and (ii) herein above cited;

    iv. the greater of 10 percent of the unbilled portion of the contract price or the unrecoverable, ongoing, fixed costs and expenses due to discontinuities in operation plus loss of reasonable anticipated profit; and

    v. interest at the rate of 1.5 percent per month on the amount of the claim as cited in (i) to (iv) inclusive, if the termination charges are not paid as invoiced.

B. The termination charges shall be payable upon presentation of Seller's invoice therefor.

EXPORT SHIPMENT

If the Seller agrees to make export shipment, all fees and expenses, including, but not limited to, those covering preparation of consular documents, consular fees, storage, marine insurance (including war risk, if available) and other insurance, ocean freight, and Seller's then current fees for such services shall be payable by the Buyer upon presentation of invoices therefor. Unless otherwise instructed by the Buyer, the Seller shall prepare consular documents according to its best judgment but without liability for fines or other charges due to error or incorrect declarations.

GOVERNMENT AUTHORIZATIONS

The Seller shall, without any assumption of liability therefor, apply for an export permit on behalf of the Buyer where a permit is required by law. In the event that an export permit is denied or revoked, the Buyer shall have the right to elect to terminate the contract subject to the payment to the Seller of termination charges determined according to the Termination Charges clause (Clause 6). The Buyer shall be responsible for obtaining any import permit, exchange permit, or other governmental authorization required by the law of the country of importation.

NUCLEAR USE

The goods sold are not intended for nor shall they be used for or as any part of any activity or process involving any use or handling of any radioactive material, including any nuclear material (as that term is defined in the Nuclear Liability Act of Canada). If the goods or any part thereof are used by the Buyer contrary to the aforesaid, the Buyer shall provide, at its own expense, insurance and indemnity satisfactory to the Seller protecting the Seller and all of its subcontractors and suppliers from all loss, expense, damages, costs, or liability of every kind, whether in contract or in tort (including negligence), and the Seller may terminate this contract. Upon such termination, the Buyer shall pay to the Seller termination charges determined according to the Termination Charges clause (Clause 6).

PATENTS

A. The Seller shall, if notified promptly in writing and given authority, information, and assistance, defend, at its own expense, any suit or proceeding brought against the Buyer so far as based on a claim that the goods, or any part thereof, sold under this contract infringe any patent of Canada, and the Seller shall pay all damages and costs awarded therein against the Buyer. In the event that the goods, or part thereof, are in such a suit held to constitute an infringement and use of the goods, or part thereof, is enjoined for the intended use, the Seller shall, at its expense and option:

    i. procure for the Buyer the right to continue using the same;
    ii. replace the same with noninfringing goods or part thereof;
    iii. modify the same so as to eliminate infringement; or
    iv. remove the same and refund the purchase price (less reasonable depreciation for any period of use) and any transportation costs and installation costs paid by the Buyer.

B. The preceding paragraph shall not apply to any goods, or any part thereof, manufactured to the Buyer's design. As to such goods, or part, the Seller assumes no liability whatsoever for infringement.
C. The rights and obligations of the parties with respect to patents or any other industrial property rights are solely and exclusively as stated herein, and the foregoing states the entire liability of the Seller for patent infringement.

WARRANTIES

A. The Seller warrants to the Buyer that the goods manufactured by the Seller will be free from defects in material, workmanship, and title and will be of the kind and quality described in the contract.
B. If a failure to meet any of the foregoing warranties, except as to title, appears within one year from the date of shipment or within one year after completion of installation, if the latter is supervised by or performed by the Seller, and provided that completion of installation is not unreasonably delayed by the Buyer, then the Buyer shall not be entitled to terminate or rescind this contract, but the Seller shall correct any such failure by either, at its option, repairing any defective or damaged part or parts of the goods or by making available, FOB Seller's plant or other points of shipment, any necessary repaired or replacement part or parts. Where a failure cannot be corrected by the Seller's reasonable efforts, the parties shall negotiate an equitable adjustment in price. In the event of a failure to meet the warranty as to title, the Buyer shall not be entitled to elect to terminate or rescind this contract but the Seller shall correct such failure. The foregoing sets out the Seller's sole obligation for failure to comply with the foregoing warranties. The Seller shall have no obligation whatsoever and the Buyer

shall have no right to make a claim against the Seller in respect of the failure to meet any of the foregoing warranties, except as to title, which appears after the one-year period set out in this clause.

C. The obligations set forth in this clause are conditional upon:

    i. proper storage, installation (except where installation is supervised by or performed by the Seller), use, maintenance, and compliance with any applicable recommendations of the Seller; and

    ii. the Buyer promptly notifying the Seller of any defect and, if required, promptly making the goods available for correction.

D. There is no warranty whatsoever with respect to goods normally consumed in operation or that have a normal life shorter than the warranty period set out in this clause.

E. With respect to goods not manufactured by the Seller (except for integral parts of the goods sold, to which the warranties given in this clause shall apply), the Seller gives no warranty whatsoever, and only the warranty, if any, given by the manufacturer shall apply.

F. The foregoing is exclusive and in lieu of all other warranties and conditions, regardless of whether they be oral, written, express, or implied by statute, including the implied conditions of reasonable fitness for purpose, merchantability, and correspondence with description.

LIMITATION OF LIABILITY

A. In no event, whether as a result of a breach of contract or a tort (including negligence), shall the Seller be liable to the Buyer for:

    i. loss of profit or revenue, loss of use, cost of capital, downtime costs, cost of substitute goods, facilities, services, or replacement power;

    ii. property damage external to the product and loss arising out of such damage;

    iii. special or consequential damages; and

    iv. any of the foregoing suffered by a customer of the Buyer.

B. Except as may be provided in the Patents clause (Clause 10), in no event, whether as a result of a breach of contract or a tort (including negligence) shall the liability of the Seller to the Buyer exceed the price of the goods, or part thereof or to the service, which gives rise to the claim.

C. If the Buyer transfers title to or leases the goods sold hereunder to, or otherwise permits or suffers use by, any third party, Buyer shall obtain from such third party a provision affording Seller and its suppliers the protection of paragraph A.

D. If the Seller furnishes Buyer with advice or other assistance that concerns the goods supplied hereunder or any system or equipment in which any such goods may be installed and which is not required pursuant to an express term of this contract, the furnishing of such advice or assistance is done without any assumption of responsibility or liability therefore, and the Buyer shall not institute a claim in contract or in tort (including negligence) arising out of or in any way connected therewith.

GENERAL

A. Unless otherwise stated in this contract, the goods shall be installed by and at the expense of the Buyer.
B. The delegation or assignment by the Buyer of any or all of its duties or rights without the Seller's prior written consent shall be void.
C. No waiver, alteration, or modification of any of the provisions of this contract shall be binding on the Seller unless it is in writing and signed by a duly authorized representative of the Seller.
D. Any goods sold shall comply with federal and provincial laws and regulations applicable to the manufacture, packing, and shipment of such goods as of the date of the Seller's proposal and shall comply with any amendments thereto that may have come into effect prior to the time such goods are shipped, provided that the price and, if necessary, delivery shall be equitably adjusted to compensate the Seller for having to comply with such amendments.
E. The invalidity, in whole or in part, of any of the foregoing clauses will not affect the remainder of such clauses or any other clauses in this contract.
F. Any reference to "goods" in this contract shall, where the context requires, be a reference to a single chattel personal or to a part of such single chattel personal.
G. No trade usage or course of dealing will be binding on the Seller unless specifically referred to in the contract.
H. This contract and any amendments thereto shall be governed in all respects including, but not limited to, validity, interpretation, and effect, by the laws of the Province of Ontario and of Canada.

EXHIBIT A. PRICE ADJUSTMENT CLAUSE (MANUFACTURING ONLY)

All prices stated herein are subject to adjustments, upon completion of this agreement, for changes in labor and material costs. Such adjustments, involving increases or decreases in the prices stated herein, are to be determined in accordance with the following.

Labor

A. For the purpose of adjustment, the proportion of the price representing labor is accepted as 50 percent thereof.
B. The above amount accepted as representing labor will be adjusted for changes in labor cost. Such adjustment will be based upon the Index Numbers of the *Average Hourly Earnings in the Electrical Industrial Equipment Manufacturing Industry,* published monthly by Statistics Canada.

Material

A. For the purpose of adjustment, the proportion of the price representing material is accepted as 40 percent thereof.
B. The above amount accepted as representing material will be adjusted for changes in material costs. Such adjustment will be based upon the *Combined Index of Wholesale Prices for Iron and Non-Ferrous Metals Groups* (excluding gold), or any similar mutually agreed-upon index published monthly by Statistics Canada.

The averages of the monthly indices for labor and material referred to above for the period from a date six months preceding shipment to date of shipment of order under this agreement will be computed separately, and percentage increases or decreases will be established for labor and material by comparison with corresponding indices in effect at the time this proposal was made in the month of _____.

The adjustments for changes in labor and material will be obtained by applying the respective percentages of increase or decrease to the amounts covering labor and material as specified above, and the results will be accepted as an increase or decrease in the aforementioned price.

If Field Construction is involved, refer to Price Adjustment Clause for Field Labor.

EXHIBIT B. PRICE ADJUSTMENT PROVISIONS

Upon completion of the work, the total contract price for the apparatus to be supplied under this contract shall be subject to an increase or decrease due to fluctuation in the cost of material and/or labor. Adjustments shall be determined in accordance with the following, and the results shall be accepted as an increase or decrease in the contract price.

Labor

A. For the purpose of adjustment, the proportion of the contract price representing labor is accepted as 50 percent.
B. The amount so accepted as representing labor will be adjusted for changes in labor costs. Such adjustment will be based upon Table 18 "Average Hourly Earnings, Machinery—Except Electrical, Canada" as shown in *Employment Earnings and Hours,* published monthly by Statistics Canada. An average of those published monthly/hourly earnings for the period from a date six months before complete shipment to the date complete shipment of the apparatus is made from the company's works will be calculated, and the percentage increase or decrease will be calculated by a comparison with such published hourly earnings for the month during which the company's tender was submitted. The adjustment for changes in labor costs will be obtained by applying such percentage of increase or decrease to the amount representing labor above mentioned.

Material

A. For the purpose of adjustment, the proportion of the contract price representing material is accepted as _____ percent hereof.
B. The amount so accepted as representing material will be adjusted for changes in material costs. Such adjustment will be based upon Table 2 "General Wholesale Index—Iron Products (1,935 2 39 5 100)" as shown in *Industry Price Indexes,* published monthly by Statistics Canada. An average of those published indexes for the period from the date six months before complete shipment to the date complete shipment of the apparatus is made from the company's works will be computed, and the percentage increase or decrease will be calculated by a comparison with such published index for the month during which the company's tender was submitted. The adjustment for changes in material costs will be obtained by applying such percentage of increase or decrease to the amount representing material previously mentioned.

Subcontract

To carry out this contract, the company will purchase the components or material listed below, which may increase or decrease in price due to increases or decreases in the cost of labor or material. The Purchaser shall reimburse the company the amount of any increase and the company shall credit the Purchaser the amount of any decrease due to such adjustment from date of submission of the company's tender.

EXHIBIT C. PRICE ADJUSTMENT CLAUSE (FIELD LABOR ONLY)

Prices stated herein applicable to construction or assembly of the equipment provided, at the Purchaser's site, are subject to adjustments upon completion of this agreement for changes in labor costs. Such adjustments, involving increases or decreases in the prices stated herein, are to be determined in accordance with the following.

Field Labor

A. For the purpose of adjustment, the proportion of the price representing labor is accepted as _____ percent thereof.
B. The above amount accepted as representing labor will be adjusted for changes in labor cost. Such adjustment will be based upon the *Average Hourly Earnings in the Construction Industry, Other Engineering Group* published monthly by Statistics Canada, for the area of _____.

The monthly average hourly earnings for labor referred to above for the period of construction under this agreement will be computed separately, and percentage increases or decreases will be established for labor by comparison with corresponding average hourly earnings in effect at the time this proposal was made in the month of _____.

The adjustments for changes in labor will be obtained by applying the respective percentage of increase or decrease to the amounts covering labor as specified above, and the result will be accepted as an increase or decrease in the aforementioned price.

Appendix I

Sample Distributorship Agreement

This Distributorship Agreement is entered into this day of between ABC
2 Company, hereinafter referred to as "Company," having its principal place
of business at Naples, Florida, and XYZ Company of Mexico City, Mexico,
hereinafter referred to as "Distributor."

DEFINITIONS

A. *Product(s):* Product or products refers to products manufactured or
   marketed by the company, that including spare parts which are listed
   in Exhibit A. Exhibit A is subject to change by mutual agreement of
   the parties.
B. *Territory:* Territory shall mean the geographical area designated under Exhibit B. Exhibit B may be revised from time to time by mutual
   agreement of the parties.
C. *Contract year:* Contract year shall mean the period commencing January
   1 and ending on December 31. The first contract year shall commence
   as of the date of this contract, and subsequent years shall commence
   on January 1 thereafter.
D. *Trade terms:* Trade terms such as FOB, CIF, etc., shall be interpreted
   according to the latest version of International Chamber of Commerce (ICC) Rules.
E. *Purchaser:* Purchaser shall mean a purchaser of goods for consumption and not for resale as a distributor.

APPOINTMENT AND ACCEPTANCE

A. Company hereby appoints Distributor as the sole importer-distributor
   of products in the territory and Distributor accepts such appointment.

Export-Import Theory, Practices, and Procedures, Second Edition

B. Company shall not appoint any third person to import, sell, or otherwise deal with products in the territory during the time when the agreement is in effect.

TERM OF THE AGREEMENT

The term of this agreement shall be from _____ to _____ unless sooner terminated or further extended as hereinafter provided.

MINIMUM ANNUAL PURCHASES

Distributor shall purchase from Company during the contract year such minimum dollar or unit amount of products as specified in Exhibit C attached thereto. Minimum sales for subsequent periods shall be specified in an addendum to this agreement. Should no agreement be reached between the parties, the minimum annual sales for the new contract year shall be deemed to be percent of the minimum annual sales for the preceding contract year.

PRICES FOR THE PRODUCTS

A. Company reserves the right to establish or revise at its sole discretion, from time to time, upon thirty days, prices and terms of its sales of products to distributor, including the right at any time to issue new price lists and to change the prices, terms, and provisions therein contained. The price to be paid by the Distributor, excluding spare parts, shall be the price quoted on the Company's current international price list, less a discount of 12 percent.
B. Company shall provide an additional discount of 3 percent when Distributor takes responsibility at the company's request to service products during the guarantee period. Company shall provide replacement parts free of charge to Distributor during the guarantee period.
C. Distributor shall bear the cost of freight, insurance, and duties for such parts. Distributor shall make no charge for the replacement parts to customer.
D. After the end of the guarantee period, spare parts shall be sold to Distributor at the company's current international price, less a discount of 20 percent.

PAYMENTS TO DISTRIBUTOR FOR DIRECT SALES

A. Where the Company sells products direct to a customer, the Company shall pay Distributor such commission as is agreed between the parties. In the event that no specific commission is agreed, company shall pay Distributor 8 percent of the net selling price for the products.
B. Any sums earned by Distributor shall be paid by Company thirty days after receipt by the Company of payment for any such order, provided that no such sums shall be payable by the Company to Distributor in respect of any orders received by the Company after termination of this agreement, except where orders are accepted from potential customers within six months after termination of this agreement and at the time of termination the Distributor has provided the Company with a written list of such potential customers, including evidence to show potential customer's communication and intent to buy the products.

GOVERNMENT LICENSES AND PERMITS

The Company shall secure the necessary licenses and permits for the sale and export of the products. It is also incumbent on the Distributor to obtain the necessary licenses and permits required for purchase and importation of the products.

INTELLECTUAL PROPERTY RIGHTS

A. The Distributor shall not remove or obliterate any marks or symbols affixed on the goods without the written permission of the Company. A small label bearing the words "supplied by" together with the name and address of the Distributor, shall be applied to the goods.
B. The Distributor shall advertise the goods solely under the trademarks of the Company. However, it shall not act in any manner, whether by advertising or other means, that might adversely affect the validity of any intellectual property rights belonging to the Company.
C. The Distributor shall, at all times, do all in its power to protect the Company's intellectual property rights and shall ensure that the same remain connected only with the products as defined in this agreement and as the Company may indicate from time to time.
D. The Distributor shall notify the Company in writing as soon as it becomes aware of any infringements of the latter's intellectual property rights in the territory. The Distributor shall bring an action to prevent

infringement of such rights at the Company's expense. However, the Company shall not be liable for any infringement caused by the actions of the Distributor.

WARRANTY AND LIABILITY

A. The Company guarantees that products sold to Distributor are free from defects in material and workmanship and agrees to reimburse all costs of repairs, including reasonably necessary related labor charges, or, at Company's option, to replace any or all defective products within the period of such warranty.
B. The period of the warranty shall extend for one year after the date of sale to the customer for products and ninety days from the date of sale to customer for parts. The Company shall not be liable for the acts or defaults of the Distributor, its employees, or its representatives.

UNDERTAKINGS BY THE DISTRIBUTOR

A. Distributor agrees to be responsible for supplying or making arrangements for supplying all necessary service to products in the territory, and this includes using its best efforts to provide the best possible service for all owners of products. The Distributor shall hire an adequate number of technicians in order to provide such services promptly.
B. Distributor shall purchase and maintain such volume and assortment of parts as may be necessary to satisfy the service needs of customers.
C. Distributor shall use its best efforts to promote the sales of the goods in its territory as well as maintain adequate staff of salespeople to carry out such responsibility.
D. If at any time during the continuance of this agreement, the Distributor shall become entitled to any development, improvement, or invention relating to any of the products, the Distributor shall give notice in writing to Company and grant to the Company a first option to acquire rights with respect to such invention.
E. The Distributor shall spend a reasonable sum each year on promoting the product in the territory. The Company may make a contribution toward such costs.
F. The Distributor shall assist the Company to produce sales literature in the language of the territory and also provide the Company any sales literature prepared by it relating to the products.

G. The Distributor shall provide Company detailed reports of sales every ninety days, general market information in the territory, and suggestions for any improvements in December of each year.

H. The Distributor shall refrain from purporting to act as an agent of the Company unless otherwise specified in the agreement. In addition, Distributor shall not make any contracts binding the company, warehouse, or advertise the goods outside its territory as well as get involved in the manufacture, production, sale, or advertising of competing goods in the territory.

I. The Distributor shall not transfer or assign the benefit of this agreement to any third party without the prior written consent of the Company.

UNDERTAKINGS BY THE COMPANY

The Company agrees to undertake the following responsibilities:

A. Assist the Distributor in advertising the goods by providing the necessary advice and literature as it considers reasonably sufficient to promote the goods in the territory.

B. Support the Distributor in its sales and technical efforts by paying regular visits to the territory of experienced personnel. In the event that a technician is sent to assist the Distributor, the Distributor shall be responsible for traveling expenses to and from the territory, all local traveling expenses, accommodation, and reasonable subsistence costs in the territory.

C. Provide the Distributor with maintenance and servicing instructions and other documentation as well as information on technical changes that are necessary and relevant in connection with the products. The Company may provide appropriate training to suitable qualified technicians of the Distributor that is necessary to install, maintain, or service the products. The parties will determine in due course where the training will take place as well as matters pertaining to expenses.

TERMINATION

This agreement may be terminated by a written instrument duly executed by the parties if any of the following situations arise:

A. Either party commits any breach of contract and in the case of a breach capable of being remedied, the party does not remedy the same within sixty days after receipt of notice in writing of such breach.

B. Either party becomes insolvent or goes into liquidation or has a receiver appointed in respect of all or a substantial part of its business.
C. Payment of any sum remains unpaid to either party for a period of thirty days after the due date.

The innocent party may forthwith, by notice in writing, terminate this agreement. Any such termination shall be without prejudice to the rights of the parties accrued up to the date of termination. Neither party will be responsible, by reason of termination of this agreement, to the other for compensation or damages on account of any loss of prospective profits on anticipated sales or on account of expenditures, investments, leases, or other commitments relating to the business or goodwill of either party.

Within thirty days after the termination or expiration of this agreement, company may, at its option, repurchase from distributor, at the latter's net warehouse cost, any or all products and/or parts that are commercially usable or salable as well as any usable advertising or promotional materials. Distributor shall return any packaging or promotional materials that were provided by Company free of charge. Distributor shall cease all use of the name and trademark of Company.

FORCE MAJEURE

The occurrence of certain events that make the continuance of this agreement impossible, such as riots, government restrictions, or other events outside the reasonable control of the party, shall not constitute a breach of this agreement.

AGREEMENT AND INTERPRETATION

A. This agreement and its annexes constitute the whole of the agreement between the Company and Distributor with respect to the products. No variation, alteration, or abandonment of any of its terms shall have effect unless made in writing by the Distributor or its duly authorized representative and by the Company or its duly authorized representative.
B. This agreement shall be construed in accordance with U.S. law.
C. The illegality or invalidity of any part of this agreement shall not affect the legality or validity of the remainder thereof.
D. The headings are for reference purposes only and shall not affect the interpretation of this agreement.

LIST OF EXHIBITS

A. Products
B. Territory
C. Minimum annual purchases
D. Price list
E. Initial order
F. Intellectual property rights

Signed for ABC Company by   Signed for XYZ distributor by

_____   _____

In the presence of   In the presence of

_____   _____

Appendix J

Sample Sales Representative Agreement

MEMORANDUM OF AGREEMENT entered into in duplicate, this _____ day of _____.

BETWEEN: _____ duly incorporated under the laws of Canada, having its head office and principal place of business at Toronto, Province of Ontario (hereinafter referred to as party of the first part, PFP).

AND: A body politic and corporate, having its head office and place of business in _____ (hereinafter called the Sales Representative).

WITNESSETH THAT in consideration of the premises and of the mutual covenant and agreements hereinafter contained, the parties hereto agree each with the other as follows:

PFP hereby engages the Sales Representative to provide services in accordance with the terms and conditions of this Agreement for the sale of proprietary products (hereinafter called Equipment) listed in Schedule attached hereto and made an integral part hereof to markets in (hereinafter called Served Market).

TERRITORY

The geographical area (hereinafter called Territory) in which the Sales Representative shall undertake the responsibilities specified in this Agreement is _____.

TERMS AND SCOPE

The term of this Agreement shall be from _____ to _____ unless sooner terminated as hereinafter provided. The provisions of this Agree-

Export-Import Theory, Practices, and Procedures, Second Edition

ment shall govern all transactions between PFP and the Sales Representative unless otherwise agreed to in writing by the duly authorized representatives of both parties.

COMPANY RESPONSIBILITIES

PFP agrees that during the term of this Agreement, it will, subject to and in accordance with the terms and conditions herein expressed:

A. keep the Sales Representative advised of new products, sales plans, and objectives with respect to Equipment for Served Market Customers in the Territory;
B. support the sales efforts of the Sales Representative by furnishing printed commercial and technical data and information and other publications that PFP may have available from time to time for export distribution; and
C. pay a commission as provided in Article 5 hereof on orders for Equipment received and accepted by PFP from Served Market Customers in the Territory as a result of the effort of the Sales Representative. As used in this Agreement, the terms "order" or "orders" include contracts for Equipment with Served Market Customers in the Territory executed by PFP.

SALES REPRESENTATIVE RESPONSIBILITIES

The Sales Representative agrees that during the term of this Agreement, it will, subject to the terms and conditions herein expressed:

A. maintain an adequate sales organization and use its best efforts to assist PFP in the sale of Equipment to Served Market Customers in the Territory;
B. maintain active contacts with Served Market Customers in the Territory;
C. keep PFP fully informed of all governmental, commercial, and industrial activities and plans that do or could affect the sale of Equipment to Served Market Customers in the Territory;
D. provide market information to PFP on Served Market Customers' and competitors' activities;
E. recommend improvements to sales plans, assist in developing strategy, and clarify the Equipment requirements of Served Market Customers in the Territory;

F. as requested, transmit proposals and technical data to Served Market Customers in the Territory, interpret customer inquiries, requirements, and attitudes, and assist in contract negotiations. (All proposals so transmitted will contain terms and conditions of sale substantially in accordance with PFP's Standard Terms and Conditions of Sale, a copy of which is attached hereto and is subject to change by PFP from time to time. No proposal shall be transmitted to a Served Market Customer unless terms and conditions of sale are approved by PFP or the Standard Terms and Conditions of Sale are incorporated in such proposal.); and

G. perform such liaison services with Served Market Customers in the Territory as PFP may from time to time direct relative to any order(s) awarded to PFP from the supply of Equipment, including assistance in the resolution of any claims or complaints of such Customers arising out of PFP's performance of said order(s).

COMPENSATION

A. As compensation to the Sales Representative for services rendered hereunder, PFP agrees to pay the Sales Representative a commission on the following orders for PFP's proprietary equipment from Served Market Customers in the Territory during the term of this Agreement:

   i. Orders that are forwarded by the Sales Representative.

   ii. Orders that the Sales Representative has specifically identified to PFP being forthcoming directly from a Served Market Customer in the Territory when, in the absolute judgment of PFP such commission may be warranted by the effort used by the Sales Representative resulting in said orders.

B. The commission, based on the net sale price (FOB factory), will be paid in accordance with the Schedule(s) attached hereto and made an integral part of this Agreement.

C. Said commission shall be disbursed in Canadian dollars to the Sales Representative within thirty days subsequent to the payment for the Equipment delivered to the Served Market Customer in accordance with the terms of payment established and accepted in the contract between PFP and the Served Market Customer.

D. No commissions will be paid on the value of technical, construction, installation, or similar services, nor on the value of insurance, bonds, interest, ocean freight, or other charges that may be included in the PFP's invoice to a Served Market Customer.

E. It is understood that if an order should be rescinded, revoked, or repudiated by a Served Market Customer for reasons beyond PFP's control or by PFP for breach of contract or by either party for force majeure causes, or it becomes invalid or inoperative due to any governmental regulation, the Sales Representative shall not be entitled to a commission with respect to such order, except pro rata to the extent of any amounts PFP may have received and retained as payment for Equipment delivered to a Served Market Customer.

F. It is further understood that no compensation, by way of commission or otherwise, shall be due the Sales Representative in connection with an order on which a commission would otherwise be payable, if as to such an order:

i. any applicable governmental law, rule, or regulation prohibits or makes improper the payment of any commission, fee, or other payment to a Sales Representative;

ii. any Served Market Customer makes it a condition that no commission, fee, or payment be made to a Sales Representative; or

iii. any action has been taken by the Sales Representative in violation of its commitments set forth in Article 6, paragraphs C and D.

RELATIONSHIP OF PARTIES AND CONTROLLING LAWS

A. PFP may assign the installation and commissioning portion of its contract to the Sales Representative but, except as aforesaid, this Agreement and any rights hereunder are nonexclusive and nonassignable, and any assignment by one party without the prior written consent of the other party shall be void. The Sales Representative is an independent contractor to PFP. It is understood that the Sales Representative or its agents, subsidiaries, affiliates, and employees are in no way the legal representatives or agents of PFP for any purpose whatsoever and have no right or authority to assume or create, in writing or otherwise, any obligation of any kind, expressed or implied, in the name of or on behalf of PFP. PFP reserves the right to determine in its sole discretion the acceptability of any order, any provisions thereof, or any condition proposed by the customer and shall in no way be obligated to bid, quote to, or negotiate with any Served Market Customer.

B. This Agreement and any services hereunder are subject to and shall be governed by all the applicable laws and regulations of Canada; the rights and obligations of the Sales Representative as well as those of PFP under or in connection with this Agreement shall be governed by such laws and regulations and by the law of the Province of Ontario, Canada.

C. The Sales Representative agrees to comply with the law applicable to the performance of its obligations under the terms of this Agreement. Without limitation to the foregoing, the Sales Representative will comply fully with the export control laws and regulations of the Canadian Government with respect to the disposition of products and the printed commercial and technical data and information and other publications supplied by PFP. Further, the Sales Representative agrees that it will not pay, nor will it make any offer or commitment to pay, anything of value (either in the form of compensation, gift, contribution, or otherwise) to any employee, representative, person or organization in any way connected with any Customer, private or governmental, where such payment is contrary to applicable law, including the laws of Canada and the laws of the country in which the Sales Representative provides services under this Agreement.

D. With respect to any transaction arising under this Agreement, it is specifically understood and agreed that neither the Sales Representative nor its employees or representatives shall receive any payments in the nature of a rebate or similar benefit paid directly or indirectly by the Customer, nor shall any employee or representative of PFP receive any such payment paid directly or indirectly by the Sales Representative or by the Customer.

EXPIRATION, RENEWAL, TERMINATION

A. This Agreement shall automatically expire at the end of the term specified in Article 2 hereof unless specifically renewed prior thereto by mutual consent given in writing by the parties hereto.

B. This Agreement may be terminated prior to the completion of the term specified in Article 2 hereof:
   i. by mutual consent given in writing by the parties hereto;
   ii. by either party at will, with or without cause, upon no less than sixty days notice in writing by registered mail, cable, or personal delivery to the other party; or
   iii. by PFP upon one day's similar notice in the event the Sales Representative attempts to assign this Agreement or any right hereunder without PFP's prior written consent; there is a change in the control or management of the Sales Representative that is unacceptable to PFP; the Sales Representative ceases to conduct its operations in the normal course of business; a receiver for the Sales Representative

is appointed or applied for or it otherwise takes advantage of an insolvency law; the Sales Representative represents other parties whose representation, in PFP's opinion, involves a conflict with the Sales Representative's obligations hereunder; or the Sales Representative breaches this Agreement or acts in any manner deemed by PFP to be detrimental to the best interest of PFP. The foregoing events shall without limitation be deemed to be cause for termination by PFP.

OBLIGATIONS UPON EXPIRATION OR TERMINATION

In the event that an order from any Served Market Customer in the Territory for the supply of Equipment is accepted by PFP prior to the date of expiration or termination of this Agreement, the obligations assumed by both parties hereunder with respect to any such order shall continue in force until fully performed. In the event this Agreement expires or is terminated, and within from the date of such expiration or termination an order from a Served Market Customer in the Territory for the supply of Equipment is accepted by PFP and is implemented within said period by financial arrangements acceptable to PFP, the Sales Representative's rights to commission payments will be fully protected, provided such purchase order is awarded in the sole opinion of PFP as a result of services performed by the Sales Representative prior to the effective date of expiration or termination. Such acceptance of an order from, or the sale of any Equipment to, a Served Market Customer after the expiration or termination of this Agreement shall not be construed as a renewal or extension hereof, but the obligations undertaken in this Article 8 shall survive such expiration or termination.

PRIVATE INFORMATION

A. The Sales Representative shall maintain in confidence and safeguard all business and technical information that becomes available to it in connection with this Agreement, the information being either of proprietary nature or not intended for disclosure to others. This obligation shall continue for five years after expiration or termination of this Agreement.

B. Knowledge or information of any kind disclosed by the Sales Representative to PFP shall be deemed to have been disclosed without obligation on the part of PFP to hold the same in confidence, and PFP shall have full right to use and disclose such information, subject to the approval of the Sales Representative, whose approval shall not be withheld without proper cause and without any compensation to the Sales Representative beyond that specifically provided by this Agreement.

COMPANY TRADEMARKS AND TRADE NAMES

The Sales Representative agrees that it will comply at all times with the rules and regulations furnished to the Sales Representative by PFP with respect to the use of and trademarks and trade names; it will express and identify properly the "Authorized Sales Representative" relationship with PFP for Equipment; it will not publish or cause to be published any statement, nor encourage or approve any advertising or practice, that might mislead or deceive any parties or might be detrimental to the good name, trademark, goodwill, or reputation of PFP or its products. The Sales Representative further agrees upon request to withdraw any statement and discontinue any advertising or practice deemed by PFP to have such effect.

LIMITATION OF LIABILITY

Neither party to this agreement shall have liability to the other with respect to the claims arising out of, in connection with, or resulting from this agreement, whether in contract, tort (including negligence of any degree), or otherwise except as provided under the terms of this agreement.

RELEASE OF CLAIMS

In consideration of the execution of this Agreement by PFP, the Sales Representative hereby releases PFP from all claims, demands, contracts, and liabilities, if any thereby, as of the date of execution of this Agreement by the Sales Representative, except indebtedness that may be owing founded upon a written contract.

FAILURE TO ENFORCE

The failure of either party to enforce at any time or for any period of time the provisions hereof in accordance with its terms shall not be construed to be a waiver of such provisions or of the right of such party thereafter to enforce each and every provision.

NOTICES

Any notice, request, demand, direction, or other communication required or permitted to be given or made under this agreement or in connection therewith shall be deemed to have been properly given or made if delivered to the party to whom it is addressed, or by registered mail, telegram, cable, or telex addressed as follows.

EXECUTION AND MODIFICATION

A. This Agreement constitutes the entire and only agreement between the parties respecting the sales representation to the Served Market of Equipment specified herein.
B. This Agreement wholly cancels, terminates, and supersedes any and all previous negotiations, commitments, and writing between the parties with respect to Equipment. No change, modification, extension, renewal, ratification, rescission, termination, notice of termination, discharge, abandonment, or waiver of this Agreement or any of the provisions hereof nor any representation, promise, or condition relating to this Agreement shall be binding upon PFP unless made in writing and signed by duly authorized personnel of PFP,

IN WITNESS WHEREOF, this agreement has been executed by both parties.

Appendix K

North American
Free Trade Agreement

Between the Government of the United States of America, the Government of Canada, and the Government of the United Mexican States (Selected Provisions) Effective January 1, 1994

PART ONE: GENERAL PART

Article 101: Establishment of the Free Trade Area

The Parties to this Agreement, consistent with Article XXIV of the *General Agreement on Tariffs and Trade,* hereby establish a free trade area.

Article 103: Relation to Other Agreements

1. The Parties affirm their existing rights and obligations with respect to each other under the *General Agreement on Tariffs and Trade* and other agreements to which such Parties are party.
2. In the event of any inconsistency between this Agreement and such other agreements, this Agreement shall prevail to the extent of the inconsistency, except as otherwise provided in this Agreement.

Document obtained from the United States Trade Representative (2007). North American Free Trade Agreement. Available at http://www.ustr.gov/Trade_Agreements/Regional/NAFTA/Section_Index.html.

Export-Import Theory, Practices, and Procedures, Second Edition

PART TWO: TRADE IN GOODS

Article 301: National Treatment

1. Each Party shall accord national treatment to the goods of another Party in accordance with Article III of the *General Agreement on Tariffs and Trade* (GATT), including its interpretative notes, and to this end Article III of the GATT and its interpretative notes, or any equivalent provision of a successor agreement to which all Parties are party, are incorporated into and made part of this Agreement.
2. The provisions of paragraph 1 regarding national treatment shall mean, with respect to a state or province, treatment no less favorable than the most favorable treatment accorded by such state or province to any like, directly competitive or substitutable goods, as the case may be, of the Party of which it forms a part.
3. Paragraphs 1 and 2 do not apply to the measures set out in Annex 301.3.

Article 302: Tariff Elimination

1. Except as otherwise provided in this Agreement, no Party may increase any existing customs duty, or adopt any customs duty, on an originating good.
2. Except as otherwise provided in this Agreement, each Party shall progressively eliminate its customs duties on originating goods in accordance with its Schedule to Annex 302.2.
3. On the request of any Party, the Parties shall consult to consider accelerating the elimination of customs duties set out in their Schedules. An agreement between two or more Parties to accelerate the elimination of a customs duty on a good shall supersede any duty rate or staging category determined pursuant to their Schedules for such good when approved by each such Party in accordance with its applicable legal procedures.
4. Each Party may adopt or maintain import measures to allocate in-quota imports made pursuant to a tariff rate quota set out in Annex 302.2, provided that such measures do not have trade restrictive effects on imports additional to those caused by the imposition of the tariff rate quota.
5. On written request of any Party, a Party applying or intending to apply measures pursuant to paragraph 4 shall consult to review the administration of those measures.

Article 305: Temporary Admission of Goods

1. Each Party shall grant duty-free temporary admission for:
   - (a) professional equipment necessary for carrying out the business activity, trade, or profession of a business person who qualifies for temporary entry pursuant to Chapter 16 (Temporary Entry for Business Persons),
   - (b) equipment for the press or for sound or television broadcasting and cinematographic equipment,
   - (c) goods imported for sports purposes and goods intended for display or demonstration, and
   - (d) commercial samples and advertising films, imported from the territory of another Party, regardless of their origin and regardless of whether like, directly competitive, or substitutable goods are available in the territory of the Party.
2. Except as otherwise provided in this Agreement, no Party may condition the duty-free temporary admission of a good referred to in paragraph 1(a), (b), or (c), other than to require that such good:
   - (a) be imported by a national or resident of another Party who seeks temporary entry;
   - (b) be used solely by or under the personal supervision of such person in the exercise of the business activity, trade, or profession of that person;
   - (c) not be sold or leased while in its territory;
   - (d) be accompanied by a bond in an amount no greater than 110 percent of the charges that would otherwise be owed on entry or final importation, or by another form of security, releasable on exportation of the good, except that a bond for customs duties shall not be required for an originating good;
   - (e) be capable of identification when exported;
   - (f) be exported on the departure of that person or within such other period of time as is reasonably related to the purpose of the temporary admission; and
   - (g) be imported in no greater quantity than is reasonable for its intended use.
3. Except as otherwise provided in this Agreement, no Party may condition the duty-free temporary admission of a good referred to in paragraph 1(d), other than to require that such good:
   - (a) be imported solely for the solicitation of orders for goods, or services provided from the territory, of another Party or non-Party;
   - (b) not be sold, leased, or put to any use other than exhibition or demonstration while in its territory;

    (c) be capable of identification when exported;

    (d) be exported within such period as is reasonably related to the purpose of the temporary admission; and

    (e) be imported in no greater quantity than is reasonable for its intended use.

4. A Party may impose the customs duty and any other charge on a good temporarily admitted duty-free under paragraph 1 that would be owed on entry or final importation of such good if any condition that the Party imposes under paragraph 2 or 3 has not been fulfilled.

5. Subject to Chapters 11 (Investment) and 12 (Cross-Border Trade in Services):

    (a) each Party shall allow a vehicle or container used in international traffic that enters its territory from the territory of another Party to exit its territory on any route that is reasonably related to the economic and prompt departure of such vehicle or container;

    (b) no Party may require any bond or impose any penalty or charge solely by reason of any difference between the port of entry and the port of departure of a vehicle or container;

    (c) no Party may condition the release of any obligation, including any bond, that it imposes in respect of the entry of a vehicle or container into its territory on its exit through any particular port of departure; and

    (e) no Party may require that the vehicle or carrier bringing a container from the territory of another Party into its territory be the same vehicle or carrier that takes such container to the territory of another Party.

6. For purposes of paragraph 5, "vehicle" means a truck, a truck tractor, tractor, trailer unit or trailer, a locomotive, or a railway car or other railroad equipment.

Article 306: Duty-Free Entry of Certain Commercial Samples and Printed Advertising Materials

    Each Party shall grant duty-free entry to commercial samples of negligible value, and to printed advertising materials, imported from the territory of another Party, regardless of their origin, but may require that:

    (a) such samples be imported solely for the solicitation of orders for goods, or services provided from the territory, of another Party or non-Party; or

    (b) such advertising materials be imported in packets that each contain no more than one copy of each such material and that neither such materials nor packets form part of a larger consignment.

Article 307: Goods Re-Entered after Repair or Alteration

1. Except as set out in Annex 307.1, no Party may apply a customs duty to a good, regardless of its origin, that re-enters its territory after that good has been exported from its territory to the territory of another Party for repair or alteration, regardless of whether such repair or alteration could be performed in its territory.
2. Notwithstanding Article 303, no Party may apply a customs duty to a good, regardless of its origin, imported temporarily from the territory of another Party for repair or alteration.
3. Annex 307.3 applies to the Parties specified in that Annex respecting the repair and rebuilding of vessels.

Article 309: Import and Export Restrictions

1. Except as otherwise provided in this Agreement, no Party may adopt or maintain any prohibition or restriction on the importation of any good of another Party or on the exportation or sale for export of any good destined for the territory of another Party, except in accordance with Article XI of the GATT, including its interpretative notes, and to this end Article XI of the GATT and its interpretative notes, or any equivalent provision of a successor agreement to which all Parties are party, are incorporated into and made a part of this Agreement.
2. The Parties understand that the GATT rights and obligations incorporated by paragraph 1 prohibit, in any circumstances in which any other form of restriction is prohibited, export price requirements and, except as permitted in enforcement of countervailing and antidumping orders and undertakings, import price requirements.
3. In the event that a Party adopts or maintains a prohibition or restriction on the importation from or exportation to a non-Party of a good, nothing in this Agreement shall be construed to prevent the Party from:
   (a) limiting or prohibiting the importation from the territory of another Party of such good of that non-Party; or
   (b) requiring as a condition of export of such good of the Party to the territory of another Party, that the good not be re-exported to the non-Party, directly or indirectly, without being consumed in the territory of the other Party.
4. In the event that a Party adopts or maintains a prohibition or restriction on the importation of a good from a non-Party, the Parties, on request of any Party, shall consult with a view to avoiding undue interference with or distortion of pricing, marketing and distribution arrangements in another Party.

5. Paragraphs 1 through 4 shall not apply to the measures set out in Annex 301.3.

Article 316: Consultations and Committee on Trade in Goods

1. The Parties hereby establish a Committee on Trade in Goods, comprising representatives of each Party.
2. The Committee shall meet on the request of any Party or the Commission to consider any matter arising under this chapter.
3. The Parties shall convene at least once each year a meeting of their officials responsible for customs, immigration, inspection of food and agricultural products, border inspection facilities, and regulation of transportation for the purpose of addressing issues related to movement of goods through the Parties' ports of entry.

CHAPTER 4. RULES OF ORIGIN

Article 401: Originating Goods

Except as otherwise provided in this chapter, a good shall originate in the territory of a Party where:

(a) the good is wholly obtained or produced entirely in the territory of one or more of the Parties, as defined in Article 415;

(b) each of the non-originating materials used in the production of the good undergoes an applicable change in tariff classification set out in Annex 401 as a result of production occurring entirely in the territory of one or more of the Parties, or the good otherwise satisfies the applicable requirements of that Annex where no change in tariff classification is required, and the good satisfies all other applicable requirements of this chapter;

(c) the good is produced entirely in the territory of one or more of the Parties exclusively from originating materials; or

(d) except for a good provided for in Chapters 61 through 63 of the Harmonized System, the good is produced entirely in the territory of one or more of the Parties but one or more of the non-originating materials provided for as parts under the Harmonized System that are used in the production of the good does not undergo a change in tariff classification because

(i) the good was imported into the territory of a Party in an unassembled or a disassembled form but was classified as an assembled good pursuant to General Rule of Interpretation 2(a) of the Harmonized System, or

(ii) the heading for the good provides for and specifically describes both the good itself and its parts and is not further subdivided into subheadings, or the subheading for the good provides for and specifically describes both the good itself and its parts, provided that the regional value content of the good, determined in accordance with Article 402, is not less than 60 percent where the transaction value method is used, or is not less than 50 percent where the net cost method is used, and that the good satisfies all other applicable requirements of this chapter.

CHAPTER 8. EMERGENCY ACTION

Article 801: Bilateral Actions

1. Subject to paragraphs 2 through 4 and Annex 801.1, and during the transition period only, if a good originating in the territory of a Party, as a result of the reduction or elimination of a duty provided for in this Agreement, is being imported into the territory of another Party in such increased quantities, in absolute terms, and under such conditions that the imports of the good from that Party alone constitute a substantial cause of serious injury, or threat thereof, to a domestic industry producing a like or directly competitive good, the Party into whose territory the good is being imported may, to the minimum extent necessary to remedy or prevent the injury:
   (a) suspend the further reduction of any rate of duty provided for under this Agreement on the good;
   (b) increase the rate of duty on the good to a level not to exceed the lesser of
      (i) the most-favored-nation (MFN) applied rate of duty in effect at the time the action is taken, and
      (ii) the MFN applied rate of duty in effect on the day immediately preceding the date of entry into force of this Agreement; or
   (c) in the case of a duty applied to a good on a seasonal basis, increase the rate of duty to a level not to exceed the MFN applied rate of duty that was in effect on the good for the corresponding season immediately preceding the date of entry into force of this Agreement.
2. The following conditions and limitations shall apply to a proceeding that may result in emergency action under paragraph 1:
   (a) a Party shall, without delay, deliver to any Party that may be affected written notice of, and a request for consultations regarding, the institution of a proceeding that could result in emergency action against a good originating in the territory of a Party;

(b) any such action shall be initiated no later than one year after the date of institution of the proceeding;

(c) no action may be maintained

(i) for a period exceeding three years, except where the good against which the action is taken is provided for in the items in staging category C1 of the Schedule to Annex 302.2 of the Party taking the action and that Party determines that the affected industry has undertaken adjustment and requires an extension of the period of relief, in which case the period of relief may be extended for one year provided that the duty applied during the initial period of relief is substantially reduced at the beginning of the extension period, or

(ii) beyond the expiration of the transition period, except with the consent of the Party against whose good the action is taken;

(d) no action may be taken by a Party against any particular good originating in the territory of another Party more than once during the transition period; and

(e) on the termination of the action, the rate of duty shall be the rate that, according to the Party's Schedule to Annex 302.2 for the staged elimination of the tariff, would have been in effect one year after the initiation of the action, and beginning January 1 of the year following the termination of the action, at the option of the Party that has taken the action

(i) the rate of duty shall conform to the applicable rate set out in its Schedule to Annex 302.2, or

(ii) the tariff shall be eliminated in equal annual stages ending on the date set out in its Schedule to Annex 302.2 for the elimination of the tariff.

3. A Party may take a bilateral emergency action after the expiration of the transition period to deal with cases of serious injury, or threat thereof, to a domestic industry arising from the operation of this Agreement only with the consent of the Party against whose good the action would be taken.

4. The Party taking an action under this Article shall provide to the Party against whose good the action is taken mutually agreed trade liberalizing compensation in the form of concessions having substantially equivalent trade effects or equivalent to the value of the additional duties expected to result from the action. If the Parties concerned are unable to agree on compensation, the Party against whose good the action is taken may take tariff action having trade effects substantially equivalent to the action taken under this Article. The Party taking the tariff

action shall apply the action only for the minimum period necessary to achieve the substantially equivalent effects.

Article 802: Global Actions

1. Each Party retains its rights and obligations under Article XIX of the GATT or any safeguard agreement pursuant thereto except those regarding compensation or retaliation and exclusion from an action to the extent that such rights or obligations are inconsistent with this Article. Any Party taking an emergency action under Article XIX or any such agreement shall exclude imports of a good from each other Party from the action unless:
   (a) imports from a Party, considered individually, account for a substantial share of total imports; and
   (b) imports from a Party, considered individually, or in exceptional circumstances imports from Parties considered collectively, contribute importantly to the serious injury, or threat thereof, caused by imports.

PART THREE: TECHNICAL BARRIERS TO TRADE

Article 904: Basic Rights and Obligations

Right to Take Standards-Related Measures

1. Each Party may, in accordance with this Agreement, adopt, maintain, or apply any standards-related measure, including any such measure relating to safety, the protection of human, animal, or plant life or health, the environment or consumers, and any measure to ensure its enforcement or implementation. Such measures include those to prohibit the importation of a good of another Party or the provision of a service by a service provider of another Party that fails to comply with the applicable requirements of those measures or to complete the Party's approval procedures.

Right to Establish Level of Protection

2. Notwithstanding any other provision of this chapter, each Party may, in pursuing its legitimate objectives of safety or the protection of human, animal, or plant life or health, the environment or consumers, establish the levels of protection that it considers appropriate in accordance with Article 907(2).

Non-Discriminatory Treatment

3. Each Party shall, in respect of its standards-related measures, accord to goods and service providers of another Party:
   (a) national treatment in accordance with Article 301 (Market Access) or Article 1202 (Cross-Border Trade in Services); and
   (b) treatment no less favorable than that it accords to like goods, or in like circumstances to service providers, of any other country.

Unnecessary Obstacles

4. No Party may prepare, adopt, maintain, or apply any standards-related measure with a view to or with the effect of creating an unnecessary obstacle to trade between the Parties. An unnecessary obstacle to trade shall not be deemed to be created where:
   (a) the demonstrable purpose of the measure is to achieve a legitimate objective; and
   (b) the measure does not operate to exclude goods of another Party that meet that legitimate objective.

Article 905: Use of International Standards

1. Each Party shall use, as a basis for its standards-related measures, relevant international standards or international standards whose completion is imminent, except where such standards would be an ineffective or inappropriate means to fulfill its legitimate objectives, for example, because of fundamental climatic, geographical, technological, or infrastructural factors, scientific justification or the level of protection that the Party considers appropriate.
2. A Party's standards-related measure that conforms to an international standard shall be presumed to be consistent with Article 904(3) and (4).

PART FIVE: INVESTMENT, SERVICES, AND RELATED MATTERS

Article 1102: National Treatment

1. Each Party shall accord to investors of another Party treatment no less favorable than that it accords, in like circumstances, to its own investors with respect to the establishment, acquisition, expansion, management, conduct, operation, and sale or other disposition of investments.

2. Each Party shall accord to investments of investors of another Party treatment no less favorable than that it accords, in like circumstances, to investments of its own investors with respect to the establishment, acquisition, expansion, management, conduct, operation, and sale or other disposition of investments.
3. The treatment accorded by a Party under paragraphs 1 and 2 means, with respect to a state or province, treatment no less favorable than the most favorable treatment accorded, in like circumstances, by that state or province to investors, and to investments of investors, of the Party of which it forms a part.

Article 1103: Most-Favored-Nation Treatment

1. Each Party shall accord to investors of another Party treatment no less favorable than that it accords, in like circumstances, to investors of any other Party or of a non-Party with respect to the establishment, acquisition, expansion, management, conduct, operation, and sale or other disposition of investments.
2. Each Party shall accord to investments of investors of another Party treatment no less favorable than that it accords, in like circumstances, to investments of investors of any other Party or of a non-Party with respect to the establishment, acquisition, expansion, management, conduct, operation, and sale or other disposition of investments.

Article 1106: Performance Requirements

1. No Party may impose or enforce any of the following requirements, or enforce any commitment or undertaking, in connection with the establishment, acquisition, expansion, management, conduct or operation of an investment of an investor of a Party or of a non-Party in its territory:
   (a) to export a given level or percentage of goods or services;
   (b) to achieve a given level or percentage of domestic content;
   (c) to purchase, use, or accord a preference to goods produced or services provided in its territory, or to purchase goods or services from persons in its territory;
   (d) to relate in any way the volume or value of imports to the volume or value of exports or to the amount of foreign exchange inflows associated with such investment;
   (e) to restrict sales of goods or services in its territory that such investment produces or provides by relating such sales in any way to the volume or value of its exports or foreign exchange earnings;

(f) to transfer technology, a production process or other proprietary knowledge to a person in its territory, except when the requirement is imposed or the commitment or undertaking is enforced by a court, administrative tribunal, or competition authority to remedy an alleged violation of competition lawsor to act in a manner not inconsistent with other provisions of this Agreement; or

(g) to act as the exclusive supplier of the goods it produces or services it provides to a specific region or world market.

Article 1107: Senior Management and Boards of Directors

1. No Party may require that an enterprise of that Party that is an investment of an investor of another Party appoint to senior management positions individuals of any particular nationality.

2. A Party may require that a majority of the board of directors, or any committee thereof, of an enterprise of that Party that is an investment of an investor of another Party, be of a particular nationality, or resident in the territory of the Party, provided that the requirement does not materially impair the ability of the investor to exercise control over its investment.

Article 1110: Expropriation and Compensation

1. No Party may directly or indirectly nationalize or expropriate an investment of an investor of another Party in its territory or take a measure tantamount to nationalization or expropriation of such an investment ("expropriation"), except:
   (a) for a public purpose;
   (b) on a nondiscriminatory basis;
   (c) in accordance with due process of law and Article 1105(1); and
   (d) on payment of compensation in accordance with paragraphs 2 through 6.

2. Compensation shall be equivalent to the fair market value of the expropriated investment immediately before the expropriation took place ("date of expropriation"), and shall not reflect any change in value occurring because the intended expropriation had become known earlier. Valuation criteria shall include going concern value, asset value including declared tax value of tangible property, and other criteria, as appropriate, to determine fair market value.

3. Compensation shall be paid without delay and be fully realizable.

Article 1114: Environmental Measures

1. Nothing in this chapter shall be construed to prevent a Party from adopting, maintaining, or enforcing any measure otherwise consistent with this chapter that it considers appropriate to ensure that investment activity in its territory is undertaken in a manner sensitive to environmental concerns.
2. The Parties recognize that it is inappropriate to encourage investment by relaxing domestic health, safety, or environmental measures. Accordingly, a Party should not waive or otherwise derogate from, or offer to waive or otherwise derogate from, such measures as an encouragement for the establishment, acquisition, expansion, or retention in its territory of an investment of an investor. If a Party considers that another Party has offered such an encouragement, it may request consultations with the other Party and the two Parties shall consult with a view to avoiding any such encouragement.

CHAPTER 12. CROSS-BORDER TRADE IN SERVICES

Article 1201: Scope and Coverage

1. This chapter applies to measures adopted or maintained by a Party relating to cross-border trade in services by service providers of another Party, including measures respecting:
   (a) the production, distribution, marketing, sale, and delivery of a service;
   (b) the purchase or use of, or payment for, a service;
   (c) the access to and use of distribution and transportation systems in connection with the provision of a service;
   (d) the presence in its territory of a service provider of another Party; and
   (e) the provision of a bond or other form of financial security as a condition for the provision of a service.
2. This chapter does not apply to:
   (a) financial services, as defined in Chapter 14 (Financial Services);
   (b) air services, including domestic and international air transportation services, whether scheduled or non-scheduled, and related services in support of air services, other than
      (i) aircraft repair and maintenance services during which an aircraft is withdrawn from service, and
      (ii) specialty air services;

(c) procurement by a Party or a state enterprise; or

(d) subsidies or grants provided by a Party or a state enterprise, including government-supported loans, guarantees, and insurance.

3. Nothing in this chapter shall be construed to:

(a) impose any obligation on a Party with respect to a national of another Party seeking access to its employment market, or employed on a permanent basis in its territory, or to confer any right on that national with respect to that access or employment; or

(b) prevent a Party from providing a service or performing a function such as law enforcement, correctional services, income security or insurance, social security or insurance, social welfare, public education, public training, health, and child care, in a manner that is not inconsistent with this chapter.

Article 1202: National Treatment

1. Each Party shall accord to service providers of another Party treatment no less favorable than that it accords, in like circumstances, to its own service providers.

2. The treatment accorded by a Party under paragraph 1 means, with respect to a state or province, treatment no less favorable than the most favorable treatment accorded, in like circumstances, by that state or province to service providers of the Party of which it forms a part.

Article 1205: Local Presence

No Party may require a service provider of another Party to establish or maintain a representative office or any form of enterprise, or to be resident, in its territory as a condition for the cross-border provision of a service.

CHAPTER 14. FINANCIAL SERVICES

Article 1403: Establishment of Financial Institutions

1. The Parties recognize the principle that an investor of another Party should be permitted to establish a financial institution in the territory of a Party in the juridical form chosen by such investor.

2. The Parties also recognize the principle that an investor of another Party should be permitted to participate widely in a Party's market through the ability of such investor to:

(a) provide in that Party's territory a range of financial services through separate financial institutions as may be required by that Party;

(b) expand geographically in that Party's territory; and

(c) own financial institutions in that Party's territory without being subject to ownership requirements specific to foreign financial institutions.

Article 1404: Cross-Border Trade

1. No Party may adopt any measure restricting any type of cross-border trade in financial services by cross-border financial service providers of another Party that the Party permits on the date of entry into force of this Agreement, except to the extent set out in Section B of the Party's Schedule to Annex VII.

Article 1405: National Treatment

1. Each Party shall accord to investors of another Party treatment no less favorable than that it accords to its own investors, in like circumstances, with respect to the establishment, acquisition, expansion, management, conduct, operation, and sale or other disposition of financial institutions and investments in financial institutions in its territory.

2. Each Party shall accord to financial institutions of another Party and to investments of investors of another Party in financial institutions treatment no less favorable than that it accords to its own financial institutions and to investments of its own investors in financial institutions, in like circumstances, with respect to the establishment, acquisition, expansion, management, conduct, operation, and sale or other disposition of financial institutions and investments.

CHAPTER 15. COMPETITION POLICY, MONOPOLIES, AND STATE ENTERPRISES

Article 1501: Competition Law

1. Each Party shall adopt or maintain measures to proscribe anticompetitive business conduct and take appropriate action with respect thereto, recognizing that such measures will enhance the fulfillment of the objectives of this Agreement. To this end the Parties shall consult from time to time about the effectiveness of measures undertaken by each Party.

2. Each Party recognizes the importance of cooperation and coordination among their authorities to further effective competition law enforcement in the free trade area. The Parties shall cooperate on issues of competition law enforcement policy, including mutual legal assistance, notification, consultation, and exchange of information relating to the enforcement of competition laws and policies in the free trade area.
3. No Party may have recourse to dispute settlement under this Agreement for any matter arising under this article.

CHAPTER 16. TEMPORARY ENTRY
FOR BUSINESS PERSONS

Article 1603: Grant of Temporary Entry

1. Each Party shall grant temporary entry to business persons who are otherwise qualified for entry under applicable measures relating to public health and safety and national security, in accordance with this chapter, including the provisions of Annex 1603.
2. A Party may refuse to issue an immigration document authorizing employment to a business person where the temporary entry of that person might affect adversely:
    (a) the settlement of any labor dispute that is in progress at the place or intended place of employment; or
    (b) the employment of any person who is involved in such dispute.

PART SIX: INTELLECTUAL PROPERTY

Article 1701: Nature and Scope of Obligations

1. Each Party shall provide in its territory to the nationals of another Party adequate and effective protection and enforcement of intellectual property rights, while ensuring that measures to enforce intellectual property rights do not themselves become barriers to legitimate trade.

Article 1705: Copyright

1. Each Party shall protect the works covered by Article 2 of the Berne Convention, including any other works that embody original expression within the meaning of that Convention. In particular:

(a) all types of computer programs are literary works within the meaning of the Berne Convention and each Party shall protect them as such; and

(b) compilations of data or other material, whether in machine readable or other form, which by reason of the selection or arrangement of their contents constitute intellectual creations, shall be protected as such.

The protection a Party provides under subparagraph (b) shall not extend to the data or material itself, or prejudice any copyright subsisting in that data or material.

Article 1711: Trade Secrets

1. Each Party shall provide the legal means for any person to prevent trade secrets from being disclosed to, acquired by, or used by others without the consent of the person lawfully in control of the information in a manner contrary to honest commercial practices, in so far as:

(a) the information is secret in the sense that it is not, as a body or in the precise configuration and assembly of its components, generally known among or readily accessible to persons that normally deal with the kind of information in question;

(b) the information has actual or potential commercial value because it is secret; and

(c) the person lawfully in control of the information has taken reasonable steps under the circumstances to keep it secret.

2. A Party may require that to qualify for protection a trade secret must be evidenced in documents, electronic or magnetic means, optical discs, microfilms, films or other similar instruments.

3. No Party may limit the duration of protection for trade secrets, so long as the conditions in paragraph 1 exist.

Article 1712: Geographical Indications

1. Each Party shall provide, in respect of geographical indications, the legal means for interested persons to prevent:

(a) the use of any means in the designation or presentation of a good that indicates or suggests that the good in question originates in a territory, region, or locality other than the true place of origin, in a manner that misleads the public as to the geographical origin of the good;

(b) any use that constitutes an act of unfair competition within the meaning of Article 10bis of the Paris Convention.

2. Each Party shall, on its own initiative if its domestic law so permits or at the request of an interested person, refuse to register, or invalidate the registration of, a trademark containing or consisting of a geographical indication with respect to goods that do not originate in the indicated territory, region, or locality, if use of the indication in the trademark for such goods is of such a nature as to mislead the public as to the geographical origin of the good.

CHAPTER 22. INSTITUTIONAL ARRANGEMENTS AND DISPUTE SETTLEMENT PROCEDURES

Article 2001: The Free Trade Commission

1. The Parties hereby establish the Free Trade Commission, comprising cabinet-level representatives of the Parties or their designees.
2. The Commission shall:
   (a) supervise the implementation of this Agreement;
   (b) oversee its further elaboration;
   (c) resolve disputes that may arise regarding its interpretation or application;
   (d) supervise the work of all committees and working groups established under this Agreement, referred to in Annex 2001.2; and
   (e) consider any other matter that may affect the operation of this Agreement.

Article 2005: GATT Dispute Settlement

Disputes regarding any matter arising under both this Agreement and the General Agreement on Tariffs and Trade, any agreement negotiated there under, or any successor agreement (GATT), may be settled in either forum at the discretion of the complaining Party.

Article 2021: Private Rights

No Party may provide for a right of action under its domestic law against any other Party on the ground that a measure of another Party is inconsistent with this Agreement.

Appendix L

Trade Documents

Appendix L.1   Proforma Invoice

Export References:		Expiration Date:
Exporter Name and Address:	Ultimate Consignee Name and Address:	Sold To Name and Address:
Intermediate Consignee/Consigned to:	Notify Party Name and Address:	Date of Shipment: AWB/BL Number: Currency: Letter of Credit Number:
Conditions of Sale and Terms of Payment: Freight (please mark): Pre-paid ___ Collect ___ Title Transfer Occurs At: Payment Terms:	Transportation method: Via: From:	Total Number of Packages: Total Net Weight (kg): Total Gross Weight (kg):

Item Number, Product Description, Tariff Classification Number, Country of Origin	Quantity	Unit Price	Total Price

Please Note: These commodities, technology, or software were exported from the United States in accordance with the Export Administration Regulations. Diversion contrary to U.S. law prohibited.

Authorized Signature:	Company:
Name:	Title:
Date: E-mail:	Telephone Number(s) Voice: Facsimile:

This invoice is for export/import purposes only and not intended for payment purposes

Export-Import Theory, Practices, and Procedures, Second Edition

Appendix L.2. Sample Document: Air Waybill (Air Consignment Note)

000 | 1234 5678   000- 1234 5678

Shipper's Name and Address   Shipper's Account Number

Not Negotiable

Air Waybill
(Air Consignment Note)
Issued by

Member of International
Air Transport Association

Copies 1, 2 and 3 of this Air Waybill are originals and have the same validity.

Consignee's Name and Address   Consignee's Account Number

It is agreed that the goods described herein are accepted in apparent good order and condition (except as noted) for carriage SUBJECT TO THE CONDITIONS OF CONTRACT ON THE REVERSE HEREOF. THE SHIPPER'S ATTENTION IS DRAWN TO THE NOTICE CONCERNING CARRIER'S LIMITATION OF LIABILITY. Shipper may increase such limitation of liability by declaring a higher value for carriage and paying supplemental charge if required.

Issuing Carrier's Agent Name and City

Accounting Information

Agent's IATA Code   Account No.

Airport of Departure (Addr of First Carrier) and Requested Routing

| To | By First Carrier | Routing and Destination | To | By | To | By | Currency | Chgs Code | WT/VAL PPD COLL | OTHER PPD COLL | Declared Value for Carriage | Declared Value for Customs |

Airport of Destination   Flight/Date   For Carrier Use Only   Flight/Date   Amount of Insurance

INSURANCE- If carrier offers insurance and such insurance is requested in accordance with conditions on reverse hereof, indicate amount to be insured in figures in box marked Amount of Insurance.

Handling Information

| No. of Pieces RCP | Gross Weight | Kg Lb | Rate Class Commodity Item No. | Chargeable Weight | Rate / Charge | Total | Nature and Quantity of Goods (Incl. Dimensions or Volume) |

Prepaid   Weight Charge   Collect   Other Charges

Valuation Charge

Tax

Total Other Charges Due Agent

Total Other Charges Due Carrier

Shipper certifies that the particulars on the face hereof are correct and that insofar as any part of the consignment contains dangerous goods, such part is properly described by name and is in proper condition for carriage by air according to the applicable Dangerous Goods Regulations.

Signature of Shipper or his Agent

Total Prepaid   Total Collect

Currency Conversion Rates   cc Charges in Destination Currency

Executed on   (date)   at   (place)   Signature of Issuing Carrier or Agent

For Carriers Use Only at Destination   Charges at Destination   Total Collect Charges

000- 1234 5678

COPY 8 - FOR FIRST CARRIER

Appendix L.3. Commercial Invoice

Export References:		
Exporter Name and Address:	**Ultimate Consignee Name and Address:**	**Sold To Name and Address:**
Intermediate Consignee/Consigned to:	**Notify Party Name and Address:**	**Date of Shipment:** **AWB/BL Number:** **Currency:** **Letter of Credit Number:**
Conditions of Sale and Terms of Payment: **Freight:** **Title Transfer Occurs At:** **Payment Terms:**	**Transportation:** **Via:** **From:**	**Total Number of Packages:** **Total Net Weight (kgs):** **Total Gross Weight (kgs):**

Line No.	Item Number, Harmonized Number, Product Description	Country of Origin	Quantity	Unit Price	Total Price

Please Note: *These commodities, technology, or software were exported from the United States in accordance with the Export Administration Regulations. Diversion contrary to U.S. law prohibited.*

Authorized Signature:	Company:
Name:	Title:
Date:	Telephone Number(s) Voice: Facsimile:

This invoice is for export/import purposes only and not intended for payment purposes.

Appendix L.4.

DOCK RECEIPT

SHIPPER / CONSIGNOR		BOOKING NUMBER	BILL OF LADING NUMBER
		EXPORT REFERENCES	
CONSIGNEE		FORWARDING AGENT - REFERENCES	
		POINT AND COUNTRY OF ORIGIN OF GOODS	
NOTIFY PARTY		DOMESTIC ROUTING / EXPORT INSTRUCTIONS (Additional Notify Party etc.)	

PRE-CARRIAGE BY	PLACE OF RECEIPT (Pre-carriage)		
EXPORTING CARRIER	PORT OF LOADING	LOADING PIER / TERMINAL	CUSTOMS CLOSING DATE
PORT OF DISCHARGE	FOR TRANSHIPMENT TO (On-carriage)	TRANSIT AT (Foreign City and Country)	CONTAINERIZED ☐ Yes ☐ No

MARKS AND NUMBERS	NUMBER OF PACKAGES	DESCRIPTION OF PACKAGES AND GOODS	GROSS WEIGHT	MEASUREMENT
CONTAINER NUMBER				
SEAL NUMBER				

ONLY CLEAN DOCK RECEIPT ACCEPTED

			SPECIAL INSTRUCTIONS
FREIGHT PAYABLE AT	NUMBER OF BILLS OF LADING REQUIRED Original Copies	DECLARED VALUE	

DELIVERED   BY:

LIGHTER
TRUCK

ARRIVED — DATE .... TIME ....

UNLOADED — DATE .... TIME ....

CHECKED IN SHIP ON DECK **LOCATION** ....

RECEIVED THE ABOVE DESCRIBED GOODS OR PACKAGES SUBJECT TO ALL THE TERMS OF THE UNDERSIGNED'S REGULAR FORM OF DOCK RECEIPT AND BILL OF LADING WHICH SHALL CONSTITUTE THE CONTRACT UNDER WHICH THE GOODS ARE RECEIVED. COPIES OF WHICH ARE AVAILABLE FROM THE CARRIER ON REQUEST AND MAY BE INSPECTED AT ANY OF ITS OFFICES.

FOR THE MASTER

BY ....

DATE ....

Appendix L.5. Ocean Bill of Lading

A RELIABLE SHIPPING LINE

(NON-NEGOTIABLE UNLESS CONSIGNED TO ORDER)

Shipper / Exporter (Complete Name and Address)	**ORIGINAL**	Bill of Lading No.
	Export References	
Consignee (Complete Name and Address)	Forwarding Agent - References	
	Point and Country of Origin of Goods	
Notify Party (Complete Name and Address)	Domestic Routing / Export Instructions (Additional Notify Party, Etc.)	

Pre-carriage By	Place of Receipt	
Vessel / Voyage No.	Port of Loading	Onward Inland Routing
Port of Discharge	For Transhipment To	

Marks and Numbers	No. of Pkgs.	Description of Packages and Goods	Gross Weight	Measurement

PARTICULARS ABOVE FURNISHED BY THE SHIPPER

Container No(s).	Seal No(s).

RECEIVED FOR SHIPMENT in apparent good order and condition unless otherwise indicated herein, the container(s) or other package(s) or units mentioned above, to be carried from the place of receipt or the port of loading to the port of discharge or for transhipment to the delivery place, subject to the terms and conditions on the reverse hereof. One of the original bills of lading must be surrendered duly endorsed in exchange for the goods or delivery order.
IN WITNESS WHEREOF, the Master or agent of said vessel has signed the number of bill(s) of lading stated below, all of the same tenor and date, one of which being accomplished, the others to stand void.

Freight & Charges	Revenue Ton	Rate	Per	Prepaid	Collect

Freight and Charges Payable At	Number of Original B(s) /L	Place of B(s)/L Issue	**A RELIABLE SHIPPING LINE**
Laden On Board the Vessel			
Dated	By	Dated	**AGENT**

Appendix L.6.

Packing List

Shipper/ Exporter:	Ultimate Consignee:	Bill To:	Intermediate Consignee

Transportation:

Commercial Invoice No.:	Total number of Packages:
Order No.:	Total Gross Weight (Lbs):
AWB/BL Number:	Total Gross Weight (Kgs):
Date Of Shipment:	Total Net Weight (Lbs):
Currency:	Total net Weight (Kgs):
Freight:	Total Cubic Feet:
	Total Cubic Meters:

Conditions of Sale and Terms of Payment:

Shipment Line No.	Item Number	Item Description, Sales Order No., Customer PO No.	Shipped Quantity	Packaging Type	Dimensions						Per package gross weight	
					Inches			centimeters			LBS.	KGS.
					L	W	H	L	W	H		

Country of Origin:
Marks:

Note: These commodities, Technology or software were exported from the United States in accordance with the Export Administration Regulation Diversion contrary to U.S. law is prohibited.

Signature: _____ Date:

Appendix L.7.

U.S. DEPARTMENT OF COMMERCE – Economics and Statistics Administration – U.S. CENSUS BUREAU – BUREAU OF EXPORT ADMINISTRATION

FORM **7525-V** (7-18-2003)

SHIPPER'S EXPORT DECLARATION

OMB No. 0607-0152

1a. U.S. PRINCIPAL PARTY IN INTEREST (USPPI)(Complete name and address)

ZIP CODE

2. DATE OF EXPORTATION

3. TRANSPORTATION REFERENCE NO.

b. USPPI'S EIN (IRS) OR ID NO.

c. PARTIES TO TRANSACTION
☐ Related ☐ Non-related

4a. ULTIMATE CONSIGNEE (Complete name and address)

b. INTERMEDIATE CONSIGNEE (Complete name and address)

5a. FORWARDING AGENT (Complete name and address)

5b. FORWARDING AGENT'S EIN (IRS) NO.

6. POINT (STATE) OF ORIGIN OR FTZ NO.

7. COUNTRY OF ULTIMATE DESTINATION

8. LOADING PIER (Vessel only)

9. METHOD OF TRANSPORTATION (Specify)

14. CARRIER IDENTIFICATION CODE

15. SHIPMENT REFERENCE NO.

10. EXPORTING CARRIER

11. PORT OF EXPORT

16. ENTRY NUMBER

17. HAZARDOUS MATERIALS
☐ Yes ☐ No

12. PORT OF UNLOADING (Vessel and air only)

13. CONTAINERIZED (Vessel only)
☐ Yes ☐ No

18. IN BOND CODE

19. ROUTED EXPORT TRANSACTION
☐ Yes ☐ No

20. SCHEDULE B DESCRIPTION OF COMMODITIES (Use columns 22–24)

D/F or M (21)	SCHEDULE B NUMBER (22)	QUANTITY – SCHEDULE B UNIT(S) (23)	SHIPPING WEIGHT (Kilograms) (24)	VIN/PRODUCT NUMBER/ VEHICLE TITLE NUMBER (25)	VALUE (U.S. dollars, omit cents) (Selling price or cost if not sold) (26)

27. LICENSE NO./LICENSE EXCEPTION SYMBOL/AUTHORIZATION

28. ECCN (When required)

29. Duly authorized officer or employee

The USPPI authorizes the forwarder named above to act as forwarding agent for export control and customs purposes.

30. I certify that all statements made and all information contained herein are true and correct and that I have read and understand the instructions for preparation of this document, set forth in the "Correct Way to Fill Out the Shipper's Export Declaration." I understand that civil and criminal penalties, including forfeiture and sale, may be imposed for making false or fraudulent statements herein, failing to provide the requested information or for violation of U.S. laws on exportation (13 U.S.C. Sec. 305; 22 U.S.C. Sec. 401; 18 U.S.C. Sec. 1001; 50 U.S.C. App. 2410).

Signature

Confidential – Shipper's Export Declarations (or any successor document) wherever located, shall be exempt from public disclosure unless the Secretary determines that such exemption would be contrary to the national interest (Title 13, Chapter 9, Section 301 (g)).

Title

Export shipments are subject to inspection by U.S. Customs Service and/or Office of Export Enforcement.

Date

31. AUTHENTICATION (When required)

Telephone No. (Include Area Code)

E-mail address

Clear fields 1 to 19

Clear Fields 20 to 26

Clear Fields 27 to 31

Clear all fields

This form may be printed by private parties provided it conforms to the official form. For sale by the Superintendent of Documents, Government Printing Office, Washington, DC 20402, and local Customs District Directors. The "Correct Way to Fill Out the Shipper's Export Declaration" is available from the U.S. Census Bureau, Washington, DC 20233.

References

CHAPTER 1

Belous, R., and Wyckoff, A. (September 1987). Trade has job winners too. *Across the Board,* 53-55.

Daniels, J., and Radebaugh, L. (2004). *International Business.* Upper Saddle River, NJ: Prentice Hall.

Davis, L. (May 18, 1992). Surge in U.S. exports supports economy, employment. *Business America,* 113(10): 27.

Fong, P., and Hill, H. (1991). Technology exports from a small, very open NIC: The case of Singapore. *World Development,* 19: 553-568.

Fugazza, M. (2004). *Export Performance and Its Determinants: Supply and Demand Constraints.* Study No. 26. Geneva: UNCTAD.

Harless, A. (2006). *Exports, Imports and Wages: What Trade Means for US Job Quality.* Washington, DC: Center for National Policy.

Kaynak, E., and Kothavi, V. (1984). Export behavior of small and medium-sized manufacturers: Some policy guidelines for international marketers. *Management International Review,* 24: 61-69.

Kletzer, L. (2001). *Job Loss from Imports: Measuring the Costs.* Washington, DC: Institute of International Economics.

Lefebvre, E., and Lefebvre, L. (2000). *Small and Medium-Sized Enterprises, Exports and Job Creation: A Firm Level Analysis* (Industry Canada. Paper No. 26). Ottawa: Research and Publications Program.

Lutz, J. (1994). To import or to protect? Industrialized countries and manufactured products. *Journal of World Trade,* 28(4): 123-145.

Rostow, W. (1978). *The World Economy: History and Prospect.* Austin, TX: University of Texas Press.

Rostow, W. (1992). *Theories of Economic Growth.* New York: Oxford University Press.

Sarmand, K. (1989). The Determinants of import demand in Pakistan. *World Development,* 17: 1619-1625.

U.S. Department of Commerce (1994). The economics of technology and trade. *Business America,* 115(8): 6-8.

U.S. Government, Securities and Exchange Commission (www.sec.gov). (2006).

Export-Import Theory, Practices, and Procedures, Second Edition

WTO (2004a). *World Trade Developments in 2004 and Prospects for 2005.* Geneva: WTO.

WTO (2004b). *Singapore Trade Review.* Geneva: WTO.

Internet Sources

World History Archives
http://en.wikipedia.org/wiki/History_of_international_trade
History of International Trade: Pre 1500 to present day.

History of International Trade
http://lsb.scu.edu/~swade/histtrad.html
This site provides a brief history of international trade since Marco Polo.

Meccan Trade and the Rise of Islam
http://www.fordham.edu/halsall/med/crone.html
This is an excerpt from a book on commerce in the Middle East and the rise of Islam.

Mountain Men and the Fur Trade
http://www.xmission.com/~drudy/amm.html
This site is an on-line research center to the history, traditions, and mode of living of the trappers, explorers, and traders known as the mountain men.

Growth of International Trade/Trade Data/Developments
http://www.wto.org/english/news_e/pres05_e/pr417_e.htm
http://www.epinet.org/briefingpapers/147/epi_bp147.pdf
http://www.factmonster.com/ipka/A0762380.html
http://www.census.gov/foreign-trade/balance/c4239.html#2005
http://www.wisegeek.com/what-countries-import-the-most.htm
http://www.infoplease.com/cig/economics/world-economies.html
http://en.wikipedia.org/wiki/Doha_round#Doha
http://www.wto.org/English/news_e/pres05_e/pr401_e.htm
http://www.infoplease.com/cig/economics/world-economies.html
http://www.census.gov/foreign-trade/Press-Release/current_press_release/ftdpress.pdf
http://www.unctadxi.org/sections/SITE/etourism/docs/Tourism0001_en.pdf.

CHAPTER 2

Archer, C., and Butler, F. (1992). *The European Community.* New York: St. Martin's Press.

Campbell, B. (July 2006). NAFTA's broken promises. http://policyalternatives.ca/monitorissues/2006/

Collins, S., and Bosworth, B. P., eds. (1994). *The New GATT.* Washington, DC: The Brookings Institution.

Das, D. (2004). *Regionalism in Global Trade.* Northampton, MA: Praeger.

Echeverri-Carroll, E. ed. (1995). *NAFTA and Trade Liberalization in the Americas.* Austin, TX: Bureau of Business Research, University of Texas.

Hoekman, B., and Kostecki, M. (1995). *The Political Economy of the World Trading System.* New York: Oxford University Press.

Hufbauer, G., and Schott, J. (1994). *NAFTA: An Assessment.* Washington, DC: Institute for International Economics.

International Monetary Fund (IMF) (2000). *World Economic Outlook.* Washington, DC: IMF.

Jackson, J. (1992). *The World Trading System.* Cambridge, MA: MIT Press.

Lederman, D., Maloney, W., and Serven, L. (2005). *Lessons from NAFTA: For Latin America and the Caribbean.* Palo Alto, CA: Stanford University Press.

Poole, P. (2003). *Europe: The EU's Eastern Enlargement.* London: Praeger.

Randall, S., Konrad, H., and Silverman, S. (1992). *North America Without Borders?* Calgary, Canada: University of Calgary Press.

U.S. Census (1993-2003). *U.S. Trade Statistics.* http://census.gov

Van Oudenaren, J. (2002). *Uniting Europe: European Integration and the Post-Cold War World.* New York: Rowman & Littlefield Publishers.

Weintraub, S. (2004). *NAFTA's Impact on North America: The First Decade.* Washington, DC: Center for Strategic and International Studies.

Wild, J., Wild, K., and Han, J. (2006). *International Business: The Challenges of Globalization.* Upper Saddle River, NJ: Prentice Hall.

WTO (2006). *Annual Report.* Geneva: WTO. http://www.wto.org

Internet Sources

The European Union
Information on the European Union and its institutions
http://europa.eu.int/institutions/council/index_en.htm

NAFTA: Economic and Commercial Information
NAFTA: The complete agreement
http://www.tech.mit.edu/Bulletins/nafta.html
http://www.policyalternatives.ca/MonitorIssues/2006/07/MonitorIssue1415/
This site provides an analysis of NAFTA
http://www.dfait-maeci.gc.ca/nafta-alena/menu-en.asp

World Trade Organization
Basic information about the WTO, its agreements, and activities
http://www.wto.org

CHAPTER 3

Albaum, G., Stradskov, J., and Duerr, E. (2002). *International Marketing and Export Management.* New York: Prentice Hall.

Albaum, G., Stradskov, J., Duerr, E., and Dowd, L. (1994). *International Marketing and Export Management.* Wokingham, UK: Addison-Wesely Publishing Co.

Anderson, R., and Dunkelberg, J. (1993). *Managing Small Business.* New York: West Publishing.

August, R. (2004). *International Business Law.* Upper Saddle River, NJ: Prentice Hall.

Beamish, P., Karavis, L., Goerzon, A., and Lane, C. (1999). The relationship between organizational structure and export performance. *Management International Review,* 39(1): 37-55.

Cheeseman, H. (2006a). *Contemporary Business and Online Commerce Law.* Upper Saddle River, NJ: Prentice Hall.

Cheeseman, H. (2006b). *Essentials of Business and Online Commerce Law.* Upper Saddle River, NJ: Prentice Hall.

Cooke, R. (1995). *Doing Business Tax-Free.* New York: John Wiley and sons.

Enderwick, P., and Ranayne, E. (2004). Reconciling entrepreneurship and organizational structure in international operations: Evidence from New Zealand specialist food exporters. *Journal of Asia Pacific Marketing,* 3(2): 53-69.

Friedman, R. (1993). *The Complete Small Business Legal Guide.* Dearbon, MI: Enterprise.

Harper, S. (1991). *The McGraw-Hill Guide to Starting Your Own Business.* New York: McGraw-Hill Inc.

Internal Revenue Service (1996a). *Business Use of Your Home.* Washington, DC: Department of the Treasury, Publication 587.

Internal Revenue Service (1996b). *Business Expenses.* Washington, DC: Department of the Treasury, Publication 535.

Internal Revenue Service (1996c). *Travel, Entertainment, Gift and Car Expenses.* Washington, DC: Department of the Treasury, Publication 463.

McDaniel, P., Ault, H., and Repetti, J. (1981). *Introduction to United States International Taxation.* Boston: Kluwer.

McGrath, K., Elias, S., and Shena, S (1996). *Trademark: How to Name a Business or Product.* Berkeley, CA: Nolo Press.

Ogley, A. (1995). *Principles of International Tax.* London: Interfisc Publishing.

Pak, S., and Zdanowicz, J. (2002). US trade with the world. http://dorgan.senate.gov/newsroom

Plender, J. (July 21-22, 2004). Counting the cost of globalisation: How companies keep tax low and stay within the law. *Financial Times,* 15.

Internet Sources

Fictitious Business Names

Fictitious Business Names: Information on filing fictitious business names
http://www.smcare.org/business/fictitious/default.asp
Tips on choosing a business name
http://www.bcentral.co.uk/startingup/planning/choose-a-business-name.mspx
Seven secrets of great business names
http://www.gmarketing.com/articles/read/133/The_7_Secrets_of_Great_Business Names.html

Information on assumed business names
http://www.leg.state.or.us/ors/648.html

Starting a Business
Starting a business: Provides answers to frequently asked questions about starting a business
http://www.irs.gov/businesses/small/article/0,,id=99336,00.html

CHAPTER 4

Ashegian, P., and Ibrahimi, B. (1990). *International Business*. Philadelphia, PA: Harper Collins.

Ball, D., Mc Culloch, W., Frantz, P., Geringer, M., et al. (2006). *International Business*. Chicago: Irwin.

Beal, M. (2000). Competing effectively: Environmental scanning, competitive strategy and organizational performance in small manufacturing firms. *Journal of Small Business Management,* 38(1): 27-47.

Cohen, W. (1995). *Model Business Plans for Product Business*. New York: John Wiley and Sons.

Czinkota, M., Ronkainen, I., and Moffett, M. (2003). *International Business*. Mason, OH: South-Western.

Schwartz, M. (July 10, 2006). ABM research finds trade shows attract buyers: Despite success of Internet, traditional advertising still pushing sales needle. *B to B,* 9: 7-10.

Silvester, J. (1995). *How to Start, Finance and Operate your Own Business*. New York: Birch Lane Press.

Subramanian, R., Fernandes, N., and Harper, E. (1993). Environmental scanning in U.S. companies: Their nature and their relationship to performance. *Management International Review,* 33: 271-275.

Tuller, L. (1994). *Exporting, Importing and Beyond*. Holbrooke, MA: Bob Adams.

U.S. Department of Commerce (1990). *A Basic Guide to Exporting*. Lincolnwood, Chicago: NTC Books.

Weiss, K. (1987). *Building an Import/Export Business*. New York: John Wiley and Sons.

Williams, E., and Manzo, S. (1983). *Business Planning for the Entrepreneur.* New York: Van Nostrand Rienhold Co.

Internet Sources

Small Business
http://www.entrepreneur.com/article/0,4621,324792,00.html
SBA information on starting, financing, and expanding a small business
http://www.sba.gov/

U.S. Export Inc.
Export Assistance to small and medium-sized firms
http://www.export.gov/
http://www.trade.gov/mas/
http://www.usda.gov/wps/portal/usdahome

CHAPTER 5

Anderson, E., and Coughlin, A. (1987). International market entry and expansion via independent or integrated channels of distribution. *Journal of Marketing,* 51(1): 80-85.

Anderson, P. (2005). Export intermediation and the Internet: An activity unbundling approach. *International Marketing Review,* 22(2): 147-164.

Anonymous (1992). EMCs/ETCs: What they are and how they work. *Business America,* 2: 3-5.

Ball, D., McCulloch, W., Frantz, P., Geringer, J., et al. (2004). *International Business.* New York: McCraw Hill-Irwin.

Bello, D., and Gilliland, D. (1997). The effect of output controls, process controls and flexibility on export channel performance. *Journal of Marketing,* 61: 22-38.

Cateora, P. (1996). *International Marketing.* New York: Irwin.

Clarke, G., and Wallsten, S. (2004). *Has the Internet Increased Trade? Evidence from Industrial and Developing Countries.* Washington, DC: World Bank Policy Research Working Paper No. 3215.

Czinkota, M., Ronkainen, I., and Moffett, M. (2003). *International Business.* Mason, OH: Thomson-South-Western.

Freund, C., and Weinhold, D. (2000). *On the Effect of the Internet on International Trade.* International Finance Discussion Paper No. 693. Washington, DC: World Bank.

International Telecommunications Union (2003). *World Telecommunication Development Report 2003: Access Indicators for the Information Society.* Geneva, Switzerland: ITU.

Kim, L., Nugent, J., and Yhee, S. (1997). Transaction costs and export channels of small and medium-sized enterprises. *Contemporary Economic Policy,* 15(1): 104-120.

Klein, S., Frazier, G., and Roth, V. (1990). A transaction cost analysis model of channel integration in international markets. *Journal of Marketing Research,* 27: 196-208.

Kogut, B. (1986). On designing contracts to guarantee enforceability: Theory and evidence from East-West trade. *Journal of International Business Studies,* 17: 47-61.

McNaughton, R. (1996). Foreign market channel integration decisions of Canadian Computer software firms. *International Business Review,* 5(1): 23-52.

McNaughton, R. (2002). The use of multiple export channels by small knowledge-intensive firms. *International Marketing Review,* 19(2/3): 190-203.

Meloan, T., and Graham, J. (1995). *International Global Marketing*. New York: Irwin.

Onkvisit, S., and Shaw, J. (1997). *International Marketing*. Upper Saddle River, NJ: Prentice Hall.

Osborne, K. (1996). The channel integration decision for small to medium-sized manufacturing exporters. *International Small Business Journal*, 14(3): 40-56.

Peterson, B., Welch, L., and Liesch, P. (2002). The Internet and foreign market expansion by firms. *Management International Review*, 42(2): 207-221.

Seifert, B., and Ford, J. (1989). Export distribution channels. *Columbia Journal of World Business*, 14-18.

Sletten, E. (1994). *How to Succeed in Exporting and Doing Business Internationally*. New York: Wiley.

Tesfom, G., Lutz, C., and Ghauri, P. (2004). Comparing export marketing channels: Developed versus developing countries. *International Marketing Review*, 21(4/5): 409-422.

Williamson, O. (1991). Comparative economic organization: The analysis of discrete structural alternatives. *Administrative Science Quarterly*, 36(2): 269-274.

Internet Sources

Information on overseas distributors and other channels
http://www.unzco.com/basicguide/c4.html
Assistance with international trade for U.S. exporters
http://www.ita.doc.gov/td/oetca/
World Business Exchange: Includes topics such as assistance with exporting, channels of distribution, market research, service exports, pricing, documentation, and financing.
http://www.wbe.net/index.phtml
Information on channels of distribution for U.S. agricultural exports
http://www.fas.usda.gov/agx/exporter_assistance.asp
International Export Guide: A Guide to Exporting
http://www.unzco.com/basicguide/toc.html

CHAPTER 6

Cheeseright, P. (November 5, 1994). Maker of reliant in receivership. *Financial Times*: 4-6.

Christopher, M. ed. (1992). *Logistics: The Strategic Issues*. London: Chapman and Hall.

Czinkota, M., Ronkainen, I., and Moffett, M. (2003). *International Business*. Mason, OH: South-Western.

Day, D., and Griffin, B. (1993). *The Law of International Trade*. London: Butterworths.

Davies, G. (1987). The international logistics concept. *International Journal of Physical Distribution and Material Management,* 17-23.

European Commission (1994). *Cross Border Payments.* Brussels: EEC.

Fabey, M. (September 1997). Software for shippers. *World Trade,* 54-56.

Green, M., and Trieschmann, J. (1984). *Risk and Insurance.* Cincinnati, OH: South-Western Publishing Co.

Guelzo, M. (1986). *Introduction to Logistics Management.* NJ: Prentice Hall.

Luesby, J. (November 5-6, 1994). Brussels calls time for EU late payers. *Financial Times*: 3-4.

Mehr, R., Cammack, E., and Rose, T. (1985). *Principles of Insurance.* Homewood, IL: Irwin.

Seyoum, B., and Morris, B. (1996). Economic and trade characteristics as discriminators of countries' payment behavior. *Journal of Global Business,* 7(12): 59-69.

Thuermer, K. (March 1998). Move 'em or wilt. *World Trade,* 11(3): 61.

Vance, W. (1951). *Handbook of the Law of Insurance.* St. Paul, MN: West Publishing Co.

Woolley, S. (March 1997). Replacing inventory with information. *Forbes,* 159(6): 2-3.

Internet Sources

Logistics World

http://www.logisticsworld.com/logistics/forumsearch.asp

http://209.51.193.25/logtalk.asp (International logistics discussion group)

Sites on Risks and Insurance

http://www.internationalbusiness.com/feb/log297.htm (cargo theft)

http://www.duke.edu/~charvey/Country_risk/pol/pol.htm (political, economic, and financial risk)

http://www.duke.edu/~charvey/Country_risk/pol/polappa.htm (Country risk)

http://www.score.org/guest (credit insurance)

CHAPTER 7

Anonymous (October 4, 1993). Price quotations and terms of sale are key to successful exporting. *Business America,* 114(20): 12-15.

Brinton, C., Christopher, J., Wolff, R., and Winks, R. (1984). *A History of Civilization,* vol. I. Upper Saddle River, NJ: Prentice-Hall.

Dussauge, P., Hart, S., and Ramanantsoa, B. (1987). *Strategic Technology Management.* New York: John Wiley and Sons.

Herman, A. (March 30, 1989). Growth in international trade law. *Financial Times,* 10.

Hiam, A., and Schewe, C. (1992). *The Portable MBA in Marketing.* New York: John Wiley and Sons.

International Chamber of Commerce (Incoterms) (1990; 2000). New York: ICC Publishing.

Martens, J., Scarpetta, S., and Pilat, D. (April 1996). Mark-up ratios in manufacturing industries. *OECD Working paper,* No. 162: 10-12.

Oster, S. (1990). *Modern Competitive Analysis.* London: Oxford University Press.

Piercy, N. (1982). *Export Strategy: Markets and Competition.* London: Unwin Hyman.

Reich, R. (1991). *The Work of Nations.* New York: Knopf.

Silberston, A. (1970). Price behavior of firms. *Economic Journal,* 80(319): 511-570.

Internet Sources

Export Pricing
http://sominfo.syr.edu/facstaff/fgtucker/ (information on export pricing)

Pricing for Profits
http://www.smartbiz.com/sbs/arts/ieb6.htm (information on pricing for an export-import business)

http://www.wbnet.com/guest4.htm (Encyclopedia of exporting including pricing, quotations, and terms)

Incoterms, 1990
http://ananse.irv.uit.no/trade_law/documents/sales/incoterms/nav/inc.html (terms of sale)

CHAPTER 8

DiMatteo, L. (1997). An international contract formula: The informality of international business transactions plus the internationalization of contract law equals unexpected contractual liability. *Syracuse Journal of International Law and Commerce,* 23: 67-111.

Hornick, R. (March, 1990). Jakarta court declares standard international sales contract illegal. *East Asian Executive Reports,* 6-14.

Lubman, S. (1988). Investment and exports in the People's Republic of China: Perspectives on the evolving patterns. *Brigham Young University Law Review,* 3: 543-565.

Rosett, A. (1982). Unification, harmonization, restatement, codification and reform of international commercial law. *North Carolina Journal of International and Commercial Regulation,* 7(1): 683-698.

Internet Sources

General Legal Information
Information on trade agreements and commercial treaties:
http://fletcher.tufts.edu/multi/secretariatslinks.html
http://fletcher.tufts.edu/inter_resources/intertrade.htm

International Commercial Law
Information on electronic commerce:
http://www.uncitral.org/uncitral/en/uncitral_texts/electronic_commerce.html
Information on international commercial law and electronic commerce:
http://www.jus.uio.no/lm/
Information is also provided on treaties, rules, and other laws pertaining to international business.
Information on international trade law:
http://www.law.cornell.edu/wex/index.php/International_trade
Guide to international economic law:
http://www.asil.org/resource/iel1.htm

CHAPTER 9

Anonymous (April 1998a). Boeing eyes commercial sector for C-17. *American Shipper,* 101.

Anonymous (April 1998b). Trackers back car con train technology. *American Shipper,* 104-105.

Department of Commerce (1990). *A Basic Guide to Exporting.* Chicago: NTC.

Federal Maritme Commission Regulations of Ocean Freight Forwarders. Part 510, 49 Federal Regulations 36297, September 14, 1984; 46 U.S. Code app. 1702-1708.

Flint, D., and O'Keefe, P. (1997). Admiralty and maritime Law. *The International Lawyer,* 31: 234-243.

Force, R. (1996). A comparison of the Hague, Hague-Visby and Hamburg rules: Much ado about nothing. *Tulane Law Review,* 70: 2051-2089.

Kendall, L. (1983). *The Business of Shipping.* Centerville, MD: Cornell Maritime Press.

Murr, A. (1979). *Export/Import Traffic Management and Forwarding.* Centerville, MD: Cornell Maritime Press.

Reyes, B., and Gilles, C. (April 1998). Lufthansa Fights Back. *American Shipper,* 94-98.

Schmitthoff, C. (1986). *Schmitthoff's Export Trade.* London: Butterworths.

Wells, F., and Dulat, K. (1996). *Exporting from Start to Finance.* New York: McGraw Hill Publishing.

Wood, D., Barone, A., Murphy, P., and Wardlow, D. (1995). *International Logistics.* New York: Chapman and Hall.

Ullman, G. (1995). *U.S. Regulation of Ocean Transportation, Under the Shipping Act of 1984.* Centerville, MD: Cornell Maritime Press.

Yancey, B. (1983). The carriage of goods: Hague, COGSA, Visby and Hamburg. *Tulane Law Review,* 57: 1238-1259.

Zodl, J. (1995). *Export-Import.* Cincinnati, OH: Betterway Books.

Internet Sources

Sites on Documentation and Shipping
http://www.ibs-ibp.com/rp01m.htm (Information on export documentation and shipping)
http://www.exportproco.com/guide.htm (An interactive guide to export documentation)
http://wisdairyexport.org/export.htm (export documentation and labeling of agricultural exports).

CHAPTER 10

CNN Money (2006). Currencies. Available at: http://money.cnn.com/data/currency. Retrieved August 21.

DeRosa, D. (1991). *Managing Foreign Exchange Risk.* Chicago: Probus; London: MacMillan.

O'Connor, D., and Bueso, A. (1990). *International Dimensions of Financial Management.* London: MacMillan.

Salvatore, D. (2005). *Introduction to International Economics.* New York: Wiley.

Internet Sources

Exchange Rates
Information on currencies, currency derivatives, and foreign exchange rates
http://www.margrabe.com/Currency.html
Information on Federal Reserve data on exchange rates, balance of payments, and trade
http://research.stlouisfed.org/fred2/categories/13

Exchange Rates and Trade
Information by the Federal Reserve on inflation and exchange rates
http://www. house.gov/jec/fed.htm

Risk Management
Guide to risk management and information related to this subject:
http://www.contingencyanalysis.com/

CHAPTER 11

Artz, R. (1991). Punitive damages for wrongful dishonor or repudiation of a letter of credit. *Uniform Commercial Code Law Journal,* 24(3): 3-48.

Barnes, J. (1994). Defining good faith letter of credit practices. *Loyola of Los Angeles Law Review,* 28: 103-107.

Cheeseright, P. (November 5, 1994). Market of Reliant in receivership. *Financial Times,* 7.

Goldsmith, H. (1989). *Import/Export: A Guide to Growth, Profits and Market Share.* Upper Saddle River, NJ: Prentice-Hall.

International Chamber of Commerce (ICC) (1993). *Uniform Customs and Practice for Documentary Credits,* No. 500. New York: ICC Publishing Co.

International Chamber of Commerce (ICC) (1995). *Uniform Rules for Collections,* No. 522. New York: ICC Publishing Co.

Kelly, J. (March 1995). Credit management. *Financial Times,* i-v.

Kozolchyk, B. (1996). The financial standby: A summary description of practice and related problems. *Uniform Commercial Code Law Journal,* 28(4): 327-374.

Macintosh, K. (1992). Letters of credit: Curbing bad faith dishonor. *Uniform Commercial Code Law Journal,* 25(3): 3-48.

Maggiori, H. (1992). *How to Make the World Your Market.* New York: Burning Gate Press.

McLaughlin, G. (1989). Structuring commercial letters of credit transactions to safeguard the interests of the buyer. *Uniform Commercial Code Law Journal,* 21(3): 318-325.

McMahon, A., Marsh, A., Klitzke, P., and Issenman, J. (1994). *The Basics of Exporting.* Austin, TX: Southern United Trade Association.

Onkvisit, S., and Shaw, J. (1997). *International Marketing.* Upper Saddle River, NJ: Prentice-Hall.

Reynolds, F. (2003). *Managing Exports: Navigating the Complex Rules, Controls, Barriers and Laws.* New York: Wiley.

Rosenblith, R. (1991). Letter of credit law. *Uniform Commercial Code Law Journal,* 21(3): 171-175.

Rubenstein, N. (1994). The issuer's rights and obligations under a letter of credit. *Uniform Commercial Code Law Journal,* 17(2): 129-174.

Ruggiero, A. (1991). *Financing International Trade.* New York: UNZ and Co.

Ryan, R. (1990). Who should be immune from the fraud in the defense in a letter of credit transaction. *Brooklyn Law Review,* 56: 119-152.

Schmitthoff, C. (1986). *Schmitthoff's Export Trade.* London: Butterworths.

Shapiro, A. (2006). *Multinational Financial Management.* New York: Wiley.

Tuller, L. (1994). *Exporting, Importing and Beyond.* Holbrooke, MA: Bob Adams.

Wells, F., and Dullat, K. (1991). *Exporting from Start to Finance.* New York: McGraw-Hill.

Internet Sources

Financing Exports

Information on letters of credit
http://www.bizhelp24.com/export-import/the-letter-of-credit-2.html
Articles and cases on letters of credit
http://www.allbusiness.com/periodicals/article/ 862988-1.html
International Financial Services Association on letters of credit

http://www.ifsaonline.org/
International Institute of Banking on financing exports and related topics.
http:// www.iiblp.org/

CHAPTER 12

Angelidis, J., Parsa, F., and Ibrahim, N. (2004). Countertrading with Latin American countries: A Compare analysis of attitudes of United States firms. *International Journal of Management,* 21(4): 435-444.

Anonymous (September 14, 1996). Philbro appoints Indonesian firm to fulfill local offsets. *Countertrade and Offsets,* 5.

Anonymous (April 14, 1997a). Dassault launches offset related aviation joint venture with Taiwan's Chenfeng. *Countertrade and Offsets,* 15(7): 5.

Anonymous (April 14, 1997b). Russian Menatep to resume Cuban oil-for-sugar swap. *Countertrade and Offset,* 15(7): 5.

Anonymous (April 14, 1997c). Saab, Lockheed and GE pledge offset in Hungary. *Countertrade and Offset,* 15(7): 2-3.

Anyane-Ntow, K., and Harvey, C. (1995). A countertrade primer. *Management Accounting,* 76(10): 47-50.

Bost, P., and Yeakel, J. (1992). Are we ignoring countrade? *Management Accounting,* 76(6): 43-47.

Bragg, A. (January 1998). Bartering comes of age. *Sales and Marketing Management,* 61-63.

Brinton, C., Christopher, J., Wolff, R., and Winks, R. (1984). *A History of Civilization,* vol. I. Upper Saddle River, NJ: Prentice-Hall.

Casson, M., and Chukujama, F. (1990). Countertrade theory and evidence. In Buckley, P., and Clegg, J., eds. *Multinational Enternprises in Less Developed Countries.* pp.11-16, London: Macmillan.

Caves, R., and Marin, D. (1992). Countertrade transactions: Theory and evidence. *Economic Journal,* 102(414): 1171-1183.

Cole, J. (1987). Evaluating offset agreements: Achieving a balance of advantages. *Law and Policy in International Business,* 19: 765-811.

Egan, C., and Shipley, D. (1996). Strategic orientations toward countertrade opportunities in emerging markets. *International Marketing Review,* 13: 102-120.

Hennart, J.F. (1990). Some empirical dimensions of countertrade. *Journal of International Business Studies,* 21(2): 243-270.

Hennart, J., and Anderson, E. (1993). Countertrade and the minimization of transaction costs: An empirical examination. *Journal of Law, Economics and Organization,* 9: 290-314.

Liesch, P. (1991). *Government Mandated Countertrade: Deals of Arm Twisting.* Brookfield, VT: Gower Press.

McVey, T. (1984). Commercial practices, legal issues and policy dilemmas. *Law and Policy in International Business,* 16: 23-26.

Office of Management and Budget (OMB) (1986). *Second Annual Report on the Impact of Offsets in Defense-Related Exports.* Washington, DC: U.S. Government Printing Office.

Roessler, F. (1985). Countertrade and the GATT legal system. *Journal of World Trade Law,* 19(6): 604-614.

Schaffer, M. (1989). *Winning the Countertrade War: New Export Strategies for America.* New York: Wiley.

U.S. Department of Commerce, Bureau of Industry and Security (2005). *Offsets in Defense Trade.* Washington, DC: U.S. Government Printing Office. www.bis.doc.gov/osies

U.S. International Trade Commission (ITC) (1985). *Assessment of the Effects of Barter and Countertrade Transactions on U.S. Industries.* Washington, DC: U.S. Government Printing Office.

Verdun, V. (1985). Are governmentally imposed countertrade requirements violations of the GATT. *Yale Journal of International Law,* 11: 191-215.

Verzariu, P. (1985). *Countertrade, Barter and Offsets: New Strategies for Profit in International Trade.* New York: McGraw-Hill.

Verzariu, P. (1992). Trends and developments in international countertrade. *Business America,* 113: 2-6.

Welt, L. (1990). Unconventional forms of financing: Buyback/compensation/barter. *Journal of International Law and Politics,* 22: 461-473.

Internet Sources

Information on global countertrade, legal and regulatory environment, and conferences pertaining to countertrade. Provides information on the American Countertrade Association.
http://www.globaloffset.org/
Information on countertrade and Incoterms, including seminars related to this subject.
http://i-b-t.net/anm/templates/trade_article.asp?articleid=206&zoneid=3
Articles on countertrade
http://www.investopedia.com/terms/c/countertrade.asp
News and Publications on countertrade
http://www.barternews.com/countertrade.htm

CHAPTER 13

Anonymous (1995). Increase services to small business, survey suggests. *Bank Management,* 71(4): 9-12.

Brewer, E., II, Genay, G., Jackson, W., III, and Worthington, P. (1996). How are small firms financed? Evidence from small business investment companies. *Federal Reserve Bank of Chicago,* 20: 1-18.

Field, A., Korn, D., and Middleton, T. (1995). How to make them give you the money. *Money*, 24(6): 94-103.

Fraser, J. (December 1996). Control those credit cards. *INC.*, 18: 128.

Gardner, L. (1994). Opportunities and pitfalls in financing during business growth. *Secured Lender*, 50: 39-42.

Grimaud, A. (June 1995). The evolution of small-business financing. *Canadian Banker*, 102(3): 36-37.

Hutchinson, R. (1995). The capital structure and investment decisions of the small owner-managed firm: Some exploratory issues. *Small Business Economics*, 7: 231-239.

Ioannou, L. (May 1995). The trade factor. *International Business*, 42-45.

Lorenz-Fife, I. (1997). *Financing Your Business*. Englewood Cliffs, NJ: Prentice-Hall.

Ring, M. (January 1993). Innovative export financing: Factoring and forfaiting. *Business America*, 114(1): 10-12.

Schleifer, A., and Vishny, R. (1992). Liquidation values and debt capacity: A market equilibrium approach. *Journal of Finance*, 47: 1343-1366.

Silvester, J. (1995). *How to Start, Finance and Operate Your Own Business*. Seacaucus, NJ: Carol Publishing Group.

Stulz, R. (1990). Managerial discretion and optimal financing policies. *Journal of Financial Economics*, 26: 3-15.

Williamson, O. (1988). Corporate finance and corporate governance. *Journal of Finance*, 43: 567-591.

Internet Sources

Small Business Financing
Information on articles and links of interest to current and prospective business owners.
http://www.hrsbdc.org/links/general.html

Other Sites for Small Businesses
http://www.creative-edgeonline.com (tips for entrepreneurs, web presence)
http://www.owi-com/netvalue/v1I1.htm (business sites on the web)
http://www.isquare.com (small business adviser)
http://www.fed.org (foundation for enterprise development)
http://www.sbaonline.sba.gov/oit/loans.html (trade finance programs)
http://www.usa.ft.com (information about companies, market and world economies)

CHAPTER 14

Economic Commission for Europe (2003). *Trade Finance for Small and Medium-Sized Enterprises in CIS Countries*. New York: United Nations.

Ex-Im Bank (1997a). *General Information.* Washington, DC: U.S. Government Printing Office.

Ex-Im Bank (1997b). *Small Business Information.* Washington, DC: U.S. Government Printing Office.

Ex-Im Bank (1997c). *Working Capital Guarantee Program.* Washington, DC: U.S. Government Printing Office.

Ex-Im Bank. www.exim.gov

IMF (2003). *International Financial Statistics.* Washington, DC: IMF.

OPIC. www.opic.gov

PEFCO. www.pefco.com

Reynolds, F. (2003). *Managing Exports: Navigating the Complex Rules, Controls, Barriersand Laws.* New York: Wiley.

Small Business Administration (2007). Programs and services to help you start, grow, and succeed. Available at: http://www.sbaonline.sba.gov.

United States Agency for International Development (USAID) (2000). *Analysis of Microfinance Supply and Demand on Russia's Market.* Moscow: USAID.

U.S. Department of Agriculture. www.usda.gov

U.S. Department of Commerce (1990). *A Basic Guide to Exporting from the United States.* Lincolnwood, IL: NTC Books.

Wells, F., and Dulat, K. (1996). *Exporting from Start to Finance.* New York: McGraw-Hill.

Internet Sources

http://www.sba.gov/INV/forentre.html (Small Business Program For Private Companies)

http://www.sbaonline.sba.gov (Small Business Administration home page)

http://www.exim.gov (Export-Import Bank of the US-programs, projects fees etc.)

http://web.ita.doc.gov/ticwebsite/tic.nsf/037197a7338428ca8525663300051710b/e597ece099a283948525663300711c40!OpenDocument (Exporting Finance Program Guide)

CHAPTER 15

Anonymous (January 28, 1995). $24.8 million penalty paid by Lockheed. *The New York Times,* Section 1, 35.

Atkinson, K., and Tillen, J. (September-October 2005). The Foreign Corrupt Practices Act: Compliance issues in the tax and customs area. *The Tax Executive,* 446-454.

Chou, W. (2005). The $4 billion question: An analysis of congressional responses to the FSC/ET. *Northwestern Journal of International Law,* 25(2): 415-451.

Clausing, K. (2005). Tax holidays (and other escapes) in the American Jobs Creation Act. *National Tax Journal,* 331-354.

Export Administration Regulations (EAR). Parts 734, 736, 740, 748, 750, 754, 760, 762, and 774.

GATT (1977). *Basic Instruments and Selected Documents.* Geneva: GATT (DOC L/4422).

Gleich, O., and Woodward, R. (2005). Foreign Corrupt Practices Act. *American Criminal Law Review,* 42: 545-571.

Gravelle, J. (2005). The 2004 corporate tax revisions as a spaghetti Western: Good, bad and ugly. *National Tax Journal,* 58(3): 347-365.

Hall, C. (1994). Foreign Corrupt Practices Act: A Competitive disadvantage, but for how long? *Tulane Journal of International and Comparative Law,* 2: 300-315.

Impert, J. (1990). A program for compliance with the Foreign Corrupt Practices Act and foreign restrictions on the use of sales agents. *The International Lawyer,* 24(4): 45-66.

Johns, R. (1988). *Colonial Trade and International Exchange.* London. Pinter publishers.

Levin, M. (2004). Tax changes in the American Jobs Creation Act of 2004. *The CPA Journal,* 54-55.

Lipman, J. (February 12, 1990). Young and Rubicam pleads guilty to settle Jamaica case. *The Wall Street Journal,* 5.

Loizeau, J. (July-August, 2004). IC-DISCs may benefit S corporation and LLC exporters. *Business Entities,* 18-27.

Moskowitz, D. (1996). Lingering Cold War Legacies. *International Business,* 9(7): 40-41.

Shenefield, J., and Stelzer, I. (1993). *The Antitrust Laws.* Washington, DC: The American Enterprise Institute.

Stein, H., and Foss, M. (1992). *An Illustrated Guide to the US Economy.* Washington, DC: The America Enterprise Institute.

Stenger, G. (1984). The Development of American Export Control Legislation. *Wisconsin International Law Journal,* 6(1): 1-5.

Walsh, K. (2002). *US Export Controls and Commercial Technology Transfers to China.* US-China Security Review Commission: Hearing on export controls and China. Washington, DC: USGPO.

Internet Sources

Bureau of Export Administration
http://www.bis.doc.gov
Export Administration Regulations
http://www.access.gpo.gov/bis/
The Foreign Corrupt Practices Act (FCPA)
http://www.usdoj.gov/criminal/fraud/fcpa/dojdocb.htm
http://www.usdoj.gov/criminal/fraud/fcpa/fcpastat.htm
Convention on Combating Bribery of Foreign Officials
http://www.oecd.org/dataoecd/7/35/35109576.pdf
U.S. Antitrust Law/Policy
http://www.usdoj.gov/
Antitrust Enforcement

http://www.usdoj.gov/atr/public/div_stats/211491.htm
U.S. Tax Reform and Opportunities for Exporters
http://www.taxpolicycenter.org
http://www.swlearning.com/tax/wft/
FAS programs
http://www.fas.usda.gov/fasprograms.html

CHAPTER 16

Rossides, E. (1986). *US Import Trade Regulation*. Washington, DC: The Bureau of
   National Affairs.
Serko, D. (1985). *Import Practice*. New York: Practicing Law Institute.
U.S. Department of Commerce (1998). *A Basic Guide to Exporting*. Lincolnwood,
   IL: NTC Books.
U.S. Department of Commerce (2003). *Importing Into the United States*. Rocklin,
   CA: Prima Publishing.
U.S. Federal Regulations, CFR 19.

Internet Sources

Information on Foreign Trade Zones
http://www.cbp.gov/xp/cgov/import/cargo_control/ftz/about_ftz.xml
http://ia.ita.doc.gov/ftzpage/tic.html
http://trade.gov/index.asp
Federal Regulations on Customs Tariffs
http://www.lawdog.com/transport/export/custom2.htm
Information on U.S. Customs and Border Protection—Importing, Exporting, NAFTA,
   and Information on the Harmonized Tariff Schedule.
http://www.customs.ustreas.gov/
Information on the U.S. Generalized System of Preferences
http://www.itds.treas.gov/gsp.html

CHAPTER 17

Buzzanell, P., and Lipton, K. (September/December 1995). Whether a pinch or a
   dash, it adds up to a growing U.S. spice market. *Food Review,* 18(3): 1-5.
Deyak, T., Sawyer, W., and Sprinkle, R. (1993). A comparison of demand for imports
   and exports in Japan and the United States. *Journal of World Trade,* 27: 63-73.
Ghymn, K. (1983). The relative importance of import decision variables. *Journal of
   the Academy of Marketing Science,* 11: 304-312.
Lindert, P., and Pugel, T. (1996). *International Economics*. Chicago: Irwin.

Lutz, J. (1994). To import or to protect? Industrialized countries and manufactured products. *Journal of World Trade,* 28(4): 123-145.

Nelson, C. (2000). *Import Export: How to Get Started in International Trade.* New York: McGraw-Hill.

Reinhart, C. (1995). Devaluation, relative prices, and international trade: Evidence from developing countries. *IMF Staff Papers,* 42: 290-312.

Sarmad, K. (1989). The determinants of import demand in Pakistan. *World Development,* 17: 1619-1625.

Shippen, B. (1999). Labor market effects of import competition: Theory and evidence from the textile and apparel industries. *Atlantic Economic Journal,* 27(2): 193-200.

Warner, D., and Kreinin, M. (1983). Determinants of international trade flows. *Review of Economics and Statistics,* 65(1): 19-104.

Weiss, K. (1987). *Building an Import Export Business.* New York: John Wiley and Sons.

Internet Sources

Finding Your Partners
Information on trade opportunities and partnerships
http://www.firstgov.gov/Business/Trade.shtml

Learn How to Trade
U.S. Customs guide to importation and planning for growth.
http://www.unzco.com/basicguide/c2.html
http://www.cbp.gov/xp/cgov/import/

Trade Shows
Information on international trade shows and conferences.
http://www.biztradeshows.com/
http://www.globalsources.com/TRADESHW/TRDSHFRM.HTM

CHAPTER 18

Bovard, J. (September 1998). Your partner: The customs service. *World Trade,* 48-49.

Buonafina,M., and Haar, J. (1989). *Import Marketing.* Lexington, MA: Lexington Books.

Code of Federal Regulations (19 CFR, 1304).

Rossides, E. (1986). *US Import Trade Regulation.* Washington, DC: The Bureau of national Affairs.

Serko, D. (1985). *Import Practice.* New York: The Practising Law Institute.

U.S. Department of Commerce (2003). *Importing into the United States.* Rocklin, CA: Prima Publishing.

Internet Sources

Import Regulations

Information on the importation of goods to the United States/ U.S. Customs rules and regulations.

http://www.cbp.gov/xp/cgov/import/infrequent_importer_info/internet_purchases.xml

http://cbp.customs.gov/linkhandler/cgov/toolbox/publications/trade/iius.ctt/iius.pdf

Site provides information on tariffs and related matters, including the U.S. Harmonized Tariff Schedule

http://www.usitc.gov/

Publications of the U.S. Customs: Entry of goods, classification, and valuation of merchandise.

http://www.customs.ustreas.gov/xp/cgov/toolbox/publications/

CHAPTER 19

Czako, J., Human, J., and Miranda, J. (2003). *A Handbook on Antidumping Investigations*. New York: Cambridge University Press.

Folsom, R., Gordon, M., and Spanogle, J. (2005). *International Business Transactions and Economic Relations*. St. Paul, MN: Thomson.

Trebilcock, M., and Howse, R. (2005). *The Regulation of International Trade*. New York: Taylor & Francis.

United States Code ss. 1337; 1677; 1862; 2436

U.S. Department of State (2005). *Trade and Economies*. (http://usinfo.state.gov/ei/Archive/2005/May/02-478072.html (accessed June 28, 2006).

U.S. International Trade Commission (USITC) (November 1996a). *Antidumping and Countervailing Duty Handbook*. Washington, DC: U.S. Government Printing Office.

U.S. International Trade Commission (USITC) (January 1996b). *Summary of Statutory Provisions Related to Import Relief*. Washington, DC: U.S. Government Printing Office.

U.S. International Trade Commission (1997). *Annual Report*. Washington, DC: U.S. Government Printing Office.

U.S. Trade Representative (USTR) (2004). *Foreign Trade Barriers*. Washington, DC: U.S. Government Printing Office.

U.S. Trade Representative (USTR) (2005). *Foreign Trade Barriers*. Washington, DC: U.S. Government Printing Office.

Internet Sources

Information provided by the U.S. International Trade Commission on antidumping and countervailing.

http://www.usitc.gov/trade_remedy/731_ad_701_cvd/index.htm

Abstract of the Judicial review of International Trade Commission determinations. http://www.questia.com/PM.qst?a=o&d=5000248716

The Heritage Foundation antidumping laws http://www.heritage.org/Research/TradeandForeignAid/BG906.cfm

Fact sheets on Special 301 and Title VII. http://hongkong.usconsulate.gov/usinfo/ustr/2000/0501.htmII)

CHAPTER 20

Ashton, T. (1988). *The Industrial Revolution.* London: Oxford University Press.

Bird, R. (2006). Defending intellectual property rights in the BRIC economies. *American Business Law Journal,* 43(2): 317-363.

Chiang, E. (2004). Determinants of cross-border intellectual property rights enforcement: The role of trade sanctions. *Southern Economic Journal,* 7(2): 424-440.

Gad, M. (2003). Impact of multinational enterprises on the multilateral rule-making: The pharmaceutical industry and the TRIPs Uruguay Round negotiations. *Law & Business Review of the Americas,* IX(4): 667-674.

Gadbaw, M., and Richards, T. (1998). *Intellectual Property Rights.* Boulder, CO: Westview Press.

Hannah, D. (2006). Keeping trade secrets secret. *MIT Sloan Management Review,* 47(3): 17-20.

Kinter, E., and Lahr, J. (1983). *An Intellectual Property Law Primer.* New York: Clark Boardman.

Ladas, S. (1975). *Patents, Trademarks and Related Rights: National and International Protection.* Cambridge, MA: Harvard University Press.

Linek, E., and Iwanicki, J. (2006). International efforts are achieving credible IP enforcement even amid chronic abuse. *Intellectual Property & Technology Law Journal,* 18(3): 4-7.

Seyoum, B. (1993). Property rights versus public welfare in the protection of trade secrets in developing countries. *The International Trade Journal,* 3, 341-359.

United States Trade Representative (2006). *Foreign Trade Barriers.* Washington, DC: GPO.

Williams, L. (1983). Transfer of technology to developing countries. *Federal Bar News and Journal,* 30: 266-267.

Wolfhard, E. (1991). International trade in intellectual property: The emerging GATT regime. *University of Toronto Faculty of Law Review,* 49: 106-151.

Internet Sources

Patents and Intellectual Property
http://members.tripod.com/~patents2/
http://iipa.com/rbi/2005
Intellectual property mall
http://www.ipmall.fplc.edu/

Intellectual Property: Copyrights, Trademarks, and Patents
http://www.brint.com/IntellP.htm
A FREE TRADE AREA FOR THE AMERICAS: Intellectual property
http://www.cptech.org/pharm/belopaper.htm
News on patent, trademark, design and copyright from Japan
http://www.okuyama.com/index-2.html
US intellectual property for non-lawyers
http://www.fplc.edu/tfield/ipbasics.htm

Index

Page numbers followed by "b" indicate boxed material; "i" indicate an illustration; "t" indicate a table.

Absolute quotas, 393
Acceptance, 181t
Accidental discrepancies, 256, 267
Accounts receivable, 307-308, 315
Actionable subsidies, 450
Active Corps of Executives (ACE), 81-82
Ad valorem duty, 309, 403
Admission Temporaire Admission (ATA) carnet
  business travel, 86
  Case 17.1, 421-422
Advance payments
  buyer financing, 307, 315
  payment arrangements, 263, 264
Advertising
  export counseling assistance, 79
  government-supported, 88
  market potential, 69-70
  overseas promotion, 87-89
  process of, 88
  service trade, 7
Affiliated groups, 47
Africa
  Ex-Im Bank, 322t
  Internet use, 120t
African Growth and Opportunity Act (AGOA) policy, 398
African Regional Industrial Property Organization (ARIPO)
PCT, 474
  regional convention, 475, 476

Agent/Distributor Service (ADS), 80b
Agricultural products
  export incentives, 375b
  import requirements, 391t
  merchandise trade, 10
  unfair trade practices, 460, 462
Air cargo rates determination, 203-204, 218
Air cargo regulation, 204b, 204-205
Air consignment note. See Air waybills
Air transportation
  advantages/disadvantages of, 202t
  growth of, 201-203, 217
  rising costs, 13
Air waybills
  documentation, 197, 204-205, 217
  logistics process, 127, 128
Aircraft sector, 321, 322t
Alcoholic beverages, 391t
All-risks policy, 137
Aluminum ladders, 68t
American Business Media, 69-70
American Credit Indemnity, 134
American Insurance Underwriters, 134
Ammunition, 391t
Andean Pact, 33t, 36
Andean Trade Preference (ATP) import policy, 398
Annecy (France) Round, GATT, 21b
Antiboycott regulations
  exceptions to, 362, 378-379
  non-reportable requests, 362b

Export-Import Theory, Practices, and Procedures, Second Edition

Antiboycott regulations *(continued)*
  penalties for noncompliance, 363, 379
  prohibitions, 361-362, 378
  purpose of, 360, 378
  reporting requirements, 362
  scope, 361, 378
Antidumping cases, countries cited, 457t
Antidumping duty (AD)
  costs of, 449b
  investigation proceedings, 453t, 453-456, 456t, 462
  proof of injury investigations, 451-452, 462
Antidumping duty (AD) laws
  international regulation, 447
  statutory remedy, 447
Antitrust regulations
  categories of, 368, 380
  checklist of practices to avoid, 371
  enforcement/penalties, 371-372, 380
  exemptions, 368, 370-371, 380
  extraterritorial applications, 371, 380
  general prohibitions, 368, 369, 380
  origins of, 368
  specific prohibitions, 368, 369, 380
Argentina
  adversative trade policies, 460
  Case 4.1, 93
  Corruption Perception Index, 364b
  IPR enforcement, 471b
  modern migration to, 3
  priority watch list, 472
  trading opportunities, 486-487
Arms sales
  import requirements, 391t
  offset transactions, 284
Asia
  Ex-Im Bank, 321, 322t, 323
  Internet use, 120t
  trading opportunities, 495-503
Asian Free Trade Area, 11-12
Asian Pacific Economic Cooperation (APEC)
  regional agreements, 33t, 36
  USFTAs, 395b

Asset specificity, 95
Asset-based financing, 301, 315
Assignment of proceeds/L/Cs, 309, 315
Association of Southeast Asian Nations (ASEAN), 33t, 36
Australia
  Corruption Perception Index, 364b
  countertrade policy, 286
  defense offsets, 292t
  Hague-Visby Rules, 208-209
  modern migration to, 3
  trading opportunities, 495-496
  USFTAs, 395b, 395-396, 403
Australian Group (AG), 350b
Authorized regular employer, 425, 439
Automated Broker Interface (ABI), 434b
Automated Clearing House (ACH), 434b
Automated Export System (AES), 358b, 434b
Automated Information Systems Security policy (AIS), 434b
Automated Manifest System (AMS), 434b
Automobile and Truck International, 88

Back-to-back letters of credit (L/Cs)
  import financing, 419
  payment arrangements, 260-261, 268
  third party financing, 309, 315
Bahamas
  adversative trade policies, 460
  watch list, 472
Bahrain, 395b
Bank accounts, 49
Bank guarantee, 191
Bank letter of credit (L/C), 328, 339
Banker's acceptance, 265, 308, 315
Bankers Association of Foreign (BAFT), 313
Banking industry
  ancient trade, 1
  countertrade departments, 272
  external financing, 300-301, 315

Banking industry *(continued)*
    letters of credit (L/Cs), 247-248,
        251, 252-254
    payment liability, 246-247
    payment role, 242-246, 266, 267
    service trade, 7
Barges, 207b
Barter
    countertrade, 276, 277i, 283i, 288
    transaction mechanics, 275b
Barter and Countertrade Unit, 286
Barter contract negotiation, 282b
Basic materials, 17t
Basic need potential, 75
Belarus, 472
Belgium
    agent contracts, 110
    countervailing duty cases, 457t
    trade volume, 10
Berne Convention, 28
Bill of exchange (draft)
    documentation, 197-198, 217
    late medieval trade, 1
Bill of lading (B/L)
    documentation, 198-199, 217
    Hague Rules, 210
    logistics process, 127, 128
Boats, 391t
Bofors-India Countertrade Deal,
        290-291
Bolivia
    import price anomalies, 68t
    watch list, 472
Bonded warehouses, 402, 404
Bonds
    export contract clauses, 190, 191,
        194
    release of merchandise, 428-430,
        430t, 440
Bovine animals, 68t
Branches (foreign), 55-56, 57, 57i
Brazil
    adversative trade policies, 460
    antidumping cases, 457t
    Corruption Perception Index, 364b
    countervailing duty cases, 457t
    Ex-Im Bank, 322t
    import barriers, 392t

Brazil *(continued)*
    modern economy, 3
    priority watch list, 472
    trading opportunities, 487-488
Brazilian Decree (No. 1298), 102b
Break-bulk, 207b
Bribery
    FCPA, 364, 365-366
    international efforts against, 368
    OECD efforts, 368
Briefs/panties, 68t
Britain. *See also* United Kingdom
    colonial trade, 2, 3
    modern trade, 3-4
British East India Company
    charter company, 2, 102b
    monopoly grant, 368
Bulgaria, 472
Bulk cargo, 207b
Bulk carriers, 207b
Bureau of Industry and Security (BIS)
    anti-boycott regulations, 360
    EAR administration, 351, 352, 357
    Office of Export Enforcement,
        359
Business angels, 305
Business International Corporation,
        132
Business locations, 49-50
Business names, 48-49
Business negotiations, 86
Business plan
    international export-import, 77-78,
        79i, 91
    sample export, 561-565, 564t, 565t,
        566t
    sample import, 567-571, 569t, 571t,
        572t
Business stage, 298, 314
Business travel
    export pricing, 155, 174
    host country knowledge, 84
    preparation, 83-84
Buy American Act, 394
Buyback transactions, 277i, 279i,
        279-280, 282b, 289
Buyer, financing arrangements, 307,
        315, 311

Buyer credit
   government programs, 319
   intermediate/long-term financing
      arrangement, 311, 316
Buyers
   countertrade benefits, 273-274, 287
   Incoterms, 161t, 162t-163t
   payment preferences, 319

California, 338, 340
Canada
   antidumping cases, 457t
Corruption Perception Index, 364b
   countervailing duty cases, 457t
   defense offsets, 292t
   Ex-Im Bank, 322t
   export price anomalies, 68t
   Hague-Visby Rules, 208-209
   impact of international trade, 8
   import barriers, 392t
   import price anomalies, 68t
   indirect marketing channels, 97-98
   lost tax revenue, 68t
   modern migration to, 3
   NAFTA, 25, 26, 30-31, 31t,
      394-395
   trading opportunities, 489-490
   U. S. tax treaty, 64
   watch list, 472
Capital, 297-298
Capital expenses, 60
Capital goods, 17t
Cargo selectivity, 434b
Caribbean Basin Initiative (CBI),
   397-398, 403
Caribbean Basin Trade Partnership Act,
   397-398
Caribbean, 120t
Caribbean Common Market
      (CARICOM), 33t, 36
Carmack Amendment, 213
Carnet, 429
Carriage and insurance paid to (CIP),
   160t, 162t-163t, 169t-170t,
   171, 176
Carriage of Goods by Sea Act
   (COGSA), 220

Carriage paid to (CPT), 160t,
   162t-163t, 169t-170t, 171,
   176
"Carrier certificate," 425
Carrier liability, 211b
Case. *See also* Minicase
Case 1.1., Limitations of Export-Led
   Growth, 15-17, 16t, 17t,
Case 2.1., Benefits and Costs of Free
   Trade, 37-38, 38t
Case 3.1., Shrinking Tax Base, 66-67,
   68t
Case 4.1., Developing Export Markets,
   92-94
Case 5.1., Export Channel Decisions,
   117-118
Case 5.2., Internet and Developing
   Countries, 118-120, 120t
Case 6.1., Marine Insurance Loss,
   147-148
Case 6.2., Inchmaree clause, 148-149
Case 7.1., Incoterms (CIF), 177
Case 7.2., Incoterms (C&F), 177-178
Case 8.1., CISG, 195
Case 8.2., *China National Products v.
   Apex Digital Inc.,* 195-196
Case 9.1., Package under COGSA, 220
Case 9.2., Container revolution, 221
Case 10.1., U. S. Dollar, 237-238
Case 11.1., Dishonoring Letters of
   Credit, 269-270
Case 11.2., Independence Principle,
   270
Case 12.1., Bofors-India Countertrade
   Deal, 290-291
Case 12.2., Offsets in U. S. Defense
   Trade, 291-294, 292t, 293t
Case 13.1., Tadoo's Sales to Belgium,
   316-317
Case 14.1., Trade Finance in Transition
   Economies, 341-342
Case 14.2., Ex-Im Bank Financing,
   342-343
Case 15.1., Export Trade Certificate of
   Review, 381-383
Case 15.2., Enforcement of Export
   Regulations, 383-385

Case 16.1., Tax Deduction for Processing in Maquilas, 406
Case 17.1., ATA Carnet, 421-422
Case 17.2., Maytags's Triad Strategy, 423
Case 18.1., Deemed Liquidation by Customs, 444
Case 18.2., Product Classification, 445
Case 19.1., Similar Products and Dumping, 463
Case 20.1., Patents for Life Saving Drugs, 477-478
Cash in advance, 258-259, 267
Central American Common Market (CACM), 33t, 36
Central banks, 226, 236
Centralization, 50-51
Certificate of origin
    documentation, 199, 217
    logistics process, 127
Certified development company (CDC), 303t, 304
Chamber of Commerce, 83t
Charter companies, 2
Chicago Prime Packers vs. Northam Trading Co., CISG, 182b
Chile
    trading opportunities, 490-491
    USFTAs, 395b
    watch list, 472
China
    antidumping cases, 457t
    Corruption Perception Index, 364b
    Ex-Im Bank, 322t
    foreign exchange reserves, 13
    import price anomalies, 68t
    international trade, 1
    IPR enforcement, 471b
    lost tax revenue, 68t
    medieval trade, 1
    priority watch list, 472
    trade volume, 10
    trading opportunities, 497-498
    U. S. tax treaty, 64
    unjustified foreign trade practices, 458, 460
    WTO membership, 11
China National Products v. Apex Digital Inc., 195-196
Chinese Foreign Trade Agency, 123
Citizens, 54-55
City agencies, 82
Clayton Act, 368, 380
Clean Air Act, 129
Clean/claused bill of lading, 198
Clean collections, 266
Clearing arrangement, 277i, 278-279, 279i, 288-289
Cocoa Association of London, 185
Colonial era
    first phase, 2
    second phase, 3
Columbia
    Corruption Perception Index, 364b
    trading opportunities, 491-493
    USFTAs, 395b
Combination carriers, 207b
Commerce Control List (CCL), 353b, 356-358, 359
Commerce export license steps, 353b, 353-359
Commercial banks, 83t
Commercial finance companies, 305, 315
Commercial invoice
    documentation, 199-200, 217
    entry documentation, 428, 439
    logistics process, 127
Commercial lenders, 300-301, 315
Commercial loan guarantees, 323, 330i, 330-331, 339
Commercial loans, 302, 315
Commercial News USA (CNUSA), 79, 80b
Commercial publications, 88
Commercial terms, 158, 159t
Common Agricultural Policy (CAP), 34
Common Market, 24b
Common markets, 11
Communications
    growth rate, 16t
    world economic integration, 12
Comparative advantages, 12-13
Competition, 124, 145

Competitive pricing, 157-158, 175
Compound duty, 309, 403
Computed value, 435, 437-438, 440
Conference lines, 206-208
Confirmed L/Cs, 253, 268
Consignment, 421
Consignment sales
    exporter financing, 307, 315
    payment arrangements, 239-241,
      265
Construction
    Ex-Im Bank, 321
    service trade, 7
Consular invoice, 199, 217
Consultants
    export decision, 71
    export pricing, 155, 174
Consumer goods
    growth rate, 16t
    import requirements, 391t
Container cargo, 13
Containers
    growth of, 221
    ocean cargo, 207b
Content requirement, 326, 336
Continental Credit Insurance, 134
Contract manufacturing, 416-417
Contractor bid, 263-264
Control
    distribution channel selection,
      98-99, 116
    export organizational issues, 51
Controlled foreign corporations (CFC),
    59-60
"Controlled group of corporations,"
    62
Convention Concerning International
    Carriage by Rail (COTIF),
    213-214, 218
Convention on Combating Bribery,
    OECD, 368
Convention on International Sale of
    Goods (CISG)
    adoption of, 180
    Chicago Prime Packers v. Northam
      Trading Co., 182b
    essential elements, 194
    and UCC, 181t

Convention on the Contract for the
    International Carriage of
    Goods by Road (CMR), 213,
    214, 218
"Convention on the limitation period in
    the International Sale of
    Goods," 184-185
Cooperative exporters (CEs), 104
Coordinating Committee for
    Multilateral Export Controls
    (COCOM)
    export control policy, 348, 349
    WA, 350b
Coordination, 51
Coproduction, 281-283, 283i, 289
Copyrights
    Customs Service registration,
      471-472
    IPRs, 465, 467-468
    Section 337 practices, 456-458, 462
    violations of, 469
Corn Laws, 3
Corporate income, 47
Corporations
    bank account, 49
    business structure, 45-47
    business/trade name, 48-49
    capital access, 297
    financing alternatives, 298
    transaction taxation, 55-56, 57
    U.S. taxation policies, 52
Corruption, international efforts
      against, 668. *See also* Foreign
      Corrupt Practices Act (FCPA)
Cosmetic import requirements, 391t
Cost, insurance, freight (CIF) terms,
    159t, 160t, 161t, 162t-163t,
    169t-170t, 174, 175
Cost and freight (CFR) terms, 160t,
    161t, 169t-170t, 171, 175
Cost in freight (CIF) value, 143
Cost-based pricing, 156, 175
Costa Rica, 364b
Counselors to America's Small
    Business (CASB), 81-82
Counterfeit goods
    Customs Service registration,
      471-472
    IPR issue, 468, 376

Counterpurchase, 277i, 280i, 280-281, 282b, 283i, 289
Countertrade
    benefits/costs, 273-274, 287, 278b
    definition of, 271, 287
    examples of, 272-273
    forms of, 276, 277i, 278-284, 279i, 280i, 283i 288-289
    GATT/WTO policies, 284-285, 289-290
    IMF policies, 285-286
    modern resurgence, 271-272
    origin of, 271
    theories of, 274-275, 287
Countervailing duty (CVD), 449b
    investigation proceedings, 453t, 453-456, 456t, 462
    proof of injury investigation, 451-452, 462
Countervailing duty cases, 457t
Countervailing duty (CVD) laws
    international regulation, 447
    statutory remedy, 447
Country-of-origins marking
    requirements, 438, 440
Court of Appeals for the Federal Circuit
    intellectual property violations, 458
    protests, 431, 440
    Section 201 appeals, 461
Court of International Trade
    AD/CVD appeals, 456
    protests, 431, 440
    Section 201 appeals, 461
Court of Justice, 35b
Coverage, 99, 116
Craft and lighter clause, 142b
Credit
    ancient trade, 1
    government financing programs, 319
    overseas customers, 306
Credit cards financing, 302, 315
Credit checks, 155
Credit information resources, 133

Credit insurance, Ex-Im Bank, 323, 326-327, 338. *See also* Export Credit Insurance Program (ECIP)
Credit reports, 265
Credit risk factors, 132-133, 146
Cross rates, 225, 226t
Crusades, 1
Cuba, 390, 393
Cumulation doctrine, 452
Cumulative presence test, 52-53
Currency, 125t
Customer characteristics, 97, 115
Customs and Border Protection (CBP)
    bond requirements, 430t
    entry processing, 426, 428
Customs brokers
    customs, 216
    entering goods, 425, 439
    license requirements, 400
    logistics process, 127, 128
    role of, 398-400, 403
Customs Cooperation Council, HTSUS, 432
Customs invoice, 127
Customs Power of Attorney, 405b
Customs Service
    import requirements, 391t
    IPR protection, 469
    IPR violation exclusions, 471-472
    voluntary reliquidation, 431
Customs Unions
    economic integration stages, 24b
    RIAs, 23t
Customs valuation process, 433, 435-438, 440
Czech Republic
    import price anomalies, 68t
    trading opportunities, 503-504

Damages clauses, 188, 189-190
Debt, 275
Debt financing
    external financing, 299, 315
    ownership structure, 298-299
Decentralization, 50-51

Decision-making, 46-47
Deductive value, 435, 436-437, 437b, 440
Deemed export license requirement, 349-350
Defense expenditures, 291-294, 292t, 293t
Deferred-payment credit, 261-262, 268
Deficiencies, 184, 194
Delay clause, 142b, 187-188
Delayed payment, 239, 240, 240i
Delivery
    contract terms, 158, 181t, 186-187, 194
    export pricing, 153, 174
Delivered duty paid (DDP) terms, 160t, 162t-163t, 169t-170t, 173-174, 176
Delivered duty unpaid (DDU) terms, 160t, 162t-163t, 169t-170t, 173-174, 176
Delivery at frontier (DAF) terms, 160t, 162t-163t, 169t-170t, 172-173, 176
Delivery ex quay (DEQ) terms, 160t, 161t, 169t-170t, 172, 173-174,176
Delivery ex ship (DES) terms, 160t, 161t, 169t-170t, 173, 176
Demand-based pricing, 157, 175
Denmark
    trading opportunities, 509-510
    world class logistics system, 128b
Deregulation, 297, 314
Design, 153, 174
Destination Control Statement (DCS)
    documentation, 200, 217
    export license determination, 357-358
Diamonds, 68t
Dillon Round, GATT, 21b
Diplomatic privileges, 1
Direct collection, 246
Direct distribution channels
    characteristics, 96, 115
    control, 98
    direct marketing, 105-106
    import marketing, 417, 421

Direct distribution channels *(continued)*
    intermediaries, 99
    marketing environment, 97-98
    marketing objectives, 96
    overseas agents, 106-107, 116
    overseas distributors, 107
    product characteristics, 97
    resources/experience, 96
    types of, 116
Direct mail, 88
Direct marketing, 116
Direct quotation, 225
Discrepancies, 255-258, 257b, 258b, 267
Dispute settlement
    claims, 143-145
    distribution agreement clause, 114-115
    GATT, 20
    NAFTA overview, 30
    TRIPS, 475
Distance, 125t
Distribution agreement sample, 585-591
Distribution channels
    financing alternatives, 298, 314
    selection factors, 96-99, 115-116
    types of, 115
Dock's receipt, 200, 217
Documentary collection
    import financing, 419, 421
    payment arrangements, 242-243, 244i, 266
    rules governing, 244, 252, 266
Documentary draft, 242-243, 244i, 265
Documentary letter of credit (L/C)
    advantages/disadvantages of, 251
    bilateral contracts, 250, 254
    definition, 251
    other types of, 259-265, 267-268
    payment arrangements, 247-250, 250i, 266
    regulations governing, 252
Documentation
    antiboycott regulations, 362
    automated systems, 434b
    business travel, 86
    entry of goods, 425-426, 426b, 428, 429, 439

Documentation *(continued)*
    export record keeping, 358-359
    frequently used, 197-201, 217
    logistics process, 126
    payment requirement, 167, 168
    sample trade documents, 619i-625i
Documents against acceptance,
    245-246
Documents against payments (D/P),
    244-245
Doha Round
    GATT, 21b
    trade barrier reductions, 11, 20
Domestic entity, 47
Domestic International Sales
    Corporation (DISC)
    export promotion, 373-374
    GATT violation, 374
    taxation of, 60
Domestic logistics, 125t
Dominican Republic, CAFTA, 11-12,
    395b, 396
Drawback entry, 427b
Drugs import requirements, 391t
Dumping, 447-448, 461. *See also*
    Antidumping duty
Dunn and Bradstreet, 133
Dutch East India Company, 101b
Dutch West India Company
    charter company, 2
    monopoly grant, 368
Duties
    entry process, 426
    export contract clauses, 190, 194
Duty to inspect, 184, 194
Dynamite, 68t

Eastern European trading opportunities,
    503-508
Economic Community of West African
    States (ECOWAS), 33t, 36
Economic factors, 132-135, 146
Economic Intelligence Unit, 132
"Effectively connected income,"
    55-56
"Efficiently connected," 55

Egypt
    adversative trade policies, 460
    agent contracts, 110
    Corruption Perception Index, 364b
    medieval trade, 1
    priority watch list, 472
    trading opportunities, 479-480
Electronic products import
    requirements, 391t
Electronic Request for Item
    Classification (ERIC), 358b
Employment
    impact of international trade, 8
    NAFTA assessment, 31
Enabling clause, 23t
Energy
    Ex-Im Bank, 321, 322t
    growth rate, 17t
Entertainment tax deductions, 61
Entrepreneurial class, 9
Entry
    CBP processing, 426, 428
    definition of, 425, 439
    documentation required, 425-426,
        426b, 428, 429, 439
    liquidation process, 430-431
    overview of process, 425, 439
    persons allowed to perform, 425,
        439
    political/legal barriers, 76
    release of merchandise, 428-429,
        440
    types of, 427b
Entry for consumption, 427b
Entry for transportation in bond, 427b
Entry for warehouse, 427b
Entry manifest, 428, 439
Entry summary, 429
Environment, 155, 175
Environmental risks, 69
Environmental subsidies, 451
Equal Export Opportunity Act of 1972,
    348
Equity financing
    external financing, 299, 315
    ownership structure, 298-299
    sources of, 305-306, 315
Escape clause, 461, 462

"Essential character," 432
Ethnocentric pricing, 156
Euro
  brief overview, 235b
  political risks, 132
  relative value, 228t
  SEA, 35
Europe
  advertising regulations, 87-88
  Ex-Im Bank, 322t
  Hague-Visby Rules, 208-209
  Internet use, 120t
European Commission, 34, 35b
European Council, 35b
European Free Trade (EFTA), 33t, 36
European Parliament, 35b
European Patent Convention, 475,
  476
European Patent Office (EPO), PCT,
  474
European Union (EU)
  adversative trade policies, 460
  economic institutions, 35b, 36
  economic integration, 32, 36
  and NAFTA, 32t
  trading opportunities, 509-518
  U. S. tax treaty, 64
Evergreen warranty, 190
Ex Store, 160-161
Ex Warehouse, 159, 159t, 160t,
  160-161, 162t-163t, 169t-170t
Ex Works, 159, 159t, 160t, 160-161,
  162t-163t, 169t-170t, 175
Exchange controls, 275, 287
Exchange rate(s)
  definition of, 225, 236
  export pricing, 155-156
  fluctuations of, 227, 228
  import volume determinant, 412,
    420
  protection against risks, 229-234
  restrictions, 229b
  trade determinant, 9
Excluded products, 73b
Export, overseas promotion, 88
Export Administration Act (EAA)
  anti-boycott regulations, 360-363
  export control policy, 348-349

Export Administration Regulations
  (EAR)
  export license determination,
    352-359, 355i, 356i, 358b,
    378
  purpose of, 351
  sanctions/violations, 359-360, 378
  scope of, 352, 378
Export business plan sample, 561-565,
  564t, 565t, 566t
Export cartels, 104
Export Certificate of Review (ETC)
  Act, 370, 380
Export commission agents (ECAs),
  102-103
Export competitiveness, 153-154, 174
Export Contact List Service, The, 88
Export contract
  additional terms, CISG, 181t
  applicable law clauses, 192-193,
    194
  basic clauses, 573-583
  cargo insurance clauses, 142b
  definition, 179, 185, 193
  dispute settlement clauses, 193, 194
  distribution agreement clauses,
    110-115
  distribution agreements, 110, 116
  Group C clauses, 159t, 160, 160t,
    161t, 162t-163t, 165-168,
    169t-170t, 171, 175
  Group D clauses, 160t, 161t,
    162t-163t, 169t-170t,
    172-174, 176
  Group E clauses, 159, 159t, 160t,
    160-161, 162t-163t,
    169t-170t, 175
  Group F terms, 159t, 160, 160t,
    161t, 161, 162t-163t,
    164-165, 169t-170t, 175
  guarantees/bonds clauses, 190-192,
    194
  harmonization motives, 179-180
  insurance, 136
  logistics process, 126
  price/delivery term clauses, 181t,
    186-187, 194

Export contract *(continued)*
quality/performance/liability
clauses, 181t, 188-190, 194
scope of work clause, 186,194
taxes/duties clauses, 190, 194
terms of sale, 158, 159t.
Export Control Act
EAR implementation, 351
export control policy, 347, 377
Export Control Classification Number
(ECCN), 353b, 356-357
Export controls
brief history of, 347-349
post September 11th policies,
349-350, 377
Export credit, 320
Export Credit Insurance Program
(ECIP)
Ex-Im Bank, 323, 326-327, 338
features of, 326-327
policies, 327i, 327-331, 330i, 331i
project finance program, 331-332
purpose of, 326
Export Development Corporation
(EDC), 313
Export leasing, 314, 316
Export level, 274, 287
Export License Application and
Information Network
(ELAIN), 358b
Export licenses, 349-350
Export management companies
(EMCs), 100-101
Export merchants, 103-104
Export packing list, 200-201, 217
Export potential, 69-71, 70t
Export prices, 273-274
Export pricing
approaches to, 156-158, 175
calculation of, 168, 169t-170t
external variables, 154, 155-156,
175
general terms of sale, 158, 159t
Group C terms, 159t, 160, 160t,
161t, 162t-163t, 165-168,
169t-170t, 171, 175
Group D terms, 160t, 161t, 162t-163t,
169t-170t, 172-174, 176

Export pricing *(continued)*
Group E terms, 159, 159t, 160t,
160-161, 162t-163t,
169t-170t, 175
Group F terms, 159t, 160, 160t,
161t, 161, 162t-163t,
164-165, 169t-170t, 175
internal variables, 154-155, 174
markups, 153-154, 174
objectives, 153, 174
policy types, 156
price determination worksheet, 166i
Export sales, 274
Export subsidies, 448, 462
Export Trade Act, 104
Export trading companies (ETCs), 101
Export Trading Company Act, 101,
102b
Export transaction, typical, 85b
Export working capital program
(EWCP), 303t, 332-333, 339
Export-import business
bank account, 49, 65
business location, 49-50
business plan, 77-78, 79i, 91
business/trade name, 48-49, 65
business travel, 77, 83-84, 86, 92
counseling assistance, 78-82, 91
export organizational issues, 50-51,
65
financing alternatives, 298-299, 314
foreign taxation, 56-57, 65
forms of, 299-301, 315
frequently used documents,
197-201, 217. *See also*
Documentation
insurance, 135-140
internal financing, 299, 300, 315
international transfer pricing, 61-64,
66
market assessment, 75-77
market research, 72-74, 91
organizational structures, 51-52
overseas promotion, 86-91, 92
ownership structure, 41-48, 65
payment arrangements, 239
private export financing, 306-315
professional services, 50

Export-import business *(continued)*
  risks of, 131-135
  selecting product/services, 69-72,
    70t, 73b, 91
  start-up costs, 298
  tax deductions/allowances, 60-61, 66
  U.S. taxation policies, 54-61, 58i
Export-Import (Ex-Im) Bank
  authorizations of, 321, 322t
  criticism of, 323
  establishment of, 320, 338
  major programs, 323
  political risks, 132
  role of, 320-322, 338
  selected cases, 342-343
  summary of programs, 537-559
Exporters
  countertrade benefits, 274, 287
  most common mistakes, 84b
  payment preferences, 319
  rights/obligations clause, 112, 116
Exporters that buy and sell, 103-104,
    116
Exporters that buy for overseas
    customers, 102-103, 116
Exporters that sell on behalf of
    manufacturer's (MEAs),
    99-101,116
Exports
  determinants, 9, 14
  domestic incentives, 373-374
  foreign taxation, 56-59, 58i
  IC-DISC, 375-376
  trade determinants, 9
Extraterritorial Income (ETI) Exclusion
    Act, 374

Factoring, 309-311, 310i, 311t, 312, 315
Family, external financing, 300, 305,
    315
Farouk Systems, 117-118
Fast track loan, SBA financing, 303t
Federal Maritime Commission (FMC)
  conference agreements, 208
  customs brokers, 216
  freight forwarders, 216-217, 219

Federal Trade Commission (FTC)
  antitrust enforcement, 371, 380
  general antitrust prohibitions, 368,
    369, 380
  import requirements, 391t
Fence posts, 68t
Fictitious name
  bank account, 49
  business/trade name, 48-49
Fidelity and Deposit Company, 134
Field trip, 77
Fifth screening, 77
Finance companies, 304-305, 315
Financial institution
  ECIP buyer credit policy, 329, 339
  ECIP supplier credit policy, 329
Financial services, export pricing, 174
Finland
  export price anomalies, 68t
  indirect marketing channels, 98
Five C's, lending decisions, 301
Flexibility
  countertrade benefits, 274
  export pricing, 154
Food and Drug Administration (FDA)
  Entry questions, 428
  import requirements, 391t
Food stuff, 391t
Force majeure
  export contract clauses, 187-188
  four categories of, 114
Fordney-McCumber Tariff, 3
Foreign content policy, 321
Foreign corporations, 55-56
Foreign Corrupt Practices Act (FCPA)
  compliance measures, 367-368,
    379
  enactment of, 363
  enforcement/penalties, 366-367,
    379
  principle objectives of, 364, 379
  responsible parties, 365-366, 379
  scope of coverage, 365, 379
Foreign dealers, 330
Foreign direct investment
  countertrade theories, 274-275, 287
  NAFTA assessment, 31, 31t
  trade determinant, 9

Foreign exchange
  economic risk factors, 135, 146
  transaction risks, 237-238
Foreign exchange market
  reasons for existence of, 236, 236
  role of, 225
  world currencies, 226-227
Foreign media, 88
Foreign persons, 55-56
Foreign Sales Corporation (FSC), 374
Foreign Trade Index, 88
Foreign travel, 410, 420
Forfaiting, 311-313, 313t, 316
Formal notice of claim, 142-143
Forms, CISG element, 183-184, 194.
  See also Documentation
Forward market hedge, 232
Forwarders, 203, 217
Fourth screening, 77
"Frachtors," 214
France
  agent contracts, 110
  antidumping cases, 457t
  CISG adoption, 180
  Corruption Perception Index, 364b
  countervailing duty cases, 457t
  lost tax revenue, 68t
  overdue payments, 133
  trading opportunities, 510-511
Free alongside ship (*named port of
    shipment*) (FAS)
  marine insurance coverage, 138
  terms, 138, 159t, 160, 160t, 161t,
    164-165, 169t-170t, 175
Free carrier (FCA) terms, 160, 160t,
    175, 161, 162t-163t, 164,
    169t-170t, 175
Free of particular average (FPA)
  contract clause, 142b
  marine insurance coverage, 138, 146
Free on board (*named port of shipment*)
    (FOB)
  marine insurance coverage, 138
  terms of sale, 159t, 160, 160t, 161t,
    165, 169t-170t, 175
Free trade areas
  economic integration stages, 24b
  establishment of, 11
  RIAs, 23t

Free Trade Agreements (FTAs),
    394-396, 395b
Free-trade zones/foreign trade zones
    (FTZ), 400-402, 404
Freight forwarders
  export pricing, 155, 174
  licensing requirements, 216-217,
    219
  logistics process, 127
  role/function of, 214-216, 219
  sea principles/practices, 211b
  selecting, 399b
French Compagme des Indes
    Orientales, 102b
Frequency, 95
Friends, external financing, 300, 305,
    315
Functional lines, 51

General Agreement on Tariffs and
    Trade (GATT)
  countertrade policy, 284-285,
    289-290
  customs valuation system, 433
  DISC violation, 374
  establishment of, 4, 19, 22
  MFN rate, 390
  principal objectives, 36
  replacement of, 10-11
  Subsidies Code, 450
  trade barrier reductions, 19-20
  unfair trade practices, 447
  unfair trade practices, 447
General and administrative expenses, 61
General average clause, 142b
General cargo vessels, 207b
Generalized System of Preferences
    (GSP), 396-397, 403
Geneva Round, GATT, 21b
Genoa, 1
Geocentric pricing, 156
Geographical lines, 51-52
Germany
  agent contracts, 110
  antidumping cases, 457t
  CISG adoption, 180

Germany *(continued)*
  countervailing duty cases, 457t
  import barriers, 392t
  lost tax revenue, 68t
  modern economy, 3
  overdue payments, 133
  taxation policies, 52
  trading opportunities, 512-513
Globalization
  emergence of world economy, 3,
  international trade's importance,
    7-8
  IPRs, 465
  small business financing, 297, 314
Gold Key Service, 80, 81b
Goods
  GATT, 20
  rejection of, 168
Government financing programs
    categorizes, 319. *See also*
    Small Business
    Administration (SBA)
Government policies
  NAFTA overview, 29
  overseas promotion, 88
  trade determinant, 9
  world economic integration, 12
Gray market
  Customs Service registration,
    471-472
  definition of, 457
  export pricing, 154
  irregular entry, 109b
Graydon America, 133
Great Depression, 4
Greece, 292t
Green-clause credit, 261, 268
Group C terms, 159t, 160, 160t, 161t,
    162t-163t, 165-168,
    169t-170t, 171, 174, 175
Group D terms, 160t, 161t, 162t-163t,
    169t-170t, 172-174, 176
Group E terms, 159, 159t, 160t,
    160-161, 162t-163t,
    169t-170t, 175
Group F, terms, 159t, 160, 160t, 161t,
    161, 162t-163t, 164-165,
    169t-170t, 175

GSM-102, agricultural export supports,
    337, 340
GSM-103, agricultural export supports,
    337, 340
Guaranteed 7a loans, 302, 303t, 304,
    304b
Guarantees
  exchange rate protection, 234
  Ex-Im Bank, 320, 321b, 322t, 323.
    See also Commercial loan
    guarantees, Working capital
    loan guarantees
  export contract clauses, 190-191, 194
  government financing programs,
    319
  ICC rules, 185, 191-192

Hague Rules, 208-211, 209b, 218
Hague-Visby Rules, 208-209, 209b,
    210, 218
Hamburg Rules, 209, 209b, 218
Handicrafts packing rules, 130b
Handling and storage, 144b
Hanover Trade Fair, 89-90
Harmonized tariff schedule of the
    United States (HTSUS),
    432-433, 433t, 440
Havana Conference, 19
Hedging, 229-231, 231t, 233-234
Holland, early modern trade, 1. *See
    also* Netherlands
Hong Kong
  export price anomalies, 68t
  NIC trade, 11
Hudson Bay Company
  charter company, 2
  monopoly grant, 368
Human resources, 128b
Hungary
  countertrade, 272
  import price anomalies, 68t
  trading opportunities, 504-505

Illinois, 338, 340
Illiteracy rate, 87

Import business plan sample, 567-571, 569t, 571t, 572t
Import risks, 413, 414b, 421
Importer common mistakes, 419b
Imports
  determinants, 9
  dutiable levies, 309, 403
  financing of, 419, 421
  GSP, 396-397, 403
  nontariff barriers, 390, 390b, 391t, 392t, 393-394, 403
  pricing products, 417, 418t
  product selection, 407-408, 420
  prohibited, 390b, 393, 403
  selection resources, 409-411
  supplier selection, 412-414, 414b, 421
  trade determinants, 9, 14
  typical transaction, 415b
  volume determination, 411-412, 420
In-bond plant contractor, 416
Inchmaree clause, 142b
Income, import determinant, 411-412, 420
Incoterms
  buyer-seller responsibilities, 162t-163t
  price calculation, 168, 169t-170t
  terms of sale, 158, 159t, 160t, 161t, 167b
Independence principle, 254-255
India
  adversative trade policies, 460
  colonial period, 2
  Corruption Perception Index, 364b
  countervailing duty cases, 457t
  export price anomalies, 68t
  IPR enforcement, 471b
  medieval trade, 1
  priority watch list, 472
  trade volume, 10
  trading opportunities, 498-500
  U. S. tax treaty, 64
Indian Copyright Act, 471b
Indirect distribution channels
  advantages/disadvantages, 105b
  CEs, 104
  channel characteristics, 95-96, 115

Indirect distribution channels *(continued)*
  control, 98
  ECAs, 102-103
  EMCs, 100-101
  ETCs, 101
  export cartels, 104
  export merchants, 103-104
  import marketing, 418-419, 421
  intermediaries, 99
  marketing environment, 97-98
  MEAs, 99-100
  resources/experience, 96
  types of, 116
Indirect quotation, 225, 226t
Indonesia
  adversative trade policies, 460
  agent contracts, 110
  Corruption Perception Index, 364b
  countertrade, 272
  countertrade policy, 287
  Ex-Im Bank, 322t
  trading opportunities, 500-501
  value of currency, 227
Industrial market economies, 10, 14
Industrial Revolution, 3
Informal entry, 427b, 431
Information technology, 297, 314
Infrastructure, 128b
Injury, AD/CVD investigations, 452, 462
Inland bill of lading, 198-199
Inland carriage
  definition, 218-219
  international rules, 213-214, 218-219
Inspection certificate, 199, 217
Inspection element, 184, 194
Institutional reform, GATT, 22
Insurance
  ancient trade, 1
  claims, 140-145
  credit risks, 134
  ECIP, 327
  elements, 135-136
  Ex-Im Bank, 322t
  exchange rate protection, 234
  government financing programs, 319

Insurance *(continued)*
  importance of, 135, 146
  late medieval trade, 1
  marine, 136-139
  OPIC, 336, 340
Insurance certificate
  documentation, 199, 217
  marine insurance, 138-139
Insurance companies financing,
    304-305, 315
Integrators, 203, 217
Intellectual property
  NAFTA overview, 29
  political/legal forces, 76
  violation remedies, 458
Intellectual property rights (IPR)
  definition of, 465, 476
  import supplier selection, 413, 414b,
    421
  issues pertaining to, 468-469
  Paris Convention, 473
  PCT, 474, 476
  priority countries, 470-472
  priority watch list, 472, 473, 476
  protection of, 469-470, 471b, 472
  red flags, 470b
  regional conventions, 475
  Super 301 clause, 358
  TRIPS agreement, 474-475, 476,
    477-478
  types of, 465-468
  Universal Copyright Convention,
    474, 476
  watch list, 472, 473, 476
Intellectual Property Committee (IPC),
    475
Interest, 319, 321
Interest-Charge Domestic International
    Sales Corporation (IC-DISC),
    375-376, 377t, 380
Intermediaries, 97, 99, 115
Intermediate financing, 319
Intermediate loans, 322t
Intermediate policies, 327i, 327-329,
    338, 339
Intermediate term financing, 299, 315
Intermodal service, 212-213

International Air Transport Association
    (IATA), 203
International Bank for Reconstruction
    and Development (IBRD), 4
International Buyer program, 90
International Chamber of Commerce
    (ICC)
  Incoterms, 158, 159t
  Rules of Conduct to Combat
    Extortion and Bribery, 368
  UCP, 244, 266
  Uniform Rules for Collection, 244,
    246, 266
  Uniform Rules for Contract
    Guarantees, 185
International Company Profiles (ICP),
    81b
International customary law, 179, 193
International Emergency Economic
    Powers Act
  EAR implementation, 351
  export control policy, 348
International Intellectual Property
    Alliance, 468
International logistics
  and domestic logistics, 125t
  steps, 126-128
International market research
  definition of, 72
  purpose, 74
  value of, 73-74
International Monetary Fund (IMF)
  countertrade policies, 285-286
  establishment of, 4
International Perspective 2.1., GATT
    Negotiations, 21b
International Perspective 2.2., Stages of
    Economic Integration, 24b
International Perspective 2.3.,
    European Union Institutions,
    35b
International Perspective 3.1., Business
    Organization Pointers, 42b
International Perspective 3.2., Transfer
    Pricing Methods, 63b
International Perspective 4.1., Selecting
    Export Products, 73b

International Perspective 4.2.,
    Programs for U.S. Exporters,
    80b
International Perspective 4.3., Common
    Exporter Mistakes, 84b
International Perspective 4.4., Typical
    Export Transaction, 85b
International Perspective 5.1., Export
    Trading Companies, 102b
International Perspective 5.2., Indirect
    Channel Structures, 105b
International Perspective 5.3., Japanese
    Distribution System, 108b
International Perspective 5.4., Parallel
    vs. Multiple Exporters, 109b
International Perspective 6.1., Danish
    World Class Logistics
    System, 128b
International Perspective 6.2., Packing
    Handicraft Exports, 130b
International Perspective 6.3., Cargo
    Insurance Contract Clauses,
    142b
International Perspective 6.4., Cargo
    Loss or Damage, 144b
International Perspective 7.1.,
    Incoterms, 167b
International Perspective 7.2.,
    Incoterms and Business
    Strategy, 168b
International Perspective 8.1., Chicago
    Prime Packers v. Northam
    Trading Co., 182b
International Perspective 8.2.,
    Acceptance of Standard
    International Contracts, 189b
International Perspective 8.3.,
    Tendering for Export
    Contracts, 192b
International Perspective 9.1., Warsaw
    Conventions, 204b
International Perspective 9.2., Ocean
    Cargo/Ocean vessels, 207b
International Perspective 9.3., Hague,
    Hague-Visby, Hamburg
    Rules, 209

International Perspective 9.4., Ocean
    Transportation Principles and
    Practices, 211b
International Perspective 10.1.,
    Exchange Restrictions, 229b
International Perspective 10.2., Euro,
    235b
International Perspective 11.1.,
    Delinquent Overseas
    Customers, 248b
International Perspective 11.2.,
    Common Letters of Credit
    Discrepancies, 257b
International Perspective 11.3.,
    Unworkable Terms in Letters
    of Credit, 258b
International Perspective 12.1.,
    Mechanics of a Barter
    Transaction, 275b
International Perspective 12.2.,
    Organizing for Countertrade,
    278
International Perspective 12.3.,
    Negotiating Countertrade
    Contracts, 282b
International Perspective 12.4.,
    Countertrade with Latin
    American Countries, 288b
International Perspective 13.1., SBA
    Loans, 304b
International Perspective 14.1., Ex-Im
    Bank Criteria for Loans/Loan
    Guarantees, 321b
International Perspective 15.1.,
    Multilateral Export Regimes,
    350b
International Perspective 15.2.,
    Commerce Export License,
    353b
International Perspective 15.3., General
    Prohibitions and License
    Exceptions, 354b
International Perspective 15.4.,
    Automated Services, 358
International Perspective 15.5.,
    Requests that are Not
    Reportable, 362b

International Perspective 15.6.,
Corruption Perception Index,
364b
International Perspective 15.7.,
*Matsushita Co. Ltd v. Zenith
Radio Corporation,* 272
International Perspective 15.8.,
Agricultural Export
Incentives, 375b
International Perspective 16.1., U.S.
Import Restrictions, 390b
International Perspective 16.2., U.S.
Free Trade Agreements, 395b
International Perspective 16.3.,
Selecting A Customs
Broker/Freight Forwarder,
399b
International Perspective 17.1., Quality
Control for Imports, 409b
International Perspective 17.2.,
International Supplier
Selection, 414b
International Perspective 17.3., Typical
Import Transaction, 415b
International Perspective 17.4.,
Advantages/Disadvantages of
Outsourcing, 416b
International Perspective 17.5.,
Common Mistakes of
Potential Importers, 419b
International Perspective 18.1.,
Avoiding Errors in Invoicing,
426b
International Perspective 18.2., Types
of Entry, 427b
International Perspective 18.3,
Automated Services, 434b
International Perspective 19.1.,
Antidumping Duties, 449b
International Perspective 19.2.,
Semiconductor Industry,
459b
International Perspective 20.1., IPR
Red Flags, 470b
International Perspective 20.2., IPR
Protection and Enforcement,
471b

International trade
ancient period, 1-2
benefit of, 7-8, 14
colonial period, 2-3
decline in, 4
definition of, 7
determinants of, 9, 14
distribution channel selection, 95
major developments, 10-13, 14
modern period, 3-4
RIAs share of, 22, 23t
volume growth, 9-10, 14
world distribution, 38t
International trade loan, 303t
International trade loan program, 333,
340
International Trade Administration
(ITA)
AD/CVD investigations, 453, 453t
export counseling assistance, 78
International Trade Commission (ITC)
investigations, 469
International Trade Court (ITC)
AD/CVD costs, 449
AD/CVD investigations, 451-452
AD/CVD proceedings, 453, 453t,
454, 455, 456, 456t
agricultural programs interference,
460
intellectual property remedies, 458
"like products," 451
WTO rulings, 447
International Trade Organization
(ITO), 19
Internet
developing countries, 118-120, 120t
overseas promotion, 88-89
Inventory, 131, 145
Inventory financing, 299, 315
Investment financing,, 299, 315
Investment return, export pricing, 153,
174
Investments
direct offsets, 283i, 284, 289
NAFTA overview, 28
Invoicing
avoiding errors, 426b
exchange rate protection, 234

Iran, 393
Ireland, 513-514
Irrevocable L/Cs, 250-251, 267
Israel
    adversative trade policies, 460
    defense offsets, 292t
    trading opportunities, 480-482
    U.S. Free Trade Agreement, 394,
        395b, 403
Italy
    antidumping cases, 457t
    CISG adoption, 180
    countervailing duty cases, 457t
    payment period, 133
    trading opportunities, 514-515

Japan
    agent contracts, 110
    antidumping cases, 457t
    Corruption Perception Index, 364b
    customer characteristics, 97
    foreign exchange reserves, 13
    Hague-Visby Rules, 208-209
    import barriers, 392t
    indirect marketing channels, 97-98
    international distribution system,
        108b
    IPR enforcement, 471b
    lost tax revenue, 68t
    trade volume, 10
    trading opportunities, 501-503
    U. S. tax treaty, 64
    unjustified foreign trade practices,
        458
    value of currency, 228t
Jordan, 395b

Kennedy Round, GATT, 21b
Kenya, 364b
Korea. *See also* North Korea
    adversative trade policies, 460
    agent contracts, 110
    antidumping cases, 457t
    countervailing duty cases, 457t
    defense offsets, 292t

Korea *(continued)*
    Ex-Im Bank, 322t
    lost tax revenue, 68t
    NIC trade, 11
    U. S. tax treaty, 64

Labeling. *See also* Marking
        requirements
    contract clause, 142b
    logistic functions, 129, 145
    logistics process, 126-127
    U.S. import policy, 393
Land transportation types, 212, 218
Latin America
    advertising regulations, 88
    agent contracts, 110
    countertrade policy, 287, 288b
    Ex-Im Bank, 322t
    Internet use, 120t
    trading opportunities, 486-488,
        490-495
Law of merchants, 158
Leasing, 329-330, 339
Lebanon, 460
Legality, 115
Letters of credit (L/Cs). *See also*
        Documentary letters of credit
        (L/Cs)
    antiboycott regulations, 361-362
    economic risk factors, 134
    import financing, 419, 421
    late medieval trade, 1
    third party financing, 308-309, 315
Liability
    air carrier, 204b, 205
    CISG element, 184
    export contract clauses, 190
    Hague Rules, 210-211
"Like products," 451
Limitation of action
    air carrier, 204b, 205
    Hague Rules, 210
Limitation period element, 184-185,
        194
Limited liability corporation (LLC),
        48-49

Limited partnership
    bank account, 49
    business structure, 44-45
    business trade name, 48
Line operation, 50
Lines of credit, 301-302, 315
Liquidation, 430-431, 440
Loan guarantees, 263, 264-265
Loans. *See also* Small Business
        Administration (SBA)
    Ex-Im Bank, 323, 331i, 339
    secured third-party financing,
        307-308, 315
Location, 155, 175
Logistics
    categories of, 121-122, 145
    definition of, 121
    external influences, 123-125, 145
    functions,129-131, 145
    importance of, 122-123, 145
    problems/solutions, 125-126
London Interbank Offered Rate
        (LIBOR), 312
Long-term financing. *See also* Small
        Business Administration
        (SBA)
    Ex-Im Bank, 322t
    external financing, 299, 315
    government programs, 319
Loss
    CIF contract, 171
    marine insurance, 143t, 144b
Low documentation loans, 303t

Maastricht, treaty of, 32, 34
Mail entry, 427b, 431
Mailing lists, 88
Major discrepancies, 256-257, 267
Malaysia
    Ex-Im Bank, 322t
    USFTAs, 395b
Management, 70, 70t
Manifest, 201, 217
Manufacture, 10
Manufacture's resources/experience,
    96, 115

Manufacturer's export agents (MEAs),
    99-100
Marginal pricing, 156-157, 175
Marine extension clause, 142b
Marine insurance
    claims, 140-141, 147
    claims procedures, 141-145, 142b,
        143t, 147
    coverage, 138
    illustration, 139
    insurance certificates, 138-139
    terms of, 136-137
    types of, 137
    types of loss, 143t
Market access, NAFTA, 26-27
Market Access and Compliance
        (MAC), 79
Market demand, 71
"Market disruption," 458
Market need, 71
Market research
    export potential, 69
    export pricing, 155, 174
    import selection resources, 409-410,
        420
    international market, 72-74
Market share, export pricing, 153, 174
Marketing
    channels, 417-419
    direct distribution channel, 103-104
    distribution channel selection,
        97-98, 116
    export potential, 69-70
    objectives, 96, 115
Marking requirements, 438-449, 440
Markups, 153-154, 174
Mass communication, 7
Material injury, 452
Materials management, 121-122, 145
*Matsushita Co. Ltd v. Zenith Radio
        Corporation,* 372b
Medical devices, 391t
Mercantilism, 3
Merchandise trade, 9, 10
Mexico
    Corruption Perception Index, 364b
    Ex-Im Bank, 322t
    export price anomalies, 68t

Mexico *(continued)*
  lost tax revenue, 68t
  NAFTA, 25, 26, 30-31, 31t,
      394-395
  trading opportunities, 493-494
  U. S. tax treaty, 64
  value of currency, 227
Microloans, 303t
Middle class growth, 10
Middle East, 322t
Minicase 16.1, 404
Minicase 18.1., 441
Minicase 18.2., 442-443
Minicase 18.3., 443
Mining, 10
Minor discrepancies, 256, 267
Missile Technology Control Regime
      (MTCR), 350b
Model tax treaties, 56
Monopolies
  colonial era, 2
  opposition to, 368
Morgan Grenfell Trade Finance
      Limited, 313
Morocco, 395b
Most-favored-nation (MFN) rate
  imported merchandise, 390
  IPR protection, 469-470
Motor vehicles, 391t
Multivitamins, 68t

National Association of Credit
      Management Corporations
      (NACM), 133
National Intellectual Property Institute
      (NPI), 471b
National Trade Data Bank (NTDB), 78
National treatment, 473, 476
Nations Commission on International
      Trade Law (UNCITRAL),
      209
Navigation Act, 3
Negotiable L/C, 268
Neo-bulk, 207b
Neo-bulk carriers, 207b
Net operating losses, 61

Netherlands
  CISG adoption, 180
  lost tax revenue, 68t
  payment period, 133
  service trade, 7
  taxation policies, 52
  trade volume, 10
  trading opportunities, 516-517
New Zealand, 64
Newly industrialized economies (NIC),
      11
Niche marketing, 73b
Nigeria
  Corruption Perception Index, 364b
  trading opportunities, 482-483
Non-vessel-operating common carriers
      (NVOCC), 215
Nondiscrimination policy, GATT, 19
Nonpayment risks, 239, 240, 240i
Nonresident aliens, 55-56
North Africa, 3
North America, 120t
North America Free Trade Agreement
      (NAFTA)
  AD/CVD appeals, 456
  assessment of, 30-31, 32t, 36
  establishment of, 11-12, 14, 25
  and EU, 32t
  merchandise exports, 23t
  negotiating objectives, 25-26
  overview of, 26-30
  scope of coverage, 36
  text, 601-618
  U.S. Free Trade Agreement,
      394-395, 403
North Korea, 390, 393
Notice, proper element, 184, 194
Nuclear Suppliers Group (NSG), 350b

Ocean carriers, 206-208, 207b
Ocean transportation
  COGSA, 220
  dominance of, 205-206
  international rules, 208-211, 209b,
      218
  principles/practices, 211b

Oceania, 120t
Office of Export Enforcement, 359
Office of Foreign Assets Control, 349
Offsets
    defense expenditures, 291-294,
        292t, 293t
    parallel transactions, 277i, 281-284,
        282b, 283i, 289
Oman, 395b
Omnibus Trade and Competitiveness
    Act, 470
Open account
    exporter financing, 306-307, 315
    import financing, 421
    sales, 239, 241-242, 263, 264, 265
Open policy, 136, 146
Opportunity cost approach, 122
Oral contracts element, 180, 181t, 183,
    194
"Order," 425
Ordinary and necessary expenses,
    60-61
Organization for Economic
    Cooperation and
    Development (OECD)
    anti-bribery recommendation,
        368
    consensus risk classification,
        341
    Convention on Combating Bribery,
        368
    export credit guidelines, 319-320
Origin rules, 438, 440
Outsourcing
    advantages/disadvantages of,
        414-415, 416b
    types of, 415-417
Overseas agents
    contracting with, 110
    evaluating, 109-110
    indirect channel, 106-107, 116
    locating, 108
Overseas distributors
    contracting with, 110
    evaluating, 109-110
    indirect channel, 107,116
    locating, 108
Overseas joint venture, 415-416

Overseas Private Investment
    Corporation (OPIC)
    credit insurance policies, 134
    government financing, 334-337, 340
Owens Online, 133
Owner, entering goods, 425, 439
Ownership
    financing alternatives, 298-299, 314
    political/legal restrictions, 76

Packaging/Packing
    export pricing, 155, 174
    logistics process, 126-127, 129,
        130b, 145
Packing list
    entry documentation, 428, 439
    logistics process, 127
Pakistan
    adversative trade policies, 460
    Corruption Perception Index, 364b
    import determinants, 9
Panama
    service trade, 7
    USFTAs, 395b
Parallel market
    export pricing, 154
    irregular entry, 109b
Parallel transactions, 279-284, 279i,
    280i, 289
Paris Convention, 473
Parole evidence element, 183, 194
Partnerships
    bank account, 49
    business structure, 43-44
    business trade name, 48
    U.S. taxation policies, 52
Patent Cooperation Treaty (PCT), 474,
    476
Patent violations, 456-458, 462, 471b
Patents, 465, 466
Penalties, export contract clauses, 188
Penetration pricing, 157, 175
Pension funds, 304-305, 315
Perfect tender rule, 181t
Performance bonds, 263-264
Perils-only policy, 137

Personal and business expenses, 61
Personal loans, 302, 315
Personal selling, 89
Personal services, 56
Personnel, 70t
Peru, 395b
Philippines
    adversative trade policies, 460
    lost tax revenue, 68t
Physical distribution, 121, 145
Piracy, 469, 471b, 476
Plastic buckets, 68t
Poland
    adversative trade policies, 460
    defense offsets, 292t
    trading opportunities, 506
Political risk factors, 131-132, 146
Polycentric pricing, 156
Population size, 412, 420
Portugal, 1
Pound sterling, 228t
Preferential trade agreements, 24b
Preferential Trade Area for Eastern and
        Southern American Common
        Market (MERCOSUR)
    establishment of, 11-12, 14
    regional agreement, 33t, 36
Preliminary notice of claim, 141
Preliminary screening, 75
Preshipment inspection, 127
Price
    CISG, 181t
    decline in world, 4
    distribution agreement clause,
        112-113, 116
    export contract clauses, 181t,
        186-187, 194
    import volume determinant, 412,
        420
Price controls
    export pricing, 155-156
    political/legal forces, 76
Pricing
    factors of, 153-154
    imported products, 417, 418t
    international transfer, 61-64
Primary market research, 74
Priority foreign country, 470-472, 476

Priority Watch List, 471b, 472, 473,
        476,
Private export assistance, 82, 83t
Private Export Funding Corporation
        (PEFCO), 337, 340
Private fleets, 206
Pro forma invoice
    documentation, 200, 217
    entry documentation, 428, 439
    logistics process, 126
Product(s)
    characteristics, 97, 115
    differentiation, 155, 174
    distribution agreement clause, 111
    export potential, 69-71, 71t
    import selection, 407-408, 420
    import selection resources, 409-411
    modification, 155, 174
    reliability, 153, 174
    selection approaches, 71-72, 73b
    U.S. Import Restrictions, 390b
Product line, 51
Production capacity, export decision, 70t
Production costs, export pricing, 174
Professional services, 50, 56
Profit remittance limits, political/legal
        forces, 76
Profits
    corporate business structure, 46-47
    export pricing, 153, 174
Progress payment, 307, 315
Promotion assistance, 79
Promotional tools, 86-87
Proof, sea principles/practices, 211b
Proper notice element, 184, 194
Protests
    liquidation process, 431, 440
    overseas delinquent accounts, 248b
Public Law 480, 337, 340
Publicity, 90-91
Purchaser, entering goods, 425, 439

Quality
    export contract clauses, 181t,
        188-190, 194
    export pricing, 153, 174

Quality assurance, 412-413, 414b, 421
Quality control, 409b
Quantity, CISG, 181t
Quotas, U.S. import policy, 393-394

Radial tires, 68t
Radioactive materials, 391t
Rail transport, 212, 218
Reactive approach, 71-72
"Red flags," 360
Red-clause credit, 261, 268
Refined Sugar Association contracts,
    185
Regional Integration agreements
    (RIAs)
    EU, 32, 32t, 34-35
    NAFTA, 25-31, 31t, 32t
    other major, 33t, 36
    WTO members, 22-24
Regulations
    export pricing, 156, 175
    harmonization motives, 179, 193
    logistic decisions, 123-124, 125t,
        145
Renewal clause, 113, 116
"Rental rights," 28
Representatives rights/obligations
    clause, 111-112, 116
Residents
    transaction taxation, 54-55
    U.S. taxation policies, 52
Retailing service trade, 7
Revised American Foreign Trade
    Definitions, 158
Revocability, CISG, 181t
Revocable L/Cs, 250, 267
Revolving agreement, 261, 268
Right of priority, 473, 476
Right to remedy deficiencies, 184, 194
Rome, Treaty of, 32, 34
Rules of Conduct to Combat Extortion
    and Bribery, ICC, 368
Russia
    adversative trade policies, 460
    copyrights violations, 469
    Corruption Perception Index, 364b

Russia *(continued)*
    priority watch list, 472
    trading opportunities, 507-508
Rwanda, Case 4.1, 93

S Corporation
    business structure, 47
    business trade name, 48-49
    U.S. taxation policies, 54
S Revision Act of 1982, 47
Safeguarding of Industries Act, 3-4
Sales
    ECIP restrictions, 326, 336
    overseas promotion, 89-90
Sales representative agreement sample,
    593-600
Saudi Arabia
    defense offsets, 292t
    Ex-Im Bank, 322t
Scope of coverage
    Ex-Im Bank, 321
    FCPA, 365, 379
Scope of work, export contract clause,
    186, 194
Screening, 75-77
Sea transportation
    COGSA, 220
    dominance of, 205-206
    international rules, 208-21, 209b, 218
    principles/practices, 211b
    rising costs, 13
Seaworthiness, 211b
Secondary market research, 74
Secondary screening, 76
Section 201, escape clause, 461, 462
Section 301
    IPR protection, 469-470, 472-473
    unjustified foreign trade practices,
        458, 462
Section 337
    IPR protection, 469
    patent, trademark, copyright
        violations, 456-458, 362
Security Exchange Commission
    corrupt practices, 363
    FCPA enforcement, 366

Selection, field trip, 77
Seller, Incoterms, 161t, 162t-163t
Semiconductor Accord, 459b
Seoul International Gift and
    Accessories Show, 90
September 11ᵗʰ, business costs, 13, 15
Service Corps of Retired Executives
    (SCORE), 81-82
Services
    export potential, 69
    NAFTA overview, 27
    new developments, 12
    RIAs, 23t
    selection approaches, 71-72
    trade volume, 10, 14
    world trade, 7
Shareholders, 47
Sherman Act, 368, 369, 380
Shipper's export declaration (SED)
    documentation, 200, 217
    export licenses, 358
Shipping, 321
Shore clause, 142b
Short-term financing
    external financing, 299, 315
    government programs, 319
Short-term loans, 322t
Short-term policies, 327i, 327-329, 339
Showcase U.S.A., 88
Silk Road, 1
Simplified Network Application
    Process (SNAP), 358b
Singapore
    CISG adoption, 180
    export determinants, 9
    Hague-Visby Rules, 208-209
    NIC trade, 11
    USFTAs, 395b
Single European Act (SEA)
    assessment, 35
    objectives of, 34
Skimming, 157, 175
Small business
    ECIP environmental policy, 339
    ECIP policy, 328, 339
    new financing factors, 297, 314
    turnover rate, 300
    undercapitalization of, 297

Small business investment companies
    (SBICs), 302, 303t, 304, 304b
Small Business Administration (SBA)
    eligibility requirements, 332, 333t
    EWCP, 303t, 332-333, 339
    export counseling assistance, 81-82
    export industries, 50
    Export Express, 333-334
    external financing, 300, 302, 303t,
        304, 315
    trade loan program, 333, 340
    working capital guarantees, 324
Small Business Development Centers
    (SBDCs), 82
Smoot-Hawley Tariff, 3
Sogo Shosha, 102b
Sole proprietorship
    bank account, 49
    business structure, 41-43
    business/trade name, 48
    U.S. taxation policies, 52-53
South Africa
    trading opportunities, 483-485
    U. S. tax treaty, 64
South African Customs Union (SACU),
    33t, 36
Southeast Asia
    foreign exchange reserves, 13
    indirect marketing channels, 97-98
Spain
    colonial trade, 2
    countervailing duty cases, 457t
    early modern trade, 1
Specific duty, 309, 403
Speculation, 226, 236
Spot market, 231-232
Standard business deductions, 61
Standby credit, 262-265, 268
Start-up costs, 60-61
State programs
    export counseling assistance, 82
    export support programs, 338, 340
Stock (corporate), 47
Storage, 131, 145
Straight letter of credit (L/C), 268
Strict compliance doctrine, 255
Subcontractor production, 283, 283i,
    289

Subsidiaries, 57-59
Subsidies
 actionable, 450
 definition of, 448, 461
 Ex-Im Bank, 320
 government financing programs,
  319
 nonactionable, 450-451
Super 301 clause, 458, 462
Supplier credit, 319
Supply/demand, 155, 175
Supreme Court
 protests, 431, 440
 Section 201 appeals, 461
Swap, 233
Swiss franc, 228t
Switch trading, 276, 277i, 278i, 288
Syria, 1
System for Tracking Export License
  Applications (STELA), 358b
Systematic approach, 71, 72
Systems approach, 122

Taiwan
 adversative trade policies, 460
 antidumping cases, 457t
 countertrade, 272-273
 defense offsets, 292t
 NIC trade, 11
Tankers, 207b
Tariff Act of 1862, national security,
  461
Tariff Act of 1930
 IPR infringement investigations,
  469
 patent, trademark, copyright
  violations, 456-458, 462
Tariff quotas, 393-394
Tariffs
 export pricing, 155-156
 levying methods, 389, 403
 MFN rate, 390
 selected countries, 392t, 535-536
Tax deductions, 60
Tax identification number, 49
Tax Reform Act, 374

Tax treaties
 common provisions, 64
 international, 63-64
Taxation
 export contract clauses, 190, 194
 general principles of, 52-54
 IC-DISC savings, 375-376, 377t,
  380
 political/legal forces, 76
Technical standards, 29
Technology
 growth rate, 16t
 logistic decisions, 124-125, 145
 small business financing, 297, 314
 trade growth, 10
 world economic integration, 12
Technology transfer
 countertrade benefits, 273
 direct offsets, 283i, 284, 289
Temporary importation under bond,
  427b
Tender, 192b
Termination clause, 110, 113-114,
  116
Territoriality
 distribution agreement clause,
  110-111, 116
 IPRs, 468
Textile, imports, 391t
Thailand, 364b
Theft, 144b
Third screening, 76
Thomas Register of Manufactures, 72
Through bill of lading, 199, 217
Time policy, 136, 146
Toilet/facial tissue, 68t
Tokyo Round, GATT, 21b, 433
Torquay (UK) Round, GATT, 21b
Total cost approach, 122
Tourism, 7
Trade
 associations, 83t
 consultants, 83t
 development, 80
 fairs/shows, 80, 410-411, 420
 harmonization motives, 179, 193
 intermediaries/services, 398-403
 NAFTA assessment, 30

Trade *(continued)*
  opportunities in selected countries, 479-518
  publications, 410, 420
  world distribution, 38t
Trade acceptance, 265, 308, 315
Trade Act of 1974
  IPR protection, 469-470
  Section 201, 461
  Section 301, 458
Trade Act of 1988, Super 301 clause, 458
Trade adjustment assistance, 460-461, 462
Trade liberalization
  GATT, 20, 21-22
  trade growth, 10
  world markets, 11
Trade missions, 90
Trade names
  Customs Service registration, 471-472
  types of, 48-49
Trade Offices, 411, 420
Trade Opportunities Program (TOP), 78-79, 81b
Trade profiles, 531-533
Trade secrets, 465, 467
Trade secret violations, 471b
Trade-related aspects of intellectual property (TRIPs)
  GATT, 20, 22
  IPR protection, 474-475, 476
  life-saving drugs, 477-478
Trade-related investment measures (TRIMs), 20, 22
Trademark violations, 456-458, 462, 471b
"Trademark-linking," 28
Trademarks
  Customs Service registration, 471-472
  IPRs, 465, 466-467
Trading companies, 83t
Traffic management, 130-131, 145
Tramps, 206
Transaction value, 435-436, 440
Transferable letter of credit (L/Cs)
  import financing, 419
  payment arrangements, 259-260, 268
  third party financing, 308-309, 315

Transparency International (TI), 368
Transport
  growth rate, 17t
  trade determinant, 9
Transportation
  Ex-Im Bank, 321
  logistics, 125t
  rising costs, 13
  service trade, 7
  via air, 201- 205, 202t, 217-218
  via land, 201, 218-219
  via sea, 201, 218
Travel
  exchange rate, 226, 236
  tax deductions, 61
Trucking, 212, 218
TRW Credit Services, 133
Turkey
  adversative trade policies, 460
  defense offsets, 292t
  Ex-Im Bank, 322t

Uncertainty, 95
Unfair trading practices
  AD/CVD, 451-453, 453t, 454, 455, 456, 456t
  agricultural programs, 460, 462
  Communist nations, 458, 462
  general description of, 447-448
  Section 337 practices, 456, 462
  unjustified foreign trade practices, 458, 460, 462
Uniform Commercial Code (UCC)
  and CISG, 180, 181t
  export contract clauses, 191-192
  L/C regulation, 252
  price determination worksheet, 166i
  terms of sale, 158
Uniform Customs Practices for Documentary Credits (UCP)
  irrevocable L/Cs, 250
  L/C regulation, 252, 266
  L/Cs, 266
Uniform Rules for Collection, 244, 246, 266
Uniform Rules for Contract Guarantees, ICC, 185, 191-192

"Uniform Rules for Demand
        Guarantees," 191-192
Unit price, 437b
United Kingdom
    antidumping cases, 457t
    countervailing duty cases, 457t
    defense offsets, 292t
    export price anomalies, 68t
    lost tax revenue, 68t
    overdue payments, 133
    trading opportunities, 517-518
United Nations, WTO, 11
United Nations Commission on
        International Trade Law
        (UNCITRAL), 180
United States
    CISG adoption, 180
    Corruption Perception Index, 364b
    countertrade policy, 286, 290
    current account deficit, 13, 15, 31
    direct marketing channels, 97-98
    direct marketing channels, 97-98
    Ex-Im Bank, 322t
    FTAs, 394-396, 395b, 403
    HTSUS, 432-433, 433t, 440
    impact of international trade, 8
    importing questions/answers,
        521-530
    IPR protection, 469-470
    modern migration to, 3
    NAFTA, 25, 25, 30-31, 31t,
        394-395, 395b
    tariffs, 3
    tax treaties, 64
    taxation policies, 52
    terms of sale, 158
    trade volume, 10
    UNCITRAL sea transportation, 209
    Uruguay Round, 20
    value of currency, 227, 228t
United States and Foreign Commercial
        Service (US&FCS), 79
United States Consumer Safety
        Commission, 391t
United States Department of
        Agriculture (USDA)
    agricultural export supports, 337
    export counseling assistance, 82
    import requirements, 391t, 393

United States Department of
        Commerce, 351
    AD/CVD investigations, 453-456
    Barter and Countertrade Unit, 286
    export counseling assistance, 78
    overseas promotion, 90
    political risks, 132
    trade adjustment assistance,
        460-461, 462
United States Department of Energy,
        391t
United States Department of Interior,
        391t
United States Department of Justice
        (DOJ)
    antitrust enforcement, 371, 380
    FCPA enforcement, 366
    import requirements, 391t
United States Department of Labor,
        460-461, 462
United States Department of State, 391t
United States Department of the
        Treasury, 391t
United States Department of
        Transportation, 391t
United States Export Assistance
        Centers (EACs), 82
United States Trade Information
        Center, 78
United States Trade Representative
        (USTR)
    discriminatory practices reviews, 458
    exported-related employment, 8
    IPR investigation, 470, 472
    market disruptions, 458
United States-Central America-
        Dominican Republic Free
        Trade Agreement (CAFTA-
        DR), 11-12, 395b, 396
Universal Copyright Convention, 474,
        476
Uruguay, 364b
Uruguay Round
    final act of, 10-11, 20
    GATT, 21b
    results of, 20-22, 36
    unfair trade practices, 447
Utilities, 17t

Vance, W. R., 135-136
Venezuela
    adversative trade policies, 460
    Corruption Perception Index, 364b
    Ex-Im Bank, 322t
    trading opportunities, 494-495
Venice, 1
Venture capitalists, 305-306
Voyage policy, 136, 146

Wages, 8
Warehouse to warehouse clause, 142b
Warehouses, bonded, 402, 404
Warranties clauses, 190
Warsaw Convention, air cargo, 204b,
    204-205
Wassenaar Arrangement (WA), 350b
Watch list, 472, 473, 476
Water damage, 144b
Wayne Engineering, 117
Webb-Pomerene Act (WPA)
    antitrust exemption, 370, 380
    intermediaries, 104
Wholly owned subsidiary, 415
Wildlife/pets, 391t
With average (WA) policy, 138, 146

Wood moldings, 68t
Working capital
    Ex-Im Bank, 322t
    external financing, 299, 315
Working capital loan guarantees
    Ex-Im Bank, 323-324, 324i, 338
    major features of, 324-326, 325t
World Intellectual Property
        Organization (WIPO)
    Copyright Treaty, 471b
    Paris Convention, 474
World trade clubs, 83t
World Trade Data Reports (WTDR), 88
World Trade Organization (WTO)
    CIT ruling on, 447
    countertrade policy, 289-290
    Doha Round, 11, 20
    establishment of, 10-11, 14, 20
    ETI violation, 374
    FSC violation, 374
    MFN rate, 390
    RIAs, 22
    TRIPS, 475
    USFTAs, 395b
Zimbabwe
    Corruption Perception Index, 364b
    trading opportunities, 485-486